Psychology
and
Work Today

■　■　■

Psychology and Work Today

An Introduction to Industrial and Organizational Psychology

■ ■ ■

SEVENTH EDITION

Duane P. Schultz
University of South Florida

Sydney Ellen Schultz

Prentice Hall
Upper Saddle River, New Jersey 07458

Library of Congress Cataloging-in-Publication Data

Schultz, Duane P.
    Psychology and work today : an introduction to industrial and
organizational psychology / Duane P. Schultz, Sydney Ellen Schultz.
— 7th ed.
       p.   cm.
    Includes bibliographical references and index.
    ISBN 0–13–636465–9
    1. Psychology, Industrial.   I. Schultz, Sydney Ellen.   II. Title.
HF5548.8.S356   1998
    158.7—DC21   97–24847
                                                           CIP

Editor in chief: Nancy Roberts
Acquisitions editor: Bill Webber
Assistant editor: Jennifer Hood
Production liaison: Fran Russello
Project manager: Marianne Hutchinson (Pine Tree Composition, Inc.)
Prepress and manufacturing buyer: Tricia Kenny
Cover design: Thomas Nery
Cover art: Jean-Pierre Stora, b. 1933. "Allees Pietonnieres." 1995. French.
Cover art photographer: The Grand Design/Superstock, Inc.
Director, Image Resource Center: Lori Morris-Nantz
Photo research supervisor: Melinda Reo
Image permission supervisor: Kay Dellosa
Photo researcher: Kathy Ringrose
Marketing manager: Michael Alread

This book was set in 10/12 Meridien by Pine Tree Composition, Inc.,
and was printed and bound by Courier Companies, Inc. The cover was printed
by Phoenix Color Corp.

© 1998 by Duane P. Schultz and Sydney Ellen Schultz

© Published by Prentice-Hall, Inc.
Simon & Schuster/A Viacom Company
Upper Saddle River, New Jersey 07458

Earlier editions, entitled *Psychology and Industry Today: An Introduction
to Industrial and Organizational Psychology,* copyright © 1973, 1977, and 1982
by Duane P. Schultz; copyright © 1986, 1990, and 1994 by Duane P. Schultz
and Sydney Ellen Schultz.

Printed in the United States of America
10 9 8 7 6 5 4 3 2 1

0-13-636465-9

PRENTICE-HALL INTERNATIONAL (UK) LIMITED, *London*
PRENTICE-HALL OF AUSTRALIA PTY, LIMITED, *Sydney*
PRENTICE-HALL CANADA INC., *Toronto*
PRENTICE-HALL HISPANOAMERICANA, S.A., *Mexico*
PRENTICE-HALL OF INDIA PRIVATE LIMITED, *New Delhi*
PRENTICE-HALL OF JAPAN, INC., *Tokyo*
SIMON & SCHUSTER ASIA PTE, LTD., *Singapore*
EDITORA PRENTICE-HALL DO BRASIL, LTDA., *Rio de Janeiro*

Brief Contents

PART FOUR

CHARACTERISTICS OF THE WORKPLACE 307

PART FIVE

ENGINEERING PSYCHOLOGY 405

PART SIX

CONSUMER PSYCHOLOGY 441

Contents

2 ■ Techniques, Tools, and Tactics   28

PART TWO

THE DEVELOPMENT OF HUMAN RESOURCES   55

3 ■ Employee Selection Principles and Techniques   57

4 ■ Psychological Testing   98

5 ■ Performance Appraisal   128

PART THREE

ORGANIZATIONAL PSYCHOLOGY   199

7 ■ Leadership   201

PART FOUR

CHARACTERISTICS OF THE WORKPLACE   307

10 ■ Working Conditions   309

11 ■ Safety, Violence, and Health in the Workplace   338

12 ■ Stress in the Workplace   371

Preface

Most of the students taking this course will work for some kind of organization. Many are already employed while attending college. Our goal in this book is to show them how industrial/organizational (I/O) psychology will directly influence their lives as job applicants, trainees, employees, managers and coordinators, and consumers. In brief, we are teaching students about the nature of work in modern society.

Our focus is on the practical and the applied rather than the scientific ideal. For example, we believe students must be introduced to topics such as training needs analysis, but they also should know that, in the reality of the workplace, training needs analyses are rarely conducted because organizations are reluctant to spend money on them.

It is important for students to learn about the major theories, models, research techniques, and findings of the science of I/O psychology, to develop an understanding of the aims and goals of the field. Students must also develop an awareness that I/O psychology in practice is often tempered by the conditions of modern organizational life. Therefore, we have chosen to discuss theories, methods, and findings within the framework of actual work situations and problems rather than as academic exercises.

Most of the research we cite deals with employees on the job, not college students performing simulated work tasks in the psychology department's laboratory. We describe I/O psychology programs in action, showing how they are developed and implemented in a variety of organizational settings with diverse groups of workers, operating in many countries throughout the world.

Thus, the seventh edition of *Psychology and Work Today* continues to present I/O psychology within the context in which work takes place. In this edition we recognize the changing composition of the work force (for example, the growing challenges of ethnic diversity), changing economic conditions, and the effects of technology on the nature and content of jobs as we approach the twenty-first century.

We have written this text primarily for students who are not psychology majors and who have little background in the field. These students make up the majority of the enrollment in courses in I/O psychology, business psychology, personnel psychology, and applied psychology in psychology departments and business schools at the community college, college, and university levels.

The changes in this edition mirror the dynamic nature of the field. All chapters have been rewritten, and several have been reorganized. More than 400 new research studies and theoretical articles have been incorporated.

Among the new topics are changing attitudes on affirmative action, impression management in selection and performance appraisal, biasing effects in interviews, selection testing for physical strength, the lack of racial or cultural bias in cognitive tests, race-banding of test scores to equalize hiring rates by race, the proactive personality, diversity training programs, the ineffectiveness of time-management training, the Golem effect, self-promotion and self-monitoring behaviors in leadership, derailment of managerial careers, accuracy of self-report absenteeism data, newcomer proactivity, resocialization, violence in the workplace, radioimmunoassay in drug testing, and the role of self-esteem and negative affectivity in stress.

Some of the current topics given expanded coverage are organizational recruitment of college seniors, realistic job previews, training disabled workers, biographical data in selection, face validity of psychological tests, the big five personality factors in selection, integrity tests, electronic performance monitoring, 360-degree feedback, pretraining characteristics of trainees, self-efficacy in training, transformational and charismatic leaders, the Pygmalion effect, management teams, sexual harassment, the relationship between job and life satisfaction, effects of layoffs, organizational commitment, labor unions, social loafing, day-care and elder-care programs, flexible scheduling, shift work, work-family conflicts, role ambiguity and stress, and burnout and workaholism.

The chapters include outlines, summaries, annotated reading lists, and key terms in boldface type. Definitions for the key terms are presented in the margins and are cumulated in a glossary at the back of the book. Chapters 3 to 14 contain case problems ("case in point"), which are brief descriptions of current on-the-job research to illustrate specific topics and research approaches. Critical thinking questions relating to the cases ask the students to analyze material from the chapter and are also suitable for class discussion and written assignments. Newsbreaks (a feature new to this edition) offer informal discussions of real-world job issues, such as job recruiting via the Internet, company liability for a dishonest letter of recommendation that results in workplace violence, virtual reality in training programs, privacy issues in company-sponsored E-mail networks, casual dress codes, anonymity in rating one's boss, and unequal pay for women and spouses. A test bank and instructor's manual is also available.

We would like to thank the many students and colleagues who took the time to write to us about the book and who offered suggestions for the new edition. In addition, several reviewers provided valuable and perceptive feedback on the manuscript, and we are most appreciative of their efforts. They include: Dr. Ladd Wheeler, University of Rochester; Dr. Diana Punzo, Earlham College; Dr. Keith Syrja, Owens Community College; and Dr. Nancy Gussett, Baldwin Wallace College.

Duane P. Schultz
Sydney Ellen Schultz

The Practice of Industrial/ Organizational Psychology

The work of industrial/organizational (I/O) psychologists will affect your attitudes, behaviors, and motivations on and off the job, whether you are seeking your first job, advancing in your career, or planning for your retirement. In Chapter 1 we review the scope of I/O psychology. In Chapter 2 we cover the research methods I/O psychologists use to collect data and draw conclusions and describe how psychologists apply their findings to problems of organizational life.

Principles, Practices, and Problems

CHAPTER 1

■   ■   ■   ■

WHAT I/O PSYCHOLOGY MEANS TO YOU

Would you work if you didn't have to? When you stop laughing, take a moment to think about it. Suppose, for example, you won $27 million in the state lottery. Would you still spend most of your adult life doing some kind of work 5 days a week? It may (or may not) surprise you to know that many people would—and do. We are not talking only about athletes and performers who continue playing and performing even though they have more than enough money on which to live comfortably for the rest of their lives. No, we are talking about people who do more traditional kinds of work.

Consider CEOs of large corporations, many of whom are paid more than $1 million a week! And yet they keep on working. Or venture capitalists or Wall Street wizards who make millions with a single deal and continue working the long hours they did before they became successful. Or software geniuses, such as Microsoft's Bill Gates, who start new companies and become immensely wealthy almost overnight. Gates, who may be the richest man in the United States, rarely takes a vacation and continues to work with the same driven intensity.

The same applies to many people in more ordinary kinds of jobs. When American, German, and Japanese employees were asked if they would continue to work even if they won a lottery and no longer needed the income from their jobs, 84% said they would (Quintanilla, 1990).

Clearly, many people get much more from their jobs than just a paycheck. Those who are fortunate enough to have found the kind of work most suited to their abilities experience a sense of personal satisfaction, fulfillment, and accomplishment that provides its own reward, distinct from the income they earn. Their work is related not only to economic well-being but also to their emotional security, self-esteem, and happiness.

Your career can offer a sense of identity and status, defining for you and for others who and what you are. Your job can give you the chance to learn new skills and master new challenges. It can bring social rewards, satisfying your need to belong to a group and providing the security that comes from being an ac-

Your work helps to define your identity and contributes to your sense of self-esteem.

cepted and valued member of a team. A job can furnish the opportunity to form friendships and to meet people of diverse backgrounds and interests.

On the other hand, work can be hazardous to your health. In addition to physical dangers in some work environments, the wrong kind of job can produce anxiety and frustration. If you are bored with your job, thwarted in your plans for advancement, or angry with your boss, you are likely to bring your discontent home at the end of the workday to influence your relationships with your family and friends.

These work-related stresses have been linked with physical and emotional health. Long-term research has found that the single greatest predictor of longevity is work satisfaction. Employees who are satisfied with their jobs tend to live longer than those who are dissatisfied with their jobs.

Selecting a job that is compatible with your interests, skills, and temperament is among the most significant decisions you will make in your life. For that reason, this course in industrial/organizational (I/O) psychology may be the most personally relevant of your college career. Regardless of the type of work you undertake or the kind of organization you join, you will find that I/O psychology will have an impact on your future from the day you approach the personnel office for an initial interview to the evening of your retirement dinner. The findings and practices of I/O psychologists, second to your own skills and motivation, will determine the position for which you are hired, the way you perform your job tasks, your rank and compensation, your level of responsibility, and the personal satisfaction you derive.

I/O Psychology and Your Job

I/O psychologists working in the area of employee selection help you initially in the difficult task of choosing a job. Your first formal contacts with I/O psychology outside the classroom are likely to be with the application blanks, interviews, psychological tests, and other selection measures I/O psychologists have devised to help employers determine whether you are the right person for the job and whether the job is the most suitable one for you.

After you have satisfied yourself and the organization about the appropriateness of the job, your advancement in the organization will depend on your performance in training programs and at work (evaluated by criteria developed by I/O psychologists) and on your performance on additional tests to determine your fitness for promotion. I/O psychologists have refined many techniques for evaluating and improving job performance.

Because of your college training, you may be qualified for management positions within the corporate hierarchy. Such positions require that you be aware of and sensitive to the diverse motivational and emotional factors that affect the people who work for you. To learn how to lead and motivate your subordinates and maintain their morale, you will need to be aware of I/O psychology research on these factors. You will probably participate in a training program established by psychologists to teach you to be an effective and responsible manager of the work of others.

Even if you have no direct subordinates—if you are an engineer, accountant, or technician, for example, working in a staff capacity—you should still master human relations skills. Knowing how to get along with others can mean the difference between success and failure.

You will want to see your employing organization grow and prosper so that it will continue to provide opportunities for employment and advancement. The company's output must be produced with as much efficiency and quality as possible. The physical plant, equipment, and working conditions must foster a productive working climate. I/O psychologists help design manufacturing and office environments to maximize efficiency and productivity. The product of a manufacturing concern must be advertised, packaged, and marketed to entice people to buy it. Psychologists play a role in all these activities.

At all levels of modern organizational life, psychologists provide essential services to employees and employers. Psychology applied to the world of work serves these two masters, you and your organization. It cannot benefit one without benefiting the other.

A note of caution, however. As vital as the field of I/O psychology is, as influential as it will be in your career, it is primarily a tool. And any tool is only as valuable as the skill of the person using it. If the methods and findings of I/O psychology are used improperly by management or are poorly understood by employees, they can do more harm than good. Proper use of this tool by competent managers and employees will profit everyone.

I/O Psychology and Your Daily Life

There is more to I/O psychology than its application to your life on the job. It also affects your attitudes and behaviors in other roles—for example, as consumer, voter, and driver. What governed your choice of toothpaste or breakfast cereal this morning? Most likely it was the psychological image created for the product, the attractiveness of the package, or the emotional need a particular brand is supposed to satisfy. Advertising tells us that we will be more popular or successful if we wear these jeans, use that cologne, or drive this car. Many of the people who identify and create these needs, and the ads and slogans to satisfy them, are psychologists.

Similar psychological techniques are used to promote and sell political candidates. Public opinion polling is used to inform political leaders about how people feel about various issues. Polling techniques are also used to determine ratings for television programs.

Psychologists assist engineers in the design and layout of displays and controls, such as those on the instrument panel of your car, to ensure that the controls are easy to use and that the visual displays are informative and easy to interpret. The shape and color of familiar highway signs resulted from I/O psychology research. Psychologists have designed aircraft cockpits, pushbutton telephones, microwave ovens, and computer monitors and keyboards to make them user-friendly and efficient.

The list of contributions I/O psychologists make to daily life is a long one. Because you are so affected by this field, both on and off the job, no matter where you are or what you do, you should know something about it—if only for self-defense.

WHAT I/O PSYCHOLOGY MEANS TO YOUR EMPLOYER

The services of I/O psychologists are used by organizations of so many different types and sizes because they work—they promote efficiency and contribute to corporate profits. Consider the problem of employee absenteeism. Workers who fail to show up cost the company money. Techniques devised and applied by psychologists to reduce absenteeism can bring substantial savings. A Canadian bank with 30,000 employees estimated that it saved $7 million in 1 year by heeding a psychologist's advice to install a computerized absentee reporting system. The psychologist's consulting fee and the cost of the system were considerably less than the amount saved.

Another costly problem in organizations is turnover. When employees quit, the company loses the investment it made in selecting and training them, and it must then hire and train replacements. At one financial brokerage house, the loss for each employee who quit was $7,000. An I/O psychologist studied the problem and suggested ways to deal with the factors that led to the high incidence of quitting. Reducing turnover by 10% saved the company in excess of $100,000 a year.

Enhancing job satisfaction is a major concern of I/O psychologists. Improving the attitudes of the work force toward their jobs and their employers can reduce grievances and other labor disputes, and it can decrease absenteeism, tardiness, turnover, work slowdowns, shoddy products, and accidents.

Appropriate personnel selection methods, designed and monitored by I/O psychologists, help to ensure that the most qualified applicants are hired. A study dealing with white-collar civil service jobs in the federal government compared employees hired on the basis of their scores on intelligence or cognitive ability tests with those hired on the basis of their level of education and work experience. The tests were found to be far superior in selecting the better and more productive employees. The increase in productivity of those selected by their test scores was valued at $8 billion over a 13-year period. Adding the tests to the overall selection program resulted in a 61% decrease in the number of poor employees hired (Schmidt, Hunter, Outerbridge, & Trattner, 1986).

In the 1980s, the Federal Aviation Administration (FAA) was forced to recruit and train thousands of air traffic controllers quickly to replace those fired because of a strike. Research by I/O psychologists showed that job applicants up to the age of 35 could be successfully trained to perform the demanding work. The previous age limit had been 30. The psychologists also found that the training program for new air traffic controllers could be reduced from 4 to 2 years, with no detrimental effects. By increasing the pool of prospective candidates and cutting the training time in half, the agency was soon able to meet the demand for this essential service.

These are only a few examples of the impact of the activities of I/O psychologists, how they contribute to the efficiency of the organization and enhance or improve the bottom line on the financial report. We remind you that the practice of I/O psychology is also of enormous benefit to you as an employee. When you are matched with the right job and when your work is meaningful and satisfying, everyone benefits.

THE NATURE OF I/O PSYCHOLOGY

I/O psychology The application of the methods, facts, and principles of the science of psychology to people at work.

Psychology is the science of behavior and mental or cognitive processes. **Industrial/organizational psychology** involves the application of the methods, facts, and principles of psychology to people at work. The fact that psychology is a science tells us how it operates. A science deals with observable facts that can be seen, heard, touched, measured, and recorded. Hence, a science is empirical, which means that it relies on verifiable observation, experimentation, and experience, not on opinions, hunches, pet notions, or private prejudices. A science is objective in its approaches and results.

It is important to remember that a science is defined by its methods, not by its subject matter. In its methods and procedures, I/O psychology attempts to be just as scientific as physics or chemistry. When psychologists observe the behavior of people at work, they do so in the best traditions of science: objectively, dispassionately, and systematically.

Because the method of the science of psychology is objective, so must be the focus of its observation. Psychologists observe overt human behavior—our movements, speech, and creative works—to understand and analyze the people they are studying. These behaviors are the only aspects of human existence that can be objectively seen, heard, measured, and recorded. Something more must be involved, however, because psychology is also the science of cognitive processes. Psychologists study intangible human aspects such as motivations, emotions, perceptions, thoughts, and feelings. These facets of our subjective inner life cannot be observed directly.

We cannot see motivation, for example. It is an internal driving force inaccessible to observation. How, then, can psychologists know anything about human motives, drives, or needs? Although it is true that motivation cannot be seen, its effects can be observed. An angry person exhibits overt behaviors such as a flushed face, rapid breathing, and clenched fists. A person with a high need to achieve behaves differently from a person with a low need to achieve, whether on the job, at a party, or in a psychology experiment.

We cannot see intelligence directly, but we can observe the overt behavioral manifestations of different levels of intelligence. Psychologists can objectively record that one person performs at a higher level than another on a test of cognitive abilities and can then infer that the first person possesses greater intelligence. Inference based on observed behavior enables us to draw conclusions regarding human states or conditions, even when we cannot see them directly.

This is how I/O psychologists function. They observe the behavior of employees on the job under well-controlled and systematic conditions. They record behavioral responses, such as the number of parts produced each hour, the number of keystrokes per minute, or the quality of managerial decisions made. They vary the conditions under which a job is performed and measure any resulting differences in performance. They use these and other techniques to seek a better understanding of human behavior, but overall they subscribe to the scientific method and observe. They look, listen, measure, and record with objectivity and precision.

A BRIEF HISTORY OF I/O PSYCHOLOGY

I/O psychology was formed and fashioned of necessity. The urgency of a practical problem needing a solution gave the initial impetus to the field, and the demands of crisis and need have continued to stimulate its growth and influence.

Early Pioneers

Industrial psychology had its formal beginning in the early years of the 20th century. The honor for sparking the development of the field is usually given to Walter Dill Scott (1869–1955). A college football player at Northwestern University, Scott graduated from a theological seminary, intending to be a missionary in China. By the time he was prepared to undertake this calling, however, he learned that there were no vacancies for missionaries in China. And so he became a psychologist instead.

Scott was the first to apply psychology to advertising, personnel selection, and management issues. In 1901 he spoke out on the potential uses of psychology in advertising. Encouraged by the response of the advertising industry, he wrote several articles and published a book entitled *The Theory and Practice of Advertising* (Scott, 1903), which is generally considered to be the first book about psychology applied to an aspect of the business world. In 1919 Scott formed the first consulting company in industrial psychology, providing services to more than 40 major corporations, primarily in the area of personnel selection.

In 1913, Hugo Münsterberg (1863–1916), a German psychologist teaching at Harvard University, wrote *The Psychology of Industrial Efficiency*. Münsterberg was an early advocate of the use of psychological tests to select employees. He conducted considerable research in real-world work situations and workplaces, with the goal of improving efficiency on the job. His writing, research, and consulting activities helped spread the influence of industrial psychology, and he became a celebrity, America's most famous psychologist of the day. A charismatic figure, Münsterberg befriended kings, presidents, and movie stars and was one of only two psychologists ever accused of being a spy (Spillman & Spillman, 1993).

World War I and the Testing Movement

The work of Scott and Münsterberg provided a beginning for the field, but it was the request of the U.S. Army during World War I that marked the emergence of industrial psychology as an important and useful discipline. Faced with the task of screening and classifying millions of recruits for military service, the army commissioned psychologists to devise a test to identify persons of low intelligence so that they could be eliminated from consideration for training programs. Two tests resulted from their efforts, the Army Alpha, for recruits who could read and write, and the Army Beta, which used mazes, pictures, and symbols for persons who could not read. The Army Beta was also suitable for immigrants who were not fluent in the English language.

Additional tests were prepared for selecting candidates for officer and pilot training and for other military classifications that required special abilities. A personality test, the Personal Data Sheet, suitable for administering to large groups, was developed to detect neuroses among the army recruits.

After the war, businesses, school systems, and other organizations that needed to screen and classify large numbers of persons clamored for more and better testing techniques. The tests used by the army were adapted for civilian use, and new ones were designed for a variety of situations. Enthusiasm for psychological testing spread throughout the United States. Soon, millions of schoolchildren and job applicants were faced with batteries of psychological tests. Thus, the initial contributions of industrial psychologists focused on issues of personnel selection—evaluating individuals and placing them in the appropriate grades or jobs.

The Hawthorne Studies

The scope of the field broadened considerably in 1924 with the commencement of a now-famous series of studies. Called the **Hawthorne studies** because they were conducted at the Hawthorne, Illinois, plant of the Western Electric Company, this long-term research program took industrial psychology beyond employee selection and placement to the more complex problems of interpersonal relations, motivation, and organizational issues (Roethlisberger & Dickson, 1939).

Hawthorne studies A long-term research program at the Hawthorne, Illinois, Western Electric Company plant that illustrated the influence of managerial and organizational factors on employee behavior.

The research began as a straightforward investigation of the effects of the physical work environment on employee efficiency. The researchers asked such questions as: What is the effect on productivity if we increase the lighting in the workroom? Do temperature and humidity levels affect production? What will happen if management provides rest periods for the workers?

The results of the Hawthorne studies surprised the investigators and the plant managers. They found that social and psychological factors in the work environment were of potentially greater importance than physical factors. For example, changing the level of illumination in a workroom from very bright to dim did not diminish worker efficiency. More subtle factors were operating to induce these workers to maintain their original production level under nearly dark conditions.

With another group of workers, lighting was increased and production levels rose. The researchers made other changes—rest periods, free lunches, a shorter workday—and with the introduction of each change, production increased. However, when all the benefits were suddenly eliminated, production continued to increase! The researchers concluded that the physical aspects of the work environment were not as important to the employees as management had assumed.

The Hawthorne studies opened up new areas for psychologists to explore, such as the nature of supervision, the formation of informal groups among workers, employee attitudes toward their jobs, communication patterns, and other managerial and organizational variables now recognized as influences on efficiency, motivation, and job satisfaction.

Although the Hawthorne studies have been criticized for a lack of scientific rigor, there is no denying their impact on the way psychologists view the nature of work and on the scope and direction of I/O psychology.

World War II and Continued Growth

World War II brought more than 2,000 psychologists directly into the war effort. Their major contribution was the testing, classifying, and training of millions of recruits in various branches of military service. Complex skills were required to operate sophisticated aircraft, tanks, and ships, and it was necessary to identify persons capable of learning these skills.

The increasingly complex weapons of war sparked the development of a new field: engineering psychology. Working closely with engineers, these psychologists supplied information on human capacities and limitations for operating high-speed aircraft, submarines, and other equipment, and thus influenced their design.

I/O psychology achieved greater stature as a result of these contributions to the war effort. Government and industry leaders recognized that psychologists were equipped to solve many practical business problems. The experience also demonstrated to many psychologists, who before the war had worked in the isolation of their university laboratories, that there were vital and challenging problems in the real world to which they could contribute solutions.

The growth of I/O psychology since the end of World War II in 1945 has paralleled the growth of American business and technical enterprise. The size and complexity of modern organizations has placed additional demands on the skills of I/O psychologists. New technologies meant that employees needed training in new skills. The advent of computers, for example, generated the need for programmers and technical support personnel and changed the way many jobs were performed. Psychologists had to determine the abilities needed for these new jobs, the kinds of persons possessing these abilities, and the best ways to identify and train them.

The demands on engineering psychologists also increased. Supersonic aircraft, missiles, and complex weapons systems required extra preparation and training for safe and efficient operation. In addition, engineering psychologists became involved in the design of industrial robots, high-tech office equipment, and the redesign of work spaces for today's automated operations.

Organizational issues also assumed greater importance (the "O" side of I/O psychology). Human relations skills have been recognized by managers and executives as vital to maintaining the job performance of their employees. The nature of leadership, the role of motivation and job satisfaction, the impact of the organizational structure and climate, and the processes of decision making are being analyzed. In recognition of the significance of organizational variables, the Division of Industrial Psychology of the American Psychological Association (APA) became the Society for Industrial and Organizational Psychology (SIOP).

THE FUTURE OF I/O PSYCHOLOGY

The changing nature of work today, together with technological advances and population changes, will alter the nature of work in our future. Any change in the way people work means new demands and responsibilities for I/O psychologists. One such change relates to the kinds and numbers of jobs that will be available.

The Continuing Loss of Jobs

Consider the statistics. Between 1978 and 1987, employment in the American automobile industry declined by 23%. Among the nation's leading corporations, the Fortune 500, nearly 3 million jobs were lost in the 1980s. Many of these positions were eliminated because the kind of work they involved was not needed. By 1992, American companies were laying off workers at the rate of 2,200 a day. Organizations can no longer be relied on to show a long-term concern for their employees.

Overall, more than 7 million American workers lost their jobs between 1987 and 1995, and those jobs were not just lost temporarily; they are gone for good as a result of changing technology and new ways of organizing and performing work. The financial and emotional costs to those who lose their jobs is staggering. Quoting several well-known business sources, I/O psychologist Wayne Cascio wrote:

> Laid-off workers who must return to the job market often must take huge pay cuts. Downward mobility is the rule rather than the exception. . . . Of roughly 2,000 workers let go by RJR Nabisco, for example, 72% found jobs subsequently but at wages that averaged only 47% of their previous pay. . . . [T]he bottom line for most reemployed workers is that both their spending power and their standards of living have dropped (Cascio, 1995, p. 929).

The problem exists not only among blue-collar workers. Downsizing has also hit the ranks of management. Beginning in the late 1980s and continuing through the 1990s, more than 5 million middle-level managers lost their jobs as companies merged, downsized, or "rightsized" to reduce their management ranks in an effort to become more competitive and cost-effective. Between 1990 and 1995 alone, more than 1.4 million executives, high-level managers, and administrative and staff professionals were laid off as companies downsized their work force (Church, 1995a).

Not even large employers such as AT&T, IBM, and Sears continued to offer the degree of job security that used to characterize management positions. In 1991, nearly 500,000 managers earning more than $40,000 a year were laid off. More than half of these men and women were forced to accept pay cuts of up to 50% in order to get a new job (Cameron, Freeman, & Mishra, 1991).

Changes in the Nature of the Job

The way in which business today conducts its business, in those jobs that remain and in the new jobs being created, is changing drastically. Different challenges and responsibilities face the employees of today and tomorrow. As we approach a new century, a great deal of work, and the way it is performed, is new. Those revolutionary changes are occurring at both blue-collar and white-collar levels.

The days when a worker was taught how to perform a single job, and told to keep doing it that way without question, are disappearing. Key words in today's workplace are "empowerment," "involvement," and "worker participation." Workers are expected to learn and master not a single job but a cluster of skills, which must be continually upgraded, and to participate in determining how work is best carried out. Workers may operate in teams, assuming increasing responsibility for their part in the production process, even including hiring new workers.

This empowering and involvement of workers necessarily changes the way managers perform their jobs. No longer can they rule by command, telling their employees what to do and when and how to do it. Now they function more as guides and mentors than traditional leaders. These changes require substantial adjustments for workers and managers, and are, in part, a response to technological change in the workplace.

New Technology in the Workplace

A radical change in the workplace stems from advances in microelectronics—in word processors, computers, and industrial robots. Work environments large and small have become automated, with advanced equipment assuming functions once performed by humans. The majority of office workers today use some sort of word-processing or data-processing equipment that eliminates clerical jobs requiring lower-level skills. Overall, more than 50 million workers now must be technically proficient in a host of equipment, systems, and procedures unknown to previous generations of employees. Computers, faxes, modems, cell phones, E-mail, the Internet, and the World Wide Web, for example, have changed the functions of many jobs and created others that never existed before.

These electronic advances are causing major dislocations in the nature of work and the knowledge, skills, and abilities workers are increasingly required to possess. A poll of the Communication Workers of America union found that 78% reported that technological change had vastly increased the skill requirements for their jobs (Cascio, 1993). As a result, there are steadily decreasing job opportunities for unskilled and illiterate persons.

New Skill Levels in the Workplace

With the reduction in manufacturing jobs and the demands of modern technology, there are fewer places in which poorly educated men and women can find

Soon, the U.S. work force will include more older workers than at any time in its history.

work. As many as 25 million Americans over the age of 17 are functionally illiterate and do not have sufficient skills to fill out an application blank for a job. Basic math skills are also lacking. One study showed that when a group of 21- to 25-year-olds were confronted with the task of calculating the change due from a two-item restaurant bill, no more than 34% of whites, 20% of Hispanics, and 8% of blacks could do so correctly.

From an employer's standpoint, it is increasingly difficult to recruit entry-level workers who have sufficient basic skills to learn how to perform many jobs. A telecommunications company in the northeastern United States had to interview and test 90,000 job applicants to find 2,000 who could be trained for a job that did not even require a high school diploma. General Motors found that workers who lacked reading, writing, and math skills had difficulty completing the training programs the company provided every few years to acquaint the employees with new manufacturing processes.

Diversity in the Workplace

Another change in the nature of the work force relates to demographics, to the changing nature of the population. The work force as a whole is aging. The baby-boom generation, born between 1946 and 1965, has been in the work force for many years. By the beginning of the new century, the United States will have more older workers than at any time in its history. Half the work force—more than 35 million people—will be over the age of 35.

A second demographic factor involves a shift in the ethnic composition of the work force. In the 1980s, minority employees accounted for 15% of the work force. By the year 2005, persons of African, Asian, and Hispanic heritage will constitute 35% of all new workers. Further, half of all new employees will be women (Hartel, 1994). White men workers today increasingly foresee themselves as becoming a minority. Organizations must become increasingly sensitive to the needs and concerns of a diverse work force.

Up to 800,000 immigrants enter the United States every year. Most of them are eager to work, but they lack English-language training and other literacy skills and are unfamiliar with corporate work habits. This presents an additional challenge to organizations of the future.

Challenges for I/O Psychology

All these changes in the workplace and the composition of the work force pose challenges for I/O psychologists in selecting and training workers, re-designing jobs and equipment, refining management practices to raise employee motivation, dealing with employee health and safety, and marketing goods and services. Thus, the needs and job opportunities for the services of I/O psychologists are certain to grow. "These challenges provide an exciting agenda with large potential payoffs for individuals, organizations, and society as psychology moves into the 21st century" (Cascio, 1995, p. 938). In addition, these opportunities suggest it is an exciting time to consider a career as an I/O psychologist.

BECOMING AN I/O PSYCHOLOGIST

Although few people believe that they are qualified to be physicists, chemists, or biologists after taking one or two courses, many people consider themselves expert psychologists even when they have had no formal training. Some think that the practice of psychology requires nothing more than common sense and a lot of time interacting with other people. This will no more make you a psychologist, however, than years of taking medicines will make you a physician.

Modern I/O psychology is a complex and demanding profession that requires university training, practical experience, and continuing study to keep aware of new developments. The minimum requirement for working as an I/O psychologist is a master's degree, which usually requires 42 semester hours and takes 2 1/2 years to complete. Most master's degree students work fulltime or parttime while in school (Lowe, 1993). Of all the graduate degrees granted in I/O psychology each year, approximately 67% are at the master's level (Koppes, 1991).

NEWSBREAK #1

Psychology Makes Top 10 of the Nation's Hottest Careers

The field of psychology is now one of the hottest career choices in America, according to a study released by the United States Department of Labor. The employment opportunities for psychologists are expected to grow faster than the average for all occupations, as projected for the period 1992–2005.

Job choices will be greatest for people with doctoral degrees in several areas, including school, clinical, counseling, health, and I/O psychology. Opportunities for master's-level psychologists are also expected to increase, particularly in government and business. So if you're looking for a hot career, here are the top ten choices.

Job	Percentage of Growth
Systems analyst	110
Physical therapist	88
Paralegal	86
Special-education teacher	74
Radiologic technologist	63
Psychologist	48
Data processing equipment repairer	45
Food service, lodging manager	44
Registered nurse	42
Veterinary-care technician	38

Source: E. Burnette, Psychology makes top 10 of country's hottest careers. *APA Monitor*, November 1994, p. 10.

A survey of I/O master's degree graduates showed that almost all found professional jobs in their specialty areas at competitive salaries in industry, government, consulting firms, research organizations, and universities. Their most marketable skills were in the areas of psychological test and survey construction and validation, personnel selection and placement, performance appraisal, fair employment practices, and employee training. Course work in motivation, job satisfaction, and organizational development were also found to be useful on the job (Erffmeyer & Mendel, 1990). Thus, a master's degree program in I/O psychology provides valuable training for a productive and rewarding career. The higher positions in corporations and universities, however, are typically held by psychologists who have earned a doctoral degree, which requires from 3 to 5 years of graduate study.

The number of graduate students in the field is continuing to grow, with the bulk of the increase being among students at the master's level. Although the number of I/O psychologists rose by 24% in the 1980s, the rate of growth may not keep pace with the increasing demand for I/O psychology services as we approach the year 2000 (Jeanneret, 1991).

A 1992–1993 survey of graduate psychology departments in the United States and Canada found a decrease in the number of applicants for graduate training in psychology in all areas except I/O psychology. At both master's and doctoral levels, the researchers found increases in applications to I/O programs, compared to the periods 1970–1971 and 1979–1980 (Norcross, Hanych, & Terranova, 1996).

The training requirements for a career in I/O psychology are difficult, but the rewards can be great. Career opportunities are excellent, and the salaries are substantial. I/O psychologists have higher salaries than any other group of psychologists. In 1994, the average income for I/O psychologists with doctoral degrees in the United States exceeded $97,000 a year. The top 10% in the field reported annual incomes greater than $150,000. For master's-degree I/O psychologists, the mean income was more than $71,000, with the top 10% earning over $125,000 (Zickar & Taylor, 1996).

In addition, the rewards of stimulating work, challenging responsibility, and continuing intellectual growth for I/O psychologists are also notable. As one leading I/O psychologist commented, it is a field in which "you can make things happen. You put in a program, and you see some results. You might see better people selected, or job satisfaction go up, or turnover go down. But you've made something happen, and that's a very exciting kind of reward."

WORKING AS AN I/O PSYCHOLOGIST

I/O psychologists work in business, industry, government agencies, service organizations, consulting firms, and universities. Many of the psychologists who teach courses in I/O psychology also undertake research and consulting activities. A survey of 647 members of the Society for Industrial and Organizational Psychology (SIOP) found that 77% of those with academic positions spent time consulting to organizations and dealing with practical, real-world problems (Borman & Cox, 1996).

The various employment settings of I/O psychologists are shown in Figure 1–1. Employment opportunities for I/O psychologists, as reflected in exam-

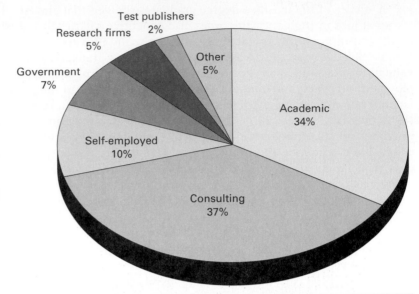

FIGURE 1–1. Employment settings of I/O psychologists. (Data from survey of SIOP members. W. C. Borman & G. L. Cox, "Who's doing what: Patterns in the practice of I/O psychology." *The Industrial-Organizational Psychologist*, 1996, 33(4), 21.)

ples of the variety of job titles, responsibilities, and organizations, are shown in Table 1–1.

Smaller organizations that cannot afford a full-time I/O psychologist rely on the services of consulting psychologists who are employed on a contract basis to fill a specific need. Consultants may evaluate candidates for employment, design a piece of equipment or an assembly line, establish a training program, conduct a survey on consumer acceptance of a new product, or try to determine why productivity in the office is declining. The value of consulting services lies not only in the technical skills I/O psychologists can apply to a problem but also in the freshness of approach and objectivity that an outsider can bring to the company.

Some specialty areas in I/O psychology are shown in Table 1–2. The majority of I/O psychologists deal with employee selection and placement and with problems of leadership and organizational development.

Almost half the I/O psychologists earning PhDs today are women. There has been a higher rate of increase in the number of women earning PhDs in I/O psychology than in any other specialty, including clinical psychology (Koppes, Landy, & Perkins, 1993). In 1973, 9.2% of women psychologists worked in business. By 1991, 39% of women psychologists had found employment as I/O psychologists (Pion et al., 1996).

Despite intensive efforts to recruit minority graduate students, blacks and Hispanics account for fewer than 4% of I/O psychologists. Most minority graduate students choose to specialize in clinical psychology.

I/O psychologists constitute more than 7% of the membership of the American Psychological Association, and they are affiliated primarily with four divisions: the Society for Industrial and Organizational Psychology, the division of Military Psychology, the Society of Engineering Psychologists, and the division of Consumer Psychology. A growing number of academic, scientific, and research-oriented psychologists are affiliated with the newer American Psychological Society, founded in 1988.

TABLE 1-1   Places of Employment and Job Responsibilities of Selected
I/O Psychologists

Human Resources Consulting Firm
Test development and validation, interview training, assessment center design,
 performance appraisal system design, career development programs, attitude surveys.

**Market Research, Consulting, and Promotional Services Firm, Marketing
 Research Project Director**
Apply social science research skills to proposal development, analysis, writing, and
 presentation.

International Airline, Assessment Center Specialist for Overseas Development
Coordinate and supervise assessment center for evaluation of employees being considered
 for promotion: Develop assessment materials, make recommendations to improve
 effectiveness, select and train staff to become qualified assessors.

Management Consulting Firm, Senior Level Manager
Oversee projects involving the systems approach to training, training technologies, and
 management/career development training.

Human Resource Research and Consulting Associates, I/O Project Manager
Work with interdisciplinary staff (psychologists, sociologists, computer science specialists,
 and educators) on information systems, test development, survey design, and equal
 employment issues, including providing expert witness testimony in selected court
 cases.

Employee Decisions Consulting Firm, Director of Human Resources
Provide services in counseling, coaching executive candidates for job interviews,
 assessment and test interpretation, and career development.

Pharmaceutical Firm, Manager of Psychological Services
Design psychological strategies for employee testing and job analysis, assess legal
 considerations in hiring, research and recommend changes in corporate compensation
 procedures, develop and monitor performance appraisal practices.

**Public Utility (Gas and Electric Company), Executive Consultant in Organization
 Planning and Development**
Work with unions, line operations, human resource departments, and senior
 management groups to redesign human resource systems and implement major
 organizational changes.

Electronics Corporation, Team Leadership and Communication Trainer
Implement self-directed production work teams: Train workers in manufacturing team
 concepts, problem-solving techniques, leadership development, communications, and
 cooperative decision making. Monitor and evaluate programs and document results.

Telecommunications Company, Human Resource Research Intern
Predoctoral internship for person admitted to doctoral candidacy at accredited university
 to conduct research on human resource programs while working with licensed I/O
 psychologists and human resource professionals.

State College, Assistant Professor of Psychology
Teach courses in organizational behavior, group processes, tests and measurements; direct
 undergraduate research projects.

TABLE 1–2 Specialty Areas of I/O Psychologists (percentage)

Employee selection	37%
Organizational development	36
Attitude surveys	29
Performance appraisal	27
Outplacement	5
Engineering psychology	4
Consumer psychology	2

Data from W. C. Borman & G. L. Cox, "Who's doing what: Patterns in the practice of I/O psychology." *The Industrial-Organizational Psychologist*, 1996, *33*(4), p. 23.

PROBLEMS OF I/O PSYCHOLOGY

No field of study is free of internal or external problems. I/O psychologists face several difficulties, all aggravated by the very factor that has made the field so successful, namely, the demand for its services.

Quacks and Frauds

More than any other science, psychology has been victimized by quackery—the illicit and fraudulent practice of psychology by persons who have little or no professional training. This problem is particularly apparent in clinical and counseling psychology, where untrained charlatans can do great harm to emotionally disturbed persons who are seeking help.

Quackery also affects I/O psychology. One I/O psychologist noted:

> A major complication in the lives of psychologists in business is the ill-trained or unscrupulous person who offers psychological-type services to companies. . . . Some of the most difficult situations I have had to cope with in my career have resulted from the actions of pseudopsychologists who have captured the ears of high-level managers (Tenopyr, 1992, p. 175).

An uninformed business organization can be just as gullible as an individual. Unethical consulting firms have sold their so-called services to industry and made quick money—and a quicker getaway—before the company realized it had been duped. Not only is such unethical behavior dangerous and unfair to business—consider, for example, all the competent people who were not hired for a job because they performed poorly on the quack's phony test—but it is also harmful to psychology as a science and profession. If a company is damaged by the charlatan's actions, the field as a whole receives the blame. The executives of an organization defrauded in the past will be reluctant to consider psychological services in the future.

The Importance of Proper Credentials

The problem of the phony practitioner is being reduced in clinical psychology because states now license or certify psychologists in the same way they license physicians. It is illegal for persons to represent themselves to the public as psychologists or to use any of the tools of psychology unless they have met the licensing or certification requirements, usually a PhD degree and satisfactory performance on an exam covering knowledge of all areas of psychology, not just the one in which the applicant is working.

These procedures were established specifically to protect the public from charlatans in the areas of clinical and counseling psychology. The question of licensing I/O psychologists is controversial within the profession. Although some 40% of the members of SIOP are licensed, SIOP takes the position that they need not be (Howard, 1990).

An organization must exercise care when seeking the services of a psychologist. It is not enough to flip through the Yellow Pages of the telephone book. The educational and professional qualifications of anyone called a psychologist must be examined carefully.

Communication

All sciences develop a specialized technical jargon that its members use to communicate with one another. This vocabulary is sometimes not understood by those outside the discipline. Because I/O psychologists must work closely with people who are not psychologists—the managers and employees of an organization—they must make the effort to communicate clearly their ideas, plans, and research results. The recommendations of I/O psychologists will be of no value to an organization if they cannot be comprehended. The reports will be filed in the nearest wastebasket. Psychologists must be able to present their contributions in a way that can be understood.

The Reluctance to Try Something New

This problem might be called, "I've always done it this way, and I'm not about to change now." Psychologists who work in business and industry often meet this attitude—a resistance to change, an unwillingness to try something new. When an I/O psychologist recommends a change in the usual way of performing a job, it is sometimes viewed by the workers as a threat. Employees who are told to alter their work habits to conform to the potentially more efficient system proposed by the psychologist may actively resist because they believe that the company is trying to get them to work harder for the same pay. Insecure workers may also feel that the company is criticizing their past job performance. This resistance to change is a serious problem at all levels, from the worker on the assembly line to the CEO at corporate headquarters.

If the findings of I/O psychologists are to have any positive impact, they must have the support of the managers and employees who will be affected by them. Psychologists need the cooperation of those employees whose jobs will be changed. They must show considerable human relations skills, patience, and persuasiveness in addition to their technical expertise.

Research or Application?

The question of research versus application continues to concern I/O psychologists in their relations with management. Some managers complain that too little of the research published in I/O psychology journals is oriented toward the practical, real-world problems with which they deal every day. Although it is true that much academic research may appear to have no immediate application or usefulness, psychologists who work directly for organizations know that the two functions, research and application, are interdependent. Without research, there would be no reliable information to apply to critical problems on the job. This point is often overlooked by managers who demand immediate solutions to specific problems and who cannot understand the hesitation of the psychologist who tells them that the answer can come only from research.

The conflict between research and application arises because organizations often need prompt answers. Production schedules and contract deadlines do not always wait for the design and execution of a research study. Managers facing time constraints may have unrealistic expectations and become impatient when the company psychologist—their so-called expert on human behavior—cannot provide a quick fix.

We are not suggesting that whenever I/O psychologists are asked a question, they run to the laboratory to begin a month-long experiment. The history of psychology provides a wealth of empirical data about human behavior in a variety of situations, and well-trained psychologists often apply these findings to specific problems in the workplace. The value of these data, however, depends on the similarity between the situations in which they were obtained and the present situation.

For example, studies about how college sophomores learn complex material are not as relevant to the learning abilities of employees in a chemical company as is research conducted on the learning abilities of employees in a steel company. The steel company research, performed in a more similar work setting, will probably provide the more useful results. But a learning study conducted in another chemical company will be even more applicable. And a study conducted on the very workers whose learning habits are in question will be the most useful of all.

Sometimes, of course, circumstances do not allow sufficient time or resources for research to be undertaken. Consider the following advice from *The Industrial-Organizational Psychologist:*

> *You can't research every question.* While it is desirable to have a body of research to support your actions, it is not always possible. When you find yourself having to make a decision in the absence of research, you have to take what you know about similar situations and use your own judgment (Campbell, 1996, p. 103).

Properly devised research can be of immense value to an organization's productive efficiency, but the exigencies of the workplace often call for compromise, patience, and understanding by both managers and psychologists. The fundamental question is not research versus application but research plus application. The two functions are compatible and complementary.

AREAS OF I/O PSYCHOLOGY

We have noted how I/O psychology affects many aspects of the relationship between you and your work. We describe here the specific interests of I/O psychologists that are covered in the following chapters.

The Tools and Techniques of Science (Chapter 2)

Psychologists study human behavior through the tools and techniques of science. To understand their work, we must have some acquaintance with the ways in which they perform research, analyze data, and draw conclusions.

Recruiting and Selecting Employees (Chapters 3 and 4)

Despite the opinion of some executives and personnel managers that they can judge job applicants by a handshake, eye contact, or the style of their clothing, selecting and evaluating employees are complex processes that continue long after initial recruitment and hiring. Throughout your career, questions of promotion and salary increases will arise. Many of the selection devices, such as interviews and psychological tests, that were used in making your first hiring decision will also be applied to these subsequent career decisions. Thus, it is important for you to understand the selection process. It is also to your advantage that your potential employer use the most valid techniques available. Improper matching of the person and the job can lead to inefficiency and dissatisfaction for employer and employee.

Evaluating Employee Performance (Chapter 5)

The periodic evaluation of the quality of your job performance will continue throughout your working career. Promotions, pay increases, transfers, and dismissals will be based on these appraisals. It is vital that these decisions be made as fairly and objectively as possible and not be based on the personal likes and dislikes of your supervisor. I/O psychologists have devised methods of appraisal for many types of jobs. Because your future depends on these appraisals, it is important that your company have a fair and appropriate system for evaluating your performance.

Employee Training and Development (Chapter 6)

Virtually every new employee receives some sort of job training. Inexperienced workers must be taught the specific operations they are expected to perform and may also need training in good work habits. Experienced workers who change jobs must be taught the policies and procedures of their new employer. Workers whose jobs are altered by changing technology require retraining. As the machinery of production and the dynamics of organizational life become more complex, the demands made on employees to learn and on employers to teach increase in scope and significance.

Organizational Leadership (Chapter 7)

One of industry's greatest challenges is selecting, training, and developing effective leaders. The problem is of concern to you for two reasons: (1) as an employee you will work under a supervisor or manager, and your efficiency and satisfaction will be affected by his or her leadership style, and (2) because most business leaders today come from the ranks of the college educated, you will most likely serve at some level of management in the course of your career.

Psychologists are concerned with the abilities of leaders in various situations and the effects of different leadership styles on subordinates. It is necessary to the continuing growth of any organization that its most competent people be placed in positions of leadership and that they exercise their skills in the most effective manner.

Motivation, Job Satisfaction, and Job Involvement (Chapter 8)

Vital to the efficiency of any organization are the motivations of its employees, the satisfactions they receive from their work, and the extent of their commitment to the company. Motivation, satisfaction, and involvement are affected by many aspects of the work environment, such as the quality of leadership, advancement opportunities, job security, and characteristics of the physical and psychological work climate.

Negative aspects of a job can produce undesirable effects, such as absenteeism, turnover, low productivity, frequent accidents, and labor grievances. I/O psychologists work to identify and modify conditions that can impair the quality of working life before they have serious psychological and economic consequences for employees and employers.

Organizational Psychology (Chapter 9)

Few people work in isolation. Whether our work is in a classroom, a department store, or a steel mill, it takes place within a particular organizational climate or culture. This culture includes the formal structure and policies of the organization, the nature of its leadership, and the informal groups that arise among workers, groups that may dictate norms and standards at variance with those imposed by the organization.

Working Conditions (Chapter 10)

The physical aspects of the work environment were the first to be studied by I/O psychologists. Much research was conducted on lighting, temperature, noise, workspace design, and working hours. Later, attention shifted to more complex social and psychological conditions of work. A job's psychological climate, including factors such as fatigue and boredom, may be more important than the physical climate because psychological effects are subject to greater individual variation.

Employee Safety and Health (Chapter 11)

In addition to the tragic physical and personal consequences of industrial accidents, economic losses cost organizations billions of dollars in lost work hours, employee compensation, and the expense of hiring and training new workers. Because the majority of accidents are caused by human error, the work of I/O psychologists is crucial in reducing the accident toll. Psychologists are also involved in efforts to deal with alcohol and drug use on the job, and with violence in the workplace.

Stress in the Workplace (Chapter 12)

Job-induced stress has widespread effects on physical and mental health. It can interfere with job performance and lead to serious illness. Many organizations attempt to deal with the effects of stress through counseling programs and by redesigning jobs to be less stressful.

Engineering Psychology (Chapter 13)

The design of the tools and equipment needed to perform a job is directly related to the physical work environment, to employee motivation and morale, and to job safety. As the machinery of the manufacturing, transportation, and service industries becomes more complex, so do the demands placed on the human operators of this equipment. It is the job of the engineering psychologist to ensure the best working relationship between person and machine by taking account of the strengths and weaknesses of both.

Consumer Psychology (Chapter 14)

The work of consumer psychologists is important to you if you are employed by a company that sells consumer products and services and if you hope to be a smart and informed buyer. Psychologists are involved in defining the markets for consumer goods, determining the effectiveness of advertising campaigns, and analyzing the motivations and needs of the buying public.

SUMMARY

Work provides a sense of identity, describes your social status, contributes to your self-esteem, and satisfies your need for belonging. **Industrial/organizational (I/O) psychology** is defined as the application of the methods, facts, and principles of the science of behavior and mental processes to people at work. As a science, psychology relies on observation and experimentation and deals with overt human behavior, that which can be observed objectively.

Industrial psychology began in the early 20th century and grew under the impetus of the two world wars. A major change in industrial psychology came with the recognition of the influence of social and psychological factors on worker behavior, as demonstrated by the **Hawthorne studies** of the 1920s and 1930s. The area of engineering psychology emerged out of the development of the sophisticated weaponry of World War II. Organizational psychology developed in the 1960s in response to a concern with the organizational climate in which most work takes place.

Continuing challenges for I/O psychologists relate to the changing age and diversity of the work force and the changing nature of work itself, such as the decline in factory and middle-management jobs and the impact of computers.

To work professionally as an I/O psychologist, you need a master's degree, but you will find a position of greater responsibility with a doctoral degree. I/O psychologists in organizations face several problems brought about, in part, by the demand for their services. These include the fraudulent practice of I/O psychology by persons who are not professionally trained; the difficulty of translating technical jargon so that ideas and research findings can be communicated to management personnel; the unwillingness of managers and workers to try a new or better way of doing things; and the necessity of balancing the need to conduct research on a company's problems with the company's desire to find a prompt solution.

Specific areas of I/O psychology discussed in the following chapters are employee selection, psychological testing, performance appraisal, training and development, leadership, motivation and job satisfaction, organizational psychology, working conditions, safety and health, the effects of stress, engineering psychology, and consumer psychology.

KEY TERMS

Hawthorne studies
Industrial/organizational (I/O) psychology

ADDITIONAL READING

The science and practice of industrial and organizational psychology; Survey of graduate programs in industrial/organizational psychology and organizational behavior; Career encounters in psychology. The first two titles are brochures from SIOP, Division 14 of the APA. The first describes research and applied interests of I/O psychologists; the second lists graduate school programs. Copies are available from the SIOP Administrative Office, 745 Haskins Road, Suite A, P.O. Bopx 87, Bowling Green OH 43402-0087. Their official newsletter, *The Industrtial-Organizational Psychologist,* is available online at http://cmit.unomaha.edu/TIP/TIP.html. The third title listed above is a 30-minute video on career opportunities; it is available from your college library or career counseling center.

Borman, W. C., & Cox, G. L. (1996). Who's doing what: Patterns in the practice of I/O psychology. *The Industrial-Organizational Psychologist, 33*(4), 21–29. Presents the results of a survey of SIOP members describing their I/O practice and consulting work.

Cascio, W. F. (1995). Whither industrial and organizational psychology in a changing world of work? *American Psychologist, 50,* 928–939. A past president of SIOP describes the changes affecting work, including global competition, information technology, reengineering of business processes, smaller companies, and the shift from a product-oriented to a service-oriented economy.

Howard, A. (Ed.). (1995). *The changing nature of work.* San Francisco: Jossey-Bass, 1995. A collection of papers reviewing changes in the workplace environment, changes in work processes, and changes in workers (such as diversity, empowerment, and skill development).

Katzell, R. A., & Austin, J. T. (1992). From then to now: The development of industrial-organizational psychology in the United States. *Journal of Applied Psychology, 77,* 803–835. Describes the history of I/O psychology since the 1900s and the current problems facing scientists and practitioners.

Sebolsky, J. R., Brady, A. L., & Wagner, S. (1996). Want an applied job?—Get experience!! *The Industrial-Organizational Psychologist, 33*(4), 65–70. A practical discussion about preparing for jobs in I/O psychology, such as networking, developing people skills, and taking the appropriate courses.

Tenopyr, M. L. (1992). Reflections of a pioneering woman in industrial psychology. *Professional Psychology: Research and Practice, 23,* 172–175. Mary Tenopyr is selection and testing director of human resources for AT&T. A noted contributor to the development of I/O psychology, she has won two awards from SIOP. She describes her career and the role of women in business today.

CHAPTER 2

Techniques, Tools, and Tactics

■   ■   ■   ■

WHY STUDY RESEARCH METHODS?

The importance of research in I/O psychology to the world of work is well established, but what is its value to you in your career? How will you benefit from learning how psychologists collect and analyze research data? Although you may not become an I/O psychologist, you will probably have to work directly with the findings of I/O psychologists. As a potential manager, you may interact with psychologists to find solutions to management problems, and you will be responsible for making decisions based in part on the recommendations of the company psychologist or of consulting psychologists your organization has hired.

Imagine, for example, that you are responsible for implementing a new manufacturing process to produce color monitors for computers. A modern production facility must be designed and built, and part of your job will be to facilitate the changeover from the old process to the new. You must consider several issues. How will the workers react to an abrupt change in the way they do their jobs? Will they be sufficiently motivated to operate the new machinery at a high level of production? Will they need retraining? How will the new process affect the company's safety record? These are just a few of the questions you would be expected to answer. If you make an incorrect decision, the cost to you and your company will be high.

Using information based on psychological research, I/O psychologists may be able to assist you. But if you are to evaluate their advice and recommendations, you must understand how they studied the problems and arrived at their conclusions. You may also be asked to decide whether the research program is worth the time and money. A knowledge of research methods will help you to make this decision more wisely.

Our goal in this chapter is not to train you to conduct research but to acquaint you with the requirements, limitations, and methods of the scientific approach. The application of the **scientific method** to problems too often dealt with by intuition or guesswork is psychology's distinctive contribution to improved management and work practices. If you understand these research tools, you will be able to ensure their proper use.

Scientific method A controlled, objective, and systematic approach to research.

REQUIREMENTS OF PSYCHOLOGICAL RESEARCH

Three requirements of scientific research are objective observation, control, and verification.

Objective Observation

A basic requirement and defining characteristic of scientific research in any discipline is objective observation. Ideally, researchers base their conclusions on objective evidence, which they view without preconceived ideas or biases. For example, when a psychologist chooses to use a particular test or training method or workspace design, that choice cannot be determined by private hunches, by the recommendations of prestigious authorities, or even by past research. The decision should be based on an objective evaluation of the facts of the present situation.

Control

A second requirement of psychological research is that observations must be well controlled and systematic. The conditions under which objective observations are made should be predetermined so that every factor that could possibly influence the outcome is known to the researcher. If, for example, we are studying the effect of background music on the efficiency of employees in word-processing jobs, we must arrange the situation so that no factors other than the music can affect worker productivity.

Duplication and Verification

The systematic control of objective observation allows for the fulfillment of a third research requirement: that of duplication and verifiability. With careful control of conditions, a scientist working at another time and place can duplicate the conditions under which the earlier experiment was conducted. We can have more confidence in research findings if they have been verified by other investigators. This verification is possible only under carefully controlled experimental conditions.

Psychological research in any setting requires systematic planning, control of the experimental situation so that the findings can be duplicated and verified, and objective observation.

LIMITATIONS OF I/O PSYCHOLOGY RESEARCH

Psychologists face many challenges in designing and executing a psychological research program within the confines of a university laboratory. But when a study is undertaken in the real-life setting of a factory or office, the problems are magnified.

Not All Behavior Can Be Studied.   One obvious limitation is that psychological research methods cannot be applied to every problem. Social psychologists, for example, cannot conduct controlled observations of how people behave in riots.

The situation is too complex and dangerous to arrange in advance. Similarly, in industry it is not feasible to conduct systematic research on some mechanical safety devices because that might expose some subjects to possible injury. There is a limit to what people should be exposed to in the interest of scientific research.

The Observation of Behavior Can Change It.   A second problem is that the act of observing people in an experiment can interfere with or change the behavior that the psychologist is trying to study. For example, if employees are asked to take a personality test as part of research on job satisfaction, they may deliberately distort their test responses because they do not want to answer personal questions or because they don't like their boss or the company psychologist. For another example, consider research to investigate the effects of jet engine noise on the efficiency of airline mechanics. The mechanics, if they are aware that they are part of a psychological research study, may deliberately work faster or slower than they would on a normal workday when they were not being observed.

The Hawthorne Effect.   Sometimes employee behavior changes because something new has been introduced into the workplace. This phenomenon was first observed during the Hawthorne experiments and so has come to be called the Hawthorne effect. Recall from Chapter 1 that one of the Hawthorne studies involved increasing the level of lighting in a work area. Production rose with each increase in illumination, and then it remained high even when the level of illumination was reduced. Whether the lighting was made brighter or dimmer, it was something new in the work environment, and that change, regardless of the level of lighting, affected worker productivity. The I/O psychologist conducting research must determine whether the differences observed in worker behavior are a result of the actual working conditions under study or of the stimulation or novelty of change itself, independent of working conditions.

Artificial Settings.   Another problem with psychological research is that some studies must be conducted in artificial settings. Management may not allow the psychologist to disrupt production by experimenting with various work procedures on the assembly line or in the office. As a result, the research may have to be conducted in a simulated job environment. In such cases, the research results will be based on performance in a situation that is not identical to the job environment in which the findings are to be applied. This artificiality may reduce the usefulness of the research findings.

College Student Subjects.   The problem of artificiality is complicated by the fact that much research in I/O psychology is conducted in universities and uses students as subjects. A review of five leading journals in the field showed that 87% of the studies published used students as subjects. A majority of the studies comparing the characteristics and behaviors of student and non-student samples have revealed important differences between the two groups. For example, a comparison of experienced business managers and college students performing the same task—evaluating applicants for a management position—showed that the students rated the applicants much higher and recommended considerably higher starting salaries than did the business managers (Barr & Hitt, 1986; Gordon, Slade, & Schmitt, 1986).

Thus, college students may behave differently from employees and managers on the job, and these differences limit the generalizability of the research findings. The situation has been described as follows: "The continued use of student samples for personnel research" is a major challenge for I/O psychology. Inferences from such studies "must be severely restricted. The inferential leap from these [college student] samples to field applications is seldom warranted" (Landy, Shankster, & Kohler, 1994, p. 289).

Although some I/O psychologists argue that research conducted in university laboratories can be generalized to employee and organizational issues (Locke, 1986), others maintain that the differences between the academic world and the world of business and industry are so great that only the most cautious generalization is acceptable (Guion & Gibson, 1988). To maximize the generalizability of the findings, we have chosen to rely primarily on research that studies employees and managers in actual work situations.

DATA COLLECTION

Several methods are available to I/O psychologists who conduct research in the workplace. Selecting the most effective technique is one of the first issues to be resolved in any research program. In most cases, the technique will be determined by the nature of the problem to be investigated. We discuss experiments, naturalistic observations, and surveys.

THE EXPERIMENTAL METHOD

Experimental method The scientific way to determine the effect or influence of a variable on the subjects' performance or behavior.

Independent variable In an experiment, the stimulus variable that is manipulated to determine its effect on the subjects' behavior.

Dependent variable In an experiment, the resulting behavior of the subjects, which depends on the manipulation of the independent variable.

The **experimental method** is simple in its basic concepts but sometimes difficult to implement. The purpose of an experiment is to determine the effect or influence of one variable on the performance or behavior of the people being studied (the subjects). Psychologists distinguish two variables in an experiment: the stimulus, or **independent variable,** the effect of which we are interested in determining, and the subjects' resulting behavior, the **dependent variable,** which is called "dependent" because it depends on the independent variable. Both variables can be objectively observed, measured, and recorded.

Designing and Conducting an Experiment

Consider the following experiment. Management is concerned about the poor production level of a group of workers who assemble television sets. Company psychologists are asked to study how output could be increased. They believe that any of a number of factors could be responsible for poor productivity, such as low pay, inadequate training, an unpopular supervisor, and obsolete equipment. After inspecting the workplace, however, the psychologists suspect that the problem is insufficient lighting. They design an experiment to test this hypothesis.

The two variables in this experiment are easy to identify and measure. The independent variable is the level of lighting. This is the stimulus variable, which the psychologists will increase during the experiment to determine its effects.

The dependent variable is the workers' response—in this case, their resulting rate of production.

The psychologists arrange for the lighting level in the workroom to be increased, and they measure production before the experiment and after 2 weeks of the brighter lighting. Prior to changing the lighting, each worker assembled an average of three television sets an hour. Two weeks later, individual production averaged eight units an hour, a considerable increase.

Why Did Production Increase?   Can we conclude that the change in the independent variable (the brighter lighting) brought about the change in the dependent variable (the greater productivity)? No. We cannot draw this conclusion on the basis of the experiment as described. How do we know that some factor other than lighting was not responsible for the higher production? Perhaps the grouchy supervisor was nicer to the workers during the 2-week experiment because he knew the company psychologists were hanging around. Maybe the workers purposely produced more because they thought their jobs were being threatened. Maybe better weather made the workers happier, or perhaps production increased because of the Hawthorne effect, the fact that a change had been introduced in the workplace. Many other factors could account for the increase in production, but the psychologists must be certain that nothing operated to influence the subjects' behavior except the stimulus being manipulated.

The Element of Control.   An essential feature of the scientific method was omitted from our experiment: the element of control. Controlling the experimental conditions would assure us that any change in the behavior or performance of the subjects was solely attributable to the independent variable.

To produce this necessary control, two groups of subjects must be used in an experiment: the **experimental group,** which consists of the subjects exposed to the independent variable, and the **control group.** The experimental and control groups are as similar as possible in every respect except that the control group is not exposed to the independent variable. Measures of productivity are taken from both groups at the beginning and end of the experimental period.

To conduct our experiment properly, then, we must divide the workers into these two groups. Their performance is measured before and after the experiment, and the production level of the control group serves as a standard against which to compare the resulting performance of the experimental group.

If the groups of workers are similar and if the performance of the experimental group at the end of the experiment is significantly higher than that of the control group, then we can conclude that the improved lighting was responsible for the increased production. Extraneous factors, such as the weather, the supervisor's behavior, or the Hawthorne effect, could not have influenced the subjects' behavior. If any of these factors had been influential, then the performance of both groups would have changed similarly.

Selecting Subjects for Experiments

The control group and the experimental group must be as similar as possible. There are two methods experimenters can use to ensure this: The **random group design** and the **matched group design.**

Experimental group In an experiment, the group of subjects exposed to the independent variable.

Control group In an experiment, the group of subjects that is not exposed to the independent variable.

Random group design A method for ensuring similarity between experimental and control groups that assigns subjects at random to each group.

Matched group design A method for ensuring similarity between experimental and control groups that matches subjects in both groups on the basis of characteristics (such as age, job experience, and intelligence) that could affect the dependent variable.

The random group design involves assigning the subjects at random to the experimental and control groups. In our experiment, if there were 100 television set assemblers, we would arbitrarily assign 50 to each condition. Because the basis for dividing the subjects into experimental and control conditions is random assignment, we may assume that the groups are essentially similar. Any possible influencing variables, such as age or length of job experience, should be evenly distributed over the two groups because these factors were not allowed to influence the assignment of the subjects.

In the matched group design, to assure similarity between experimental and control groups, subjects in one group are evenly matched with subjects in the other group on the basis of characteristics that could affect the dependent variable. For our experiment we could find pairs of subjects who are matched on age, job experience, intelligence, and supervisor ratings, and then we could assign one member of each pair to each group. In this way, the experimental and control groups would be as alike as possible.

Although desirable, the matched group technique is costly and difficult to carry out. To find enough pairs of subjects, we would need an even larger pool of potential subjects from whom to choose. Also, it becomes extremely complicated to equate pairs of subjects on more than one factor. Matching subjects on length of job experience alone presents few problems, but matching them on several factors at the same time is cumbersome.

A Sample Experiment: The Effect of Training on Turnover and Productivity

As an example of a typical experiment, let us consider the research conducted in a factory that produced women's lingerie (Lefkowitz, 1970). Management had asked a consulting psychologist to find out why 68% of the sewing machine operators quit within a year. After taking a survey of employee attitudes and interviewing the supervisors, the psychologist suspected that the reason for the high turnover was insufficient job training.

It was decided to study the effects of several training conditions on both the rate of turnover and the rate of productivity. Note that the initial problem leading to the research was the high number of people quitting. In the process of designing an experiment to investigate this problem, the psychologist realized that with little extra effort, data could also be secured on a second dependent variable: the level of production.

Subjects and Experimental Design.   The subjects were 208 women employees hired in 1 year as trainees. The dependent variables were (1) job turnover, defined as the percentage of workers who quit in their first 40 days on the job, and (2) productivity, defined in terms of daily output figures in the first 40 days on the job. The psychologist chose the 40-day period because company records showed that most terminations occurred during that time. The dependent variables were easy to observe, measure, and record with precision.

The independent variable was the level of training. The psychologist specified four training periods. The company's standard practice was to provide 1 day of training for new employees, conducted in a special training facility. This 1-day training was designated as the control condition, against which other training periods would be compared.

Trainees assigned to Group I took the standard 1-day training course. Group II received 2 days of training in the training facility, and Group III received 3 days of training in the training facility. Group IV had 3 days of training, but part of it was conducted in the training room and part of it took place on the job.

The subjects were assigned to each of the four conditions on the basis of the date of their initial employment with the company. Those hired during the first month of the study were placed in Group I, those hired during the second month in Group II, and so on, repeating the cycle throughout the year the study was in progress. Statistical comparisons of each group's initial performance demonstrated their similarity.

Results.   The results of the turnover study revealed that the longer the training received in the training facility (Groups I, II, and III), the lower the rate of turnover (see Figure 2–1). The 3-day training period combining on-the-job experience with the training facility (Group IV) did not reduce the turnover rate when it was compared to that of the 3-day training period wholly in the training facility (Group III). As you can see, however, comparing Groups I and III shows that the additional days of training reduced the turnover rate from 53% to 33%.

The second part of the study (the effect of training on productivity) produced unexpected complications. The data indicated that the longer the time spent in the training facility, the lower the average daily rate of production (see Figure 2–2). The 3 days of training in the facility and on the job (Group IV) led to greater productivity than did the 3 days of training in the facility alone (Group III).

Thus, the independent variable (the different training levels) produced conflicting results on the dependent variables. Greater time in the training room resulted in lower turnover, but it also yielded lower productivity. It is at this point—interpreting the research results—that the training and experience of the I/O psychologist are put to their most severe test. Experiments do not always turn out as the researcher hoped. Research results are not always clear and consistent, and considerable interpretive skill is necessary to relate the data to the job or the problem being studied.

The psychologist conducting this experiment considered the productivity and turnover data and concluded that the 3-day integrated training condition (Group IV) would be the most profitable for the company. It yielded a close second-highest level of production and a close second-lowest rate of turnover.

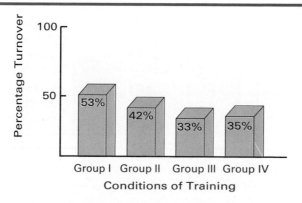

FIGURE 2–1. Turnover rates of four training conditions.

In summary, we must keep in mind that I/O research proceeds on two levels: (1) designing the experiment and (2) interpreting and implementing the results. In both stages, psychologists must depend on the cooperation of managers who understand the requirements of psychological research.

NATURALISTIC OBSERVATION

Naturalistic observation
The scientific observation of behavior in its natural setting, without any experimental manipulation of the independent variable.

In the study of human behavior at work, it is not always possible to bring the relevant variables under the precise control required by the experimental method. Also, it may be more useful to study behavior as it occurs in real life. We mentioned that one of the weaknesses of the experimental method is artificiality. To avoid this, psychologists sometimes prefer to observe behavior in its natural setting without introducing any manipulation of the independent variable. This is the essence of the method of **naturalistic observation.** Although this method does not involve the manipulation of the independent variable, the psychologist is still able to maintain some control over the situation.

One advantage of naturalistic observation is that the behavior being observed and the situation in which it is observed are typical of what occurs in everyday life. The findings of naturalistic observation can be more readily generalized and applied to real life because that is where they were obtained. After all, our ordinary daily activities occur in situations that are not under the stringent control necessary in the experimental method.

This advantage is also a major weakness. Because researchers do not manipulate the independent variable, it is sometimes difficult to conclude with any assurance precisely what brought about the resulting change in the subjects' behavior or performance. Another limitation is that the observation cannot be repeated. It is impossible to duplicate the exact conditions that prevailed during the initial observation.

The experimental method is not without problems, as we noted. Nevertheless, when it can be used, it is a better choice than naturalistic observation because the experimenter can control and systematically manipulate the independent variable. However, both methods, when applied with precision and interpreted with care, are valuable in the study of human behavior in the workplace.

FIGURE 2–2.   Production levels of four training conditions.

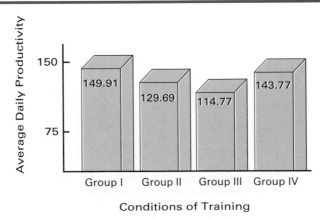

A Sample Naturalistic Observation:
Friendly Behaviors of Convenience Store Clerks

A nationwide chain of convenience stores instituted a training program to teach its clerks to be friendly toward customers. The company wanted to determine whether the friendly behaviors would lead to an increase in sales (Sutton & Rafaeli, 1988). Arranging an experiment would have been difficult and might not have been informative. The company could have compared sales at two groups of stores, one of which had clerks trained to be friendly whereas the other did not, but that might have meant a loss in sales in the control group stores and the possible alienation of customers.

The company could have designed a laboratory experiment in which people would pose as courteous clerks and rude clerks. Subjects playing the role of customer would be asked if they thought they would buy more from the courteous clerks than from the rude clerks, but that would have been too artificial a situation. Also, the results would not tell the company anything about the impact of friendly behavior on actual sales.

Design of the Study.   The psychologists decided to conduct a naturalistic observation in which the behavior of 1,319 clerks in 576 convenience stores was secretly watched by trained observers in 11,805 transactions with customers. Clerks knew that their level of courtesy would be monitored at some time, but they were not told when the observations would take place.

The observers, chosen to fit the profile of a typical customer, pretended to be making purchases. They spent from 4 to 12 minutes in each store, depending on how many customers were present. The more crowded the store, the longer the observers could linger without causing the clerks to be suspicious. Observers reported that they thought clerks were suspicious of them in fewer than 3% of the observations; these data were excluded from consideration. The clerks' friendly behaviors, as recorded by the observers, included smiling at customers, greeting customers, thanking customers, and maintaining eye contact with customers. These behaviors, along with the sales figures for each store, were the dependent variables.

Although no independent variables were manipulated, factors that might have influenced behavior and sales were controlled. The proportion of women to men clerks was considered in order to control for variation in courteous behaviors by sex; past research suggested that women tend to be more courteous than men in any setting. The proportion of women to men customers was also recorded to control for sex differences in purchasing behavior. If some stores were patronized primarily by women, for example, and if women made more purchases than men did, then sales figures for those stores would be higher, independent of the clerks' behavior.

The stores for the observations were selected at random, but all were in heavily populated urban districts. None was from a suburban or rural area where the sales pattern might differ from that of an urban area. Recognizing that people in various regions of the United States behave differently, independent of the company's training program, the data from four sectors—Northeast, South, Midwest, and West—were analyzed separately. Thus, taking the research out of the laboratory and conducting it in the real world still permitted the psychologists to control relevant variables and make objective observations.

Results.   To the surprise (and consternation) of the researchers, the findings showed that the greater the incidence of courteous behaviors, the lower the sales. Analysis of the data revealed that a store's level of sales influenced the clerks' behaviors, and that the courteous behaviors taught in the training program did not lead to increases in sales. The busier the store (the higher the sales), the less time the clerks had to exhibit the courteous behaviors. In stores with lower sales, clerks had time to be more friendly and so did customers. The results also confirmed that women clerks were more courteous than men clerks and that clerks in the western region were more friendly than those in the northeast.

The behavior being observed in this example was not as well controlled as it could have been under laboratory conditions, but the greater realism afforded by the use of the real-life situation offset this disadvantage. In many cases, the nature and complexity of the phenomena under investigation determine the most appropriate method of study. In other instances, the psychologist must decide whether to sacrifice some measure of control for greater applicability.

SURVEYS AND POLLS

Survey research method
Interviews, behavioral observations, and questionnaires designed to sample what subjects say they think or how subjects say they will behave in a given situation.

Surveys and opinion polls rely on the observation of behavior as it is revealed in the subjects' responses to personal interviews and questionnaires. The focus in the **survey research method** is not on what subjects do (as in experiments or naturalistic observations) but on what they say they will do.

Survey questionnaires and interviews have many applications in I/O psychology. Psychologists use surveys to ascertain factors that contribute to job satisfaction and morale. Some large organizations maintain a staff of poll-takers to conduct periodic employee surveys on a variety of work-related issues. This polling gives employees the chance to air gripes and complaints (a form of upward communication), assesses reactions to changes in work procedures and policies, and provides the opportunity for employees to participate in policy making.

As a result, surveys have the potential for raising employee morale, reducing turnover, and avoiding costly union grievance procedures. In some plants, maintaining an open channel of communication between employees and employers has prevented unionization altogether. Workers who believe their opinions are heard and valued by management are less likely to feel the need for union representation.

Advertising and motivation research firms use survey techniques to uncover consumer preferences. For example, Campbell Soup questioned more than 100,000 consumers to determine their food likes and dislikes. On the basis of the survey results, the company changed the seasonings in its frozen food dinners and introduced a line of low-salt soups.

In addition, public opinion polls are routinely used in political campaigns to assess voter reaction to candidates and to the issues in their platforms.

Even the best polling organizations have problems, however, with the precise measurement of personal opinions and attitudes. One difficulty is that some people deliberately lie when they are asked questions in surveys. They may say they will do one thing and then do something else. Sometimes they change their

The focus of the survey method is on what people tell interviewers they will do rather than on what they actually do.

minds, for example, telling an interviewer in October that they will vote Republican and then voting Democratic in the November elections.

People may say they prefer a particular brand name or product because they believe this choice will make them appear sophisticated. They may claim to drink an expensive European beer, for example, but if interviewers could look in the refrigerator, they might find cans with an inexpensive domestic label instead.

Sometimes people express an opinion in response to a survey question even when they do not have one, because they do not want the interviewer to think they are uninformed. In a poll designed to document this effect, people were asked if they favored "the new monetary control bill now being considered by Congress." There was no such bill, but more than 25% of the respondents expressed an opinion about it anyway (Jaroslovsky, 1988).

An analysis of 37 surveys found that 64% of the respondents claimed to have read the particular magazine article the poll-takers were questioning them about. In reality, no such article had ever been published! The researchers were appalled at the extent of the deception in responses to the most innocuous questions. The results also showed that people were more likely to be honest in their responses when they completed a questionnaire in private than when they were asked the same questions in a face-to-face interview (Wentland, 1993).

Another complication, particularly with telephone surveys, is the increasing difficulty in finding people to respond. Many people are annoyed by junk telephone callers pretending to take a survey when the real purpose is to sell land or dance lessons. Also, some people are no longer willing to spend their time responding to surveys. Although it is relatively easy to poll retired people and full-time homemakers, it is more difficult to reach an adequate sample of office workers, young adults, and high-income people. Surveying these groups requires considerable time and effort.

NEWSBREAK #2

"Push Polls" Can Win Elections

Public opinion polls not only collect information from voters but they can also provide information, some of it false or distorted information about a political candidate that can ruin his or her chances of winning. These polls are called **push polls** because they are designed to see if certain negative information can push voters away from one candidate to support the candidate who is paying for the poll.

Here's how they work. A polling firm hired by Congressperson Green, let us say, calls several thousand registered voters in the congressional district. The callers are asked if they intend to vote for Green or for the opponent, Candidate Brown. Those voters who say they plan to vote for Brown or who have not yet made up their minds are asked a question of this type: "If I told you that Brown was once arrested for fraud—for cheating senior citizens out of their life savings—would that make a difference in your vote?"

Note how the question is phrased. The pollster is not saying that Brown had actually been arrested on such charges—which, in truth, he had not—but merely by raising the issue, the *implication* is that Brown had been arrested. In this way, thousands of people in the voting district can be fed false information about an opposition candidate in the otherwise innocent guise of taking a poll.

Push polls have been used by candidates of both major political parties at all levels of government. Their use has raised questions for ethical professional polling experts. Pollster Brian Tringali, for example, has criticized this questionable practice. Writing in the trade journal *Campaign Elections*, in 1995, Tringali noted: "The truth is that polls are being used in today's campaigns as much to shape public opinion as to simply report it. Some polling may be used to mislead the public by skewing questions or reporting results out of proper context."

In the world of public opinion polling, the results may not always be what they seem.

These difficulties with the survey method can explain some lost elections, failed businesses, and bad management decisions. The problem lies not with the method itself but with the complex, subjective, and sometimes perverse nature of human attitudes, preferences, and behaviors. Keep in mind, however, that properly designed surveys can be highly accurate and that they succeed more often than they fail.

Personal Interviews

Three basic ways to collect survey data are personal interviews, questionnaires, and telephone surveys. The personal interview, the most expensive and time-consuming technique, requires a face-to-face meeting with the respondents.

Finding and training capable interviewers is vital because their appearance, manner, and behavior can influence the way people cooperate with them and answer their questions. Research has shown that subjects respond differently to interview questions, depending on the interviewer's age, race, and sex. More subtle interviewer variables can also affect survey results. For example, if an interviewer asking questions about drug use shows by smiling or frowning apparent agreement or disagreement with what the respondent is saying, that person may change subsequent answers because of the perception of the interviewer's opinion about drugs.

Assuming a competent, well-trained interviewer and a cooperative subject, the personal interview offers advantages over telephone and questionnaire surveys. It yields the highest response rate—80 to 95%—and can provide more complete and accurate information.

The major disadvantage is the high cost in time and money of training interviewers and conducting the interview sessions. It is considerably more expensive and time-consuming to contact, say, 500 individuals in person than to telephone them or mail them a questionnaire. Additional problems are the safety of interviewers in some neighborhoods, the difficulty of finding people at home, and the influence of the interviewers' personal biases. In general, interviewers are not highly paid. Some have been known to make up answers to interview questions rather than take the trouble to actually conduct the interview.

Questionnaires

Questionnaires offer a cheaper and more convenient way to obtain information from large numbers of people over a wide geographical area. In I/O psychology today, questionnaires are the most frequently used survey technique for collecting information from employees. Because employees can remain anonymous, they are more likely to respond freely and openly, and because they can take their time responding, they can formulate their answers more carefully than in a personal interview.

The major disadvantage of questionnaire surveys is that the response rate is typically only 40 to 45%. Since it is usually not possible to determine how those who respond differ from those who fail to respond, generalizations based on these relatively small returns must be made with caution.

Research has shown that the source of the questionnaire can affect the rate of return. In one study, a questionnaire identified as coming from a prestigious university had a 52% response rate, whereas one from a private research firm brought only a 42% response rate (Albaum, 1987). Another study found no difference in response rate when a questionnaire with a postage-paid return envelope was mailed to 3,800 employees throughout the United States. Half the employees received a reply envelope addressed to company headquarters. The other employees received a reply envelope with the name and address of a fictitious consulting firm. The rate of return for both groups was 40% (Armstrong, 1991).

Follow-up procedures are sometimes used to try to secure additional returns. A reminder letter or postcard can be mailed to all questionnaire recipients explaining the importance of the survey and requesting cooperation. Letters sent by registered mail and follow-up telephone calls can also be used. Some companies offer incentives to employees for responding to a survey. A few hold contests with valuable prizes as an inducement to return the questionnaires. Most

Telephone surveys offer a low cost per interview and the likelihood that an interviewer can contact hundreds of people in the course of the workday.

companies offer only a token payment, such as a dollar bill, which is often sufficient to make respondents feel guilty if they take the money and do not answer the questions.

The order in which questions are asked can affect the response rate. A 95-item attitude survey distributed to 1,188 office personnel yielded an astonishingly high 96% return among the group whose questionnaires dealt first with questions about the employees' most pressing concerns, as determined by their elected employee representatives. In another experimental condition, in which the questionnaires gave those issues a lower priority (they appeared later in the questionnaire), the response rate fell to 78%. The response rate was higher when personal information (age, sex, education, number of years with the company) was requested at the end of the questionnaire rather than at the beginning. The researchers suggested that personal items at the beginning of a questionnaire might be perceived as more of a threat to the respondents' anonymity (Roberson & Sundstrom, 1990).

A high-tech method of conducting questionnaire surveys uses electronic mail (E-mail) in which questions are asked and answers obtained through the company's computer system. One E-mail survey in the research and development division of a major corporation brought a response rate of 73%, and the time required to receive the replies was less than a week (Sproull, 1986).

Telephone Surveys

Telephone surveys offer the advantage of a low cost per interview and the possibility that a single interviewer can contact several hundred people a day. With perseverance, it is possible to reach most of the people in the sample by continuing to phone until they answer. Telephone surveys have been aided by computerized phone systems that speed up the process. These surveys cost approximately half as much as personal interviews and obtain comparable data.

For surveys of voters, television viewers, and shoppers, the telephone approach is the major data collection technique even though the refusal rate is higher than for personal interviews (Groves, 1990). Poll-takers expressed concern that the popularity of telephone answering machines would limit their ability to reach a representative sample of subjects, but research has shown that this may not be a problem. An automated random-digit dialing of nearly 5,000 residential telephone numbers was followed by either a brief or a lengthy questionnaire. A maximum of three call attempts was made for each household. Answering machines were found to be used more on weekends than weekday evenings, and owners of answering machines were found to be just as reachable and willing to participate in surveys as residents of homes without answering machines (Tuckel & Feinberg, 1991).

Survey Questions

With any survey, regardless of the method used to collect the data, two basic problems must be resolved: (1) what questions will be asked, and (2) who will be questioned. In general, surveys use two types of questions: open-end questions or fixed-alternative questions.

With **open-end questions,** which are similar to the essay questions you have faced on college exams, respondents are allowed to present their views in their own words without any restrictions. They are encouraged to answer in their own way and to take as much time as needed. If there are many open-end questions, this approach will be time-consuming. The usefulness of the replies depends on how skillfully the subjects can verbalize their thoughts and feelings. Open-end questions place considerable pressure on interviewers to be accurate and complete in recording the answers.

Open-end questions Questions for which respondents state their views in their own words; similar to essay questions on college examinations.

Fixed-alternative questions, like the multiple-choice exam questions you are familiar with, limit a person's answer to a specific number of alternatives. A typical open-end question might be: How do you feel about raising taxes to provide money for schools? A fixed-alternative question on the same topic might be: With regard to raising taxes to provide more money for schools, are you in favor _____, opposed _____, or undecided _____? Thus, the person is faced with a finite number of possible choices and a restricted way in which to answer.

Fixed-alternative questions Similar to multiple-choice questions; respondents must limit their answers to the choices or alternatives presented.

Fixed-alternative questions simplify the survey, allowing more questions to be asked in a given period of time. Also, answers can be recorded more easily. A disadvantage is that the limited number of alternatives may not accurately reflect the respondent's opinion. A person could be in favor of higher school taxes under some circumstances and opposed to them under others. When their answers are restricted to yes, no, or undecided, people cannot make these feelings known to the interviewer. If enough people in the sample have such unexpressed reservations, the results will be misleading.

Often it is necessary to pretest the questions on a small sample of respondents to make sure that the questions are understandable. If subjects misinterpret a question or find unintended meanings, the results may be biased. For example, the annual survey by the National Center for Health Statistics routinely questioned Americans about "abdominal pain" until poll-takers discovered that many people did not understand the phrase or know where the abdomen was located. When respondents were shown a diagram of the body and the specific area was pointed out, their answers turned out to be quite different.

The wording of survey questions presents a serious problem for I/O psychologists because approximately 25% of the American work force is functionally illiterate. Researchers have also found that questionnaire responses are affected by the respondents' level of intelligence. In one study, 347 U.S. Army reservists were given a general test of mental ability and a questionnaire designed to assess their current job duties, their satisfaction with their job, and their degree of commitment to the army reserve. The researchers found that the lower the level of cognitive ability, the greater the number of unanswered questionnaire items. They concluded that people who cannot read and comprehend a questionnaire's items and instructions will not be motivated to complete it and may not have the ability to do so properly even if they wanted to (Stone, Stone, & Gueutal, 1990).

Subject Sampling

Suppose a researcher wants to determine the opinions of automobile owners in Texas about a proposed change in the driver license fee. To question every car owner would be tedious and difficult even with sufficient time and money, and it would not be possible to locate and personally interview everyone. Nor is it necessary. With proper care, a representative sample of the population will provide the desired information and predict the responses of the total population.

To select a sample of car owners in Texas, we could question people at shopping centers, gas stations, or busy intersections. However, this would not guarantee that the people we asked would be representative of all car owners in the state. The people found at an exclusive shopping center in the suburbs of a large city, for example, would be more likely to represent a particular income bracket rather than the total population.

Probability sampling A method for constructing a representative sample of a population for surveys or polls; each person in the population has a known probability or chance of being included in the sample.

Two ways to construct a representative sample of a population are probability sampling and quota sampling. In **probability sampling,** each person in the population has a known probability or chance of being included in the sample. By securing from the state department of motor vehicles a list of all automobile owners, we can select every 10th or 25th name, depending on how large a sample we need. In this way, every person in the population of registered car owners has the same chance (1 in 10, or 1 in 25) of being included in the sample.

This method is satisfactory as long as there is a list of everyone in the population. If we wanted to study eligible voters in the United States, this method would not be useful because only registered voters are listed.

Quota sampling A method for constructing a representative sample of a population for surveys or polls; because the sample must reflect the proportions of the larger population, quotas are established for various categories such as age, gender, and ethnic origin.

In **quota sampling,** the researcher attempts to construct a duplicate in miniature of the larger population. If it is known from census data that in Texas 10% of all car owners are college graduates, 50% are men, 40% are of Hispanic origin, and so on, then the sample must reflect these proportions. Interviewers are given quotas for people to interview in the various categories and must find appropriate respondents. Because the persons questioned are chosen by the interviewers, their personal feelings and prejudices can affect the selection of the sample. An interviewer may prefer, for example, to talk to people who appear well dressed and friendly or to call on people who live in upscale neighborhoods.

DATA ANALYSIS

In psychological research, as in research in any science, collecting the data is only the first step in the scientific approach to problem solving. If we have conducted an experiment to measure the productivity of, say, 200 workers, or have given an aptitude test to 200 employees, we are left with 200 numbers—the raw scores. Now it is necessary to analyze and interpret these data, and to do so we draw on the principles of statistics. Statistics is a tool to help us summarize and describe masses of data and to enable us to draw inferences or conclusions about their meaning.

DESCRIPTIVE STATISTICS

You are already familiar with the word *descriptive*. When you describe a person or an event in words, you try to convey a mental picture or image. Similarly, when psychologists use **descriptive statistics,** they are trying to describe or represent their data in a meaningful fashion. Let us examine some research data and see how statistics can describe them.

Descriptive statistics Ways of describing or representing research data in a concise, meaningful manner.

To evaluate a new test for job applicants that was designed to predict their success in selling life insurance, a corporate psychologist administered the test to 99 applicants. The test scores are shown in Table 2–1. Looking at this swarm of numbers should tell you why it is important to have a way to summarize and describe them. It is not possible to make sense of the data as they are. You cannot

TABLE 2–1   Raw Scores of 99 Job Applicants on Life Insurance Sales Test

141	91	92	88	95	113
124	119	108	146	120	123
122	118	98	97	94	89
144	84	110	127	81	120
151	76	89	125	108	90
102	120	112	89	101	118
129	125	142	87	103	147
128	94	94	114	134	114
102	143	134	138	110	128
117	121	141	99	104	127
107	114	67	110	124	122
112	117	144	102	126	121
127	79	105	133	128	118
87	114	110	107	119	133
156	79	112	117	83	114
99	98	156	108	143	99
96		145		120	

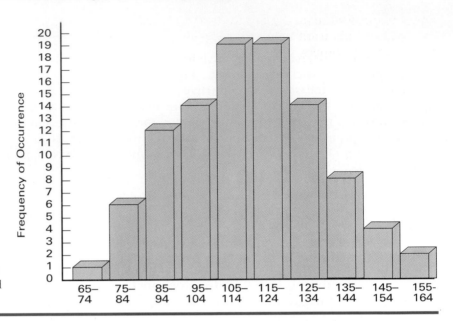

FIGURE 2–3. Distribution of life insurance sales test scores (grouped data).

formulate a useful prediction or make a meaningful evaluation of the potential job performance of these applicants as a whole by looking at the table of individual numbers.

Frequency distribution A graphic representation of raw data that shows the number of times each score occurs.

One way to describe the data is to construct a **frequency distribution** or a bar graph, plotting the number of times each score occurs (see Figure 2–3). For convenience in dealing with so many scores, we can group them into equal intervals. Grouping the data is not necessary, but it does make them easier to work with. The graph offers a clearer idea of the test performance of our group of job applicants than does the table of raw scores alone. Also, the graph provides useful information about group performance by showing that most of the subjects who took the test scored in the middle range.

Mean, Median, and Mode

Central tendency In statistics, a quantitative representation of a group of raw scores.

Scientific analysis requires that the raw scores also be summarized and described quantitatively. We must be able to represent the data with a single number, a measure of **central tendency.** To find the typical or average score in this distribution of scores, we can calculate the mean, median, or mode.

Mean The arithmetic average; a way of describing the central tendency of a distribution of data.

The most common and useful measure of central tendency is the arithmetic average, or **mean,** which is calculated by adding the scores and dividing the resulting sum by the total number of scores. The mean for our group of 99 job applicants is 11,251 divided by 99, or 113.6. Thus, averaging reduces our raw data to a single number. The mean provides the basis for many higher-level statistical analyses.

Median The score at the midpoint of a statistical distribution; half the scores fall below the median and half above.

The **median** is the score at the midpoint of the distribution. If we arrange the 99 scores in order from lowest to highest, the median is the score obtained by the fiftieth person. Half the job applicants scored higher than the median, and half scored lower. In our sample, the median is 114, which is close to the mean. The median is a useful measure when dealing with skewed distributions.

Mode The most frequently obtained score in a distribution of research data.

The **mode** is the most frequently obtained score in the distribution; a distribution may have more than one mode. With our data, the mode is 114. The mode is seldom applied to describe data but is useful in certain work situations.

For example, a store manager concerned with stocking an adequate inventory of stereo sets would want to know which components were being purchased more frequently than others.

Normal Distributions and Skewed Distributions

In Figure 2–3 you can see that most of the job applicants achieved test scores in the middle of the distribution and that only a few scored very high or very low. Many measurements approximate this kind of distribution. In general, such a distribution occurs when a large number of measurements are taken of a physical or psychological characteristic. Whether we measure height, weight, or intelligence, for example, a sample of sufficient size will yield a distribution in which most scores fall near the middle and few fall at the extreme low and high ends. This bell-shaped distribution is called the normal distribution.

The **normal distribution** is predicated on the random nature and size of the sample tested. If the sample is not representative of the population but is biased in one direction or another, the distribution will not approximate a normal curve.

Suppose we administered an IQ test to a group of school dropouts, persons with little formal schooling and little experience in taking standardized tests. Such a group is not typical or representative of the general population, so the distribution of their test scores will not look like the normal curve. When measurements are taken from specially selected groups, the distribution will most likely be an asymmetrical distribution, or **skewed distribution** (see Figure 2–4).

In dealing with skewed distributions, the median is the most useful measure of central tendency. The mean is affected by a few extreme scores in either direction and thus may provide a misleading description of the data. The median is less affected by extreme scores.

You have no doubt heard people say that statistics lie. Although statistics can be misleading, the fault is usually with the person applying them inappropriately, not with the techniques themselves. Consider the data in Figure 2–5, which represent median and mean awards in corporate liability cases between 1960 and 1984. The mean or average awards increased dramatically from about $60,000 to $250,000. The median awards decreased slightly.

Normal distribution A bell-shaped distribution of data in which most scores fall near the middle and few fall at the extreme low and high ends.

Skewed distribution An asymmetrical distribution of data with most scores at the high or low end.

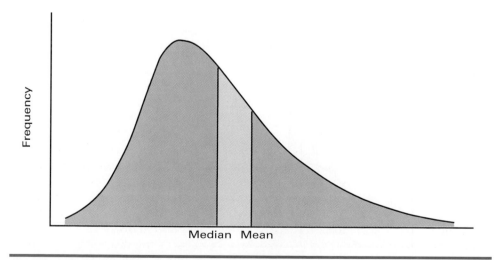

FIGURE 2–4. A skewed distribution.

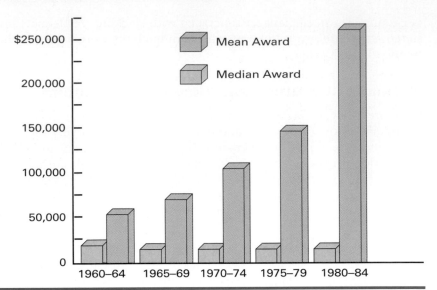

FIGURE 2–5. Median and mean liability awards, 1960–1984. (Data from Institute for Civil Justice, Rand Corporation; *New York Times,* April 13, 1986.)

A controversy erupted over how to interpret these data. Lawyers, who benefit from larger liability awards to their clients, argued that the liability judgments did not increase over the 24-year period. Insurance companies, who have to pay these liability awards, argued that there had been a fivefold increase. The lawyers were using *median* liability awards; the insurance companies were citing *mean* liability awards. Both sides were technically correct, although the median is the better measure with a skewed distribution. As an employee, manager, voter, and consumer, you will find that it pays to be skeptical when you hear about "average" figures. Ask which average is being used—the median or the mean.

Variability and the Standard Deviation

Having calculated and diagrammed the central tendency of a distribution, you may not be happy to learn that more analysis is needed to provide a comprehensive description of a distribution of scores. It is not sufficient to know the central tendency; we must also have a numerical indication of the spread of the scores around the measure of central tendency.

Consider the normal distributions in Figure 2–6. If we take the mean or the median as the measure of central tendency of these distributions, we would con-

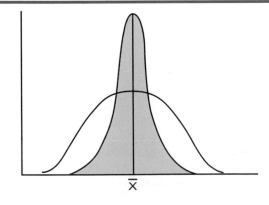

FIGURE 2–6. Normal curves with the same central tendency but different variability.

clude that the distributions are identical: The means and medians are the same for both curves. You can see, however, that the distributions are not identical. They differ in their spread, or **variability.**

The basic measure of variability is the **standard deviation** (SD), a precise distance along the distribution's baseline. Once we determine this distance, we can learn a great deal about the data and describe them more meaningfully.

Let us examine the distribution of IQ scores presented in Figure 2–7. The data form a normal curve with a mean of 100 and a standard deviation of 15. Knowing that the SD is 15 tells us that an IQ score of 115 is 1 SD unit or distance above the mean of 100. An IQ score of 130 is 2 SD units above the mean, and so on. Similarly, an IQ score of 85 is 1 SD distance below the mean (−1 SD).

With the standard deviation, we can determine the percentage of scores in the distribution that fall above or below any particular raw score. Tables based on the mathematical formula for the normal distribution give us the percentage of cases, or frequency of scores, between standard deviation units. For example, 99.5% of the population have IQ scores below 145, 97.5% below 130, and 84% below 115. These percentages hold for any variable measured as long as the distribution of the data follows the normal curve. If we know the standard deviation of a distribution, we can determine precisely the meaning of any particular score. We can tell where it falls in terms of the performance of the group as a whole.

Suppose we develop an aptitude test for dental school students that we will use to measure the motor skills needed to manipulate the implements used in dental surgery. Your roommate takes the test and obtains a score of 60. This number tells us nothing about that student's aptitude relative to that of all the other students. However, if we know that the distribution of test scores is normal, that the mean is 50, and that the standard deviation is 10, then a score of 60 (+1 SD from the mean) indicates that only 16% of the students scored higher and 84% scored lower. Your roommate might make a pretty good dentist after all.

There is a method by which raw scores can be converted to standard deviation scores, allowing us to interpret each raw score in the distribution. The standard deviation also permits us to compare the performance of individuals on two or more measures that use different scoring systems. By converting the distributions on all tests to standard deviation units, we can compare performance on one test with performance on another test because the scores will be expressed in the same terms.

Variability The spread of a distribution of data around the measure of central tendency.

Standard deviation A precise distance along the baseline of a distribution of data; a measure of variability.

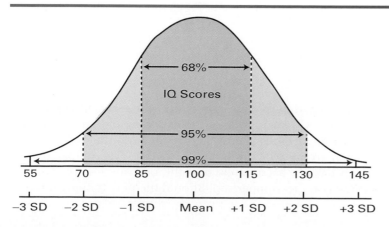

FIGURE 2–7. Normal distribution of IQ scores showing standard deviation units.

Correlation: The Relationship Between Two Variables

We have been discussing the statistical treatment of one variable at a time, such as a set of test scores from a group of job applicants. I/O psychologists frequently are concerned about the relationships between two or more variables. Any situation in which a prediction must be made about whether a person is likely to succeed on the job involves matching two or more variables. For example, an employee's performance on a selection test must be compared with a later measure of actual job performance. That is the only way the psychologist can determine whether the selection technique is choosing the best people for the job. Psychologists use the correlational method to investigate the relationships among variables.

Correlation The relationship between two variables.

A **correlation** tells the researcher two things: (1) the direction of the relationship between the variables, and (2) the strength of that relationship. The direction of the relationship may be positive or negative, depending on whether high scores on one variable are accompanied by high or low scores on the other variable. In a positive relationship, increasing scores on one variable are accompanied by increasing scores on the other variable. For example, a positive correlation between employees' test scores and supervisors' ratings of the employees' job performance tells us that the higher the test score, the higher the supervisory rating. As one variable increases, so does the other. We can predict that job applicants who do well on the test will tend to do well on the job. In other words, applicants who earn a high test score are likely to get a high rating from their supervisor.

In a negative correlation, increasing scores on one variable are accompanied by decreasing scores on the other. In our example, applicants who got high scores on the selection test would be likely to receive low ratings from their supervisors. In other words, those who do well on the test tend to do poorly on the job.

Correlation coefficient A measure of the strength and direction of the relationship between two variables.

Through the application of the statistical formula for the **correlation coefficient,** we can calculate the direction and strength of the relationship between the variables. Positive correlations range from zero to +1.00; negative correlations range from zero to −1.00. A correlation coefficient of −1.00 indicates just as strong a relationship or correspondence as a coefficient of +1.00. Only the direction is different. In both cases, performance on one variable, such as job ratings, can be predicted from performance on the other variable, such as test scores. The closer the correlation coefficient is to +1.00 or −1.00, the more accurately we can predict performance on one variable from performance on the other. Correlation is a valuable and widely used tool in I/O psychology, and we shall see its use in many examples throughout this book.

INFERENTIAL STATISTICS

In the typical psychology experiment, researchers are interested in comparing the performance levels of at least two groups—the experimental group and the control group. In an experiment to test the value of a new training method, for example, the experimental group, which has had the training, is compared with the control group, which has not been exposed to the new method of training. An important decision rests on this comparison. Should the new training method be implemented throughout the organization? The decision hinges on the size of the difference between the two groups on their job performance (the dependent variable).

Levels of Significance

How do I/O psychologists know when the difference between the two groups is large enough to justify the cost of establishing the training program for the entire company? They must determine the level of **statistical significance** of the difference between the means of the two groups. Their answer will be expressed in terms of probabilities rather than certainties. The problem is this: Is the difference between the means of the groups large enough so that it is unlikely it could have occurred by chance?

Statistical significance The level of confidence we can have in the results of an experiment; based on the calculation of probability values.

Probability

Applying techniques of **inferential statistics** to the data from the experimental and control groups, we can calculate a **probability** value for the difference between the means. This number represents the probability that the difference could have occurred by chance. Psychologists recognize two levels of statistical significance: a probability (p) of .05 and a p of .01. A p value of .01 means that a difference as large as that obtained in the experiment would occur by chance only 1 time out of every 100. Thus, a difference of this level of significance could be attributed to the new training method used with the experimental group and not merely to chance. If the p value was .05, we would have a little less confidence in the results, because this would tell us that there was a probability of 5 in 100 that the difference could have occurred by chance.

Inferential statistics Methods for analyzing research data that express relationships in terms of probabilities.

Probability The idea that the differences between the means of experimental and control groups could have occurred by chance.

Meta-Analysis

This approach to significance testing has been challenged by psychologists who favor the technique of meta-analysis (Hunter & Schmidt, 1990). The prefix *meta-* refers to something beyond or higher than something else; in I/O psychology, **meta-analysis** is a level of analysis higher than significance testing. Meta-analysis, which involves the large-scale reanalysis of previous studies to determine overall trends, has been adopted by many psychologists as a way of reaching more objective conclusions about issues on which a considerable body of research data exists. The technique of meta-analysis has been used in many areas of psychology and in fields as diverse as economics and medical research (Johnson, Mullen, & Salas, 1995). Its popularity in I/O psychology has even led to the development of meta-analysis computer software packages.

Meta-analysis The large-scale reanalysis of previous research studies.

Regardless of the specific techniques applied, statistics help the I/O psychologist to reach informed decisions and recommendations about crucial problems in business and industry. The use of statistics does not eliminate the need for human decision making, but it does help to guide the researcher, manager, or executive in that task. Statistical tools are means to an end, not an end in themselves.

SUMMARY

In psychological research, observations must be objective, well controlled and systematic, and capable of being duplicated and verified. Research has several limitations. For example, some problems are too complex to investigate by psychological research methods. The act of observing some behaviors may interfere with them. The novelty of change may alter behavior more than the actual change itself (the Hawthorne effect). Also, some research must be conducted in artificial settings, limiting the generalizability of the findings.

In the **experimental method,** psychologists investigate one influencing variable while holding all others constant. The variable being investigated is the **independent variable;** the behavior that results is the **dependent variable** (it depends on the independent variable). In an experiment, two groups of subjects are used: the **experimental group** and the **control group.** The groups must be as similar as possible, a condition brought about by random group design (assigning subjects at random to the two groups) or by matched group design (matching the subjects in the groups on a number of personal characteristics).

Naturalistic observation involves observing behavior in its everyday setting. The experimenter can control the independent variables but cannot manipulate them with the precision permitted by the experimental method.

Survey research focuses on attitudes and opinions. Three survey techniques are personal interviews, telephone surveys, and questionnaires. Electronic mail (E-mail) questionnaires ask questions and obtain responses through an organization's in-house computer system. The personal interview is the most expensive and time-consuming technique, but it is likely to secure the most useful information. Survey questions can be **open-end,** allowing respondents to answer in their own words, or they can offer **fixed alternatives,** restricting respondents to a few choices. Representative samples of the people to be questioned in a survey can be selected through **probability sampling,** in which each person in the population has a known probability of being included in the sample, or through **quota sampling,** in which a replica in miniature of the larger population is constructed.

The raw data obtained in a research project can be summarized, described, and analyzed by **descriptive statistics.** Data can be presented in graphs or reduced to a few meaningful numbers. Three ways to measure the central tendency of a distribution of data are the **mean**, **median,** and **mode.** When sufficient data are collected from a representative sample of the population, they form a bell-shaped or **normal distribution,** in which most of the scores fall in the center or average range. To measure a distribution's **variability,** psychologists use the **standard deviation—**a distance along the distribution's baseline. The standard deviation provides information on the percentage of scores that fall above or below any particular raw score. The **correlation coefficient** denotes the direction and strength of the relationship between two variables. Correlation coefficients range from −1.00 (a perfect negative relationship) through zero to +1.00 (a perfect positive relationship). Correlation coefficients enable psychologists to predict performance on one variable from performance on another variable.

Inferential statistics are used to determine the level of **statistical significance** of the difference between the means of two groups by indicating whether the difference is so large that it is unlikely to have occurred by chance. Psychologists use two levels of significance: a **probability** of .05 (5 chances in 100 that the difference occurred by chance) and a probability of .01 (1 chance in 100 that the difference occurred by chance). **Meta-analysis** is a technique for averaging the results of a large number of studies.

KEY TERMS

central tendency

control group

correlation

correlation coefficient

dependent variable

descriptive statistics

experimental group

experimental method

fixed-alternative survey questions

frequency distribution

independent variable

inferential statistics

matched group design

mean

median

meta-analysis

mode

naturalistic observation

normal distribution

open-end survey questions

probability

probability sampling

push polls

quota sampling

random group design

scientific method

skewed distribution

standard deviation (SD)

statistical significance

survey research methods

variability

ADDITIONAL READING

Frank, H., & Althoen, S. C. (1994). *Statistics: Concepts and applications.* New York: Cambridge University Press. An introductory statistics textbook.

Goodwin, C. J. (1995). *Research in psychology: Methods and design.* New York: Wiley. A basic methods textbook that includes numerous case studies, application exercises, and first-hand accounts of research.

Leary, M. R. (1995). *Introduction to behavioral research methods* (2nd ed.). Pacific Grove, CA: Brooks/Cole. An undergraduate research methods textbook that emphasizes statistics.

Levin I. P., & Hinrichs, J. V. (1995). *Experimental psychology: Contemporary methods and application.* Madison, WI: Brown and Benchmark. An introductory textbook that presents various methodological approaches for specific research areas in psychology. Includes a chapter on how to write a research report.

The Development of Human Resources

The areas of application of I/O psychology referred to as **personnel** or **human resources psychology** include selecting, training, and evaluating new and current employees. People applying for a job undergo an extensive selection process. An organization may use

Personnel psychology The study of personnel issues including employee recruitment, selection and placement, training, and performance evaluation.

techniques ranging from application blanks to sophisticated psychological tests. Once hired, new employees must be trained to perform their jobs efficiently. The same selection and training techniques are used when employees are being considered for promotion. A similar process of matching employee skills with job requirements is undertaken. Employees who are promoted to more responsible jobs must be trained for their new roles. Periodically, the performance of all employees must be evaluated by their supervisors. Ideally, these appraisals are fair and objective and provide feedback to employees about their progress on the job.

Employee selection, training, and appraisal methods determine the kind of job for which you will be hired and the way in which you will perform your duties. Chapters 3 and 4 deal with problems of selection. Chapter 3 discusses selection techniques (application blanks, interviews, letters of recommendation, and assessment centers). Chapter 4 describes intelligence, interest, aptitude, personality, and integrity tests used for selection purposes. Methods of performance appraisal are covered in Chapter 5, and training techniques are considered in Chapter 6.

Employee Selection Principles and Techniques

■   ■   ■   ■

When you leave college to take a full-time job, there is a 50% chance that you will quit your first job within 3 to 5 years. For a variety of reasons, half the students in your college graduating class will not find enough satisfaction in their work to remain with the first organization they join. They may find the job to be different from what they were told by the company recruiter or the interviewer in the personnel department. Or they may find that they did not know themselves so well, that their abilities and interests were not what they thought or that they were socially or temperamentally unsuited to a particular kind of work.

Whatever the reasons for dissatisfaction with the job, it is an unfortunate situation in which the employee and the organization both lose. The dilemma emphasizes the importance of employee selection principles and practices. Improper matching of the person and the job, of the person's skills and characteristics with the job's demands and requirements leads to unhappiness and poor performance in the work situation.

Because improper selection is so costly, in both financial and personal terms, management should make better use of all available psychological tools and techniques to ensure that the majority of the people they hire will work to the ultimate advantage of themselves and the company.

Before you enter the personnel office of a potential employer—before you complete an application blank or take a psychological test—certain preselection factors will influence your choice of job. Some of these are internal, such as your preferences about the kind of work you want to do and your expectations about the organization. Other factors are external, such as the nature of the recruiting effort that brought you in contact with the organization and the amount of realistic information you are given about your possible place in it. I/O psychologists describe these preselection issues as problems of organizational entry.

ORGANIZATIONAL ENTRY

Your entry into an organization is of immense importance not only for the immediate satisfaction it brings you—or fails to bring you—but also for your long-term happiness. Just as the nature of your first love affair can influence your subsequent emotional relationships, so your first job experience can affect your expectations about future jobs and your performance throughout your career. Whether troubling or successful, your first love affair or first job can affect similar experiences for some time to come. A study of managerial, professional, and technical employees of a large oil company found that those who demonstrated success early in their career were more likely to be promoted than those who were less successful early in their career (Dreher & Bretz, 1991). In other words, employees who started out well, who had positive experiences early in their working life, continued to do well.

The amount of challenge your first job provides influences your feelings of commitment to your work, your level of achievement, and your motivation to perform well on the job. The positive impact of initial job challenge stimulates a high level of performance and technical competence that leads to continued success. I/O psychologists have demonstrated this relationship between the level of initial job challenge and later success in employees in many organizations for a variety of occupations.

Finding the right amount of challenge is of major importance in your organizational entry process. It is vital that the challenge offered by your first job be compatible with your expectations and preferences. Indeed, it is crucial to you and your employer that everything about your initial job comes close to satisfying your needs. That is why employers try to learn all they can about the expectations and preferences of potential employees.

EMPLOYEE PREFERENCES

What are you looking for in a job? High salary? Ample fringe benefits? Short working hours? Although there may be a single answer for you as an individual, there is no single answer for all employees. I/O psychologists have identified several job characteristics likely to be important to employees. Some of these are as follows. How would you rank these for yourself?

___ Challenging, interesting, and meaningful work
___ High salary
___ Opportunities for advancement
___ Job security (no danger of being fired)
___ Satisfactory working hours
___ Pleasant working conditions
___ Compatible co-workers
___ Feeling of being respected and appreciated   (continued on page 60)

_____ Opportunity to learn new skills
_____ Fair and loyal supervisor
_____ Being asked one's opinion on work issues
_____ Assistance with personal problems

In a study of 49 business students, the subjects were presented with job listings for fictitious companies and asked to indicate their interest in signing up for an interview. This experimental attempt to uncover employee preferences revealed that the most important consideration for these students was the company's location. Almost half of the subjects said they would not interview a company if they disliked its location. Also ranking high on the list of preferences were salary and fringe benefits (Barber & Roehling, 1993).

Another factor that affects employee preferences is level of education. College graduates have different expectations from those of high school graduates, who in turn have different preferences from those who did not complete high school. Not all college graduates have the same preferences. Engineering majors differ from liberal arts majors, and A students differ from C students. Younger workers' preferences differ from those of older workers, white-collar workers from blue-collar workers, and technical personnel from managerial personnel.

Employee preferences change as a function of economic conditions. In times of hardship when jobs are difficult to obtain, new employees in the job market may be more interested in pay and job security. In a better economic climate when jobs are plentiful, issues such as challenging work or the opportunity to develop new skills rank higher than security or salary.

Preferences have also been found to vary as a function of race. A survey using open-end questions to compare the job preferences and expectations of black and white women college students found that more blacks than whites wanted a high-paying job rather than interesting work (Murrell, Frieze, & Frost, 1991).

Many people enter an organization with unrealistic or inflated expectations about the nature of the job and the company, which may explain why so many people leave their first job. The discrepancy between expectations and reality is too great.

Expectancies begin to meet realities when you have your first contact with a potential employer, typically at your initial meeting with the company recruiter. This marks the first opportunity for each to size up the other, and it is an important step in the preselection process of organizational entry.

THE RECRUITMENT PROCESS

Several issues in the recruiting process are sources of potential employees, recruiter characteristics, college campus recruiting, and the kinds of information to provide to job recruits.

Sources for Recruiting

The traditional recruiting sources available to organizations include help-wanted ads in newspapers, referrals from employees, employment agencies and search services, placement services of professional associations, job fairs, and outplace-

NEWSBREAK #3

Online Recruiting

One night Jerry Baker sat down at his computer and found a job. Baker had been looking for work in the health care field for 4 months with no luck. But that night, surfing the Internet, he chanced upon the high-tech way to search for employment, the latest way for companies to recruit new employees.

Baker spotted job listings on the career center Web site maintained by a large commercial online service provider. Within a few minutes he had responded to the job listing. The next day he heard from the company recruiter and, 2 months later, he had the job.

Several major newspapers, including the *New York Times*, the *Washington Post*, and the *Chicago Tribune*, jointly began an online career employment service, currently carrying up to 50,000 help wanted ads. Another online service claims to list up to 15,000 new ads each week. One Web site reports generating nearly two million hits each month from people looking for jobs. With millions of computer-literate job applicants conducting job searches online in a way that's cheap, easy, and fast, can online interviews be far behind?

Source: Finding a paycheck online. *New York Times,* January 7, 1996.

ment agencies. Another popular source for recruiting is the college campus. Almost half of all large corporations actively recruit managerial and professional employees through on-campus interviews.

In addition to these formal sources, informal sources are available, such as contacting friends and acquaintances. In general, informal sources provide more accurate and detailed information about a job than do formal sources. Also, informal sources more often lead to hiring. Research has shown that informal sources are an important aspect of any employment search.

A study of 186 students at universities and vocational training schools found that the longer the job search, the less the students used formal recruiting sources. However, those who remained unemployed 3 months after the study began significantly increased their use of formal sources. Thus, the use of formal sources was high in the early stages of a job search and again later if the search proved unsuccessful (Barber, Daly, Giannantonio, & Phillips, 1994).

In following the job search of 467 nurses, researchers found that those applicants who used at least one informal recruiting source acquired more information about potential employers than did applicants who relied exclusively on formal recruiting sources (Williams, Labig, & Stone, 1993).

Recruiter Characteristics

I/O psychologists have conducted considerable research on the behavior and personal characteristics of recruiters to determine how these influence college seniors in the choice of a job. The psychologists have found that characteristics

THEY'LL BE PROUD TO BE HERE.

The Army offers young people great opportunities to learn self-discipline, confidence and teamwork, qualities they need throughout life.

WE'LL BE PROUD TO SEND THEM THERE.

And they can earn up to $40,000 to go to college if they qualify for the Montgomery GI Bill plus the Army College Fund.

C A L L   1 - 8 0 0 - U S A - A R M Y   w w w . g o a r m y . c o m

Organizations of all types spend considerable time and money recruiting suitable employees. (Army materials courtesy of the U.S. Government, as represented by the Secretary of the Army)

A corporate recruiter meets with business students at a job fair in Philadelphia. Almost half of all large U.S. corporations actively recruit new employees on college campuses.

likely to induce graduating seniors to accept a job offer include behaviors such as smiling, nodding, maintaining eye contact, demonstrating empathy and warmth, and showing thoughtfulness, competence, and personableness (Harn & Thornton, 1985; Harris & Fink, 1987; Liden & Parsons, 1986).

College men expressed the same likelihood of job acceptance whether their recruiter was male or female, but college women said they would be much more likely to accept a job offer if the company recruiter was male (Taylor & Bergmann, 1987).

Later research showed that 50% of the college senior women interviewed were offended by gender-related comments made to them by male recruiters about their personal appearance. They also resented receiving mail addressed to "Mister," even after the interview, failing to meet women employees during a visit to the company office, and being told that women would not advance as rapidly as men. This was considered surprising behavior in light of corporate efforts to eliminate gender bias (Rynes, Bretz, & Gerhart, 1991).

Other research on job applicants in an on-campus placement center showed that college seniors preferred recruiters to spend the interview period providing information about the company, soliciting information about the applicant, and answering applicant questions. When the college seniors thought corporate recruiters were spending too much time talking about irrelevant topics, they were significantly less likely to accept a job offer (Macan & Dipboye, 1990).

Another study dealt with 379 college seniors who had successfully completed the campus interview and then had been invited to visit the company offices. The purpose of the research was to determine the aspects of the site visits that were most influential for the job applicants. The major factors found to be important in determining whether the college seniors accepted a job offer were (1) the likability of the corporate host and how comfortable the applicant felt in his or her presence, and (2) whether the company's location provided access to cultural, recreational, and social activities (Turban, Campion, & Eyring, 1995).

Success of Campus Recruiting

College recruiting may not be living up to its potential, and companies may not be realizing full value from their recruitment programs. Research has shown that an applicant's degree of interest in a particular job is not greatly affected by the recruiter (Powell, 1991). One explanation for this finding is that fewer than half of the corporate recruiters had received training in the proper techniques for interviewing job applicants. Recruiters tended to form a positive or negative impression about an applicant's qualifications in the first few minutes of an interview—hardly sufficient time to collect enough information on which to base a recruiting decision—and to spend more time with applicants they considered to be qualified (Macan & Dipboye, 1990). They often do not agree on the topics that should be covered in an interview and sometimes fail to discuss important issues with applicants. All these points reflect a lack of interviewing skills.

In an effort to reduce campus recruiting costs, many organizations are turning to computerized recruitment databases, compilations of student résumés. Résumés in the database can be retrieved by subscribers who are searching for candidates with particular qualifications. Approximately 200 colleges and universities now maintain online résumés of graduating seniors. Some of the databases and database networks available to students include computerized listings of available positions and detailed descriptions of the companies that are hiring. In others, students can access information about alumni who will serve as mentors.

More than 100 universities currently offer computerized videoconferencing facilities in which companies can conduct long-distance interviews with college seniors. Recruiters can meet students without leaving their offices, and students can consider many organizations that otherwise might not schedule interviews on campus. A recruiter for Procter and Gamble told a *New York Times* interviewer: "It's a no-lose situation for us. We get a form of interactivity between the students and the recruiter, and we also get access to schools we might not visit."

Whatever technique is used, one major difficulty faced by corporate recruiters on campus is finding job candidates who have a realistic view of the business world. This is another reason why college recruiting often produces less than satisfactory results, leading half of all college graduates, as we noted, to leave their first job within 3 to 5 years.

Part of the reason for dissatisfaction on the part of new graduates can be traced to the campus recruitment interview. Many students obtain a false picture of the job and the organization, sometimes because they have had no experience in corporate life and, therefore, do not know what questions to ask the recruiter.

They want to make a good impression and may tend to hide attitudes and characteristics they think the recruiter might not like.

Another reason for the misleading image is the fault of the recruiters. Their job is to find people with promise for their company, and to accomplish this, they may paint an idealized picture of their organization and of the new graduate's first job in it.

Thus, each side may be guilty of misleading the other, and the result, when they turn out to be a less-than-perfect match, is likely to be dissatisfaction. The obvious solution is greater honesty, with each party being open about good and bad points. Some corporations have recognized this problem and try to present a realistic preview of the job as part of their organizational entry procedures.

Realistic Job Previews

Realistic job previews provide information that is as accurate as possible about all aspects of a job. Such information can be supplied through a brochure or other written description of the job, through a film or videotape, or through an on-the-job sample of the work to see if the applicant can perform the required tasks. The purpose of realistic job previews is to acquaint prospective employees with both positive and negative aspects of the job. The hope is that this practice will reduce overly optimistic or unrealistic expectations about what the job involves.

> **Realistic job previews** A recruitment technique that acquaints prospective employees with positive and negative aspects of a job.

Research indicates that realistic job previews correlate positively with job satisfaction, job performance, and reduced turnover rates. Realistic job previews have also been found to reduce the number of applicants accepting jobs, because potential employees can learn, before starting a job, whether certain aspects of the work situation are unappealing or otherwise not appropriate for them.

The effects of realistic job previews vary as a function of the prior exposure applicants have had to the job in question. For example, a study of 1,117 applicants for positions as correctional officers found that applicants with previous experience at prison work were far less likely to accept employment offers after watching a realistic job preview on videotape. Applicants who had no such prior work experience were more likely to accept the job offers (Meglino, DeNisi, & Ravlin, 1993). Apparently, this realistic job preview, which focused on negative aspects of the job, reminded the applicants with prior experience of the unpleasant and dangerous nature of the work.

After the recruiting process has been completed and applicants and organizations have decided that each meets the other's needs, the selection process formally begins.

AN OVERVIEW OF THE SELECTION PROCESS

There is more to proper selection methodology than simply placing an advertisement in the newspaper, having the people who appear in the personnel office complete an application blank, and then questioning them in a brief interview. A successful selection program involves several additional procedures.

Let us suppose that the head of the human resources department is told that 200 new employees must be hired to operate the complex machinery that is being installed to produce fax machines. How are these workers to be found?

Job and Worker Analyses

First, I/O psychologists must investigate the nature of the job. The organization will not know what abilities potential employees should have unless it can describe in detail what they are expected to do to perform the job effectively. A process called **job analysis** is undertaken to determine the specific skills necessary to the job. From the job analysis, a profile of worker qualifications can be developed.

Job analysis The study of a job to describe in specific terms the nature of the component tasks performed by the workers.

Once these abilities have been specified, the human resources manager must determine the most effective means of identifying these characteristics in potential employees. Does the job require the ability to read complicated diagrams? To manipulate small component parts? To have a knowledge of electronics? And how will the company find out whether an applicant has these skills?

The necessary background characteristics and aptitudes, as determined from the job and worker analyses, must be assessed or evaluated in each applicant. Cutoff scores or levels for the various abilities will be established. A minimal score on a test or a fixed number of years of education or experience will be proposed, and no one who falls below that level will be hired. It may be necessary for the I/O psychologist to study present workers in the same or similar jobs to determine where the cutoff scores should be set.

Recruitment Decisions

Recruitment decisions are next. Should the company recruit new employees through ads in newspapers or trade journals? Through an employment agency? Through referrals from current employees? The number of potential employees recruited affects the caliber of those who will be selected. If ads and referrals bring in only 250 applicants for the 200 jobs, the company must be less discriminating in hiring than if there were 400 applicants to choose from. I/O psychologists call this the **selection ratio,** the relationship between the number of people to be hired and the number who are available to be hired. Thus, the potential labor supply directly affects the stringency of the requirements established for the job. If there is a shortage of applicants and the jobs must be filled within a few weeks, some requirements (perhaps the cutoff score on an intelligence test) will have to be changed.

Selection ratio The relationship between the number of people to be hired and the number available to be hired (the potential labor supply).

A shortage of job applicants may also force the company to expand its recruiting campaign and to offer higher wages, enhanced benefits, or improved working conditions to attract and retain new employees. Thus, the size of the labor supply can greatly influence not only recruitment and selection procedures but also features of the job itself .

Selection Techniques

Selecting the new employees and classifying them as suitable or unsuitable for the job are accomplished by a variety of techniques, including application blanks, interviews, letters of recommendation, assessment centers, and psychological tests. Hiring decisions usually are not based on a single technique but on a combination of methods. In addition, testing for drug use is now widespread for all types of jobs. We deal with this issue in detail in Chapter 12, but it is important to note here that you will probably be asked to submit to a drug test as a condition of employment. An analysis of the preemployment drug screening of more than 5,000 job applicants estimated that the organizations involved achieved substantial financial savings, in terms of reduced absenteeism and turnover, by not hiring anyone who failed the drug tests (Normand, Salyards, & Mahoney, 1990).

Concern about AIDS in the workplace has led some organizations to screen applicants for human immunodeficiency virus (HIV). In the future, scientists suggest, genetic testing may be applied to identify applicants who may be sensitive to certain chemicals used in the workplace and to predict those individuals who are likely to develop specific diseases.

Testing the Selection Techniques

The next step in the selection process is to test the selection procedures. After the initial 200 workers in our example have been hired, the human resources manager must follow their progress to see how many of them succeed on the job. This is the major test of the worth of the selection program.

Every new selection program must be investigated to determine its predictive accuracy or validity. This is done by evaluating the performance of the employees selected by the new procedures. For example, after 6 months on the job, the supervisors of the 200 new workers can be asked to rate their job performance. By comparing these ratings with performance on the selection techniques, we can determine how the two measures correlate. We want to know whether the selection techniques were able to predict which of the applicants turned out to be the better workers.

Suppose we learn that the employees who received high ratings from their supervisors had performed an average of 10 points above the cutoff score on a test of manual dexterity and had earned a high school diploma. Employees who received low ratings from their supervisors performed within 1 or 2 points of the cutoff score on the manual dexterity test and had not completed high school. These findings tell us that the two factors (manual dexterity and a high school diploma) were able to distinguish between potentially good and potentially poor workers. In the future, then, the human resources manager can use these techniques with confidence to select the best people for these jobs.

Keep in mind that to evaluate the selection process we must have some measure of job performance with which to compare performance on the selection techniques. The ways of appraising work performance, of determining these job performance measures, are discussed in Chapter 5.

THE CHALLENGE OF FAIR EMPLOYMENT PRACTICES

Successful selection has been rendered more difficult by the regulations of the Equal Employment Opportunity Commission (EEOC), established in 1972. All job applicants, regardless of race, religion, sex, or national origin, are guaranteed equal opportunities for employment. Not only is such discrimination in employment unethical and immoral, it is also illegal. The Civil Rights Act of 1964 and the enforced guidelines of the EEOC make it against the law to discriminate against job applicants. (The impact of the 1991 Civil Rights Act on psychological testing in employee selection is noted in Chapter 4.)

Adverse Impact

When any minority group of job candidates is treated markedly worse than the majority group, that minority group is said to be the target of **adverse impact** in the selection process. Any selection rate for a minority group that is less than 80% of the selection rate for the majority group is evidence of adverse impact.

Let us say that a company had 100 job applicants (50 blacks and 50 whites) and hired 50 of them (10 blacks and 40 whites). In this instance, 80% of the white applicants were hired but only 20% of the black applicants. The selection rate for blacks was only one fourth, or 25%, of that for whites, much less than the 80% rule for showing adverse impact. The company could be challenged in court for maintaining these vastly different rejection rates for minority and majority applicants.

A 1989 decision by the U.S. Supreme Court ruled that statistical documentation of racial imbalance in a work force may not be sufficient to establish adverse impact. This judicial finding has eased the employer's burden of proof of discrimination, but it has also led to the use of more valid selection procedures.

Discriminatory Questions

Interviews and application blanks as selection techniques have been greatly affected by antidiscrimination legislation. Questions that discriminate against a particular group can lead to lawsuits. For example, no questions can be asked that identify applicants' national origin, race, creed, or color. Applicants cannot be asked to name their birthplace or that of their relatives, to identify their religious affiliation, if any, or to give the maiden names of female relatives. It is also unlawful to inquire about the clubs or societies to which applicants belong and to ask them to submit photographs with their employment applications. Not only can such questions be discriminatory, they also have no relation to an applicant's potential for success on the job.

In addition, employers cannot ask applicants if they have ever been arrested for any crime, because members of certain minority groups are much more likely to be arrested on suspicion of wrongdoing. It is lawful, however, to ask applicants if they have ever been convicted of any crime. Conviction could be considered relevant to job performance in certain instances, such as when a person convicted of embezzlement applies for a job as a bank teller.

Reverse Discrimination

The impetus to recruit, hire, and promote members of minority groups and to implement EEOC rulings has sometimes resulted in discrimination against members of the majority group. An organization may be so intent, for example, on increasing the number of women in its ranks to meet federal guidelines that it denies opportunities to men. In 1992, a white male medical school professor in Florida filed a discrimination lawsuit charging that the university unfairly had denied him a salary increase because the money available for pay raises was distributed only to women and minority faculty. This phenomenon, called **reverse discrimination,** has also occurred in graduate and professional schools, where some white applicants have been denied admission in favor of minority applicants whose grades and test scores were not as high as those of the white applicants.

Reverse discrimination may operate in promotion decisions in other organizations, too. A 4-year survey of 13,509 employees in scientific and engineering occupations found that women and blacks had greater promotion opportunities than equally qualified white men. The author of this longitudinal study concluded that the result was caused by the companies' deliberate efforts to promote minority employees (Shenhav, 1992).

These efforts can stigmatize those persons who are hired or promoted on an affirmative action basis. A survey of 184 white men showed that they viewed co-workers who they presumed had been hired or promoted solely because of race or gender as being less competent to perform the job than those not associated with an affirmative action program (Heilman, Block, & Lucas, 1992).

The issue of reverse discrimination is complex and controversial. The intent of the civil rights laws was to prevent preferential treatment for any group. Yet, when an otherwise qualified applicant is denied educational or job opportunities because institutions must by law include more persons of a specified sex or ethnic background, those persons are also receiving preferential treatment.

Supreme Court decisions in the 1980s upheld charges of reverse discrimination, noting that the rights of the majority group must not be unnecessarily restrained in the effort to help minorities and that minorities should not be hired or promoted solely on the basis of percentages or some other quota system. The Court ruled that only fully qualified minority employees should be hired or promoted.

The Impact of Fair Employment Legislation

"Affirmative action and related race relations programs have done much to integrate women and minorities more fully into the economy," wrote psychologist Linda Gottfredson, an expert on diversity in the workplace. "But," she added, "they have fallen short of expectations. Affirmative action dramatically increased the hiring of women and minorities, but it has done less to ensure their promotion or retention" (Gottfredson, 1992, pp. 281–282).

In addition, affirmative action programs have created the impression among majority-member employees that, as we noted earlier, preferential hiring practices for women and for minorities have led to the hiring of unqualified people. As a result, many white men feel resentful and neglected. In the 1990s, some degree of backlash has been expressed by political leaders, employers, and employees.

A survey of 349 college students found sharp opposition to affirmative action in general among white males, although women, blacks, and Hispanics were more favorably disposed to the idea. Interestingly, however, all forms of preferential treatment of minorities in hiring, as well as the forced hiring of unqualified applicants to fill racial quotas, was opposed by all surveyed groups—white, black, and Hispanic. Thus, even those who would benefit from this preferential treatment may oppose it (Kravitz & Platania, 1993).

We close our brief discussion of this complex and emotionally-charged issue with the disturbing findings of two additional studies. The first, an analysis of earlier studies, found that increasing the percentage of minorities hired by organizations resulted in a loss in overall job performance and that the amount of loss was positively accelerated. In other words, the more minorities hired, the higher the performance loss (Silva & Jacobs, 1993).

Second, observations of the placement of 369 new clerical employees hired by a bank found that although many white employees were assigned to white supervisors, twice as many black employees were assigned to black supervisors. When the employees were reassigned 5 months later, four times as many blacks

NEWSBREAK #4

It's No Longer the Back of the Bus, But . . .

We are unable to get taxis to pick us up in front of office buildings. We are frisked and detained on suburban commuter trains. We are watched in department stores and mistaken for coatcheck clerks and restroom attendants while lunching in the best restaurants. We are directed to freight elevators and delivery windows by receptionists who fail to recognize us in our own company offices.

We are black professionals in corporate America in the 1990s.

Although I am at my desk each morning facing the same corporate challenges as my white co-workers, a great deal of my job-related stress comes from sources totally unrelated to my job. My father dreamed of the day when his son would work in a towering office with a city view. What he didn't know was that arriving there would not be the end of the struggle for black Americans.

Even though I have been the beneficiary of affirmative action, I can acknowledge some of its flaws—its tendency to create resentment among white men and its potential for generating a sense of "group entitlement" among minorities and women. But my experiences as a corporate lawyer, professor, and black professional in a mostly white environment have shown me that workplace bias in America, even today, is so intractable that it justifies establishing affirmative action as a permanent policy. . . .

For those who believe I am overzealous in suggesting the permanent enforcement of affirmative action, I offer an incident that took place soon after I started a new job as a corporate lawyer in Manhattan.

A receptionist with a security guard in tow came running past my secretary's desk just as I was joining a conference call with a client in my office.

"Excuse me, Larry, but I've got security here," the receptionist said breathlessly, interrupting our call. "Did you see a delivery boy get past reception and come through here with a purple bag?"

I looked to the corner where a Bergdorf Goodman bag sat with a hat that I had bought for my wife.

"That's the boy!" shouted the security guard, pointing to me.

When the receptionist saw the shopping bag, recognition and relief washed over her face. "That's so funny," she laughed while closing the door. "We thought you were a delivery boy. Sorry to bother you."

The client looked at me with the slightest hint of skepticism as we turned back to our documents.

Source: Quoted from Lawrence Otis Graham, The case for affirmative action. *New York Times,* May 21, 1995.

were assigned to black supervisors, a phenomenon that resulted in de facto segregation on the job. Management claimed to be unaware of this segregation of employees by race and had no idea how it came about.

The psychologist who had noticed the situation found that employee ability, job performance, employee qualifications, and supervisor racial animosity had no effect on the placement. He attributed the phenomenon to what he called "ethnic drift," which he defined as a benign instance of like attracting like, of people of similar backgrounds being assigned to the same work units in order to make their work adjustment easier (Lefkowitz, 1994).

The resulting placement was, indeed, a form of segregation and discrimination, but the question remains as to why it happened. Was it racism, or simply an attempt to place new employees in units where they would more readily fit in with current workers? What do you think?

Other Targets of Discrimination

Older Workers.   The work force in the United States is aging. One American out of four is now age 50 or older, and one in eight is over 65. By the beginning of the 21st century, nearly half of all Americans will be over 45, and 36 million people will be over 65.

However, management still prefers to hire younger workers, despite consistent evidence from I/O psychology research that older workers are as productive, and sometimes more so, as younger workers and have lower absenteeism and turnover rates. A meta-analysis of 96 studies involving nearly 39,000 employees found no relationship between age and job performance for professional and nonprofessional jobs (McEvoy & Cascio, 1989). A survey of human resource managers showed that they believed older workers to be more loyal to the organization and just as punctual as younger workers (Blocklyn, 1987). In general, older employees do not suffer from poorer health, diminished vigor, or declining mental abilities when compared with younger employees.

Studies of some 24,000 persons in nonmanagerial jobs in the manufacturing, clerical, and service sectors of the work force found that age was positively related to performance in highly complex and cognitively challenging jobs and that performance declined with age only in less demanding jobs such as low-level clerical or repetitive assembly-line work (Avolio, Waldman, & McDaniel, 1990). Research on employee ratings of their supervisors, who ranged in age from the twenties to the seventies, found no significant differences in leadership effectiveness as a function of age (Gilbert, Collins, & Brenner, 1990).

The stereotypes about older workers persist, however. Older workers tend to receive more negative performance evaluations than younger workers, appraisals that are based more on age than on actual work performance (Gordon, Rozelle, & Baxter, 1988). A meta-analysis of studies of ratings of older employees found that workers 34 years old and younger tended to give less favorable ratings to workers age 55 and older than they did to younger workers. Younger workers were rated as having higher job qualifications and more potential for development and as being more qualified for physically demanding work (Finkelstein, Burke, & Raju, 1995).

Older workers are protected by law against ageism, this form of discrimination in hiring and promotion. The Age Discrimination in Employment Act of 1967 legislated against such discrimination against persons in the 40- to 65-year age bracket. The act was amended in 1978 to raise the age at which employees could be forced to retire from 65 to 70.

Workers With Disabilities.   Employees with physical and mental disabilities are protected by federal laws against job discrimination. The Vocational Rehabilitation Act of 1973 made it mandatory for organizations to recruit, hire, and promote qualified disabled persons. The 1990 Americans with Disabilities Act prohibits employers, state and local governments, employment agencies, and labor unions from discriminating against qualified individuals with disabilities in job application procedures, hiring, firing, advancement, compensation, job training, and other conditions of employment. The act requires employers to make reasonable accommodations to the physical or mental impairments of a qualified applicant or employee with a disability if it would not impose an undue hardship on normal business operations.

Since the law took effect, disabled persons have filed almost 6,000 discrimination complaints with the EEOC, and that figure is projected to increase (Hall & Hall, 1994). Despite the growing number of complaints filed against organizations for discriminating against disabled persons, the number of such persons entering the work force has increased only marginally in the years since the law was passed. In 1986, 4 years before the enactment of the Americans with Disabilities Act, 33% of disabled persons between ages 16 and 64 held full-time or part-time jobs. In 1996, 6 years following the passage of the law, the figure had increased only to 34.6%. In addition, workers with disabilities were employed primarily in part-time, low-status jobs in which they earned up to 35% less than nondisabled employees (Stone & Colella, 1996).

Some 43 million people in the United States experience some mental or physical impairment. Approximately 17% of the U.S. population shows severe

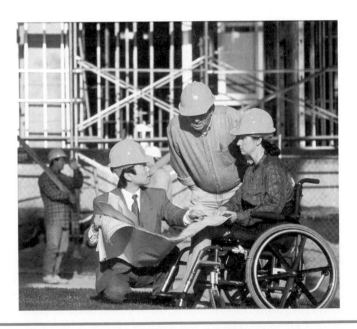

The Americans with Disabilities Act of 1990 prohibits employers from discriminating against qualified persons who have disabilities.

sensory impairment (vision or hearing disabilities), motor impairment, or cognitive impairment (learning disabilities, speech impairment, or mental retardation).

Defining the term *disability* has proven difficult and requires some 60 pages of government regulations. In general, a person is considered disabled if he or she has a physical or cognitive impairment that limits one or more major life activities.

The prejudice against hiring disabled workers is at variance with their actual job performance. Research by I/O psychologists in a variety of organizations shows that disabled employees perform as well as or better than nondisabled employees. Many large U.S. corporations, such as Du Pont, 3M, and McDonnell Douglas, routinely hire disabled workers because they have found that they make good employees.

Job opportunities for disabled persons also vary as a function of type of disability. People with impairments of vision, hearing, or motor skills experience greater difficulty obtaining employment than people with less disabling conditions.

Women Workers. Women face discrimination in the workplace, particularly when they apply for what are still considered to be traditionally male jobs. Evidence indicates that employment discrimination against women, although frequent, is not as pervasive as discrimination against ethnic minorities. Once hired, however, women receive lower wages than men with similar skills and qualifications who are performing the same jobs. Gender-based wage discrimination— lower pay for **comparable worth**—has been found in organizations in several countries; for example, in a study of 5,000 employees in a telecommunications corporation in Israel, the gap between men and women in rank and salary was found to be largely attributable to sex discrimination (Haberfeld, 1992). Thus, discrimination against women today may occur less in the hiring process but more in terms of pay and promotion.

Comparable worth The idea that jobs that require comparable or equivalent skills should receive comparable compensation.

Discrimination Based on Sexual Orientation. Gay men and lesbian women face discrimination in hiring in public agencies and private companies. To date, no federal civil rights legislation protects homosexuals from workplace discrimination. Since 1989, however, six states have included sexual orientation among the protected categories in their civil rights laws and more than 85 cities have passed ordinances forbidding job discrimination against gay people.

An increasing number of U.S. corporations are developing antidiscrimination policies with regard to gay persons. Some companies, such as AT&T, Xerox, Lockheed, and Levi Strauss, actively sponsor support groups and networks for their gay employees. In most companies, however, gay workers continue to face discrimination and the threat of losing their job, which is a major reason why many choose to keep their sexual orientation a private matter.

Discrimination Based on Physical Attractiveness. Some job applicants have a more pleasing appearance than others in terms of currently accepted cultural standards. This type of judgment, called *beautyism* by some, affects hiring and promotion decisions in the business world.

Many people believe that physically attractive persons also possess more desirable personality and social traits, an attitude summed up by some I/O psychologists as "what is beautiful is good." A meta-analysis of 76 laboratory studies found only moderate support for this stereotype (Eagly, Ashmore, Makhijani, & Longo, 1991). Another analysis of 78 studies involving 4,727 subjects concluded that physically attractive persons were believed by others to be more sociable, dominant, sexually warm, mentally healthy, and socially skilled than less attractive persons (Feingold, 1992).

Some people also believe that attractive persons are better qualified and more successful than less attractive persons. In a study of corporate recruiters who interviewed 350 graduating MBA students from an Ivy League business school, the recruiters' first impression about an applicant's physical attractiveness and height contributed to the overall judgment about which applicants were suitable for employment with their firm (Rynes & Gerhart, 1990).

In a simulated hiring situation, 112 managers (46 men and 66 women) evaluated résumés, to which photographs were attached, for male and female job applicants. The photographs had been judged by human resources personnel as being either highly attractive or slightly below average in attractiveness. Not surprisingly, the more physically attractive candidates were preferred to the less attractive candidates. This bias was found to decrease with the managers' length of job experience; in other words, the more experienced the manager, the less tendency he or she exhibited toward discriminating among potential workers on the basis of physical appearance. However, even among the most experienced managers, the less attractive female job applicants received the lowest ratings on suitability for hiring (Marlowe, Schneider, & Nelson, 1996).

Research on one component of attractiveness studied the possibility of bias against overweight job applicants. The subjects were 320 college students who observed simulated job interviews. The results showed a prejudice against hiring applicants (especially women) who appeared to be overweight (Pingitore, Dugoni, Tindale, & Spring, 1994).

JOB ANALYSIS

Job analysis The study of a job to describe in specific terms the nature of the component tasks performed by the workers.

The purpose of **job analysis** is to describe in specific terms the nature of the component tasks performed by workers on a particular job. A job analysis includes information about the tools or equipment used, the operations performed, the education and training required, the wages paid, and any unique aspects of the job such as safety hazards. We mentioned earlier the value of job analysis in employee selection. Unless the company knows precisely what is required for the successful performance of a job, it will have no way of knowing what qualities to seek in applicants for that job.

Job analysis has other important uses in organizational life. To establish a training program for a particular job, for example, the nature of the job must be known. A company cannot expect to train a person to perform a job unless the tasks and operations required for job success can be described. Job analysis can aid in efforts to design a job or a workspace for more efficient performance. If a job analysis reveals that a lathe operator has to walk 50 yards from the machine to the storage shelves every time it is necessary to replenish the supply of raw material, this wasted time and effort can be eliminated by redesigning the work area. Job analysis can also uncover safety hazards or dangerous operating procedures.

Job analyses are also applied to the development of job evaluations, which are used to determine appropriate wages for various jobs. The issue of wage equity and comparable worth has forced a reexamination of pay scales in recent years. To determine fair pay, it is necessary to collect and evaluate data from large numbers of employees on such job-related factors as the specific skills required, the level of education, the level of responsibility, and the consequences of making errors. These judgments are usually made by a panel of experts and are based on the job analyses.

There are two basic approaches to job analysis: the job-oriented approach and the worker-oriented approach. The job-oriented approach focuses on the specific tasks involved in performing a job and on the job outcome or level of productivity. The worker-oriented approach focuses on worker behaviors on the job and on the specific skills, abilities, and personal traits needed to perform the job. Most job analyses involve a combination of job-oriented and worker-oriented data.

I/O psychologists have devised a number of techniques for conducting job analyses (see, for example, Levine, Sistrunk, McNutt, & Gael, 1988; Levine, Thomas, & Sistrunk, 1988; Spector, Brannick, & Coovert, 1989). Published analyses are available for many jobs, but there are limitations to using them because the jobs described, no matter how similar, may not be identical to the one in question. A standard and comprehensive published list of jobs is the *Dictionary of Occupational Titles* (DOT), issued by the U.S. Department of Labor. This periodically updated work gives brief definitions of some 22,000 jobs. The revised version of the fourth edition was published in May 1991. The listings are not as detailed as a job analysis should be, but they serve to familiarize researchers with a job's general aspects and requirements. They also include information on physical demands and on general educational and vocational training requirements. A few of the job definitions from this sourcebook are listed in Table 3–1.

TABLE 3–1   Sample Job Descriptions

Bowling-Ball Finisher
Tends buffing machine that removes scratches and polishes surface of bowling balls.

Clip Coater
Coats tips of sunglass clips with protective plastic and cures coated clips in oven.

Dog Bather
Bathes dogs in preparation for grooming.

Hair Stylist
Specializes in dressing hair according to latest style or period, following instructions of patron.

Maturity Checker
Tends machine that mashes peas and registers force required to crush them to ascertain hardness (maturity).

Potato-Chip Sorter
Observes potato chips on conveyor and removes chips that are burned, discolored, or broken.

Sequins Stringer
Strings plastic sequins on thread for use as decoration on wearing apparel.

Squeak, Rattle, and Leak Repairer
Drives automobiles of service customers to determine origin of noises and leaks, and repairs or adjusts components to eliminate cause of complaint.

Note. From *Dictionary of Occupational Titles* (4th ed., rev.), 1991, Washington, DC: Government Printing Office.

Interviews.   The use of interviews for job analysis involves extensive meetings with the persons directly connected with the job—the workers currently performing the job and their supervisors (the subject matter experts), and sometimes the instructors who trained the workers for the job. Job analysts may supplement interviews with questionnaires. The persons being interviewed should be told the purpose of the interview and why it is important to answer the questions fully and honestly. The questions should be carefully planned and clearly worded to elicit as much information as possible.

Questionnaires.   Two types of questionnaires are used in job analysis: the unstructured questionnaire and the structured questionnaire. In the unstructured or open-end approach, the subject matter experts (workers and their supervisors) describe in their own words the components of the job and the tasks performed.

When the structured questionnaire approach is used, workers and supervisors are provided with descriptions of tasks, operations, and working conditions and are asked to rate the items or to select those items that characterize their jobs. Research has shown, however, that many subject matter experts are careless in providing ratings, perhaps because of boredom, which can lead to less-than-accurate job analyses.

A study of several hundred police officers who were given 2 weeks to complete a checklist questionnaire showed that the content of a job analysis varied as a function of length of job experience. For example, when the officers were asked to rate the specific job tasks in a given work period, it was found that those with greater experience chose to spend less time dealing with traffic offenses than did officers with fewer years of experience. Level of education and gender were found to have only minimal effects on most job analysis task ratings (Landy & Vasey, 1991). A study of 100 women clerical workers in state government agencies used a 5-point rating scale questionnaire to document job tasks. The researchers found that the specific typing, filing, and communications tasks reported by the workers differed by the workers' race and by whether an employee had co-workers of the same or a different race (Veres, Green, & Boyles, 1991). Thus, the possible effects of such variables as race and job experience should be considered by the job analysts.

A widely used questionnaire is the Position Analysis Questionnaire (PAQ), which consists of 194 job elements related to specific behaviors. The job elements are organized into six categories of job behavior: information input, mental processes, work output, relationships with other persons, job context, and other job activities and conditions. Subject matter experts rate each element for its importance to the job in question. Such quantifiable ratings have an obvious advantage over the kind of information yielded by the unstructured questionnaire.

For some occupations, however, the PAQ may pinpoint only commonsense beliefs or stereotypes about the components of a job. For example, PAQ ratings obtained from subject matter experts showed a high positive correlation with the ratings made by college students (considered naive rather than expert raters). The college students based their ratings on job titles or brief job descriptions, not on any personal familiarity with the jobs. The researchers suggested that if naive raters could provide ratings similar to those of the subject matter experts, then the PAQ may be reflecting common knowledge about the jobs rather than a detailed description and ranking of job tasks (DeNisi, Cornelius, & Blencoe, 1987).

Direct Observation.   A third approach to job analysis is the direct observation of the workers on the job. Because people may behave differently when they know they are being watched, it is necessary for the job analysts to remain as unobtrusive as possible. Also, they should observe a representative sample of workers and make observations at various times throughout the workday to take account of changes caused by such factors as fatigue.

Systematic Activity Logs.   With systematic activity logs, workers maintain a detailed written record of their activities during a given period. If prepared with care, these logs can reveal details not otherwise obtainable.

Critical Incidents.   The **critical-incidents technique** is based on the identification of those incidents or behaviors that are necessary to successful job performance. The goal is to have subject matter experts indicate the behaviors that differentiate good from poor workers. The critical-incidents technique focuses on specific actions that lead to desirable or undesirable consequences on the job. A single critical incident is of little value, but hundreds of them can effectively describe a job task sequence in terms of the unique behaviors required to perform it well.

Critical-incidents technique A means of identifying specific actions or behaviors that lead to desirable or undesirable consequences on the job.

Research comparing the effectiveness of various approaches to job analysis indicates that they vary in their usefulness. The choice of a specific technique must depend on the organization's reasons for conducting the analysis in the first place. Unfortunately, most job analyses seem to be undertaken without specific goals in mind. Unless a job analysis is targeted toward a definite objective, such as refining an employee selection or training program, much of the data collected by the interviews, questionnaires, and other methods of job analysis will be useless. Unless the purpose of the job analysis is stated, the company cannot make an informed decision about which technique to use or what kind of information to seek. When a job analysis is conducted for a clearly defined purpose, a combination of methods rather than a single technique provides for the most accurate and comprehensive job descriptions.

Job analysis continues to be an important part of the employee selection process (Borman, Hanson, & Hedge, 1997). Every employing organization must be able to justify each of its job requirements to show that whatever it asks of a job applicant is related directly to the ability to perform the job. It must not set arbitrary qualifications that can be used to discriminate against groups of workers and to deny them equal opportunity for employment. A detailed job analysis provides justification for determining specific job requirements. For example, if a company is charged with sex discrimination because women employees are paid less than men employees for what appears to be the same job, the company would have to show that the men are performing different tasks that justify the greater pay. A job analysis can provide that information. Therefore, organizations take seriously the task of job analysis. Equal employment opportunity and successful selection programs are not possible without it.

Let us now consider some specific employee selection techniques currently in use: biographical information forms, interviews, references and letters of recommendation, assessment centers, polygraphs, integrity tests, and handwriting analysis. Psychological tests for employee selection are described in Chapter 4.

BIOGRAPHICAL INFORMATION

The collecting of biographical information, sometimes called biodata, on the backgrounds of job applicants is a common method of employee selection. The rationale for this technique is the belief that our past experiences or characteristics can be used to predict the direction of our career. Because many of our behaviors, values, and attitudes remain consistent throughout life, it is not unreasonable to assume that our behavior in the future will be based on our behavior in the past.

People responsible for hiring decisions place great importance on the kinds of past behaviors routinely described on application blanks. For example, a sample of 113 recruiters for 17 companies was surveyed about their judgments of the usefulness of the following information from application blanks and résumés: work experience, education, extracurricular activities, and honors. The results showed that the recruiters assessed this life history data as reflecting both the applicants' formal abilities (such as language or math skills) and less tangible attributes (such as leadership qualities, motivation, and interpersonal skills) (Brown & Campion, 1994). Thus, we can conclude that initial determinations about your suitability for employment are likely to be based on the information you supply on a company's application blank.

I/O psychologists have refined two major techniques for collecting biographical information: the standard application blank and the biographical inventory.

Standard Application Blanks

Application blanks A technique for compiling biographical information about a job applicant.

Rarely is anyone hired by an organization at any level of employment without being asked to complete an **application blank.** The information routinely solicited on applications includes biographical data such as name, address, education, and work experience. It can also cover medical history, specific skills, and criminal convictions. For higher-level positions, applicants might be asked to describe their interests and hobbies, reading habits, and career goals.

The crucial problem in the construction of employment applications is deciding what information to ask. What does the employer need to know to determine whether the applicant is suitable for the job? Beyond basic biographical data, the company must ascertain those facts about the candidate that correlate with subsequent successful performance of the job.

If research shows, for example, that most successful executives are college graduates who maintained grade point averages of 3.5 or better and who served in the student government association, then this is the kind of information the human resources department will want to elicit about an applicant early in the selection process. If the completed application blank indicates that the candidate does not possess these qualities, then the company will not have to pursue the process and undertake the expense of administering a battery of psychological tests or arranging for the candidate to visit the company headquarters.

The utility of the information obtained depends on the thoroughness of the research conducted to develop the items on the application blank. Each relevant item must be correlated with a later measure of job success. If a high positive correlation is found, then that item can be used with confidence to select new employees.

Honesty of Responses.   One problem with applications is the honesty of the applicant's responses. Is the information the applicant supplies complete and correct? Did he actually graduate from the college indicated on the form? Did she really supervise 50 workers in her previous job? Was the previous annual salary $40,000, or is that an exaggeration? A sizable number of job applicants provide misleading or fraudulent information, especially about their previous job title, pay, and degree of responsibility.

A large government agency in New York State reported that one third of its job applicants lied about their prior work experience. Other research suggests that up to two thirds of all applicants may falsify some aspect of their background (Shaffer, Saunders, & Owens, 1986). Some of this faking can be reduced by follow-up interviews and by issuing advance warnings to the effect that the information provided on an application blank is subject to verification.

Many organizations attempt to confirm the accuracy of biographical information by contacting former employers and the persons named as references. Nowadays, however, many companies are reluctant to release personal information for fear of lawsuits. A former employee may sue a company for providing unfavorable information, claiming libel or slander. Therefore, many employing organizations hesitate to supply more than limited factual data, such as job title and dates of employment. Few give evaluative information, such as performance ratings and responsibilities, or answer questions such as why the employee left or whether the company would rehire the employee. Thus, it is difficult for an organization to verify certain kinds of information obtained from an application.

Biographical Inventories

The **biographical inventory,** or biographical information blank, is a more systematized form of application blank (Owens & Schoenfeldt, 1979). Biographical inventories are typically much longer than application blanks and cover information on an applicant's life in much greater detail. The rationale for this extensive probing is that on-the-job behavior is related to past behavior in a variety of situations as well as to attitudes, preferences, and values. For example, whereas a standard application blank might ask for the name of your college, your major field, and the dates you attended, a biographical inventory might ask the following questions about your college experience:

> **Biographical inventories**
> An employee selection technique covering an applicant's past behavior, attitudes, preferences, and values; these questionnaires are longer and more extensive than standard application blanks.

- How often did you have problems with other students because of different social groups or cliques?
- How often have other students come to you for advice?
- How often have you set a goal to do better than anyone else at something?
- How often did you feel you needed more self-discipline?

Other sample biographical inventory items are shown in Table 3–2.

Considerable research is required to determine the background experiences that correlate with job success. The process of validating the items on a biographical inventory is similar to that for any selection technique. Each item is correlated with a measure of job performance.

Research on biographical inventories has confirmed their high predictive value, equal to that of cognitive ability tests and assessment centers (Childs &

TABLE 3–2   Sample Biographical Inventory Items

Habits and Attitudes
  How often do you tell jokes?
     1. Very frequently.
     2. Frequently.
     3. Occasionally.
     4. Seldom.
     5. Can't remember jokes.

Human Relations
  How do you regard your neighbors?
     1. Not interested in your neighbors.
     2. Like them but seldom see them.
     3. Visit in each others' homes occasionally.
     4. Spend a lot of time together.

Personal Attributes
  How creative do you feel you are?
     1. Highly creative.
     2. Somewhat more creative than most in your field.
     3. Moderately creative.
     4. Somewhat less creative than most in your field.
     5. Not creative.

Self-impressions
  Do you generally do your best?
     1. At whatever job you are doing.
     2. Only in what you are interested.
     3. Only when it is demanded of you.

Values, Opinions, and Preferences
  Which one of the following seems most important to you?
     1. A pleasant home and family life.
     2. A challenging and exciting job.
     3. Getting ahead in the world.
     4. Being active and accepted in community affairs.
     5. Making the most of your particular ability.

Adapted from *Biographical Data in Industrial Psychology* by W. A. Owens & E. R. Henry, 1966, Greensboro, NC: Richardson Foundation.

Klimoski, 1986; Drakeley, Herriot, & Jones, 1988). A meta-analysis of one biographical inventory, in which the items chosen had predicted success in 79 companies, showed that its predictive value could be generalized across organizations. Approximately 11,000 first-line supervisors were involved. The researchers concluded that the same inventory could be used to select successful employees in a large number and variety of organizations. As a result, the costly process of devising separate inventories for each company could be avoided (Rothstein, Schmidt, Erwin, Owens, & Sparks, 1990).

A study involving 2,535 U.S. Army recruits found that many of the items asked on a biographical inventory could be grouped into four personality factors: rugged/outdoors, solid citizen, team sports/group orientation, and intellectual/achievement orientation. The individual responses or scores on these factors showed a strong positive correlation with the recruits' identification with military service and their later decision to leave the army before their term of enlistment was up. Thus, the scores on these factors could be used prior to enlistment to predict who would succeed in the military and who would not (Mael & Ashforth, 1995).

In a study of 1,523 college graduates, their responses on a biographical inventory taken as first-year college students proved to be valid predictors of occupational status 16 to 21 years later. The data of greatest predictive value included academic achievement, scientific interests, popularity, and social activity (Snell, Stokes, Sands, & McBride, 1994).

The Problem of Faking. Some I/O psychologists recommend that biographical inventory questions be restricted primarily to external events that are verifiable and deal with unique personal experiences. These kinds of items seldom elicit false answers. For example, studies on employees in a large international manufacturing company showed that faking on biographical inventories was low (Becker & Colquitt, 1992).

Faking does occur, however, and applicants can deliberately distort their responses by giving answers they believe are more socially acceptable or desirable, or that will present them in a more favorable light. In one experiment, a 171-item biographical inventory was given to 2,262 salespersons employed by a large office equipment company. The employees were told they were participating in a research project and that their responses would be confidential and would have no bearing on their careers.

A second group, comprising 2,726 applicants for salesperson positions, were given the same biodata questionnaire and told that the results would determine whether or not they were hired. You can probably guess the outcome. The incidence of faking—of giving socially desirable responses—was significantly higher for the job applicants. The group of current employees could afford to be honest; they already had jobs (Stokes, Hogen, & Snell, 1993)

Faking on biographical inventories can be reduced by warning people that their answers will be checked or by telling them that a scale to detect faking is built into the questionnaire or that a special scoring system will lower their scores if they answer dishonestly.

The effect of the latter condition was demonstrated in a study of 429 applicants for the job of nurse's assistant in a nursing home. Half of the applicants were told that dishonest responses would be detected and subtracted from their total score, so they would not increase the chances of getting a job. The other applicants were given no such warning. The results showed that faking was considerably reduced among those who received the warning (Kluger & Colella, 1993).

As we noted, biographical inventories have been found to be valid predictors of job success. Unfortunately, the technique is seldom applied in the world of work. A survey of 248 personnel directors suggested several reasons for this situation (Hammer & Kleiman, 1988). First, slightly more than half said they did not know much about biographical inventories. Many more said that their organizations lacked the time, money, and human resources to develop and update them. More than one fourth reported that they did not think biographical inventories were valid. It appears that the I/O psychologists working for these companies or conducting research on biographical inventories have not been effective in communicating the success of these techniques to the persons in a position to implement them.

This situation illustrates the gap that sometimes arises between research and application in I/O psychology, as we discussed in Chapter 1. In this case, researchers have developed a highly successful employee selection tool, but it is seldom used in the workplace. What is needed now are data persuading management that the use of such a valid procedure to select the best employees will save more money in the long run than the costs of developing and implementing it.

INTERVIEWS

The personal interview is a widely used employee selection technique in the United States and many other countries. Regardless of any other techniques that are part of an organization's selection program, almost every prospective employer wants the chance to meet an applicant in person before making the offer of a job. Interviews may range from a handshake and a cursory meeting of a few minutes to more elaborate sessions lasting a few days. It is important to remember that the employment interview, like the college recruiting interview, is a two-way process. Its purpose is to provide a situation for the evaluation of a candidate's suitability for employment. But it also offers the opportunity for candidates, if they ask the right questions, to determine whether the company and the job are right for them.

The purpose of the interview helps determine how useful it is to a job applicant for obtaining information about a prospective employer. For example, research has shown that an interview conducted solely for the purpose of recruiting, in which the goal is to convey information about the job, resulted in substantially greater information acquisition about the employer than when applicants were told the interview was for the purpose of selection (Barber, Hollenbeck, Tower, & Phillips, 1994).

First Impressions

The impression you make during an interview will be a decisive factor in whether the organization offers you a job. I/O psychology research has shown that interviewers' assessments of job applicants often are influenced more by their subjective impressions of the applicants than by such factors as work history, academic qualifications, or extracurricular activities. Personal qualities, such as perceived attractiveness, likability, and skill at self-promotion, were the key applicant factors in the interviewers' hiring recommendations.

Impression management
Acting deliberately to make a good impression, to present oneself in the most favorable way.

Of course, as you probably know from your own experience, it is possible to act deliberately so as to make the right impression; that is, to present yourself in the most favorable light. I/O psychologists have described this situation as **impression management** and have noted two approaches job applicants can take: ingratiation and self-promotion (Stevens & Kristof, 1995). Ingratiation refers to behaviors that attempt to persuade the interviewer to like you. For example, you may praise the interviewer or appear to agree with his or her opinions, values, and attitudes. Self-promotion tactics include making laudatory comments about your accomplishments, character traits, or goals. Research has shown that impression management techniques are effective in significantly influencing interviewers' judgments. Self-promotion tactics are used more frequently than ingratiation behaviors.

The personal interview is part of virtually every employee selection program.

Unstructured Interviews

Three kinds of interviews used in the business world are the standard or unstructured interview, the patterned or structured interview, and the situational interview.

The **unstructured interview** is characterized by a lack of advance planning. It could even be described as little more than a general conversation. The format and the questions asked are left to the discretion of the interviewer. It is possible, therefore, that five interviewers conducting separate unstructured interviews with the same applicant will receive five different impressions.

Thus, a basic weakness of the unstructured interview is its lack of consistency in assessing candidates. Interviewers may be interested in different aspects of an applicant's background, experience, or attitudes, and the results of the interview may then reflect more of the biases and prejudices of the interviewers than the objective qualifications of the applicants.

A now-classic study in this area, published in 1929, asked 12 interviewers independently to rate 57 applicants on their suitability for a sales job (Hollingworth, 1929). Although the interviewers were experienced sales managers who had conducted many interviews with job applicants, there was a significant lack of agreement among them. Some applicants who were ranked first by one interviewer were ranked last by another. The results of the judgments made about a single applicant are shown in Figure 3–1. You can see that the ratings for this one person range from a low of 1 to a high of 55. If the person responsible for making the decision about hiring this individual was given this interview information, it would be of little help because it offers no firm basis on which to decide about the person's suitability.

Unstructured interviews
Interviews in which the format and questions asked are left to the discretion of the interviewers.

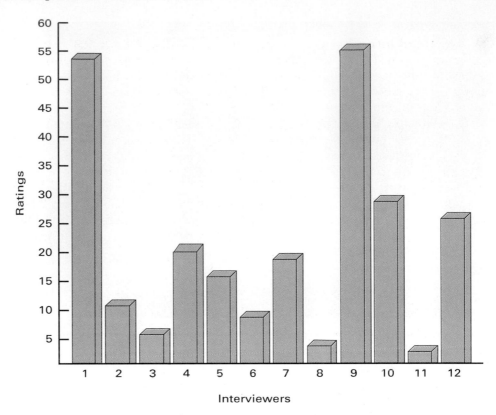

FIGURE 3–1. Ratings of 1 applicant by 12 interviewers. (Data from H. L. Hollingworth, *Vocational psychology and character analysis.* New York: Appleton, 1929.)

This same weakness was demonstrated in a more recent study of 29 professional interviewers for a large financial services (banking and insurance) company. Their level of effectiveness was rated by 427 supervisors of the people hired by the interviewers. The I/O psychologists found substantial differences in the interviewers' decision-making strategies. Even though they all worked for the same company and presumably knew what qualities were being sought among job applicants, they applied more than a dozen different patterns of applicant qualifications in their hiring recommendations. The researchers concluded that the company was not getting consistency in employee selection decisions based on interviews, because the same applicants were being evaluated in different ways by different interviewers (Graves & Karren, 1992).

In addition to the lack of consistency, or reliability, of the unstructured interview, is the finding that its predictive validity is low. This was demonstrated decades ago by Walter Dill Scott, mentioned in Chapter 1 as a founder of the field of industrial psychology (Scott, 1915). Scott's conclusion has been supported by subsequent empirical research (see, for example, Arvey & Campion, 1982).

Despite the recognized limitations of low reliability and validity, unstructured interviews are still used far more frequently by employing organizations than other interview techniques that demonstrate greater validity.

Structured Interviews

The **structured interview** uses a predetermined list of questions that are asked of every applicant. Thus, the interview procedure is standardized so that the resulting assessment of job candidates is less open to interviewer bias. Although subjective and personal factors can still affect an interviewer's judgment, they are less of a problem in the structured interview.

In conducting the structured interview, the interviewer uses a printed form that contains the questions to be asked. The applicant's responses are recorded on the same form. The interview session is sometimes described as more like an elaborate application blank that the interviewer completes on the basis of what the applicant says.

The following structured interview questions are typical of those used by an organization selecting college graduates for management positions. Because they deal with work experience, they are intended for graduates who have held at least one job since graduation:

1. What was your first job after completing college?
2. What were your major accomplishments on that job?
3. What were some of the things you did less well, things that point to the need for further training and development?
4. What did you learn about yourself on that job?
5. What aspects of the job did you find most challenging?
6. What sort of work would you like to be doing five years from now?

Because all applicants are asked the questions in the same sequence, there is a firmer basis for comparison of candidates than with the random questioning procedures of the unstructured interview.

You can see that structured interviews are a considerable improvement over unstructured interviews and have the potential for higher predictive validity. Many research studies have verified this judgment and report validities as high as +.62, twice that of unstructured interviews (see, for example, Huffcutt, 1990; Wiesner & Cronshaw, 1988; Wright, Lichtenfels, & Pursell, 1989). I/O psychology research has also shown that structured interviews can be as valid predictors of job success as a battery of intelligence or cognitive ability tests. Not surprisingly, structured interviews are high in reliability as well (Campion, Campion, & Hudson, 1994; Campion, Pursell, & Brown, 1988; Conway, Jako, & Goodman, 1995; Huffcutt & Arthur, 1994; McDaniel, Whetzel, Schmidt, & Maurer, 1994). Thus, the interview can be made a more useful selection device if it is formalized and structured.

Situational Interviews

A third kind of interview, the **situational interview,** is developed specifically to meet the needs of a particular job. The interview questions are not designed to inquire about general work experience or personal characteristics and abilities but, rather, about the behaviors needed for successful performance of the job in question. These behaviors are determined by a job analysis conducted by the critical-incidents technique.

Structured interviews Interviews that use a predetermined list of questions that are asked of every person who applies for a particular job.

Situational interviews Interviews that focus not on personal characteristics or work experience but on the behaviors needed for successful job performance.

The first step in developing the situational interview is to prepare a list of critical incidents that differentiate between successful and unsuccessful employees currently on the job. These incidents are typically identified by supervisors who have a comprehensive knowledge of the job. The supervisors determine benchmarks for scoring the incidents, assigning a score of 5 to those behaviors displayed by successful employees, 3 to behaviors displayed by average employees, and 1 to behaviors displayed by poor employees. The incidents are rephrased as questions to be used in the situational interview, and therefore they represent items that are directly related to how the applicant would behave on the job. The numerical benchmarks make it possible to score the interview objectively.

Once constructed, situational interviews are quick and easy to administer and interpret. Because the questions are clearly and directly related to job behavior, this type of interview can increase the motivation of job applicants to answer the questions accurately.

Situational interviews have been used to select workers for skilled and semi-skilled factory jobs, for sales jobs, and for first-line supervisory positions. Situational interview results have been found to correlate positively with measures of later job performance and to be more valid than structured interviews (see, for example, Maurer & Fay, 1988; McDaniel, Whetzel, Schmidt, & Maurer, 1994). However, one study found that interview questions about an applicant's past behavior on the job were more valid predictors of job performance than situational questions dealing with the ways in which applicants would cope with hypothetical situations (Pulakos & Schmitt, 1995). Nevertheless, the preponderance of evidence favors the situational interview approach and justifies the suggestion that the best kind of interview for predicting job success would be both situational and structured (Landy, Shankster, & Kohler, 1994).

Other Approaches to Interviews

Another way to increase the predictive utility of interviews is to have them conducted by a panel of three to five interviewers instead of by one person. Combining the judgments about a prospective employee has been shown to improve reliability and validity and temper the possible biasing effects of personal characteristics that are not job-related.

An innovation in interviewing uses computer software to conduct the initial interviews. In computer-assisted interviewing, applicants answer a fixed sequence of multiple-choice questions at a computer terminal. In this high-tech structured interview, all applicants for a given position are asked the same questions in the same order. Questions on sensitive issues can be included, if appropriate, whereas in the traditional interview situation, many interviewers are hesitant to ask about personal matters. Corporate users of computer-assisted interviews indicate that applicants do not feel threatened by the computer and are willing to respond with honesty and candor. However, some applicants for high-status executive jobs may resent the impersonality of computer-assisted interviews.

Biasing Effects in Interviews

We discuss three factors that can bias an interviewer's judgment about a job applicant: (1) prior information, (2) the contrast effect, and (3) interviewers' prejudices. All of these factors can be reduced or minimized by training interviewers to recognize their effects.

Prior Information.   Interviewers generally have some prior information about a job candidate, such as recruiter's evaluations, data supplied on an application blank or biographical inventory, or the results of psychological tests. The nature of that prior information can predispose an interviewer to have a favorable or unfavorable attitude toward an applicant before he or she shows up for the interview.

A sample of 577 candidates for jobs as life insurance sales agents filled out comprehensive biographical inventories prior to being interviewed. The results showed that interviewers gave considerably less weight to how candidates behaved during their interviews when those candidates had scored high on the inventory. Interviewers gave more weight to interview performance for candidates who had scored low on the inventory. In both cases, the prior information influenced the emphasis interviewers placed on the candidates' behavior while being interviewed (Dalessio & Silverhart, 1994).

In another study, three interviewers for a large energy corporation received application blank and test score data on 79 applicants prior to their interviews. Toward applicants the interviewers were impressed with because of this prior information (as indicated by ratings of how qualified they thought each applicant was), the interviewers behaved differently than they did toward those applicants they found not so impressive. Interviewers showed more positive regard for the candidates whose prior information was favorable; they agreed with them more, laughed, and were more encouraging, warm, understanding, approving, and friendly. Interviewers also spent more time selling the company and providing job information to the more impressive applicants, as well as less time soliciting information from them, than they did to applicants who had scored low on the tests (Dougherty, Turban, & Callender, 1994).

The Contrast Effect.   Interviewers see many job applicants, often one after another, and how they evaluate a particular applicant may depend on their standards of comparison; that is, the characteristics of the applicants they have interviewed previously. For example, after having interviewed three undesirable candidates, an interviewer may rate the next candidate in line as more favorable than the candidate's qualifications merit. The same average candidate may be rated less favorably if the previous candidates have all been highly qualified.

Not only does this tendency highlight the importance of your place in an interviewer's schedule, it also means, as we saw earlier, that interviewers often do not have objective standards for the type of person considered to be a suitable employee. Applicants are not evaluated on an absolute basis but are judged relative to the other applicants interviewed that day or that week. How good you appear to be depends on how good or poor the others are. Thus, the standard for the acceptable employee may frequently change.

Interviewers' Prejudices.   Another characteristic of interviewers that affects their judgment is their personal likes and dislikes. For example, men interviewers sometimes think that women employees are incapable of performing certain jobs. Interviewers of both sexes are more likely to hire women for so-called traditional female jobs, such as schoolteacher or nurse, than for traditional male jobs. Older job applicants and persons with disabilities tend to receive lower evaluations from interviewers (Raza & Carpenter, 1987).

Some research has shown that interviewer ratings of black and white job applicants do not differ on the basis of color (see, for example, Arvey & Faley,

1988). However, a study of racial effects in structured, two-person panels responsible for interviewing approximately 3,000 applicants for custodian jobs in an urban West Coast school district found a bias toward recommending persons of the same race as the interviewers. That bias was reduced when the interview panel included people of different races, such as one black and one white interviewer, or one white and one Hispanic interviewer (Lin, Dobbins, & Farh, 1992).

A study of four-member panel interviews of 153 police officers applying for promotion also showed a same-race biasing effect. With racially balanced interview panels (2 black raters and 2 white raters), individual interviewers gave significantly higher ratings to candidates of the same race. When the majority of the panel members were white, white candidates received significantly higher ratings from both black raters and white raters. When the majority of the panel members were black, black candidates received higher ratings from both black raters and white raters, although, in this instance, the differences were not statistically significant (Prewett-Livingston, Feild, Veres, & Lewis, 1996).

Thus, interviewers may prejudge applicants who display certain qualities or traits and refuse to consider their other characteristics. They may also hire applicants merely because they exhibit some quality the interviewers like, even though it may bear no relation to job performance.

Halo effect   The tendency to judge all aspects of a person's behavior or character on the basis of a single attribute.

The phenomenon of generalizing from one trait or characteristic to the entire person in a positive or a negative direction is called the **halo effect,** and it operates whenever people make personal judgments about others.

As difficult and error-prone as the standard interview is, it remains part of virtually every selection program in business, industry, education, and government. The danger lies in placing too much emphasis on its results. If used wisely, however, the interview can assist both organization and applicant. Its predictive accuracy can be greatly improved by the use of structured and situational interviews and by careful training of interviewers.

REFERENCES AND LETTERS OF RECOMMENDATION

At one time, selection programs routinely involved obtaining information about job applicants from persons who knew something about their background, skills, and work history, such as former teachers, employers, co-workers, and friends. The purpose was to examine other people's impressions of the applicants and to verify the information the applicants reported.

A major limitation of letters of recommendation was that they often presented a false picture of the applicant. The person providing the reference—whether in a letter, in person, or in a telephone interview—sometimes deliberately responded in a misleading manner for several reasons. Past employers wanted to be kind and to say only favorable things about former employees. Current employers who hoped to get rid of undesirable employees wrote glowing letters of recommendation. Professors wrote positive letters because they knew that students would be able to read their files in the university placement center.

A more important limitation on the usefulness of letters of recommendation is that many organizations are no longer willing to supply evaluative information

NEWSBREAK #5

A Deadly Letter of Recommendation

Around the Allstate Insurance Company office in Tampa, Florida, where he worked, Paul Calder had frequently seemed to be acting weird. He told people he was an alien. He wrote *blood* and other strange words on his computer screen and refused to let the boss see them. He threatened to kill a masseuse who refused to give him a refund. And then he brought a gun to work

"I was reasonably sure I had a total lunatic on my hands," his boss said. "A nut case."

The boss was afraid to fire Calder because he believed the employee was capable of killing him and others in the office, but he knew somehow he had to get rid of Calder. So he made up a story about a corporate restructuring that would eliminate Calder's job and offered him severance pay if he would resign. When Calder chose to resign, the boss wrote him a letter of recommendation that was bland and innocuous, as most such letters are nowadays. It did not indicate that there was anything at all wrong with Paul Calder.

The letter said Calder resigned because of organizational restructuring and that his resignation "is in no way a reflection upon Paul's job performance."

To do otherwise—to put an employee's faults and failings on paper—is to open yourself and your organization to a lawsuit for libel or slander. It has become prudent in corporate life today to say nothing about an ex-employee but the bare facts: job title and dates of employment.

Paul Calder found a job with another Tampa insurance company, but his bizarre behavior continued and he was fired. Several months later, he returned to that office to see the people who had fired him. He carried a 9mm handgun. He killed three men and wounded two women, then drove to nearby Clearwater and killed himself.

The families of the murdered employees filed a multimillion-dollar lawsuit against Allstate—Calder's original employer—for failing to disclose the problems with Calder's behavior. Allstate is being sued for writing a misleading letter of recommendation, which, ironically, it wrote out of fear of being sued.

Source: L. Dougherty. Shooting victims' families can sue Allstate. *St. Petersburg (FL) Times*, August 8, 1995.

about former employees for fear of lawsuits. If a company makes a false statement about why a former employee was fired, for example, the employee can sue the company for defamation of character. Thousands of such lawsuits have been filed against U.S. corporations. The mere threat of legal action has prevented many companies from cooperating in even the most ordinary reference checking effort. Companies are advised to refuse to reveal any information about former employees beyond dates of employment, job title, and final salary. If a company chooses to discuss the poor job performance of a fired employee, it should have for its own protection written evidence from objective performance appraisals citing specific instances that can be documented by date, time, and place. In addition, managers and supervisors should assume that anything they include in a letter of recommendation may one day be scrutinized by a judge and jury.

Even though the amount and kind of information obtained from references is minimal, many employers still make at least a cursory attempt to check references. Because of the legal complications, however, they are used less frequently today as a selection technique than in the past.

ASSESSMENT CENTERS: SELECTION BY SIMULATION

Assessment centers A method of selection and training that involves a simulated job situation in which candidates deal with actual job problems.

Situational testing An early term for the assessment-center approach to employee selection and performance appraisal in which subjects act in a simulated job setting so that their behavior under stress can be observed and evaluated.

The **assessment center** is a method of selection that places new job applicants and candidates for promotion in a simulated job situation so that their behavior under stress can be observed and evaluated. This approach, initially called **situational testing,** was developed and used by the German army in the 1920s to select officer candidates of high quality. It was first used extensively in the United States by psychologists during World War II when it was adopted as a selection technique by the Office of Strategic Services (OSS), the forerunner of today's Central Intelligence Agency (CIA).

The use of situational testing in industry was pioneered by AT&T in the mid-1950s, and the technique has since been adopted by more than 2,000 organizations, including IBM, Ford, and Kodak. Assessment-center testing can now be found in many countries, such as Britain, Australia, Brazil, and Japan. The technique has been used most frequently to select persons at the executive and managerial levels, but it is being increasingly applied to the selection of nonmanagerial employees.

Assessment centers usually involve 6 to 12 candidates at a time who are evaluated as they work through a series of exercises over several days. Candidates are interviewed extensively and may be given intelligence and personality tests, but most of their time is devoted to exercises that are designed to simulate the actual problems of high-level jobs. The major techniques for eliciting these work samples are the in-basket exercise and the leaderless group discussion.

The In-Basket Technique

In-basket technique An assessment center exercise that requires job applicants to process memos, letters, and directives found in a typical manager's in-basket.

The **in-basket technique** presents each applicant with the sort of in-basket that is found on virtually every managerial desk. It contains the typical problems, questions, and directives that managers would expect to find when they returned to the office from vacation. The applicants must process this material in a fixed period of time, demonstrating precisely how they would handle the questions and problems on the job. After the exercise, they may be required to justify their decisions during interviews with the assessors.

The program at AT&T relies heavily on the in-basket exercise. Each candidate, playing the role of a manager, must process 25 items (memos, orders, and correspondence) in 3 hours. The assessors observe the candidates to see if they are systematic, establish priorities, decide to delegate authority to subordinates, or become en-meshed in trivialities. In-basket exercises can be scored with a high degree of relia-bility, and their validity for predicting managerial success is moderate (see, for ex-ample, Brannick, Michaels, & Baker, 1989; Schippmann, Prien, & Katz, 1990).

The Leaderless Group Discussion

In the **leaderless group discussion,** the applicants meet as a group to discuss an actual business problem. For example, they may be given information about a group of subordinates from among whom they must select one for promotion. As the meeting proceeds, the behavior of the candidates is observed to see how they interact and what leadership and communications skills each person displays.

> **Leaderless group discussion** An assessment center exercise in which job appli-cants meet to discuss an actual business problem under the pressure of time; usually, a leader emerges from the group to guide the discussion.

In a leaderless group discussion exercise at AT&T, a group of six candidates are told that they are managers of a corporation and are directed to increase profits in a fixed period. They are given information about the company and the market, but no one is appointed leader and no rules are established about how to accomplish their goal. Usually, one candidate assumes the leader's role, and that person's capabilities can be evaluated. The other group members are assessed on their cooperation in performing the tasks assigned to them by the leader.

To induce additional pressure, participants are notified of changes in prices or costs every 20 minutes, sometimes immediately after the total problem has been solved. The new information must be processed and incorporated into the planning. All the while, the clock is ticking, the assessors are watching, and the stress is mounting. Some participants become angry, and their behavior can dis-rupt the group's ability to function cohesively. The contrast between those who can operate well under stress and those who cannot becomes obvious.

The assessment-center method sometimes uses oral presentations and role playing. In the oral presentation exercise, candidates are given a packet of infor-mation about some aspect of corporate operations, such as the development of a new product or a new sales campaign. They must organize this material and pre-sent it to the group, a task typical of today's executive responsibilities. In role playing, the candidate acts out the role of manager in a simulated job situation, showing, for example, how he or she would conduct a job interview, fire an in-competent worker, or deal with an irate boss.

Predictive Validity of Assessment Centers

Although researchers are not certain which attributes or dimensions of behavior are being evaluated through assessment-center techniques, the predictive validi-ties for assessment centers as a whole have been found to be in the moderate range (see, for example, Gaugler, Rosenthal, Thornton, & Bentson, 1987).

A study at the Bell System of 506 employees promoted to the first level of management on the basis of their assessment-center evaluations found that more than 90% received very high performance appraisals from their superiors. In addition, there was a marked improvement in the general quality of manage-ment at the first level. When this group of managers was compared with em-ployees who had been promoted to first-level management positions before the assessment center was established, it was found that almost twice as many man-agers in the first group (who had received high assessment-center ratings) demonstrated the potential to advance to the next level of management (Camp-bell & Bray, 1993).

A 10-year follow-up study of 206 managers at a large insurance company found that their assessment-center ratings for career motivation predicted their actual career advancement more effectively than did ratings of their knowledge and skills (Jones & Whitmore, 1995).

Although such research indicates support for the predictive validity of assessment centers, not all organizations bother to evaluate their programs. A survey of 215 companies found that more than 20% made no attempt to calculate the worth of their assessment centers (Spychalski, Quiñones, Gaugler, & Pohley,1997).

Reactions to Assessment-Center Experiences

Some job candidates, particularly those who perform poorly, resent assessment-center exercises. Many people believe that a poor evaluation in an assessment center marks the end of their career, no matter how excellent a record they have compiled in their years with the company. Some candidates believe that success in the assessment center depends more on being articulate and personable than on actual competence at managerial tasks. There may be some truth to these charges. Interpersonal skills do count strongly in these assessments, and active and forceful participation is rewarded. However, as we noted, assessment-center ratings are also based on organizational and decision-making skills, as well as on motivation.

Participation in assessment centers can lead to changes in candidates' perceptions of their interpersonal and administrative skills. Those who perform well tend to believe they have the ability to develop and refine their skills. Those who do poorly tend to have lowered expectations for promotion (Noe & Steffy, 1987). In this sense, assessment centers serve as a realistic job preview, demonstrating to applicants what life as a manager or executive would be like. The assessment-center experience also serves as a training exercise. Managerial and interpersonal skills are developed and refined by the feedback candidates receive from the assessors.

Computers and video cameras are being used in today's assessment centers as a way of reducing costs. The information needed for the exercises can be presented on a computer terminal, and the candidates' behaviors can be videotaped for later and more careful evaluation by the assessors. A less expensive modification involves presenting candidates with a written description of a hypothetical job problem and having them select from among five alternatives the ways they would most likely and least likely respond to the situation. Research conducted in seven telecommunications companies to compare this method of obtaining assessment-center ratings with the traditional method showed that they correlated similarly with later ratings of job performance (Motowidlo, Dunnette, & Carter, 1990).

OTHER SELECTION TECHNIQUES

Tests of Physical Strength

Not everyone works at a desk all day, staring at a computer screen. Many jobs require heavy physical labor, and it is necessary to test applicants for those jobs to determine if they have sufficient strength to perform the work. For example, part of the selection process for firefighters must involve a test of strength because the job requires them to be able to carry people out of burning buildings.

One study dealt with the use of isometric tests, which involve pitting one muscle against another or against an immovable object. Using relatively simple equipment, such as a hand dynamometer and a lifting bar, isometric tests have been shown to be safe, efficient, and precise ways of measuring strength.

A sample of 1,364 individuals was given four isometric strength tests as part of the application procedures for a number of physically demanding jobs, including firefighter, law enforcement officer, pipefitter, and utility worker. The strength test results showed high positive correlations with both supervisor ratings of physical performance and applicant performance in simulated work situations. Thus, the tests were found to be valid selection techniques for a number of jobs requiring physical strength (Blakley, Quiñones, Crawford, & Jago, 1994).

As with the development of all selection techniques, it is necessary first to undertake a job analysis to determine the physical requirements of the tasks to be performed. I/O psychologists conducting job analyses of physical abilities have suggested that occupational tasks can be described in terms of three components: (1) muscular strength, (2) cardiovascular endurance, which includes aerobic capacity and general fitness, and (3) movement quality, which includes flexibility, balance, and coordination (Hogan, 1991). These and similar findings have been used to establish measures of physical ability related to successful job performance.

Polygraphs

American businesses lose some $40 billion each year to employee theft, embezzlement, espionage, computer tampering, and other forms of dishonesty. In an effort to control this problem during the 1980s, approximately 20% of U.S. corporations used **polygraphs** (so-called lie-detector machines) to test job applicants and employees.

Polygraphs So-called lie-detector machines that purport to measure deception and dishonesty; they have no predictive value for employee selection.

The polygraph purports to assess deception and dishonesty by measuring changes in physiological functions such as heart rate, blood pressure, breathing rate, and the galvanic skin response (the electrical conductivity of the skin). Although supporters of the apparatus claim accuracy rates up to 90%, a U.S. government study concluded that the polygraph has no predictive value for employee selection and screening. The British Psychological Society reached a similar conclusion. Research has shown that the polygraph can easily be defeated through the use of such simple mental and physical countermeasures as pressing the toes against the floor or counting backward by seven (Anderson & Schackleton, 1986; Honts, Raskin, & Kircher, 1994).

In 1988, the U.S. Congress passed the Federal Employee Polygraph Protection Act, forbidding private employers, but not the federal government, from using the polygraph to test job applicants and employees. Exceptions were allowed for drug companies, private security firms, and organizations whose work involves public health, safety, and national security. The legislation was supported by the APA, which provided expert witnesses to testify at hearings and briefings. The use of polygraphs for employee selection has since been virtually eliminated, replaced by the **integrity test,** a paper-and-pencil selection technique (see Chapter 4).

Integrity tests Paper-and-pencil tests to predict and detect employee dishonesty.

Graphology The study of handwriting; although proponents claim that graphology is a valid predictor of job success, scientific research does not support this claim.

Graphology

Although most I/O psychologists believe that **graphology,** the study of handwriting, is unscientific, it is being used as a method of employee selection in the United States and several other countries. It is estimated that 2,000 to 3,000

American companies currently use handwriting analysis, as well as some 50% of the European and Israeli companies surveyed (Fowler, 1991; Johns, 1993; Sackhaim, 1991).

Proponents claim that graphology is a valid predictor of job success, but their evidence is primarily anecdotal. Carefully controlled research has demonstrated that graphologists do no better than chance at predicting job success. One meta-analysis found validity to be near zero (Neter & Ben-Shakhar, 1989). Here is another instance in which improved communication is needed between researchers and the managers who apply their findings. I/O psychologists need to make it known to management that the value of handwriting analysis as an employee selection technique has been refuted by scientific research.

No matter which selection technique is preferred, it should not be relied on exclusively. No method is infallible. An employee selection program should include a combination of techniques to maximize the chances of matching the right person with the right job.

Assessment Centers for Selection

We noted in Chapter 3 that performance on assessment-center exercises can be a highly valid predictor of job success, particularly for managers and executives. Candidates in assessment centers are observed by trained assessors (usually company managers) while they perform a variety of tasks that simulate on-the-job problems. They are interviewed extensively and usually given personality and cognitive ability tests.

The assessment-center technique is expensive and time-consuming. Managers must take time away from their regular duties to be trained in observation and assessment techniques and, later, for the time they devote to evaluating candidates. These demands on managers led three I/O psychologists to ask whether similarly valid results could be obtained if candidates assessed themselves and their peers instead of being assessed by company managers.

To answer this question the psychologists monitored the progress of 394 men and women employees of a large oil company who had been nominated by their immediate supervisors to participate in an assessment center. The assessment-center exercises were designed to identify management potential early in an employee's career. The candidates were from different divisions of the company, and the majority of them did not know one another before attending the assessment center. Thus, they had few, if any, preconceived notions about the abilities of the other participants.

The candidates participated in group and individual exercises and completed tests of reasoning, quantitative ability, reading speed and comprehension, and personality. Their performance on the assessment-center exercises was rated by three trained manager-assessors on a 5-point scale from 1 (low) to 5 (high). The candidates rated their peers (in groups of 6 or 12) on six dimensions, plus an overall evaluation ("best bet for top management responsibility"). The candidates made self-rankings on the same dimensions, assigning themselves to the top, middle, or lower third of the group.

Source: Based on T. H. Shore, L. M. Shore, & G. C. Thornton III. (1992). Construct validity of self- and peer evaluations of performance dimensions in an assessment center. *Journal of Applied Psychology, 77,* 42–54.

Assessors did not use peer ratings or self-ratings to determine a candidate's management potential. They used their own performance ratings and the cognitive ability test scores in deciding whether to recommend a candidate for promotion. The criterion used by the psychologists to measure job advancement was the job level attained 5 to 10 years after the assessment-center evaluation.

The results showed that the peer assessments were the best predictor of job advancement. These evaluations had been based almost solely on the candidates' contact with one another during the assessment-center experience. Further, the candidates had been given no training in assessment methods.

The I/O psychologists suggested that one reason for the greater predictive validity of peer assessments was that the behavior of the candidates in the exercises directly influenced the behavior of their peers. In other words, the candidates, as members of the same work group, were in a position to see how effective or ineffective the others in their group were in handling management situations and how the actions of each group member then affected the candidates personally.

Manager-assessors, on the other hand, were observing the candidates' behavior without being directly affected by it. Thus, the peer experience may have led to more useful insights into what it would be like to work with each person. The results raise the following question: If such peer ratings can effectively predict management potential and job advancement, are trained manager-assessors really necessary?

Critical Thinking Questions

1. If you were in charge of the assessment center for your organization, would you eliminate, on the basis of the results of this study, the use of managers as assessors and substitute peer evaluations? Why or why not?
2. Based on our discussion of the experimental method (Chapter 2), what criticisms would you make of this study? How would you design a study to investigate assessor, peer, and self-ratings in assessment centers?
3. What factors other than assessment-center performance could have influenced the peer

evaluations? What factors can influence ratings made by manager-assessors?

4. What are the advantages of using managers as assessors?

5. If you were a candidate for promotion and knew that your career advancement depended on your performance in the assessment center, would you prefer to be evaluated by your peers or by trained assessors? What are the reasons for your choice?

6. What are the advantages and disadvantages of assessment centers for selecting employees?

SUMMARY

The proper selection of employees—matching the right person with the right job—is a vital and complex process. Problems of organizational entry, which involve the job applicant's preferences and expectations as well as the nature of the company's recruiting efforts, are among the first to be dealt with. Because our first job experience influences the rest of our working life, it is important that our expectations match the realities of the job. This can be accomplished through a **realistic job preview.**

An employee selection program requires (1) job analysis, (2) worker analysis, (3) establishing minimal requirements and cutoff scores for the selection techniques, (4) recruiting applicants, (5) administering selection devices, and (6) validating the selection devices by determining how they correlate with a measure of subsequent job performance.

Equal employment opportunity legislation mandates specific fair employment practices in hiring. Selection techniques should be job-related and should minimize **adverse impact** on minority groups. Companies must also try to prevent **reverse discrimination** against qualified members of the majority group.

Job analysis involves a detailed description of the component tasks performed on a job. Job analysis can be undertaken by referring to published analyses, by interviewing in person or through questionnaires the persons directly concerned with the job, by observing workers performing the job, by having workers keep a systematic log of their activities, or by recording critical incidents that are vital to successful job performance. On the basis of the information collected, a job specification can be written that defines the characteristics to be sought in job applicants.

Application blanks can provide information about job candidates that can be directly related to their probability of success on the job. Weighted application blanks and **biographical inventories** have been useful in predicting job success; they are similar to psychological tests in their objectivity and types of questions. Because many companies are reluctant to release information on former employees for fear of lawsuits, it can be difficult to confirm the accuracy of the information people provide on applications.

Although the interview consistently receives unfavorable evaluations in research on employee selection, most companies continue to use it. The weakest type of interview is the **unstructured interview;** the **structured interview** is a more valid predictive device. If interviews are conducted by a panel rather than a single interviewer, their usefulness increases. Some weaknesses of interviews are the failure of interviewers to agree on the merits of a job candidate, the failure of interviews to predict job success, the subjectivity of interviewers' standards of comparison, and interviewers' personal prejudices. In the **situational interview,** questions relating to actual job behaviors are developed from a critical-incidents job analysis; this may be the most valid type of interview for predicting an applicant's potential for success on the job.

Letters of recommendation are part of most employee selection programs, despite the recognized tendency of the writers to be overly kind and the reluctance of employers to reveal more than basic, factual information in order to avoid lawsuits.

In **assessment centers,** used primarily to select persons for managerial and executive positions, job candidates perform a series of exercises that realistically simulate problems found on the job. Using the **in-basket technique,** the **leaderless group discussion,** oral presentations, and **role playing,** applicants are assessed by trained managers on their interpersonal skills and their leadership and decision-making abilities. Isometric tests of strength are valid predictors of success in jobs requiring physical strength.

Paper-and-pencil **integrity tests** are replacing the **polygraph** (the so-called lie detector) as a way of predicting employee honesty. **Graphology** (handwriting analysis) is also being used for employee selection, despite research showing its lack of validity.

KEY TERMS

adverse impact

application blanks

assessment centers

biographical inventories

comparable worth

critical-incidents technique

graphology

halo effect

human resources psychology

impression management

in-basket technique

integrity tests

job analysis

leaderless group discussion

personnel psychology

polygraphs

realistic job previews

reverse discrimination

role playing

selection ratio

situational interview

situational testing

structured interview

unstructured interview

ADDITIONAL READING

Borman, W. C., Hanson, M. A., & Hedge, J. W. (1997). Personnel selection. *Annual Review of Psychology, 48,* 299–337. Reviews the literature on equal employment opportunity issues, personnel selection for work groups, and applicant reactions to selection procedures.

Hall, F. S., & Hall, E. L. (1994). The ADA: Going beyond the law. *Academy of Management Executive, 8*(1), 17–26. Examines attitudes toward employees with disabilities and describes corporate initiatives to accommodate these employees in the work force.

Levine, E. L. (1983). *Everything you always wanted to know about job analysis.* Tampa, FL: Workforce Dynamics. An enjoyable and informative guide to job analysis, based on current research and practice.

Santy, P. A. (1994). *Choosing the right stuff: The psychological selection of astronauts and cosmonauts.* Westport, CT: Praeger/Greenwood. Reviews the U.S. space program and the changing problems of selecting astronauts for sustained space flight and for maintaining cooperative living and working relationships with space flight personnel from other countries.

Snell, A. F., Stokes, G. S., Sands, M. M., & McBride, J. R. (1994). Adolescent life experiences as predictors of occupational attainment. *Journal of Applied Psychology, 79,* 131–141. Describes a study of 1500 first-year college students in which biographical information was correlated with their occupational status some 20 years later.

CHAPTER 4

Psychological Testing

CHAPTER OUTLINE

As you know from your own experience, psychological tests are widely used at all levels and stages of life. Public school systems periodically give intelligence, aptitude, and interest tests. If students are having academic or social difficulties, they are likely to be referred to a school psychologist who will administer other psychological tests to help diagnose the problem.

Nearly all of you attending college were admitted partly on the basis of your performance on college entrance examinations. If you plan to continue your education in a graduate or professional school, you must take additional competitive examinations. Those headed for military service will find tests given for almost every job and rank. In the world of work, tests are used to select employees for all levels of corporate responsibility, from apprentice to CEO. Organizations also administer tests to employees already on the job to determine who shows the highest potential for promotion.

Many employing organizations stopped using psychological tests during the 1970s and 1980s, despite their high predictive values, because of the threat of legal action arising from equal employment opportunity legislation. Companies relied instead on other selection methods, which were less valid for predicting job success than the best psychological tests. By the middle to late 1980s, however, psychological testing was regaining importance as a method of employee selection.

Today, psychological tests are once again in frequent use. I/O psychologists generally agree that no other selection technique is superior to intelligence or cognitive ability tests for selecting the best employees. These tests carry fewer risks of adverse impact in hiring decisions, and they are good predictors of performance on the job and in training programs for many kinds of occupations. Even NFL football teams administer psychological tests to prospective players. For example, the New York Giants team has used personality tests to detect whether a player would tend to be overly aggressive, undisciplined, or likely to cause trouble on or off the field (*New York Times*, April 22, 1997)

CHARACTERISTICS OF PSYCHOLOGICAL TESTS

Carefully developed and researched psychological tests have several characteristics that set them apart from the tests published in the Sunday newspaper, the ones that ask "Are You a Good Spouse?" or "What Is Your Sex Quotient?" A good test involves more than a list of questions that appear to be relevant to the variable being measured. A proper psychological test is standardized, objective, based on sound norms, reliable, and valid.

Standardization

Standardization refers to the consistency or uniformity of the conditions and procedures for administering a test. If we expect to compare the performance of many job applicants on the same test, then they must all take that test under identical circumstances. This means that every person taking the test reads or listens to the same set of instructions, is allowed the same amount of time in which to respond, and is situated in a similar physical environment.

Any change in testing procedure may produce a change in individual test performance. For example, if the air conditioning system in the testing room

Standardization The consistency or uniformity of the conditions and procedures for administering a test.

breaks down during a summer day, the people taking a test that day may not perform as well as people who took the test under more comfortable conditions. If an inexperienced or careless tester fails to read the complete instructions to a group of job applicants, then those applicants are not taking the test under the same conditions as other applicants.

The appropriate testing procedures can be designed into a test by its developers, but maintaining standardized conditions is the task of the persons administering the test. Therefore, the training of test administrators in proper procedures is vital. An excellent test can be rendered useless by an untrained tester.

Objectivity

Objectivity refers primarily to the scoring of the test results. For a test to be scored objectively, it is necessary that anyone scoring the test be able to obtain the same results. The scoring process must be free of subjective judgment or bias on the part of the scorer.

Objective tests Tests for which the scoring process is free of personal judgment or bias.

In your college career you have taken both objective and subjective examinations. With **objective tests**—those containing multiple-choice and true-false items—scoring is a mechanical process that requires no special training or knowledge. A clerk in a company's human resources department, an undergraduate grader in the psychology department, or a computer can score an objective test accurately as long as a scoring key with the correct answers has been provided.

Subjective tests Tests that contain essay questions; the scoring process can be influenced by the personal characteristics and attitudes of the scorer.

Scoring **subjective tests**—such as those containing essay questions—is more difficult, and the final grade or result can be influenced by the scorer's personal characteristics, including a like or dislike for the person who took the test. For fair and equitable assessments of job applicants, then, objective tests are the more desirable.

Test Norms

Test norms The distribution of test scores of a large group of people similar in nature to the job applicants being tested.

To interpret the results of a psychological test, a frame of reference or point of comparison must be established so that the performance of one person can be compared with the performance of others. This is accomplished by means of **test norms,** the distribution of scores of a large group of people similar in nature to the job applicants being tested.

Standardization sample The group of subjects used to establish test norms; the scores of the standardization sample serve as the point of comparison for determining the relative standing of the persons being tested.

The scores of this group, called the **standardization sample,** serve as the point of comparison in determining the relative standing of the applicants on the ability being tested. Suppose a high school graduate applies for a job that requires mechanical skills and achieves a score of 82 on a test of mechanical ability. This score, alone, tells us nothing about the level of the applicant's skill, but if we compare that score of 82 with the test norms—the distribution of scores on the test from a large group of high school graduates—then we can ascribe some meaning to the individual score.

If the mean of the test norms is 80 and the standard deviation is 10, we know immediately that an applicant who scores 82 has only an average or moderate amount of mechanical ability. With this comparative information, we are in a better position to evaluate objectively the applicant's chances of succeeding on the job relative to the other applicants tested.

The most widely used psychological tests have sets of norms for different age groups, races, sexes, and levels of education. The adequacy of a test's norms can determine its usefulness in employee selection.

Reliability

Reliability refers to the consistency or stability of response on a test. If a group takes a cognitive ability test one week and achieves a mean score of 100, and repeats the test a week later and achieves a mean score of 72, we would have to conclude that something is wrong. We would describe the test as unreliable because it yields inconsistent measurements. It is common to find a slight variation in test scores when a test is retaken at a later date, but if the fluctuation is great, it suggests that something is amiss with the test or the scoring method.

The **test-retest method** for determining reliability involves administering a test twice to the same group of people and correlating the two sets of scores. The closer the correlation coefficient (called, in this case, the reliability coefficient) approaches a perfect positive correlation of +1.00, the more reliable the test is considered to be. This method has several limitations. It is uneconomical to ask employees to take time from their jobs to take the test twice. The effects of learning (remembering the test questions) and the influences of other experiences between the two testing sessions may cause the group to score higher the second time.

The **equivalent-forms method** for determining reliability also uses a test-retest approach, but instead of using the same test a second time, a similar form of the test is administered. The disadvantage of the equivalent-forms method is that it is difficult and costly to develop two separate and equivalent tests.

Another approach to determining test reliability is the **split-halves method.** The test is taken once, the number of items divided in half, and the two sets of scores are correlated. This method is less time-consuming than the other methods because only one administration of the test is required. There is no opportunity for learning or recall to influence the second score.

In choosing a test for employee selection, the reliability coefficient ideally should exceed +.80, although, in practice, a coefficient of approximately +.70 is considered acceptable.

Validity

Validity is the most important requirement for a psychological test or any other selection device; that is, the test or selection device must be shown to measure what it is intended to measure. I/O psychologists consider several different kinds of validity.

Criterion-Related Validity.   Suppose that an I/O psychologist working for the Air Force develops a test of radar operator proficiency. The test will be considered valid if it measures those skills needed for competent performance on the job. One way to determine this is to correlate test scores with some measure of subsequent job performance. If persons who score high on the radar operator proficiency test also perform well on the job and if those who score low on the test perform poorly on the job, then the correlation coefficient (called, in this case, the validity coefficient) between test scores and job performance will be high. We will know that the test truly measures the skills needed to be a good radar operator and can be considered a valid predictor of job success. Validity co-

Reliability The consistency or stability of a response on a test.

Test-retest method A method for determining test reliability that involves administering a new test twice to the same group of subjects and correlating the two sets of scores.

Equivalent-forms method A method for determining test reliability that involves administering similar forms of a new test to the same group of subjects and correlating the two sets of scores.

Split-halves method A method for determining test reliability that involves administering a new test to a group of subjects, dividing in half the total number of items, and correlating the two sets of scores.

Validity The determination of whether a psychological test or selection device measures what it is intended to measure.

efficients of +.30 to +.40 are considered acceptable for employee selection tests. It is rare to find a test with a validity coefficient greater than +.50.

This approach to defining and establishing validity is called **criterion-related validity.** It is not concerned with the nature or properties of the test itself but only with the relationship between test scores and later job performance.

A meta-analysis of 138 criterion-related validity studies published in two leading I/O journals found that psychologists working in industry reported significantly higher validities from their research than did psychologists conducting research in universities. In addition, researchers undertaking validity studies to comply with EEOC guidelines reported significantly higher validities than researchers testing an academic theory. In both instances, the psychologists with practical, real-world reasons for conducting validation research found higher validities. The authors of the meta-analysis attributed this to the different reward contexts for psychologists employed in industry as compared to psychologists employed in academia (Russell et al., 1994).

Personnel psychologists have developed two approaches to establishing criterion-related validity: predictive validity and concurrent validity. **Predictive validity** involves administering the new test to all job applicants for a specified period and hiring them all, regardless of their test scores. At a later date, when some measure of job performance, such as production figures or supervisor's ratings, can be obtained on each worker, the test scores and the job performance criteria are correlated to determine how well the test predicted job success. In most corporations, top management is not in favor of this approach because some of the people hired will turn out to be poor workers.

Concurrent validity is used more frequently. It involves giving the test to employees already on the job and correlating the scores with job performance data. The disadvantage of this method is that by testing current workers, the validation sample contains only the better employees. Poorer workers will have already quit or been fired, demoted, or transferred. Therefore, it is difficult to establish by using concurrent validity whether the test is discriminating between good and poor workers.

Another problem is that applicants for a job and employees already on the job have different motivations and are likely to perform differently on psychological tests. A study of highway maintenance workers showed that applicants demonstrated significantly higher levels of effort and motivation to perform well on an employment test than did current workers (Arvey, Strickland, Drauden, & Martin, 1990).

The job performance measure, or criterion, most often used in the establishment of criterion-related validity is ratings assigned by a supervisor to an employee's present level of job performance. Such ratings are made routinely as part of the employee performance appraisal process (see Chapter 5). A meta-analysis of research studies compared supervisor ratings of job performance with quantitative measures, such as quantity of production, for the purpose of validating 10 types of cognitive, perceptual, and motor ability tests. The ratings and the quantitative measures produced similar validity coefficients. This result suggests that supervisor ratings, even though they may be influenced by subjective factors, can be assumed to be as valid predictors of job success as more objective measures (Nathan & Alexander, 1988). However, because the average performance of a group of workers has been found to decline as a function of time between performance appraisals, periodic reap-

Criterion-related validity A type of validity concerned with the relationship between test scores and job performance.

Predictive validity An approach to establishing criterion-related validity in which a new test is administered to all job applicants; all applicants are hired, regardless of test scores, and at a later date their test scores are correlated with a measure of job performance.

Concurrent validity A type of validity that involves administering a test to employees on the job and correlating their scores with job performance data.

praisals will be necessary when these are used for validation purposes (Deadrick & Madigan, 1990).

Rational Validity.   I/O psychologists are also interested in **rational validity,** the kind of validity that relates to the nature, properties, and content of a test, independent of its relationship to measures of job performance. In some employment situations it is not feasible to establish criterion-related validity, perhaps because the company is too small to support the expensive and time-consuming process or because the job has no precedent. In the selection procedures for the original U.S. astronauts, for example, before any space flights had taken place, there were no measures of job performance that could be correlated with test scores.

Two approaches to establishing the rational validity of a test are content validity and construct validity. In **content validity,** the test items are assessed to ensure that they adequately sample the knowledge or skills the test is designed to measure. This assessment can be accomplished by conducting a job analysis and determining if the test items are related to all those abilities needed to perform the job. For a job involving word processing, for example, test questions about word-processing computer software are job-related, whereas questions about mechanical abilities may not be. In the classroom, if your professor says you will be tested on the first three chapters of this book, questions about information from other chapters would not be considered content valid.

Construct validity is an attempt to determine the psychological characteristics measured by a test; that is, what the test really measures. How do we know that a new test developed to measure intelligence or motivation or emotional stability really does so? One way to determine construct validity statistically is to correlate scores on the new test with scores on established tests that measure these variables or constructs. If the correlation is high, then we can have some confidence that the new test is measuring the trait it claims to measure.

Some psychologists suggest that the term *validity* should be applied only to construct validity because, more than any other approach, construct validity deals with the meaningfulness of a test. Other psychologists argue that all validity is really construct validity (Anastasi, 1986; Carrier, Dalessio, & Brown, 1990). For these reasons, the use of construct validity is increasing.

Face Validity.   **Face validity** is not a statistical measure but a subjective impression of how well the test items seem to be related to the job in question. Experienced airline pilots would not think it unusual to take tests about mechanics or navigation because these topics are directly related to the job they expect to perform, but they might balk at being asked if they loved their parents. The question might be related to emotional stability, but it does not appear to be related to flying an airplane. If a test lacks face validity, applicants may not take it seriously, and this may lower their test performance.

A survey of 390 job applicants showed that they considered selection techniques that were high in face validity to be the most useful and worthwhile (Rynes & Connerley, 1992). A study of 154 managers and recruiters found that cognitive ability tests containing concrete items such as vocabulary and mathematical word problems were judged to be significantly more job-related (higher in face validity) than personality tests or cognitive ability tests with abstract items (Smither, Reilly, Millsap, Pearlman, & Stoffey, 1993). The same researchers found, in a study of 460

Rational validity The type of validity that relates to the nature, properties, and content of a test, independent of its relationship to measures of job performance.

Content validity A type of validity that assesses test items to ensure that they adequately sample the skills the test is designed to measure.

Construct validity A type of validity that attempts to determine the psychological characteristics measured by a test.

Face validity A subjective impression of how well the items on a psychological test appear to be related to the requirements of the job.

applicants for civil service jobs, that people who perceived the selection tests to be high in face validity also rated the organization as more attractive and reported they were more willing to recommend the organization to others as a place to work.

A group of 259 college students in the United States and in France was asked to rate the effectiveness and fairness of 10 selection procedures, to assess the students' degree of favorability toward them. The procedures included personality, ability, honesty, and work-sample tests, as well as interviews, résumés, biodata, references, personal contacts, and graphology. The single strongest correlate of favorable ratings was the face validity of the selection techniques (Steiner & Gilliland, 1996).

The best psychological tests include in their manuals the results of validation studies. Without this information, the personnel or human resources manager can have little confidence that the tests in the company's employee selection program are actually measuring the qualities and abilities being sought in new employees. The average cost of test validation has been estimated at more than $400,000, and the process requires over a year to complete. However, validation procedures will more than pay for themselves.

Validity Generalization

Until the late 1970s, I/O psychologists followed a doctrine of "situational specificity," which recommended validating a test in every situation for which it was chosen as a selection device, whether for a different job or a different company. Tests were said to be differentially valid. A test valid in one situation was not automatically considered to be valid for another. Therefore, no test could be used for employee selection without first determining its validity in the given instance, no matter how valid the test had proven for other, similar jobs.

Validity generalization The idea that tests valid in one situation may also be valid in another situation.

This idea of situational specificity or differential validity has been replaced by **validity generalization.** On the basis of large-scale reanalyses of previous validation studies, I/O psychologists have concluded that tests valid in one situation may also be valid in another situation. In other words, once established, the validity of a test can be generalized (Burke, 1984; Schmidt et al., 1993).

If a test is valid for one job, it will be valid for others of the same or similar nature. A test valid in one company will be valid in other companies. A test valid for one ethnic group will be valid for other ethnic groups. This generalizability has been verified by meta-analyses involving thousands of job applicants in a variety of job categories (Cornelius, Schmidt, & Carron, 1984). For example, a reexamination of more than 500 validation studies conducted by the U.S. Employment Service covered some 12,000 jobs. The tests in question measured cognitive, perceptual, and psychomotor abilities. All the tests were found to be valid predictors of job success and success in training programs for many kinds of jobs (Hunter, 1980).

Similar results were obtained from studies involving employees in clerical, supervisory, computer programming, law enforcement, and power plant operator jobs (Dunnette, 1989; Hirsh, Northrop, & Schmidt, 1986; Hunter & Hunter, 1983; Hunter & Schmidt, 1983). In one study, the same cognitive ability tests were used by 70 companies for six types of jobs held by some 3,000 workers. The tests were found to be equally valid for all the jobs and companies (Dunnette et al., cited in Zedeck & Cascio, 1984). In a study involving a meta-analysis of 80 criterion-related validity studies of technical jobs in a telecommunications company, the validities of cognitive ability tests were shown to generalize across a variety of skilled and semiskilled jobs (Levine, Cannon, & Spector, 1985).

Controversy and Impact. As impressive as these findings are, the notion of validity generalization has not been accepted by all psychologists. Some critics question the feasibility of meta-analysis in general as well as the procedures for carrying it out. Others cast doubt on the accuracy and the conclusions drawn from validity generalization studies. Still others suggest that the findings of the early validity generalization studies were overly optimistic (see, for example, Bangert-Drowns, 1986; Kemery, Roth, & Mossholder, 1987).

Despite such criticisms, the Society for Industrial and Organizational Psychology (SIOP) supports validity generalization. And proponents can legitimately claim, on the basis of empirical research, that meta-analytic methods in validity generalization have been widely accepted, extending "beyond ability and aptitude tests to biodata, assessment centers, interviews, integrity tests, and other predictors" (Schmidt, Ones, & Hunter, 1992, p. 661).

Many large corporations and government agencies routinely base their selection testing programs on the concept of validity generalization. It has also been endorsed by the National Academy of Sciences and is included in the Standards for Educational and Psychological Testing of the APA.

The concept of validity generalization has important practical implications for psychological testing as an employee selection technique. The resurgence of interest in tests, especially cognitive ability tests, has been spurred by validity generalization research. If tests no longer require expensive validation procedures for every job in every company, then organizations can improve their selection programs while saving time and money.

PSYCHOLOGICAL TESTING AND FAIR EMPLOYMENT PRACTICES

One result of fair employment legislation has been an increase in validity research to document whether a test is discriminatory. If studies show that applicants of all races who score below a certain level on a test perform poorly on the job, then the test is not discriminatory by race. I/O psychology research confirms that tests with high validity coefficients have relatively low levels of adverse impact (Maxwell & Arvey, 1993). Criterion-related validation procedures (correlating test scores with job performance measures) are required, when feasible, by the guidelines of the Equal Employment Opportunity Commission (EEOC). Rational validation procedures may also be used to meet EEOC requirements.

We noted that differential validity is no longer believed to apply to ethnic groups. A test found to be valid for one group is expected to be valid for another. Research has demonstrated that racial differences among average test scores are not the result of test bias but arise from educational, social, and cultural differences. Particularly for cognitive ability tests, there is an "emerging consensus among testing experts . . . that cultural bias in the IQ tests themselves is no more than a minor source of group IQ difference" (Rowe, Vazsonyi, & Flannery, 1994, p. 409). An even stronger statement was signed by 52 scientists, experts in intelligence and related fields:

Intelligence tests are not culturally biased against American blacks or other native-born, English-speaking peoples in the U.S. Rather, IQ scores predict equally accurately for all such Americans, regardless of race and social class (*Wall Street Journal*, December 13, 1994).

A report prepared by the American Psychological Association's Board of Scientific Affairs concluded that cognitive ability tests "do not seem to be biased against African Americans" (Neisser et al., 1996, p. 93). In other words, the tests do not discriminate against minority groups. Rather, they reflect in quantitative terms the discrimination that has been created by a society over time.

However, the empirical demonstration of validity does not guarantee that a test will not be declared discriminatory and barred from further use. This occurred with the Professional Administration and Career Exam (PACE), banned as a selection test after 1984. Although it had been used as a selection device for more than 100 occupations within the federal government, the government determined that insufficient numbers of black applicants were being hired. This result demonstrated adverse impact, and the test was declared illegal even though it was a valid predictor of job success.

A similar problem arose with the General Aptitude Test Battery (GATB) used by the U.S. Employment Service. The GATB is a test of cognitive functioning; it also assesses manual and finger dexterity. More than 750 validity studies have confirmed the high validity of the test as a screening instrument for employment (Vevea, Clements, & Hedges, 1993). Test validities for whites and minorities were comparable, although minorities showed lower average scores and hence were less likely to be hired.

Race Norming and Banding

Race norming A controversial practice, now outlawed, of boosting test scores for minority job applicants to equalize hiring rates.

To avoid the adverse impact that would result from continued use of the test, the U.S. Employment Service adopted the controversial practice of **race norming.** Scores for minority applicants were adjusted upward to equalize hiring rates. Thus, political, social, and legal imperatives were given precedence over scientific ones. The 1991 Civil Rights Act prohibits the practice of race norming, specifically banning any form of score adjustment on the basis of race, color, religion, sex, or national origin (Brown, 1994b; Gottfredson, 1994).

Banding A controversial practice of grouping test scores for minority job applicants to equalize hiring rates.

With race norming outlawed, attention has turned to the technique of **banding,** an attempt to equalize hiring rates by race by compensating for the consistently lower scores obtained by minorities on cognitive ability tests. Let us consider a simplified example: A company's human resources director, or the psychologist supervising the employee selection program, could examine the test scores and decide to band or group together all applicant scores between, say, 91 and 100, calling the range of scores "band 1." Band 2 would encompass all scores between 81 and 90, band 3 the scores between 71 and 80, and so on. Of course, any bandwidth could be selected; that is, band 1 might just as easily include all scores between 81 and 100.

For the purpose of hiring equality by race, then, all applicants included in band 1 would be considered equal in terms of the ability being tested. In the last example, then, no distinction would be drawn between the applicant with a score of 100 and the applicant with a score of 81. Thus, all applicants in band 1 would be eligible for selection.

Further, the order of selection within a band would not necessarily be by test score (the 100-scorer in preference to the 81-scorer) but, rather, could be by race.

> Because all individuals within the band are viewed as interchangeable ... a firm might choose to select members of a minority group in the interests of diversity. Thus, under a strict minority preference approach, all members of a minority group who fall within a band are screened in before turning to members of the majority group. In the extreme, it is conceivable that the result could be that only members of the minority group are screened in if the number of openings to be filled is equal to or less than the number of minority group members in the top band (Sackett & Wilk, 1994, p. 938).

Testing for Disabled Persons

Discrimination against disabled job applicants and employees has been substantially reduced in recent years as a result of EEOC regulations and the Americans with Disabilities Act of 1990. Many psychological tests have been adjusted or modified for disabled persons. I/O psychologists conduct empirical validation studies on these modified tests before they are used for employee selection.

For visually handicapped persons, test questions can be presented orally, in large print, or in braille, and people can be allowed more time in which to complete the test. Test questions relating to color, shape, and texture cannot be used with persons who were born without sight and have never seen colors and objects. Applicants with hearing disabilities can be given written instead of oral test instructions.

In 1994 and 1995, the EEOC ruled that medical examinations for applicants, which might indicate the presence of a disability, can be conducted only after an offer of employment has been made. These determinations have affected the use of personality tests in hiring, because the EEOC considers personality tests to be medical examinations under the following conditions: if they are administered and interpreted by a health care professional (a category that includes psychologists) and if the test provides evidence that can lead to the identification of a mental disorder or impairment, which, therefore, indicates the presence of a disability. When these conditions apply, personality tests can be given to applicants only after a job offer has been made.

If these limitations are upheld in court challenges, they will severely restrict an employer's ability to gather information on a job applicant's personality characteristics, information that could be crucial in determining a person's ability to perform the job (Brown, 1994a, 1996).

ESTABLISHING A TESTING PROGRAM

The basic steps in establishing a testing program are essentially those necessary for any kind of employee selection program. The first requirement is to investigate the nature of the job for which testing will be used. Once job and worker analyses have been conducted, the appropriate tests to measure the behaviors and abilities necessary for job success must be carefully chosen or developed.

Where do I/O psychologists find appropriate tests? They can use tests already available or develop new tests specifically for the job and company in question. The best tests include information on reliability, validity, and test norms. Additional evaluative information is provided by the periodically revised *Mental Measurements Yearbook*, the twelfth edition of which was published in 1995.

There are several issues to consider in deciding whether to use a published test or develop a new one. Cost is always important. It is less expensive to purchase a test than to construct one, especially if only a small number of employees are to be selected. Time is also important. If the organization needs qualified workers as soon as possible, management may be unwilling to wait for a test to be developed.

If an organization decides to develop its own test for a particular job, the I/O psychologist overseeing the project will prepare a list of suitable test items. Then the test must be validated to determine whether it measures what it is supposed to measure. The psychologist will conduct an item analysis to evaluate how effectively each test item discriminates between those who score high on the total test and those who score low. This evaluation involves correlating a person's response on each item with the response on the test as a whole. A perfectly valid test question is one that was answered correctly by everyone who scored high on the complete test and was answered incorrectly by everyone who scored low. Only items with a high correlation coefficient will be retained for the final version of the test.

The level of difficulty of each item must be determined. If the majority of the test questions are too easy, most people will obtain high scores. The resulting range of scores will be too narrow to distinguish those who are high on the characteristic or ability being measured from those who are moderately high. A test on which most items are too difficult presents the opposite problem. It will be difficult to distinguish between those who possess extremely low ability and those who possess moderately low ability.

Much of this validity research requires the determination of some measure of job performance, a criterion with which the test scores can be correlated. Ideally, the test will be administered to a large group of applicants and all will be hired regardless of the test scores. At this point, the value of the test is unknown, so it makes little sense to base hiring decisions on its results. Later, after workers have been on the job long enough to develop some competence, their job performance will be assessed, and these ratings will be compared with the test scores.

Economic and time constraints usually preclude this approach to establishing predictive validity; the more common method is to test workers already on the job. The content validity of a test should also be demonstrated; it must be shown that the items deal with abilities that are directly related to the job. A survey of 1,200 organizations in Britain found that only 22% always attempted to verify the validities of the psychological tests used for hiring decisions. Some 20% never examined test validities, and 58% reported doing so only some of the time. Thus, these tests were often being used as selection techniques by employing organizations in the absence of validity data (Baker & Cooper, 1995).

Once validity and reliability of a new test have been found to be satisfactory, a cutoff score must be set; no one scoring below this level will be hired. The cutoff score depends partly on the available labor supply. The greater the number of applicants, the more selective a company can be. The higher the cutoff score, the higher the quality of the applicants hired. However, by being increasingly selective, the organization must spend more money to recruit and evaluate more applicants to find sufficient numbers who meet or exceed the cutoff score. Researchers have determined a point of diminishing returns at which the increase in the quality of new hires is less than the cost of recruitment and selection (Law & Myors, 1993; Martin & Raju, 1992).

Most of the procedures for establishing cutoff scores involve job analyses and criterion-related validity studies to determine the minimum acceptable level of job performance. One frequently used technique, for example, asks subject matter experts to assess the probability that a minimally competent person would answer each test item correctly.

TYPES OF PSYCHOLOGICAL TESTS

I/O psychologists categorize tests in two ways: (1) how they are constructed and administered, and (2) the skills and abilities they are designed to measure.

Individual and Group Tests

Some tests are designed so that they can be administered to a large number of people at the same time. These **group tests** can be given to 20, 200, or 2,000 applicants simultaneously. The only limitation is the size of the testing facility.

Group tests Tests designed to be administered to a large number of people at the same time.

Because individual tests are costly and time-consuming to administer, they are used mostly for vocational counseling and for selecting management personnel.

Individual tests Psychological tests designed to be administered to one person at a time.

Individual tests are administered to one person at a time. Because this makes them more costly than group tests, they are used less frequently by employing organizations, usually only for selecting senior management personnel. Individual tests are more popular for vocational guidance and counseling and for diagnostic work with patients.

Computer-Assisted Tests

Computer-assisted tests A means of administering psychological tests to large groups of applicants in which an applicant's response determines the level of difficulty of succeeding items.

Designed for large-scale group testing, **computer-assisted tests** provide an individual testing situation in which the applicant takes the test at a video display terminal. This approach has sometimes been called tailored testing because the test is tailored or adapted to the person taking it.

If you were given a standard cognitive ability test in the paper-and-pencil format, you would have to answer questions designed to sample the full range of your intelligence. Some questions would be easy because your level of intelligence is higher than the level at which the questions are targeted, whereas other questions would be more difficult because they are at or above your level of intelligence. To complete the test, you must take the time to answer all questions, even the simple ones.

In computer-assisted testing, you do not have to waste time answering questions below your level of ability. The computer program begins with a question of average difficulty. If you answer correctly, it proceeds to questions of greater difficulty. Had you answered incorrectly, it would then have given you a less difficult question.

Another advantage of computer-assisted testing is that the testing can be done at any time in the selection process. It is not dependent on finding a qualified test administrator and scheduling a testing session. Because a range of abilities can be measured in a relatively short time, there is less opportunity for the applicant's interest and motivation to diminish. Fatigue and boredom in the testing situation are reduced, and immediate results are available to the human resources department.

Comparisons of the same tests given in paper-and-pencil format and computer-administered versions show little difference in the resulting scores. In one study, 874 college students took four work-related noncognitive tests; half of the group received the computerized version and half the paper-and-pencil version. No significant differences were found in test performance (King & Miles, 1995). In a similar study, 326 students enrolled in a military academy in the Netherlands took the General Aptitude Test Battery; half received the computerized format and half the paper-and-pencil format. On several of the subtests, the computerized version yielded faster and less accurate responses, most notably on simple clerical tasks. On overall scores, however, the differences were negligible (Van de Vijver & Harsveld, 1994).

Tests on which there is a time limit (see speed tests, in the next section) do show less valid responses for computerized formats. However, psychologists have found that using an electronic stylus or light pen to respond to test items, instead of making keyboard entries, tends to equalize any differences between computerized and paper-and-pencil versions (Overton, Taylor, Zickar, & Harms, 1996).

Research has shown that most people react favorably to computer-assisted testing (Schmitt, Gilliland, Landis, & Devine, 1993). On personality tests, they tend to provide more accurate information (Burke & Normand, 1987). Some research suggested that the relative anonymity of the testing situation led test-takers to be less likely to give socially desirable responses; that is, to try deliberately to make a good impression (Lautenschlager & Flaherty, 1990). Other research failed to find any difference in giving socially desirable responses in computer-assisted versus paper-and-pencil testing situations (Booth-Kewley, Edwards, & Rosenfeld, 1992).

For high-level managerial jobs, an organization may have an I/O psychologist prepare a summary of the test scores and, based on those scores, a description and judgment of the applicant's abilities. Computer-generated reports are also available. These are compiled from standard phrases or sentences designed to interpret the scores. Computerized test interpretation eliminates the possibility of personal bias in evaluating the test results.

Speed and Power Tests

The difference between speed tests and power tests is the time allotted for completion of the tests. A **speed test** has a fixed time limit, at which point everyone taking the test must stop. A **power test** has no time limit; applicants are allowed as much time as they need to complete the test. A power test often contains more difficult items than does a speed test. Large-scale testing programs often include speed tests because all test forms can be collected at the same time.

Speed tests Tests that have a fixed time limit, at which point everyone taking the test must stop.

Power tests Tests that have no time limit; applicants are allowed as much time as needed to complete the test.

For some jobs, working speed is an important component of successful performance. A test for a computer keyboarding job would contain relatively easy questions. Given enough time, most people would be able to respond correctly. The important predictive factor for keyboarding or word processing is the quality of the work that can be performed in a given period: in this case, data entry accuracy and speed. A power test would not be able to evaluate this skill properly.

Paper-and-Pencil and Performance Tests

Paper-and-pencil tests are the kind with which you are most familiar. The questions are in printed form, and your responses are recorded on an answer sheet. Most standard group tests of cognitive abilities, interests, and personality are paper-and-pencil tests.

Paper and pencil tests Psychological tests in printed form; answers are recorded on a standard answer sheet.

Some behaviors or characteristics are not so easily evaluated by paper-and-pencil means. For example, the mechanical skills of applicants applying for jobs with an appliance repair company are better tested by having the applicants perform the appropriate mechanical operations than by having them answer questions about the nature of those operations.

Performance tests may take longer to administer than paper-and-pencil tests and may require an individual testing situation. For the assessment of more complex skills, expensive testing equipment may be needed.

Performance tests The assessment of complex skills, such as word processing or mechanical ability, for which paper-and-pencil tests are not appropriate.

TESTS OF KNOWLEDGE, SKILLS, AND ABILITIES

A more familiar distinction among psychological tests for employee selection is in terms of the characteristics or behaviors they are designed to measure. The basic categories are tests of cognitive abilities, interests, aptitudes, motor skills, and personality.

Cognitive Abilities

Cognitive ability tests
Tests of intelligence or mental ability.

Cognitive ability tests (intelligence tests) are widely used for employee selection. For example, a survey of personnel practices in departments of law enforcement found that 92% used intelligence tests to select police officers (Ash, Slora, & Britton, 1990). Group intelligence tests, the kind given most often, are a rough screening device. They are brief, take little time to complete, and can be administered to large groups. They are rapidly and easily scored by hand or machine.

A large number of research studies involving thousands of people in the military services and in civilian life, in a wide variety of jobs, have shown consistently that cognitive ability tests are highly valid for predicting success in job training programs and in actual job performance (Olea & Ree, 1994; Ree, Carretta, & Teachout, 1995; Ree, Earles, & Teachout, 1994). Data from representative studies are shown in Table 4–1. Validity coefficients of +.30 to +.40 are considered acceptable for selection tests. You can see that many of the validities in Table 4–1 exceed that.

Cognitive ability tests correlate highly with measures of job performance such as supervisor ratings, production quantity and quality data, and work samples. Also, the high predictive validities of cognitive ability tests have been shown to remain stable up to 5 years (Nathan & Alexander, 1988; Schmidt, Hunter, Outerbridge, & Goff, 1988). In addition, cognitive ability is a valid predictor of employee mobility. A study of more than 11,000 employees between the ages of 24 and 30 found that over a 5-year period, people tended to gravitate to jobs that suited their level of cognitive ability, whether high or low (Wilk, Desmarais, & Sackett, 1995).

The following cognitive ability tests are among the most commonly used by employing organizations today.

The Otis Self-Administering Tests of Mental Ability has been found useful for screening applicants for jobs such as office clerk, assembly-line worker, and first-line supervisor. The test is group administered and takes little time to complete. It is less useful for professional or high-level managerial positions because it does not discriminate well at the upper range of intelligence.

TABLE 4–1   Validities of Cognitive Abilities Tests for Predicting Success in Training Programs and Success on the Job

Occupation	Job Success	Training Success
Salespersons	+.61	—
Clerks	.54	.71
Managers	.53	.51
Waiters and waitresses	.48	.66
Construction workers	.46	.65
Police officers	.42	.87
Unskilled industrial workers	.37	.61
Bus and truck drivers	.28	.37

Note. Adapted from "Cognitive Ability, Cognitive Aptitudes, Job Knowledge, and Job Performance" by J. E. Hunter, 1986, *Journal of Vocational Behavior*, 29, p. 343.

Mazes *ask examinees to mark the shortest distance through a maze without crossing any lines (1.5 minutes)*

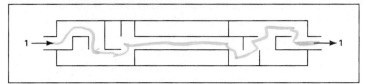

Coding *requires labeling figures with their corresponding numbers (2 minutes)*

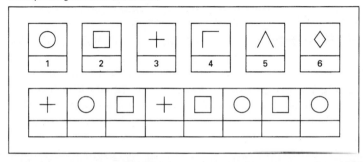

FIGURE 4–1. Sample items from Revised Beta Examination, Second Edition (Beta-II). (Reproduced by permission. Copyright 1978 by The Psychological Corporation, San Antonio, TX. All rights reserved.)

(see notes)

The Wonderlic Personnel Test, a reliable 50-item measure of general mental ability, is a popular individual or group test for selection, placement, promotion, and reassignment for more than 140 jobs in business and industry, such as flight attendant, bank teller, store manager, and industrial engineer. Because the test has a 12-minute time limit, it is an economical screening device. Test items measure ability to understand instructions, to solve job-related problems, and to propose ideas that can be applied to new work situations. Test norms are based on more than 450,000 working adults. Computer and hand scoring versions are available.

Wonderlic scores show a high positive correlation with scores on the Wechsler Adult Intelligence Scale, a longer and more complex individual test. A hiring kit to facilitate employer compliance with the Americans with Disabilities Act of 1990 offers large-print, braille, and audiotape versions of the test.

A nonverbal measure of cognitive ability, the Revised Beta Examination, Second Edition (Beta-II), a 15-minute group or individual test, is designed for use with people who read poorly or who cannot read at all. Instructions are provided for English-speaking and Spanish-speaking job applicants. The test has been used extensively for occupational rehabilitation programs in correctional facilities and for unskilled workers in large-scale manufacturing job retraining programs. The six timed subtests include mazes, coding, paper form boards, picture completion, clerical checking, and picture absurdities (see Figure 4–1). The Beta-II can be scored for professional, managerial, technical, clerical, sales, crafts, and service occupations.

The Wechsler Adult Intelligence Scale-Revised (WAIS-R) is a lengthy (approximately 75 minutes), individually administered test used primarily for jobs requiring a comprehensive psychological assessment, such as senior management personnel. Its administration, scoring, and interpretation require a well-trained and experienced clinical examiner. The WAIS-R includes 11 subtests, as follows: the verbal subtests are information, digit span, vocabulary, arithmetic, comprehension, and similarities; the performance subtests are picture completion, picture arrangement, block design, object assembly, and digit symbol. Separate verbal and performance measures of cognitive ability can be obtained as well as an overall IQ score. Computer scoring and interpretation are available.

Interests

Interest tests Psychological tests to assess a person's interests and preferences; used primarily for career counseling.

Interest tests include items about daily activities from among which applicants select their preferences. The rationale is that if a person exhibits the same pattern of interests and preferences as people who are successful in a given occupation, then the chances are high that the person will find satisfaction in that occupation.

It is important to remember that just because a person shows a high degree of interest in a particular job, it is no guarantee that he or she has the ability to be successful in that job. What interest tests scores show is that the person's interests are compatible with the interests of successful people in that career. If a test shows that a person has no interest in a field, then the chances of succeeding in it are limited.

Two frequently used interest tests are the Strong Interest Inventory and the Kuder Occupational Interest Survey.

The Strong is a 317-item, computer-scored group test that covers occupations, school subjects, work-related activities, leisure activities, types of people, and work preferences. Items are rated as "like," "indifferent," or "dislike." Scales for more than 100 vocational, technical, and professional occupations are grouped around six themes on which test-takers are ranked from low interest to high interest. These themes are: artistic, conventional, social, realistic, investigative, and enterprising. In addition, many of the test's occupational scales are gender-differentiated; that is, they have separate male and female norms.

Research on the Strong Interest Inventory has shown that people's interests tend to remain stable over time. For example, a group of 162 adolescents with high measured IQs took the Strong in 1978 and in 1993. The correlations between the two sets of scores, obtained 15 years apart, were high (Lubinski, Benbow, & Ryan, 1995). One possible explanation for this stability of interests may be related to genetics. Interest inventories measuring vocational and recreational interests were given to 924 pairs of twins reared together, and 92 pairs of twins separated in infancy and reared apart (hence subject to different environmental influences). The results showed that approximately 50% of the interests measured were influenced by heredity (Lykken, Bouchard, McGue, & Tellegen, 1993).

The Kuder Occupational Interest Survey items are arranged in 100 groups of three alternative activities. Within each forced-choice triad, applicants must select the most preferred and least preferred activities. The test can be scored for more than 100 occupations. Typical groups of items are as follows:

Visit an art gallery.	Collect autographs.
Browse in a library.	Collect coins.
Visit a museum.	Collect butterflies.

When the two numbers or names in a pair are exactly the same, make a check mark on the line between them.

66273894 _____ 66273984
527384578 _____ 527384578
New York World _____ New York World
Cargill Grain Co. _____ Cargil Grain Co.

FIGURE 4–2. Sample items from Minnesota Clerical Test. (Reproduced by permission. Copyright 1933, renewed 1961, 1979 by The Psychological Corporation, San Antonio, TX. All rights reserved.)

Both of these interest inventories are used primarily for vocational counseling, where the focus is on trying to select the right kind of occupation for an individual. One problem with using them for employee selection is the possibility of applicants' faking their responses to make themselves appear more suitable for a particular job. Presumably, when a person is taking an interest test for the purpose of career counseling, he or she will answer more honestly because the results will be used to select a broad area of training and employment rather than a particular job.

Aptitudes

For many jobs, **aptitude tests** must be designed to measure special skills, but there are also many published tests that measure more general clerical and mechanical aptitudes.

> **Aptitude tests** Tests to measure specific abilities such as mechanical or clerical skills.

The Minnesota Clerical Test is a 15-minute individual or group test in two parts: number comparison (matching 200 pairs of numbers) and name comparison (see Figure 4–2). Applicants are instructed to work as fast as possible without making errors. The test measures the perceptual speed and accuracy required to perform various clerical duties. It is useful for any job that requires attention to detail in industries such as utility companies, financial institutions, and manufacturing.

The Revised Minnesota Paper Form Board Test measures those aspects of mechanical ability that require the capacity to visualize and manipulate objects in space, necessary skills for occupations with mechanical or artistic orientation, such as industrial designer or electrician. Applicants are presented with 64 2-dimensional diagrams of geometric shapes cut into two or more pieces and are given 20 minutes to picture how the figures would look as whole geometric shapes (see Figure 4–3). Research shows that the test successfully predicts performance in production jobs, electrical maintenance work, engineering shopwork, power sewing machine operation, and various other industrial tasks. Hand and machine scoring options are provided. A French-language edition is available.

The Bennett Mechanical Comprehension Test uses 68 pictures with questions about the application of physical laws or principles of mechanical operation (see Figure 4–4). Tape-recorded instructions are provided for applicants with limited reading skills. The Bennett is designed for individual or group administration. It takes 30 minutes to complete. The test is used for jobs in aviation, construction, chemical plants, oil refineries, utilities, glass manufacturing, steel, paper and plywood manufacturing, and mining.

The Computer Competence Tests include five individual or group subtests containing multiple-choice items to assess an applicant's level of knowledge of basic computer terminology and ability to operate computers in the workplace. A typical question is as follows: Which component of a computer system is used to perform arithmetic operations? (a) Input device; (b) Output device; (c) Storage

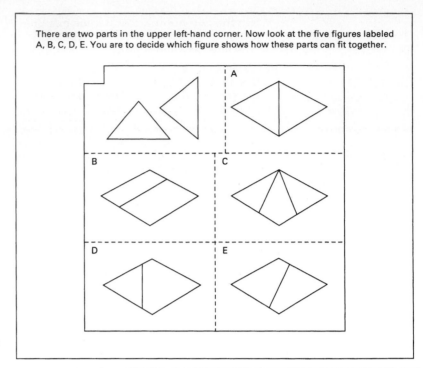

There are two parts in the upper left-hand corner. Now look at the five figures labeled A, B, C, D, E. You are to decide which figure shows how these parts can fit together.

FIGURE 4–3. Sample item from Revised Minnesota Paper Form Board Test. (Reproduced by permission. Copyright 1941, renewed 1969, 1970 by The Psychological Corporation, San Antonio, TX. All rights reserved.)

unit; (d) Processing unit. The test is useful for any job that requires personal computer expertise.

Motor Skills

Many jobs in industry and the military require abilities involving muscle coordination, finger dexterity, and eye-hand coordination.

The Purdue Pegboard is a performance test that simulates assembly-line conditions and measures fingertip dexterity and eye-hand coordination neces-

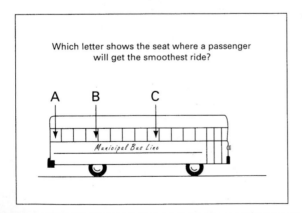

Which letter shows the seat where a passenger will get the smoothest ride?

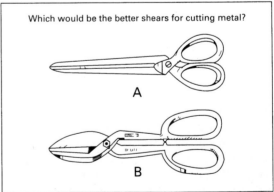

Which would be the better shears for cutting metal?

FIGURE 4–4. Sample items from Bennett Mechanical Comprehension Test. (Reproduced by permission. Copyright 1940, renewed 1967; 1941; renewed 1969; 1942, renewed 1969; 1967, 1968, 1980 by The Psychological Corporation, San Antonio, TX. All rights reserved.)

sary for assembly tasks, general factory work, and vocational rehabilitation. The task is to place 50 pegs in a series of holes in a pegboard as rapidly as possible, first with one hand, then the other, then both. Each task is limited to 30 seconds. The test also includes a 1-minute task involving the simultaneous use of both hands to assemble pegs, collars, and washers.

The O'Connor Finger Dexterity Test and the O'Connor Tweezer Dexterity Test measure how fast an applicant can insert pins into small holes by hand and by the use of tweezers. These tests are standard measures of finger dexterity and have proven to be useful in predicting job success for occupations that require precise manipulative skills.

Personality

Certain personality characteristics can contribute to job satisfaction and job performance. For example, empathy and nurturance are important traits for counselors to have; autonomy and persistence are vital to investigative reporters; and orderliness and precision are needed by accountants. **Personality test** scores have been found to correlate with job success. The predictive validities of personality test scores can be as high as those for assessment centers (Goffin, Rothstein, & Johnston, 1996). Personality researchers have concluded that "well-constructed measures of normal personality are valid predictors of performance in virtually all occupations" (Hogan, Hogan, & Roberts, 1996, p. 469). Personality tests are popular selection techniques, and their use is expected to increase. Two approaches to personality assessment are self-report inventories and projective techniques.

Personality tests Assessments of personal traits and feelings.

Self-report personality inventories include items dealing with specific situations, symptoms, or feelings. Applicants are asked to indicate how well each item describes themselves or how much they agree with each item.

Self-report personality inventories Personality assessment tests that include questions dealing with situations, symptoms, and feelings; applicants are asked to indicate how well each item describes themselves or how much they agree with each item.

Honesty of the applicants' responses was assumed to be the major difficulty with self-report personality tests. Test questions are often transparent, and people can usually figure out how to respond to make themselves appear to possess whatever qualities they believe the organization wants. Research suggests, however, that few job applicants deliberately distort their responses in a socially desirable direction and that validity measures remain stable regardless of any possible distortion (Hough, Eaton, Dunnette, Kamp, & McCoy, 1990; Ones, Viswesvaran, & Reiss, 1996). Thus, faking may not be as great a problem as previously believed.

Projective techniques for personality testing present applicants with an ambiguous stimulus such as an inkblot. The task is to tell what is seen in the figure or picture. The rationale is that people will project their thoughts, wishes, and feelings onto the stimulus in an effort to give it meaning. These tests cannot be faked because there are no right and wrong answers. The best known projective technique is the Rorschach Inkblot Test, in which subjects are shown 10 standardized inkblots and asked to describe what they see in the figures. In the Thematic Apperception Test (TAT), subjects are asked to respond to 30 ambiguous pictures of people and situations.

Projective techniques A personality assessment technique in which applicants project their feelings onto an ambiguous stimulus such as an inkblot.

Projective tests are time-consuming and must be administered individually. Examiners must be thoroughly trained and experienced. Because few of the tests have objective scoring keys, there is ample opportunity for subjective bias to affect the scoring and interpretation of the results. Although projective techniques are used for employee selection at the executive level, research shows that they have low validity.

Self-Report Inventories.   The Guilford-Zimmerman Temperament Survey is a widely used paper-and-pencil personality test. The items are statements rather than questions, and the applicant responds by checking "yes," "?," or "no." Three sample items are the following:

You start work on a new project with a great deal of enthusiasm.
You are often in low spirits.
Most people use politeness to cover up what is really cutthroat competition.

The test yields separate scores for 10 independent personality traits. As a check against faking or carelessness in responding, there are three falsification scales based on answers to selected items.

The Minnesota Multiphasic Personality Inventory (MMPI), first published in 1943 and revised in 1989, is the most frequently used personality test for employee selection and for clinical diagnostic work. The test is widely used in screening for jobs that require a high level of psychological adjustment, such as police officer, firefighter, air traffic controller, and airline flight crew member (see, for example, Butcher, 1994).

The 1989 revision of the MMPI, the MMPI-2, consists of 567 statements answered by "true," "false," or "cannot say." The items cover physical and psychological health; political and social attitudes; educational, occupational, family, and marital factors; and neurotic and psychotic behavioral tendencies. A number of items can be scored to determine whether the person taking the test was faking, careless, or misunderstood the instructions.

One problem with any test as popular as the MMPI-2 is that some people will take it more than once, should they apply to different organizations that use it. Among a sample of 1,997 workers in the nuclear power industry, more than 200 were found to have taken the MMPI four times, 102 had taken it five times, 26 had taken it six times, and 3 had responded to all 567 items seven times.

The scores of these examinees showed that repeated administrations of the test resulted in less extreme scores. One reason for this finding is that the job applicants became more "test-wise" with each additional exposure to the test. The psychologists who conducted this survey concluded that

> the usefulness of the Inventory appears to decrease with an increasing number of administrations. . . . It becomes increasingly difficult to identify unfit employees with the Inventory (Kelley, Jacobs, & Farr, 1994, p. 575).

This problem is not unique to the MMPI; it applies to any psychological test used by a large number of employers.

The California Psychological Inventory, developed in 1957 and revised in 1987, consists of 462 items calling for "true" or "false" responses. It provides scores on 17 personality dimensions and has been shown to be useful for predicting success in teaching and in health care occupations (physicians, dentists, and nurses). The test has scales to identify leadership and management potential, creative potential, and social maturity.

Predictive validities for self-report personality tests are generally in the low to moderate range. However, research using self-report inventories to assess the so-called Big Five factors of personality have shown much higher validities. These basic factors have been identified as extraversion, agreeableness, conscientiousness (or the will to achieve), neuroticism, and openness to experience.

Two of those factors, conscientiousness and extraversion, have been found to be particularly effective in predicting job performance. Conscientiousness includes such characteristics as being responsible and dependable, able to plan, organized, and achievement-oriented. Conscientiousness has been found to be a valid predictor for many occupations, including managerial, sales, professional, law enforcement, and skilled and semiskilled jobs.

Extraversion, which includes the characteristics of sociability, talkativeness, ambition, assertiveness, and high activity level, correlates highly with success for salespersons and managers. A third factor, openness to experience, has been found to predict training proficiency for all tested occupations (Barrick & Mount, 1991; Tett, Jackson, & Rothstein, 1991).

Much research is being conducted on the role of conscientiousness and extraversion in job performance. In a study involving 146 civilian managers employed by the U.S. Army, conscientiousness and extraversion were found to be more valid predictors of job performance for managers whose jobs offered a high degree of autonomy than for managers whose jobs offered low autonomy.

> Managers who are responsible, persevering, dependable, and achievement oriented (Conscientious) and those who are sociable, outgoing, and assertive (Extraverted) perform better in jobs when given a great deal of discretion in selecting the appropriate work behaviors to be performed (Barrick & Mount, 1993, p. 117).

A study of 91 sales representatives employed by a large appliance manufacturer found that salespersons who were high in conscientiousness were more likely to set goals and to be committed to them. This, in turn, was linked to higher sales volume and higher supervisor ratings of their job performance (Barrick, Mount, & Strauss, 1993). A study of 130 resort hotel employees found that conscientiousness correlated significantly with self-direction; that is, the performance of desirable on-the-job behaviors undertaken at the worker's own initiative (Stewart, Carson, & Cardy, 1996). Research on 286 long-distance truck drivers found that conscientiousness was a valid predictor of an employee's decision to leave a job (voluntary turnover), and of supervisor ratings of performance (Barrick & Mount, 1996). And a meta-analysis of 36 studies conducted in several countries in Europe showed conscientiousness to be a valid predictor of job performance in professional, police, managerial, sales, and skilled labor jobs (Salgado, 1997). In view of these and similar studies, it is clear that conscientiousness is a desirable characteristic for employees to show and for employers to seek in job applicants.

Studies of managers who make hiring decisions confirm that conscientiousness (along with general mental ability) is the most important attribute related to hirability (Dunn, Mount, Barrick, & Ones, 1995). Other research found that ratings of conscientiousness and extraversion made by supervisors, co-workers, and customers of 105 salespeople were valid predictors of job performance (Mount, Barrick, & Strauss, 1994). Thus, whether conscientiousness and extraversion are assessed by self-report inventory or by ratings given by others, both correlate positively with high job performance.

Some psychologists urge caution in the use of conscientiousness and extraversion as predictors of job performance. These critics point to research findings indicating that the frame of reference an applicant adopts when taking a test that measures the Big Five personality factors can affect their score. Whether they interpret the items as being relevant *only* to job performance or in terms of overall life experiences will produce different results. Applicants who adopt a work-related context or frame of reference have been found to score higher, particularly on conscientiousness (Schmit, Ryan, Stierwalt, & Powell, 1995). Those who try to project their image of the ideal employee in their responses on a personality test score differently from those who do not try to present such an image. This ideal-employee factor affects the majority of items assessing conscientiousness (Schmit & Ryan, 1993).

Keep in mind, however, that this research does not invalidate the extraordinary predictive utility of the factors of conscientiousness and extraversion. What it suggests is that personality researchers and human resources managers must remember that an applicant's frame of reference or mindset can influence the test results, even on tests designed to measure such stable predictors of job performance as conscientiousness and extraversion.

Inventories have been developed to measure other specific personality characteristics, such as introversion, self-esteem, sociability, emotional maturity, and proactivity. Proactivity refers to a tendency to take action to try to influence or change one's environment. "Proactive personalities identify opportunities and act on them; they show initiative, take action, and persevere until they bring about meaningful change" (Crant, 1995, p. 532).

The Proactive Personality Scale consists of 17 items to which respondents indicate the extent of their agreement or disagreement (Bateman & Crant, 1993). A sample item is the following: "No matter what the odds, if I believe in something I will make it happen." People who express a high degree of agreement with statements such as that should perform well in certain jobs, particularly those involving sales. A study of 131 real-estate agents found a high positive correlation between high scores on the Proactive Personality Scale and such objective measures of job performance as commission income, number of homes sold, and number of new listings obtained. In this case, the factor of proactivity was more relevant to job performance than scores on conscientiousness and extraversion (Crant, 1995).

Integrity Tests

We noted in Chapter 3 that American companies lose billions of dollars every year to theft, embezzlement, and other forms of employee dishonesty. The polygraph (the so-called lie detector) has been discredited as an effective means of detecting employee theft. Many private employers have discontinued its use.

A more valid way to predict and detect employee dishonesty is with **integrity tests,** a paper-and-pencil approach developed as an alternative to the polygraph. Integrity tests are less expensive to administer and can be used in situations in which the polygraph has been banned. I/O psychologists estimate that

Integrity tests Paper-and-pencil tests to predict and detect employee dishonesty.

every year more than 15 million employees and job applicants take integrity tests. Currently, some four dozen such tests are in use.

There are two types of integrity tests: overt integrity tests, which directly assess attitudes toward theft, and personality-oriented integrity tests, which measure general delinquency, impulse control, and conscientiousness. Both types of test appear to be valid predictors of theft and of such counterproductive behaviors as absenteeism, drug abuse, and malingering. They have also been found predictive of general job performance as assessed by supervisor ratings (Bernardin & Cooke, 1993; Cunningham, Wong, & Barbee, 1994; Ones, Viswesvaran, & Schmidt, 1993, 1995).

A report by an American Psychological Association task force on integrity tests in employee selection was generally favorable toward integrity testing (Goldberg, Grenier, Guion, Sechrest, & Wing, 1991). Other research evidence strongly suggests that most integrity tests are probably measuring the Big Five factor of conscientiousness, which would explain why the tests are such valid predictors of job performance (Ones, Viswesvaran, & Schmidt, 1993, 1995).

LIMITATIONS OF PSYCHOLOGICAL TESTING PROGRAMS

Uncritical Use.   A continual danger with psychological tests is their uncritical or inappropriate use by trusting human resources managers who may be taken in by slick brochures and promises of instant success in solving problems of employee selection and equal employment opportunity. A personnel manager may choose a test because it is new, without investigating the test's norms, reliability, or validity. A test may continue to be used despite negative information about its dependability because the employment office is unaware of the research. Often, there are no data to support a test because no research has ever been conducted on it. The harm generated by an improper testing program affects not only the organization but also applicants who may be unfairly disqualified from a job by an ineffective test.

Rejection of Qualified Applicants.   Even the best psychological tests are not perfectly valid. No validity coefficients for tests reach a perfect positive correlation of +1.00. There is always some margin for error in the prediction of job success. Sometimes unqualified persons will be hired, and sometimes otherwise qualified applicants will be incorrectly identified as unqualified or ineligible on the basis of their test performance. (This error of prediction also exists with other selection techniques.) Research has shown that these false-positive errors, although unfortunate, are considerably reduced when tests with the highest predictive validities are used (Martin & Terris, 1991).

To minimize these errors, an employee selection program should not be based on a single technique. The use of several techniques allows for the compilation and evaluation of as much information as possible about an applicant.

Faking.   We have mentioned that faking of responses on personality tests may be less a problem than previously believed and that it may have a negligible effect on validity. This suggestion was confirmed by a study of 495 assessment center candidates in a forestry products company. Some of the candidates were already employed by the organization; others were applying for jobs. All took the 16 PF Test, a self-report personality inventory that has two scales designed to detect faking. The researchers found that correcting the test scores for faking had only a negligible effect on criterion-related validity (Christiansen, Goffin, Johnston, & Rothstein, 1994). Nevertheless, organizations using tests for employee selection must be sensitive to the possibility of faking.

Suppose you are in desperate need of a job and apply for a sales position. You are given a test that includes the following questions:

I enjoy meeting new people.	Yes_____	No_____
I get along well with most people.	Yes_____	No_____
I find it easy to talk to people.	Yes_____	No_____

You can anticipate the way the company expects salespersons to answer. Unless these characteristics apply to you, however, your answers will provide the company with a false impression. You may be hired, but you probably will not be successful or satisfied with the job because it requires abilities that you do not possess. In the long run, then, faking test responses works to your disadvantage, but it is hard to convince some avid job seekers of this in advance.

Attitudes Toward Testing.   Psychological tests have never been popular with people who are required to take them and whose future is dependent on the outcome. But most of us have little choice. We can refuse to take the tests an organization wants to administer, but refusal often means that we will not be considered for the job.

Many applicants experience considerable test anxiety. A large-scale survey of the attitudes of job applicants found significantly more test anxiety among female and older job applicants than among male and younger applicants (Arvey, Strickland, Drauden, & Martin, 1990). Labor union members typically hold negative attitudes toward tests, believing that testing serves the company, not the employee. We have seen, however, that a carefully researched and administered testing program can be of tremendous value to employees by guiding them into the kind of work for which they are best suited.

Effects of Negative Attitudes.   Applicants who react negatively to psychological tests that are administered as part of a selection procedure may become so offended that they withdraw from the application procedure and develop a hostile attitude toward the organization. They may spread that attitude to friends and acquaintances, possibly causing a number of potential applicants to avoid that company.

Negative feelings about selection tests and about the organization that forced the tests on job seekers may even lead rejected applicants to file a lawsuit against the company. Further, negative attitudes toward psychological tests may lower applicants' motivation to perform well on the tests, which, in turn, reduces the predictive validity of the tests.

One study of 80 job applicants at a property management company found that a personality test that contained mostly job-related items, deliberately worded to be inoffensive, nonetheless managed to offend a sizable number of applicants. However, those subjects who took the personality test along with a cognitive ability test that has a high degree of face validity (the Wonderlic Personnel

NEWSBREAK #6

Target Stores Sued Over Personality Test

When Sibi Soroka applied for a job as a security guard at Target Stores in California, he didn't know he would be asked about his religious beliefs or his sex life. And he didn't like it when he was. As part of the employment screening process, he had to take *Psychscreen*, a personality test used by Target, which contains items from two well-known psychological tests, the Minnesota Multiphasic Personality Inventory and the California Psychological Inventory.

Soroka felt that his privacy had been invaded when he was asked if he believed there was a devil and a hell in an afterlife. He was also asked whether he was strongly attracted to members of his own sex, or if he dreamed a lot about sex. Questions like these were entirely too personal, he said—and besides, what did his religious beliefs or sexual behavior have to do with being a security guard? Soroka sued Target for violating his right to privacy.

The trial judge denied Soroka's motion for an injunction to prohibit further use of the personality test by Target Stores and ruled that *Psychscreen* was not an unreasonable device for screening job applicants. Soroka appealed his case to the California Court of Appeals, which ruled in his favor. *Psychscreen*'s questions about religion and sex, wrote the judges in a 39-page decision, violated a job applicant's right to privacy, unless the company could prove that such information was directly related to job performance.

The appeals court ruling did not object to the psychological screening of the store's security guards; it clearly acknowledged that Target had a legitimate and justifiable interest in hiring only the most emotionally stable applicants. Nor did the court find fault with the idea of using personality tests to select guards.

What it did criticize was the asking of questions about sex and religion when Target Stores could not provide any empirical demonstration of a compelling interest in that kind of personal information about an applicant.

Although Target Stores appealed to the California Supreme Court, it made an out-of-court settlement with Soroka before a decision could be rendered. Between the legal fees and the undisclosed amount of the settlement, plus the public notoriety, the use of *Psychscreen* turned out to be an expensive selection technique for this company.

Sources: Brown, D. C. (1993). Target Stores settle out of court in Soroka v. Dayton Hudson. *The Industrial-Organizational Psychologist, 31*(2), 88–89. Jacison, D. N., & Kovacheff, J. D. (1993). Personality questionnaires in selection: Privacy issues in the Soroka case. *The Industrial-Organizational Psychologist, 30*(4), 45–50.

Test) exhibited a significantly less negative attitude toward the overall selection process (Rosse, Miller, & Stecher, 1994).

Another study of 3,984 applicants for factory jobs found that an assessment-center experience had greater face validity for them than did cognitive ability tests. In addition, applicants who had more favorable attitudes toward both selection techniques were significantly more satisfied with the selection process as a whole, as well as with the job and the company (Macan, Avedon, Paese, & Smith, 1994).

Ethical Issues. The APA is concerned about the ethical practices of all psychologists, whether they are engaged in clinical practice, in academic laboratory research and teaching, or in employee selection. Principles for proper conduct state that psychologists must protect the dignity, worth, and welfare of the persons with whom they deal. Unfortunately, this ideal is sometimes violated in applying psychological tests to employee selection. The APA ethics code describes the proper safeguards for the distribution and use of psychological tests (American Psychological Association, 1992, 1996).

1. Test users. Persons who administer and interpret psychological tests should be aware of the principles of psychological measurement and validation and the limitations of test interpretation. They must avoid bias and should always consider more than one means of assessment. They must adhere to standardized test administration procedures and make every effort to achieve accuracy in recording and scoring test results.
2. Test security. Actual test questions should never be reprinted in a public medium such as a newspaper or magazine. It is permissible to publish sample questions (similar to real questions) but not items used in the actual scoring of a test. (The examples in this chapter are sample questions.) Tests should be sold only to professionals who will safeguard their use.
3. Test interpretation. Test scores should be given only to those qualified to interpret them. They should not be given to anyone outside the human resources department, such as the applicant's potential supervisor, unless the supervisor has the training necessary to interpret the scores. The person being tested has the right to know the test score and what it means.
4. Test publication. Tests should not be released for use without adequate background research to support the test developers' claims. Informative and current test manuals containing reliability, validity, and normative data should be made available. Advertisements should describe tests accurately, without emotional or persuasive appeals.

Privacy Issues. One aspect of psychological testing that has come under attack is the use of questions about personal or intimate issues. Critics charge that such personal probing is an unnecessary invasion of privacy. Individual freedom is violated when organizations request or require information that cannot be shown to be related to performance of the job for which the person is applying. Few people question the right of an organization to investigate the background, training, abilities, and personality of job applicants. But personal questions about sex, religion, political beliefs, and health have been successfully challenged in court as unwarranted invasions of privacy. Even if such questions could be shown to be related to job performance, there remains the issue of just how much of ourselves we should be required to reveal to a potential employer.

Attitudes Toward Psychological Tests

Our attitude toward a task can affect how well or how poorly we perform it. Sometimes, attitudes are more decisive than our physical or mental abilities for achieving or completing the task. In addition, our motivations, feelings, and anxieties affect task performance. These factors apply to all types of tasks—taking a course, participating in sports, working in an office, or answering questions on a psychological test when we seek employment.

To measure attitudes and opinions of test-takers, several I/O psychologists developed the Test Attitude Survey (TAS), a questionnaire of 45 items to which respondents indicate their level of agreement or disagreement on a 7-point scale. The items were designed to measure nine components of test taking, such as motivation, concentration, belief in the usefulness of tests, feeling of ease at taking tests, amount of preparation for taking a test, and belief that test results will influence job status. For example, the statement "Doing well on this test is important to me" was designed to measure motivation; the statement "I am not good at taking tests" was designed to measure anxiety.

To determine whether the TAS was valid—that is, whether it actually measured motivational components of test-taking—it was administered to several groups of subjects, including 86 psychology students and 535 U.S. Army recruits. The results indicated that the TAS had sufficient construct validity to be used as an assessment device.

The psychologists proceeded with two studies. In the first instance, 301 applicants for the job of highway maintenance worker completed the TAS and three employment tests (mechanical knowledge, shop math, and tool use). Next, 179 persons, currently employed as highway maintenance workers, took the same tests; they were told that the tests were for research purposes only and that the results would have no bearing on their wages or conditions of employment.

Source: Based on R. D. Arvey, W. Strickland, G. Drauden, & C. Martin (1990). Motivational components of test taking. *Personnel Psychology, 43,* 695-716.

Significant differences between the two groups were found on seven of the nine motivational components of the TAS. Job applicants exhibited greater effort, motivation, and preparation and a stronger belief that the tests would directly affect their employment status than did current workers.

To evaluate the importance of this finding, recall that a frequently used approach to validating a new employment test involves administering the test to employees already on the job (concurrent validity). The present study provides evidence that current employees do not display a level of effort and motivation on employment tests comparable to that of job applicants. Does this suggest that the concurrent validity approach provides a distorted measure of the appropriateness and usefulness of a new test?

In their second study with the TAS, the I/O psychologists administered the scale to 337 applicants for a county office worker job. The applicants were also given a speed test (comparing names and numbers), an arithmetic test, and a 1-hour work sample test. The purpose of this investigation was to document any race, gender, or age differences in test-taking motivations and attitudes.

The results showed that men reported significantly less test anxiety and significantly greater test ease than did women. Older applicants (over 25) scored higher in test anxiety and lower in test ease than did younger applicants (under 25). White applicants showed significantly greater motivation to work hard on the tests than did black applicants. Whites also expressed a stronger belief that the tests would affect their future. Blacks scored significantly higher on test preparation, indicating that they had spent considerably more time than whites preparing for the tests. The results led the psychologists to ask whether a portion of the race, gender, and age differences found in the test scores of job applicants might be accounted for by the differences in their attitudes and feelings about tests.

Critical Thinking Questions

1. Do you think a person's attitude toward tests can influence his or her performance on the TAS?
2. How would you determine the validity of the TAS? Why do some psychologists argue that

the term *validity* should be applied only to construct validity?

3. How would you establish the reliability of the TAS?

4. Can we conclude from this research that tests cannot be used to predict job performance of older job applicants, women applicants, or black applicants because of their relative unease about test-taking? Explain your answer.

5. What approach would you take to changing the test-taking attitudes of a group of job applicants? Would you enlist the help of high schools or colleges? Of employers?

SUMMARY

I/O psychologists report a resurgence of interest in psychological tests as employee selection devices, largely because research has shown that cognitive ability (intelligence) tests are excellent predictors of success in training programs and on the job.

Psychological tests must meet the following criteria: standardization, objectivity, norms, reliability, and validity. **Standardization** refers to the consistency of procedures and conditions under which people take tests. **Objectivity** involves accurate and consistent test scoring that is unbiased by the scorer's personal characteristics and beliefs. **Test norms** are the scores of a group of people who are similar to persons taking the test; norms serve as a point of comparison for individual test scores. **Reliability** refers to the consistency of responses; it can be determined by the test-retest, equivalent-forms, or split- halves methods. **Validity** is concerned with how well a test measures what it is intended to measure. **Criterion-related validity** is determined by the methods of **predictive** or **concurrent validity**. **Rational validity** is established by **content** or **construct validity**. The concept of face validity refers to how valid or relevant the test appears to the person taking it. **Validity generalization** indicates that a test that is valid for one job may be valid for other jobs, and a test valid for one ethnic group may be valid for others.

Fair employment legislation prohibits the use of any test to discriminate against job applicants because of their race, color, religion, sex, or national origin. A valid test may be declared discriminatory if adverse impact on minority groups can be demonstrated.

To establish a testing program, I/O psychologists conduct job and worker analyses, find or develop suitable tests, conduct an item analysis of each test question, determine the level of difficulty of each question, establish the test's reliability and validity, and set cutoff scores.

Psychological tests differ in terms of how they are constructed and administered and in terms of the type of behavior they measure. Categories include **individual** and **group tests**, **speed** and **power tests,** and **paper-and-pencil** and **performance tests**. **Computer-assisted tests,** designed for large groups, involve individual interaction with a computer. Some tests can be scored and interpreted by computer software programs that produce a narrative description of a person's abilities. Psychological tests can measure **cognitive ability, interests, aptitudes, motor skills,** and **personality.** Personality characteristics are assessed by **self-report inventories** or **projective techniques**. **Integrity tests** are designed to predict and detect employee dishonesty.

Psychological tests can be of great value in employee selection because of their objectivity and validity. Limitations of tests include uncritical use, unfair rejection of applicants, and faking of responses. Ethical issues include invasion of privacy and confidentiality of test questions and answers.

KEY TERMS

aptitude tests
banding
cognitive ability tests
computer-assisted tests
concurrent validity
construct validity
content validity
criterion-related validity
equivalent-forms method
face validity
group tests
individual tests
integrity tests
interest tests
motor skills tests
objective tests
paper-and-pencil tests
performance tests

personality tests
power tests
predictive validity
projective techniques
race norming
rational validity
reliability
self-report personality inventories
speed tests
split-halves method
standardization
standardization sample
subjective tests
test norms
test-retest method
validity
validity generalization

ADDITIONAL READING

Borman, W. C., Hanson, M. A., & Hedge, J. W. (1997). Personnel selection. *Annual Review of Psychology, 48,* 299–337. Reviews current issues in personnel selection including personality tests as predictors of job performance.

Geisinger, K. (Ed.). (1992). *Psychological testing of Hispanics.* Washington, DC: American Psychological Association. Discusses issues such as cultural traditions and English-as-a-second-language that affect the testing of Hispanics for educational placement and employment status purposes.

Landy, F. J., Shankster, L. J., & Kohler, S. S. (1994). Personnel selection and placement. *Annual Review of Psychology, 45,* 261–296. Reviews the literature on personnel selection and placement including tests of cognitive ability, personality, and physical abilities; computerized testing; and issues in construct validity and validity generalization.

Murphy, K. R. (1993). *Honesty in the workplace.* Pacific Grove, CA: Brooks/Cole. Discusses issues of employee honesty and dishonesty, summarizes relevant research, and offers suggestions about encouraging honest behaviors and discouraging dishonest behaviors in the workplace.

Walsh, W. B., & Betz, N. E. (1995). *Tests and assessment* (3rd ed.). Englewood Cliffs, NJ: Prentice Hall. An informative, well-written undergraduate textbook on the foundations of psychological and educational testing.

Performance Appraisal

CHAPTER OUTLINE

■   ■   ■   ■

Nothing in organizational life these days is guaranteed, except, perhaps, a performance review. Whether one is at the very bottom of the organization or at the senior most level, someone somewhere is evaluating your performance. . . . In this time of massive staff reductions, reengineering, and continuous improvement efforts, however, the evaluation of employee work behavior has become an even more pressing and important function (Church, 1995b, p. 57).

Throughout your career, your performance will be monitored and appraised, and your level of salary, rank, and responsibility will depend on how well you satisfy the established criteria for job performance. Of course, **performance appraisal** is nothing new to you. It has been going on since you started school. Your performance has been appraised continuously through classroom examinations, term papers, standardized tests, and oral presentations—all techniques designed to gauge or assess the quality of your work. In principle, they are similar to the techniques used on the job, and the results of these evaluations obviously have an important bearing on your future.

> **Performance appraisal** The periodic, formal evaluation of employee performance.

Although you may not take formal examinations during your years with an organization, performance appraisals at work are just as important as those in college. Your pay raises, promotions, and job duties affect not only your income and standard of living but also your self-esteem, emotional security, and general satisfaction with life. Performance appraisals can also determine whether you keep your job. In a sense, then, you are never finished passing tests; once you have been evaluated and hired by a company, your performance will continue to be assessed.

It is important to remember that performance appraisal can be as beneficial to you as to your company. Just as classroom tests show where you stand and where you need improvement, so the effective performance appraisal program can help you to assess your competence and personal development on the job. Performance appraisal will reveal your strengths and weaknesses, enhancing your self-confidence in some areas and encouraging you to strive to improve your performance in others.

PERFORMANCE APPRAISAL AND FAIR EMPLOYMENT PRACTICES

The Equal Employment Opportunity Commission (EEOC) guidelines apply to any selection procedure that is used for making employment decisions, not only for hiring but also for promotion, demotion, transfer, layoff, discharge, or early retirement. Therefore, performance appraisal procedures must be validated like tests or any other selection device. A study of age discrimination complaints decided by federal courts showed that employers who based their personnel decisions on the results of well-designed performance review programs that included formal appraisal interviews were much more likely to be successful in defending themselves against claims of discrimination (Miller, Kaspin, & Schuster, 1990).

In addition, a study of 295 U.S. Circuit Court decisions in employment discrimination cases showed that organizations were more likely to win such cases when their performance appraisal programs included formal job analyses and written instructions to the appraisers, and allowed employees to review the results (Werner & Bolino, 1997).

Racial Bias. Most performance evaluation programs are based on supervisor ratings, which are subjective human judgments that can be influenced by personal factors and prejudices. Race discrimination is known to persist in job assignment, pay, promotion, and other personnel decisions. For example, an analysis of ratings given by 20,000 supervisors showed that both black supervisors and white supervisors gave higher ratings to subordinates of their own race (Mount, Sytsma, Hazucha, & Holt, 1997).

An analysis of performance ratings from a variety of military and civilian jobs found that black workers received lower performance appraisals than did white workers from both white and black raters (Sackett & DuBois, 1991). I/O psychologists who examined employment data from more than 21,000 workers in 10 major job categories concluded that the lower performance ratings assigned to blacks by both white and black raters may reflect the "somewhat lower job-related ability and experience levels of blacks. The ability and experience measures were all related to job performance; the supervisors may be accurately representing performance differences due to ability or experience" (Waldman & Avolio, 1991, p. 901). Therefore, the lower ratings may not have resulted from any alleged racial bias on the part of the raters but rather from the different life experiences of the workers.

Gender Bias. Sex bias in performance appraisal has been reported more often in laboratory studies that simulate work situations than in research conducted on the job. In the workplace, many studies have reported that appraisal ratings for the same job do not differ significantly by sex (see, for example, Drazin & Auster, 1987; Shore & Thornton, 1986). However, an analysis of biographical data, test scores, and job performance measures for 486 work groups in a variety of blue-collar and clerical jobs found that women received lower performance appraisal ratings than did men when they constituted less than 20% of a work group. When women made up more than half of a work group, they were rated more highly than men. This "tokenism" effect was found to operate only for women workers, not for men or black workers (Sackett, DuBois, & Noe, 1991). We see in Chapter 7 that women in managerial and professional jobs also face discrimination.

Age Bias.   The evidence with regard to age bias shows that older workers tended to receive significantly lower ratings than younger workers on measures of self-development, interpersonal skills, and overall job performance. We have noted that job proficiency does not necessarily decline with age. In some cases, then, raters may be basing their assessments on their expectations of an older worker's skills rather than on his or her actual job performance.

Criteria for Compliance.   Performance appraisal systems, which depend on having one person evaluate another, provide opportunities for unfair treatment in terms of pay, promotion, and other job outcomes. For organizations to ensure compliance with fair employment practices, performance appraisals should be based on job analyses to document those critical incidents and specific behaviors that are related to successful job performance. The appraisers should focus on these actual job behaviors rather than on personality characteristics. They should review the ratings with the employees who are being evaluated and offer training and counseling to employees who are not performing well.

In addition, appraisers should be trained in their duties, have detailed written instructions about how to conduct the evaluation, and observe the workers on the job. It is vital that all relevant notes, records, and supporting documentation be well organized and maintained to ensure the accuracy and objectivity of the appraisals and to support the company's position in any future challenges from workers who claim they were treated unfairly.

PURPOSES OF PERFORMANCE APPRAISAL

The overall purpose of performance appraisal is to provide an accurate and objective measure of how well a person is performing the job. On the basis of this information, decisions will be made about the employee's future with the organization. In addition, performance evaluations are often used to validate specific selection techniques. Thus, there are two broad purposes for conducting performance appraisals: (1) administrative, for use with personnel decisions such as pay increases and promotions, and (2) research, usually for validating selection instruments.

Can the purpose of an appraisal affect the results? In other words, do supervisors give different appraisals to their employees when they know that their evaluations and judgments will directly affect their subordinates' careers, than when the appraisals are to be used solely for research or validation purposes? The answer is yes. In a study of 223 first-line supervisors in a Fortune 500 company, the results showed that the supervisors gave significantly more lenient ratings when they knew those ratings would be used for administrative or personnel decisions affecting their subordinates' jobs (Harris, Smith, & Champagne, 1995). Let us consider the purposes of performance appraisal in more detail.

Validation of Selection Criteria

We noted in the chapters on employee selection that to establish the validity of selection devices, they must be correlated with some measure of job performance. Whether we are concerned with psychological tests, interviews, application blanks, or some other technique, we cannot determine their usefulness until we examine the subsequent performance of the workers who were selected and hired on the basis of those techniques. Therefore, a major purpose of performance appraisal is to provide information for validating employee selection techniques.

Training Requirements

A careful evaluation of employee performance can uncover weaknesses or deficiencies in knowledge, skills, and abilities that once identified can be corrected through additional training. Occasionally, an entire work crew or section is found to be deficient on some aspect of the work routine. Documenting information of this sort can lead to the redesign of the training program for new workers and the retraining of current workers to correct the shortcomings. Performance appraisal can also be used to assess the worth of a training program by determining whether job performance improved after the training period.

Employee Improvement

Performance appraisal programs should provide feedback to employees about their job competence and their progress within the organization. I/O psychologists have found that this kind of information is crucial to maintaining employee morale (Derven, 1990). Appraisals can also suggest how employees might change certain behaviors or attitudes to improve their work efficiency. This purpose of performance appraisal is similar to that of improving training requirements. In this instance, however, a worker's shortcomings can be altered through self-improvement rather than through retraining. Workers have a right to know what is expected of them—what they are doing well, and how they might improve.

Pay, Promotion, and Other Personnel Decisions

Most people believe they should be rewarded for above average or excellent performance. For example, in your college work, fairness dictates that if your performance on an exam or term paper is superior to that of others taking the course, you should receive a higher grade. If everyone received the grade of C regardless of academic performance, there would be little incentive for continued hard work.

In employing organizations, rewards are in the form of salary increases, bonuses, promotions, and transfers to positions providing greater opportunity for advancement. To maintain employee initiative and morale, these changes in status cannot depend on a supervisor's whim or personal bias but must be based on a systematic evaluation of employee worth. Performance appraisals provide the foundation for these career decisions and also help to identify those employees with the potential and talent for contributing to the company's growth and expansion.

OPPOSITION TO PERFORMANCE APPRAISAL

Not everyone is in favor of formal performance appraisal systems. Many employees—especially those affected most directly by such ratings—are less than enthusiastic about them. The list of critics also includes labor unions and managers.

Labor Unions

Labor unions, which represent 16% of the U.S. work force, require that seniority (length of service) rather than any assessment of employee merit be taken as the basis for promotion. However, length of job experience alone is no indication of the ability to perform a higher-level job. For example, a worker with 10 years of experience in an auto body plant may know everything about the assembly line, but unless the company has a formal, objective evaluation of that worker's competence—say, the ability to get along with people or the verbal skills to write reports for management—there is no basis for concluding that the worker will make a good supervisor.

Senior people should be given the first opportunity for promotion, but they should be qualified for that promotion on the basis of their skills, not solely because of length of service. Performance evaluations can provide a reliable basis for these decisions.

Employees

Few of us enjoy being tested or evaluated, particularly if we believe we may receive an unfavorable rating. Not many people are so confident of their skills and abilities that they expect consistently to receive praise and tributes from their superiors. And few of us welcome criticism, no matter how objective is its basis or how tactfully it is offered. Because many of us would rather not be assessed and told of our weaknesses or deficiencies, we may react with suspicion or hostility to the idea of performance appraisals.

Managers

Managers who have had unsatisfactory experiences with inadequate or poorly designed appraisal programs are skeptical about their usefulness. Some managers dislike playing the role of judge and are unwilling to accept responsibility for making decisions about the future of their subordinates. This tendency can lead them to inflate their assessments of the workers' job performance. Also, managers may be uncomfortable providing negative feedback to employees and may lack the skills to conduct the postappraisal interview properly.

Despite the opposition to performance appraisal, it remains a necessary activity in organizational life. Its critics overlook the point that some form of appraisal is inevitable. Some basis must be established for employee selection and training and other personnel decisions. These determinations should not be based on personal likes and dislikes. Job competence must be measured in a way that reflects, as objectively as possible, the qualities and abilities required to do the job.

TECHNIQUES OF PERFORMANCE APPRAISAL

I/O psychologists have developed a number of techniques to measure job performance. The specific technique used depends on the type of work being evaluated. The abilities needed to work satisfactorily on an assembly line differ from those required on a sales job or a high-level administrative position. The performance measures chosen must reflect the nature and complexity of the job duties. For example, repetitive assembly-line work can be assessed more objectively than the daily activities of a bank executive.

Two categories of performance measures are (1) objective methods and (2) judgmental methods. Proficiency on production jobs is more readily appraised by objective performance and output measures. Assessing competence on nonproduction, professional, and managerial jobs, however, requires more judgmental and qualitative measures. We shall see examples of both types of performance measures in the next sections.

The question of the comparability or equivalence of objective and subjective measures remains controversial. For example, a validation study of 212 unionized maintenance, mechanical, and field service workers in a gas utility company compared an objective performance appraisal measure (production quantity) with a judgmental measure (supervisor ratings). The researchers found that the two methods yielded similar validity coefficients (Hoffman, Nathan, & Holden, 1991). In this study, then, the two types of measures yielded results that could be considered generally equivalent. However, with a meta-analysis of 40 studies involving 50 samples of workers, the results demonstrated that objective and subjective performance measures were not equivalent and could not be used interchangeably (Bommer, Johnson, Rich, Podsakoff, & Mackenzie, 1995).

OBJECTIVE PERFORMANCE APPRAISAL METHODS

The measurement of performance on production jobs is relatively easy in principle. It typically involves recording the number of units produced in a given time period. Such measures of quantity are widely used in industry in part because production records are readily available. In practice, performance appraisal of production jobs is not so simple, particularly for nonrepetitive jobs. Quality of output must also be assessed.

Quantity and Quality of Output

Consider the productivity of two employees doing word processing. One enters 70 words a minute, and the other enters 55 words a minute. If we use quantity as the sole measure of job performance, we must give the first worker the higher

Some routine production jobs can be evaluated in terms of the number of units produced in a given period.

rating. However, if we examine the quality of their work, we find that the first worker averages 20 errors a minute and the second makes none. We must now adjust the performance evaluations to reflect the quality of output, and the second worker should receive the higher rating.

Even though we have corrected the output data to compensate for the different quality of performance, we must consider the possibility that other factors can influence or distort the performance measure. Perhaps the employee who made so many keyboard errors works in a vast, open room surrounded by many other employees and a lot of noisy office equipment. The other employee may have a private office and few distractions. Or perhaps one produces only short, routine business letters and the other transcribes technical reports from the engineering department. It would be unfair to assign performance ratings without correcting for differences in office environment and level of difficulty of the job tasks.

Another possible contaminating factor is length of job experience. In general, the longer employees are on a job, the greater is their productivity. The performance appraisals of two otherwise identical workers doing the same job may be expected to differ if one has 2 years of experience and the other 20 years.

Therefore, many factors have to be recognized in evaluating performance on production jobs. The more of these influences that must be taken into account, the less objective is the final appraisal because the impact of these extraneous factors requires raters to make personal judgments. Thus, even with production jobs in which a tangible product can be counted, performance appraisal may not always be completely objective. In repetitive jobs, such as much assembly-line work, subjective judgments may have less impact. In these instances, a straightforward record of quantity and quality of output suffices as a measure of job performance.

Electronic Performance Monitoring

Work performed at video display terminals can be thought of as a kind of electronic assembly line. Computers are part of the work environment of more than 20 million people in word-processing, data-entry, insurance, and customer-service jobs in the United States. Many organizations have programmed their computers to monitor employees' on-the-job activities. Every time a worker produces a unit of work—for example, a keystroke on the keyboard—it is automatically counted and stored, providing an objective measure of job performance. Computers can record the number of keystrokes per unit of time, the incidence of errors, the pace of work over the course of a shift, and the number and length of work breaks or rest pauses. More than half of all workers who use computer terminals are subject to this continuous monitoring and evaluating of their job performance by the "electronic supervisor," the machine that is always watching and detects and remembers everything.

Computers are also used to assess workers whose jobs involve telecommunications, such as airline and hotel reservations agents and telephone operators. An airline based in San Diego, California, monitors its reservations agents throughout the work period, timing their calls and comparing performance with company standards for the number of seconds spent on each inquiry and the number of minutes allotted for rest breaks. Employees who exceed the standards receive demerits and unfavorable ratings.

In computerized performance appraisal, the data entries made by employees such as these stock exchange clerks are monitored and evaluated automatically.

Attitudes Toward Electronic Performance Monitoring.

> Computer monitoring has a bad name. Consider the titles of some recent articles in the business press: Big Brother Is Counting Your Keystrokes, How Companies Spy on Employees, Employee Computer Monitoring . . . or Meddling? The Dark Side of Computing, The Boss That Never Blinks. These titles capture the primary way in which computer monitoring has been used in the workplace—as a surveillance technique to control employee behavior (Griffith, 1993, p. 73).

Think about it for a moment. How would you like to have your movements during the workday monitored and recorded? Would it bother you? It may surprise you to learn that a lot of employees, perhaps the majority, are not bothered by electronic performance monitoring. Some of them like it and prefer it to other forms of performance appraisal. Psychologists have found that a person's reaction to electronic monitoring depends on how the information compiled on their job performance is used.

When the information is used to help employees develop and refine their job skills (instead of punishing them for taking long rest breaks, for example), most workers hold a favorable attitude toward electronic monitoring. A survey of Internal Revenue Service employees found that more than 90% favored electronic monitoring as long as the results were used to help them perform their jobs better (Chalykoff & Kochan, 1989).

Many employees like this high-tech performance appraisal technique because it ensures that their work will be evaluated objectively, not on the basis of how much their supervisor may like or dislike them. Employees who support electronic monitoring "also point out that what is being measured is factual, and that many workers favor such systems because they allow diligent workers to legitimately argue a case for better pay or benefits, with the case not relying on personal opinions or personalities" (Hedge & Borman, 1995, p. 460).

Stress and Electronic Performance Monitoring. Having noted that many employees like electronic performance monitoring, it may seem contradictory to report that many employees also find it to be stressful—or so they claim in surveys asking whether electronic performance appraisal causes stress. Employee responses on self-report inventories have shown that approximately 80% report feeling stressed by the use of this technique (Aiello & Shao, 1993; Carayon, 1993).

Keep in mind, as we try to reconcile these disparate findings, that the research results may not be contradictory after all. It is quite conceivable that many employees like electronic monitoring—that they prefer it over other, more subjective, forms of performance appraisal—yet still find it stressful. Indeed, it would be surprising if some workers did not claim that *all* forms of appraisal are stressful to some degree. (If you were asked on a questionnaire whether you find college exams to be stressful, you would probably answer yes.)

There are additional points to be made about the topic of stress and electronic monitoring. First, the monitoring of individual job performance is far more stressful for that employee than when the performance of the work group as a whole is monitored. In the latter case, the individual's performance is combined with that of other group members.

Second, both field and laboratory studies show that people who work alone experience greater stress from electronic monitoring than people who work as part of a cohesive group, even when they are monitored individually. The social support provided by the other members of a close-knit work group serves to reduce the stress (Aiello & Kolb, 1995a).

Third, the stress of continuous monitoring (of knowing that *every* action one takes or fails to take is being recorded) is known to lead workers to focus more on the quantity of their output than the quality. Thus, the stress of electronic monitoring can lead to a reduction in work quality, which has a negative effect on overall job performance and satisfaction.

As with many innovations in the workplace, electronic performance monitoring has both advantages and disadvantages. Let us sum these up as follows (Aiello & Kolb, 1995b).

Advantages of Electronic Monitoring. It provides immediate and objective feedback; reduces bias in performance evaluation; helps identify training needs; facilitates goal setting; and may lead to productivity gains.

Disadvantages of Electronic Monitoring. It invades privacy; may increase stress and reduce job satisfaction; may lead workers to focus on quantity of output at the expense of quality; may transform the work environment into a sort of electronic sweatshop.

Job-Related Personal Data

Another objective approach to performance appraisal involves the use of personal data, such as absenteeism, earnings history, accidents, and advancement rate. It is usually less difficult to compile job-related personal information from the files in the personnel office than to measure and assess production on the job. I/O psychologists have found that personal data may provide little information about an individual worker's ability on the job, but these data can be used to distinguish good from poor employees. The emphasis here is on a semantic dis-

How would you evaluate the job performance of a documentary filmmaker?

tinction between *workers* and *employees*. Highly skilled and experienced machine operators who are prone to excessive absenteeism and tardiness may be outstanding workers when they are actually on the job, but they are poor employees because the company cannot rely on them to show up regularly and contribute to the efficiency of the organization. Job-related personal data have a use in assessing the relative worth of employees to an organization, but they are not substitutes for measures of job performance.

JUDGMENTAL PERFORMANCE APPRAISAL METHODS

Jobs on which employees do not produce a countable product—or one that makes sense to count—are more difficult to assess. How would you evaluate the performance of firefighters? Should we count the number of fires they put out in a day? How would you appraise brain surgeons? By the number of brains they operate on each week? And for business executives, do we tally the number of decisions they make each month? In each of these cases, I/O psychologists must find some way to assess the merit of the person's work, not by counting or keeping a precise record of output but by observing work behavior over a period of time and rendering a judgment about its quality. To determine how effective or ineffective an employee is, we must ask people who are familiar with the person and the work, usually a supervisor, but sometimes colleagues, subordinates, and the employee.

Written Narratives

Although some organizations use written narratives—brief essays describing employee performance—as the sole means of performance appraisal, most also use numerical rating procedures. Although both narrative and rating approaches are subjective, the narrative technique is more prone to personal bias. An essay written by a supervisor can be ambiguous or misleading when describing an employee's job performance. Sometimes these misstatements are inadvertent, and sometimes they are deliberate, to avoid giving a negative appraisal. An article published in the *Harvard Business Review* listed some common expressions used in written performance appraisals—and suggested what the rater really meant (Jackall, 1983).

"Exceptionally well qualified" (Has committed no major blunders to date)
"Tactful in dealing with superiors" (Knows when to keep quiet)
"Quick thinking" (Instantly offers plausible-sounding excuses for errors)
"Meticulous attention to detail" (A fussy nitpicker)
"Slightly below average" (Stupid)
"Unusually loyal to the company" (No one else wants them!)

In an attempt to reduce ambiguity and personal bias, various merit rating techniques have been developed to provide greater objectivity for judgmental performance appraisal methods.

Merit Rating Techniques

In many everyday situations we make judgments about the people with whom we come in contact. We may assess them in terms of their appearance, intelligence, personality, sense of humor, or athletic skills. On the basis of these informal judgments, we may decide whether to like or dislike them, hire them, become friends with them, or marry them. Our judgments are sometimes faulty; a friend can become an enemy, or a spouse an adversary in divorce court. The reason for errors in judgment lies in the fact that the process is subjective and unstandardized. We do not always judge people on the basis of meaningful or relevant criteria.

Merit rating Objective rating methods designed to yield an objective evaluation of work performance.

The process of judgment in **merit rating** is considerably more formalized and specific in that job-related criteria are established to serve as standards for comparison. There is still opportunity for raters to impose their prejudices on the process, but that is not the fault of the method. Merit rating is designed to yield an objective evaluation of work performance compared with established standards.

Rating Technique

Rating scales A performance appraisal technique in which supervisors indicate how or to what degree each relevant job characteristic is possessed by a worker.

Performance **rating scales** are the most frequently used merit rating method of performance appraisal (Borman, White, Pulakos, & Oppler, 1991). The supervisor's rating task is to specify how or to what degree each relevant job characteristic is possessed by the worker. In rating quality of work based on observations of the worker's performance, the supervisor expresses a judgment on a rating scale such as the following. The worker in this example has been judged to exhibit a slightly above average level of task proficiency.

1	2	3	4	5
Poor		Average		Excellent

Some companies rate employees on specific job duties and on broader factors such as cooperation, supervisory skills, time management, communications skills, judgment and initiative, and attendance. In addition, many organizations compare current employee performance with previous evaluations, asking supervisors to indicate whether employees have improved, worsened, or shown no change since the last appraisal.

Supervisors are asked to note particular strengths and to explain any extenuating circumstances that might have affected a worker's performance. Some companies ask employees to add their own written comments to the evaluation form. A portion of a typical performance review form is shown in Figure 5–1.

Ratings are a popular way of evaluating performance for two reasons: They are relatively easy to construct, and they attempt to reduce personal bias.

Ranking Technique

Ranking technique A performance appraisal technique in which supervisors list the workers in their group in order from highest to lowest or best to worst.

In the **ranking technique,** supervisors list their workers in order from highest to lowest or best to worst on specific characteristics and abilities and on overall job proficiency. You can see a major conceptual difference between rating and ranking. In ranking, each employee is compared with all others in the work group or department. In rating, each employee is compared with his or her past performance or with a company standard. Ranking is not as direct a measure of job performance as is rating.

Name _____ Position _____ Time in Position _____ Date _____

Department _____ Location _____ Evaluator (Name/Title) _____

Type of Evaluation: Initial 6 Months ☐ Annual ☐ Other _____ Evaluation Period Dates _____

INSTRUCTIONS: Place a check mark (✓) in the box corresponding to the appropriate performance level. Possible elements to consider in evaluation are suggested.

PERFORMANCE RATING LEVELS _____

Commendable (C) Performance exceeded expectations for the position in most areas and results were fully accomplished in all other areas. Assignments always produce results above "good" performance standards established for this position.

Good (G) Performance met most of the expectations for the position. Overall performance was satisfactory. Assignments and major job duties are accomplished with minimal supervision and direction.

Needs Improvement (NI) Performance is below expectations. Work may lack consistency or require more frequent and closer supervision than normally expected. Attitude or attendance may affect performance.

Unsatisfactory (U) Performance does not meet minimum expectations. This may include below standard performance, lack of ability, lack of application, or disruptions in the workplace. After a final warning and if performance does not improve, the employee will be terminated.

PERFORMANCE RATING FACTORS (Use additional paper if necessary) _____

Specific Responsibilities and Duties _____	(C)	(G)	(NI)	(U)
1.				
2.				
3.				

PERFORMANCE RATING FACTORS (Continued) — (NA) Does Not Apply (S) Satisfactory (NI) Needs Improvement (U) Unsatisfactory

General Responsibilities and Requirements _____	(NA)	(S)	(NI)	(U)
1. Cooperation. Ability to demonstrate a spirit of willingness and interest when working with superior(s) and co-workers.				
2. Supervision. Ability to direct, control and train subordinates. Also consider degree to which assistants are helped to establish work objectives.				
3. Time Management. Ability to organize time effectively. Also consider ability to set priorities, anticipate problems, estimate time requirements, and meet deadlines.				
4. Communication. Ability to explain, convince and be understood in oral and written communications with employees at all levels. Also consider evidence of an understanding of people's views and of the effect of own actions on others.				
5. Judgment and Initiative. Ability to identify and appropriately solve or refer problems. Willingness to expand responsibilities.				
6. Attendance. Attendance and timeliness meet acceptable standards.				

Days Absent _____ Days Late _____

FIGURE 5–1.   Performance appraisal form. (*continued on page 142*)

COMPLETE THIS SECTION

Principal Strengths _____

Areas for Development _____

Comments: _____

_____

Overall Performance Rating: ☐ Commendable   ☐ Good   ☐ Needs Improvement   ☐ Unsatisfactory

Last Performance Review: ☐ Exceptional   ☐ Commendable   ☐ Good   ☐ Needs Improvement   ☐ Unsatisfactory

Date _____

Evaluated by (Name/Title): _____   _____   _____
                                    Please print   Signature   Date

   Signature of Reviewer: _____   _____
                                                                          Date

   Signature of Employee: _____   _____
                                                                          Date

Note: Employee's comments, if any, should be attached to this form.

FIGURE 5–1.   *continued*

An advantage of the ranking technique is its simplicity. No elaborate forms or complicated instructions are required. It can be accomplished quickly and is usually accepted by supervisors as a routine task. Supervisors are not being asked to judge workers on factors such as initiative or cooperation that they may not be competent to assess.

Disadvantages.   Ranking has its limitations when there are a large number of employees to appraise. Supervisors would have to know all the workers on their shifts quite well in order to make comparative judgments of their efficiency. With a group of 50 or 100 subordinates, it becomes difficult and tedious to rank them in order of merit. Another limitation is that because of its simplicity, the ranking technique supplies less evaluative data than does the rating technique. Worker strengths and weaknesses cannot be readily determined, and there is little feedback or information to provide to workers about how well they are doing or how they might improve their job performance.

The ranking technique for performance appraisal also makes it difficult to indicate similarities among workers. In ranking 10 workers, for example, a supervisor may believe that three are equally outstanding and two are equally poor, but there is no way to indicate this. The supervisor is forced to rank the workers from highest to lowest; only one of the three outstanding workers can be at the top of the list even though all three deserve it.

These limitations make the ranking technique a crude measure of performance appraisal. It is usually applied only when a small number of workers are involved and when little information is desired beyond an indication of their relative standing.

Paired-Comparison Technique

The **paired-comparison technique** requires that each worker be compared with every other worker in the work group or section. It is similar to ranking, and the result is a rank ordering of workers, but the comparative judgments are more systematic and controlled. Comparisons are made between two people at a time, and a judgment is made about which of the pair is superior. If specific characteristics are to be rated, the comparisons are repeated for each item. When all possible comparisons have been made, an objective ranked list is obtained that is based on the worker's score in each comparison. If a supervisor evaluates six workers by this technique, comparing each worker with every other worker, 15 paired comparisons must be made because there are 15 possible pairs. The following formula is used; N represents the number of persons to be evaluated.

$$\frac{N\,(N-1)}{2}$$

Paired-comparison technique A performance appraisal technique that compares the performance of each worker with that of every other worker in the group.

Advantages.   An advantage of the paired-comparison approach over the ranking technique is that the judgmental process is simpler. The supervisor has to consider only one pair of workers at a time. Another advantage is that it is possible to give the same rank to those of equal ability.

Disadvantages.   The disadvantage lies in the large number of comparisons required when dealing with many employees. A supervisor with 60 employees would be required to make 1,770 comparisons. If the performance evaluation called for the appraisal of, say, five separate traits or factors, each of the 1,770 comparisons would have to be made five times. The use of the technique is necessarily restricted to small groups and to a single ranking of overall job effectiveness.

Forced-Distribution Technique

The **forced-distribution technique** is useful with somewhat larger groups. Supervisors rate their employees in fixed proportions, according to a predetermined distribution of ratings. The standard distribution is as follows:

Forced-distribution technique A merit rating technique of performance appraisal in which supervisors rate employees according to a prescribed distribution of ratings; analogous to grading on a curve.

Superior	10%
Better than average	20%
Average	40%
Below average	20%
Poor	10%

If your college instructors grade on a curve, then you are already familiar with forced distribution. The top 10% of the class receives a grade of A, regardless of their specific test scores. The next 20% receives Bs, and so on, until all grades are forced into the categories of the distribution resembling the normal curve.

Disadvantages.   A disadvantage of the forced-distribution technique is that it compels a supervisor to use predetermined rating categories that might not fairly represent that particular group of workers. All workers in a group may be better than average or superior in job performance, and all deserve good ratings. However, the forced distribution technique dictates that only 30% can be rated as above average.

Forced-Choice Technique

One difficulty with the merit rating techniques we have discussed is that raters are aware of whether they are giving good or poor ratings to employees. This knowledge may permit their personal biases, animosities, or favoritism to affect the ratings. The **forced-choice technique** prevents raters from knowing how favorable or unfavorable a rating they are assigning to employees.

In the forced-choice technique, raters are presented with a series of descriptive statements in groups of two, three, or four, and are asked to select the phrase that best describes an employee or is least applicable to that employee. The phrases within each group are designed to appear equally positive or equally negative. For example, raters may be asked to choose one statement in each of the following pairs that best describes a subordinate.

1. Is reliable
2. Is agreeable

1. Is careful
2. Is diligent

Next, raters may be asked to select one statement in each of these pairs that least describes the subordinate.

1. Is arrogant
2. Is not interested in the job

1. Is uncooperative
2. Is sloppy on the job

Given a number of sets of statements, it is difficult for supervisors to distinguish the items that represent desirable or undesirable characteristics. Therefore, they are less likely to deliberately assign favorable or unfavorable ratings.

When I/O psychologists develop statements for forced-choice rating scales, they correlate each item with a measure of job success. Although the statements in each pair may appear to be equally favorable or unfavorable, they have been found to discriminate between more efficient and less efficient workers.

Disadvantages.   Although the use of this technique limits the effect of personal bias and controls for deliberate distortion, it has several disadvantages and is unpopular with raters. Considerable research is necessary to determine the predictive validity for each item. Thus, the technique is more costly to develop than other merit rating methods. The instructions are difficult to understand, and the task of choosing between similar alternatives in a large number of pairs is tedious.

Behaviorally Anchored Rating Scales (BARS)

Behaviorally anchored rating scales (BARS) attempt to evaluate job performance in terms of specific behaviors that are important to success or failure on

Forced-choice technique A merit rating technique of performance appraisal in which raters are presented with groups of descriptive statements and are asked to select the phrase in each group that is most or least descriptive of an employee.

Behaviorally anchored rating scales (BARS) A performance appraisal technique in which appraisers rate critical employee behaviors.

the job rather than in terms of general attitudes or factors such as communications skills, cooperativeness, or common sense. The usual way to develop behavioral criteria is through the critical-incidents technique described in Chapter 3 as a method of job analysis.

Supervisors familiar with the job observe the performance of their workers and note those behaviors necessary to effective job performance. A series of critical-incident behaviors are established, some associated with superior performance and others with unsatisfactory performance. These behaviors, based on actual job behaviors, are used as standards for appraising worker effectiveness. The BARS items can be scored objectively by indicating whether the employee displays that behavior or by selecting on a scale the degree to which the employee displays that behavior. A BARS scale to appraise supermarket checkout clerks is shown in Figure 5–2. Although there are not many applicants for the position of Superman or Wonder Woman, one I/O psychologist developed a BARS scale for that job (Figure 5–3).

Much of the success of the BARS approach depends on the observational skill of the supervisors in identifying behaviors that are truly critical to successful or unsuccessful performance on the job. If the list of critical incidents is inade-

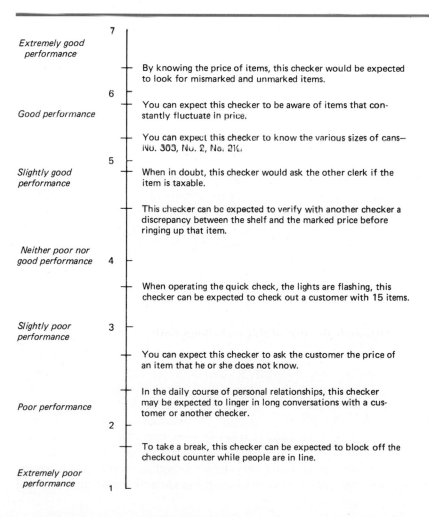

7 — *Extremely good performance*	
	By knowing the price of items, this checker would be expected to look for mismarked and unmarked items.
6 — *Good performance*	You can expect this checker to be aware of items that constantly fluctuate in price.
	You can expect this checker to know the various sizes of cans—No. 303, No. 2, No. 2½.
5 — *Slightly good performance*	When in doubt, this checker would ask the other clerk if the item is taxable.
	This checker can be expected to verify with another checker a discrepancy between the shelf and the marked price before ringing up that item.
4 — *Neither poor nor good performance*	
	When operating the quick check, the lights are flashing, this checker can be expected to check out a customer with 15 items.
3 — *Slightly poor performance*	You can expect this checker to ask the customer the price of an item that he or she does not know.
	In the daily course of personal relationships, this checker may be expected to linger in long conversations with a customer or another checker.
2 — *Poor performance*	To take a break, this checker can be expected to block off the checkout counter while people are in line.
1 — *Extremely poor performance*	

FIGURE 5–2.   Critical incident behaviors associated with job performance for supermarket checkout clerks. (Adapted from L. Fogli, C. L. Hulin, & M. R. Blood, "Development of first-level behavioral job criteria." *Journal of Applied Psychology*, 1971, 55, 6.)

Area of Performance	Degree of Performance				
	Far Excels Job Requirements	Exceeds Job Requirements	Meets Job Requirements	Needs Improvement	Does Not Meet Minimum Requirements
Quality of work	Leaps tall buildings in a single bound	Leaps tall buildings with running start	Can leap over houses, if prodded	Often stumbles into buildings	Is often knocked down by buildings
Promptness	Is faster than a speeding bullet	Is as fast as a speeding bullet	Would you believe a slow bullet?	Misfires frequently	Wounds self when handling a gun
Initiative	Is stronger than a locomotive	Is as strong as a bull elephant	Almost as strong as a bull	Shoots the bull	Smells like a bull
Adaptability	Walks on water	Strong swimmer	A good water treader	Favorite haunt is the water cooler	Passes water in emergencies
Communication	Talks with God	Talks with the angels	Talks to self	Argues with self	Loses most of these arguments

FIGURE 5–3. Behaviorally anchored rating scale (BARS). (Adapted by Hurd Hutchins from *The Industrial-Organizational Psychologist,* 1980, *17*(4), 22.)

Behavioral expectation scales (BES) A performance appraisal technique in which appraisers rate critical employee behaviors in terms of expectations.

quate, any performance appraisal based on these behaviors may be misleading. In some applications of the BARS technique, behaviors are listed in terms of expectations; in this instance, the instrument is called a **behavioral expectation scale** (BES). One advantage of BARS and BES approaches to performance appraisal is that they meet federal fair employment guidelines. The criteria on which workers are assessed are job related because they derive from actual job performance. Research on the effectiveness of BARS has yielded mixed results. Some studies show that they are no more objective or free of bias than scales that do not have specific behavioral anchors (Murphy & Constans, 1987).

Behavioral Observation Scales (BOS)

Behavioral observation scales (BOS) A performance appraisal technique in which appraisers rate the frequency of critical employee behaviors.

In the **behavioral observation scale** (BOS) approach to performance appraisal, employees are also evaluated in terms of critical incidents. In that respect, it is similar to BARS. However, the BOS appraisers rate subordinates on the *frequency* of the critical incidents as they are observed to occur over a given period (Latham & Wexley, 1977). The ratings are assigned on a 5-point scale, similar to the example for supermarket checkout clerk shown in Figure 5–4. The evaluation yields a total score for each employee by adding the ratings for each critical incident. The behavioral incidents for the rating scale are developed in the same way as for BARS: through identification by supervisors or other subject matter experts. Similarly, BOS meet equal employment opportunity guidelines because they are related to behaviors required for successful job performance.

I/O psychology research comparing BARS and BOS techniques has been inconclusive. Some studies demonstrate the superiority of one technique over the other; other studies fail to confirm these findings (Kane & Bernardin, 1982; Latham & Wexley, 1981). A survey of managers who conduct performance appraisals showed that they preferred BOS over BARS and that BARS were considered no more effective than merit rating scales that measured general traits. However, the managers reported that BOS allowed them to justify low employee ratings and to improve the quality of the feedback they gave employees. Attorneys specializing in employee dis-

Knows the price of competitive products

Never	Seldom	Sometimes	Generally	Always
1	2	3	4	5

FIGURE 5–4.   Sample item from behavioral observation scale (BOS) for supermarket checkout clerks.

crimination cases believed that the BOS approach was more defensible in court than BARS or other merit rating systems (Wiersma & Latham, 1986).

Management by Objectives (MBO)

Management by objectives (MBO) involves a mutual agreement between employees and supervisors on goals to be achieved in a given time. Instead of focusing on abilities or characteristics as in merit rating, or on job behaviors as in BARS and BOS, management by objectives focuses on results—on how well employees accomplish specified goals. The emphasis is on what employees do rather than on what their supervisors think of them or perceive their behaviors to be. Further, MBO actively involves employees in their own evaluations. They are not simply graded or rated by others.

MBO consists of two phases: goal setting and performance review. In goal setting, employees meet individually with supervisors to determine the goals for which they will strive in the time before the next appraisal, usually 1 year, and to discuss ways of reaching those goals. The goals must be realistic, specific, and as objective as possible. For example, it is not sufficient for salespersons to say that they will try to sell more products. A fixed number of items or a dollar volume must be established as the goal.

In performance review, employees and supervisors discuss the extent to which the goals were met. Again, this is a mutual process involving both parties. The performance appraisal is based on job results, not on characteristics such as initiative or general skills.

Employees in MBO programs may feel pressured to set higher goals with each appraisal to show evidence of improvement or progress. A supervisor may not accept last year's quota as a sufficient goal for this year's job performance. Thus, the goals may become increasingly unrealistic. Also, MBO is not appropriate for jobs that cannot be quantified. It would be silly to expect research chemists to agree to make five more scientific breakthroughs this year than last.

The MBO technique satisfies fair employment guidelines and is popular in private and public organizations. It has been found to be effective in increasing employee motivation and productivity. A meta-analysis of 70 studies revealed an average gain in productivity of 44.6% in all but two studies (Rodgers & Hunter, 1991). Thus, MBO can be a valuable tool for appraising and improving job performance.

Management by objectives (MBO) A performance appraisal technique that involves a mutual agreement between employee and manager on the goals to be achieved in a given period.

PERFORMANCE APPRAISAL OF MANAGERS

The performance appraisal of managerial personnel presents problems not faced in the assessment of other employees. Merit rating techniques are often used to evaluate low- and middle-level supervisory personnel, but additional methods of appraisal are also required. Paradoxically, senior executives are rarely evaluated. They seldom receive feedback or judgments about the quality of their job performance unless the company faces a crisis. Interviews with top executives have shown that at higher levels of management, performance reviews are less systematic and informative.

The Assessment-Center Technique

Assessment centers (discussed in Chapter 3 as an employee selection technique) are a popular method of performance appraisal. Managers participate in simulated job tasks such as management games, group problem solving, leaderless group discussions, in-basket tests, and interviews. Recall that assessment centers do not assess actual job behavior but, rather, a variety of activities that are like those encountered on the job. Research has shown high reliability and validity of assessment-center evaluations when they are used for performance appraisal (see, for example, Klimoski & Brickner, 1987).

Evaluation by Superiors

The most frequently used technique for the performance appraisal of managers is assessment by their superiors in the organization. Standard rating sheets are rarely used. Typically, the rater writes a brief descriptive essay about the individual's job performance. An evaluation by an immediate superior is often supplemented by the judgments of executives at higher levels.

Evaluation by Colleagues: Peer Rating

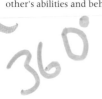

Peer rating A performance appraisal technique in which managers or executives at the same level assess one another's abilities and behaviors.

Peer rating (also called "buddy rating") was developed during World War II. It is a technique for having managers or executives at the same level assess one another in terms of their general ability to perform the job or their specific traits and behaviors. Although peer ratings tend to be higher than ratings given by superiors, research shows a positive correlation between high peer ratings and subsequent promotion. "On the whole, both field and laboratory studies indicate that peer assessment is a valid and reliable evaluation procedure" (Saavedra & Kwun, 1993, p. 450). Peer ratings also show high reliability and a focus on job-related abilities.

Attitudes toward peer rating among managers are generally positive. However, research has shown that managers are significantly more favorable toward peer rating when the evaluations are used for development or improving job skills, than when they are used for promotion or other career decisions (McEvoy & Buller, 1987).

Peer rating for lower-level employees has received mixed research support. A study of U.S. Army enlisted personnel compared supervisor ratings and peer ratings for 18 job categories, including combat engineer, tank crewman, radio operator, and food service specialist. The data were taken from a long-term project to improve the selection and classification system for army assignments. The researchers found that supervisor ratings showed a greater relationship to actual job behaviors than did peer ratings (Oppler, Campbell, Pulakos, & Borman, 1992).

Self-Evaluation

Another approach to managerial performance appraisal is to ask individuals to assess their own abilities and job performance. One technique is similar to management by objectives (MBO), discussed earlier in this chapter. Managers and their superiors meet to establish goals for managerial performance—not specific production targets but personal skills to be developed or deficiencies to be corrected. After a time, the managers meet again with their superiors to discuss their progress.

Self-ratings tend to be higher than evaluations by superiors and to show greater leniency. Self-ratings were found to focus more on interpersonal skills, whereas ratings by superiors emphasized initiative and specific job skills (Hoffman, Nathan, & Holden, 1991; McEnery & McEnery, 1987). Leniency can be reduced if raters are told that their self-evaluations will be validated against more objective criteria.

Self-ratings A performance appraisal technique in which managers assess their own abilities and job performance.

Cultural differences in the leniency of self-evaluations have also been investigated. A study conducted in the Republic of China (Taiwan) surveyed more than 900 employees and supervisors in a variety of organizations—a hospital, a hotel, a shoe manufacturer, a fast-food chain, an automobile manufacturer, a government-owned oil company, and several advertising agencies. The questionnaire response rate was 85%. The employees were found to rate their own job performance less favorably than did their supervisors, showing what the researchers called a socially acceptable "modesty bias" (Farh, Dobbins, & Cheng, 1991).

A replication of this study, using another sample of Asian workers (367 employees in 7 workshops and factories in mainland China), failed to confirm this so-called modesty bias. In the replication, self-ratings were significantly higher than supervisor ratings, results similar to those typically obtained from research on employees in the United States (Yu & Murphy, 1993).

Managers who overestimated their abilities—whose self-ratings differed greatly from the ratings they were given by their superiors—were found to perform more poorly on the job than managers whose ratings of their own abilities were more accurate. For the latter group, self-ratings coincided with ratings by superiors (Bass & Yammarino, 1991). Other research on self-awareness studied squad leaders at the U.S. Naval Academy and lieutenants who were recent USNA graduates. It was found that effective leadership behavior was positively related to self-ratings for personnel whose self-ratings agreed with the ratings of their superiors but not for personnel who overestimated their abilities (Atwater & Yammarino, 1992).

A study of 357 male recruits for the Israeli army found that self-appraisals had a low but statistically significant validity for predicting success in training programs. The self-ratings also correlated positively with ratings made by peers and superiors (Fox & Dinur, 1988).

Although self-ratings can be a useful part of a performance appraisal program, their value as the sole technique is questionable. A meta-analysis of research on self-ratings, peer ratings, supervisor ratings, and subordinate ratings suggests that self-ratings in general do not correlate highly with supervisor ratings (Harris & Schaubroeck, 1988).

Evaluation by Subordinates

Another approach to the performance appraisal of managers involves evaluation by subordinates. This technique, described as upward feedback, is similar to having students evaluate their classroom instructors (Bernardin, Dahmus, & Redmon, 1993; Hedge & Borman, 1995).

Upward feedback is effective in developing and improving leadership abilities. In one global corporation, more than 1,500 employees completed two behavioral observation scales 6 months apart to rate 238 managers. Managers who received top scores in the first rating did not show improvement at the second rating; they were already seen to be performing well. Managers who received moderate to low ratings initially did show improved leadership effectiveness by the second rating. Thus, the managers who needed to improve did so, most likely in response to the upward feedback from subordinates (Smither, London, Vasilopoulos, Reilly, Millsap, & Salvemini, 1995). A study of 92 managers also found improvement in performance ratings in an upward feedback program. The improvement was documented more than two years later (Reilly, Smither, & Vasilopoulos, 1996).

At the U.S. Naval Academy, where students and their cadet officers live and work together, 978 leaders were rated by 1,232 followers 8 weeks and 14 weeks after the beginning of the academic year. Overall, the behavior of the cadet officers improved following the evaluations by their subordinates. When the leaders then rated themselves, however, the self-ratings of those who had received negative feedback from their subordinates declined, whereas the self-ratings of those who had received positive feedback increased. Apparently, the cadet officers placed great importance on the ratings their subordinates had given them (Atwater, Roush, & Fischthal, 1995).

Subordinate appraisals have shown a higher validity for predicting managerial success than assessment-center performance. However, the combined use of subordinate ratings and assessment-center ratings is better than either technique alone. Subordinate ratings also correlated positively with supervisor ratings and with self-ratings (Bernardin, 1986).

In a study of the agreement between subordinate ratings and self-ratings, data were collected from 86 managers with nearly 500 subordinates on 48 items relating to leadership and to manager/subordinate relations. The correlation between subordinate ratings and self-ratings on these items was found to be higher for women managers than for men managers, suggesting to the researchers that because women show greater self-understanding, their self-perceptions are more likely to agree with other people's perceptions of them. The correlations between subordinate ratings and self-ratings was higher in larger work groups, supporting the hypothesis that the greater the number of raters, the more reliable the ratings. Agreement between subordinate and self-ratings increased over time, perhaps because managers attempted to work more closely with their subordinates and focused more on building a relationship with them (London & Wohlers, 1991).

Anonymity.   In appraisal programs that use evaluations by subordinates, it is vital that the raters are not identified. A survey of employees and managers in a large telecommunications company reported that 88% of the employees said they could not be candid or straightforward in their evaluations of their superiors if they had to put their names on the evaluation forms (Bernardin, 1986). A survey in another company showed that 24% of the employees would have rated their managers differently if the survey had not been anonymous (London, Wohlers, & Gallagher, 1990).

Multisource Feedback

A newer approach to performance appraisal involves combining evaluations from several sources into an overall appraisal. Any number of individual ratings

#7

Rating Your Boss: No Names, Please!

You know the drill. About every 6 months or so, your boss calls you in for a chat about how you're doing at your job. It's called a performance appraisal. You sit there, perhaps seething inside, while the boss tells you what you're doing wrong and how you could improve. And you're thinking how you'd like to tell the boss a thing or two about how he or she is doing.

Nowadays, some employees *can* talk back. Growing numbers of companies are asking workers to participate in an upward-appraisal process, that is, to appraise the performance of their supervisors and managers. These appraisals or ratings are then used to help determine promotions and pay raises. Sounds great, doesn't it? A chance to get back at unfair bosses? Maybe get them fired?

Suppose, however, you had to sign your name on the appraisal form? Would that influence your comments? Most likely, unless, of course, you had already lined up another job. To test this hypothesis, a management professor at the University of Wisconsin asked 183 employees at an insurance company to rate 38 managers. The employees were all volunteers for the task and were told that no reprisals would be taken by the managers, regardless of what the employees reported. To further assure the employees, they were given the telephone number of a contact in the company's human resources department in the event of any backlash.

Half the employees in the study appraised their bosses anonymously. The other half put their names on the performance appraisal forms. Did the act of identifying themselves make a difference in the ratings? You bet it did! Employees who signed their names to the appraisal forms gave higher ratings to their managers than did the employees who were doing the ratings anonymously. All employees reported they would feel much more comfortable rating their bosses on the condition that they remained anonymous.

This kind of upward appraisal can be an effective tool for improving manager effectiveness. Just don't sign your name to the form.

Source: Antonioni, D. (1994). The effects of feedback accountability on upward appraisal ratings. *Personnel Psychology, 47,* 349–356.

sources can be so combined, but the ultimate multisource approach is called 360-degree feedback. It combines the full circle of ratings from all sources—from superiors, subordinates, peers, and self, and even evaluations by the organization's customers or clients who have dealings with the person being rated.

Multisource feedback can provide information that would not otherwise be available about the ratees because it provides data from unique perspectives. Subordinates and peers, for example, have different experiences and relationships with their managers than do the managers' bosses. Evaluations from customers provide yet another view of how well managers are performing their jobs.

Multisource feedback may also reduce many forms of bias. If all parties are told that their ratings will be compared with those assigned by others, they are likely to be more objective in their assessments. We have noted some research that supported high positive correlations between various combinations of ratings, but other research has reported low correlations. The level of agreement appears to vary as a function of type of job, being generally lower for managerial and professional employees than for employees in blue-collar and service jobs (Harris & Schaubroeck, 1988).

When combined ratings are consistent, decisions about a manager's future with the organization can be made with greater confidence. Also, if ratings show a high level of agreement, a manager may be more willing to accept criticism because it comes from sources other than the immediate supervisor. When ratings disagree, however, the manager may be reluctant to accept and act on criticism.

Multisource feedback is obviously more expensive than appraisals from a single source, but there are indications that the combination approach is growing in popularity despite its cost. The appraisals obtained from multiple sources are used primarily for development purposes—that is, for making managers more effective—but some organizations are also using them for pay and promotion decisions (Bracken, 1994; London & Smither, 1995; Tornow, 1993).

SOURCES OF ERROR IN PERFORMANCE APPRAISAL

Regardless of the sophistication of the techniques used, performance appraisal still involves one human being judging, assessing, or estimating the characteristics or performance of another. This inevitably means that human biases and prejudices can affect the judgments. Some common sources of error that can distort employee performance appraisals include the halo effect, constant or systematic bias, most-recent-performance error, inadequate information error, average rating error, and the rater's cognitive processes.

The Halo Effect

Halo effect The tendency to judge all aspects of a person's behavior or character on the basis of a single attribute.

The **halo effect** involves the familiar tendency to judge all aspects of a person's behavior or character on the basis of a single attribute. For example, if we find a person to be physically attractive, we may tend to think of that person also as friendly, likeable, and easy to get along with, generalizing from one attribute to personality characteristics and other abilities. A supervisor who scores an employee high on one factor of a merit rating scale may tend to grade that person high on all other factors. This distortion is particularly likely to occur when a high rating is given on one or two traits and the other traits to be rated are difficult to observe, unfamiliar, or not clearly defined.

One way to control for the halo effect is to have more than one person rate a worker, on the assumption that any personal biases will tend to cancel each other out. Another way is to have supervisors rate all subordinates on one trait or characteristic at a time instead of rating each person on all items at once. When workers are judged on a single characteristic, there may be less opportunity for one rating to carry over to other traits.

I/O psychology research suggests that the halo error may be less a problem than previously thought. For example, a study of 294 clerical workers in a large petrochemical company was designed to validate tests of clerical, verbal, and numerical ability. The researchers found that the greater the halo effect in subsequent job performance ratings, the higher the validity coefficients between test scores and those ratings. When statistical manipulation removed the effect of the halo error, validity and rating accuracy were reduced. This apparent paradox suggested to the researchers that the halo effect served to ensure that raters considered "the employee as a whole when conducting performance ratings rather than attending too much to specific, but unrepresentative, critical incidents" (Nathan & Tippins, 1990, p. 296). More recent research also suggested that the halo effect deals with the rater's general impression of the ratee rather than with specific behaviors (Lance, La Pointe, & Stewart, 1994).

A number of I/O psychologists have drawn the following conclusions (Murphy, Jako, & Anhalt, 1993):

1. The halo effect is not as common as previously thought;
2. It does not detract from the quality of ratings;
3. It often cannot be detected; and
4. It may, in many cases, be illusory—caused by irrelevant factors such as errors of memory or observation, or deficiencies in measurement.

These findings have led to "an emerging consensus (or at least a popular plea) to abandon halo measures as indicators of the psychometric integrity of performance ratings. . . . [Halo] should not be used to evaluate the adequacy of a rating device or process until we know more about what halo is and how it should be measured" (Landy, Shankster, & Kohler, 1994, p. 284).

Constant or Systematic Bias

Constant or **systematic bias** as a source of performance appraisal error has its basis in the standards or criteria used by the raters. Some raters or supervisors expect more than others from their employees. Similarly, in college some professors are known as easy graders and expect less from their students than those known as hard graders. The constant biasing error means that a top rating given by one supervisor may not be equivalent to a top rating given by another supervisor, just as an A from one professor may not mean the same as an A from another professor as an evaluation of merit or ability.

Constant bias A source of error in performance appraisal based on the different standards used by raters.

Constant bias can be corrected by requiring supervisors to distribute ratings in accordance with the normal curve. However, as we noted with the forced-distribution technique, this means that some workers will receive ratings that are undeserved.

Most-Recent-Performance Error

Performance appraisals are usually made every 6 or 12 months. There is an understandable tendency to base ratings on the workers' most recent behavior, without considering their performance throughout the period since the last appraisal. It is natural for memory to be clearer about events that have occurred more recently, but recent behavior may be atypical or distorted by extraneous factors. For example, if a worker performs poorly in the weeks just before the evaluation because of illness or marital problems, the result may be a distortion of a previous record of exemplary job performance. If a worker is aware that a performance evaluation is due, he or she may strive to work more efficiently just before the rating. In both cases, performance is not typical of the workers' overall job behavior, and a falsely low or high rating will result.

One way to reduce this **most-recent-performance error** is to require more frequent appraisals. By shortening the time between performance reviews, there is less tendency to forget a worker's usual behavior. Making supervisors aware of the possibility that this type of error can occur can also be effective in reducing it.

Most-recent-performance error A source of error in performance appraisal in which a rater tends to evaluate a worker's most recent behavior rather than behavior throughout the period since the last appraisal.

Inadequate Information Error

Supervisors are required to rate employees at specified intervals whether or not they know enough about the employees to do so fairly and accurately. To admit to their superiors that they lack adequate knowledge of their subordinates can be construed as a personal failing. The resulting appraisals will be worth little to the organization and to the employees because they will not be based on a comprehensive knowledge of worker behavior. An examination of two-person ratings made of 9,975 first-line supervisors from 79 organizations found a strong positive relationship between the opportunity to observe the employees (which ranged from less than 3 months to nearly 20 years) and the level of interrater reliability. The researcher suggested that ratings of employees observed by their bosses for less than a year are not likely to be reliable (Rothstein, 1990).

A way to deal with this **inadequate information error** is to train raters on the value of performance appraisals and the harm done by ratings based on incomplete information. Supervisors should be given the opportunity to refuse to rate employees about whom they have little knowledge and the assurance that they will not be penalized for such refusal.

Inadequate information error A potential source of error in performance appraisal in which supervisors rate their employees even though they may not know enough about them to do so fairly and accurately.

Average Rating or Leniency Error

Some raters are reluctant to assign extreme scores in either direction. The tendency is to be lenient and to assign average ratings to all workers. Particularly when dealing with a small number of workers, it is not unusual to find their ratings clustered around the middle of the scale, separated by no more than 1 or 2 points. Thus, the range of abilities indicated is restricted, and the ratings are so close that it is difficult to distinguish between good and poor workers. This **average rating** or **leniency error** does not reflect the range of differences that exist among workers, and the ratings provide no useful information to the company or to employees.

Research involving three real-world appraisal situations dealt with the following groups of subjects: 38 police sergeants rating 328 patrol officers, 31 head nurses rating 243 nurses, and 44 supervisors rating 376 social workers. The results showed that the leniency error is a stable rater characteristic, independent of rating format or situational and personal variables (Kane, Bernardin, Villanova, & Peyrefitte, 1995). Some supervisors, then, will always tend to give more lenient evaluations than others. The challenge for employers is to identify the raters who express this tendency and take it into consideration when making personnel decisions based on their appraisals of subordinates.

Average rating error In performance appraisal, the reluctance of a rater to assign very good or very poor ratings. Consequently, most ratings fall in the middle of the rating scale.

Cognitive Processes of Raters

Performance appraisals can be affected by the **cognitive,** or thought, **processes** of the raters that underlie their judgments of worker effectiveness. We discuss four cognitive variables that can influence evaluations of employee performance: category structures, beliefs, interpersonal affect, and attribution.

Cognitive processes Our processes of thought and judgment; in performance appraisal, a rater's cognitive processes can influence the judgments made about the employees he or she is evaluating.

Category Structures.   The category structures that supervisors or managers use in evaluating their employees can affect their assessments. When an appraiser thinks about a worker as belonging to a particular category, the information he or she recalls about that worker will be biased toward that category. Suppose that an employee is perceived to be a team player; this becomes a category in the rater's mental picture. The employee's performance on the job is likely to be observed, interpreted, and remembered in terms of how a typical team player is expected to behave rather than in terms of how that employee actually behaves.

Beliefs.   A related cognitive variable that can influence performance appraisal involves raters' beliefs about human nature. These ideas can lead raters to make evaluations in terms of how they view people in general rather than in terms of specific worker characteristics and behaviors. For example, supervisors who believe that people are basically good and trustworthy may give more generous ratings than those who believe that people are mean and conniving. Supervisors who accept the idea of individual differences among people and who are tolerant of those differences may give ratings that are different from those of supervisors who believe that most people are alike.

Interpersonal Affect.   The cognitive variable of **interpersonal affect** refers to one person's feelings or emotions toward another person. Common sense suggests that, except for those raters who can maintain impartiality and objectivity toward their employees, ratings will be influenced by the personal relationship between rater and ratee. In general, I/O psychology research supports the hypothesis that raters who have positive emotions or affect toward the persons they are rating give higher marks than raters who have negative affect (Judge & Ferris, 1993; Varma, DeNisi, & Peters, 1996).

Interpersonal affect Our feelings or emotions toward another person; in performance appraisal, interpersonal affect—the emotional tone of the relationship between rater and employee—can influence the assigned ratings.

For example, a study of 367 employees of a telephone company found that those who were in trusting and high-quality relationships with their supervisors received high performance ratings from them, regardless of the actual quality of the employees' work (Duarte, Goodson, & Klich, 1994).

It is possible to manipulate interpersonal affect through impression management techniques. A study of 111 pairs of subordinates and supervisors found that "other-enhancement" impression management strategies—such as flattery, doing favors for one's supervisor, and agreeing with the opinions of one's supervisor—significantly affected how much the supervisor liked the worker. This, in turn, led to higher performance ratings. The other impression management strategy, "self-presentation," which includes such assertive behaviors as boasting about one's abilities, did not influence the level of liking of supervisors for subordinates (Wayne & Liden, 1995).

These findings probably coincide with our everyday experiences. We tend to be more lenient, forgiving, and generous toward people we like, and there are few reasons we should expect the situation to be different in the workplace.

However, interpersonal affect, or liking, may not influence ratings in all situations. An analysis of the ratings of 631 soldiers by their supervisors found that rater dependability was a more powerful influence on ratings than ratee friendliness and likability. In the military, then, agreement with such statements about a ratee as "I can count on this soldier to back me up if I really need it," or "I can trust and depend on this soldier," were more important in rating job performance than was interpersonal affect (Borman, White, & Dorsey, 1995, p. 171).

Attribution.   The concept of **attribution,** another cognitive influence on performance appraisal, derives from social psychology research on the way we form impressions of other people. In performance appraisal, one person forms an impression of the abilities and characteristics of another. The rater mentally attributes or assigns reasons to the ratee's behavior. These beliefs about why an employee behaves in a particular way can affect the rater's evaluation. For example, a supervisor may observe that two employees frequently seem tired. That supervisor may be lenient and understanding toward the tired employee who has young children but less forgiving of the tired employee who is known to enjoy late-night partying.

Supervisors can attribute employee behavior to external causes such as luck or task difficulty or to internal factors such as health, skills, and effort. Research has shown that high performance ratings correlate with attributions of employee behavior to internal causes (Hogan, 1987; Schmitt & Robertson, 1990). Therefore, performance appraisals can depend in part on the factors the supervisor believes account for the level of job performance.

Attribution can also be influenced by interpersonal affect. Managers have been shown to attribute poor employee performance to internal factors, such as lack of motivation or inadequate skills, when they disliked or had negative affect toward the person being rated (Dobbins & Russell, 1986). In other words, the managers appeared to believe that the poor performance of the workers they did not like was the fault of the workers themselves, whereas the poor performance of the workers they did like was a result of external factors such as bad luck, a heavy work load, or equipment failure.

The attribution error can be reduced by having supervisors spend time performing the job they are evaluating. This experience exposes them to the kinds of external factors that can influence job performance. Raters should also be made aware of how their perceptions of a worker's behavior on the job can differ from the worker's own point of view.

Role Conflict

One final factor that may introduce error into performance appraisals is the amount of role conflict experienced by the supervisor. **Role conflict** refers to the disparity or contradiction between the job's demands and the supervisor's standards of right and wrong. Sometimes the nature of a job requires supervisors to compromise those standards; we shall see in Chapter 12 that role conflict is a recognized source of job stress.

Self-report measures of role conflict, and of the tendency to deliberately inflate performance ratings, were obtained from two groups totaling 177 supervisors. Those who scored high in role conflict tended to deliberately inflate the ratings they gave to their subordinates. The researchers suggested that the supervisors who experienced role conflict may have given the inflated ratings for several reasons (Fried & Tiegs, 1995):

1. as a way of establishing control over the work situation;
2. as a way of avoiding the confrontation with subordinates that might have resulted from giving them lower ratings;
3. as a way of obtaining their subordinates' gratitude and goodwill.

Whatever the reasons, it is clear from this and similar research that role conflict, and the stress associated with it, may lead supervisors to give higher-than-justified performance ratings. These findings are part of a growing body of evidence showing that managers may inflate performance appraisals as a way of satisfying personal needs and dealing with organizational pressures.

IMPROVING PERFORMANCE APPRAISALS

The fact that performance appraisals can be so easily biased is no reason to abandon hope of achieving more objective evaluations. We have noted various steps that can be taken to reduce some sources of error. In addition, providing training and feedback to raters can decrease errors and increase accuracy.

Training.   Training the persons who conduct performance appraisals involves (1) creating an awareness that abilities and skills are usually distributed in accordance with the normal curve, so that it is acceptable to find broad differences within a group of workers, and (2) developing the ability to define objective criteria for worker behaviors—the standards or average performance levels against which workers can be compared. I/O psychology research supports the suggestion that rater training can reduce errors in performance appraisal, particularly errors of leniency and halo.

The type of training provided for appraisers is important because not all training methods yield an improvement in performance appraisal. The more actively the raters are involved in the training process, the greater the positive effects. Having raters participate in group discussions and in practice sessions to provide feedback to ratees generally produces better results than having raters attend lectures about the rating process.

Providing Feedback to Raters.   Providing feedback to raters can also improve performance appraisal. In one study, marketing managers in a large high-tech company received feedback from trained raters about the evaluations those managers had given their subordinates. The feedback included information about how each manager's ratings differed from the ratings given by other managers. When these marketing managers evaluated their subordinates a year later, they assigned lower ratings than did a control group of marketing managers who had received no feedback about their earlier ratings. More than 90% of the managers in the experimental group said that the feedback had influenced their second set of ratings. The researchers concluded that the feedback had reduced the leniency error (Davis & Mount, 1984).

THE POSTAPPRAISAL INTERVIEW

We have noted that two goals of performance appraisal programs are to supply information to management for personnel decisions and to diagnose strengths and weaknesses of employees and provide them with the means for self-improvement. To fulfill the second goal, the job performance ratings and the recommendations of the appraisers must be communicated to the employees.

Offering Feedback.   Offering feedback to employees is usually accomplished during a postappraisal interview between worker and supervisor, a situation that can easily become antagonistic, even hostile, especially when a performance evaluation contains criticism. Negative feedback during a postappraisal interview can make employees angry and lead them to reject any criticism. Employees may attempt to shift the blame for any alleged deficiencies in job performance by dismissing the usefulness of the appraisal, downgrading the importance of the job, or criticizing the supervisor.

Reaction to Criticism.   The primary purpose of the postappraisal interview is to stimulate employees to improve their job performance. This expectation may be wishful thinking. Some workers, when criticized, will act to exaggerate their faults—coming to work late or missing more days of work as an imagined means of revenge. If workers are told that they ask for assistance too frequently, they may stop doing so and, as a result, make more mistakes. In such instances, criticism can lead to a deterioration in motivation and job performance. It may also be unrealistic to expect that a brief meeting every 6 or 12 months will provide sufficient impetus for employees to change. In addition, it may be unwise to believe that supervisors, unless they are specially trained, possess the insight and the skill to diagnose the reasons for a worker's unsatisfactory job performance and to prescribe a program for improvement.

If feedback on employee performance were provided more frequently and competently and were not restricted to the formal postappraisal interview, employee motivation to change job behavior and to persist in that behavior could be enhanced. A review of the research literature supports the suggestion that feedback has a greater impact when employees are allowed to ask for feedback from their supervisors at any time rather than having to wait until it is provided at the postappraisal interview (Morrison & Bies, 1991).

Improving Postappraisal Interviews.   Despite the limitations and problems of postappraisal interviews, they can be structured to fulfill the purposes for which they are intended. I/O psychology research has identified several factors related to successful postappraisal interviews. Employees are more likely to be satisfied with postappraisal interviews and to follow their supervisors' suggestions about improving job performance under the following conditions (Dorfman, Stephan, & Loveland, 1986; Giles & Mossholder, 1990; Greenberg, 1986; Nathan, Mohrman, & Milliman, 1991).

1. Employees should be allowed to participate actively in the appraisal process.

In the postappraisal interview, the supervisor should be positive and supportive and should focus on specific job behaviors rather than on the employee's personal qualities.

2. The postappraisal interviewer should adopt a positive, constructive, and supportive attitude.
3. The interviewer should focus on specific job problems rather than on the employee's personal characteristics.
4. The employee and the supervisor should establish jointly specific goals to be achieved in the period before the next appraisal.
5. The employee should be given the opportunity to question, challenge, and rebut the evaluation without fear of retribution.
6. Discussions of changes in salary and rank should be linked directly to the performance appraisal criteria.

PERFORMANCE APPRAISAL: A POOR RATING?

Performance appraisal may be one of the least popular features of organizational life. Many managers think that their performance appraisal programs are ineffective. Two British psychologists offered the following judgment:

There is evidence that the appraisers as well as the appraised do not consider traditional performance appraisal systems to be sufficiently important to merit their time and attention. A typical response from a manager in a recent study we conducted summed up the attitude to performance appraisal in his organization thus: "The general attitude to performance appraisal is 'Oh my God, it's appraisal time again. I suppose we had better do it.' But what the hell are we doing it for?" (Redman & Snape, 1992, p. 36).

Why do performance appraisal programs get such a poor rating? We have discussed the opportunities for personal bias and other errors to enter into the evaluations. There are other reasons as well.

A Poor Rating from Supervisors.   Consider the supervisor. Despite a great deal of impressive research supporting the benefits of performance appraisal from other sources, such as subordinates or peers, the fact remains that on the job, most performance appraisal ratings are still made by supervisors or managers.

Performance appraisal requires time and effort from supervisors who already are subject to considerable demands. They must spend many hours observing their subordinates to develop sufficient knowledge on which to base their assessments. They spend additional hours completing the performance appraisal forms and, in some companies, yet more time in rater training programs.

In practice, supervisors may resist appraisal programs and fill out the forms only when pressured by their superiors. The evaluations are often not thorough and systematic but are compiled in haste. Many supervisors loathe the idea of judging employees and taking responsibility for their progress in the organization, and therefore they are reluctant to give low ratings, even for poor performance.

Further, supervisors may deliberately delay providing feedback, particularly when the evaluation is negative, and they may inflate the ratings or suppress unfavorable information. By pretending that the employee is performing at a higher level than actual job performance justifies, the supervisor eliminates the potential for confrontation and reduces the negative impact of an unfavorable appraisal.

A Poor Rating from Employees.   Employees do not like performance appraisals, although most recognize that some means of evaluating job performance is necessary. We noted that when appraisal results are communicated ineptly to employees, the result can be a decrease in performance and in job satisfaction. Employees also express concern about the effect of performance assessments on their career, apprehensive that a supervisor will use the appraisal to exaggerate misunderstandings or highlight personality clashes that have nothing to do with job competence. Employees are often not sufficiently informed about the criteria by which they are being judged or even precisely what is expected of them on the job. In addition, employees are often given low ratings for faults that may lie within the organization or in the way jobs are structured. These are matters over which employees have no control but for which they may be blamed.

A survey of employees at General Electric, conducted over a 30-year period, showed that most employees were more uncertain about the status of their job performance after a postappraisal interview than before. The implication is that the supervisors were not clear and direct about communicating the appraisal results and that the results conflicted with informal feedback the employees had received from their supervisors in the period between appraisals. Another survey of 200 large corporations found that 70% of the employees were more "confused than enlightened" by their appraisals (Meyer, 1991, p. 70).

In many organizations, the results of performance appraisal programs are never used to help make decisions about promotions or to help employees improve their skills, the major purposes for which such programs were developed. Interviews with a representative sample of the 600 employees of a natural gas utility company showed that they judged their performance appraisals to be meaningless because merit pay increases were not given until 6 months after the appraisals. They saw no connection between performance appraisals and pay (Guinn & Corona, 1991). Findings such as these reinforce the negative attitudes of employees and supervisors toward the appraisal process.

In sum, then, the system of performance appraisal as practiced in most organizations today is unsatisfactory, which may help to explain why correlations between ratings and results-oriented job performance criteria (such as sales and output data) are relatively low. However, performance appraisal must be carried out in some manner. Appraisals of job ability at all levels of employment are necessary. The question is not whether to use an employee appraisal system but, rather, which is the most effective approach to use.

Stress and Electronic Performance Monitoring

Electronic monitoring of the job performance of employees who work at computer terminals and in telecommunications can provide comprehensive and accurate measures of output and competence. This type of monitoring is becoming more widespread in business and industry, not only for employee surveillance and control but also for performance appraisal. Some employees like the computer-aided approach because it yields an objective evaluation of job performance. Others find it to be stressful and object to the continuous monitoring of their work.

To investigate the relationship between stress and electronic performance monitoring, a study was conducted at the Work Stress Laboratory of the National Institute for Occupational Safety and Health (NIOSH). The subjects were 47 women data-entry operators with a mean age of 24 recruited from a temporary employment agency. They were paid $7.55 an hour for the 3-day study. Each workday consisted of six 40-minute work periods. To ensure the work would be demanding, no subject was selected who was able to exceed the performance standards of 200 keystrokes per minute and no more than six errors per minute.

The subjects were required to enter numbers from bogus IRS tax forms using the numeric keypad of an IBM M3163 VDT. On the first workday, the subjects performed the data-entry task at their usual work pace; there was no monitoring of their performance. On the second and third days, the subjects were randomly assigned to one of two conditions: half had their work monitored electronically, and the other half continued to work as they had on the first day, with no monitoring of their performance.

Source: Based on L. M. Schliefer, T. L. Galinski, & C. S. Pan (1995). Mood disturbance and musculoskeletal discomfort effects of electronic performance monitoring in a VDT data-entry task. In S. L. Sauter & L. R. Murphy (Eds.), *Organizational risk factors for job stress* (pp. 195–203). Washington, DC: American Psychological Association.

The electronic performance monitoring (EPM) group received feedback on their video screens following each 40-minute work period. Those subjects who did not meet the speed and accuracy standards of 200 keystrokes a minute and no more than six errors a minute received a negative-feedback message informing them that they had not met the performance criteria and that their work was unsatisfactory. Those who met the standards received a positive message, indicating that their performance was satisfactory. The no-EPM group received no feedback. At the end of each work period, subjects in both groups completed questionnaires assessing their level of irritation, perceived time pressure, tension, workload dissatisfaction, boredom, and fatigue.

In the group whose performance was monitored electronically, the workers reported significant increases in irritation, tension, perceived time pressure, and workload dissatisfaction from the beginning to the end of the 3-day study period. The researchers also found among the EPM group a significant increase in reported discomfort in the right hand (the hand used for data-entry by all subjects). They concluded that electronic performance monitoring was highly stressful.

Critical Thinking Questions

1. Do you think this study is a realistic simulation of actual working conditions for employees? In what ways might the simulation differ from the conditions of a real job?

2. Based on our discussion of survey research in Chapter 2, how would you devise a survey on computer-aided performance appraisal? Would you use interviews or mailed questionnaires? Open-end or fixed-alternative questions? Probability sampling or quota sampling?

3. In what ways, other than computer-aided monitoring, can the job performance of IRS employees be appraised objectively?

4. We discussed in Chapter 5 several sources of error in the performance appraisal process. Even with objective measures, such as those provided by computer-aided monitoring, can

these sources of error affect performance appraisals? Explain your answer for each potential source of error.

5. If you were a company manager, what would you do about employees who opposed computer-aided monitoring on the grounds of invasion of privacy? Would you refuse to promote them? Transfer them to another department? Evaluate their performance by some other means? Why?

SUMMARY

Performance appraisal programs are used to validate selection criteria, determine the need for and success of training programs, improve employee behavior, determine promotions and pay raises, and identify employees with promotion potential. To ensure compliance with EEOC guidelines, performance appraisals must be based on job analyses, must focus on job behaviors rather than personal traits, and must be reviewed with the person being evaluated.

Labor unions oppose performance appraisal because of their commitment to seniority as the basis for personnel decisions. Employees dislike performance appraisal because few of us like to be judged or criticized. Supervisors do not like making appraisals that will affect their subordinates' careers.

Two approaches to performance appraisal are objective and judgmental. Objective measures include quantity and quality of output, computerized appraisal, and data on accidents, salary, advancement, and absenteeism. Judgmental methods involve having supervisors assess their workers' ability to perform the job. These assessments are made by **merit rating** techniques including **rating, ranking, paired comparisons, forced distribution,** and **forced choice,** techniques that involve one person judging the abilities or characteristics of another. The **BARS** and **BOS** approaches to merit rating attempt to evaluate performance in terms of specific behaviors that are critical to success or failure on the job. BARS and BOS meet EEOC guidelines and can reduce rating errors. **Management by objectives** (MBO) involves mutual agreement between supervisors and subordinates about setting and achieving specific goals.

Evaluating managerial performance may be accomplished through assessment centers or evaluation by supervisors, colleagues (peers), subordinates, or **self-ratings.** Combining ratings into an overall appraisal is of particular value.

Sources of rater error include the **halo effect, systematic bias, most-recent-performance error, inadequate information error, average rating error (leniency error),** the rater's **cognitive processes,** and **role conflict.** Two ways to improve performance appraisals are through better training for raters and providing feedback to raters.

The results of performance appraisals must be communicated to employees to provide them with information about their strengths and weaknesses. Feedback should be given with tact and sensitivity, particularly when criticism is involved, because it can lead to defensiveness and a decline in job performance. Feedback sessions should be informal and frequent and focus on specific goals. Workers should be allowed to participate freely in the discussions.

KEY TERMS

attribution
average rating error
behavioral expectation scales (BES)
behavioral observation scales (BOS)

behaviorally anchored rating scales (BARS)
cognitive processes
constant bias

forced-choice technique
forced-distribution technique
halo effect
inadequate information error
interpersonal affect
leniency error
management by objectives (MBO)
merit rating
most-recent-performance error

paired-comparison technique
peer rating
performance appraisal
ranking technique
rating scales
role conflict
self-ratings
systematic bias

ADDITIONAL READING

Griffith, T. L. (1993). Teaching Big Brother to be a team player: Computer monitoring and quality. *Academy of Management Executive,* 7(1), 73–80. Describes the electronic performance monitoring system at Hughes Aircraft and how it is used to improve performance and employee development in a diverse work force.

Murphy, K. R., & Cleveland, J. (1991). *Performance appraisal: An organizational perspective.* Needham Heights, MA: Allyn & Bacon. Highlights legal issues in performance appraisal and reviews research on the cognitive processes of raters.

Murphy, K. R., & Cleveland, J. (1995). *Understanding performance appraisal: Social, organizational, and goal-based perspectives.* Thousand Oaks, CA: Sage. Describes the history of performance appraisal, purposes of performance appraisal, and influential environmental and organizational contextual variables that affect the performance appraisal process.

Swan, W. S. (1991). *How to do a superior performance appraisal.* New York: Wiley. Covers the basics of conducting a performance appraisal, with emphasis on developing listening skills and coping with defensiveness in the postappraisal interview.

Training and Development

■   ■   ■   ■

THE SCOPE OF ORGANIZATIONAL TRAINING

"When I look at the money we spend on education and training," said a chemical company executive, "I wonder whether we're running a chemical business or a college!" From the high school dropout to the college graduate, from the long-time unemployed to the high-level executive, millions of people today are participating in some form of organizational training in their workplace. Employers spend some $30 billion annually on formal training programs and another $180 billion on informal on-the-job instruction.

Training is big business and it begins at an elementary level, often teaching basic literacy and mathematics skills before offering instruction in specific job skills. When Motorola geared up to meet global competition by converting a plant from radio to cellular technology, the company found that 60% of its work force had trouble with simple arithmetic and with reading and understanding English. Without remedial training in these skills, the employees could not be taught to perform their jobs (Wiggenhorn, 1990). Polaroid spent $700,000 to offer basic language and math instruction to 1,000 employees. Domino's Pizza teaches reading and math so that employees can follow instructions for making pizza dough (Goldstein & Gilliam, 1990).

A 1994 survey by the National Association of Manufacturers found that 30% of the companies were unable to reorganize their work procedures to make them more efficient because employees lacked the basic language and math skills to learn the new ways of carrying out their job tasks. Further, 25% of the companies reported that they were unable to upgrade their products for the same reason. Employee illiteracy is a costly problem for both employers and employees.

NEWSBREAK #8

Illiteracy in the Workplace: Employees Who Can't Read the Directions

Cindy Marano forgot her glasses when she left her office to go to lunch, otherwise she would never have noticed it. Marano, who directs a job-training program in Washington, DC, could not read the menu posted on the wall of the local sandwich shop without her glasses.

She asked the middle-aged woman behind the counter to read it to her. At first, the woman pretended not to hear, then she became flustered and rude before asking another waitress to read the menu aloud. "Suddenly, the light went on for me," Marano said: The woman was unable to read! And Marano knew, from her work with the job-training program, that many of the 40 million Americans who have trouble reading and writing are able to fake it on the job and conceal their handicap, as the waitress had done.

Marano also knew how expensive employee illiteracy is, costing the American economy some $225 billion a year in lost productivity. Someone else very much aware of that cost is Peter Coors, CEO of Colorado's Coors Brewing Company. He calls employee illiteracy a crisis for American industry, and he has taken the lead in promoting corporate awareness and creating industry-based training programs to teach employees how to read.

How do workers who cannot read get jobs in the first place? How do they fill out application blanks? By indulging in the same kinds of tricks they use to keep the jobs once they are hired. They tell the personnel director they forgot their glasses, or they're in a hurry and will complete the application form at home. Or they can ask a friend or family member to do it and so can be hired without the employer's knowing of their inability to read.

But with today's increasingly high-technology jobs, it is becoming harder to apply these subterfuges, to pretend you can read when you can't. Coors found that out in 1990 when the company instituted a computerized inventory-control system. The new system required forklift operators to punch information into a computer, and it soon became obvious that many of them could not do the job. Why? Because they could not recognize the letters on the computer keyboard or read the product codes on the items to be inventoried.

Even low-tech companies lose money to illiteracy. The Outback Steakhouse chain found that some of their cooks were mistakenly preparing more expensive instead of less expensive steaks because they could not read the waiters' orders. Outback started a training program to teach all employees a list of abbreviations, so that even workers for whom English was a new language could do their jobs without making costly mistakes. Other restaurant and fast-food chains use symbols instead of words on their computer screens.

(continued)

> Every company would operate more efficiently if all their employees could read. It would be better for the employees, too. Sharon Thomas, a 34-year-old high school dropout living in Washington was on welfare for 15 years, until she learned to read and was hired for a well-paid job in construction. "I had a lot of hurdles to get over," she said, "but once I was in the work force, I was so happy. I feel good about myself."
>
> *Source:* K. D. Grimsley. Battling against workplace illiteracy. *Washington Post,* September 29, 1995.

Training for skilled high-tech jobs is a priority today in industry, government, and the military. Aerospace, telecommunications, and defense-related industries now rely on reprogrammable robots, multifunctional machines, and computer-assisted design and manufacturing equipment. The companies need a highly trained work force to design, operate, and maintain this sophisticated equipment.

As we described in Chapter 1, the nature of work as we approach the 21st century is changing. We can no longer count on learning one job and keeping it until retirement. As we approach the new century, we must learn to think not only of a single chosen career over a lifetime, but of several careers from which we master a cluster of skills that must be continually upgraded. Careers of the future will require lifelong learning, which means that training will become even more vital in your working lives than it was for previous generations.

New employees find themselves back in the classroom to learn about company policies.

One final point about the scope of training in the world of work today. Although training programs are offered for employees at all levels, they are more prevalent for noncollege and nonmanagerial personnel. It is the technician more than the executive who is more likely to receive training. Also, formal training programs are typically found only in larger companies, those with more than 10,000 employees. Thus, training is a vital aspect of career and corporate growth, but "only 16% of American employees have ever had any training from their employer" (Carnevale, 1995, p. 246). That figure is expected to increase as training becomes more necessary for the workplace of tomorrow.

A Sample Training Program

Let us describe an example of a high-level organizational training program. Western Electric Company established a company college, the Corporate Education Center, to provide instruction in engineering and management. The facility contains state-of-the-art equipment and offers more than 300 courses on a 190-acre campus, complete with dormitories. Newly hired engineers participate in 6-week orientation programs, one during the first 6 months of employment and a second during the next 6 months. Engineers may choose among various courses in their specialty areas, classes designed to keep them up-to-date. Supervisors may select courses to upgrade their technical knowledge and managerial skills. The center provides management training at several levels to persons with promotion potential; courses range from planning and interdepartmental relations to urban affairs and I/O psychology.

This ambitious venture is not unusual in American business. Training centers are maintained by such organizations as IBM, Xerox, General Electric, and Avis Rent A Car. So, do not be surprised if, during your first month on the job and periodically throughout your career, you find yourself back in the classroom.

Cooperative Education Programs

Some of you may already be involved in business-sponsored training while attending college. **Cooperative education programs,** or work-study programs, in which students alternate periods of full-time college instruction with full-time employment, are increasingly popular. They involve some 1,000 colleges and more than 200,000 students (Murray, 1996). Cooperating companies in these earn-while-you-learn programs hire students to work a portion of each year in their field of study, thus giving students money for college expenses as well as valuable job experience. After graduation, many students are offered permanent jobs with the company they worked for during college. For example, General Motors hires 95% of the students in its cooperative education program when they graduate.

Cooperative education programs Business-sponsored training programs in which college students alternate periods of full-time college instruction with full-time employment.

Training for Disabled Employees

Many organizations provide specialized training for disabled employees. At McDonald's, more than 9,000 workers with visual, hearing, orthopedic, or learning disabilities, or mental retardation, have been trained for various jobs at the company's fast-food restaurants. In an attempt to dispel stereotypes and to make all employees sensitive to the problems of being disabled, training is provided not only for the disabled employees but for the other employees who will be working with them. Over a 10-year period, more than 90% of the disabled persons who began training in a "McJobs" program completed it and became productive employees. The company believes that people with disabilities constitute a large pool of under-used labor. As the special employment manager at McDonald's noted, "We're going to let them do whatever they are capable of doing" (Laabs, 1991, p. 57).

Training and Fair Employment Practices

Organizational training programs may have an adverse impact on minority employees because performance in a training program is often used as a basis for career decisions about promotion, transfer, or dismissal. Any technique that results in personnel decisions has the potential for discriminating against ethnic minority, women, older, or disabled employees. Therefore, training programs must meet equal employment opportunity guidelines and must be clearly related to job performance before their results can be applied to career decisions.

OBJECTIVES OF TRAINING PROGRAMS

The first step in establishing a formal training program is the precise formulation of objectives. These objectives must be stated in terms of specific behavioral criteria, the acts or operations employees must perform on the job and the way they should perform them to maximize job efficiency. It is impossible to determine what the training program should include unless the organization knows what the program is supposed to accomplish. In other words, what knowledge, skills, and abilities are critical to learning to perform the job successfully?

Needs assessment An analysis of corporate and individual goals undertaken before designing a training program to achieve them.

Needs Assessment.   The goals of the training program should be derived from the needs of the organization and the employees. A **needs assessment** should be conducted to determine corporate and individual goals and how a training program would help to achieve them. Such assessments, more ideal than real in organizational life today, are used to determine specific job components and the skills required to perform them.

There are situations in which the need for a training program is obvious. For example, a company that automates a manufacturing process, eliminating a number of jobs, may choose to retrain its employees for other work. Rapid expansion that creates new jobs requires a program to train workers to fill the positions. A high accident rate in one department may call for additional safety training. Frequent complaints from dissatisfied customers may lead to employee training in human relations skills. In the absence of a clear indication that training is needed, however, it is management's responsibility to analyze its operations periodically to determine if any aspect could benefit from additional training.

Organizational Analysis.   A general organizational analysis can suggest broad training needs that can then be translated into specific needs of employees or groups of employees. The next step is a task analysis to identify the specific tasks performed on a job and the knowledge, skills, and abilities needed for those tasks. An employee analysis is undertaken to determine which workers need retraining and what kind of training is necessary. These evaluations can be accomplished by job analysis methods, critical incidents, performance appraisal techniques, or self-assessments.

Job analysis is the most frequently used technique for determining training needs and objectives. It yields a detailed list of the characteristics needed to perform a job successfully and the sequence of operations required. From a job analysis, the company can determine how new training procedures can improve job performance.

The critical-incidents technique (discussed in Chapter 3), which focuses on specific desirable or undesirable job behaviors, provides information on how employees are equipped to cope with significant workday events. For example, how do assembly-line workers deal with jammed machinery? How do supervisors handle disputes among subordinates? How do managers deal with charges of sexual harassment? An analysis of critical incidents can alert the training director to areas in which additional training or instruction is needed.

Performance appraisals are an obvious source of information on training needs. They can document employee weaknesses and lead to recommendations for retraining to correct specific deficiencies. Self-assessment is based on the assumption that the person who is performing a job well is a good source of information about the skills needed to do that job and the areas in which training may be desirable.

THE TRAINING STAFF

The quality of an instructor can have a tremendous impact on your performance as a student. Some teachers are able to bring the subject matter to life, to organize and present it with enthusiasm, and to inspire interest among the class

The best instructors are trained in teaching methods as well as job skills.

members. Other instructors teaching the same material can make the classroom experience frustrating, tiring, and boring. The most important factor in teaching anything at any level seems not to be competence or expertise in the subject matter. Although competence is necessary, the instructor must also have the ability to teach, to impart information in a clear and compelling manner.

The same principle holds for organizational training. Too often, corporate training is conducted by people who have vast experience in the task or skill to be taught but no instruction in how to communicate that skill effectively to others. The solution is to use professional instructors, persons trained in teaching methods and in job skills. Some large organizations maintain full-time teaching staffs equipped to teach a number of subjects or job skills.

THE PRETRAINING ENVIRONMENT

The pretraining environment established by an organization includes those decisions and cues, communicated directly or indirectly to employees by supervisors and peers, that indicate the value management places on training programs. These factors may include organizational policies, supervisor attitudes toward training, resources available for training, and employee participation in needs assessments. These cues influence the effectiveness of training programs because they tell employees how supportive the company is of training efforts.

The more training opportunities a company offers, the more likely its employees are to believe that training as an important and relevant activity for their careers. Trainees are also more likely to regard training as worthwhile and to be more motivated to achieve in training programs when they know their supervisors support training, know their post-training skills will be assessed, and are given a realistic picture of what the training involves. When these conditions are not met—when the organization's pretraining attitude or climate is perceived as unsupportive—a training program is likely to be rendered ineffective before it even begins.

PRETRAINING ATTRIBUTES OF TRAINEES

A number of psychological characteristics or attributes of trainees can influence both their desire to learn from a training program and the amount and kind of material they are capable of learning from a training program. These attributes include individual differences in ability, pretraining expectations, motivation, job involvement, locus of control, and self-efficacy.

Individual Differences in Ability

Individual differences in training ability can be predicted through cognitive ability tests, biographical data, and performance in an initial training experience, such as a work sample. A study of more than 78,000 U.S. Air Force enlisted personnel analyzed scores from a widely used vocational aptitude test battery. The researchers found that the measure of general cognitive ability was the best predictor of performance in a job training course. Measures of specific abilities, such as word knowledge, mechanical principles, and electronic and scientific facts, were not important in predicting job training success.

Trainability tests, such as work samples or minicourses, are also valid predictors of performance in a full course of training. Work samples, when used as measures of trainability, offer a short period of formal job skill instruction followed by a test of job performance in a training facility. A meta-analysis of studies of the work sample approach found that they predict performance in full-scale training programs and subsequent performance on the job in most situations (Robertson & Downs, 1989).

Pretraining Expectations

Employees' expectations about the outcome of training can influence the program's effectiveness. Structured interviews with 113 midcareer managers from financial services firms found that those with a low sense of self-efficacy (a low expectation that they could master new job skills) were unreceptive to the idea of participating in a corporate retraining program. Managers high in self-efficacy—who believed that they were capable of learning new work-related skills—were more amenable to the prospect of midcareer retraining (Hill & Elias, 1991).

I/O psychologists have also found that when a training program fails to live up to trainees' expectations, they are less likely to complete the program. Trainees whose expectations are not met but who do complete the program are likely to be dissatisfied on the job, to have a low sense of commitment to the organization, and to have a high rate of job turnover. A study of 666 U.S. Navy recruits surveyed their training expectations and desires before and after an 8-week training course. Trainees whose pretraining expectations were met by the training program developed greater organizational commitment, a higher sense of self-efficacy, and enhanced motivation to succeed than those whose expectations were not met (Tannenbaum, Mathieu, Salas, & Cannon-Bowers, 1991).

Motivation

The motivation or desire to learn is vital to employees' success in a training program. Learning will not occur unless trainees truly want to learn, regardless of their ability. In every occupation we can find examples of people who have achieved success with less than an optimal level of ability but with a great drive or motivation to succeed.

Research has shown that trainees with higher motivation learn more in training programs than do trainees with lower motivation. Trainees who are highly motivated are more likely to complete the program and to apply their training on the job. When 106 junior-level managers in a British company were studied over a 4-month training program, their pretraining levels of motivation (as measured by questionnaires) were found to be significantly related to the amount of learning that occurred. The direction of the relationship was clear: the higher the pretraining motivation, the higher the learning (Warr & Bunce, 1995).

Management can increase trainees' motivation by involving them in decisions about the training program, allowing them to participate in the needs-assessment process, and giving them a choice of training courses. For example, a study involving 242 trainees assigned them at random to three choice or no-choice conditions. Choice was based on written descriptions of four 2-hour training seminars on practical business skills. The researchers found that trainees whose choice of programs was satisfied showed greater motivation to learn. Those whose choice of programs was not satisfied were less motivated and learned less than those given no choice at all. It is interesting that there were no significant differences in actual learning outcomes between trainees who received their choice of seminars and those who were not given a choice (Baldwin, Magjuka, & Loher, 1991).

Other research has shown that previous negative events or experiences can increase motivation to learn. For example, trainees in an assertiveness training course who had experienced undesirable incidents—when being more assertive might have helped them—were more motivated to learn the training material (Smith-Jentsch, Jentsch, Payne, & Salas, 1996).

Job Involvement

Trainees who show greater job involvement—whose sense of self-identity is closely linked with their work—show higher motivation to learn than do trainees who are less involved. Long-term career plans are also a factor. I/O psychologists have suggested that training opportunities may be wasted on employees who display low job involvement and a lack of career interest because their motivation to learn is likely to be low. Further, employees with low job involvement have low potential for showing improvement in job performance as a result of their training. Pretraining programs to increase job and career involvement may be desirable for some employees (Noe & Schmitt, 1986).

Locus of Control

Another variable that affects trainee motivation is locus of control. People identified as having an internal locus of control believe that job performance and such work-related rewards as pay and promotion are under their personal control—dependent on their own behaviors, abilities, and efforts. People with an external locus of control believe that life events in and out of the workplace are beyond their control—dependent on such outside forces as luck, chance, or whether their boss likes them.

Employees who have an internal locus of control are likely to be highly motivated to succeed in a training program because they believe that mastering the job skills is under their control and within their capabilities. They are more likely to accept feedback during training and to take action to correct deficiencies. They also show higher levels of job and career involvement than do employees with an external locus of control.

Self-Efficacy

Another factor that influences employee motivation to succeed in training programs is self-efficacy, mentioned earlier in the section on pretraining expectations. Self-efficacy is the belief in one's capacity to perform a task; that is, a sense of adequacy, efficiency, and competence in coping with life's demands. The relationship between self-efficacy and motivation to learn, and between self-efficacy and actual success in training programs, has been amply demonstrated. One study, using a highly realistic computer-based Naval Air Defense simulation training task, found a significant positive relationship between pretraining level of self-efficacy and the subjects' expressed motivation to learn (Quiñones, 1995).

The study also showed that experimentally enhanced self-efficacy resulted in higher learning.

Another study of 115 college students, which dealt with a realistic air traffic control computer simulation, found that subjects higher in self-efficacy reached significantly higher final task performance levels than subjects lower in self-efficacy (Eyring, Johnson, & Francis, 1993).

Other research has also demonstrated that people high in self-efficacy have strong beliefs about their ability to succeed in training programs and that they outperform people who are low in self-efficacy. For example, in a study of managers and administrators undergoing training in the use of computer software, the researchers found that high self-efficacy trainees learned more during training, persevered in the face of difficulties, and scored higher on post-training measures than did trainees low in self-efficacy (Gist, Schwoerer, & Rosen, 1989).

Self-efficacy has been shown to increase a person's perception of the value of a training program. Surveys were taken of 118 U.S. Air Force mechanics at 8 and 12 months following a formal training program. The trainees higher in self-efficacy gave significantly higher ratings on a scale recommending the training program for other mechanics than did trainees lower in self-efficacy (Ford, Smith, Sego, & Quiñones, 1993). A review of the literature on self-efficacy and organizational behavior concluded that an employee's level of self-efficacy is positively related to job performance (Gist & Mitchell, 1992). Thus, self-efficacy can affect performance in the training program and, later, on the job.

In turn, self-efficacy can be affected by training. For example, telling trainees that the skill they are trying to learn can be acquired through practice may increase self-efficacy, as was demonstrated with a group of 76 university employees taking a microcomputer training course. Trainees who were told that computer skills could be readily acquired through practice showed a significant increase in their efficacy beliefs, compared to trainees who were told that the inability to acquire computer skills was a reflection of their personal competence (Martocchio, 1994).

Training-enhanced self-efficacy can have long-term effects beyond the duration of the training program, effects that influence more than just the skills acquired during the program. An analysis of 112 newly-hired accountants at 10 accounting firms found that the increase in self-efficacy that resulted from training had beneficial effects on socialization and adjustment to the new job during the first year of employment. Those accountants with higher post-training self-efficacy scored higher on such measures as ability to cope, job satisfaction, and job commitment than those lower in self-efficacy (Saks, 1995).

PSYCHOLOGICAL FACTORS IN LEARNING

Psychologists have devoted considerable effort to the study of learning. The published literature in the field contains thousands of research reports on human and animal learning under various conditions. Although psychologists do not pretend to have all the answers about this complex activity, they have observed and described several factors that can facilitate or hinder learning. In this section we deal with those factors that relate to teaching methods and to the nature of the material to be learned.

Active Practice

Practice may not always make perfect, as the saying goes, but it does help. For learning to be most effective, trainees must be actively involved in the learning process, not merely passive recipients of information. For example, it is not sufficient to read about the operation of a construction crane or to watch a videotape of someone operating it. The training program should provide the opportunity for the trainee to sit in the operator's cab and have hands-on practice of the skills required to perform the job.

Imagine learning to drive an automobile only by listening to a lecture and memorizing traffic regulations. This can make you a better driver, but you will not actually learn how to drive the car until you sit in the driver's seat and start practicing. The same principle holds for academic material. Actively taking notes during lectures, highlighting and outlining the textbook, and discussing questions with classmates facilitate learning much more than sitting passively in the lecture hall soaking up the professor's words like a sponge.

Mental practice, the cognitive rehearsing of a task prior to performing it, can have a positive and significant effect on the actual performance of the task. This was demonstrated by a meta-analysis of 100 studies conducted between 1934 and 1991. The results confirmed that mental practice is effective for both physical and cognitive tasks, though it is less effective than overt physical practice. Thus, mentally rehearsing a task can help to learn it, but actively performing it helps more (Driskell, Copper, & Moran, 1994).

Massed and Distributed Practice

Some tasks are learned more readily when the training program schedules one or a few relatively long practice sessions (massed practice). Other tasks require a large number of relatively short practice sessions (distributed practice). In general, distributed practice results in better learning, particularly for motor skills.

A British company compared massed and distributed practice sessions in a training program for word-processor operators. Both groups received a 60-minute training course. The massed practice group had a single uninterrupted session; the distributed practice group had a 35-minute session and a 25-minute session, interrupted by a 10-minute break. Performance tests were given immediately after the training course and again 1 week later. On both tests, the distributed practice trainees worked significantly faster and more accurately than did the massed practice trainees (Bouzid & Cranshaw, 1987).

The research evidence is less clear for the learning of verbal skills. Massed practice may be more useful, but much depends on the nature and complexity of the task to be mastered or the material to be learned. Short, simple material can be learned well by massed practice because the sessions do not have to be too long for the trainees to absorb the content. More difficult material must be divided into shorter units and learned by distributed practice.

Whole and Part Learning

The concept of whole or part learning refers to the relative size of the unit of material to be learned. The training course content can be divided into small parts, each of which is studied individually, or the material can be learned as a whole. The decision depends on the nature and complexity of the material and the ability of the trainees. More intelligent trainees are more capable of rapidly learning larger units of material than are less intelligent trainees. However, when slower learners are offered the chance to learn the same material in smaller units, they may be able to master it better than when forced to apprehend it as a whole.

Some skills are obviously better suited to the whole learning method. For example, when learning to drive a car, it serves no useful purpose to divide driving behavior into component skills and to practice separately such movements as fastening the seat belt, turning on the ignition, releasing the emergency brake, adjusting the rearview mirror, and moving the gearshift lever from park to drive. Driving is an interdependent flow of movements and actions that can be learned more effectively as a whole.

When a task requires the initial learning of several subskills, the part method is more efficient. For example, piano students confronting a new piece of music may choose at first to practice the right-hand and the left-hand parts separately. Trainees can practice these various subskills until a particular level of efficiency has been achieved before integrating the subskills into the total behavior or operation.

Transfer of Training

Organizational training often takes place in an artificial setting, a training facility that may differ in several important ways from the actual job environment. This discrepancy between training and job situations must be bridged. The training program must ensure that there will be a transfer of training—a carryover of the skills mastered during the training program—to the job itself.

The issue is one of relevance: Is the information provided during the training program relevant and meaningful to actual job performance? Is there a correspondence between the behaviors and attitudes taught in the training sessions and the behaviors and attitudes needed to perform the job successfully? Can all the knowledge, skills, and abilities mastered in the training facility be applied in the production facility or the office? In many instances, the answer to these questions is no.

If there is close correspondence between training requirements and job requirements, positive transfer will develop. The material learned during training will aid or improve job performance. The greater the similarity between the training and work situations, the greater will be the transfer. This question of similarity is becoming increasingly important in view of the growing use of computer simulations of work environments for training purposes. Does training on a computer simulator transfer to the actual job?

For 58 aviation cadets in the air force of Israel, the answer was yes. Some of the cadets received 10 hours of training in a computer game, Space Fortress, before beginning flight training. The game simulated the kinds of activities a pilot would be called on to perform in the cockpit of an actual fighter aircraft. The results showed that cadets who trained first on the computer game performed significantly better in flight training than cadets who did not have the computer game pretraining (Gopher, Weil, & Baraket, 1994).

If there is little similarity between training situations and work situations, negative transfer will result. In that case, the skills learned in the training program will hamper or interfere with job performance. In negative transfer, these skills or behaviors must then be unlearned or modified before employees can perform the job in question.

I/O psychologists have found that several conditions in the post-training environment can facilitate positive transfer. The most important is supervisor support for and reinforcement of the behaviors and skills taught in the training program. Also influential are the opportunity to apply on the job the skills learned in the training program and a follow-up discussion or assessment shortly after completing the training program. Another important factor is the overall organizational culture or climate. The more supportive it is of training, the greater the opportunities for transfer of training to the work situation (Rouiller & Goldstein, 1993; Tracey, Tannenbaum, & Kavanagh, 1995).

Feedback

People learn more readily when they are given a clear idea of how well they are doing. Feedback (sometimes called knowledge of results) indicates to the trainees their level of progress. Feedback is also important in maintaining motivation. If trainees were not provided with feedback during a training program, they might persist in learning and practicing inappropriate behaviors and incorrect techniques of job performance.

To be maximally effective, feedback must be offered as soon as possible after the inappropriate behavior occurs. If a sequence of operations is being practiced incorrectly, the desired change is more likely to be brought about if the trainees are told immediately. Overall training progress is greater when the program allows for frequent feedback. The more specific and detailed the feedback, the more useful it will be.

Feedback also influences self-efficacy, which, as we saw, is positively related to learning. A sample of 86 university employees taking microcomputer software training was divided into two groups. One group received feedback attributing their training performance to factors within their control. The other group received feedback attributing their performance to factors beyond their control. Trainees who believed their performance was due to factors within their control scored significantly higher in self-efficacy and also demonstrated greater learning (Martocchio & Dulebohn, 1994).

Reinforcement

The greater the reward that follows a behavior, the more easily and rapidly that behavior will be learned. The reward, or reinforcement, can take many forms—a good test grade, a gold star on a chart, a pat on the back from a supervisor, or a promotion for successful completion of a training program. By establishing a program of reinforcement, management can maintain employee motivation and effectively shape behavior by rewarding only those actions that the trainees are supposed to learn and display.

Reinforcement should be provided immediately after the desired behavior has occurred. The longer the delay between behavior and reinforcement, the less effective the reinforcement will be because the trainee may fail to perceive the connection between the correct behavior and the reward for having behaved in that way.

In the early stages of a training program, reinforcement should be given every time the desired behavior is displayed. Once some learning has taken place, continuous reinforcement is no longer necessary. Then, a partial reinforcement schedule will be effective—for example, one that rewards the trainees every third or every tenth time they display the desired behavior.

TRAINING METHODS IN THE WORKPLACE

Now that we have described the pretraining attributes of trainees and the psychological factors that affect learning, let us consider specific organizational training techniques. Each technique offers advantages and disadvantages, depending on the goals of the training program, the abilities of the trainees, and the nature of the material to be learned.

On-the-Job Training

One of the oldest and most widely used training methods takes place directly on the job for which the worker is being trained. Under the guidance of an experienced operator, supervisor, or trained instructor, trainees learn while working. They operate the machine or assembly process in the production facility and have the opportunity to develop proficiency while they work.

Advantages. The **on-the-job training** approach offers certain advantages. Management asserts that the primary one is economy because the organization does not have to establish, equip, and maintain a separate training facility. If workers and supervisors can serve as trainers, even the cost of a professional instructor is saved. A more obvious advantage is positive transfer of training. There is no concern about whether job performance in a training situation will carry

On-the-job training Training that takes place directly on the job for which the person has been hired.

In an on-the-job training program at a window screen factory, new employees practice job skills under the supervision of an experienced worker.

over to the actual work situation because training and job situations are the same. In terms of other psychological factors, active practice is provided from the outset. Motivation to learn should be high because the training situation is clearly relevant to the job situation. Feedback is immediate and visible; good performance will elicit praise, and poor performance will show in a faulty part or product.

Disadvantages.   On-the-job training can be expensive in the long run. Workers and supervisors must take time from their regular jobs to train new employees. This can lead to an overall reduction in productivity. Additional costs come with the slower productivity of the trainees and any damage they cause to equipment or product because of their inexperience. On certain jobs, permitting untrained workers to operate machinery may be hazardous not only to trainees but also to other employees. Accident rates for trainees on the job are typically higher than for experienced workers. Using current workers or supervisors as trainers does not ensure adequate training for new employees. Just because a person performs a job competently or has been on the job for a considerable time does not mean that person has the ability to teach the job to someone else. On-the-job training is often haphazard and inadequate, amounting to no more than the supervisor's saying to the trainees, "Go ahead and start. If you have any questions, come see me."

Managerial Training.   I/O psychologists have recognized that on-the-job training is also important at the management level. Much managerial and executive training and development occurs through informal and unstructured on-the-job experiences. Indeed, on-the-job experiences may contribute more significantly to the development of managerial ability than any formal classroom instruction. Also, a study of 692 managers suggested that on-the-job learning for managers is most likely to occur when they are forced to deal with challenging situations (McCauley, Ruderman, Ohlott, & Morrow, 1994).

Vestibule Training

Vestibule training Training that takes place in a simulated workspace.

Because on-the-job training has the potential for disrupting the production process, many companies prefer **vestibule training;** that is, establishing a simulated workspace in a separate training facility. (A vestibule is a hallway or entrance foyer between the outer door of a building and its main rooms. In the early days of American industry, vestibule schools were organized just inside the doors of industrial plants to introduce new workers to their jobs with a few weeks of specialized training. The word *vestibule* is used in this context to denote that the training program is like an entryway or passageway the employee must traverse before getting to the job itself.)

Using the same kind of equipment and operating procedures as the actual work situation, a vestibule training program relies on skilled instructors, rather than experienced workers and supervisors, to teach new workers how to perform their jobs.

Advantages.   There are several advantages to vestibule training. Because its sole purpose is training, there is no pressure to maintain a given level of productivity. Trainees do not have to be concerned about making costly or embarrassing errors or about damaging production equipment. They can concentrate on learning the skills necessary to be successful on the job.

Disadvantages. The greatest disadvantage of vestibule training is the cost. The organization must equip the facility and maintain a teaching staff. This expense is particularly burdensome when there are not enough new workers to make full use of the training facility. If the training situation does not correspond closely to the work situation, negative transfer of training will occur, and the trainees may need informal, on-the-job instruction once they start to work. This problem can be aggravated by the common business practice of using obsolete equipment, retired from the production floor, in the training facility. However, it is important to note that if a vestibule training program is properly designed, staffed, and equipped, it can be a very effective training technique.

Apprenticeship

Perhaps the earliest recorded training method still in use today is the **apprenticeship** program for skilled crafts and trades in private-sector industries such as construction and manufacturing. Programs are available for plumbers, carpenters, electronics technicians, painters, and auto mechanics, among others. Conducted in the classroom and on the job, apprenticeship involves extensive background preparation in the craft as well as actual work experience under the guidance of experts.

> **Apprenticeship** A training method for skilled crafts involving classroom instruction and on-the-job experience.

Apprenticeships average 4 to 6 years. The standard procedure is for the trainees to agree to work for a company for a fixed period in return for a specified program of training and a salary, usually half that earned by skilled and licensed craftspersons.

Trainees must complete their apprenticeship before they are allowed to join a union. Membership in a labor union is necessary to securing employment. Thus, apprentice programs constitute a joint effort by industry and organized labor to maintain an adequate supply of trained workers.

In recent years, apprenticeships in the public sector have grown in popularity. A number of federal, state, and local government agencies have adopted them for skilled, blue-collar jobs in civilian and military programs, such as building maintenance worker, highway maintenance worker, prison correctional officer, and firefighter. Even the Smithsonian Institution in Washington, DC, operates an apprenticeship program for carpenters, electricians, and plaster masons to build displays for their museums.

Programmed Instruction

Programmed instruction involves several techniques, ranging from printed paper-and-pencil booklets to interactive videotapes to complex computer software. All techniques depend on self-instruction—the trainees proceed at their own pace.

> **Programmed instruction** A teaching method in which the material to be learned is presented in small, sequential steps.

Detailed programmed information is presented in sequence to the trainees, who are required to make frequent and precise responses. The material begins at a low level and gradually becomes more complex. The increments of increasing difficulty are designed to be small so that slower learners can progress with rela-

NEWSBREAK #9

Victims of a Changing Economy Learn New Skills

At age 37, Cathlene Turner lost her inventory control job to a computer. Elaine Hargroves, age 46, lost her job inspecting eyeglass lenses when her factory relocated from Florida to Mexico. Rex Merhal, 51, suddenly found himself out of work when his midlevel management insurance company job was eliminated.

At the time of life these employees expected to be working at financially secure jobs, planning to put their children through college, and thinking about retirement, these three residents of Tampa, Florida, had to start all over again. And they were the lucky ones. They were able to enroll in a federally funded job-retraining program. Turner is now a nurse, Hargroves is training to become a medical transcriptionist, and Merhal is learning computer skills.

If not for this taxpayer-funded program, these workers, and countless others, would have been devastated, because none of their former employers offered retraining. And that is the typical corporate response, according to Harvard professor Shoshana Zuboff. Only a handful of companies have been willing to help their employees learn new skills.

In Tampa and other U.S. cities, government programs are available to those who have lost jobs because of changing technology and economy dislocations.

"We can offer them up to a two-year program of retraining at junior colleges or trade school," said Jean-Marie Moore, head of the local center called Workforce. "We are seeing more and more dislocated workers," she added. "People who made their living in banking, manufacturing, defense, and midlevel managements have been streaming through Workforce's door. By they time they arrive, often months after losing their jobs, they're in bad shape, emotionally and financially."

But by the time they've completed their retraining for different kinds of work, 80% of them are able to find new jobs, thanks to the new skills they have learned. Even in these days of severe cutbacks and layoffs, jobs are out there for those with the right skills. IBM has laid off 180,000 workers since 1987, but now they are looking desperately for 10,000 new employees a year for the computer services division. As IBM's chief financial officer put it, "Our major constraint is finding these 10,000 people." They are out there—and many are former IBM employees now undergoing retraining in job skills for the future.

Sources: T. Burney. Second chances. *St. Petersburg [FL] Times,* January 14, 1996. Economic anxiety. *Business Week,* March 11, 1996. pp. 50–52. Is all that angst misplaced? *Business Week,* March 11, 1996. pp. 52–53.

tive ease. Faster learners are allowed to proceed more rapidly. The rate of learning is determined by the trainee's motivation and cognitive ability.

Two approaches to presenting programmed material are linear and branching. In the linear program, all trainees follow the same program in the same sequence. The learning steps are so small and simple that errors are rare, thus permitting trainees to receive frequent positive feedback. The branching program takes account of individual differences in ability. Trainees may skip intervening questions and advance to a more difficult section of material if they show that they are learning the material well. If they make mistakes and show that they are not learning well, they are directed for remedial assistance to a new set of questions on the same or earlier material.

Advantages. Programmed instruction provides active participation, immediate and continuous feedback, and positive reinforcement, and takes account of individual differences. Programmed instruction also eliminates the need for an instructor. In booklet form, the method can be used by trainees wherever they choose; a training facility and expensive equipment are not required. The course content is standardized for all trainees, and a complete record of the trainees' progress is maintained.

Disadvantages. The kind of material that can be taught by programmed instruction is limited. The method is appropriate for teaching only certain items of knowledge, particularly those that require rote memorization, but it is less effective for teaching complex job skills. Because instructional materials can be costly to develop, programmed instruction is usually restricted to training programs that involve very large numbers of trainees who are required to learn a job within a short time. Initial acceptance of programmed instruction is usually high, but enthusiasm often fades as trainees proceed robotlike through the lengthy series of small steps. Research on learning effectiveness suggests that programmed instruction provides for faster learning of certain types of material, but it does not appear to improve the quality of learning.

Computer-Assisted Instruction

Computer-assisted instruction (CAI), sometimes called computer-based training (CBT), is a derivative of programmed instruction that is widely used by private- and public-sector organizations. In CAI, the program of instruction, which is stored on computer disks, serves as the teacher. Trainees interact with the material on personal computer terminals. Trainees' responses are recorded and analyzed automatically, and the difficulty of each item presented is based on the correctness of the response to the previous item.

Computer-assisted instruction (CAI) A computer-based training method in which trainees learn material at their own pace and receive immediate feedback on their progress.

One of the most widespread uses of computer-based training is to teach computer literacy skills. With more than 20 million American workers now using computers daily on the job, and another 3 million jobs incorporating computer use each year, the development of computer operating skills is critical.

Another widespread use of CAI is the software used by airlines for training flight crews. The program presents displays and touch-panel graphics to simulate the buttons, switches, dials, and signal lights in the cockpit of the Boeing 767. This type of instruction has been found to reduce the number of hours pilots and copilots would otherwise have to spend in a more expensive flight simulator.

Trainees learn computer skills in a classroom equipped with personal computers and an overhead projector.

Advantages.   Trainees are actively involved in the learning process and work through the material at their own pace. They receive immediate feedback on their progress and reinforcement for displaying mastery of a skill. Another advantage of CAI is that it offers considerably more individualized instruction than does programmed instruction. CAI is not unlike being tutored privately by an excellent teacher who has a comprehensive knowledge of the subject and never becomes impatient with the student. The computer responds instantly to the progress of each trainee without showing annoyance, prejudice, or error. Because CAI assumes record-keeping functions and maintains a current performance analysis on each trainee, the instructional staff is free to devote time to any unusual learning problems that arise.

Computer-assisted instruction can be used with a small number of trainees so that the company does not have to make them wait until there is a sufficient number to fill a classroom and schedule a course. It can also be provided to a large number of trainees simultaneously in different locations.

Studies conducted in a variety of employing organizations have shown that computer-assisted instruction can decrease training time by as much as 50% while providing levels of retention and transfer of training equivalent to traditional classroom instruction (Weiss & Craiger, 1997).

Behavior Modification

The use of positive reinforcement to change behavior has many applications to organizational training. An assessment called a **performance audit** is conducted first, to determine the problems or behaviors that can be modified for more efficient job performance. A program of positive reinforcement is then introduced to reward employees for displaying the desired behaviors, such as reducing errors or production time per unit. Punishment or reprimands are not used. Although they may eliminate an undesirable behavior, they may leave in its place anxiety, hostility, and anger. Providing positive reinforcement is much more effective in improving employee productivity and job behavior.

A classic program of **behavior modification** in industry was developed at Emery Air Freight, where the behavioral changes induced were directly connected to job performance (Feeney, 1972). A performance audit revealed two problem areas: (1) despite the employees' belief that they were responding within 90 minutes to 90% of customer telephone inquiries, they were actually responding to only 30% of the inquiries within that time; (2) employees were combining packages into containers for shipment only 45% of the time, whereas management expected containers to be used almost 90% of the time. The goals of the behavior modification training program were to have employees respond faster to customer inquiries and to use containers for shipment whenever possible.

Managers were taught 150 recognitions and rewards to bestow on employees as reinforcers, ranging from a smile and a nod to specific praise for a job well done. Financial incentives to improve performance were not used. Praise and recognition were found to be sufficient reinforcers for improving job performance and for bringing about the desired behaviors. Managers were told to reinforce desirable behaviors as soon as they occurred and gradually to shift from constant to intermittent reinforcement.

Employees were required to keep a detailed record of their accomplishments so that they could compare their performance with the company standards. This record keeping provided daily feedback on their progress.

The company estimated that the improved productivity and response time saved $3 million in 3 years, considerably more than the cost of instituting the behavior modification program.

Job Rotation

Job rotation is a popular management training technique. It exposes trainees to different jobs and departments to acquaint them with all facets of their organization. It is frequently used with new college graduates who are just beginning their working careers. Through job rotation, trainees gain perspective on various aspects of organizational life. They have the opportunity to see and be seen by higher management in different departments, and to learn through direct experience where they might best apply their knowledge, abilities, and interests.

The rotation phase of a management career may last several years, taking employees from one department to another, one plant or office to others in the United States, and perhaps to offices in other countries as well. Such changes can promote the development of flexibility, adaptability, and self-efficacy as employees learn to deal successfully with new challenges. Job rotation programs are also

Performance audit An analysis undertaken prior to implementing a behavior modification training program to determine the problems or employee behaviors that can be modified for more efficient job performance.

Behavior modification A training program of positive reinforcement to reward employees for displaying desirable job behaviors. Behavior modification techniques are also effective in dealing with stress.

Job rotation A management training technique that assigns trainees to various jobs and departments over a period of a few years.

used for skilled and semiskilled jobs. They allow workers to increase their skill levels in diverse occupations, and they serve to alleviate the boredom that can result from years of performing the same tasks.

A study of 255 employees of a major pharmaceutical manufacturer, which practiced job rotation as part of its career development program for all employees, obtained the following results (Campion, Cheraskin, & Stevens, 1994):

1. The average rotation was 2 to 3 years between job changes.
2. Younger employees were more interested than older employees in rotating jobs.
3. Executives used rotation as a reward for their better employees.
4. Workers with a high rotation rate believed it led to greater improvement in their job-related skills and knowledge.

Overall, the majority of employees and executives were highly pleased with job rotation as a training technique.

Disadvantages.   There are disadvantages to job rotation. Frequent moves can disrupt family life and interrupt a spouse's career. If the rotation period is too brief, there may not be sufficient time to become fully acquainted with a particular job. If top management is more interested in management trainees as temporary office help, instead of the rising group of managers in need of mentors, the trainees will not have the opportunity to acquire the necessary skills to transfer to upper-management positions. This can defeat the purpose of the program.

Case Studies

Case studies A method of executive training in which trainees analyze a business problem and offer solutions.

The use of **case studies,** a method developed by the Harvard University School of Business, is popular in executive training programs. A complex problem, or case, of the kind faced daily by managers and executives, is presented to the trainees prior to a general meeting. The trainees are expected to familiarize themselves with the information and to find additional relevant material. When they meet as a group, each member must be prepared to interpret the problem and offer a solution. Through the presentation of diverse viewpoints, the trainees come to appreciate different perspectives on a problem and, consequently, different approaches to solving it. Usually, the cases have no one correct solution. The group leader does not suggest an answer. The group as a whole must reach a consensus and resolve the problem.

Disadvantages.   A limitation of the case study method is that it is not related to job requirements. There may be a discrepancy between the theoretical solution to the case problem and the solution that is practical for the organization. Therefore, actions taken on the basis of the case study solution proposed in the training program may not transfer positively to actions that can be taken on the job.

Business Games

Business games A training method that simulates a complex organizational situation to encourage the development of problem-solving and decision-making skills.

Business games attempt to simulate a complex organizational situation. They are intended to develop problem-solving and decision-making skills and to provide practice in using those skills in a situation in which a trainee's mistake will not prove costly or embarrassing to the organization. More than half of the largest U.S. corporations use business games for management training.

Trainees compete in teams, each team representing a separate, hypothetical business organization. The team companies are given detailed information about the operation of their organization, including data on finances, sales, advertising, production, personnel, and inventories. Each group must organize itself and assign various tasks and responsibilities to each member. As the teams deal with corporate problems, their decisions are evaluated by an instructor. They may be required to consider additional problems based on the outcomes of their initial decisions.

Because the business problems presented to the trainees are so realistic, many trainees form an emotional commitment to their company. They gain experience in making decisions on real-life problems under the twin pressures of time and the actions taken by rival organizations. For new employees, business games may provide their first exposure to the actual job tasks and stresses managers face. This type of realistic job preview persuades some trainees that they would be happier in another line of work.

In-Basket Training

The in-basket technique was discussed in Chapter 3 as a method of employee selection. The same technique is used to train prospective managers. Each trainee

In a typical business game, management trainees operate a fictitious company and make decisions about human resources, productivity, and finances.

NEWSBREAK #10

Virtual Training

You've seen it in the movies. A jet fighter eases its way upward, below and behind a mammoth flying tanker loaded with aviation fuel. A long thin tube with a funnel extends from the rear of the tanker airplane. The fighter pilot has to maneuver the jet so that its fuel tank port connects with that tiny funnel, while traveling at more than 500 miles an hour. It's called in-flight refueling, and it's a tricky, delicate, and dangerous operation every fighter pilot has to learn.

Lt. Charlie Howard, a newly graduated 26-year-old pilot, is trying to perform the maneuver for the first time. He listened to the lectures, read the operating manual, and paid close attention to the video showing a pilot's eye view of making that connection, but now he feels his fear mount as he closes in on the monster plane overhead.

He never takes his eyes off the funnel. It's only 20 feet away. He draws closer. Suddenly, his plane is buffeted by gusty winds, and his body is shoved down in the seat as the fighter bounces on an updraft. Frantically, Charlie forces the control stick forward, but it is too late. The wind whips faster than he can react, and his plane smashes into the tanker.

"Boom," rings a voice in his ear. "You're dead, Charlie. And so's everybody in the tanker. OK, let's try it again."

Charlie Howard was flying in a simulator, wearing a head-mounted virtual reality generator that provided lifelike computer-generated images. The only damage he suffered was to his ego, and now he can try the maneuver again, until he gets it right. Only then will he be permitted to try it in a real airplane.

The U.S. military is investing millions of dollars in virtual training for pilots, air-traffic controllers, and tank commanders, so they can learn their jobs without inflicting harm on themselves and others or damaging expensive equipment.

Virtual reality "works because it allows researchers to mold the training to people's specific needs," said U.S. Air Force psychologist Wesley Regian. "For example, people can practice one part of a more complicated task. Or, simulations can start out easy—as with removing the wind in the refueling simulation—and increase in difficulty as a student grasps basics."

One day Lieutenant Howard will practice refueling in a real plane under real wind conditions, but thanks to the psychological research on virtual reality simulation devices, he will be well trained by then. He will have performed the required maneuvers many times—and survived, thanks to virtual reality.

Source: Azar, B. (1996a, March). Training is enhanced by virtual reality. *APA Monitor*, p. 24.

is given a stack of letters, memos, customer complaints, requests from subordinates, and other items that present various problems faced by managers on the job. The trainees must take action on each item within a specified period. After completing the tasks, the trainees meet with a trainer to discuss their decisions and receive feedback on the outcomes.

Role Playing

In role playing, management trainees pretend to act out a particular role, displaying whatever behaviors they believe are appropriate in a given situation. For example, they may be asked to imagine themselves to be a supervisor who must discuss a poor performance appraisal with a subordinate. They act out these situations in front of a group of trainees and instructors, who offer comments on their performance. In one instance, a trainee may play the role of supervisor. Then the situation will be reversed and the same trainee will play the role of employee. Sessions can be videotaped for later analysis. Many people feel foolish or awkward at first about pretending or acting in front of a group, but once they begin, most people develop a sensitivity for the role and try to project their feelings and beliefs onto it.

Role playing can be a valuable learning device. It enables trainees to become sensitive to their subordinates' views and to the roles the trainees will be expected to play as managers. It provides practical experience as well as feedback from other trainees and instructors. Trainees have the opportunity to practice job-related behaviors in a situation in which mistakes or inappropriate behaviors will not jeopardize interpersonal relations on the job.

Behavior Modeling

The behavior modeling approach to management training involves having trainees attempt to imitate or model their behavior on examples of exceptional job performance. It is one of the more popular techniques for teaching interpersonal and leadership skills. Behavior modeling is usually conducted with groups of 6 to 12 supervisors or lower-level managers. Sessions may last 2 to 4 hours a week for up to 4 weeks. In the intervals between training sessions, the trainees are on the job, applying what they have learned, which provides them with feedback from their subordinates.

The usual procedure is for a trainer, using a prepared script, to provide a general introduction to the nature of the training. Then the trainees watch a videotape of a manager who is acting out appropriate procedures and behaviors for handling a particular job situation with a subordinate—for example, discussing poor job performance, excessive absenteeism, or low morale. The trainees engage in behavior rehearsal, practicing the behaviors they saw the model perform. Trainees are not being asked to play a role; instead, they are imitating the actual behaviors they will use on the job, the behaviors the model has displayed. The trainer and the other trainees provide feedback by telling each trainee how closely he or she imitated the model's behavior and where the behavior diverged. This social reinforcement helps trainees gain confidence in their ability to display the appropriate behavior.

Advantages. The interpersonal and leadership behaviors learned by behavior modeling will transfer to the job. Because the modeled situations between manager and subordinate are actual job situations, the behaviors should carry over to job performance. Thus, there is a high degree of relevance between behavior modeling as a training technique and job requirements, a condition that increases trainees' motivation to accept and apply the training.

Reports from more than 300 organizations using behavior modeling have been enthusiastic. A meta-analysis of more than 70 management training studies shows that behavior modeling has been effective in raising employee morale, improving communication with customers, increasing sales, decreasing absenteeism, enhancing supervisory skills, improving production quantity and quality, and reducing employee resistance to change (Burke & Day, 1986).

Diversity Training

We described in Chapter 1 how the nature of the work force is changing to include more women and ethnic minority workers. Economic forecasters expect white males to become a minority of the work force in the new century. To aid workers in coping with an increasingly diverse work force, organizations are instituting diversity training programs to teach employees to confront personal prejudices that could lead to discriminatory behaviors. Through lectures, videos, role playing, and confrontational exercises, employees are learning, in a way, how it feels to be a female worker being sexually harassed by a male boss, or a Hispanic worker receiving an unsatisfactory performance appraisal from a Black supervisor. Trainees are forced to deal with their own sexist and racist attitudes, and to learn to be more sensitive to the concerns and viewpoints of others.

A survey of 785 human resources personnel found that the development of diversity training programs and their perceived success depended on several factors: support from management, mandatory attendance, the size of the organization, and the hiring of so-called diversity managers. Larger organizations with strong support from top executives, a staff of diversity specialists, and required attendance for all employees were the most likely to have successful diversity training programs.

When these human resources managers were asked how successful they thought their programs were, 33% said successful, 18% said unsuccessful, and almost 50% gave a mixed evaluation. It is important to remember that these data represent the subjective opinions of the people surveyed. No objective studies of the success of their diversity training programs were conducted. Fewer than one third of the companies attempted to evaluate the worth of their courses or conduct follow-up research (Rynes & Rosen, 1995). However, this lack of outcome evaluation for diversity training is not unique; few training programs receive systematic evaluation.

Anecdotal evidence from participants in diversity training suggests that many programs foster negative reactions as well as charges that the programs are offered only because it appears to be the politically correct thing to do (Nemetz & Christensen, 1996).

CAREER DEVELOPMENT AND PLANNING

We have discussed specific training methods designed to improve employees' knowledge, job skills, and interpersonal relations. Most training programs are mandatory and oriented toward a specific job or a specific career stage, such as the entry-level worker, the employee who needs retraining, or the midcareer manager. Many organizations also offer personal development opportunities throughout an employee's career. These career development and planning efforts, which are strictly voluntary, involve a lifelong learning approach.

Organizations as diverse as General Electric, AT&T, Merrill Lynch, TRW, and Xerox operate career development centers. They provide information on company career paths and opportunities and offer counseling and self-analysis programs so that employees can determine how their personal goals coincide with organizational goals. Many companies sponsor workshops to assist employees in career planning and in the development of human relations skills. Employees are encouraged to set career objectives—for example, specifying where they hope to be within the corporate hierarchy in 5 years' time—and to review these goals periodically. Some companies offer tuition refund plans that enable employees to return to college or graduate school to upgrade job skills or to learn new skills. Employees are also encouraged to participate in in-house training courses.

The Importance of Lifelong Learning

We noted in Chapter 1 and at the beginning of this chapter that part of the changing nature of work today is the decline of the idea of a lifetime career. Increasingly, we may choose to or be forced to change careers several times during the course of our working lives and to continually enhance and upgrade our skills. This necessity for lifelong learning increases the importance of career development and planning efforts. Some research has been conducted on the factors that influence employee decisions to participate in the voluntary learning opportunities provided by employers. A survey of 1,035 employees of a health maintenance organization (HMO), a bank, and an engineering firm found that employees' motivation to learn and the social support offered by managers and peers were the most significant influences on the decision to take advantage of these programs (Noe & Wilk, 1993).

A survey of 1,360 clerical, technical, and sales employees of a large corporation found several factors significantly and positively related to participation in company-sponsored voluntary training activities. These factors included organizational and supervisor support, career insight, perceived need for skill enhancement, job involvement, and self-efficacy (Maurer & Tarulli, 1994).

Career Development and Life Stages

Psychologists have long recognized individual differences in people's values, goals, and needs at different ages and stages of life. The job or lifestyle that is appropriate in our twenties may be inappropriate for our thirties or fifties. Three distinct career stages have been proposed (Super & Hall, 1978):

1. *Establishment.* During this stage, approximately ages 20 to 40, people are getting established in their careers and adjusting to work routines. Toward the middle of this period, they learn whether they are going to be successful, through promotions and a sense of personal satisfaction, or through an unwanted transfer or dismissal. If they are successful, they develop feelings of self-efficacy and organizational commitment. If they are unsuccessful, self-analysis, counseling, and a revision of career plans may be necessary.

2. *Maintenance.* This stage lasts from approximately age 40 to 55, the time of the so-called midlife crisis. People become aware that they are aging. They have either approached or reached their goals or they know they will never reach them. It is a time of self-examination, which may lead to a change in interests, values, and lifestyles. Some people seek challenge and satisfaction in new jobs, hobbies, or relationships. Some organizations offer counseling to their managerial personnel to help them through this period.

3. *Decline.* From age 50 or 55 through retirement, employees confront the end of the career to which they devoted their adult life. They must consider the prospect of living on a reduced income and of diminished physical capacity. Retirement brings not only the loss of work and a sense of identity, but also the loss of colleagues with whom to socialize. Additional counseling may be required to assist employees in planning for retirement.

I/O psychologists have found that career stage is related to attitudes toward work, job performance, and job satisfaction. A study of 466 salespersons showed that job satisfaction and job performance increased during the maintenance stage and fell during the decline stage (Cron & Slocum, 1986). Follow-up research on salespersons reported that those in the establishment stage were more concerned with promotion than were those in the maintenance and decline stages. Maintenance-stage employees were the most productive in terms of sales volume. Decline-stage employees had the lowest sales volume and the lowest belief in future promotions. They reported the greatest agreement with statements such as "I would like to cut down on work hours" and "I would like to develop more hobbies" (Cron, Dubinsky, & Michaels, 1988).

A survey of 600 human resources managers from various organizations found that they cited loss of motivation as the major correlate of middle- and late-stage career problems. They attributed the cause of this motivational decline to career plateaus, those points at which employees realize that further advancement is unlikely. This is also when employees come to believe (perhaps correctly) that their job skills are obsolete (Rosen & Jerdee, 1990).

Career development and planning efforts at each stage of working life involve responsibilities shared by employers and employees. Organizations must offer opportunities for personal growth and development. Employees must make effective use of these programs. They should be willing periodically to reanalyze their abilities and job performance and to formulate realistic career development plans. Their future depends on their willingness and ability to do so.

EVALUATING TRAINING AND DEVELOPMENT PROGRAMS

Regardless of how impressive and sophisticated a training program or facility may appear, it is necessary that the outcomes or results be evaluated in systematic and quantitative terms. One proposed model for assessing the success of a training program measures actual changes in *cognitive outcomes,* such as the amount of information learned, *skill-based outcomes,* such as changes in quantity or quality of production, and *affective outcomes,* such as changes in attitudes or motivation (Kraiger, Ford, & Salas, 1993). Unless such evaluative research is conducted, the organization will not know how worthwhile or effective is its investment of time and money.

Are employees learning the skills needed for their jobs? Are productivity, safety, and efficiency rising? Have communications and leadership skills improved? Have the attitudes of majority-group employees toward minority-group employees changed? To answer these questions, comparisons must be made of trained and untrained workers in the same job. Or the same workers before and after training must be compared with a control group of workers that were not exposed to the training. Only through such research can the organization determine whether its training program should be modified, extended, or eliminated.

Even with such a substantial investment at stake, most organizations do not make systematic efforts to evaluate their training programs. If evaluation is undertaken at all, it is usually subjective or intuitive. A survey conducted by the American Society of Training and Development showed that, although most large organizations recorded trainees' reactions to training programs, only 10% of the companies investigated whether training led to changes in job behavior (Tannenbaum & Yukl, 1992). Thus, most organizations do not have a clear idea whether the millions of dollars they spend on training is worthwhile.

This failure to evaluate the worth of training programs is increasingly expensive as more and more training is conducted by electronic technology. One psychologist noted the acceleration of technological changes but warned:

> ...the research base necessary for evaluating the usefulness of these technologies has lagged behind. Developers are often seduced by the technology and forget to measure the extent to which trainees are actually learning anything (Quiñones, 1996, p. 9).

Evaluative research itself is costly, but other factors contribute to the lack of assessment of the effectiveness of training programs. Many training directors do not have the skills to conduct such research, and they also may tend to overestimate the usefulness of programs they have initiated and designed. Some organizations establish training programs not because management believes in them or expects them to meet specific corporate goals but because their competitors have them.

Some training programs are established because a so-called new technique has become newsworthy and produced a flood of anecdotal reports in the media attesting to its value. One example from the 1980s is "time management," supposedly a method for learning to use one's time in the most efficient manner. Supporters claimed time management increased job performance and satisfaction and reduced stress. With the growing number of magazine articles and television reports about the success of time management, more and more companies hired time-management consultants to train employees in this latest miracle cure for the ills of the workplace. The only problem was, time management did not work. This was not demonstrated convincingly, however, until 1994, when an I/O psychologist conducted research with 353 state civil service employees and 341 college students. The documented conclusion was that time-management training was ineffective (Macan, 1994). No one knows how many companies established expensive time-management training programs and maintain them in the absence of data on their effectiveness.

Assessing behavioral changes following training can be difficult. If a worker operates a simple machine or assembles a part, the goal of the training program and the measurement of the outcome are relatively straightforward. The number of items produced per unit time by trained and untrained workers or by workers trained by different techniques can be determined objectively and compared. At this work level, training programs have been shown to be effective. When dealing with human-relations, problem-solving, or other management behaviors, it is far more difficult to assess the effects of training programs.

A meta-analysis of 70 managerial training studies showed that, on the average, training appeared to be only moderately effective (Burke & Day, 1986). A 4-year investigation of 18 training programs in a large pharmaceutical company found that management training was less effective in changing behavior (as measured by performance ratings) than was sales or technical training (Morrow, Jarrett, & Rupinski, 1997). Yet, the face validity of management training programs is high—the programs are popular, everyone says they are necessary, and management looks good for providing them—but the question remains: Are they truly worthwhile?

Training directors defend their programs by pointing out that management trainees are subsequently promoted to higher levels of responsibility. This is not a valid or sufficient measure of the value of management training programs because it is usually only the most capable and promising candidates who are chosen to participate in management training initially. These trainees are the most promotable individuals anyway, even without the training programs. Training directors also like to boast that employees like training programs. Although it is nice when trainees enjoy the experience, these subjective reactions are not sufficient indication that training results in better job performance.

Problems of organizational training provide many challenges for I/O psychologists: to identify the abilities required to perform more complex jobs; to provide opportunities for unskilled workers; to assist supervisors in the management of an ethnically diverse work force; to retrain workers displaced by changing economic, technological, and political forces; and to remain competitive in the international marketplace. Organizations must be encouraged to expend the resources necessary to evaluate their elaborate training and development programs. It makes little sense to continue to support such activities without empirical evidence of their worth.

Transfer of Training: The Importance of the Work Environment

Regardless of how well designed and rigorous a training program is, if employees cannot carry over or transfer their newly learned skills to actual job duties, the training efforts will have been less than maximally effective. We noted in Chapter 6 that the degree of similarity between the training situation and the work situation affects transfer of training. Transfer is aided when supervisors show support for employees who use new skills and when employees are given the opportunity to apply those skills on the job. Therefore, transfer of training depends on more than the quality of the training program itself. It also depends on the overall culture or climate of the organization.

This was demonstrated in a study of 505 supermarket managers from 52 stores who participated in a 3-day training program on basic supervisory behaviors and skills. The mean age of the supervisors was 32; 57% of them were women. Training dealt with *interpersonal skills,* such as customer and employee relations, and *administrative skills,* such as purchasing and shift scheduling.

Three weeks prior to the training program, the managers and their superiors completed questionnaires assessing the managers' level of knowledge of supervisory skills and behaviors. (The specific behaviors and skills covered were taken from the curriculum content of the training program.) The same questionnaires were retaken by managers and supervisors 6 to 8 weeks after the training program. The difference in scores for the managers between this posttraining test and the pretraining test would constitute a measure of how well they had learned the new skills. The difference between the pretraining and posttraining scores given by supervisors would provide a measure of how well the managers were actually applying their newly acquired skills on the job.

Source: Tracey, J. S., Tannenbaum, S. I., & Kavanagh, M. J. (1995). Applying trained skills on the job: The importance of the work environment. *Journal of Applied Psychology, 80,* 239–252.

At the completion of the training period, the managers filled out two additional questionnaires dealing with their work environment. One questionnaire assessed the organization's transfer of training climate. It dealt with such issues as the following:

- The extent to which supervisors and coworkers encouraged and set goals for trainee-managers to use new skills and behaviors acquired in training
- The extent to which trainees were openly discouraged from using new skills and behaviors acquired in training
- The extent to which trainees received extrinsic and intrinsic rewards for using newly learned skills and behaviors

The second questionnaire assessed organizational support for continuous learning, such as the extent of social support from supervisors and coworkers in encouraging learning and using new skills, and the extent to which the company promoted efforts to be innovative and progressive.

The results showed that the trainees demonstrated significantly more knowledge of supervisory skills and behaviors and that they used these skills on the job to a greater extent after the training than before. Also, the findings from the transfer-of-training questionnaire and the organizational-support questionnaire were significantly related to posttraining behavior. The extent of support provided by the work environment directly influenced the application of the managers' newly acquired skills and knowledge. The work environment facilitated the transfer of training from the training situation to the job.

Critical Thinking Questions

1. What factors other than those studied can affect transfer of training?
2. If employees do not have the opportunity to perform on the job the tasks for which they have been trained, how might this affect their job satisfaction, turnover intentions, self-efficacy, and job performance?

3. What weaknesses, flaws, or omissions do you find in the study as described? How would you redesign the experiment to improve it? Would you include a control group? Why or why not?

4. If you were the training director of a large corporation, what steps would you take to maximize transfer of training among your employees?

SUMMARY

Training and development take place at all levels of employment, from unskilled teenagers who need remedial work in basic math and English skills to seasoned corporate vice presidents, from the first day on a job to the final months before retirement. For college students, **cooperative education programs** are increasingly popular; students alternate college course work with jobs related to their field of interest.

Fair employment legislation affects training programs because decisions on placement, promotion, retention, and transfer are often based on performance during training. Therefore, training has the potential to be discriminatory.

The first step in establishing a training program is to specify the training objectives. A **needs assessment** based on organizational, task, and worker analyses is conducted using job analysis, critical incidents, performance appraisal, and self-assessment techniques. The training staff must be carefully selected and trained. Trainers should be knowledgeable in their subject matter, be able to communicate effectively, and have the requisite interpersonal skills.

Pretraining characteristics of trainees can influence how much they will benefit from a training program. These attributes include individual differences in ability, pretraining expectations, motivation, job involvement, locus of control, and self-efficacy. Psychological factors in learning include active practice of the material, massed or distributed practice, whole or part learning, transfer of training, feedback, and reinforcement.

In **on-the-job training,** trainees learn while actually working at the job. **Vestibule training** takes place in a simulated work area. In **apprenticeship,** trainees undergo classroom instruction and work experience under the guidance of skilled craftspersons. In **programmed instruction,** information is presented in easy steps to facilitate comprehension. In **computer-assisted instruction,** trainees interact with computer software that presents the material to be learned. In **behavior modification,** trainees are reinforced, or rewarded, for displaying the desired behaviors.

Job rotation exposes trainees to various jobs at their level of employment. In **case studies,** management trainees analyze, interpret, and discuss a complex business problem. **Business games** require groups of trainees to interact in a simulated business situation. The **in-basket technique,** also a simulation, asks trainees to respond individually to letters, memos, and other office tasks. In **role playing,** trainees act out the problems of workers and managers. **Behavior modeling** asks trainees to pattern their behavior on that of successful managers. In **diversity training,** employees learn to confront and deal with racist and sexist attitudes.

Career development and planning is a lifelong learning approach to enhancing job skills and abilities and to fostering personal development. Through self-analysis and company counseling and training programs, employees are assisted through three career stages: establishment, maintenance, and decline.

Companies rarely undertake systematic or quantitative evaluation of their training programs. Many training programs are continued because of subjective beliefs about their effectiveness rather than empirical evidence of actual behavior changes that result from training.

KEY TERMS

apprenticeship

behavior modification

business games

career development and planning

case studies

computer-assisted instruction (CAI)

cooperative education programs

job rotation

needs assessment

on-the-job training

performance audit

programmed instruction

vestibule training

ADDITIONAL READING

Gopher, D., Weil, M., & Bareket, T. (1994). Transfer of skill from a computer game trainer to flight. *Human Factors, 36*, 387–405. Describes a study of air force cadets to determine whether training on the computer game Space Fortress transferred to job performance and attention control in subsequent test flights.

Jacobs, R. L., & Jones, M. J. (1995). *Structured on-the-job training: Unleashing employee expertise in the workplace.* San Francisco: Berrett-Koehler. Describes the creation, implementation, and evaluation of formal on-the-job training programs emphasizing the involvement, preparation, and support of the people who will be conducting the training.

Leong, F. (Ed.). (1995). *Career development and vocational behavior of racial and ethnic minorities.* Mahwah NJ: Erlbaum. Reviews research and theory on career counseling and career development for African Americans, Hispanic Americans, Asian Americans, and Native Americans. Focuses on unique cultural factors that facilitate or inhibit career intervention programs.

Tannenbaum, S. I., & Yukl, G. (1992). Training and development in work organizations. *Annual Review of Psychology, 43*, 399–441. Reviews research on pretraining and posttraining work environments, training methods and needs assessments, and the evaluation of training programs. Considers trainee characteristics such as skills and abilities, motivation, attitudes, and expectations.

Organizational Psychology

PART III

Organizational psychology is concerned with the social and psychological climate at work. Few people work alone. Most of us work in groups, such as a crew on an assembly line or a department in a corporate office. We develop informal cliques that generate and reinforce standards, values, and attitudes that may differ from those of the organization. We are also influenced by the formal structure of the company that employs us. Like informal groups, these formal groups generate a psychological climate or culture of ideals and attitudes that affect our feelings about our job and the way we perform it. Thus, employee attitudes and work behaviors are influenced by the social climate of the organization and the psychological characteristics of its members. Organizational psychologists study the relationships between these two sets of factors.

Organizational psychology The study of the social and psychological climate of the workplace.

Leadership (Chapter 7) is a major influence on work attitudes and behaviors. Organizational psychologists study the impact of various leadership styles and the characteristics and responsibilities of leaders.

Motivation, job satisfaction, and job involvement (Chapter 8) relate to employee needs and the ways organizations can satisfy them. We discuss the nature of employee identification with a job and with organizational goals and how this identification affects job performance and satisfaction.

The chapter on the organization of the organization (Chapter 9) discusses formal and informal groups and their psychological climate. We describe participatory democracy, adaptation to social and technological change, the socialization of new employees, and efforts to improve the quality of work life.

Organizational psychology affects your working career directly—your motivations, the style of leadership under which you function best, the style of leadership you may display, and the structure of the organization for which you work. These factors determine the quality of your work experience, which, in turn, influences your general satisfaction with life.

Leadership

CHAPTER OUTLINE

■   ■   ■   ■

Organizations today place great emphasis on selecting and training leaders at all levels, from first-line supervisors to chief executive officers. I/O psychologists understand that the success or failure of any organization depends largely on the quality of its leaders. The basic difference between a successful and an unsuccessful organization can often be explained in terms of leadership.

We have seen the importance of management support for the successful implementation of any change in organizational procedures. To add another example, consider a meta-analysis of 18 studies that found a significant gain in job satisfaction as a result of a new MBO program (Rodgers, Hunter, & Rogers, 1993). However, that improvement occurred only when the program received the active support of top management. Without proper leadership, then, very little in the organization will work well.

Half of all new business ventures fail within their first 2 years. Only one third survive 5 years. In most cases, the business failures can be related to poor leadership. Other factors dependent on leadership include morale, turnover, insubordination, and job performance. It is not surprising that organizations are greatly concerned with selecting, developing, and supporting their managers and executives and in making the best use of their leadership abilities on the job.

In addition to selection and training efforts, I/O psychologists have conducted considerable research on leadership. They have explored the qualities and behaviors of successful and unsuccessful leaders, the effects of different leadership styles on subordinates, and the techniques for maximizing leadership abilities.

Anything that affects the economic fortune and prospects of an organization also affects its employees. Regardless of the level of your job, the quality of leadership at your place of employment will have a daily impact on the quality of your life. Until you become the company's president or CEO, you must take orders from someone else. Your motivation, enthusiasm, expectations, and job performance will be influenced by the ways in which your bosses carry out their responsibilities.

As college graduates, most of you will eventually hold leadership positions. What you make of that opportunity ultimately determines your salary, rank, responsibility, and sense of identity.

NEWSBREAK #11

A Bad Boss Can Ruin Your Day

We've all worked for someone like Ellen Brower at some time in our lives, or we've known someone who did. She's arrogant, abrasive, and abusive. She gets angry at the slightest provocation and chews out her employees in front of their colleagues, berating them as incompetent and stupid—and a lot worse. No matter how hard you work, no matter how good a job you do, it's never good enough. She's never satisfied.

You dread going to work, and maybe you have a headache or an upset stomach by the time you reach the office. You have trouble sleeping because of all the stress at work, thanks to her. You plan to quit as soon as you can, but until then, you're likely to remain an unhappy employee, getting little from your job but a paycheck. And no amount of money, you tell yourself every day, is worth having to put up with a boss like her.

If you do work for someone like Ellen Brower, you're not alone. Psychologist Robert Hogan of the University of Tulsa says that as many as 7 out of every 10 managers are incompetent, exploiting, domineering, irritable, and untrustworthy. They refuse to delegate authority and have poor decision-making skills. In short, they are lousy bosses.

Hogan, drawing on years of psychological research on the leadership process, concluded that managerial incompetence in American business is widespread. The research shows that the base rate for managerial incompetence ranges from 50% in the aerospace industry to 60% in hospitals, and up to 75% in some other industries. Even in the best run companies, then, half the managers are probably not performing their jobs properly. As a result, some 60 to 75% of American workers believe that the worst thing about their jobs—the greatest single cause of stress—is their boss. The most common complaints from workers are that managers are unwilling to exercise authority, tyrannize subordinates, and treat employees as if they were stupid.

How did such incompetent people get to be bosses? Hogan says it's because many companies select their best workers on the job and promote them to supervisory positions. The catch is that being the best worker may have nothing to do with having the kinds of skills and abilities needed for leadership. "What these bad guys are good at," Hogan claims, "is sucking up to their boss. These people have good social skills. That's how they got their jobs, interviewing well." It takes a lot more than social skills to make a good boss, though, as you know if you work for someone like Ellen Brower.

Sources: A. Barciela. How to keep the bad guy from making good. *St. Petersburg Times,* December 5, 1994. Hogan, R., Curphy, G. J., & Hogan, J. (1994). What we know about leadership: Effectiveness and personality. *American Psychologist, 49,* 493–504.

CHANGING VIEWS OF LEADERSHIP

The ways in which leaders behave—the specific acts by which they play out their leadership roles—are based on certain assumptions about human nature. Consciously or unconsciously, leaders operate on the basis of some personal theory of human behavior, a view of what their subordinates are like as people. For example, managers who exercise close supervision on the job—who watch to make sure that their employees are doing the work exactly as they have been told—hold a different view of human nature from that of managers who give their subordinates the freedom to work in whatever way they think best.

Scientific Management

In the early years of the 20th century, foremen—the first level of supervisor over production workers—were promoted from the ranks of the workers and received little formal training for their leadership role. These turn-of-the-century supervisors had complete control over their subordinates' work lives. Foremen hired and fired, determined production levels, and set pay rates. There were few reins on their authority—no labor union, no industrial relations department, no human resources or personnel manager, no one to whom a worker could complain. As one I/O psychologist recounted, "Foremen generally hired friends and relatives or selected unskilled workers from the masses who waited anxiously outside the factory gates. In a Philadelphia factory, a foreman tossed apples into a throng and gave a job to any man who caught one" (Howard, 1995a, pp. 9–10). Foremen applied a combination of autocratic behavior, aggressiveness, and physical intimidation to force their workers to produce.

Scientific management A management philosophy concerned with increasing productivity that regarded workers as extensions of the machines they operated.

The management philosophy during that period was called **scientific management,** an approach promoted by Frederick W. Taylor, an engineer. Taylor's concern was with finding ways to increase productivity, with getting the workers and the machines they operated to run faster.

Scientific management regarded workers simply as extensions of the machines they operated. No consideration was accorded employees as human beings, as people with different needs, abilities, and interests. Workers were considered to be lazy and dishonest and to have a low level of intelligence. This view was reinforced by research that psychologists were then conducting on the general level of intelligence in the United States. The psychologist H. H. Goddard argued that people with low intelligence required supervision by people with greater intelligence. "Laborers," Goddard said, "are but little above the child [and] must be told what to do and shown how to do it" (quoted in Broad & Wade, 1982, p. 198). The only way for an organization to increase productivity and efficiency was to have workers submit to the dictates of their leaders and the requirements of the manufacturing equipment.

The Human Relations Approach

Human relations approach The approach to leadership that regards employee needs as a legitimate corporate responsibility.

It is difficult to imagine people working under the scientific management system. Most modern organizations regard the satisfaction of employee needs as a legitimate corporate responsibility. This changed viewpoint is called the **human relations approach** to management. It arose in the 1920s and 1930s under the impact of the Hawthorne studies, which focused attention on workers instead of on production.

One change introduced into the work situation in the Hawthorne studies was style of leadership. Workers were routinely treated harshly by supervisors who berated them for dropping parts, talking on the job, and taking breaks. As we noted, workers were treated like children who needed to be watched, shouted at, and punished. In the Hawthorne experiments, a new type of supervisor acted differently, allowing workers to set their own production pace and to form social groups. They were permitted to talk to one another on the job, and their views about the work were solicited. The new supervisor treated them like human beings, not interchangeable cogs in some giant production machine.

Theory X and Theory Y

The scientific management and human relations approaches to leadership behavior were given formal expression by Douglas McGregor as Theory X and Theory Y (McGregor, 1960). The **Theory X** approach to management assumes that most people are innately lazy and dislike work, avoiding it whenever they can. They must be coerced, watched, and scolded on the job to make them work hard enough to meet organizational goals. Theory X assumes that most people have no ambition, avoid responsibility, and prefer to be led and directed; they would not work at all without a dictatorial leader.

Theory X is compatible with scientific management and with the classic organizational style known as **bureaucracy.** It is incompatible with current theories of human motivation, such as the work of psychologist Abraham Maslow, who argued that our ultimate goal is self-actualization, or the fulfillment of all our human capacities. Maslow's conception of human nature reflects McGregor's **Theory Y,** which proposes that most people seek inner satisfaction and fulfillment from their work. Control and punishment are not necessary to bring about good job performance. According to Theory Y, then, people are industrious and creative and seek challenge and responsibility on the job. They function best under a leader who allows them to participate in setting and working toward personal and organizational goals.

The Theory Y viewpoint is compatible with the human relations movement in management and with the participative, democratic style of organization. An example of the application of Theory Y is the management by objectives (MBO) approach to performance appraisal. We have noted that MBO involves a high degree of employee participation in setting goals for job performance and personal growth.

Theory X/Theory Y The Theory X approach to management assumes that people are lazy and dislike work and therefore must be led and directed; Theory Y assumes that people find satisfaction in their work and function best under a leader who allows them to participate in working toward their goals.

Bureaucracies A formal, orderly, and rational approach to organizing business enterprises.

THEORIES OF LEADERSHIP

Leadership theories recognize that effective leadership depends on the interaction of three factors: the traits and behaviors of the leaders; the characteristics of the followers; and the nature of the situation in which leadership occurs. We describe several theoretical explanations of leadership: contingency theory, cognitive resource theory, path-goal theory, normative decision theory, and the leader-member exchange.

Contingency Theory

Contingency theory An approach to leadership in which leadership effectiveness is determined by the interaction between the leader's personal characteristics and aspects of the situation.

In **contingency theory,** developed by Fred Fiedler (Fiedler, 1978), leadership effectiveness is determined by the interaction between the leader's personal characteristics and aspects of the situation. Leaders are classified as primarily person-oriented or task-oriented. The type of leader who will be the more effective depends on the leader's degree of control over the situation.

Control is contingent on three factors: the relationship between the leader and followers, the degree of task structure, and the leader's authority or position power. If leaders are popular, are directing a highly structured or routine task, and have the authority or power to enforce discipline, then they have a high degree of control over the situation, a condition we may describe as favorable. For example, army sergeants who get along well with the soldiers in their squad are high-control and effective leaders. On the other hand, an unpopular president of a social club that has no formal goals and who has no authority to require attendance or collect dues is a low-control leader in an unfavorable situation.

According to contingency theory, the task-oriented leader will be more effective in extremely favorable or extremely unfavorable situations. When the situation is moderately favorable, the person-oriented leader will be more effective.

Contingency theory has stimulated a great deal of research, some of which is supportive and encouraging (see, for example, Schriesheim, Tepper, & Tetrault, 1994). However, most of that research was conducted in laboratory settings, not on the job. The validity of contingency theory remains in dispute, and it has not been determined whether the laboratory findings can be generalized to the workplace (Peters, Hartke, & Pohlmann, 1985). In response to these criticisms of contingency theory, Fiedler offered the cognitive resource theory of leadership, which is an outgrowth of his earlier work.

Cognitive Resource Theory

Cognitive resource theory An approach to leadership that focuses on the interaction between a leader's cognitive resources (intelligence, technical competence, and job-related knowledge), job performance, and stress.

The **cognitive resource theory** of leadership focuses on leaders' cognitive resources: that is, their intelligence, technical competence, and job-related knowledge. The leader's level of cognitive ability is related to the nature of the plans, decisions, and strategies that will guide the actions of a work group. The better the leader's abilities, the more effective the plans, decisions, and strategies. If the group supports the leader's goals and if the leader is not under inordinate stress, then the leader's programs are likely to be implemented.

The cognitive resource theory is based on the following hypotheses (Fiedler & Garcia, 1987):

1. When leaders are under stress, their cognitive abilities are diverted from the task and they focus instead on problems and activities that are less relevant. As a result, group performance will suffer.
2. The cognitive abilities of directive leaders will show a higher positive correlation with group performance than will the cognitive abilities of nondirective leaders.
3. Plans and decisions cannot be implemented unless the group complies with the leader's directives. Therefore, the correlation between a leader's cognitive resources and group performance will be higher when the group supports the leader than when it does not.

4. The leader's cognitive abilities will enhance group performance only to the degree to which the task requires those abilities: that is, the degree to which the task is intellectually demanding.
5. The leader's directive behavior will be partly determined by the nature of the relationship between leader and followers, the degree of task structure, and the leader's control over the situation (elements of the contingency theory, described earlier).

Cognitive resource theory describes the interaction between cognitive resources, job performance, and stress. The emphasis on stress has practical implications because it is partially under the leader's control. Through stress-management techniques, a leader's cognitive resources can be developed and applied more effectively. A major source of stress for leaders arises from their own superiors in the organization. When managers have a stressful relationship with their boss, they tend to rely on responses or behaviors that worked for them in the past rather than on their cognitive resources. When leaders are free of stress, they rely on their intelligence instead of being constrained by past experiences.

Fiedler has presented impressive research support for the cognitive resource theory, although most of his work was conducted in the laboratory, not in the workplace. The generalizability of the theory remains in question. Other research has been less supportive, resulting in a spirited exchange of views, charges, and countercharges in the pages of the *Journal of Applied Psychology*. This debate demonstrates that scientists are not devoid of passion, particularly when their own work is under attack (see Fiedler, Murphy, & Gibson, 1992; Vecchio, 1990, 1992).

Path-Goal Theory

The **path-goal theory** of leadership focuses on the kinds of behaviors a leader exercises to allow subordinates to achieve their goals. The theory states that leaders can increase their subordinates' motivation, satisfaction, and job performance by administering rewards that depend on the achievement of particular goals. In other words, effective leaders will help employees reach personal and organizational goals by pointing out the paths they should follow and by providing them with the means to do so.

Path-goal theory A theory of leadership that focuses on the kinds of behaviors leaders should exercise to allow their subordinates to achieve personal and organizational goals.

Four styles that leaders can adopt to facilitate employee attainment of goals are as follows (House, 1971; House & Mitchell, 1974):

- Directive leadership—the leader tells subordinates what they should do and how they should do it.
- Supportive leadership—the leader shows concern and support for subordinates.
- Participative leadership—the leader allows subordinates to participate in decisions that affect their work.
- Achievement-oriented leadership—the leader sets challenging goals for subordinates and emphasizes high levels of job performance.

The leadership style that will be most effective depends on characteristics of the situation and of the subordinates. Leaders must be flexible and adopt whichever style is called for. For example, employees who have low levels of the skills required to perform a task will function better under directive leadership. Employees who have high skills need less direction and will function better under supportive leadership. Leaders must be able to perceive the nature of the situation and the characteristics of their subordinates and respond with the most appropriate approach.

Research findings on the path-goal theory are contradictory, but in general the support is weak. It is a difficult theory to test experimentally because basic concepts, such as "path" and "goal," are hard to define in operational terms.

Normative Decision Theory

Normative decision theory
A theory of leadership that focuses on the correct norms or standards of behavior for leaders to follow.

Normative decision theory focuses on a single aspect of leadership—decision making—and attempts to prescribe specific behaviors for leaders to follow. The word *normative* refers to those norms or standards of behavior considered to be correct. The theory is concerned with the extent to which leaders allow their subordinates to participate in making decisions (Vroom & Jago, 1988).

Normative decision theory proposes five styles on a continuum of leader behavior ranging from autocratic—in which decisions are made by the leader—to complete participation—in which decisions are reached through consensus. The most effective style of leadership depends on the importance of the decision, the degree to which it is accepted by subordinates, and the time required to make the decision. A decision reached through participation might be better accepted by subordinates than a decision made by their leader, but sometimes the demands of the job require a faster response than can be provided by the participatory decision-making process.

Leaders must be flexible in selecting the decision-making approach that yields maximum benefits in terms of quality, acceptance, and time constraints. Several factors of the work situation have been proposed as an objective basis for helping leaders to choose the best approach to decision making.

Normative decision theory has empirical support to show that some decisions reached through prescribed procedures for a given situation were more effective than decisions reached in other ways (Field, 1982; Field & House, 1990; Jago & Vroom, 1980). Other research questions the applicability of those decision-making procedures in the workplace (Pate & Heiman, 1987).

Leader-Member Exchange

Leader-member exchange
An approach to leadership that encompasses the ways in which the leader-follower relationship affects the leadership process.

The **leader-member exchange** model (formerly the vertical dyadic linkage theory) deals with the ways in which the leader-follower relationship (the leader-member exchange, or LMX) affects the leadership process (Graen & Schliemann, 1978). The proponents of this model criticized other leadership theories for focusing on average leadership styles or behaviors and for ignoring individual differences among subordinates. The relationship between each leader-subordinate pair, or dyad, must be considered separately because leaders behave differently with each subordinate.

Subordinates are of two types: the in-group employees, whom the supervisor views as competent, trustworthy, and highly motivated; and the out-group employees, whom the supervisor views as incompetent, untrustworthy, and poorly motivated.

The LMX model also distinguishes two leadership styles: supervision, in which leadership is based on formal authority, and leadership, in which influence is exerted through persuasion. With out-group subordinates, leaders use supervision and assign tasks requiring low levels of ability and responsibility. There is little personal relationship between leaders and out-group members.

With in-group subordinates, leaders practice leadership rather than supervision and assign members important and responsible tasks that require high levels of ability. Leaders and in-group members establish personal relationships in which in-group subordinates provide support and understanding.

On-the-job research conducted in the United States and in Japan has generally supported the leader-member exchange model for various levels of management (see, for example, Crouch & Yetton, 1988; Graen, Novak, & Sommerkamp, 1982; Graen & Wakabayashi, 1986). Other research has shown that the quality of the leader-subordinate relationship can be improved through training, resulting in the display of more leadership than supervision. Significant improvements in job satisfaction and productivity and decreases in errors have been found among subordinates as a result of training to improve the quality of the LMX (Graen, Scandura, & Graen, 1986; Scandura & Graen, 1984). Additional research suggests that supervisor career mentoring behavior toward subordinates may form part of the LMX and may be responsible for promotions and improvements in performance (Scandura & Schriesheim, 1994).

Other investigations have focused on factors that might influence the LMX. In a rare longitudinal study, three psychologists analyzed the development over time of LMXs between 166 newly hired employees and their immediate supervisors. The subjects were employees at two universities, in nonacademic jobs such as secretary, electrician, librarian, admissions counselor, and computer programmer. The results showed that the expectations of workers and supervisors toward each other (what each thought the other would be like), when measured in the first 5 days of their LMXs, predicted the nature of those LMXs 6 weeks later. In addition, workers' expectations of their supervisors predicted how the workers assessed those supervisors 6 months later. In short, those who had high expectations in the beginning of the relationships reported high-quality LMXs later, which suggests that the LMX develops early in the life of the relationship. Workers and supervisors who reported early a high liking for, and similarity with, one another developed high-quality LMXs later (Liden, Wayne, & Stilwell, 1993).

A study of 84 nurses and their supervisors showed that the closer their attitudes on such issues as family, money, careers, and life goals, the higher the quality of their LMXs. The level of extraversion of the nurses was also significantly related to the quality of the LMXs; the higher the extraversion, the higher the quality of the relationship (Phillips & Bedeian, 1994).

Questionnaire data from 102 hospital employees and 26 supervisors found that the more the leader-member exchanges were based on interpersonal affect, as well as mutual trust, loyalty, and respect, the more the subordinates were likely to engage in behaviors that were not required duties but were voluntary behaviors that helped coworkers and the organization (Settoon, Bennett, & Liden, 1996).

A study of bank employees found that subordinates who displayed positive behaviors, such as verbal praise toward their bosses, enhanced the supervisors' liking for them. This condition improved the quality of the LMX and led to greater employee job satisfaction and productivity (Wayne & Ferris, 1990). Thus, employees are able to influence the quality of their relationship with their supervisors, which, in turn, affects the way their leaders treat them. This is another example of how the behavior of leaders can vary as a function of the behavior of their followers. These on-the-job research findings give the leader-member exchange model a practical advantage over most other leadership theories.

LEADERSHIP STYLES

Much I/O psychology research focuses on leadership styles and the behaviors by which they are manifested on the job. We discuss the differences between authoritarian and democratic leaders, and transactional and transformational leaders.

Authoritarian and Democratic Leaders

Authoritarian leadership The situation in which the leader makes all decisions and tells followers what to do.

Democratic leadership A leadership style in which leader and followers discuss problems and make decisions jointly.

Leadership in the workplace involves various styles along a continuum. The continuum ranges from a highly **authoritarian leadership** style, in which the leader makes all decisions and tells followers what to do, to a highly **democratic leadership** style, in which the leader and the group of followers discuss problems and jointly make all decisions that affect their work. The style that is most effective depends on the nature of the situation and the needs and characteristics of the followers.

A meta-analysis of studies comparing the effects of authoritarian and democratic leaders on employee job satisfaction indicated that 60% of the employees surveyed reported greater satisfaction with the democratic leadership style. Some

For police officers, who hold stressful jobs that require rapid decision-making skills and efficient job performance, authoritarian leadership is desirable. Often, law-enforcement situations do not allow time for a more democratic approach.

9% showed greater satisfaction with the authoritarian style; these employees were not interested in worker participation and preferred to be told what to do. Approximately 30% of the employees reported no difference in job satisfaction under the two leadership styles. However, when actual job performance instead of job satisfaction was studied, the results did not favor the democratic style so strongly. Of the studies analyzed, 22% showed that productivity was higher under some degree of democratic leadership, but 56% of the studies reported no difference in job performance between democratic and authoritarian leadership styles. Job performance was higher under authoritarian leadership in 10% of the studies (Locke & Schweiger, 1978).

In stressful work situations that require unusually rapid and highly efficient job performance, productivity and satisfaction are more likely to be maintained under authoritarian leadership. I/O psychologists suggest that these employees recognize that the nature of their work does not allow time for a participatory democracy approach. For example, firefighters must respond to a fire alarm immediately and follow the directions of their chief. They do not have time to hold a committee meeting to determine the best way to deal with the fire.

Transactional and Transformational Leaders

Transactional leaders focus on the social transactions or exchanges between leaders and followers. The leaders' freedom to act is constrained by their followers' perceptions of them. The key to this interaction is the followers' perceptions of and expectations about the leaders' abilities, competence, and source of authority. In other words, the behavior of transactional leaders depends on what their followers think of them. Transactional leaders conduct their business by identifying the needs of their followers and bestowing rewards to satisfy those needs in exchange for a certain level of performance.

Transactional leadership Leadership that focuses on the social interactions between leaders and followers; based on followers' perceptions of and expectations about the leader's abilities.

Transformational leaders have more latitude in their behavior. They are not limited by their followers' perceptions. Rather than believing that they must act in accordance with their followers' expectations, transformational leaders work to change or transform their followers' needs and redirect their thinking (Bass, 1985).

Transformational leadership Leadership in which leaders are not constrained by their followers' perceptions but are free to act to change or transform their followers' views.

Transformational leaders challenge and inspire subordinates with a sense of purpose and excitement about what can be accomplished. These leaders create a vision of what the corporate culture can be and communicate it to their employees, stimulating them to develop their abilities while accepting feedback and suggestions.

Three components of transformational leadership have been identified:

1. Charismatic leadership—the level of confidence and inspiration engendered by the leader
2. Individualized consideration—the amount of attention and support the leader supplies to the followers
3. Intellectual stimulation—the extent to which leaders persuade followers to think differently about how they perform their jobs

There is some research support for these three factors showing them to correlate highly with one another (Bycio, Hackett, & Allen, 1995).

Studies of business executives, high-ranking military officers, and high-level administrators in government and universities have found that those who were described by their subordinates as transformational leaders were more effective on the job, had better relations with superiors, and made greater contributions to organizational goals than did those described as transactional leaders. Employees reported that they expended more effort on the job for transformational leaders than for transactional leaders. The greater effectiveness of transformational leaders has been demonstrated in a wide range of employing organizations in several countries including the United States, India, Spain, Japan, China, and Austria (Bass, 1997). In addition, a 1-year study of 78 bank managers in Canada found that the degree of the transformational leadership of their superiors was significantly related to the extent to which the managers reached their annual productivity goals. The research also showed that the variable of locus of control was positively related to transformational leadership; transformational leaders tended to internal rather than external locus of control (Howell & Avolio, 1993).

High-performing executives rated higher on the component of individualized consideration of subordinates than did executives whose performance was average. Entrepreneurs, whose success in new business ventures depends on innovation, commitment, and persistence, scored significantly higher on facets of transformational leadership than did leaders of established businesses (see, for example, Hater & Bass, 1988). Entrepreneurs also scored high on the needs for personal achievement, innovation, and goal-setting (Miner, Smith, & Bracker, 1994).

Often, transformational leaders exhibit **charismatic leadership,** mentioned above as one of three components of this type of leadership. Charismatic leaders have a broad knowledge of their field, a self-promoting personality, a high energy level, and a willingness to take risks and use unconventional strategies. They use their power effectively to serve others and inspire their trust. Charismatic leaders stimulate their followers to think independently and to ask questions. They maintain open communication with subordinates and freely share recognition with them. Reviews of 35 studies on charismatic leaders found a significant positive relationship between this leadership style and high job performance and positive work attitudes on the part of their followers (Bass & Avolio, 1993; Shamir, House, & Arthur, 1993).

Three facets of charismatic leadership have been suggested: communicating a vision; implementing the vision; and displaying a powerful communication style, such as using a captivating tone of voice, animated facial expressions, and a dynamic way of interacting with other people.

A study of 282 college students performing an assembly-line task under the supervision of trained actors playing the roles of different types of leaders found that communicating and implementing a vision influenced job performance but that communication style did not (Kirkpatrick & Locke, 1996). Charismatic leaders can be heroes, launching new businesses, directing organizational change, and stimulating impressive gains in employee productivity. But charismatic leaders can also misuse their power in unethical ways. They can be insensitive to the needs of their followers and act only for personal gain (Howell & Avolio, 1992).

Charismatic leadership A leadership style characterized by a self-promoting personality, a high energy level, and a willingness to take risks; charismatic leaders stimulate their followers to think independently.

THE ROLE OF POWER IN LEADERSHIP

Among the issues relating to the role of power in leadership behavior are (1) the power leaders have over their subordinates and (2) the ways in which leaders are motivated by power. Leaders may use different kinds of power, depending on the situation, the nature of their followers, and their personal characteristics.

Types of Power

Psychologists have proposed five types of power (Yukl & Taber, 1983). The first three are:

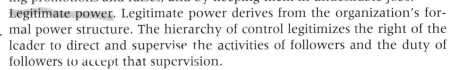

1. Reward power. Organizational leaders have the ability to reward their subordinates with pay raises and promotions. This power gives leaders a means of control over employees and can affect employee behavior.
2. Coercive power. Organizational leaders have an equally strong source of power in their ability to punish subordinates by firing them, by withholding promotions and raises, and by keeping them in undesirable jobs.
3. Legitimate power. Legitimate power derives from the organization's formal power structure. The hierarchy of control legitimizes the right of the leader to direct and supervise the activities of followers and the duty of followers to accept that supervision.

element of democracy

These three sources of power are derived from and defined by the formal organization to which leaders and subordinates belong. They are types of power dictated or prescribed by the organization. The last two types of power derive from the leaders themselves and are earned or merited by the leaders' personal characteristics as these are perceived by followers. We might call these attributes "respect" as well as power.

4. Referent power. Referent power refers to the degree to which employees identify with their leaders and the leaders' goals, accept those goals as their own, and work with their leaders to achieve the goals.
5. Expert power. Expert power refers to the extent to which leaders are perceived to have the skills necessary to attain the group's goals. If employees recognize their leader's expertise, then those employees are more likely to become willing and supportive subordinates.

Effects and Uses of Power

The effects of these types of power were investigated in a study of 251 middle-level managers. The dependent variables were (1) job satisfaction, (2) satisfaction with their superior's technical skills, (3) satisfaction with their superior's human relations skills, and (4) organizational commitment. The results showed that legitimate, referent, and expert power correlated positively with all four measures. Reward power correlated positively with the first three but not with organizational commitment. Coercive power showed a strong negative correlation with all measures of satisfaction and commitment and thus was viewed negatively by the managers. This finding suggests that leaders who rely primarily

Leaders born not made?

on coercive power are less likely to be effective than are leaders who exercise the other types of power (Hinkin & Schriesheim, 1988).

A survey of managers in various small and large businesses confirmed that the threatening tactics of coercive power led more often to failure on the job than to success. The managers reported that their most widely used influence tactic was expert power (Keys & Case, 1990). Another study surveyed managers' subordinates and peers in pharmaceutical, chemical, and financial services companies to rate the managers' effectiveness. It was found that legitimate power, expert power, and referent power were cited as the most important reasons for complying with managers' requests (Yukl & Falbe, 1991).

Some I/O psychologists question the relationship between the five types of power and the dependent variables that have been studied. They urge that the findings be interpreted with caution because the ranking and rating scales used may not adequately sample all aspects of power (Schriesheim, Hinkin, & Podsakoff, 1991).

What are the uses of power in motivating organizational leaders? High-level executives and middle-level managers often show a great personal need for power. It has been found that effective managers demonstrate a greater need for power than do less effective managers. However, the most effective managers do not seek power for personal gain. Their power need is directed toward the organization and is used to achieve organizational goals. As a result, they are usually successful in establishing and maintaining a good work climate, high morale, and high team spirit among their subordinates. Managers motivated by the need for personal power serve themselves rather than their organization. They are capable of creating loyalty among subordinates, but it is a loyalty toward themselves, not toward the organization. These managers are more effective than those who show no need for power, but they are not as effective as those whose power is oriented toward the organization.

THE ROLE OF LEADERS' EXPECTATIONS

Leaders' expectations about their employees' job performance can influence that performance. For example, managers who expect high performance tend to get high performance, and those who expect poor performance tend to get poor performance.

The Pygmalion Effect

This instance of a self-fulfilling prophecy was first observed in the classroom. In a now-classic demonstration, teachers were told that some of their students had a high level of potential and others had a low level of potential. Of course, there were no such differences between the two groups. The differences existed only in the teachers' expectations, as created by the experimental situation. Yet, the group of students with the allegedly high potential later scored significantly higher on IQ tests than the other group. The teachers had subtly communicated their expectations to their students (Rosenthal & Jacobson, 1968).

This expectancy effect was labeled the **Pygmalion effect,** named after Pygmalion, a king of Cyprus who fell in love with an ivory statue of a beautiful woman named Galatea. In answer to Pygmalion's prayers, the statue came alive, turning his fantasy into reality.

The self-fulfilling prophecy has been widely demonstrated in the workplace. For example, platoon leaders in the Israel Defense Forces were told that some of

Pygmalion effect A self-fulfilling prophecy in which managers' expectations about the level of their employees' job performance can influence that performance.

their trainees had unusually high potential for command. These trainees later scored significantly higher on all training measures than did a control group whose platoon leaders had been given no such information and thus could not communicate their expectations to their subordinates (Eden, 1990).

To test for the Pygmalion effect among females, the phenomenon was studied in the classroom. No gender differences were found; the effect was found to occur with both boys and girls. However, sex differences in the Pygmalion effect emerged with adult subjects. A meta-analysis of 14 expectancy studies revealed that when women constituted the majority of the subjects studied, no such effect was demonstrated (Hall & Briton, 1993).

A study of 172 engineers, scientists, and technicians in a large corporation investigated the role of leader expectations on innovative behavior; 92% of the subjects were men. The results showed that the managers' expectations influenced the technicians' innovative behavior, suggesting support for the Pygmalion effect among this group (Scott & Bruce, 1994). The more highly educated engineers and scientists did not appear to be affected by leader expectations, perhaps because their work was already considered to be innovative. Gender differences were not noted.

The Golem Effect

The reverse of the Pygmalion effect has been termed the **Golem effect,** describing the situation in which low expectations affect performance. (*Golem* is the Hebrew word for a zombie or automaton.) To test for the Golem effect, I/O psychologists in Israel studied army squad leaders, telling them that some of their male paratrooper trainees, who had received low scores on a physical fitness test, should perform just as well in training as the trainees who had obtained higher scores on the fitness test. Leaders in the control group squads were told nothing about the physical potential of the low scorers under their command. Thus, expectancies were established about some of the low scorers (the Golem) but not about others.

The results showed that low-scoring trainees in the experimental groups improved significantly more than low-scoring trainees in the control groups. The researchers concluded that "raising expectations led the leaders to expect more and to demand more; subordinates of whom more was demanded performed better and enjoyed themselves more" (Oz & Eden, 1994, p. 751). Low-scoring control group trainees, whose leaders had no expectations about their performance, made significantly smaller gains.

LEADERSHIP FUNCTIONS

A comprehensive research program to identify the functions of leaders began in the late 1940s at Ohio State University. A host of leader behaviors were grouped into two categories of functions called **consideration** and **initiating structure** (Fleishman & Harris, 1962).

Consideration functions Leadership behaviors that involve awareness of and sensitivity to the feelings of subordinates.

Initiating structure functions The leadership behaviors concerned with organizing, defining, and directing the work activities of subordinates.

The Consideration Dimension

The functions in the consideration dimension involve awareness of and sensitivity to the feelings of subordinates; these functions are allied with the human relations approach to management. Leaders high in consideration understand and accept subordinates as individuals with unique motivations and needs. Success-

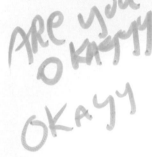

ful leaders must relate to each employee by being considerate of that person's feelings. This necessity places a great demand on the sympathy, warmth, and understanding of managers because they also must maintain production levels and deal with other organizational concerns.

There is a similarity between the consideration leadership function and the leadership styles proposed by the theories discussed earlier. High consideration relates to the person-oriented leader in contingency theory, to participative leadership in path-goal theory, to complete participation in the normative decision theory, and to the leadership condition in the leader-member exchange model.

The Initiating Structure Dimension

The functions in the initiating structure dimension include tasks traditionally associated with a leadership role—organizing, defining, and directing the work activities of subordinates. Sometimes this aspect of a manager's job conflicts with the demands of the consideration dimension. To accomplish a job (to initiate structure), managers must assign specific tasks to employees, direct the way in which the tasks are to be performed, and monitor the work to ensure that it is being done properly.

These work activities may call for some authoritarian behavior, and there may not be time or opportunity for leaders to consider their subordinates' needs or feelings. A certain amount of work must be accomplished at a specified level of quality in a fixed period of time. The organization's survival and the manager's job depend on meeting these standards consistently. Managers are often forced to walk a thin line between the demands of consideration and of initiating structure.

Effective managers balance consideration functions (sensitivity to subordinates' personal needs) with initiating structure functions (providing a framework within which the organization's productivity goals can be met).

TABLE 7–1 Daily Work Activities of Managers

Activity	Percentage of Work Time
Conversing with staff and subordinates	41%
Writing reports	19
Reading reports	18
Clerical duties	5
Operating equipment	5
Engaging in personal activities	5
Thinking	3
Traveling	2
Inspecting products	1
Processing data	1

Note. Adapted from "Are the Classical Management Functions Useful in Describing Managerial Work?" by S. J. Carroll and D. J. Gillen, 1987, *Academy of Management Review, 12,* p. 41.

The leadership functions in the initiating structure dimension are similar to those of the task-oriented leader in contingency theory, directive leadership in path-goal theory, autocracy in normative decision theory, and supervision in the leader-member exchange model.

On-the-Job Tasks

What specific tasks do managers perform as they carry out the functions of consideration and initiating structure? Psychologists have conducted considerable research on this issue, observing managers at work, interviewing them about their activities, and having them complete questionnaires about their job behaviors. The results of one analysis are shown in Table 7–1. You can see that more than 40% of a manager's work time is spent interacting with other people, almost as much time as is devoted to paperwork, with little time available for thought and reflection. Most managers are kept quite busy tending to routine tasks and problems.

The Operant Supervisory Taxonomy and Index (OSTI) has been used to measure managerial behaviors. It includes seven categories that encompass the daily activities of managers (Komaki, Zlotnick, & Jensen, 1986).

1. Performance consequences—providing feedback on performance to employees
2. Performance monitoring—collecting data about employee performance
3. Performance antecedents—providing instructions, goals, and expectations for employees
4. Own performance—gathering information about personal goals and discussing them with superiors
5. Work-related activities involving job tasks but not employee performance
6. Non-work-related conversations and activities
7. Solitary activities—reading, thinking, and planning

LEADERSHIP CHARACTERISTICS

The characteristics required for successful leadership vary with the manager's level in the organizational hierarchy. The CEO of an automobile manufacturing company performs different functions and needs different abilities from those of a supervisor on the auto painting assembly line. In general, the higher the position on the corporate ladder, the fewer consideration activities and the more initiating structure activities are required. A high-level executive needs fewer human relations skills than a supervisor, because the executive typically controls and interacts directly with fewer subordinates. The corporate vice president may deal only with a half-dozen department heads, whereas the first-line supervisor may have 50 or more workers to manage. Therefore, leaders at different levels have different functions, characteristics, and problems on the job.

First-Line Supervisors

I/O psychology research on first-line supervisors suggests that supervisors with the most productive work groups have the following qualities:

1. They are person-centered. Successful supervisors are higher in the consideration function than are unsuccessful supervisors.
2. They are supportive. Effective supervisors are more helpful to employees and more willing to defend them against criticism from higher management.

A first-line supervisor at an automobile plant meets with subordinates before the work shift begins to discuss problems and hear grievances.

3. They are democratic. Effective supervisors hold frequent meetings with employees to solicit their views and encourage participation. Less effective supervisors are more autocratic.
4. They are flexible. Effective supervisors allow employees to accomplish their goals in their own way whenever possible. Less effective supervisors dictate how a job is to be performed and permit no deviation.

A study comparing effective and ineffective supervisors was undertaken at two manufacturing plants, one with a participative organizational climate and the other with an authoritarian climate. The data showed that effective supervisors at both plants operated similarly, despite the differences in organizational structure and climate. Effective supervisors were found to be more competent, caring, and committed to their work and to their subordinates, thus ranking high on the consideration dimension. They emphasized quality, provided clear directions, and gave timely feedback to their workers. Effective supervisors described themselves more as coaches than directors. They freely shared with subordinates information about organizational policies and procedures and the reasons for their own decisions (Klein & Posey, 1986).

A study of 570 soldiers operating as first-line supervisors in the U.S. Army found that a primary requisite for successful job performance was high cognitive ability. Supervisors with high cognitive ability were more likely to be given supervisory responsibilities earlier in their careers than supervisors with lower cognitive ability (Borman, Hanson, Oppler, Pulakos, & White, 1993).

Managers and Executives

At higher levels of an organization, managers and executives engage in fewer consideration behaviors and more initiating structure behaviors. In other words, they are less people-oriented and more work-oriented. Successful executives share other characteristics. We discuss background factors, the role of power, the importance of self-promotion, and the stability of certain characteristics over time. We also note the characteristics of unsuccessful executives.

Background Characteristics. A 1988 investigation of the background characteristics of 425 successful executives found that 98% had attended college and 89% had graduated. In contrast, in a similar study of executives conducted in 1952, 24% of the executives had not attended college, and 13% had not completed high school. The percentage of successful male executives whose fathers had been executives or business owners, and thus in a position to help their sons' careers, declined from the 1950s to the 1980s from 31% to 28% (Ross & Unwalla, 1988).

Two longitudinal studies of AT&T executives rated as successful on the job also found that college attendance correlated positively with later job success. Employees who had gone to college showed, at the time of hiring, greater potential for middle- and upper-management positions than those who had not gone to college. Eight years later the differences between these two groups were even more pronounced. The college sample rose faster and higher in management ranks than the noncollege sample (Bray, 1964; Howard, 1986; Howard & Bray, 1988).

College grades correlated positively with assessment-center ratings of management potential and later advancement on the job. People who had earned higher grades in college showed greater potential for promotion, obtained their first promotion earlier in their careers, and rose higher in management than those who had earned lower college grades. The quality of the college attended was found to be a less useful predictor of later job performance, although assessment-center ratings were higher for managers who had attended what was considered a better-quality college.

A more valid predictor of potential and actual promotion was the college major. Those who had majored in humanities and social sciences received superior ratings in assessment-center exercises and job performance and moved faster and farther up the corporate ladder. Those who had majored in business administration ranked second. Mathematics, science, and engineering majors were third. Humanities and social science majors were shown to excel in decision making, creativity in solving business problems, intellectual ability, written communications skills, and motivation for advancement. They, and the business majors, also ranked higher in interpersonal skills, leadership ability, oral communications skills, and flexibility than the math, science, and engineering majors.

Some collegiate activities, such as student government, student newspaper, and debating society, correlated positively with measures of management potential, although they were not related to actual job advancement. Participation in sports showed no relationship to management potential.

A study of more than 200 managers in a variety of organizations identified other demographic factors that correlated positively with managerial success. Sex, marital status, and length of time with one organization (organizational tenure) were found to be important. More likely to advance to high levels of management were married men who had been with their company a shorter rather than a longer time (Gattiker & Larwood, 1990).

A more recent study of 1,388 top executives, all men, found that those who were the most successful were more likely to have graduated from prestigious Ivy League colleges, to be married to women who did not hold jobs outside the home, and to display a high commitment to their work. It should be noted that not *all* the executives considered successful had graduated from Ivy League schools. However, those who had done so earned substantially higher salaries. Those with law degrees earned substantially more than those who held degrees in other fields (Judge, Cable, Boudreau, & Bretz, 1995).

The Role of Power.   We noted that power was an important motivating force for successful executives. Psychologist David McClelland proposed a leadership motive pattern (LMP) that is informally described as "empire building." Executives with a high LMP are believed to be effective managers. They have a high need for power, a lower need for affiliation with other people, and a great amount of self-control. They have a greater need to influence people than to be liked (McClelland, 1975).

Longitudinal studies of managers at 8- and 16-year intervals after their LMPs were first measured showed that this personality pattern was highly predictive of success for managers in nontechnical jobs. The managers' need for achievement (the need to perform well) also predicted success in nontechnical jobs. However, the LMP characteristics were not found in successful managers in technical and engineering jobs. Managers high in the LMP appear to prefer jobs that are high in prestige and status (McClelland & Boyatzis, 1982).

Self-Promotion. People who are good at promoting themselves, so that they acquire the support or sponsorship of their superiors, are often the ones more likely to advance within the corporate hierarchy. This was demonstrated in a study of mentoring. A mentor is a coach or counselor who provides support and advice to a younger protégé. Those fortunate enough to have had good mentors were shown to be far more likely to receive pay increases and promotions, compared to those who had no mentors (Scandura, 1992).

Survey data collected from 147 college graduates during their early years of employment showed that employees themselves can influence the amount of mentoring they receive. Specifically, people high in internal control, emotional stability, and self-monitoring (the ability to be sensitive to social cues so that they can alter their behaviors to fit various situations) were much more likely to initiate a mentoring relationship with a senior manager. The data also confirmed the positive relationship between mentoring and career achievement (Turban & Dougherty, 1994).

The factor of self-monitoring was involved in a study investigating the first 5 years on the job for 139 MBA graduates. Those who scored high on a questionnaire to measure self-monitoring answered yes to such questions as "How can I become the kind of person this situation requires?" High-scorers were found to be changeable and flexible, adapting themselves to any environment. Low-scorers maintained more consistent and stable attitudes, values, and behaviors, often refusing to change to fit the demands of changing situations or different supervisors. High self-monitors advanced further in the company than low self-monitors (Kilduff & Day, 1994).

Stability of Managerial Characteristics. I/O psychologists have investigated whether the characteristics of successful managers are stable over a manager's working career or whether they vary with age and rank. A longitudinal study of these issues began at AT&T in 1956 as the Management Progress Study, designed to determine and analyze personal characteristics as managers progressed through their careers (Bray, 1964, 1982; Howard & Bray, 1988).

The primary means of studying the AT&T managers was the assessment-center technique. Managers and their superiors were also interviewed extensively. The findings suggested that managerial success is highly predictable and is based on the following factors:

1. Administrative skills
2. Leadership skills
3. Advancement orientation
4. Cognitive ability
5. Stability of performance
6. Work motivation
7. Independence of others

Six personality variables were identified as being highly related to job success: leadership motivation, ambition, impulsivity, affability, self-esteem, and optimism. "The most promising managers are those who want to lead and advance, who reject dependency on others, who are self-confident and optimistic, energetic, and work-oriented" (Bray, 1982, p. 186).

Four of the six personality variables were found to change over a 20-year period. Leadership motivation increased, but ambition decreased, a decline related to a similar decline in the factor of advancement orientation. The managers lost interest in further promotions either because they believed they had reached a satisfactory level or because they knew they were unlikely to receive additional promotions. However, they remained interested in managing and in achieving on the job. Among the other personality variables, affability declined and impulsivity rose. The managers also appeared to become more cynical and selfish. Self-esteem and optimism remained unchanged; these variables correlated positively with job and life satisfaction.

The Management Progress Study is following these managers to retirement. This research program is a monumental and all-too-rare undertaking that has provided considerable practical benefits to the organization. It has contributed to our understanding of the nature of leadership.

Unsuccessful Executives.   It is just as important for organizations to know what characteristics lead some managers to fail as it is to understand what makes others succeed. Such failure is usually referred to as derailment, such as when a train unexpectedly leaves the track.

In an analysis of executives who once showed management potential but who were later dismissed or retired early, it was found that the primary explanation for their derailment was related to personality factors rather than job performance. The failed executives were judged by their superiors to lack consideration behaviors. Insensitive, arrogant, and aloof, they displayed an abrasive and domineering leadership style and were overly ambitious to attain personal rather than organizational goals (McCall & Lombardo, 1983).

These findings have been supported by considerable research: Executive failure is related to personality factors. Interviews with 20 senior executives from U.S. companies and 42 senior executives from European companies revealed that the major reason for executive derailment was poor interpersonal relations—that is, an inability to get along with other people (Van Velsor & Leslie, 1995).

A review of derailment research described the failed executive in the following terms:

> Many managers who are bright, hardworking, ambitious, and technically competent fail (or are in danger of failing) because they are perceived as arrogant, vindictive, untrustworthy, selfish, emotional, compulsive, over-controlling, insensitive, abrasive, aloof, too ambitious, or unable to delegate or make decisions (Hogan, Curphy, & Hogan, 1994, p. 499).

MANAGEMENT TEAMS

In large organizations, management functions are increasingly being performed by groups of managers rather than a single manager. I/O psychologists are studying the composition and effectiveness of these management teams under different corporate conditions.

An analysis of 87 Fortune 500 companies found that firms that underwent changes in diversification strategy over a 3-year period to respond to market changes had management teams that showed similar characteristics. The team executives were younger, had been with the company a shorter time, had a higher educational level and training in the sciences, and had been team members longer than had executives in companies that underwent less change. The responsive teams were more receptive to change, more willing to take risks, and more creative in their decision making. The result was that their companies became more successful and diversified (Wiersema & Bantel, 1992).

Another study compared top management teams in different kinds of organizations, specifically, 26 computer firms and 21 natural gas distribution companies (Haleblian & Finkelstein, 1993). Successful computer companies were found to be dynamic, constantly changing and growing, adaptable and responsive to fluctuating market conditions. Their corporate climate is considered to be turbulent because of the constant pressures under which their management teams must function. In contrast, natural gas distribution companies are highly regulated, stable, relatively unchanging, and operating under fairly constant market conditions; therefore, they may be described as nonturbulent. We would expect such different corporate environments to require different types of management teams.

The results of the study showed that large management teams and teams with less dominant CEOs were far more effective in the turbulent computer industry environment than in the more stable, nonturbulent natural gas company environment. The latter situation was found to be so stable and regulated that there was little discretion available to the management teams and they had little effect on their environment.

Turnover in management teams is a problem that threatens their continuity and stability. Studies of organizational turnover in the United States and in Japan have found that demographic characteristics are a greater factor in turnover in Japan than in the U.S. (Wiersema & Bantel, 1993; Wiersema & Bird, 1993). Greater heterogeneity of age, team tenure, and prestige of university attended were significantly related to turnover on Japanese management teams but not on American management teams.

Another problem for management teams relates to self-limiting behaviors in decision making; that is, a tendency for people on management teams to deliberately limit their involvement. Individual self-limiting behaviors reduce the decision-making capability of the team as a whole because not all members will be committed to participation in the process.

A survey of 569 managers revealed that they limited their input in more than half of the teams in which they participated (Mulvey, Veiga, & Elsass, 1996). Their reasons for limiting their behavior are shown in Table 7–2. In addition, self-limiting behaviors were found to increase with group size. It should be disturbing

TABLE 7–2   Reasons for Self-Limiting Behavior

	Frequency (percent)
The presence of someone with expertise	73%
The presentation of a compelling argument	62
Lack of confidence in one's ability	61
An unimportant or meaningless decision	52
Pressure from others to conform to the team's decision	46

Adapted from "When Teammates Raise a White Flag" by P. W. Mulvey, J. F. Veiga, & P. M. Elsass, 1966, *Academy of Management Executive, 10*(1), p. 44.

to top executives to realize how often their managers are failing to participate in decision making, thus reducing their ability to offer dynamic leadership.

PRESSURES AND PROBLEMS OF LEADERSHIP

Just as leader characteristics vary with a manager's level in the organizational hierarchy, so do the pressures and problems.

First-Line Supervisors

In some ways, supervisors have more difficult jobs than executives, yet they receive less formal training in how to manage other people. In fact, supervisors may receive no training at all, and they are not selected as carefully as people who enter higher-level management positions. Often, the most competent workers are selected to be supervisors, without any assessment of their leadership potential.

Supervisors promoted from the ranks face conflicting demands and loyalties. Before promotion, they were accepted by those who worked with them and shared their attitudes and values, and they may have socialized with co-workers off the job. Their work group gave them a sense of identity and belonging that provided a measure of emotional security. After they become supervisors, they can no longer enjoy the same relationship with co-workers and friends. Even if they try to remain part of the group, their former co-workers do not react to them in the same way because of the changed relationship. This costs newly promoted supervisors the emotional security that comes from group affiliation and identification.

Supervisors are the point of contact between management and workers, trying to weigh the conflicting needs of both sides. If supervisors expect to establish and retain the loyalty and cooperation of their workers, they must present management's needs and decisions to the workers and must present the workers' needs to management, serving as a buffer and an open channel of communication. In practice, it is often necessary for supervisors to be more responsive to the demands of their superiors if they hope to keep their jobs. A study of 160 first-line supervisors in a pharmaceutical plant showed that pressure from higher management to exercise strict supervision over employees resulted in harsh and punitive supervisory behavior (Hammer & Turk, 1987).

The trend toward greater worker participation in industry complicates the job of first-line supervisors. They stand to lose what little autonomy they have by being forced to share leadership and decision-making power with subordinates. **Self-managing work groups** are another threat to supervisory power and autonomy. In these programs, instead of sharing power, supervisors must abandon their traditional responsibilities and act as resource persons rather than leaders. If the work groups are less effective than expected, the supervisor will be blamed. If the work groups are effective, top management usually attributes the favorable results to the workers, not to the supervisor.

Computer technology in the workplace has made supervision more difficult. First-line supervisors are responsible for hardware they often are not trained to understand. Computers can control and monitor quantity and quality of production and provide top management with data on employee performance, output,

Self-managing work groups Employee groups that allow the members of a work team to manage, control, and monitor all facets of their work, from recruiting, hiring, and training new employees to deciding when to take rest breaks.

and other aspects of office or manufacturing processes, thus bypassing any input from the first-line supervisor.

Managers and Executives

A department or section head faces stresses that are different from those of the CEO. Middle-level managers, despite comfortable salaries and fringe benefits, typically express considerable discontent. A frequent complaint is the lack of influence in formulating company policy, policy they are expected to implement without question. Middle managers also complain about having insufficient authority and resources to carry out company policy. They must fight for recognition from superiors and compete for support for their ideas and projects. As a result, middle managers often experience considerable frustration as they vie for the few top management slots in the hierarchy.

Another source of dissatisfaction is the feeling of obsolescence that comes to characterize middle-level managers in their late thirties and early forties. Most of them have reached a plateau and will receive no additional promotions. That realization often becomes part of a general midlife crisis, a period of self-examination for middle managers who feel threatened by younger subordinates, by changing values, and by redefined organizational goals. Their productivity, creativity, and motivation may decline, and they may in effect retire on the job, making little further contribution to the organization. A survey of 3,000 managers in their forties found that most expressed eagerness to learn new skills and undertake new assignments but felt denied the chance to do so. Fully 45% reported that they had received no training opportunities in the previous 5 years, and 36% believed they faced age barriers to future promotions (Lewis & McLaverty, 1991).

The trend toward employee participation is a source of stress for middle managers. Although they have no influence in decisions affecting their own jobs, they see that assembly-line, production, and office workers have gained the right to participate in decision making and job design. Participatory democracy leads to drastic changes in the ways managers can exert control over their employees. Shared leadership results in a loss of managerial authority, status, and power. Democratization may also eliminate traditional management perquisites, such as reserved parking spaces, corporate dining rooms, and private offices.

Because of the corporate mergers, acquisitions, and buyouts, as well as the competitiveness of the world economy and the changes in the nature of work, several million middle-management jobs have been lost over the last decade. These massive layoffs have created a motivational crisis among middle-level managers. Seeing that their companies were less loyal and supportive of co-workers than they had expected, they may feel less organizational commitment in return. The layoffs also mean fewer opportunities for promotion and more competition for the available positions. Since 1980, the time between promotions for even the most promising managers has doubled, and the chances for salary increases have diminished. It is not surprising that a survey of 700 managers reported that 70% were dissatisfied (Northcraft, Griffith, & Shalley, 1992).

A source of stress more common among high-level managers is the intense commitment of time and energy to the organization. It is not uncommon for executives to work 60-hour weeks and to bring work home for evenings and weekends. With portable electronic equipment, such as cell phones, beepers, laptop computers, and fax machines, executives can work at home and while traveling, rarely escaping the demands of the office.

A study of 30 CEOs of major corporations found that their extensive organizational commitment and job involvement resulted in an imbalance in their personal lives, leaving little time for their families. When questioned, 60% said they desired a greater balance between work and family life (Piotrowski & Armstrong, 1989). This finding was confirmed in a later survey of 1,309 male executives, which revealed that their average level of work-family conflict was substantially higher than for lower-level employees (Judge, Boudreau, & Bretz, 1994).

The potential rewards of an executive position—power, money, status, challenge, and fulfillment—are great, but so are the demands. Still, there are more positive aspects to life at the top of the organizational hierarchy. Although middle managers are not a particularly happy group, top executives report great job satisfaction. Surveys show that most upper-level executives would remain on the job even if they were financially independent. Their work provides much more than financial satisfaction.

WOMEN IN MANAGEMENT

The number of women currently in management jobs has risen from 24% to over 40% in the last decade. However, most of these jobs are at entry and middle-management levels. Only 5% of women employed outside the home hold senior management jobs. Further, only half of the large corporations in the United States include women on their boards of directors. And of course, at all levels of management, women tend to be paid less than men for the same work.

I/O psychology research on women in the workforce shows consistently that the continuing underrepresentation of women in higher-level management jobs has several consequences: increased performance pressures on women, isolation from the informal social networks available to men, lack of role models and fe-

NEWSBREAK #12

Women in the Workplace: Less Pay for the Same Job

Lisa Sutton is a 32-year-old manager for a large utility company and is in charge of a group of 50 subordinates. She earned her MBA degree 6 years ago and has been with the company 3 1/2 years. She works hard, often coming into the office on Saturdays to catch up on paperwork. Her boss thinks she does a great job and gave her top ratings in every category in her last performance appraisal.

Just down the hall, Bob Taylor, also 32, manages another department of 50 people. Thus, Bob and Lisa are at the same level in the company hierarchy. He received his MBA 6 years ago and joined the company the same month she did. He works just as hard and his performance ratings are also excellent.

Lisa and Bob are among the best midlevel managers the firm has, and they are both on the fast track for promotion. They are equal in almost all things, including the size of their offices. There is only one important difference: Bob's salary is $42,000 a year; Lisa's is $36,000.

Unfair? You bet! Unusual? Not at all. Women typically are paid less, regardless of the type of employer, level of education, or job performance ratings. Take a look at your own college. According to a *Working Woman* magazine survey, the average annual salary for men college deans is $126,000; for women deans it is $104,000. Men employed as hospital managers average $44,000, women $30,000. A study of attorneys in Colorado found that women lawyers with 10 years' experience earned approximately $68,500 a year; men with comparable experience earned $90,500. And so it goes.

According to the U.S. Bureau of Labor Statistics, women earn about 74 cents for every dollar earned by a man. Women corporate vice presidents (and there aren't many of those) earned 42% less than men at the same level. Women graduates of the top business schools earn 12% less than men with the same academic record. A study of 205 MBA graduates found no differences between men and women in their propensity or ability to negotiate for a higher starting salary, but men still received higher offers.

So, women begin their working careers at lower starting salaries, and most of them never catch up. A comparison of 1,029 men and women managers at 20 large companies found that salary increases for women were slower than for men, despite similar educational achievements, work backgrounds, and a willingness to transfer geographically in order to accept a promotion.

There are a few signs of change, particularly in engineering and computer companies. In 1995, a woman engineer with 5 years on the job earned an average annual salary of $49,100. A man in the same job was paid $50,000. Although there is still a difference, the gender gap in salary is beginning to narrow, at least in some fields. Of course, the remaining disparity shows that the day of equal pay for equal work is a long way off for the majority of working women. And who knows, maybe by then they will not have to also cope with discrimination in hiring and promotion, being excluded from the "old boy" networks of power, and sexual harassment on the job. But that's another story. Women have come a long way in the workplace, but they still have a long way to go to achieve full equality.

Sources: Women still face bias as lawyers, report says. *St. Petersburg [FL] Times,* January 9, 1996. Women still suffer wage gap, poll says. *St. Petersburg [FL] Times,* January 16, 1996.

male mentors, and sex stereotyping. We deal in this section with some of the factors that differentially affect women in management.

Women managers are often stopped in their career progress by the so-called glass ceiling, an impenetrable barrier that allows them to view the rewards and responsibilities of upper management but prevents them from advancing to it.

Women managers are often restricted to staff jobs in departments such as human resources and public relations.

One of the few organizations to shatter the glass ceiling is the federal government. An analysis of promotion decisions by the Senior Executive Service in a cabinet-level department found that women had an advantage because of the federal commitment to equal employment opportunities (Powell & Butterfield, 1994). However, this commitment to hiring women for senior positions is not nearly as widespread in the private sector. There, many women managers are restricted to staff jobs in departments that are low in status, such as human resources, public relations, and consumer affairs, instead of line jobs in more powerful departments such as engineering, manufacturing, and marketing.

A similar segregation is seen even for women at the top, those who do serve on corporate boards of directors. An analysis of 1,940 men and 175 women directors for 133 companies showed such differences in the ways committee assignments were made. Men were far more likely to be selected for the powerful compensation, executive, and finance committees, whereas women were far more likely to be chosen for the less powerful public affairs committee (Billimoria & Piderit, 1994). Work in areas such as public affairs, public relations, and human resources at any level is seen as requiring more social sensitivity and human relations skills than general leadership abilities, and they represent a sort of velvet ghetto for women managers. A study of 338 men managers over a 10-year period showed that the power of the department in which they entered the company influenced their promotion and salary progress. Those who started their career in a powerful department tended to advance more rapidly than those who started in a less powerful department (Sheridan, Slocum, Buda, & Thompson, 1990).

A common sex stereotype is being applied here—discrimination against women managers by keeping them in jobs that require so-called feminine attributes such as empathy and sensitivity. So-called masculine attributes, such as aggressiveness, ambition, and self-reliance, are seen as more suited to line jobs in manufacturing and sales. It is the line departments that are the stepping-stones to top management. When women do succeed on the job, their superiors (usually men) are likely to attribute that success to luck or other external conditions, not to personal ability. When men succeed, it is usually attributed to personal ability.

Women managers are assessed differently from men managers on their leadership behaviors. When men and women managers display assertiveness, women are typically judged as pushy. These judgments are made by women as well as by men. A woman lawyer wrote:

> There's nothing men hate more—especially men in power—than a woman who is [too much] like a man. It's a very negative thing. There was a very well-qualified woman who interviewed at our firm for a position. She had years of experience in the exact practice area that we were recruiting for, but when she showed up at the doorstep . . . people hated her. Men and women alike said, "She's too mannish." . . . She didn't get the job (Ely, 1995, p. 617).

This attitude was confirmed in a meta-analysis of 61 leadership studies that found that women were negatively evaluated by both men and women when they exhibited so-called masculine, autocratic leadership characteristics. However, the men exhibited a stronger tendency to make such evaluations (Eagly, Makhijani, & Klonsky, 1992).

Men managers expect women managers to be assertive but will tolerate that assertiveness only up to a point. They expect women managers to take risks but always be outstanding, to be tough and ambitious but not "masculine," and to take responsibility but follow the advice of others. In other words, women managers are expected to perform better than men managers, but they should not expect better, or even equal, treatment. The higher the management position in the corporate hierarchy, the more traditionally masculine characteristics managers of both sexes are expected to display (Fagenson, 1990).

A meta-analysis of 96 studies of leader effectiveness found that men and women leaders were rated as equally effective in laboratory studies and in research conducted on the job. However, these ratings differed by gender when the jobs were judged to required different abilities. For example, women were rated as more effective leaders in situations that required the ability to cooperate and get along with other people. Men were rated more effective in situations requiring the ability to direct and control subordinates. Despite these differences, in general, men and women leaders were rated equally effective (Eagly, Karau, & Makhijani, 1995).

A comparison of 100 women managers and 270 men managers on personality and interest variables showed that women were more autonomous and understanding. These were the only sex differences found (Hatcher, 1991). A review of research on managerial effectiveness found no sex differences on subordinates' ratings of men and women managers and in task-oriented and people-oriented behaviors of managers (Powell, 1990).

Men and women managers performed similarly on assessment-center exercises, demonstrating the ability to lead, influence, and motivate subordinates.

They showed equal levels of the leadership functions of consideration and initiating structure, and they attained similar performance appraisal ratings. Although ratings of leadership effectiveness were found to differ in laboratory studies (men scored higher), no differences in effectiveness ratings were found in research conducted on the job (Dobbins & Platz, 1986).

Other research on men and women managers in various industries reported less assertiveness on the part of women managers, along with a higher drive to succeed. No sex differences were found in job performance. Women were rated high by men in three so-called masculine areas: decision making, controlling emotions, and the ability to withstand criticism. The researchers suggested that women may be making extra efforts on the job to behave in ways that dispel feminine stereotypes. The men surveyed believed that women managers brought new insights and viewpoints to management problems (Ottaway & Bhatnagar, 1988).

Some laboratory and on-the-job research indicates that the style of leadership practiced by women is more democratic and participative than that shown by men. A survey of the second generation of women managers suggests that they may develop a unique leadership style called interactive leadership; it involves actively promoting interactions with subordinates in a positive way. Interactive leadership encourages employee participation and the sharing of information and power. Interactive leaders energize their subordinates and enhance their sense of self-worth. Researchers suggest that women are practicing transformational leadership, whereas men are displaying transactional leadership (Eagly & Johnson, 1990).

Ratings of 582 men and 219 women managers in the top three management ranks at six Fortune 500 companies showed that women were rated significantly higher than men on charisma, being inspirational, and showing individual consideration, all aspects of transformational leadership. The women were also rated by both male and female subordinates as more effective in their jobs than the men managers, and as more satisfying to work for (Bass & Avolio, 1994).

Job satisfaction is higher for women executives than for women in middle- and lower-level management positions. Overall, women managers report greater job satisfaction than do women employees in nonmanagerial positions. Job satisfaction among women managers is not diminished by the fact that most of them believe they have been discriminated against and must work harder than men to achieve the same level of success. Women managers may make a more intense commitment to their careers than men managers. The AT&T Management Continuity Study found that women managers were higher in positiveness, affability, poise, flexibility, and self-confidence (Howard & Bray, 1988).

Contrary to expectations, studies of women managers have also found that they experienced the same frequency of mentoring from higher-level managers as did men managers. This equal access to mentors, who are vital in assisting upward mobility in an organization, was also found in a group of professional women in research and development organizations (Dreher & Ash, 1990; Ragins & Cotton, 1991). These findings suggest that women are achieving some degree of acceptance from top management.

In addition to receiving mentoring, higher-level women managers are also willing to provide mentoring for younger women managers. A comparison of 80 men and 80 women managers found no significant differences in their willingness to be mentors (Ragins & Scandura, 1994).

Other developmental activities are less open to women managers. Comparisons of men and women managers consistently show that both formal training programs and on-the-job growth experiences (such as high-profile, challenging assignments that increase one's visibility to senior management) are less available to women. Also, women managers appear to receive considerably less encouragement from superiors than men managers at the same level (Ohlott, Ruderman, & McCauley, 1994; Stroh, Brett, & Reilly, 1992; Tharenou, Latimer, & Conroy, 1994).

Women employees at all levels face the problem of sexual harassment, ranging from suggestive comments and lewd jokes to actual physical assault. In 1995, the Equal Opportunity Employment Commission (EEOC) received more than 15,000 complaints of sexual harassment, more than twice the number received in 1991. Surveys show that women employees subjected to repeated harassment have a higher incidence of eating disorders, a fear of men, and a greater anxiety about coping with new situations (DeAngelis, 1991).

Other research suggests that employees most subject to sexual harassment on the job are younger women in low-level jobs, single or divorced, who work in a predominantly male environment or for a male supervisor. The most frequent harassers are immediate co-workers. The most frequently reported harassment is verbal abuse (Lengnick-Hall, 1995).

Federal law requires organizations to develop policies to prevent sexual harassment. For example, AT&T and Du Pont deal aggressively with sexual harassment and make it clear by their policies and actions that the practice will not be tolerated. Du Pont provides a telephone hotline so that employees can report anonymously any incidents of harassment. The company also offers a training program on preventing sexual harassment.

Some women managers become discouraged by their lack of progress and opportunity relative to that of men managers and decide to leave the corporate world. By 1994, some 4 million U.S. women had started their own companies. In the 1980s, five times as many women as men left organizational life to start their own businesses. A comparison of the reasons given by men and women managers for quitting their jobs found that women were far more likely than men to leave because they believed their expectations for their work had not been met (Rosin & Kobarik, 1995). Other research has shown that both men and women entrepreneurs had negative experiences working for other people, which motivated them to become self-employed (Powell, 1993). However, even working for themselves, women face discrimination. Women-owned businesses tend to operate in certain occupational categories, notably retail sales, education, and personal services. Women entrepreneurs tend to be as successful as men entrepreneurs. A study of 411 small businesses over a 3-year period found that 16% of the firms owned by men failed, compared to 15% of the firms owned by women (Kalleberg & Leicht, 1991).

MINORITY EMPLOYEES IN MANAGEMENT

Although minority employees have access to management positions in increasing numbers, they face stereotypes, prejudice, and unique problems and challenges. Like women managers, black and other minority managers meet a glass ceiling that effectively bars them from attaining top management jobs. That ceiling may be lower for minorities than for women. Most minority employees in management are black; few are Hispanic or Asian-American. Virtually all of the I/O psychology research on minority personnel in management jobs has studied black subjects.

Blacks must usually work harder than whites to prove themselves, and their job performance may be evaluated more stringently. They may find that white employees resent their presence, believing they were hired or promoted with fewer qualifications in order to meet equal employment opportunity requirements. Racist attitudes openly expressed can make everyday interactions with superiors, co-workers, and subordinates unpleasant. Some minority managers quit in frustration. Corning Glass found that black managers were leaving the company at three times the rate of white managers. Monsanto Chemical reported that the major reasons black managers gave for quitting were problems with superiors, a sense of not belonging, and a lack of challenge.

A study of 828 managers in communications, banking, and electronics found that black managers felt less accepted than white managers. Black managers believed that they had less discretion in their jobs and that they received lower ratings on job performance and promotability. They reported lower job satisfaction and were more likely to have reached career plateaus. It is important to note that, although these differences favor white managers, the size of the difference on each factor was modest and no racial differences were found in sponsorship or mentoring activities (Greenhaus, Parasuraman, & Wormley, 1990).

Later research contradicted this finding on racial differences in mentoring. A survey of 1,018 managers who received MBA degrees around 1982 found that black and Hispanic managers were significantly less likely to have established mentoring relationships with white managers than their white colleagues. Those who did not have white male mentors earned significantly less than those who did have such mentors (Dreher & Cox, 1996).

Results of the AT&T Management Continuity Study showed that black managers scored lower than white managers on characteristics such as positiveness, impulsivity, poise, and flexibility. Blacks scored higher on affability and motivation for advancement (Howard & Bray, 1988).

A study of 63 middle-level managers (46 whites, 12 blacks, 3 Hispanics, 2 Asian-Americans) found that nonwhites who had the highest potential for promotion made more social and work-related contacts outside their ethnic groups (Ibarra, 1995).

Conflict may arise when a black manager is promoted over an equally qualified white manager. The common reaction of those passed over for promotion is that the black person was given the job on the basis of race. This attitude can create hostility on both sides. Black managers may also have difficulties dealing with other minority employees. Hispanic Americans and Asian Americans often believe that blacks receive preferential treatment. This perception presents problems when black managers must conduct performance appraisals of subordinates. Minority employees of all races expect black managers to be more lenient than white managers. Black managers may be pressured by black subordinates to give them special consideration or overlook poor job performance. Any perceived display of favoritism on the part of a manager can create animosity, which, in turn, can affect the work group's performance.

As we noted in Chapter 6, many companies offer workplace diversity training, programs designed to reduce discrimination and prejudice on the job and to teach employees of all races to display greater sensitivity to the needs, values, and concerns of all groups.

Leader Expectations for Women Workers

Leaders who expect more from their subordinates tend to be rewarded with better performance, whereas leaders who expect less tend to get less. This example of a self-fulfilling prophecy, called the Pygmalion effect, has been demonstrated in classroom situations and in the workplace. When teachers or managers are told that some of their students or employees are exceptionally talented or qualified, they develop higher expectations for the performance of these subordinates and communicate their expectations, often unconsciously, in subtle ways. They may give the "better" students more opportunities to speak out in class or allow the "better" employees to assume greater responsibility. The results are often just what the leaders expected—superior performance from subordinates believed to be superior.

However, as we saw earlier, the Pygmalion effect does not seem to apply to adult women in training programs. That was confirmed by two studies conducted in the Israeli Defense Force. One group of army trainees consisted of female officer cadets led by female squad leaders. Another group consisted of male trainees led by men, women trainees led by men, and women trainees led by women. The last mixture is the same as in the first study. There were no groups in which men were led by women.

The experimental procedure was the same for all groups. Squads were randomly assigned to the Pygmalion condition or the control condition. All trainees were 18- to 20-year-old high school graduates, and all had been selected because they had shown in previous training and on psychological tests a high aptitude for leadership. Thus, they were assumed to be equally qualified.

To confirm that the leaders' expectations in the Pygmalion groups were raised, squad leaders rated the command potential (CP) of each cadet in their squad on a 9-point scale. These ratings were made during the first, fourth, and sixth weeks of the 7-week officer training course. The trainees' level of performance in the training program was assessed by multiple-choice tests.

Before the squad leaders in the Pygmalion condition met their trainees, they were told that on the basis of aptitude and ability tests, as well as ratings by previous commanders, their trainees had a much higher-than-normal command potential. As a result, so the leaders were informed, they could expect a better-than-average level of achievement from their cadets.

The results showed that the Pygmalion manipulation was effective. Squad leaders in the Pygmalion condition rated the CP of their trainees significantly higher than did squad leaders in the control condition. Results also showed that when the squad leader was a man, a significant Pygmalion effect was produced in every case, whether the trainee was male or female. When the squad leader was a woman, however, no Pygmalion effect occurred. The expectations of the women leaders had been raised by the Pygmalion instructions, but those expectations did not translate into increased performance on the part of their trainees. Thus, the Pygmalion effect was produced in women trainees, but it could not be brought about by women leaders.

Critical Thinking Questions

1. Why do you think the Pygmalion effect was not produced by women leaders in this study? Can you suggest additional instructions or other forms of manipulation that might result in the Pygmalion effect being produced by women leaders?

2. What factors other than those described in this study might account for the Pygmalion effect?

3. What ethical and moral considerations are involved in applying the Pygmalion effect in the workplace? What are the practical objections to its use?

Source: Dvir, T., Eden, D., & Banjo, M. L. (1995). Self-fulfilling prophecy and gender: Can women be Pygmalion and Galatea? Journal of Applied Psychology, 80, 253–270. [16]

4. How might leader expectations of the performance of ethnic minority employees affect productivity and job satisfaction?

5. If research has shown that the Pygmalion effect is effective in increasing job performance, then why has it not been applied more widely?

SUMMARY

The **scientific management** philosophy was concerned solely with production and was replaced in the 1920s and 1930s by the **human relations approach,** concerned with satisfying the personal growth needs of employees as well as maintaining production. McGregor's **Theory X** holds that people dislike work and need strong, directive, and punitive leadership. **Theory Y** holds that people are creative, industrious, and responsible, and function best under leaders who allow them to participate in decisions that affect their work.

Contingency theory suggests that leader effectiveness is determined by the interaction between the leader's personal characteristics and aspects of the situation. **Cognitive resource theory** focuses on leaders' cognitive abilities—intelligence, technical competence, and job-related knowledge. **Path-goal theory** emphasizes the leadership behaviors that allow subordinates to achieve their goals. **Normative decision theory** deals with the extent to which leaders allow subordinates to participate in making decisions. **Leader-member exchange** is concerned with ways in which leaders behave toward subordinates.

Authoritarian and **democratic leaders** differ in the degree of participation they extend to subordinates. **Transactional leaders** are constrained by their followers' expectations. **Transformational leaders** inspire subordinates and redirect their behavior through personal charisma, intellectual stimulation, and consideration.

Leaders may display reward, coercive, legitimate, referent, or expert power. Through the **Pygmalion** and **Golem effects,** leaders' expectations can affect their subordinates' behavior in a kind of self-fulfilling prophecy. Leadership functions may be grouped into two categories: **consideration** and **initiating structure.** Consideration behaviors are concerned with subordinates' personal feelings. Initiating structure behaviors are concerned with achieving organizational productivity goals.

Leadership characteristics vary with the level of leadership; the higher the level, the fewer consideration functions and the more initiating structure functions are required. Successful first- line supervisors are person-centered, supportive, and loyal to the company and to subordinates. They exercise a democratic supervisory style. Effective executives need decision-making and technical skills more than they need human relations skills. Self-promotion behaviors influence the amount of mentoring managers receive from their superiors. Self-monitoring behaviors result in higher promotion rates. Derailment (executive failure) is related more to personality factors than job performance.

Management teams have problems with turnover and self-limiting behavior in decision making. Other leadership problems also vary with level. First-line supervisors may be poorly trained in supervisory skills and face conflicts between organizational demands and demands of subordinates. Participative management, **self-managing work groups,** and computer technology are stressful for supervisors. Middle managers have lost authority because of participative management and may find themselves obsolete at midcareer. Executives face long working hours yet show greater job satisfaction than do persons at lower levels of leadership.

Women managers are often restricted to staff jobs and low-status departments because of sexist stereotypes; the glass ceiling is often a barrier to promotion. Black managers face similar problems of stereotyping and discrimination and may have difficulties dealing with white and other minority subordinates.

KEY TERMS

authoritarian leadership
bureaucracy
charismatic leadership
cognitive resource theory
consideration functions
contingency theory
democratic leadership
Golem effect
human relations approach
initiating structure functions

leader-member exchange
normative decision theory
organizational psychology
path-goal theory
Pygmalion effect
scientific management
self-managing work groups
Theory X/Theory Y
transactional leadership
transformational leadership

ADDITIONAL READING

Chemers, M. M., & Ayman, R. (Eds.). (1993). *Leadership theory and research: Perspectives and directions.* San Diego, CA: Academic Press. Discusses research and theory on leadership issues including teamwork, ethical accountability, gender and cultural diversity, responses to stress, follower commitment, and decision-making.

Heckscher, C. (1995). *White-collar blues: Management loyalties in an age of corporate restructuring.* New York: Basic Books. Explores changes in leadership structure and functioning resulting from downsizing, layoffs, and corporate re-engineering. Based on interviews with more than 250 middle managers from 14 major manufacturing organizations

Hogan, R., Curphy, G. J., & Hogan, J. (1994). What we know about leadership: Effectiveness and personality. *American Psychologist, 49,* 493–504. Presents a definition of leadership and discusses the major practical decisions to be made about appointing, evaluating, and terminating leaders.

Kanigel, R. (1997). *The one best way: Frederick Winslow Taylor and the enigma of efficiency.* New York: Viking. A biography of Taylor (1856–1915), who promoted the management philosophy called scientific management, which depicted workers as extensions of the industrial machinery they were hired to operate.

Powell, G. N. (1993). *Women and men in management.* Newbury Park, CA: Sage. A literature review covering the working relationships between men and women at the management level. Discusses the link between gender stereotypes instilled in childhood and subsequent adult attitudes and behavior toward colleagues of the opposite sex.

CHAPTER 8

Motivation, Job Satisfaction, and Job Involvement

CHAPTER OUTLINE

■　　■　　■　　■

One of the most pressing problems facing organizations today is how to motivate employees to work more productively and to increase their feelings of satisfaction, involvement, and commitment. All around us we see examples of shoddy and imperfect work in products such as automobiles with faulty parts or in careless mistakes made in government offices. Manufacturers, retail stores, and service industries echo the complaint. Too many employees do not seem to care about doing a good job.

Organizations have made tremendous strides in applying the findings of I/O psychology to recruit, select, and train their workers and to provide effective leadership. But none of these functions can improve the quality of the work being performed if employees are not motivated to do the best job possible.

The study of motivation is of concern to you for two reasons. First, as a consumer, you are often the victim of dissatisfied workers who produce faulty products or who process your requests improperly. Second, and more important, is the fact that you will likely spend one third to one half of your waking hours at work for 40 to 45 years. That is a long time to be frustrated, dissatisfied, and unhappy, especially since these feelings will carry over to your family and social life and affect your physical and emotional health.

I/O psychology theory and research on motivation, job satisfaction, job involvement, and organizational commitment offer options for making your work life satisfying and fulfilling instead of dull and disappointing.

THEORIES OF MOTIVATION

I/O psychologists have proposed various theories to explain **motivation**—why people behave as they do on the job. Some of these theories emphasize the impact of factors in the workplace. Other theories focus on personal characteristics of the employees. The theories have stimulated a great deal of research and have spawned a number of techniques to modify work behavior.

Motivation Workplace factors and personal characteristics that explain why people behave the way they do on the job.

We discuss here two types of motivation theories: content theories and process theories. Content theories focus on the importance of the work itself and the challenges, growth opportunities, and responsibilities work provides for employees. Thus, these theories deal with the content of motivation, that is, with the specific needs that motivate and direct human behavior. Process theories do not focus directly on the work but rather deal with the cognitive processes we use in making decisions and choices about our work.

CONTENT THEORIES OF MOTIVATION

We describe five content theories: achievement motivation, needs hierarchy, ERG, motivator-hygiene (two-factor), and job-characteristics.

Achievement Motivation Theory

Achievement motivation
McClelland's theory that emphasizes the need to accomplish something, to do a good job, and to be the best.

We described the need for achievement, or **achievement motivation,** as a characteristic of successful executives. This desire to accomplish something, to do a good job, and to be the best typifies many people, not only business leaders. People who have a high degree of the need for achievement derive great satisfaction from working to accomplish some goal and they are motivated to excel in whatever they undertake.

Since the early 1950s, achievement motivation theory has been studied intensively by David McClelland and his colleagues (Atkinson & Feather, 1966; McClelland, Atkinson, Clark, & Lowell, 1953). Their research, conducted in several countries, shows that successful business managers consistently display a high need to achieve. For example, in Poland, which was then a Communist country, the level of concern for achievement was almost as high as in the

People high in the need for achievement are motivated to excel. They derive satisfaction from working hard to accomplish their goals.

United States. McClelland has demonstrated that the economic growth of organizations and of whole societies can be related to the level of the need for achievement among employees and citizens (McClelland, 1961).

McClelland's research identified three major characteristics of people who have a high need to achieve:

1. They favor a work environment in which they are able to assume responsibility for solving problems.
2. They tend to take calculated risks and to set moderate, attainable goals.
3. They need continuing recognition and feedback about their progress so that they know how well they are doing.

Studies have found a high positive correlation between the achievement motivation scores of executives and the financial success of their companies. Research also shows that managers high in the need to achieve have more respect for their subordinates. They are more receptive to new ideas and are more accepting of participative management programs than are managers low in the need to achieve. Later research findings indicate that the need for achievement is positively related to subsequent promotions among middle- and upper-level managers. Also, both men and women entrepreneurs have been found to score significantly higher in the need to achieve than men and women employees who are not entrepreneurs (Langan-Fox & Roth, 1995; McClelland, 1987).

The need for achievement is also important for employees who are not in managerial positions. An investigation of the job behaviors of 141 salespersons working on commission for a retail furniture chain found that their work behavior varied with their level of achievement motivation. Salespersons high in the need to achieve were more effective and were more likely to undertake tasks beyond their formal job duties, tasks that would benefit the organization. For example, they would routinely assist other salespersons and keep display areas tidy. Salespersons low in the need for achievement exhibited more counterproductive behavior, such as lateness, unauthorized breaks, complaints about company policy, and taking sales away from co-workers (Puffer, 1987).

Psychologists studied 268 telephone reservations agents working for an airline, a job that provides little opportunity to satisfy the need for achievement. For employees who scored high in the need to achieve, job performance declined the longer they remained on the job (Helmreich, Sawin, & Carsrud, 1986).

Although not all research supports the achievement motivation theory, the idea provides a plausible explanation for the motivation of some employees. It is considered to have widespread application in the workplace.

Needs Hierarchy Theory

Abraham Maslow, a founder of humanistic psychology, developed the **needs hierarchy theory** of motivation in which human needs are arranged in a hierarchy of importance (Maslow, 1970). According to Maslow, we always want what we do not yet have. Consequently, the needs that we have already satisfied no longer provide any motivation for our behavior and new needs must rise to prominence. Once we have satisfied our lower-level needs, we can pay attention to higher-level needs. The needs, from lowest to highest, are as follows:

Needs hierarchy theory A theory of motivation encompassing physiological, safety, belonging, esteem, and self-actualization needs.

1. Physiological needs: the basic human needs, including food, air, water, and sleep, and the drives for sex and activity
2. Safety needs: the needs for physical shelter and for psychological security and stability
3. Belonging and love needs: the social needs for love, affection, friendship, and affiliation that involve interaction with and acceptance by other people
4. Esteem needs: the needs for self-esteem and for esteem, admiration, and respect from other people
5. Self-actualization need: the need for self-fulfillment, for achieving one's full potential and realizing one's capabilities

These needs should be satisfied in the order presented. People who are hungry or who fear for their physical safety are too busy attempting to satisfy these needs to be concerned about self-esteem or self-fulfillment. In economic recessions, when jobs are scarce, most people are so intent on survival that they cannot attend to higher needs such as self-actualization. However, once we reach a sufficient level of physical and economic security, we can move on; that is, we will be motivated to satisfy the next level of needs.

The belonging needs can be important motivating forces on the job. Workers can develop a social support network and a sense of belonging through interactions with co-workers. Esteem needs can be satisfied by buying a bigger house or car, which contributes to the feeling that we are successful, and through on-the-job rewards such as praise from the boss, an office with a window, or a reserved parking space. To satisfy the **self-actualization need,** employees should be provided with opportunities for growth and responsibility so that they can exercise their abilities to the utmost. A routine and boring job will not satisfy the self-actualization need, no matter how high the salary.

Maslow's theory has received little research support and is judged to have low scientific validity and applicability. Its complexity makes it difficult to test empirically. However, the self-actualization concept became popular with managers and executives who accepted this high-level need as a potent motivating force.

Self-actualization need The need for self-fulfillment, for achieving one's full potential and developing all one's abilities.

ERG Theory

ERG theory A theory of work motivation based on three categories of needs: Existence, Relatedness, and Growth.

Existence needs Physical survival needs, satisfied on the job through pay, fringe benefits, a safe working environment, and job security.

Relatedness needs The needs for social relationships that bring emotional support, respect, and recognition, satisfied on the job by interactions with co-workers and mentors.

Growth needs The needs for personal growth and development, satisfied on the job through the maximum use of our knowledge, skills, and abilities.

Related to Maslow's needs hierarchy theory is the **ERG theory** of work motivation developed by Clayton Alderfer. He proposed three basic needs: Existence needs, Relatedness needs, and Growth needs. These needs encompass the needs proposed by Maslow and they can be satisfied within the work environment (Alderfer, 1972). **Existence needs,** the lowest level of needs, are concerned with physical survival. They include the needs for food, water, shelter, and physical safety. Companies can satisfy these needs through pay, fringe benefits, a safe working environment, and job security. **Relatedness needs** involve interactions with other people and the satisfactions these social relationships bring in terms of emotional support, respect, recognition, and belonging. The relatedness needs can be satisfied on the job by interactions with co-workers and mentors and off the job by family and friends. **Growth needs** focus on the self, such as our need for personal growth and development. These needs can be satisfied by using our skills and abilities to the fullest. Growth needs include Maslow's self-esteem and self-actualization needs. A job can satisfy the growth needs if it involves challenge, autonomy, and creativity.

The ERG needs are not arranged in a hierarchy; all of the needs can influence us at the same time. Therefore, satisfaction of one set of needs does not automatically lead to the emergence of higher needs. However, frustration of the relatedness or growth needs can lead to a reversion to the existence needs. Whereas Maslow believed that a person will persevere to satisfy a need, Alderfer suggested that a person will give up on that need and refocus attention on a more basic need. For example, if employees cannot find emotional support or recognition on the job (the relatedness needs), they may demand higher pay or better health care coverage (existence needs) as compensation for failing to satisfy the other needs.

Maslow suggested that once a need is satisfied, it no longer motivates the individual. By contrast, Alderfer said that satisfying a need may increase its strength. For example, if a job provides a great deal of challenge and creativity, the growth needs might become stronger, leading the employee to seek greater challenges. The ERG theory has an intuitive appeal and it is more directly applicable to employee motivation than the needs hierarchy theory. The ERG theory also has greater empirical support (see, for example, Rauschenberger, Schmitt, & Hunter, 1980; Wanous & Zwany, 1977).

Motivator-Hygiene (Two-Factor) Theory

The **motivator-hygiene,** or two-factor, theory, which deals with both motivation and job satisfaction, was proposed by Frederick Herzberg. The theory has stimulated a great deal of research, although the results have not been consistently supportive. The scientific validity of the theory is low, yet it has led to a redesign of many jobs (Herzberg, 1966, 1974).

According to Herzberg, there are two sets of needs: the motivator needs, which produce job satisfaction, and the hygiene needs, which produce job dissatisfaction. The **motivator needs** (the higher needs) motivate employees to high job performance. Motivator needs are internal to the work itself. They include the nature or content of the job tasks and the person's level of responsibility, achievement, recognition, advancement, and career development and growth. The motivator needs are similar to Maslow's self-actualization need and Alderfer's growth needs. They can be satisfied by stimulating, challenging, and absorbing work. When these conditions are met, job satisfaction will result. However, when these conditions are not met, the result is not necessarily job dissatisfaction.

Job dissatisfaction is produced by the **hygiene needs** (the lower needs). The term *hygiene* relates to the promotion and maintenance of health. Hygiene needs are external to the tasks of a particular job and involve features of the work environment, such as company policy and administration, supervision, interpersonal relations, working conditions, and salary and benefits. When the hygiene needs are not satisfied, the result is job dissatisfaction. However, when the hygiene needs are satisfied, the result is not necessarily job satisfaction, merely an absence of dissatisfaction. The hygiene needs are similar to Maslow's physiological, safety, and belonging needs. Both Maslow and Herzberg insisted that these lower needs be satisfied before a person can be motivated by higher needs.

Herzberg's theory focused attention on the importance of internal job factors as motivating forces for employees. If the motivator needs stimulate employees

Motivator-hygiene theory A two-factor theory to explain motivation and job satisfaction in terms of job tasks and workplace features.

Motivator needs Work characteristics—such as job duties, level of responsibility, and organizational recognition—that motivate employees to maximum job performance.

Hygiene needs Characteristics of the work environment—such as company policy, quality of leadership, and salary—which are external to a job's actual requirements and can lead to job dissatisfaction.

Job enrichment An effort to expand a job to give employees a greater role in planning, performing, and evaluating their work.

to perform at their best and to foster a positive attitude toward the job, then why not redesign the job to maximize opportunities to satisfy motivator needs? This effort, called **job enrichment,** expands jobs to give employees a greater role in planning, performing, and evaluating their work, thus providing an opportunity to satisfy the motivator needs. Herzberg suggested the following ways of enriching a job:

1. Remove some management controls over employees and increase their accountability and responsibility for their work, thus increasing employee autonomy, authority, and freedom.
2. Create complete or natural work units where possible—for example, allow employees to produce a whole unit instead of one component of that unit. This policy increases the likelihood that employees will regard their work as meaningful in the total process.
3. Provide regular and continuous feedback on productivity and job performance directly to employees instead of through their supervisors.
4. Encourage employees to take on new, challenging tasks and to become experts in a particular task or operation.

All these proposals have the goals of increasing personal growth, fulfilling the needs for achievement and responsibility, and providing recognition. Proper job enrichment, therefore, involves more than simply giving the workers more tasks to perform. It means expanding the level of knowledge needed to perform the job. This was demonstrated in a 2-year study of 445 clerical employees in a financial services firm (Campion & McClelland, 1993). Simply enlarging the tasks had negative consequences such as reduced job satisfaction and efficiency as well as increased errors. In contrast, expanding the knowledge needed to perform the job resulted in enhanced job satisfaction and efficiency and fewer errors

NEWSBREAK #13

The Work Ethic: Is That What Drives Us?

On September 8, 1995, a baseball player made history. And he did it by showing up for work. In fact, Cal Ripken, Jr., showed up exactly 2,131 times, every time his team, the Baltimore Orioles, played a major league baseball game. He has never recorded a single absence, and as of this writing, he still hasn't.

The 42,000 fans in the Oriole Park at Camden Yards stadium went wild the night Ripken broke the previous record, held by Lou Gehrig, for the longest streak of consecutive games played. The President of the United States witnessed the historic moment and praised Ripken's "discipline, determination, and constancy." A television reporter summed up the excitement that gripped the nation when he described Ripken as "a paragon of the work ethic."

The *work ethic* is a term we hear a lot, and it's been a guiding rule and way of life for generations of American workers. It drives, pushes, goads, and motivates them to work hard like Cal Ripken—to do the best job they can, to be on time, and to show up for work every day. If you are curious about the great driving force of the 19th and 20th centuries that led to unimaginable heights of industrial, agricultural, and commercial productivity and economic success, then the work ethic is where you should begin. To most progressive economies, work is not a four-letter word.

It wasn't always that way. There was a time when people were not motivated to perform a job well, or even to do it at all. To the ancient Greeks and Romans, there was nothing noble about work. They saw it as a curse of the gods that brutalized the mind and ruined an otherwise good day. The early Hebrews agreed. Work was a punishment from God, although it was also a necessary evil, a way of improving society and atoning for sin.

It was the early Christians who put a more positive spin on work, viewing it as a way to serve God by sharing the proceeds of one's work with people who were less fortunate. Wealth was a means to charity. Work became holy, and idleness sinful.

But it was John Calvin, the 16th-century French Protestant leader, who gave us the ultimate work ethic. Work alone pleases God, he declared, but to achieve that end, work must be methodical and disciplined. "Not leisure and enjoyment but only activity serves to increase the glory of God."

To Calvin, and others who refined what came to be called the Protestant work ethic, work was an "emblem of faith." And so was wealth. It was OK to make a lot of money and not feel guilty about it, as long as you did not enjoy it. Old fashioned, puritanical, nose-to-the-grindstone, toil for its own sake became the motivation that drove millions of people to work hard all their lives and to feel virtuous for doing so. And it still drives millions of us each and every day to do the best job we can. And to show up for every game.

Sources: R. Todd. All work, no ethic. *Worth Magazine*, January, 1996, pp. 78–84. J. Bair., & S. J. Sherer. What happened to the work ethic? *College Park Magazine*, Fall, 1995, pp. 18–22.

in job performance. Enhancing the mental requirements for a job, therefore, increases the worker's level of responsibility and challenge, which may, in turn, lead to the satisfaction of Herzberg's motivator needs.

The job enrichment movement led psychologists to consider more carefully the specific job characteristics that could be enriched. To deal with this issue, two psychologists proposed the job-characteristics theory of motivation.

Job-Characteristics Theory

The **job-characteristics theory,** developed by J. Richard Hackman and G. R. Oldham, grew out of research on objective measures of job characteristics that would correlate with employee satisfaction and attendance (Hackman & Oldham, 1976, 1980). Evidence suggested that certain characteristics can influence behavior and attitudes at work, but these characteristics do not affect all employ-

Job-characteristics theory
A theory of motivation that states that specific job characteristics lead to psychological conditions that lead to increased motivation, performance, and satisfaction, if employees have a high need for growth.

ccs in the same way. The research pointed to individual differences in the need for growth. People with a high growth need were found to be more affected by changes in job characteristics than were people with a low growth need. Also, changes in these job characteristics did not seem to influence employee attitudes and behavior directly but were filtered by the employees' cognitive processes—their perceptions of the changes.

The presence of positive job characteristics causes employees to experience a positive emotional state when they perform their job well. This condition motivates them to continue to perform well, on the expectation that good performance will lead to good feelings. The strength of one's motivation to perform well depends on the strength of the need to grow and develop. The stronger the need, the more one will value the positive emotional feelings that result from good job performance. Thus, the job-characteristics theory states that specific job characteristics lead to psychological conditions that lead to greater motivation, performance, and satisfaction—if employees have a high growth need to begin with.

The core job characteristics identified by Hackman and Oldham are as follows:

1. Skill variety: the extent to which workers use various skills and abilities on the job. The more challenging a job, the more meaningful it will be.
2. Task identity: the unity of a job—that is, whether it involves doing a whole unit of work or completing a product instead of making only part of a product on an assembly line.
3. Task significance: the importance of a job to the lives and well-being of co-workers or consumers. For example, the job of aircraft mechanic affects the lives of more people in a more significant way than does the job of postal clerk.
4. Autonomy: the amount of independence employees have in scheduling and organizing work.
5. Feedback: the amount of information employees receive about the effectiveness and quality of their job performance.

Jobs can be redesigned to maximize these characteristics in a manner similar to that proposed earlier by Herzberg:

- Combine small, specialized tasks to form larger work units; this enhances skill variety and task identity.
- Arrange the tasks in natural, meaningful work units to make the worker responsible for an identifiable unit; this enhances task identity and task significance.
- Give workers responsibility for direct contact with clients or end users; this enhances skill variety, autonomy, and feedback.
- Give workers authority, responsibility, and control over the job tasks; this increases skill variety, task identity, task significance, and autonomy.
- Arrange for workers to learn regularly how well they are performing the job; this increases feedback.

Hackman and Oldham developed the Job Diagnostic Survey (JDS) to measure the three major aspects of the theory: (1) employee perceptions of the job characteristics, (2) employees' level of the need for growth, and (3) job satisfaction (Hackman & Oldham, 1975). The JDS is a self-report inventory consisting of short descriptive phrases on the various job characteristics. Respondents rate how accurately each statement describes their job. A revised version, using positively worded items only, has been found to be more valid than the original version (Corderey & Sevastos, 1993; Idaszak & Drasgow, 1987).

Research suggests that the JDS provides useful information about perceptions of job characteristics but that other measures are needed for complete assessment of the objective nature of a job. Additional job characteristics that need consideration include cognitive demand and production responsibility in dealing with such developing technologies as computer-controlled machine tools (see, for example, Jackson, Wall, Martin, & Davids, 1993; Spector & Jex, 1991; Taber & Taylor, 1990).

The job-characteristics theory continues to stimulate research. A meta-analysis of 200 studies confirmed a positive relationship between actual and perceived job characteristics and provides support for the idea that job characteristics are related to satisfaction and performance (Fried & Ferris, 1987). However, not all the characteristics are similar in their effect. Improvements in productivity were related mostly to task identity and feedback. Reduced absenteeism was related to skill variety, autonomy, and feedback. Job attitudes were related to skill variety, task significance, autonomy, and feedback. Feedback was the only characteristic associated with both job satisfaction and job performance. These results should be viewed with caution because they relied on job characteristics measures that may not be equivalent to the JDS (Fried, 1991).

Another meta-analysis involved nearly 7,000 workers in 876 jobs in 56 organizations. The findings challenge some of the core dimensions in the job-characteristics theory, suggesting that task identity and feedback are legitimate but that the other three could be combined in a single factor. The five core characteristics were found to vary with age, education, and job level and may not be applicable to all workplaces or types of workers (Fried & Ferris, 1986).

Studies on job enrichment programs that followed the principles of job-characteristics theory have been more supportive. The redesign of 11 clerical jobs for more than 500 employees in a financial services company showed that adding challenge, complexity, and responsibility to the jobs resulted in greater job satisfaction (Campion & McClelland, 1991). A job enrichment study of 526 bank tellers found no change in performance 6 months after their jobs were redesigned to make them more professional and rewarding. However, performance increased significantly when measured 24 and 48 months after the jobs were enriched (Griffin, 1991). These findings suggest the importance of waiting a sufficient period before assessing the impact of a major change in the nature and content of a job. Had the study ended after 6 months, the conclusion would have been that the job enrichment intervention had no effect on performance.

PROCESS THEORIES OF MOTIVATION

We describe four process theories: valence-instrumentality-expectancy (VIE), equity, goal-setting, and high performance cycle.

Valence-Instrumentality-Expectancy (VIE) Theory

The **VIE theory,** originated by Victor Vroom, asserts that people make choices that are based on their perceived expectancy that certain rewards will follow if

Valence-instrumentality-expectancy (VIE) theory A theory of motivation asserting that people make choices that are based on their perceived expectations that certain rewards will follow if they behave in a particular way.

they behave in a particular way (Vroom, 1964). In the workplace, employees will choose to perform at the level that results in the greatest payoff or benefit. They will be motivated to work hard if they expect this effort to lead to positive outcomes such as a promotion or higher pay and if those outcomes will be instrumental in leading to other desired outcomes.

The psychological value, or valence, of the reward varies with the individual; in other words, our perception of the importance of the outcome determines its strength as a motivator. A high salary and increased responsibility have a positive valence for many people. Dangerous working conditions have a negative valence for most people. The outcome may not be as satisfying as we expected, but it is the level of expectancy that determines whether we will work hard to obtain that outcome.

The three facets of the VIE theory are related as follows. First, employees must decide whether they expect certain job behaviors—such as coming to work on time, following safe procedures, or increasing productivity—to have a high probability of leading to a particular outcome (expectancy). Second, employees must determine whether that outcome will lead to other outcomes—for example, whether a good attendance record leads to a bonus (instrumentality). Third, employees must decide whether those outcomes have sufficient value to motivate them to behave a certain way (valence).

The VIE theory has received a great deal of research support (see, for example, Tubbs, Boehne, & Dahl, 1993). It appears to agree with personal experience and common sense; the greater our expectation of receiving a reward, assuming it is of sufficient value, the harder we will work for it.

Equity Theory

J. Stacy Adams advanced the equity theory, the notion that motivation is influenced by our perception of how equitably or fairly we are treated at work (Adams, 1965). He proposed that in any work environment—whether office, shop, factory, or classroom—we assess our inputs (how much effort we put into the work) and our outcomes (how much reward we receive for the work). We calculate, perhaps unconsciously, the ratio of outcome to input and mentally compare it with what we believe are the ratios for our co-workers. If we think we are getting less than other people, the feeling of tension or inequity that results motivates us to act—to do something to bring about a state of equity. If we perceive that we are receiving the same ratio of reward-to-effort that others are receiving, then a state of equity exists.

Other psychologists extended the equity theory, suggesting three behavioral response patterns to situations of perceived equity or inequity (Huseman, Hatfield, & Miles, 1987). These three types are benevolent, equity sensitive, and entitled. The level of reward received by each type affects motivation, job satisfaction, and job performance. *Benevolent* persons, described as altruistic, are satisfied when they are underrewarded compared with co-workers and feel guilty when they are equitably rewarded or overrewarded. *Equity-sensitive* persons, the type described by the equity theory, believe that everyone should be rewarded fairly. They feel distressed when underrewarded and guilty when overrewarded. *Entitled* persons believe that everything they receive is their due. They are satisfied only when they are overrewarded and distressed when underrewarded or equitably rewarded. A study of 2,617 employees from the banking and the public utility industries confirmed that these three types varied in the importance they placed on work outcomes (Miles, Hatfield, & Huseman, 1994).

It seems intuitively correct to state that if we believe we are being treated fairly in comparison to others, in accordance with our expectations, then we will be motivated to maintain our level of job performance. In contrast, if we think we are being treated unfairly, then we will try to reduce that inequity.

A study that supported these assumptions involved 198 employees of a large insurance company. Because of extensive office renovations, the employees were moved to temporary office quarters for a 2-week period and randomly assigned to offices of higher, lower, or the same status as their regular offices. Status was defined in terms of number of employees sharing an office, presence or absence of an office door, amount of space per employee, and size of desk. Employees assigned to high-status offices showed improvements in job performance in terms of the number of insurance cases completed. Employees in same-status offices showed no change in job performance. Employees assigned to low-status offices, who perceived themselves to be treated unfairly, showed a decline in job performance. The size of the change in job performance was directly related to the magnitude of the change in office status (Greenberg, 1988).

A study of employee theft in three manufacturing plants that produced small parts for aerospace and automotive industries also supported predictions based on the equity theory. Workers received a pay cut, which some perceived as an underpayment inequity; they believed their inputs (efforts) were greater than the outcomes or rewards they were receiving. These workers attempted to correct or compensate for that inequity by increasing their rate of theft, stealing more than twice as much as when they perceived that their pay had been fair. Employees in another group, who were given an adequate explanation for the pay cut, stole less than before; they did not feel that they were being treated inequitably (Greenberg, 1990).

Major league baseball players (fielders) who had their salaries cut or who lost at arbitration during their first year as free agents performed at lower levels during the following season. They reduced their inputs (batting averages and runs batted in) when they thought their outcomes (salaries) were too low. Additional research also related perceived underpayment inequity to performance decrements but only to the extent that the players believed their performance would not adversely affect future rewards (Harder, 1991; Lord & Hohenfeld, 1979).

Goal-Setting Theory

Developed by Edwin Locke, **goal-setting theory** also has a commonsense appeal and is clearly relevant to the workplace. Locke argues that our primary motivation in a work situation is defined in terms of our desire to achieve a particular goal (Locke, 1968; Locke & Latham, 1990b). The goal represents what we intend to do at a given time in the future. For example, we may set the goal of graduating from college with honors, or achieving the highest sales record in the company, or getting a pay raise within a year so we can buy a new house.

Setting specific and challenging performance goals can motivate and guide our behavior, spurring us to perform in more effective ways. Research has shown that having goals leads to better performance than not having goals. Specific goals are more powerful motivating forces than general goals. Goals that are

Goal-setting theory A theory of motivation based on the idea that our primary motivation on the job is defined in terms of our desire to achieve a particular goal.

difficult to attain are greater motivators than goals that are easy to attain. However, difficult goals may spur greater achievement motivation toward attaining the goals at the expense of other behaviors, such as helping co-workers; this response has the potential for reducing overall organizational effectiveness. In addition, goals that are too difficult, perhaps beyond our capabilities, are worse than having no goals in terms of their impact on motivation and job performance (Wright, George, Farnsworth, & McMahan, 1993).

An important aspect of the goal-setting theory is individual goal commitment; that is, the strength of our determination to reach our goal. That commitment is influenced by external factors, interactive factors, and internal factors (Locke, Latham, & Erez, 1988). The external factors that affect goal commitment are authority, peer influence, and external rewards. Complying with the dictates of an authority figure such as a boss has been shown to be an inducement to high goal commitment in laboratory and in field studies. Goal commitment increases when the authority figure is physically present, supportive, and trusted. Peer group pressure and external rewards such as pay increases also strengthen goal commitment.

The interactive factors that influence our commitment to reaching our goals are competition and the opportunity to participate in setting goals. These factors have been shown to be an inducement to setting higher goals and to working harder to reach them. Internal cognitive factors that facilitate goal commitment are self-administered reward and our expectation of success. Commitment to the goal is reduced when our expectation of achieving it declines.

Other personal and situational influences on goal commitment have been suggested. The need for achievement, endurance, aggressiveness, and competitiveness (so-called Type A behavior), success in achieving difficult goals, high self-esteem, and an internal locus of control have all been related to high goal commitment. Situational variables linked with high goal commitment include the extent to which others are aware of our goals and information about the performance of others in pursuit of the same or similar goals (Hollenbeck & Klein, 1987).

What holds true for individual goal commitment has also been found to apply to group commitment to a goal. A meta-analysis of 26 studies showed that the mean performance level on a variety of tasks of work groups and management teams that set goals was significantly higher than the mean performance level of groups that did not set goals (O'Leary-Kelly, Martocchio, & Frink, 1994).

The goal-setting theory has generated considerable supportive research. Goal setting has been found to produce substantial increases in employee output. A meta-analysis of 72 on-the-job studies found that the motivating effects of setting goals were strongest for easy tasks and weakest for more complex tasks. These effects were shown to generalize across a variety of organizations, jobs, and tasks (Wood, Mento, & Locke, 1987). Also, the theory is high in scientific validity and in applicability on the job.

The High Performance Cycle

Research on the goal-setting theory led to the formulation of a more comprehensive theory to account for motivation and job satisfaction. This refinement and extension of the goal-setting theory expands the role of cognitive factors and describes the relationship between motivation and satisfaction (Locke & Latham,

1990b). Called the **high performance cycle,** this model is conceptually more complex than goal-setting theory.

The cycle begins with the demands, goals, or challenges provided by the job. This is the goal-setting theory, which asserts that goals motivate employees to improve job performance. In addition to the goals we set for ourselves, challenges can come from authority figures (supervisors or managers), from participation (joint decisions between subordinates and superiors), from peer pressure to produce, or from role models. Whatever the source, these specific, attainable, and difficult goals do not automatically produce high performance. Rather, they lead to an increase in work motivation. Having challenging goals does not guarantee high performance, but they will lead to high performance if other factors, called moderators, are present.

Moderators affect the strength of the relationship between goals and job performance. A specific and challenging goal will enhance motivation and lead to high job performance when the employee has the following:

- Commitment to the goal
- Feedback demonstrating progress toward the goal
- High self-efficacy or expectation of performing well
- A task that is not too difficult

Assuming, then, the existence of challenging goals and demands and the moderators just listed, the next step in the cycle is how goals actually affect performance. This occurs through mediating mechanisms called universal task strategies, which are necessary to the accomplishment of a task. The strategies are direction of attention, effort, and persistence. "Virtually every individual learns at an early age that you perform better on a task if you pay attention to it, exert effort on it, and persist at it over time than if you do not do so" (Locke & Latham, 1990b, p. 11).

Given challenging demands, the moderators that facilitate job performance, and the mediating strategies that translate goals into action, then employee performance will be high. The rewards that follow can serve as an incentive to maintain job performance. Rewards can be external, such as pay raises, promotions, or other organizational recognition, or internal and self-administered, such as feelings of achievement, self-efficacy, and pride in one's accomplishments. There are also noncontingent rewards that are based on simply having a job, such as fringe benefits, job security, and affiliation with co-workers. Noncontingent rewards do not motivate performance directly as moderators do, but they can encourage people to remain on the job.

If the internal and external rewards, which are contingent on high job performance, satisfy employee needs and values, employees will have high job satisfaction. If the rewards do not satisfy these needs, then the result is dissatisfaction. High satisfaction leads to greater organizational commitment and a willingness to accept new goals and challenges; this illustrates the cyclical nature of the high performance model. High satisfaction results from high performance rather than causes it; that is, high performance comes first. Once satisfaction is experienced, it is related indirectly to future performance by the strength of the organizational commitment and by the employee's willingness to work toward new goals.

The high performance cycle has a commonsense feel and is applicable to many work situations. Research supports the importance of moderators and me-

High performance cycle A theory of motivation and job satisfaction that suggests that goals affect level of job performance, depending on the kind of task and the abilities of the worker.

diators in job performance and the impact of rewards on job satisfaction. The influence of cognitive factors such as self-efficacy as mechanisms by which goals affect performance have also been demonstrated (see, for example, Earley & Lituchy, 1991; Wood & Bandura, 1989). The high performance cycle suggests that motivation and job satisfaction can be affected by the same factors.

JOB SATISFACTION: A MEASURE OF THE QUALITY OF WORKING LIFE

Job satisfaction Our positive and negative feelings and attitudes about our jobs.

Job satisfaction refers to the positive and negative feelings and attitudes we hold about our jobs. It depends on many work-related factors, ranging from where we have to park to the sense of fulfillment we get from our daily tasks. Personal factors can also influence job satisfaction. These factors include age, health, length of job experience, emotional stability, social status, leisure activities, and family and other social relationships. Our motivations and aspirations and how well these are satisfied by our work also affect our attitudes toward our jobs.

For some employees, job satisfaction is a stable, enduring characteristic, independent of the features of the job. Changes in job status, pay, working conditions, and goals have little effect on the job satisfaction of these people. Their personal tendency toward happiness (satisfaction) or unhappiness (dissatisfaction) varies little over time and circumstances.

I/O psychologists have suggested, on the basis of research conducted on twins, that attitudes toward work and the outcomes or satisfactions we want from it may be inherited. These attitudes and outcomes may be influenced more by our genetic endowment than by features of our work environment. Research indicates that between 30 and 40% of job satisfaction may be related to genetic factors (Arvey, Bouchard, Segal, & Abraham, 1989; Bouchard, Arvey, Keller, & Segal, 1992; Keller, Bouchard, Arvey, Segal, & Dawis, 1992). However, the notion of an inherited predisposition toward satisfaction or dissatisfaction has drawn criticism, and additional research is needed before the issue is resolved (Cropanzano & James, 1990; Newton & Keenan, 1991). For example, a study in Sweden involving 540 pairs of twins, some reared together and some reared apart, failed to find a significant genetic influence on job satisfaction (Hershberger, Lichtenstein, & Knox, 1994).

Related research suggests that different satisfaction patterns, involving both work-related and personal attitudes, may characterize different people. A study of 390 male college graduates, tested after they had held full-time jobs for 5 or 6 years, suggested that some people are generally more satisfied with life. They score high on both work and nonwork satisfaction (Shaffer, 1987).

A number of studies have confirmed that job satisfaction is related to satisfaction with all aspects of life. People who have positive attitudes toward their work are likely to have positive feelings about their personal and family life. Data from national surveys of middle-aged black men, black women, white men, and white women found that for all four groups job satisfaction was positively related to life satisfaction (Crohan, Antonucci, Adelmann, & Coleman, 1989).

It is generally accepted that job satisfaction and life satisfaction are positively related, but which one causes the other? Or are both influenced by some third factor? To explore this relationship, a sample of 804 employees, selected to be representative of the workforce in the United States, was interviewed and given questionnaires to assess job and life satisfaction. The results showed a positive and reciprocal relationship between job and life satisfaction in the short term; that is, each influenced the other. Over time, the effect of life satisfaction on job satisfaction was significantly stronger, indicating that general life satisfaction may be the more influential of the two factors (Judge & Watanabe, 1993). However, it does not follow that attempts to enhance job satisfaction are futile. Remember that the two are interrelated; job satisfaction still has an effect on life satisfaction.

Measuring Job Satisfaction

The approach used most often to measure employee attitudes is the anonymous questionnaire, typically distributed to employees in their offices or mailed to their homes. Many companies also use E-mail, in which questions are asked and responses are given through the in-house computer network. Because questionnaire responses are anonymous and participation is voluntary, not all workers will complete a questionnaire. There is no way of knowing which employees responded and which did not, or how those who failed to respond differ from those who did respond. For example, it might make a difference if more good workers than poor workers completed the questionnaires.

Two popular attitude surveys are the Job Descriptive Index (JDI) and the Minnesota Satisfaction Questionnaire (MSQ). The JDI contains scales to measure five job factors: pay, promotion, supervision, the nature of the work, and the characteristics of one's co-workers. It can be completed in 15 minutes and has been published in several languages (Smith, Kendall, & Hulin, 1969, 1987). The MSQ is a rating scale for various levels of satisfaction and dissatisfaction, ranging from very satisfied to very dissatisfied. It covers 20 job facets including advancement, independence, recognition, social status, and working conditions. The MSQ takes 30 minutes to complete; a 10-minute form is also available (Weiss, Dawis, England, & Lofquist, 1967). These questionnaires show high construct validity.

Research on telephone operators showed a high correlation between JDI ratings and objective measures of work behavior that indicate job satisfaction, such as work speed, absenteeism, and tardiness. The subjects were asked two open-end questions: to describe what they liked or were satisfied with about their jobs, and to describe what they disliked or were dissatisfied with about their jobs. The answers were assessed by 11 independent judges. The employees' responses on the JDI showed a high positive correlation with these clinical assessments of job satisfaction (Taber, 1991).

Personal interviews are sometimes used in conjunction with questionnaires. In these interviews, employees discuss aspects of their jobs with supervisors or interviewers from the organization's human resources department. Another method of measuring job attitudes is the sentence completion test. Employees are presented with a list of phrases to complete; for example, "My job is _____" or "My job should be _____." In the critical-incidents technique for evaluating job satisfaction, employees are asked to describe job incidents that occurred at times when they felt very good or very bad about their jobs.

Job Facet Satisfaction

Many I/O psychologists suggest that data on overall job satisfaction may not be an adequate measure of the full range of employees' positive and negative attitudes toward all aspects of the work situation. Employees may be satisfied with certain conditions and dissatisfied with others. For example, you may like your work and be comfortable in your office, but you may dislike your boss or your company's health insurance program. A measure of overall job satisfaction fails to represent these differences. For this reason, more psychologists are focusing on the measurement of facets of job satisfaction.

The Job Descriptive Index and the Minnesota Satisfaction Questionnaire measure job facet satisfaction. To derive a measure of total satisfaction, scores for each facet are added. In one study, 185 employees took the short form of the MSQ. They were interviewed about their jobs and asked two general questions about job satisfaction. The results showed a low correlation between the sum of the MSQ facets and the general questions about job satisfaction. The researchers concluded that the simple summation of the job facet scores failed to encompass all aspects of job satisfaction. Therefore, the questionnaires may not be measuring all possible job elements or all variables that affect job satisfaction (Scarpello & Campbell, 1983).

This conclusion was upheld by the results of the interviews, which uncovered five facets not measured by the questionnaire: flexibility in scheduling work hours, tools and equipment, workspace, the ability of co-workers to facilitate one's work, and the perceived pleasantness of social interactions in the workplace. Satisfaction with these facets was found to correlate positively with other

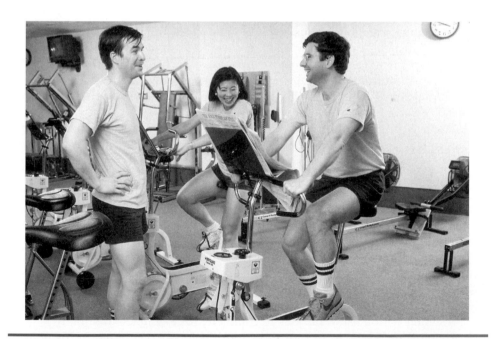

Job satisfaction is related to workplace conditions. For some employees, a wellness center with state-of-the-art exercise equipment fosters a positive attitude toward the job.

measures of overall job and life satisfaction. This study and others demonstrate empirically the complexity of job satisfaction. I/O psychologists are continuing to investigate numerous job facets. Some facets appear to apply over all types of jobs and organizations, whereas others are present in only certain job categories.

Extent of Job Satisfaction

Every year since 1949, the Gallup Poll has asked a representative sample of U.S. workers the following question: On the whole, would you say you are satisfied or dissatisfied with the work you do? The results have shown consistently that only 10 to 13% of the workers questioned each year say that they are dissatisfied with their jobs. These findings were confirmed in a 1995 Gallup Poll of a representative sample of 657 adults. The results indicated that 88% of the respondents were "very satisfied" or "somewhat satisfied" with their jobs. The remaining 12% expressed dissatisfaction with their jobs. Thus, for nearly 50 years, the reported overall job satisfaction data have been consistent.

However, when more specific questions are asked about job satisfaction, the results are different. For example, when blue-collar workers are asked if they would like to change jobs, many say yes, even though they say they are satisfied with their present jobs. When people say they are satisfied, often they really mean that they are not dissatisfied. When examining data on job satisfaction, then, we must consider the kinds of questions asked.

Some job satisfaction studies survey a representative national sample of workers. Others deal with targeted populations, such as the workers in a particular industry, or with specific components of job satisfaction. Job satisfaction

Assembly-line workers such as these at a computer manufacturing plant may have lower job satisfaction than workers who are not employed on assembly lines. Routine, repetitive work offers little opportunity for personal growth and fulfillment.

varies with type of occupation. For example, an anonymous questionnaire survey of 209 women in nonmanagerial jobs in a food-processing plant found that assembly-line workers were significantly less satisfied with their jobs than were office workers (Clegg, Wall, & Kemp, 1987).

A survey of more than 800 senior U.S. Civil Service managers found extremely low morale and job satisfaction. Almost 70% said they would advise intelligent young people not to work for the federal government. When asked if they would seek work elsewhere if they could start their careers over, 66% said yes (Posner & Schmidt, 1988). Other studies comparing job satisfaction of government and private-sector employees confirmed these attitudes. A survey of 240 high-level managers in public and private organizations in Israel found significantly higher levels of satisfaction for private-sector managers (Solomon, 1986).

In Britain, a comparison of 557 senior civil service managers and 1,056 senior managers in private industry found job dissatisfaction to be significantly higher among the government managers. Also, their mental and physical health were reported to be poorer than for their counterparts in the private sector (Bogg & Cooper, 1995). This consistency of results over time and over different cultures can be interpreted to suggest serious organizational and morale problems in government employment.

Personal Characteristics and Job Satisfaction

Many characteristics of the job and the workplace affect job satisfaction. By redesigning job and work environments, it is possible for management to raise job satisfaction and productivity. For example, by redesigning jobs to maximize opportunities to satisfy the needs for achievement, self-actualization, and personal growth and development, and by enriching jobs to enhance the motivator needs and the core job characteristics, job satisfaction can be increased.

Personal characteristics that can influence job satisfaction include, among others, age, sex, race, intelligence, use of skills, and job experience. Although these factors cannot be altered by employing organizations, they can be used to predict satisfaction among various groups of workers.

Age.   In general, job satisfaction increases with age; the lowest job satisfaction is reported by the youngest workers. This relationship holds for blue-collar and white-collar employees and for men and women employees. Many young people are disappointed with their first jobs because they fail to find sufficient challenge and responsibility. Why does job satisfaction tend to increase with age when our reaction to our first job is often disappointment? Three possible explanations are the following:

1. The most strongly dissatisfied young workers may drop out of the work force or change jobs so frequently in their search for satisfaction that they are no longer counted in surveys. This means that the older the sample of employees studied, the fewer dissatisfied people are likely to be included.
2. A sense of resignation may set in as employees grow older. They may give up looking for fulfillment and challenge in their work and seek these satisfactions elsewhere. Therefore, they may tend to report less dissatisfaction with their jobs.

3. Many older workers have greater opportunities to find fulfillment and self-actualization on the job. Age and experience usually bring increased confidence, competence, esteem, and responsibility, leading, in turn, to a greater sense of accomplishment. In other words, older workers are more likely to have better jobs than are younger workers.

Gender.   The research evidence about possible differences in job satisfaction between men and women employees is inconsistent and contradictory. Even when differences in work values and job satisfaction have been shown, there is disagreement about the causes. A large-scale questionnaire study of more than 6,000 employees in nine Western European countries found no clear pattern of differences between males and females in job satisfaction (de Vaus & McAllister, 1991). Other studies have shown that the sources of job satisfaction differ for women who voluntarily choose a career in the business world and women who are forced to enter the work force to support their families.

It may not be gender, as such, that relates to job satisfaction as much as the group of factors that vary with sex. For example, women are typically paid less than men for the same work, and their opportunities for promotion are fewer. Most women employees believe that they have to work harder and be more outstanding on the job than men employees before they receive comparable rewards. Obviously, these factors influence job satisfaction.

Race.   In general, more white than nonwhite employees report satisfaction with their jobs. However, before a person can be concerned with job satisfaction, he or she must have a job. Although there is a large, thriving middle class among black and ethnic minority employees, large numbers of persons who want to work are unemployed, are employed irregularly, or are too discouraged to seek employment. Many who have full-time work are confined to low-level jobs that offer marginal pay and little opportunity for advancement or fulfillment. Thus, the primary concern for many workers is not satisfaction but finding a job that pays a decent wage.

Cognitive Ability.   Cognitive ability does not appear to be a significant determinant of job satisfaction, but it may be important when considered in relation to type of work. For many jobs, there is a range of intelligence associated with high performance and satisfaction. People who are too intelligent for their work may find insufficient challenge, which leads to boredom and dissatisfaction. People in jobs that require a higher level of intelligence than they have may become frustrated because they are unable to handle the job's demands.

A factor sometimes related to intelligence is level of education. Some studies have shown that education has a slight negative relationship to job satisfaction; the higher the level of formal education, the more likely a person is to be dissatisfied with the job. One explanation is that better-educated persons have higher expectations and believe that their work should provide greater fulfillment and responsibility. Most jobs do not satisfy these expectations. Employees with college degrees are somewhat more satisfied with their jobs than employees who attended college but did not graduate. This finding may be related to the fact that many higher-level positions are open only to college graduates. It may also be related to a generalized dissatisfaction with life on the part of people who did not complete college.

Job Experience.   During the initial stage of employment, new workers tend to be satisfied with their jobs. This period involves the stimulation and challenge of developing skills and abilities, and the work may seem attractive just because it is new. However, this early satisfaction wanes unless employees receive evidence of progress and growth. After a few years on the job, discouragement is common, often being brought on by the feeling that advancement in the company is too slow.

Research on the first 4 years of employment for 625 British engineers found that those who changed jobs reported significantly greater job satisfaction than those who remained with their initial employer. Changing jobs brought feedback on progress and growth and provided increased opportunities for advancement (Newton & Keenan, 1991). A study of 124 salespersons from seven companies showed that they became more dissatisfied with their jobs over time. More experienced workers did not believe that job performance led to rewards. Their sense of challenge and job involvement had diminished, and they showed lower organizational commitment (Stout, Slocum, & Cron, 1987).

Job satisfaction appears to increase after a number of years of experience and to improve steadily thereafter. The relationship between job satisfaction and length of work experience parallels the relationship with age. They may be the same phenomenon under different labels.

Use of Skills.   A common complaint, particularly among college graduates in engineering and science, is that their jobs do not allow them to exercise their skills or apply the knowledge acquired during their college training. Surveys of engineers show high dissatisfaction with job facets such as pay, working conditions, supervisors, and opportunities for promotion (Rynes, Tolbert, & Strausser, 1988). Other studies show that people are happier at work if they have the chance to use the abilities they believe they possess. Interviews with workers on an automobile assembly line in Sweden revealed that a major factor in their job satisfaction was the opportunity to perform their work with high quality. When working conditions or the actions of co-workers interfered with work quality, job satisfaction declined (Eklund, 1995).

Job Congruence.   Another study investigated the relationship between job satisfaction and **job congruence.** The subjects were 792 men and 1,077 women who were questioned during their first year at college and again 6 years after graduation. Those with the highest congruence—that is, the best match between their abilities and job demands—had aspired to their present jobs early in college and had majored in a field leading directly to the job. Thus, they were using skills acquired and developed in college. They were more satisfied with income, fringe benefits, and promotion opportunities than were persons with low congruence. Those with the lowest congruence—that is, the poorest fit between their abilities and their jobs—had not aspired to their present jobs while in college, nor had they majored in a field leading to that job (Elton & Smart, 1988).

Additional research involved a survey of 253 college graduates in a variety of full-time jobs studied over a 7-year period and a survey of 345 bank tellers studied for 4 months on the job. The results of both investigations support the relationship between job congruence and job satisfaction. The better the fit between the subjects' abilities and the job requirements, the higher the job satisfaction (Fricko & Beehr, 1992; Gottfredson & Holland, 1990). Another study of per-

Job congruence The match between one's abilities and the requirements of one's job.

son/organization fit questioned nearly 15,000 schoolteachers and 356 principals. The researchers found that agreement about organizational goals (goal congruence), such as increasing students' basic skills or upgrading physical resources, was positively related to job satisfaction and negatively related to intention to quit (Vancouver & Schmitt, 1991).

Personality.   Research suggests that employees who are more satisfied in their work are better adjusted and more emotionally stable. Although the relationship seems clear, the cause-and-effect sequence is not. Which comes first, emotional stability or job satisfaction? Emotional instability or job dissatisfaction? Emotional instability can cause discontent in every sphere of life, and prolonged job dissatisfaction can lead to poor emotional adjustment.

Two personality factors related to job satisfaction are alienation and locus of control. Employees who feel less alienated and who have an internal locus of control are more likely to be high in job satisfaction, job involvement, and organizational commitment (King, Murray, & Atkinson, 1982; Stout, Slocum, & Cron, 1987). A study of 117 life insurance salespersons in South Africa identified two dimensions of the **Type A personality** that are related to job satisfaction. *Achievement striving* (the extent to which people work hard and take their work seriously) was positively related to job satisfaction and high job performance. The factor of *impatience/irritability* (intolerance, anger, hostility, and a sense of time urgency) was negatively related to job satisfaction. The higher the impatience scores, the lower the job satisfaction (Bluen, Barling, & Burns, 1990).

Type A/Type B personalities Personality factors related to one's ability to tolerate stress; Type A persons have been associated with heart disease, anger, hostility, time urgency, and depression; Type B persons work as hard as Type As but show fewer stress effects.

A study of 1,473 employees in the United States used questionnaire data and 1-hour interviews to investigate the relationship between job satisfaction and social attitudes. The researchers found that job satisfaction was highest among employees who expressed a high degree of social and institutional trust; that is, who believed that people and government institutions are fair and helpful and can be trusted. The research also supported the spillover hypothesis: the argument that satisfaction with one aspect of life carries over to other aspects of life (Liou, Sylvia, & Brunk, 1990).

Among 231 clerical employees at a large university it was found that those with dysfunctional thought processes, of the kind leading to depression, scored low in job and life satisfaction. They were likely to believe that "life is no good, and that things will never change for the better" (Judge & Locke, 1993, pp. 484–485).

Occupational Level.   The higher the occupational or status level of a job, the higher the job satisfaction. Executives express more positive job attitudes and feelings than do first-line supervisors, who, in turn, are usually more satisfied than their subordinates. The higher the job level, the greater is the opportunity for the satisfaction of motivator needs and the greater are the autonomy, challenge, and responsibility of the work. Satisfaction of Maslow's esteem and self-actualization needs also increases with each level in the organizational hierarchy.

Job satisfaction also varies with job categories. High job satisfaction scores have been found among entrepreneurs (self-employed persons) and employees in technical, professional, and managerial jobs. A comparison of 62 self-employed and 115 organizationally employed male college graduates found a significantly higher positive relationship among job, life, family, and self-satisfaction for self-employed persons (Thompson, Kopelman, & Schriesheim, 1992). According to national surveys, the least satisfied employees are in manufacturing and service industries and in wholesale and retail businesses.

Losing One's Job

There can be no job satisfaction without a job. As we noted, millions of employees at all occupational levels have lost their jobs in recent years as a result of reorganizations and the inability of some industries to remain competitive in the world market. I/O psychology research confirms the obvious. Losing one's job or being laid off is stressful for employees and their families. In Japan, layoffs are considered so traumatic and personally debilitating that they are referred to as *kubi kiri,* which means "beheading." Specific consequences of layoffs can include feelings of guilt, resentment, and anxiety about the future, as well as physical complaints, alcohol abuse, drug abuse, divorce, spouse and child abuse, and thoughts of suicide. Finding a job tends to reverse most of these negative effects.

Employees with higher-level jobs appear to suffer more greatly from unemployment; employees with lower-level jobs seem to be more adaptable. Executives, managers, and professionals tend to become defensive and self-critical. Losing a job requires a transformation in lifestyles, expectations, goals, and values. The unwritten psychological contract these employees believed they had with their employer has been breached. The agreement specifying that if they worked hard and showed loyalty to the company, they would receive steady, secure employment and pay raises and promotions, can no longer be relied upon. Many people who lost their jobs in the 1980s and early 1990s report a sense of betrayal.

Comparisons of employed and unemployed men and women found that unemployed persons scored higher on measures of depression and scored lower on measures of self-esteem than did employed persons. Unemployed persons showed greater external locus of control. Employed persons who did not like their jobs showed emotional and psychological distress similar to that of unemployed persons (Feather, 1990; Wincfield & Tiggemann, 1990; Winefield, Tiggemann, Winefield, & Goldney, 1991).

A survey of laid-off workers found that almost 50% found other jobs within 14 weeks, but 30% were out of work for more than a year. Blue-collar workers took longer to find new jobs than white-collar and service workers. Workers older than 40 were less likely to find new jobs than workers younger than 40 (Wanberg, Watt, & Rumsey, 1996). Women were usually unemployed for longer periods than were men. Interviews with men and women executives in outplacement counseling programs who were faced with the loss of their jobs found that it took women up to 38% longer than men to find suitable new employment (Phelps & Mason, 1991).

Those high in self-efficacy, or whose self-efficacy was enhanced by training in job-seeking behaviors, were significantly more likely to find reemployment than those low in self-efficacy (Eden & Aviram, 1993; Vinokur, Van Ryn, Gramlich, & Price, 1991). Those who attributed their job loss to internal causes (the internal locus of control factor) were less likely to find new jobs than those who attributed their unemployment to external causes, beyond their control (Prussia, Kinicki, & Bracker, 1993).

Unemployment can lead to anxiety and resentment that may persist even after a new job has been found.

Interviews with 53 laid-off professionals (such as engineers) found that those who were able to openly express their thoughts and emotions in creative essays were significantly more likely to find reemployment than those who did not have access to such outlets for their feelings (Spera, Buhrfeind, & Pennebaker, 1994).

How do company layoffs affect the workers who remain on the job? One study compared attitudes and feelings of engineers who worked for companies that had experienced mild layoffs (2 to 4% of the work force over 2 years) with those who worked for companies that had experienced severe layoffs (25 to 70% of the work force). In the mild layoff condition, employees high in the work ethic showed greater job involvement than employees low in the work ethic. In severe layoff situations, a high work ethic was not sufficient to protect employees from feelings of stress and a deterioration in job involvement (Brockner, Grover, & Blonder, 1988).

Surveys 13 months apart of 207 assembly-line workers who had survived rounds of layoffs showed that the extended period of job insecurity was related to significant decreases in job satisfaction and increases in feelings of stress (Heaney, Israel, & House, 1994). In addition, a 1995 report for the U.S. Department of Labor noted that half of the layoff survivors questioned reported increased job stress. Also, 60% reported greatly increased workloads. Half the companies involved in layoffs found reduced morale and job commitment among their remaining workers (Seppa, 1996).

NEWSBREAK #14

Stop Blaming Us! The Lament of the Layoff Survivor

Peter Thornton is afraid. And he's also angry. The 36-year-old systems engineer at a telecommunications company has lived through three downsizings in the last 5 years. He's seen a lot of his friends and co-workers fired, for the purpose—they were told—of saving the company.

When he's not worrying about whether he'll survive the next round of layoffs, he's mad as hell at the company for screwing everything up. Corporate profits did not rise, as the CEO promised they would (although that same CEO received a $1.2 million bonus last year, in addition to his $3 million salary). And the employees who still have jobs have to take up the slack left by the downsizing. "I'm doing the work that used to be done by three engineers," Peter said. "I'm putting in 60-hour weeks and I still can't catch up."

Last week his supervisor told him he would need to be more productive if he wanted the company to survive. She made him feel as if it was all his fault—the layoffs, the low morale, the backlog of work.

"Stop blaming us!" he said, though only to this interviewer; he did not dare complain aloud to his boss. "We've been loyal to the company. We've worked hard and did everything we were told. We've moved for the company; we've traveled for the company; and we've taken on extra work for the company. And now you say the problem was caused by the way we organized and performed our work.

"Hell, you told us to do it that way. Management told us to do it! And the company did pretty well all those years while we did it that way. But then the economy changed and technology changed and management didn't react fast enough to those changes and now they say it's all our fault. Stop blaming us!"

Peter Thornton is not alone in his anger. International Survey Research, a Chicago polling firm, surveyed 312,742 managers working for companies that underwent major restructuring between 1991 and 1995. A third of the managers said they worried a great deal about getting laid off, an increase of 17 percentage points from a similar survey conducted 5 years earlier. Only 31% approved of the way top management had handled the restructuring, down 12 percentage points from 1991. Less than half believed their co-workers trusted top management, down 6 points from 1991.

And those are the opinions of the *survivors* of layoffs. They're scared and they're mad. So it is not very surprising their job satisfaction has plummeted.

Sources: S. Berkeley. Researchers see the downside of downsizing. *St. Petersburg [FL] Times*, January 7, 1996. O'Neill, H. M., & Lenn, D. J. (1995). Voices of survivors: Words that downsizing CEOs should hear. *Academy of Management Executive*, 9(4), 23–34.

Job Satisfaction and Job Behavior

We have described factors that can influence job satisfaction. Now let us consider those aspects of our behavior at work that can be affected by our level of satisfaction.

Productivity.   Research suggests a positive, although weak, relationship between satisfaction and productivity. However, it has not been demonstrated consistently in the laboratory or in studies conducted on the job. Part of the problem is that some jobs lend themselves more readily than others to objective assessments of performance. In other words, different measures of productivity are appropriate for different jobs.

Some I/O psychologists have offered an interesting interpretation of the relationship between job satisfaction and productivity (Lawler & Porter, 1967). Instead of suggesting that job satisfaction leads to improved performance, improved performance may cause job satisfaction. (Recall that this idea was formalized as the high performance cycle.) Satisfaction derives from the fulfillment of our needs. If our work meets those needs, then we can, in effect, administer our own rewards by improving our job performance.

This notion may be more applicable to managers than to lower-level employees. Managers have more opportunities on the job to express and fulfill their needs for self-actualization, achievement, and personal growth. Workers in clerical or assembly-line jobs have little control or opportunity to fulfill these higher-order needs.

Prosocial and Counterproductive Behavior.   High job satisfaction has been related to **prosocial behavior**—that is, to helpful behavior directed at customers, co-workers, and supervisors to the benefit of employees and their organization. Does it follow that low job satisfaction is related to antisocial actions or to counterproductive behavior that may thwart organizational goals? Negative employee behavior can interfere with production and lead to faulty products, poor service, destructive rumors, theft, and sabotaged equipment. Employees may view these behaviors as a way of striking back at an organization because of real or imagined grievances.

Prosocial behavior Employee behaviors directed toward supervisors, co-workers, and customers that are helpful to an organization.

Studies have shown a positive relationship between job dissatisfaction and counterproductive behavior for workers over the age of 30. This does not mean that older workers engage in more negative behaviors than do younger workers; the *frequency* of negative behaviors is higher for employees under 30. What the research indicates is that only in older workers has counterproductive behavior been related to job dissatisfaction (McNeely & Meglino, 1994; Organ & Ryan, 1995).

Absenteeism.   Absenteeism is widespread and costly for organizations. On any given workday in the United States, 16 to 20% of employees do not show up for work. Absenteeism accounts for more time lost from work than do strikes and lockouts, and it costs businesses up to $30 billion a year.

Absenteeism has plagued industry since the invention of machines. In textile mills in Wales in the 1840s, the absenteeism rate was approximately 20%. During the 2-week period following each monthly payday, absenteeism often reached 35%. Throughout the 19th century in England, workers typically took off Mondays—"Saint Monday," they called it—to recover from weekend drinking bouts. Factory owners levied stiff fines and dismissed many workers, but that had no impact on attendance.

A relatively small percentage of employees accounts for a disproportionate share of absences. A survey of 1,292 employees of a public utility company found that 25% of them accounted for all the avoidable absences (Dalton & Mesch, 1991). The primary excuse for missing work is illness. However, interviews with 40 state government employees revealed that only 5% of their reported illnesses were legitimate (Latham & Frayne, 1990).

Accuracy of Self-Report Absenteeism Data.   Suppose you were filling out a questionnaire dealing with your job performance. One of the questions asked how many days of work you missed last year. Would you answer accurately? Or would you underreport the number of times you were absent? Would you say you missed only 2 days when the actual number was nearer to 10? Many people are not always honest about reporting absenteeism.

Studies with diverse groups of workers consistently demonstrate a significant underreporting of their absences by as much as 4 days a year. Managers also tend to underreport the extent of absenteeism in their work groups. Some 85 to 95% of employees report above-average attendance records (Harrison & Shaffer, 1994; Johns, 1994a, 1994b). Clearly, many of us are less than honest about admitting the amount of time we lose from work.

If self-report absenteeism data are sometimes inaccurate, then why not use a company's personnel records to get a true indication of absenteeism? That's a good idea in theory, but it does not work well in practice. Many companies do not compile attendance data in any systematic fashion; for managers and professional employees, such as engineers and scientists, such data are rarely collected at all. So when you read a study about absenteeism and learn that the data come from self-reports, you know that the actual number of absences is likely to be higher.

Not surprisingly, the more liberal an organization's sick-leave policy, the higher its absenteeism rate. Absenteeism is also high in companies that do not require proof of illness, such as a doctor's note. High-paying manufacturing industries have higher absenteeism rates than do low-paying industries. The more money employees earn, the more likely they are to feel entitled to take time off. Workers in routine jobs often have a higher absence rate than workers in more interesting, challenging jobs.

Societal values may foster absenteeism, as is evident in the variations in absentee rates for different countries. In Japan and Switzerland, where job attendance is considered to be a duty, absenteeism rates are low. In Italy, where societal attitudes toward work are more permissive, companies routinely hire 15% more workers than needed to make certain that enough people report to work each day to maintain operations. Absenteeism declined in the United States during World War II because it was considered unpatriotic to miss a day of work.

Management often contributes to an organizational climate that appears to condone absenteeism by failing to enforce company policy. If management is believed to be lenient and unconcerned about absences, some employees will take advantage of the situation. For example, a study of 800 clothing factory workers and their 41 supervisors revealed a significant negative relationship between supervisory standards of acceptable absenteeism and actual absenteeism rates. Supervisors who supported high standards (who tolerated few absences in their work group) had lower absenteeism rates than supervisors who had low standards. In other words, supervisors who were more tolerant of absences, and so created a climate that seemed to condone absenteeism, had—as you would expect—more absences among their workers (Markham & McKee, 1995). It is interesting to note that in this study the companies kept accurate records so that self-reported absences could be verified.

Economic conditions can influence absentee rates. A study of 17 textile plants over a 5-year period reported that as the local unemployment rate increased and more workers lost their jobs, absenteeism declined up to 48%. The researchers concluded that when co-workers are being laid off and jobs are scarce, fewer people are willing to risk the disciplinary action that might result from frequent absences (Markham & McKee, 1991).

Both avoidable and unavoidable absences appear to be inversely related to age. Meta-analyses of studies of employee attendance show that younger workers are much more likely to have higher absenteeism rates than are older workers (Hackett, 1990; Martocchio, 1989).

A 70-month study of 419 U.S. government civil service employees found that job satisfaction was a valid predictor of absenteeism. The higher the job satisfaction, the lower the number of absences. Extent of job involvement was also a valid predictor of absenteeism (Steel & Rentsch, 1995).

A study of tardiness among 381 hospital employees and 448 bank workers noted a strong positive relationship between lateness for work and absenteeism. In other words, employees who frequently showed up late for work also missed more workdays than employees who seldom came late. Frequently tardy workers also scored low in job satisfaction, job involvement, and organizational commitment (Blau, 1994).

Turnover. Turnover is also costly for organizations. Every time someone quits, a replacement must be recruited, selected, and trained, and permitted time on the job to gain experience. Evidence relating high turnover to high job dissatisfaction is strong. For example, studies of nurses and of managers confirmed that both intended and actual turnover could be attributed to dissatisfaction with various aspects of the job (Bretz, Boudreau, & Judge, 1994; Lee, Mitchell, Wise, & Fireman, 1996). A study of 234 nurses, medical assistants, and laboratory technicians found that employees who were dissatisfied with their jobs but high in general life satisfaction were the most likely employees to quit (Judge, 1993a).

Another factor related to turnover is organizational commitment. Meta-analyses of I/O psychology research studies have found that the higher the commitment, the lower the turnover rate (Jaros, Jermier, Koehler, & Sincich, 1993; Tett & Meyer, 1993). A study of 315 newly hired clerical workers found that those with high organizational commitment remained on the job almost three times longer than those with low organizational commitment (Kline & Peters, 1991).

Age does not seem to be a factor that affects turnover. A meta-analysis of 46 samples involving a total of 46,625 employees found virtually no relationship between these two variables (Healy, Lehman, & McDaniel, 1995).

Turnover is higher in times of low unemployment and expanding job opportunities than it is in times of high unemployment and limited opportunities. When people perceive that the economic climate is good and the economy is growing, they find it easier to consider changing jobs in the hope of increasing their job satisfaction.

Turnover also depends on the seriousness of an employee's intentions about changing jobs. An investigation of job-searching behavior among 339 nurses and 234 insurance company employees confirmed that those who engaged in only preparatory job-searching activities (such as finding out if other desirable jobs were available) were far less likely to quit than were employees actively applying for other jobs (Blau, 1993).

There is a crucial difference between absenteeism and turnover. Whereas absenteeism is almost always harmful to the organization, turnover is not necessarily detrimental. Sometimes it is the unsatisfactory employees who leave the company. I/O psychologists distinguish between **functional turnover,** when poor performers quit, and **dysfunctional turnover,** when good performers quit. A study of 143 salespersons in a large department store found that their turnover was largely functional: More than half the employees who quit their jobs had been rated marginal or unsatisfactory in their performance appraisals (Hollenbeck & Williams, 1986).

A meta-analysis involving more than 7,000 employees in various jobs and organizations confirmed that employees with high job performance were significantly less likely to quit than were employees with low job performance (McEvoy & Cascio, 1987). Another meta-analysis, involving 15,138 employees, also found a significant relationship between low job performance and high turnover (Williams & Livingstone, 1994).

In research involving 194 salespersons, studied during a period of corporate downsizing, it was found that involuntary turnover (a polite way of saying, "you're fired") was significantly related to job performance. Employees who performed better on the job, as indicated by performance appraisals, were the least likely to be fired (Barrick, Mount, & Strauss, 1994).

An organization's records on employee turnover may be incomplete or inaccurate, making it difficult to determine precisely why some employees quit. Questionnaire data were collected from several hundred former employees of a large university and from their supervisors. The results showed that in one third of the cases the reasons given by employees at the time of quitting disagreed with the reasons given by the same employees and by their former supervisors several months later (Campion, 1991).

Functional turnover The situation that arises when poor employees quit their jobs; this type of turnover is not necessarily detrimental to the organization.

Dysfunctional turnover The detrimental situation that arises in an organization when good employees quit their jobs.

PAY AS A SOURCE OF MOTIVATION AND SATISFACTION

Considerable research has demonstrated a positive relationship between pay and job satisfaction.

Perceived Pay Equity

The perceived equity or fairness of one's pay can be more important than the actual amount. Data from a national sample of 1,297 adults questioned about their economic and subjective well-being confirmed the importance of the perceived equity of one's pay. Survey respondents who believed that people with similar qualifications earned more than they did reported more dissatisfaction with their

NEWSBREAK #15

If Your Spouse Has a Job, You May Pay a Price

Bob and Tom could be twins. Not that they look alike, but in all other respects they are. Both married with two kids, they hold similar jobs as midlevel managers with the same company, have the same education and number of years on the job, and have received the same ratings from their supervisors. There the similarity ends. Bob's wife has a paying job outside the home. Tom's wife is a homemaker raising the kids. And that's why Bob makes $8,000 a year less than Tom for the same work.

Women aren't the only managers facing salary discrimination. A survey of 350 managers at 20 Fortune 500 companies revealed salary discrimination against men whose wives work outside the home. At the beginning of the study, in 1984, men with children whose wives worked received 11% less in pay raises than men with children whose wives did not work outside the home. Five years later, the pay raise gap had increased to 70%.

Another survey, conducted of 695 business school graduates (MBAs) contacted from 12 to 17 years after graduation, also found that men managers whose wives worked outside the home earned 20% less, on the average, than colleagues whose wives remained at home fulltime to rear the children.

The psychologists who conducted the survey are not sure why this disparity exists. Perhaps top managers believe that working fathers whose wives stay home with the children are more productive employees and therefore deserve higher salaries. Or perhaps they figure that men whose wives have paying jobs don't need to earn as much money themselves. After all, they have two incomes, don't they?

Not only is the employee whose wife has a job paid less, but she is earning less on her job than a man doing the same work. So the working couple is penalized twice. An I/O psychologist concluded, "Dual-earner dads may be the latest victims of salary discrimination in the nineties."

Sources: Barrett, M. W. (1995). Dual-earner dads may be the latest victims of salary discrimination. *Academy of Management Executive, 9*(2), 71–72; Schner, J. A., & Reitman, F. (1993). Effects of alternate family structures on managerial career paths. *Academy of Management Journal, 36,* 830–843.

pay; they thought they were being paid less than they deserved. In a mail survey of 2,000 managers and executives in a federal government agency, it was found that the managers and executives had more favorable attitudes toward the organization's pay system when they believed that their salaries were higher than those of their colleagues (Miceli, Jung, Near, & Greenberger, 1991; Sweeney, McFarlin, & Inderrieden, 1990).

Most people develop personal standards of comparison that are based on the minimum salary we consider acceptable, the pay we believe our job deserves, and the amount we think our co-workers are being paid. Thus, satisfaction with pay is determined by the discrepancy between our standards and our actual salary, a view that has received much research support (see, for example, Rice, Phillips, & McFarlin, 1990).

Of course, as we have seen, for some groups in American society there is no pay equity, either actual or perceived. Women are paid less than men for the same work, and many ethnic minority employees are paid less than whites. When the pay rates of 197 Hispanic, black, and white men and women workers were compared, the results were clear. Women and minorities earned significantly less than white men. Further, the older the workers, the greater the income gap (Barnum, Liden, & Ditomaso, 1995).

Measuring Pay Satisfaction

We have seen that I/O psychologists have developed questionnaires and other types of self-report inventories to measure many aspects of job performance and behavior and our attitudes and feelings about them. Pay satisfaction is one of these aspects. The Pay Satisfaction Questionnaire (PSQ) is an 18-item inventory dealing with various pay issues, including fringe benefits, raises, salary policies, administrative procedures, and the influence of one's supervisor in determining employee salaries (Heneman & Schwab, 1985).

Research with the PSQ has identified four dimensions of pay satisfaction: pay level, pay raises, fringe benefits, and structure and administration. Studies have also shown that employees may be satisfied with one dimension (such as fringe benefits), but dissatisfied with another (perhaps pay raises). Therefore, an overall or global measure of pay satisfaction could be misleading, causing a company's executives to misjudge how the employees feel about their pay (Judge, 1993b; Judge & Welbourne, 1994).

Merit Pay

Merit pay A wage system in which pay is based on level of performance.

The notion of **merit pay,** or pay for performance (with the better performers paid more), is fine in theory but does not translate well to the realities of the workplace. I/O psychologists have studied influences on the size of pay increases given under merit pay plans. They have found widespread disagreement among managers about the employee job behaviors that should be important in making decisions about pay. A worker in one department might receive a sizable raise for job behaviors that bring no recognition in another department. Supervisors who receive substantial pay raises tend to recommend larger raises for their subordinates than do supervisors who receive smaller pay raises.

Pay raises are also related to the degree to which managers depend on their subordinates' expertise and support and whether managers consider such dependence a threat. For example, a manager who is low in self-esteem may rely on subordinates to provide praise or positive feedback and therefore may be reluctant to give them low pay increases. The manager may fear that if subordinates do not receive a sufficient salary, they will withhold their support or reduce their productivity to make the manager look bad (Bartol & Martin, 1988, 1990). A study of 171 job-seeking college students found that most of them said they would prefer a merit pay arrangement, in which salary increases are based on evaluations of individual achievement (Cable & Judge, 1994).

Wage-Incentive Pay Systems

There are also problems with **wage-incentive systems,** the primary pay scheme for production workers. Through a time-and-motion analysis of a production job, an average or standard number of units produced in a given time can be determined. The wage-incentive system is based on this rate. In theory, the system provides an incentive for high job performance—the more units produced, the higher the wage—but it seldom works in practice. (We will discuss this issue more fully in Chapter 9.) Many work groups establish their own standard for a good shift's production. Regardless of the incentive offered they will not produce more but will spread out the work to comfortably fill the hours. Surveys show that most workers prefer a straight hourly payment system.

Wage-incentive systems
The primary pay system for production workers in which the more units produced, the higher the wage.

piecemeal

JOB INVOLVEMENT

Closely related to motivation and job satisfaction is **job involvement**—the intensity of a person's psychological identification with the job. Usually, the higher one's identification or involvement with a job, the greater is the job satisfaction. Job involvement depends on personal characteristics, job characteristics, and social factors.

Job involvement The intensity of one's psychological identification with the job.

Personal Characteristics.   Personal characteristics important in job involvement are age, growth needs, and belief in the traditional work ethic. Older workers are usually more involved with their jobs, perhaps because they have more responsibility and challenge and more opportunity to satisfy growth needs. Older workers are also more likely to believe in the value of hard work. Younger workers, typically in entry-level positions, hold less stimulating and challenging jobs.

Job Characteristics.   Because growth needs are important in job involvement, it follows that the job characteristics most relevant to job involvement are stimulation, autonomy, variety, task identity, feedback, and participation—the characteristics that allow for satisfaction of the growth needs.

Social Factors.   Social factors on the job can also influence job involvement. Employees who work in groups report stronger job involvement than employees who work alone. Participation in decision making is related to job involvement, as is the extent to which employees support organizational goals. Feelings of success and achievement on the job enhance one's level of job involvement.

The relationship between job involvement and job performance is unclear. Employees with high job involvement are more satisfied with, and more successful at, their jobs. Their rates of turnover and absenteeism are lower than those of employees with low job involvement. However, we cannot state with certainty that high job involvement correlates with high performance.

ORGANIZATIONAL COMMITMENT

Organizational commitment The degree of one's psychological identification with or attachment to the organization for which one works.

Another variable allied with motivation and job satisfaction is **organizational commitment;** that is, the degree of psychological identification with or attachment to the organization for which we work. Organizational commitment has been found to have the following components (Mowday, Porter, & Steers, 1982):

- Acceptance of the values and goals of the organization
- Willingness to exert effort for the organization
- Having a strong desire to remain affiliated with the organization

Organizational commitment is related to both personal and organizational factors.

Personal Factors

Older employees who have been with a company more than 2 years and who have a high need to achieve are more likely to rate high in organizational commitment. A study of 119 bank employees in New Guinea showed that organizational commitment developed as early as 6 months after joining the company. Further, high organizational commitment was found to be positively related to job satisfaction (O'Driscoll, 1987).

A survey of 338 salespersons from two companies found that the relationship between job performance and organizational commitment was higher for those with fewer financial pressures. This finding suggests that personal financial difficulties may weaken an employee's commitment to the organization (Brett, Cron, & Slocum, 1995).

Employees of U.S. companies who work in other countries may develop dual organizational commitments: to the parent company at home and to the local plant or office abroad. A study of 321 American managers on international assignment in European or Pacific Rim countries found that high tenure with the parent company, low role conflict, and a high level of training for the overseas job were associated with high organizational commitment to the parent firm (Gregersen & Black, 1992).

Scientists and engineers appear to have less organizational commitment than do employees in other occupational groups. Employees who have reached a career plateau—who have held the same position for 5 years and believe they are less marketable and have fewer promotion opportunities—show a decline in organizational commitment (Stout, Slocum, & Cron, 1988).

A comparison of 1,418 employees in private and public sector organizations in Australia showed that those who worked for government agencies had significantly lower organizational commitment (Zeffane, 1994). Recall the earlier study showing that government employees were also low in job satisfaction.

Organizational Factors

Organizational factors associated with high organizational commitment include job enrichment, autonomy, opportunity to use skills, and positive attitudes toward the work group. A study of white-collar employees showed that their level of organizational commitment was influenced by their perception of how committed the organization was to them. The greater the perceived commitment to employees, the higher employees' expectations that if they work to meet organizational goals, then they will be equitably rewarded (Hutchison & Sowa, 1986). A questionnaire survey of several occupational groups (high school teachers, brokerage firm clerks, factory workers, insurance salespersons, and police officers) found a positive relationship between perceived organizational support and organizational commitment, diligence, innovative management, job performance, and attendance (Eisenberger, Fasolo, & Davis-LaMastro, 1990).

A study involving 383 employees of a large multinational firm and their managers found a positive relationship between perceived organizational support and organizational citizenship behaviors (Shore & Wayne, 1993). Thus, organizational commitment goes both ways. Employees will not feel attached to their employers unless they have reason to believe their employers are committed to them. That belief is increasingly hard to maintain during massive layoffs and downsizings when workers lose their jobs regardless of how well they are performing them.

Another organizational factor involves the increasing diversity of the workforce. A study of 1,705 supervisory and nonsupervisory personnel at a state government agency and two large private firms found that the greater the diversity of the work group, the lower the level of organizational commitment of the majority white male employees. Racial differences had the greatest impact. The more ethnic minority employees in the work group studied, the less committed were its white workers. The reverse did not hold true. Organizational commitment of minority employees was not affected by the number of white employees in their work group. However, an extensive research review concluded that, in general, minority employees in work groups tend to exhibit lower levels of organizational commitment (Milliken & Martins, 1996).

Research has also been conducted on sex differences. The more women in the work group, the lower the commitment of the men. With women, however, the reaction was the opposite. The more men there were in a work group, the higher the level of organizational commitment among the women (Fagenson, 1993).

Relationship to Job Satisfaction and Performance

A meta-analysis of empirical studies on organizational commitment found that it correlated positively with job satisfaction and attendance and negatively with turnover. It had little direct influence on job performance (Mathieu & Zajac, 1990). This finding was supported by a study of 469 recent college graduates. Although the researchers found no significant relationship between job performance and commitment to the organization, a relationship was noted between job performance and commitment to one's immediate supervisor. These results suggest that commitment may be directed in different ways, one of which would be loyalty to one's boss (Becker, Billings, Eveleth, & Gilbert, 1996).

A survey of 588 Army and Navy ROTC cadets found that there was a mutual interaction between commitment to their military units and satisfaction with their job duties but that the influence of satisfaction on commitment was the stronger (Mathieu, 1991). A survey of 440 employees of a military supply company found that employee commitment to top management was a better predictor of job satisfaction than was employee commitment to the organization as a whole (Becker, 1992). This finding highlights again the need to determine the specific aspects of the organization to which employees feel committed.

A study of 82 hospital employees conducted during a time of tightening budgets, closing of hospital units, and rumors of layoffs showed that employees' degree of organizational commitment eased the effects of the stress engendered by the corporate changes. The stress of the turmoil increased job dissatisfaction primarily in those employees low in organizational commitment (Begley & Czajka, 1993).

Types of Organizational Commitment

I/O psychologists have identified three kinds of organizational commitment: affective or attitudinal commitment, behavioral or continuance commitment, and normative commitment (Dunham, Grube, & Castañeda, 1994; Meyer & Allen, 1991; Meyer, Allen, & Smith, 1993). In affective commitment, the type we have been discussing, the employee identifies with the organization, internalizes its values and attitudes, and complies with its demands. Affective commitment correlates highly with perceived organizational support (Shore & Tetrick, 1991). Psychologists have found that managers perceive those employees who are high in affective commitment as having greater management potential than those high in behavioral commitment (Shore, Barksdale, & Shore, 1995).

In behavioral commitment, the employee is bound to the organization only by peripheral factors such as pension plans and seniority, which would not continue if the employee quit. There is no personal identification with organizational goals and values. Research suggests that affective commitment is positively related to job performance and behavioral commitment is negatively related to job performance (Meyer, Paunonen, Gellatly, Goffin, & Jackson, 1989).

Normative commitment involves a sense of obligation to remain with the employer, a feeling that develops through receiving benefits such as tuition reimbursement or specific skills training. In summary, psychologists have concluded the following:

> Employees with a strong affective commitment remain with the organization because they want to, those with a strong [behavioral] commitment remain because they need to, and those with a strong normative commitment remain because they feel they ought to do so (Meyer, Allen, & Smith, 1993, p. 539).

Employee Commitment and Job Performance

We saw that employees who are high in organizational commitment are also high in job satisfaction and attendance, and low in turnover. In other words, these people like their jobs, are seldom late or absent, and don't want to quit. In view of these highly positive findings about organizational commitment, you may find it surprising that I/O psychologists have documented no relationship between organizational commitment and employee performance.

That puzzling finding led one group of researchers to suggest that an employee's commitment to an organization may comprise different components, rather than being a global, unitary tendency. One of those factors might be the employee's supervisor, because it is the immediate supervisor, rather than the organization as a whole, who creates and promotes norms of job performance and rewards employees for reaching or exceeding them.

To determine the effect on job performance of commitment to one's supervisor, questionnaires were mailed to 1,803 members of the 1993 graduating class of a large university. Usable data were obtained from 469 respondents. The mean age was 24. Of the 469 subjects, 55.1% were women, 85.5% white, 2% Hispanic, and 4.2% Asian. Fewer than 2% were African-American or Native American. All graduates had been working for approximately 11 months at the time they were surveyed. The subjects were asked for permission to contact their supervisors. A survey was then sent to the 355 supervisors identified, asking them to rate the job performance of the graduate. Usable data were received from 315 supervisors, an impressive 88.7% return.

The researchers wanted to assess the employees' degree of identification with their supervisor and with the organization, as well as the extent to

Source: Becker, T. E., Billings, R. S., Eveleth, D. M., & Gilbert, N. L. (1996). Foci and bases of employee commitment: Implications for job performance. *Academy of Management Journal, 39,* 464–482.

which they internalized the values and goals of both supervisor and organization. To measure identification and internalization, the employees were asked questions such as the following; they checked which of the two items in the brackets applied to them.

1. When I talk about [my supervisor, this organization], I usually say "we" rather than "they."
2. When someone criticizes [my supervisor, this organization], it feels like a personal insult.

To assess internalization of values and goals, items such as the following were asked.

1. If the values of [my supervisor, this organization] were different, I would not be as attracted to [my supervisor, this organization].
2. Since starting this job, my personal values and those of [my supervisor, this organization] have become more similar.

The results showed that commitment to the supervisors was significantly and positively related to job performance. There was no significant correlation between commitment to the organization and job performance. No significant differences were found between performance and commitment based on identification with either supervisor or organization and commitment based on internalization of organizational values. Employee commitment to their supervisors was clearly related to job performance; commitment to the organization was not.

Critical Thinking Questions

1. Define organizational commitment and distinguish it from job involvement.
2. What personal and organizational factors are related to high organizational commitment?
3. What weaknesses or limitations can you find in this study? How would you design an exper-

iment to study organizational commitment and its components?

4. In what ways might the results have been different if older subjects, who had been with an organization for many years, had been studied? Explain your answer.

5. If you were the CEO of an organization, how would you attempt to switch your employees' commitment from their immediate supervisors to the organization as a whole?

SUMMARY

Content theories of motivation deal with internal needs that influence behavior. Process theories focus on cognitive processes involved in making decisions. **Achievement motivation** theory posits the need to accomplish something and to be the best in whatever one undertakes. **Needs hierarchy theory** proposes five needs (physiological, safety, belonging, esteem, and **self-actualization**), each of which must be satisfied before the next becomes prominent. **ERG theory** posits three needs (existence, relatedness, and growth). The growth needs include self-actualization. **Motivator-hygiene theory** proposes motivator needs (the nature of the work and its level of achievement and responsibility) and hygiene needs (aspects of the work environment such as pay and supervision). An outgrowth of motivator-hygiene theory is **job enrichment,** the redesign of jobs to maximize motivator factors. **Job-characteristics theory** posits individual differences in growth needs and suggests that employee perceptions of job characteristics influence motivation.

The **valence-instrumentality-expectancy (VIE) theory** describes a person's perceived expectation of the rewards that will follow certain behaviors. **Equity theory** deals with the perceived ratio of outcome to input and how equitably that ratio compares with those of co-workers. **Goal-setting theory** suggests that motivation is defined by one's intention to achieve a particular goal. The **high performance cycle** suggests that goals affect performance through moderators and mediators.

Job satisfaction can be measured through questionnaires and interviews. It may be partly an inherited characteristic reciprocally related to overall life satisfaction. Job facet satisfaction refers to individual aspects of the job that can influence employee attitudes. Job satisfaction increases with age, length of job experience, and occupational level. Sex differences in reported job satisfaction are inconsistent. Race differences have been found to be statistically significant only at the managerial level, where whites report greater job satisfaction than do blacks. Job satisfaction appears to be unaffected by cognitive ability, assuming that the job is sufficiently challenging. Losing one's job can be damaging to self-esteem and health. Large-scale layoffs also affect those workers remaining on the job.

The relationship between job satisfaction and productivity is inconsistent. High performance may lead to job satisfaction, or job satisfaction may lead to high performance. Job dissatisfaction can result in antisocial behavior as well as counterproductive behavior (sabotage, shoddy work, and theft) that interferes with organizational goals. Absenteeism is higher among younger workers and in companies with liberal sick-leave policies. Absenteeism is high in low-status jobs and in high-paying jobs. Turnover is allied with low job involvement, low organizational commitment, poor promotion opportunities, and dissatisfaction with pay and supervision. In functional turnover, low performers quit; in dysfunctional turnover, high performers quit.

There appears to be a positive relationship between pay and job satisfaction. An important factor in pay satisfaction is its perceived equity and relation to job performance. Blue-collar workers on **wage-incentive systems** and managers on **merit pay** systems report pay dissatisfaction. Merit pay can lower work motivation because of perceived unfairness; one's true abilities may not be sufficiently rewarded.

Job involvement (intensity of psychological identification with work) is related to job satisfaction. Involvement is affected by personal characteristics such as age, high growth needs, and belief in the work ethic, and by job characteristics such as level of challenge and opportunity for employee participation.

Organizational commitment is related to motivation and satisfaction and is greater among older employees and those high in achievement motivation. Also contributing to organizational commitment are job enrichment, autonomy, perceived organizational support, opportunity to use skills, and a positive attitude toward the work group. Three types of commitment are affective commitment, behavioral commitment, and normative commitment.

KEY TERMS

achievement motivation	job satisfaction
dysfunctional turnover	merit pay
equity theory	motivation
ERG theory	motivator-hygiene theory
existence needs	motivator needs
functional turnover	needs hierarchy theory
goal-setting theory	organizational commitment
growth needs	prosocial behavior
high performance cycle	relatedness needs
hygiene needs	self-actualization need
job-characteristics theory	Type A personality
job congruence	valence-instrumentality-expectancy (VIE)
job enrichment	theory
job involvement	wage-incentive systems

ADDITIONAL READING

Adams, S. (1996). *The Dilbert Principle: A cubicle's-eye view of bosses, meetings, management fads and other workplace afflictions.* New York: Harper Business. Dilbert is a comic-strip character, an employee in a tiny office cubicle, coping with a parody of a dull-witted boss and idiotic management policies. The book is a composite of comic strips, E-mail messages the author has received from hundreds of real employees, and the author's commentary on issues affecting worker motivation and job satisfaction.

Barnum, P., Liden, R. C., & Ditomaso, N. (1995). Double jeopardy for women and minorities: Pay differences with age. *Academy of Management Journal, 38,* 863–880. Considers differential pay rates based on age for white, black, and Hispanic men and women workers in public-sector and private-sector organizations.

Judge, T. A., & Watanabe, S. (1993). Another look at the job satisfaction-life satisfaction relationship. *Journal of Applied Psychology, 78,* 939–948. Analyzes the interrelationship of job satisfaction issues (such as pay, work hours, working conditions, and promotion opportunities) and life satisfaction issues (such as marital status, health, and age).

Locke, E. A., & Latham, G. P. (1990). *A theory of goal setting and task performance.* Upper Saddle River, NJ: Prentice Hall. Reviews the theoretical and research work and the extensions and applications of 20 years of goal-setting theory.

O'Neill, H. M., & Lenn, D. J. (1995). Voices of survivors: Words that downsizing CEOs should hear. *Academy of Management Executive, 9*(4), 23–34. Presents interviews with middle managers focusing on their emotional responses to the policy of downsizing; includes a response from a senior corporate manager.

The Organization of the Organization

CHAPTER OUTLINE

All of us live and work within the framework of some kind of organization, a context that provides written and unwritten, formal and informal rules and guidelines about how its members conduct themselves. You grew up in an organization called a family. A climate or culture was established by your parents that defined the rules by which the family functioned—the acceptable attitudes, values, and behaviors that blended to make your family a unique organization, different from the families of your friends and acquaintances.

Perhaps a family in the house across the street had a culture based on orthodox religious beliefs and unusually strict standards of behavior, whereas a family next door was more moderate in its beliefs or reared the children more permissively. These families operated within different organizational styles. They established a culture based on a specific set of expectations, needs, and values that were expected to hold for all family members.

Various organizational styles are also evident in your college classes. One professor may be stern, even dictatorial, allowing no student participation. Another may operate in a more democratic fashion, asking students to participate in decision making about course content and requirements.

Differences in organizational style in the workplace range from the rigid, hierarchical bureaucracy of the military and the civil service to the open, participatory plan that fosters high employee involvement. Bureaucracies regulate and prescribe what workers do and how they do it. Little or no deviation is tolerated.

The trend toward the humanization of work has led to a modification of many bureaucracies. Increasing numbers of organizations are treating their employees as integral members of the company and allowing them to participate in planning and decision making. This shift in organizational style has brought about radical changes in the way work is organized and performed and has led to an improvement in the quality of work life for many employees.

Organizational psychologists study these changing trends in organizational life to determine their impact on employees. We have described how the nature of leadership and the motivations of workers can affect job satisfaction, job performance, and organizational efficiency. In this chapter we describe the impact of organizational factors.

CLASSIC AND MODERN ORGANIZATIONAL STYLES: CHANGES IN COMMUNICATION AND DECISION-MAKING PROCESSES

Two extremes in organizational style are represented by the bureaucratic approach and the participatory approach.

Bureaucracy

Bureaucracies A formal, orderly, and rational approach to organizing business enterprises.

We tend to think of **bureaucracies** in negative terms, as bloated, inefficient structures, top-heavy with layers of management and wrapped in miles of red tape that frustrates creativity. As we know from our everyday experiences trying to deal with organizations of this type, there is much truth to this view. Yet, the bureaucratic organizational style was once as revolutionary as the modern participative style, and it was considered just as humanistic in its intentions. Bureaucracies were devised to improve the quality of work life, and for a time, they did.

The few executives at the top of the organization chart have little contact with lower-level employees and thus may have little awareness of their working conditions and personal concerns.

As a movement of social protest, bureaucracy was designed to correct the inequities, favoritism, and cruelty that characterized organizations at the beginning of the Industrial Revolution. Companies were owned and managed by their founders, who had absolute control over the terms and conditions of employment. Employees were at the mercy of the owners' whims, prejudices, and decrees.

To correct these abuses, Max Weber, a German sociologist, promoted a new organizational style that would eliminate social and personal injustice (Weber, 1947). Bureaucracy was to be a rational, formal structure organized along impersonal and objective lines—an orderly, predictable system that would function like an efficient machine, unaffected by the prejudices of the factory owners. Workers would have the opportunity to rise from one organizational level to the next on the basis of their ability, not because of their social class or whether the boss liked them. Bureaucracy was a tremendous improvement over the earlier system and served in its day to humanize the workplace.

Organization Charts.   The first practical application of the bureaucratic organizational style appeared in the United States even before Weber published his ideas on bureaucracy. The organization chart, which may be the most famous symbol of the bureaucratic approach, came into being in the 1850s. A general superintendent for the New York & Erie Railroad, Daniel McCallum, prepared a chart for his company and insisted that all workers abide by it (Chandler, 1988). McCallum's idea—formalizing the position and status of all employees in a hierarchical structure—quickly became popular, and by 1910 it had been adopted by most American companies. Thus, when Weber formally proposed the rules by which bureaucracies should function, he was describing an organizational style already widely accepted in the United States.

Weber's ideas about bureaucracy, as depicted on the organization chart, involved breaking down or decentralizing the organization into component parts and operations. Each operation would be linked to others in a fixed rank order of control. The concept of division of labor, fostered by the scientific management approach, simplified jobs and made them more specialized. Responsibility or authority for each operation was delegated downward through the hierarchy, and communication flowed upward through the same channels. This arrangement effectively cut employees off from contact with other levels and sectors of the organization (see Figure 9–1).

Although organization charts look nice and give managers the feeling that their employees are in their proper places and that the organization is running smoothly, these neat lines and boxes on paper do not always reflect daily operations on the job. There is, as we shall see, an organization within the organization—an uncharted complex of informal social groupings of workers—that can interfere with the most rigid rules of the most dictatorial structure. And it is often through these informal groups and networks that the work of an organization is (or is not) accomplished.

Problems With Bureaucracies.   Bureaucracies ignore human needs and values. They treat employees as inanimate, impersonal squares on the chart, as interchangeable as the machines they operate. Bureaucracies do not recognize human motivations, such as the needs for personal growth, self-actualization, and participation in decision making.

Employees within a bureaucracy have no individual identity and no control over their work or over the organizational policies that influence the quality of their working life. The ideal employees for a bureaucracy are docile, passive, de-

FIGURE 9–1.   A typical bureaucratic organization.

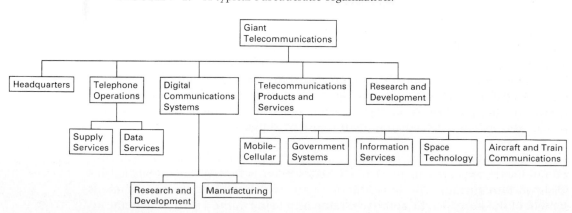

pendent, and childlike. Decisions are made for them, for their own good, because they are considered incapable of deciding for themselves. By being forced to channel all communication through their immediate supervisor, workers are isolated from higher management and prevented from making suggestions about company practices that affect their jobs and well-being. Recall from Chapter 8 that workers in these situations score low on measures of job satisfaction and organizational commitment.

Bureaucracies can be criticized not only for their smothering effects on workers but also for their harmful effects on themselves. Just as they prevent personal growth for employees, bureaucracies minimize opportunities for organizational growth, in part because of the barriers to upward communication. Bureaucracies foster rigidity and permanence and do not adapt quickly or well to the kinds of changing social conditions and technological innovations characteristic of today's workplace. The orderly bureaucratic structure was designed to preserve existing conditions. New developments are viewed as threats. For all its initial revolutionary fervor and humanistic intentions, then, the bureaucratic style has not been successful in meeting human needs and changing times.

Participatory Democracy

We noted that a major criticism of bureaucracy is its tendency to treat workers as docile, passive, and dependent. The modern **participative organizational style** holds a totally different view of human nature, summarized by the Theory Y position of McGregor's Theory X/Theory Y formulation (McGregor, 1960). Theory X describes a view of human nature compatible with the rigid requirements of a bureaucracy, which stifles individual motivation and the potential for growth. Workers need controlling, dictatorial leaders because they are incapable of acting on their own initiative. This traditional bureaucratic approach is also known as the low-involvement organization in which "the line worker performs the organization's work, middle managers control that work, and top management plans, designs, and leads the organization" (Mohrman & Cohen, 1995, p. 369).

> **Participative organizational style** Emphasis on the behaviors and needs of employees instead of a rigid focus on job tasks.

In contrast, Theory Y assumes that employees are motivated to seek and accept responsibility for their work. The theory attributes to people a high level of creativity, commitment, and need for personal growth. Theory Y and other motivational conceptions supporting a participatory democracy approach suggest that organizations must decrease workers' dependency and subordination in order to take better advantage of their potential. Jobs and organizations must become less rigid in design and structure, allowing employees to help determine how best to perform their tasks. Jobs can be enriched to increase challenge and responsibility. Leaders should become less autocratic and more responsive to employee input. Decision making should involve participation at all levels. And organizations must become more flexible, capable of changing in response to employee needs and to social, technological, and economic conditions.

High-Involvement Management. This **high-involvement management** style of the participative organization rests on three assumptions about people, participation, and performance (Lawler, 1986).

> **High-involvement management** The management style necessary for the modern organizational approach of participatory democracy.

NEWSBREAK #16

The Workers Are Taking Over!

It's happening everywhere you look. Workers are taking on more and more responsibility and making decisions only their bosses used to make. Jobs have been enlarged, expanded, and enriched, and employees have been empowered, given the freedom to do their work in their own way.

Take the case of a major department store. A salesperson overheard a customer tell a companion that the suit she had bought 3 weeks ago was now on sale. She wished she had waited for the sale so she could have bought it for less. The alert salesperson asked for the customer's name and credited her account with the difference between the sale price and what she had paid 3 weeks before. The salesperson acted on his own initiative, without asking his supervisor for an OK. Without even telling his supervisor! He was empowered to make these decisions for himself.

Nordstrom, the department store that prides itself on both customer and employee satisfaction, posts the following rules for its new employees:

Rule #1: Use your good judgment in all situations.
There will be no additional rules.

The rule says to use *your* good judgment. That means decisions and the responsibility for them are in the hands of the employees, not the supervisors. This is nothing short of a revolution in the way we work.

A commercial printing company in Wisconsin encourages its printing press operators to make their own decisions. A company spokesperson explained:

Just as each lawyer is a partner and runs his own part of the business, I said each pressman is going to run his own press. I'd rather have 50 people out there thinking independently than for me to sit up here from the top and say, "This is the way we're going to do it."

At Compaq Computers, three-person teams assemble and test the new computers. Each worker is capable of performing different tasks and coping with challenges. Previously, the computers were built on an assembly line, with each worker performing one small task repeatedly. Under the new system, the number of completed units per worker increased 50%. Profits improved, and the employees reported greater satisfaction with their jobs. They feel important—and they are. The workers are taking over!

Sources: D. P. Levin. Compaq storms the PC heights from its factory floor. *New York Times,* November 13, 1994. Pfeffer, J. (1995). Producing sustainable competitive advantages through the effective management of people. *Academy of Management Executive, 9*(1), 55–70. T. Burney. Layoff survivors need training. *St. Petersburg [FL] Times,* March 10, 1996. M. Lefkoe, Corporate culture and worker health. *New York Times,* May 24, 1992.

Susan Pacheco-Baker,
Ford Mechanical Engineer.

"Some of our best customer input comes from employees."

Because our employees are customers too, they want the same thing in a car or truck as you do. So at Ford Motor Company we encourage everyone, in every area of the company, to share their ideas. And it's this kind of thinking that has resulted in vehicles like our Ford Explorer having one of the highest customer satisfaction ratings in the industry. People know a good idea when they see it.

Ford • Lincoln • Mercury • Ford Trucks

QUALITY IS JOB 1.^{SM} IT'S WORKING.

Buckle up–Together we can save lives.   Always insist on genuine Ford Motor Company collision repair parts.

Modern organizations invite employee participation in decision making. (Courtesy of Ford Motor Company.)

1. *Human relations.* People should be treated fairly and with respect. People want to participate, and when they are allowed to do so, they will accept change and become more satisfied with and committed to the organization.
2. *Human resources.* People are a valuable resource because they have knowledge and ideas. When they participate in decision making, the result is better solutions to organizational problems. Organizations must promote the personal development of their employees because it makes them more valuable to the company.
3. *High involvement.* People can be trusted to develop the knowledge and skills to make important decisions about the management of their work. When people are allowed to make such decisions, the result is an improvement in organizational performance.

Quality-of-work-life (QWL) programs Organizational programs based on active employee participation in decision and policy making.

High-involvement management calls for active employee participation in decision and policy making at all levels and can lead to greater opportunities for personal growth and fulfillment and increased organizational effectiveness. These changes in organizational style have been expressed in various **quality-of-work-life (QWL) programs.** A questionnaire survey of 171 CEOs of small, midsize, and large U.S. firms revealed that the greatest challenge they faced was the need for more employee involvement and participative management (Harper, 1992). However, even the strongest proponents of high-involvement management concede that it has not totally transformed the workplace. The majority of employees are not yet working in high-involvement, participative situations.

QUALITY-OF-WORK-LIFE PROGRAMS

LTV Steel established labor-management participation teams in the early 1980s to break down barriers between union and management and to involve employees in efforts to solve work-related problems. Each team consists of 8 to 10 members who meet weekly to deal with problems in their area of responsibility. A facilitator trains the team members in team-building exercises, problem-solving techniques, and communication skills.

The company reports that this team approach to problem solving has reduced production costs and improved product quality and job satisfaction. Some LTV labor-management teams work with teams from automobile manufacturers (LTV's major customer) to discuss mutual problems such as the quality of the steel being supplied. One LTV team designed a system to improve the paperwork flow within the company, which resulted in an annual savings in excess of $70,000.

Another ambitious quality-of-work-life program was undertaken by General Motors with the support of top management and the United Auto Workers union. The program began in 1973 when company and union officials agreed to form a labor-management committee to assess QWL projects (Miller, 1978). All projects had to consider extrinsic factors (physical working conditions) and intrinsic factors (employee involvement and satisfaction). Teams of I/O psychologists, managers, and employees were empowered to enlarge jobs, redesign production facilities, and revise the old low-involvement organizational structure.

Consider the GM assembly plant in Fremont, California. The company closed the plant in 1982 because the quality of the cars assembled there was exceptionally poor. Absenteeism stood at 20%, on-the-job use of alcohol and illicit drugs was widespread, and more than 800 grievances had been filed against the company. The plant reopened 3 years later as New United Motors Manufacturing Incorporated (NUMMI), a joint venture of GM and Toyota that was committed to participative management.

NUMMI employees work in teams of four to six members and perform various tasks throughout the workweek. Cars are built on the traditional assembly line, but employees rotate from one job to another, mastering new skills in the process. They solve production problems and devise ways to increase productivity on their own, without being told what to do by their supervisors.

Artificial status barriers have been eliminated. Workers and managers eat in the same cafeteria, and all begin the workday with a group exercise period. The majority of the employees who worked in the old GM plant like the participative organizational style, and the quality of the cars produced has improved markedly. Labor productivity is reported to be at least 50% higher than at other GM plants and nearly as high as at Toyota plants.

Encouraged by NUMMI's success, General Motors adopted the participatory approach for its new Saturn Motors plant in Spring Hill, Tennessee, which opened in 1990. Workers are organized into teams of about a dozen members, and they make all major decisions about their work, including the hiring of new employees. Management perks, such as reserved parking places, were eliminated, and communication is encouraged across all levels without employees having to obtain permission from supervisors or union shop stewards. Absenteeism is reported to be less than 1%, a rate similar to that of Japanese auto plants, and less than a tenth of other U.S. auto plants. A 1991 *New York Times* survey found the quality of the Saturn cars to be higher than any other GM car.

Why Some Programs Fail

There are many reports of successful QWL programs, but it should be noted that some have failed. Consider Volvo, which has been building cars by the team approach for more than 20 years. Although productivity is lower than at standard assembly plants, the participative approach resulted in substantial improvements in quality and reductions in turnover and absenteeism (Gyllenhammar, 1977). Volvo expanded the concept of worker participation at a new car assembly factory in Sweden in 1988. Instead of having employee teams build a portion of each car, which then moves on to the next team, the teams at the new plant build an entire car. The results were dismal. It took 50 hours to assemble a car at the new plant, compared to 37 hours using the older team approach. At a Volvo plant in Belgium that uses the traditional assembly line, it takes 25 hours to assemble a car. Absenteeism is high because many employees did not realize the demands the job would entail. In addition, the training period to provide workers with the skills to assemble an entire car turned out to be longer than anticipated.

Other QWL programs have failed because some employees have no desire to participate in decision making or to assume responsibility for determining the best way to perform their jobs. Some workers prefer, or need, more rather than less direct supervision. Also, QWL efforts can be doomed when managers continue to try to control their subordinates instead of working with them to share power and authority. QWL programs have a high probability of failure when they do not have the forceful advocacy and commitment of senior executives and when supervisors and shop stewards view such programs as a threat to their power. Managers and supervisors must give up some of the power and authority by which they once directed and controlled their subordinates. They must also learn to share power and to function willingly as coaches, guides, mentors, and resource persons. Many managers find this a difficult adjustment to make.

The Effects of Worker Participation Programs

An analysis of QWL programs at 20 plants led one psychologist to conclude that in general QWL programs can lead to improvements in job satisfaction, quantity and quality of output, and work procedures, and to an enhanced ability to attract and retain competent workers. Some QWL programs have also been shown to lead to reductions in the need for staff and supervisory support and in the number of union grievances filed against the organization (Lawler, 1986).

A meta-analysis of 47 studies on the effectiveness of employee participation programs found that they had a greater impact on job satisfaction than on productivity, although the programs did influence both factors. Workers reported that being offered the opportunity to participate in decision making was just as important as the actual participation itself (Miller & Monge, 1986). A more recent meta-analysis of 52 studies and 10 other research reviews on the effects of worker participation showed that it had small but statistically significant positive effects on work performance and job satisfaction (Wagner, 1994).

Some questions about employee participation remain unresolved. Will employees, once allowed some input into decision making, insist on greater and greater power? Will there be a worker-management struggle for organizational control? Will changing economic circumstances and high unemployment reduce the desire for employee participation? The QWL movement arose in the 1970s in response to three trends: employee interest in increased challenge and personal fulfillment; the recognition that boring, routine, and oversimplified jobs were dehumanizing; and the problems of low productivity and high absenteeism and turnover when jobs were plentiful. Adverse economic circumstances may temporarily replace the desire for a challenging job with an interest in finding any kind of job.

Quality Control Circles

Quality control circles Employee groups organized to deal with specific production problems.

Quality control circles, based on the work of Maslow, McClelland, and Herzberg, are concerned not so much with the overall quality of work life but with specific ways to improve the finished product and the level of production. Quality circle programs also have the potential to raise employee satisfaction and morale and contribute to personal growth and development, although these are by-products of the process. The overall goal is enhanced quantity and quality of production.

Quality control circles require that workers be given greater responsibility for their work and be allowed to participate in decisions affecting the nature of the work and the way it is performed. A quality control circle typically consists of 7 to 10 employees from the same section or department. Membership is voluntary, and meetings are usually held once a week. Members are trained in human relations skills and problem-solving techniques before they are permitted to deal with specific problems relating to productivity.

Although quality control circles afford workers the opportunity to advise management and to participate in the decision-making process, they do not affect the majority of organizational decisions. They typically have an impact only on their organizational unit. The hierarchical structure of the organization remains untouched. Managers do not share power with quality control circles, as they do with large-scale employee participation programs.

Companies using quality control circles have reported savings in money and time, increases in production and satisfaction, and decreases in absenteeism and turnover. A meta-analysis of 33 studies on the effectiveness of quality control circles reported that 49% showed positive results (Barrick & Alexander, 1987). In a large public utility company, the quality control circle program, in place for 7 years, encompassed 8% of the work force in 200 circles over all major departments. A comparison of 118 members with 118 nonmembers found that in the year following their participation, quality control circle members received significantly higher job performance ratings and were promoted more frequently than were nonmembers (Buch & Spangler, 1990). One explanation for the job success of quality control circle members is the greater visibility provided by weekly interactions with supervisors and higher-level managers.

Under the quality-of-work-life program at this plant, small teams of workers meet periodically to deal with problems of productivity and employee involvement.

I/O psychologists have found that the longer a quality control circle operates, the more likely it is to yield benefits for the organization. Management initiated quality circles appear to solve more problems, and solve them faster, than do worker-initiated programs. Quality circles whose members are high in self-esteem are more successful than circles whose members are low in self-esteem (Brockner & Hess, 1986).

One problem with quality control circles is that not all eligible workers volunteer to participate in the programs. For example, a study of 47 quality control circles in a Tennessee factory found that less than 7% of the work force agreed to join. Other research showed that those who join quality control circles want a greater degree of job involvement than those who decline to participate. No differences were reported between quality circle members and nonmembers on the variables of age or length of job experience (Tang, Tollison, & Whiteside, 1987).

Another difficulty is that some quality circles disband after a period of time. Reasons for these terminations include a lack of support from management or resistance from midlevel managers who have difficulty accepting suggestions from their subordinates. Failure to implement workers' suggestions and ideas can lower employees' expectations and willingness to continue to participate. Other quality control circles have become victims of their own success. Having solved major problems and maximized productivity, there is no longer any reason for them to continue. For these reasons, then, evidence suggests that quality control circles, although still operating in many organizations, are losing their popularity.

Self-Managing Work Groups

Self-managing work groups Employee groups that allow the members of a work team to manage, control, and monitor all facets of their work, from recruiting, hiring, and training new employees to deciding when to take rest breaks.

Self-managing work groups allow the members of a work team to manage, control, and monitor all facets of their work, from recruiting, hiring, and training new employees to deciding when to take rest breaks. These autonomous work groups have become highly popular; one estimate suggests that up to 80% of organizations with more than 100 employees are using self-managing work teams. In addition, 50% of the employees in these companies are reported to be members of at least one team (Gordon, 1992).

An analysis of self-managing work groups yielded the following behavioral characteristics (Hackman, 1986):

1. Employees assume personal responsibility and accountability for the outcomes of their work.
2. Employees monitor their own performance and seek feedback on how well they are accomplishing their tasks and meeting organizational goals.
3. Employees manage their performance and take corrective action when necessary to improve their performance and the performance of other group members.
4. Employees seek guidance, assistance, and resources from the organization when they do not have what they need to do the job.
5. Employees help members of their work group and employees in other groups to improve job performance and raise productivity for the organization as a whole.

Self-managing work groups require a level of employee maturity and responsibility not called for in supervisor-managed groups. Self-managing work groups also need clear direction from the organization about production goals, a support staff to provide technical expertise, and adequate material resources. In some cases, engineers and accountants are added to the self-management teams so that they can deal with a full range of problems, operating, in effect, as minibusinesses within the larger organization.

Self-managing work groups also depend on the maturity and responsibility of managers, who must be willing to surrender authority to their subordinates. When a wholesale distributor of architectural, engineering, and commercial art supplies decided to initiate the self-managing team approach, I/O psychologists interviewed the managers to determine their reactions. The managers' initial response was suspicion, uncertainty, and resistance to the prospect of losing their power. That attitude changed in time when managers accepted the idea that their employees were competent to handle the increased responsibility. The interviewers wrote: "These managers gradually switched from questioning their employees' competence to exploring ways of empowering them with the authority to perform management tasks" (Manz, Keating, & Donnellon, 1990, p. 20). Only then were the managers able to drop their traditional autocratic leadership role and become facilitators, helping rather than directing their groups.

A survey of 80 work groups involving 391 employees and 70 managers in a large financial organization found that employees considered management support to be the most critical variable in work group effectiveness. The extent of managerial support was also highly predictive of employee satisfaction (Campion, Medsker, & Higgs, 1993). A replication of this study, conducted in the same company but with higher-level professional employees, also demonstrated the importance of managerial support in the success of self-managing work groups (Campion, Papper, & Medsker, 1996).

At a telephone company in Arizona, a staff of 100 operators ran the facility full time without direct supervision. The operator work teams were responsible for finances, employee training, service quality, office procedures, and discipline. The self-management system resulted in lower absenteeism, fewer grievances, fewer customer complaints, and increased productivity (Taylor, Friedman, & Couture, 1987).

When self-managing work groups were introduced at a new minerals refining and processing plant in Australia, turnover and absenteeism increased initially. (This may be partially explained by the fact that the new location of the plant meant a longer commute for many workers.) Questionnaire responses from shift workers and maintenance workers 8 and 20 months after the program began showed higher job satisfaction among self-managing work groups than among supervisor-managed groups (Corderey, Mueller, & Smith, 1991).

A study of 72 self-managing work groups involving nearly 1,500 employees in an electronics firm and a manufacturer of hand tools assessed the effectiveness of the groups through questionnaires and interviews. The researchers concluded that the success of the team concept was positively related to three factors: the degree to which team members were given access to information needed to solve problems; the variety of skills the members were capable of performing; and the size of the team, up to a limit of approximately 50 members (Magjuka & Baldwin, 1991).

Other studies of self-managing work groups confirm the positive effects on productivity, quality of work, turnover, and job satisfaction (see Applebaum & Batt, 1994; Banker, Field, Schroeder, & Sinha, 1996; Cohen & Ledford, 1994; Kalleberg & Moody, 1994). "Ample evidence indicates that team-based forms of organizing often bring about higher levels of organizational effectiveness in comparison with traditional, bureaucratic forms" (Guzzo & Dickson, 1996, p. 330).

Self-managing work groups are not without problems however. Converting from traditional management to self-management is difficult, expensive, and time-consuming, and many organizations misunderstand the extent of the investment required. In particular, they underestimate the amount of training and meeting time involved and have unrealistic expectations about how soon self-managing groups can become productive. The need to monitor and review the progress of self-managing work groups can also dampen the initial enthusiasm for this approach.

The experience of a Texas chemical plant points to another problem with self-managing work groups: Not all employees like them. The Texas facility was organized to operate without supervisors. Members of the work teams were trained in technical and business skills so that they could perform various jobs. The more tasks they mastered, the higher their pay. The teams managed and monitored all phases of the work and conducted performance appraisals in open meetings. However, during the first 2 years of the program, nearly 50% of the employees quit. Improved employee selection procedures eventually reduced turnover to less than 5%, but until the work force stabilized, productivity remained low (Wagel, 1987).

INTRODUCING CHANGE IN ORGANIZATIONS

The employee participation programs we have discussed call for radical changes in organizational style. We have noted, however, that bureaucratic organizations by definition are resistant to change. When a structural change is to be introduced into an organization, it often meets with hostility, production slowdowns, strikes, or increased absenteeism and turnover. Whether the change involves new equipment, work schedules, procedures, office layout, or reassignment of personnel, it will usually be resisted at first.

Some organizations are able to change with the cooperation and support of employees and managers. The factor most responsible for determining whether change will be received positively or negatively is the way in which change is proposed and implemented. If change is imposed on employees in an autocratic manner and they are given no explanation or opportunity to participate, then they are most likely to react negatively. However, when managers make an effort to explain the nature of the change, the reasons for implementing it, and the benefits workers and management can expect from it, then workers are more likely to respond positively and accept the change.

This effect was demonstrated in the corporate merger of two companies engaged in light manufacturing. A merger is a stressful change for employees at all levels because they face an uncertain future. Employees at one of the company's plants were given realistic information about the merger and its consequences, and attempts were made to answer all their questions fully. Thus, employees were given a chance to express their concerns. At another plant, employees received only a brief letter from the CEO announcing the merger. Using rating scales to measure uncertainty and stress, job satisfaction, and organizational commitment, data were collected 3 days after the merger announcement and again 4 months later. They showed that employees who received more information about the merger experienced less uncertainty than those who received less information about the merger. The employees also expressed a greater belief that management was trustworthy, honest, and caring (Schweiger & DeNisi, 1991).

Another study dealt with 173 salaried employees whose wages had been frozen for a year and whose morale and job satisfaction had declined. In a series of workshops, half the employees were informed of the reason for the pay freeze: that the alternative would have been widespread layoffs and that the action had been taken to affect all employees equally. The other half of the employees (the control group) were given no such explanation. The employees who received the explanation showed significant increases in job satisfaction and organizational commitment, and a decrease in turnover intentions. Thus, in this instance, providing detailed reasons for this organizational change had beneficial effects, even when given long after the change had been implemented (Schaubroeck, May, & Brown, 1994).

Another organization instituted a smoking ban. They provided considerable information in a sensitive manner to their 732 clerical employees, making clear the reasons for the decision. The researcher concluded that heavy smokers (those most affected by this change in the conditions at the work site) accepted the ban more readily than if the company had simply announced the ban with no explanation or understanding about the problems it might cause (Greenberg, 1994).

Are the positive effects of worker participation permanent, or do they disappear once the researchers leave the office or factory? To study this question, two I/O psychologists visited a plant more than 4 years after it had undergone a radical change from a typical centralized bureaucracy to a flexible, innovative, participatory democracy. The change had been guided by the company president (a psychologist), with full worker participation, and was considered successful in terms of increased corporate profits, productive efficiency, and employee satisfaction. The consulting psychologists in this now-classic study found that the benefits were evident 4 years later and that some of the effects were even greater than during the period immediately following the change. The increase in job satisfaction was accompanied by a higher concern with maintaining production levels (Seashore & Bowers, 1970). When properly introduced, then, a change in work procedures or in the entire organizational climate can have long-lasting positive effects.

Organizational Development (OD)

I/O psychologists have focused considerable attention on the problems of total organizational change and on systematic ways to bring about planned change. This effort, called **organizational development (OD)**, involves techniques such as sensitivity training, role playing, group discussion, and job enrichment as well as survey feedback and team building.

In the **survey feedback technique,** surveys are conducted periodically to assess employee feelings and attitudes. The results are communicated to employees, managers, and work teams throughout the organization. Their task is to provide feedback to higher management by suggesting explanations for the questionnaire findings and by recommending ways to correct the problems identified in the surveys.

The **team building technique** is based on the fact that many organizational tasks are performed by small work groups or teams. To enhance a team's morale and problem-solving abilities, OD consultants (called **change agents**)

Organizational development (OD) The study and implementation of planned organizational changes.

Survey feedback technique An organizational development technique in which surveys are conducted periodically to assess employee feelings and attitudes; the results provide feedback to higher management.

Team building technique An organizational development technique that works with small groups or work teams to enhance team morale and problem-solving abilities.

Change agents Organization development facilitators who work with business groups to implement change and develop group confidence and effectiveness.

work with the groups to develop self-confidence, group cohesiveness, and working effectiveness.

Outside consultants or change agents are usually able to view an organization's structure, functions, and culture with greater objectivity than in-house managers. Change agents' first task is diagnosis, using questionnaires and interviews to determine the organization's problems and needs. They evaluate strengths and weaknesses and develop strategies for solving problems and for coping with future changes. However, they must be cautious about introducing changes without allowing employees to participate in the process.

The implementation of the recommended strategies, or intervention, begins with top management. Unless organizational change has management support, the chance of success is small. The specific intervention techniques depend on the nature of the problem and on the organizational climate. The OD process is flexible and can be adapted to the needs of the situation. In general, regardless of the specific techniques applied, the OD process helps to free the typical bureaucratic organization from its rigidity and formality, allowing more responsiveness and open participation.

OD techniques have been applied by many public and private organizations. Although research results are mixed, some significant increases in productivity have been documented. Job satisfaction seems to be negatively related to the OD process, however, perhaps because the emphasis is on improvements in productivity.

THE SOCIALIZATION OF NEW EMPLOYEES

Organizations are constantly undergoing change through the addition of new employees at all levels of the work force. New workers come with different levels of ability, motivation, and desire to perform their job well. They bring various needs and values that affect the organizations for which they work. Our concern here is not with the effect of new employees on the organization but with the impact of the organization on the new employees. New employees have much to learn beyond the necessary job skills. They must learn their role in the hierarchy, the company's values, and the behaviors considered acceptable by their work group.

Socialization The adjustment process by which new employees learn their role in the organizational hierarchy, their company's values, and the behaviors considered acceptable by their work group.

This learning and adjustment process is called **socialization,** and it is not unlike a rite of passage in which members of a society enter new stages of life. Those who successfully cope with this rite of passage are generally happier and more productive employees. This was demonstrated in a study of 594 engineers and managers during their first 3 years of employment. Those who were better socialized in the company's values and goals rated higher in career involvement and job satisfaction than those who did not become as well socialized (Chao, O'Leary-Kelly, Wolf, Klein, & Gardner, 1994).

Poor socialization to an organization—a negligent or haphazard introduction to the company's policies and practices—can undermine the accomplishments of the most sophisticated employee selection program. An organization can recruit and hire qualified people and lose them in the early stages of employment because of an inadequate reception. Improper socialization can foster frustration, anxiety, and dissatisfaction for new employees, which can lead to low job involvement and organizational commitment, low motivation and productivity, and to dismissal or quitting.

Positive interactions between current and new employees should be part of a company's socialization program.

Socialization involves several organizational strategies. Ideally, the company should provide new employees with challenging jobs that offer opportunities for growth and development, the mastery of skills, self-confidence, success experiences, positive interactions with superiors, feedback, and co-workers who have high morale and a positive attitude toward the organization. A study of 295 business school graduates, surveyed after 4 months and 10 months on a new job, confirmed that formal socialization programs had induced the newcomers to accept and conform to organizational goals, methods, and values (Ashforth & Saks, 1996).

Although institutionalized socialization strategies are effective in teaching new hires about the organization, most new employees are not passive learners in this rite-of-passage stage. Studies of accountants in their first 6 months of employment showed that they were highly proactive, taking an active role in seeking the information they believed they needed to adapt to their work environment. For example, when they needed technical information, they sought assistance from supervisors; when they needed social information on the company's standards of acceptable behavior, they sought help from co-workers (Morrison, 1993a, 1993b).

A study of 103 young managers (mean age 27 years), during their first 6 months on the job, found that those with a high desire for control actively sought greater information, socialized more, networked more with colleagues in other departments, and negotiated more job changes than those with a low desire for control (Ashford & Black, 1996).

It is important that newcomers' expectations about their jobs be met. A meta-analysis of 31 studies involving more than 17,000 employees showed that fulfilled expectations correlated positively with job satisfaction, organizational commitment, and the intention to remain with the company (Wanous, Poland, Premack, & Davis, 1992). A study of 128 MBA graduates over their first 2 years of employment found that the obligations they felt toward their employers declined when they perceived that employers were not fulfilling their commitments in terms of expected advancement, training, and pay (Robinson, Kraatz, & Rousseau, 1994).

A comparison of 257 new college graduates in their first jobs confirmed the importance of meeting expectations during their initial 12 months on the job. This research also demonstrated that providing a positive work experience—in terms of stimulation, feedback, and opportunity to develop—was even more important to job satisfaction than meeting expectations (Irving & Meyer, 1994).

Other research on employee expectations found that the potential detrimental effects of unmet expectations could be reduced by establishing positive, high quality relationships with co-workers and supervisors (Major, Kozlowski, Chao, & Gardner, 1995). Expectations were also found to affect turnover. Providing realistic job previews, which served to define or clarify employee expectations, resulted in a higher turnover during the first month on the job for 61 low-level workers at a hospital and a fast-food chain (Waung, 1995). Presumably, the employees knew what to expect from the job and found it not to their liking.

College graduates in their first year with an insurance company were paired with supervisors who served as mentors. Questionnaire responses from both groups indicated that the stronger the relationship, the higher the employees' level of job performance and organizational commitment (Blau, 1988).

I/O psychologists have suggested that socialization occurs more quickly when there is greater interaction between new and established employees. Interactions can include asking questions, having informal conversations, and taking coffee breaks as well as formal activities such as mentoring and performance appraisals. However, some evidence indicates that socialization programs should not rely on the employees who are being replaced by the newcomers. There is the possibility that departing employees will teach their successors established and perhaps inefficient job performance techniques and thus discourage innovation. A study of MBA graduates surveyed 6 and 12 months after beginning a new job suggested that they were unlikely to question job attitudes and behaviors they had been taught during the socialization period (Allen & Meyer, 1990).

Role Ambiguity and Role Conflict

Role ambiguity A situation that arises when job responsibilities are unstructured or poorly defined.

Role conflict A situation that arises when there is a disparity between job demands and the employee's personal standards.

Psychologists have identified two factors that relate to socialization: **role ambiguity** (when the employee's work role is poorly structured or defined) and **role conflict** (when there is a disparity between job demands and the employee's personal standards). High levels of role ambiguity and role conflict are associated with low levels of job satisfaction, satisfaction with supervisor, and organizational commitment, and with a high rate of turnover. To resolve role ambiguity and role conflict, many new employees act on their own to obtain information about the job and organization from their co-workers and supervisors.

Resocialization

Most of the research we have described in this section has dealt with new college graduates entering their first full-time jobs. Most people can expect to change jobs several times during their working life. This means that, throughout your career, you are likely to experience new rites of passage, new socialization experiences—or resocialization—every time you join a different organization.

Common sense suggests that having had one or more prior jobs should make socialization to the next job easier. Also, it is expected that performance, job satisfaction, and organizational commitment will be higher among workers who have had previous jobs because of their experience in adjusting to different organizations. However, that expectation was *not* confirmed in a study of 171 mental health specialists starting new jobs. There were no significant differences on performance, job satisfaction, or commitment between those with prior work experience and those for whom this was their first employment (Adkins, 1995). This study shows the importance of careful I/O research. Sometimes, our commonsense expectations and intuitive beliefs are not supported by scientific study.

ORGANIZATIONAL CULTURE

A major organizational factor to which new employees must be socialized is the culture of the group they are joining. Just as nations have cultural characteristics—beliefs, customs, and behaviors that distinguish them from other nations—so do organizations. **Organizational culture** may be defined as a general pattern of beliefs, expectations, and values, some conscious and some unconscious, that are expected to guide the behavior of all members of an organization.

Organizational culture The organization's pattern of beliefs, expectations, and values as manifested in company and industry practices.

An organization's culture is influenced by the type of industry of which it is part; different companies within the same industry can be expected to have a common organizational culture. For example, steel manufacturers share cultural characteristics that are distinct from those of publishers, insurance companies, hospitals, or movie studios because of different market conditions, competitive environments, and customer expectations. Also, society expects different services from, say, an electric power company and a furniture manufacturer; there is a greater societal need for continuous and uninterrupted service from the former than from the latter. Different departments within a company, such as research, engineering, and marketing, can develop their own subcultures that may differ from that of the dominant organizational culture (see Gordon, 1991; Chatman & Jehn, 1994).

Some I/O psychologists use the terms organizational *culture* and organizational *climate* interchangeably, arguing that the concepts share a fundamental similarity (Denison, 1996). Others note that climate is the surface manifestation of culture. Organizational climate is what we perceive when we observe the way a company functions, whereas organizational culture relates to deeper issues, the causes of an organization's operational style.

From our descriptions of various participatory management programs, you have seen that organizational culture can influence a company's effectiveness. In an analysis of the financial performance of more than 2,000 companies, those with a culture of high involvement and high participation consistently outperformed those that did not favor employee involvement and participation (Denison, 1990).

Person-Organization Fit

The concept of **person-organization fit** has been widely investigated by I/O psychologists. This concept can be defined as the degree of congruence between an employee's values and the organization's values (Kristof, 1996). That agree-

Person-organization fit The degree of congruence between an employee's values and organizational values.

ment can be maximized through recruitment, selection, and socialization procedures. In a study of 171 entry-level auditors in eight public accounting firms, whose careers were followed for 2½ years, it was found that employees whose values as recruits matched company values adjusted to the job more quickly than did employees whose values did not match. Employees who received extensive socialization in company values and culture (based on number of socialization events, hours of formal training, and time spent with mentors) fit those values after 2½ years on the job better than did those who did not receive rigorous socialization. New employees whose values coincided with the company's values were found to be the most satisfied with their jobs (Chatman, 1991).

The values of the auditors in this study were assessed by the Organizational Culture Profile (OCP), which was devised to measure person-organization fit. The test contains 54 value statements to be sorted into nine categories ranging from "most desirable organizational values" to "least desirable organizational values" (O'Reilly, Chatman, & Caldwell, 1991). Examples of these value statements are given in Table 9–1. Validation studies on the OCP show that it predicts job satisfaction, organizational commitment, and turnover for accountants, MBA students, and government employees. The higher the person-organization fit, as measured by this test, the higher the job satisfaction and organizational commitment and the lower the turnover. Another way to assess person-organization fit is the structured interview (see Karren & Graves, 1994).

The Performance Priority Survey, a 40-item self-report inventory, has been shown to be a valid measure of **person-environment congruence,** a concept related to person-organization fit. Person-environment congruence refers to the match between an employee's perception of the job requirements and the requirements of the organization (Barrett, 1995).

Person-environment congruence The match between an employee's perception of the requirements and the actual requirements of the organization.

Job tenure—simply staying with a company for a long period of time—will tend to assure a closer person-organization fit. Employees who cannot accept the company's values may have quit or been fired, whereas employees who remain on the job are likely to have internalized the company's values and attitudes.

TABLE 9–1   Organizational Value Statements

Being rule-oriented

Being team-oriented

Being people-oriented

Being achievement-oriented

Being competitive

Being socially responsible

Providing opportunities for professional growth

Providing high pay for good performance

Providing security of employment

Providing a low level of conflict

Note. Adapted from "People and Organizational Culture: A Profile Comparison Approach to Assessing Person-Organization Fit" by C. A. O'Reilly, III, J. Chatman, and D. F. Caldwell, 1991, *Academy of Management Journal, 34,* p. 516.

Some organizational psychologists advocate a more comprehensive approach to employee selection, suggesting that companies should evaluate not only whether the applicants' knowledge, skills, and abilities are suitable for a particular job but also whether the applicants fit the organization's culture.

LABOR UNIONS

One aspect of organizational life that helps to define a company's culture is the presence or absence of labor unions, in which workers act collectively to protect and promote their interests. Union members form a subculture within the larger organizational culture. Membership in a union can contribute to job satisfaction and productivity and can have a powerful influence on employees' attitudes toward their jobs and their employers.

Our attitudes toward labor unions may be learned from our parents, as was demonstrated in a study of 87 college students and their parents. The students' attitudes toward unions correlated significantly with those of their parents (Kelloway & Watts, 1994).

Socialization of Union Members

The socialization of new members of a union is similar to the process of becoming acclimated to any new organization. Unions offer formal institutionalized socialization as well as informal individual socialization. The formal procedures include orientation lectures and training programs. Informal procedures involve such acts as being invited by a co-worker to attend a union meeting, being introduced to the shop steward, or having a work problem solved by the union. A study of 305 new members of the letter carriers' union, in which they were surveyed twice over a 1-year period to obtain presocialization and postsocialization attitudes, found that individual socialization practices produced a higher level of commitment to the union. More formal socialization procedures had little effect on commitment and had a negative impact on participation in union activities (Fullagar, Gallagher, Gordon, & Clark, 1995). At least for that union, then, formal socialization procedures were found to be counterproductive.

A study of 377 members of a government employees' union in Canada found that the extent of participation in union activities was significantly related to the degree of union commitment. In turn, the degree of union commitment was at least partially dependent on the effectiveness of socialization to the union (Kelloway & Barling, 1993).

As we saw earlier, our commitment to any organization depends on the degree of commitment and support we believe we receive from that organization. To measure the extent to which union members perceived that their unions were committed to them, I/O psychologists developed the 15-item Perceived Union Support Scale (Shore, Tetrick, Sinclair, & Newton, 1994).

Sex Differences in Union Membership

Almost one third of union members in the United States are women, yet they hold only 8% of the elected offices and are less likely to serve on committees or participate in union activities. Research shows that women are more likely to get involved in local union activities under the following conditions (Mellor, 1995; Mellor, Mathieu, & Swim, 1994):

- When more rather than fewer women hold office in the union
- When the local union is more formalized in its rules and procedures
- When the local union is receptive to participatory democracy in decision making

Despite the claim of union leadership to represent all its members, a study of employees in two high-tech companies in Israel (one unionized and the other not) found that union membership did not protect women members from facing discrimination in pay and promotion. Women who worked at the unionized company experienced as much gender bias as did women who worked in the nonunion company (Bamberger, Admati-Dvir, & Harel, 1995). If unions expect to recruit and retain the ever-growing number of women in the work force, they will have to pay more attention to the issues facing *all* of their members.

Effects of Union Membership

A review of pay scales in the United States shows that unionized employees are paid wages up to 33% greater than nonunion workers (Jackson & Schuler, 1995). In addition to higher pay, membership in a labor union can also result in better and safer working conditions, job security, and fringe benefits, thus contributing to satisfaction of what Maslow called the lower-order needs. It can also satisfy the higher-order needs for status, belonging, and esteem and can provide a sense of power through the knowledge that unionized employees have an important bargaining tool: the threat of a strike. Some union members report a greater loyalty to their union than to their company.

Unions initially resisted quality-of-work-life programs because they feared such efforts would erode union loyalty. This resistance has been declining as more union members participate in and support QWL programs and other forms of participatory democracy. A study of more than 600 union members employed by a large public utility showed that more than 85% wanted the union to be involved in QWL programs. After participating in a QWL program designed jointly by union and management representatives, union members expressed the belief that the union had come to have influence in areas with which it had not previously been involved, such as implementing technological change and improving customer service. Union members who believed the QWL program was successful gave equal credit for that success to union and to management. The few union members who considered the program to be unsuccessful blamed management for its failure (Thacker & Fields, 1987).

The same researchers conducted a study of 412 union workers in a public utility involved in a QWL program that established joint problem-solving teams composed of workers and supervisors. Measures of organizational commitment, job satisfaction, union commitment, and perceived QWL success were taken 12 months and 32 months after the program began. The psychologists found that organizational commitment increased only when the workers believed the program was successful. Commitment to the union increased regardless of whether members believed the program was successful (Fields & Thacker, 1992). In both studies, the union won support for sponsoring a QWL program, even when the program was judged not to be a success.

Union Grievances

Another aspect of union activity that affects employee attitudes and behaviors is the **grievance process.** Specified in union contracts, the grievance process establishes a formal mechanism for airing and resolving worker complaints. The number and focus of worker grievances serve as an indication of job dissatisfaction and can pinpoint the causes of problems in the workplace. Grievance procedures provide employees with a means of upward communication to management and an approved way of venting frustrations that might otherwise be expressed in work slowdowns, stoppages, or sabotage. Thus, the grievance process can be useful for both workers and managers.

The number of grievances varies with the nature of the job. Monotonous and repetitive assembly-line jobs performed under uncomfortable conditions by unskilled workers are associated with a high grievance rate. Social factors are also important. Highly cohesive work groups tend to file more grievances than do groups that lack a sense of unity. First-line supervisors who are low in consideration behaviors are the targets of more grievances than are supervisors who are high in consideration. An analysis of 324 grievances showed that when a complaint was resolved in favor of the worker, job satisfaction rose, along with the perception that the grievance system was fair and unbiased. When the grievance was settled in favor of management, labor-management relations deteriorated (Gordon & Bowlby, 1988).

A study of grievances over an 8-year period found that absenteeism increased when complaints were filed over matters of policy; that is, when the grievance was related to management's interpretation of the union contract. Absenteeism decreased when complaints were related to disciplinary matters, such as when an employee had been reprimanded for breaking a company rule. The researchers suggested that in the latter case workers were motivated to improve their behavior to avoid further disciplinary action (Klaas, Heneman, & Olson, 1991).

Organized labor currently faces a crisis in the decline of its membership. At the end of World War II, in 1945, more than 35% of the U.S. workforce belonged to unions. By 1994, that figure had fallen to less than 16%. In the private sector, only 11% of U.S. workers are union members, and the percentage is expected to fall to 5% by the year 2000. Questionnaire surveys of 20 United Steel Workers local unions found that the locals that suffered greater membership losses due to layoffs reported a higher union commitment from its members than did locals that experienced smaller membership losses. In other words, the greater the threat of job loss, the greater the union commitment—the union being the only organization from which the workers could expect help. Workers in locals with less severe membership losses reported higher satisfaction with the union and with their employer, perhaps reflecting the workers' relief at still having a job (Mellor, 1990, 1992).

Grievance process A formal mechanism for airing and resolving complaints between unionized employees and management.

Informal work groups develop in every organization. The workers are apt to have similar backgrounds, interests, and lifestyles and may determine for themselves an acceptable standard of productivity, which may differ from the one set by management.

INFORMAL GROUPS: THE ORGANIZATION WITHIN THE ORGANIZATION

Informal work groups Cohesive groups within an organization that are not sanctioned or controlled by management.

Informal work groups develop within every organization. These groups have tremendous power to shape employee attitudes, behavior, and productivity. Workers come together informally to establish and promote a set of norms and values, a subculture within the larger organizational culture. These informal groups do not appear on the organization chart and are beyond the control of management. Often, management is not aware of their existence. Informal groups determine for new employees how they will come to perceive management and other aspects of organizational life. These groups can work for or against the organization by encouraging cooperation with company policies and procedures or by thwarting productivity and management goals.

The Hawthorne Studies

The classic Hawthorne studies provided empirical evidence of informal work groups. A team of 14 workers in the telephone bank wiring room of the Western Electric plant was observed for 6 months. The observer noticed that the group had developed its own standards of behavior and production. The workers shared many interests, engaged in rough but friendly teasing, and stood ready to help one another on the job. They valued one another's friendship and acceptance and displayed many of the characteristics of a family. They avoided doing anything that might bring disapproval from the group.

In terms of productivity, the group determined what it considered to be a fair and safe day's output. Management had set one standard, with an incentive to be paid for meeting or exceeding the daily level (an employee could make more money by working faster). But the group had set its own standard, which was below the company's level. The workers believed that if they met or exceeded management's demands, the company would raise the standard and force them to work harder. Therefore, they set a leisurely, easily attainable production goal, willing to forgo the opportunity to earn extra money. The workers admitted to the observer that they were capable of producing more, but to do so would have defied the group's norms. The group had assumed such prominence in the workers' lives that they considered group acceptance more important than extra pay.

Social Loafing

Another effect of informal work groups is the phenomenon known as **social loafing,** which is the idea that people do not work as hard in a group as they do when working alone (Latané, Williams, & Harkins, 1979). One explanation for social loafing is that people believe they can get lost in a crowd and that their slower work pace will not be noticed. Also, people tend to expect, on the basis of past experience, that others in the group will goof off, so they might as well do so, too. Research supports both explanations. Studies by social psychologists show that when college student subjects were told that their individual output would be identified and when they were told what others in the group were expected to produce, social loafing was considerably reduced (Brickner, Harkins, & Ostrom, 1986).

Social loafing The idea that people do not work as hard in a group as they do when working alone.

Studies conducted on the job tend to confirm these findings. For example, an examination of the behavior of more than 200 salespersons for a large retailer showed that social loafing was less likely to occur when workers believed that their supervisors were aware of how hard they worked as individuals. Social loafing was more likely to occur when salespersons believed that their personal efforts were not recognized by their supervisors. The study also found that the greater an employee's sense of job involvement, as measured by the Job Diagnostic Survey, the lower the amount of social loafing (George, 1992).

A meta-analysis of 78 laboratory and field studies confirmed the social loafing phenomenon in work groups. Although the magnitude of social loafing was found to be smaller in on-the-job studies than in laboratory studies, it was still statistically significant. Men were more likely to engage in social loafing than were women. Further, employees from Eastern cultures (which are more collectivist or group-oriented) were less likely to practice social loafing than employees from Western, more individualistic, cultures.

This analysis also showed that workers were likely to engage in social loafing under the following conditions (Karau & Williams, 1993):

1. When their individual outputs could not be evaluated
2. When working on tasks that were not meaningful or personally involving
3. When working with strangers
4. When they expected their co-workers to perform well on the task

In addition, the researchers found that experimental subjects were unwilling to admit they had been loafing on a group task.

Group Cohesiveness

Informal groups exist in virtually every type of organization. They are characterized by personal interactions that occur over an extended period because frequent interactions are necessary to the development of closeness and a commonality of interests. Groups must also have a focus, such as workers in the same department who share a physical workspace. The groups cannot be too large, or the sense of personal and direct contact will be lost.

Most of us have a need for affiliation and companionship, and this need can be satisfied by an informal work group. The group also serves as a source of information about work procedures and about what constitutes an acceptable day's output. Observations made over a 15-month period of 26 crews of coal miners revealed that productivity was lower when work group members were infrequently assigned together and thus were unfamiliar with one another's habits (Goodman & Leyden, 1991).

Group closeness was also found to influence employee perceptions of organizational issues. A study using interviews and questionnaires for 64 employees of an accounting firm found that employees who had formed personal relationships interpreted organizational events in a similar way. Employees in other informal groups interpreted the same events in a different way (Rentsch, 1990).

Group norms and standards are pervasive throughout organizational and personal life. The group can influence political and racial attitudes, style of dress, even where to eat or go on vacation. Because group membership satisfies so many needs, employees strive to be accepted by group members. Deviant behavior is rarely encountered, except from new workers who need time to absorb the group's ways.

Informal groups tend to attract and retain people with similar personality characteristics and to take on a consistent affective or emotional tone. An investigation of 26 work groups of department store salespersons confirmed that individual affect was consistent within groups; that is, group members tended to have similar moods and feelings about their work. A group's affective tone influenced the group's behavior. Negative affective tone was related to a low level of helping behaviors, manifested in rude and uncooperative behavior toward customers. Positive affective tone was found to be related to a low level of absenteeism (George, 1990).

A literature review concluded that positive affective tone was positively related to organizational spontaneity, which includes such behaviors as helping coworkers, protecting the organization, making constructive suggestions, developing one's abilities, and spreading good will. Positive affect in a group is likely to be stronger when the group is small, the members work in physical proximity, and the leader is energetic and enthusiastic (George & Brief, 1992).

Group cohesiveness The degree of closeness within a work group.

The degree of closeness within a group is called **group cohesiveness.** The greater the cohesiveness, the greater is the group's power over its members and the greater the pressure on group members to conform. Several factors influence cohesiveness. As the group gets larger, and there is less opportunity for frequent contact among group members, cohesiveness declines. Larger groups generally splinter into subgroups or competing groups. Diversity of background, interests, and lifestyles reduces group cohesiveness.

Working conditions are also important. Workers under a wage-incentive system that rewards on an individual rather than a team basis find that the resulting personal competition reduces feelings of closeness. Team rewards en-hance group cohesiveness by encouraging cooperation; everyone works for a common goal.

Outside pressures and threats affect group cohesiveness. Just as citizens of a na-tion under attack usually cooperate to submerge personal or regional differences, so will a work group faced with an unfair supervisor or an unpopular policy.

COMPUTER TECHNOLOGY AND ORGANIZATIONAL STRUCTURE

The widespread use of computer-aided manufacturing and office equipment has changed the ways in which daily work is performed and the formal and informal structure of organizations. Computer technology creates the need for greater co-ordination and integration of an organization's basic units, which requires the development of new reporting hierarchies. For example, at one plant in which operations were computerized, the engineering staff had to be reorganized so that it reported to the marketing department, a unit with which it previously had had no direct contact. The change was necessary to coordinate customers' needs (marketing) and the development of new products (engineering).

Computer technology requires greater formalization of work procedures. Rules for entering data into computer files must be precise; they permit no em-ployee discretion or deviation. These formal procedures reduce opportunities for individuality in structuring and organizing work. Computers also change the locus of decision-making authority, although the direction of the change is not always clear. In practice, automating an office or a manufacturing plant some-times results in greater centralization of decision making, restricting it to fewer levels on the organization chart. In other cases it results in decentralization, giv-ing greater decision-making authority to the worker at the video display termi-nal. For some jobs, the computer operators may be more knowledgeable than their supervisors about the equipment's capabilities. This shift in power from su-pervisors to employees can disrupt traditional working relationships and leave managers with a reduced understanding of the work they are supposed to be managing.

Computers are also changing the procedures for the meetings that result in corporate decisions. Instead of asking a group of employees to sit around a table and discuss a problem, some organizations hold electronic meetings in which the interaction is through computers. Participants express their ideas simultaneously and anonymously and comment on one another's work. Anecdotal evidence from organizations as diverse as hotel chains, banks, plastics companies, and air-craft manufacturers indicates that electronic meetings are shorter and less stress-ful. Leaders are able to stick to an agenda because employees do not digress or waste time at the computer to the extent they do in person. Reports also suggest that **electronic brainstorming**—the generation of ideas by the group—im-proves substantially at electronic meetings.

Electronic brainstorming The generation of ideas by a group in which interaction takes place through individual computer workstations instead of in a face-to-face meeting.

Laboratory research with undergraduate and MBA student subjects in the United States and in Canada has consistently supported the usefulness and pro-ductivity of electronic brainstorming for groups of up to 12 participants. These groups were found to generate more unique and better ideas than did traditional

NEWSBREAK #17

E-Mail: Beware of Big Brother

It pays to be careful when you log on at work these days. What you say could get you fired. That was the painful lesson learned by Michael Smyth, who used to be a sales manager at The Pillsbury Company until he messaged his boss one day and referred to the boss's supervisor as a "back-stabbing bastard."

Smyth thought his E-mail was private and personal, just like sending a letter through the regular mail. But it wasn't. Not when a co-worker found printouts of the message and brought it to the attention of the "back-stabbing bastard." Smyth was fired right away. He sued for wrongful discharge, arguing that his communication was private, but a judge turned down his claim.

The judge ruled that Smyth forfeited any and all reasonable expectations of privacy when he used the company network, even though his message was clearly intended for only one person. A lawyer for the company pointed out that a warning appears on the screen every time employees log on, reminding them that their mail might be intercepted and read by anyone else on the network.

So be careful what you say on line. You don't know who might be monitoring your mail.

Sources: L. Light. E-mail: Beware of big brother. *Business Week,* March 4, 1996. P. D. Samuels. Who's reading your E-mail? Maybe the boss. *New York Times,* May 12,

face-to-face groups or nominal groups (the same number of people working alone whose ideas are then pooled) (Dennis & Valacich, 1993; Gallupe, Cooper, Grisé, & Bastianutti, 1994; Valacich, Dennis, & Connolly, 1994). With very small groups (groups with only three members), a significantly greater number of ideas was produced by face-to-face groups. However, there was no significant difference in the quality of the ideas generated by computer-mediated or face-to-face groups (Straus & McGrath, 1994). Members of electronic brainstorming groups also reported that they were more satisfied with the process than were members of traditional groups (Gallupe, Dennis, Cooper, Valacich, Bastianutti, & Nunamaker, 1992).

Early research suggested that communicating by computer might lower the social inhibitions and status barriers present in face-to-face groups. For example, high-level managers tend to dominate group meetings and informal conversations. It was thought that electronic communication would reduce or eliminate this phenomenon. However, one series of studies showed that high-status group members continued to dominate group discussions whether conducted via computer or face-to-face (Weisband, Schneider, & Connolly, 1995).

Computers can force changes in the organization's informal structure by disrupting traditional lines of communication and power. For example, in companies where clerical workers have desks side by side, they communicate freely and easily about work-related and personal matters. Where such jobs have been automated, workers are often separated by partitions that inhibit talking and socializing.

Reducing the chances for personal interaction reduces the group's cohesiveness. Even though workers have found ways to use their computers for informal communication, this approach lacks the closeness and the privacy afforded by face-to-face contact. Also, some companies routinely monitor the messages on their internal E-mail system, an action that discourages the use of E-mail for promoting the personal relationships necessary to maintain group cohesiveness.

Participatory Democracy in Russia

We have discussed examples of positive outcomes of participatory democracy programs in various U.S. companies. Benefits typically include improvements in productivity, job satisfaction, job involvement, and organizational commitment, as well as reductions in rates of turnover and absenteeism. Employee participation programs have also been successful in several Western countries that are characterized by the democratic tradition of citizen participation in government through free elections. It is popularly assumed that participative management has universal applicability—that what works in the United States will work in other countries.

I/O psychologists from the states of Washington and Nebraska wanted to determine whether a worker participation system could be applied successfully in Russia with workers who had no experience with democracy. Russian industry has for decades operated along strict bureaucratic lines. The study was conducted at a large textile factory, the Kalinin (now Tver) cotton mill, 90 miles northwest of Moscow. Ninety-nine male workers in the weaving mill served as subjects, 33 from each of three work shifts. Each was randomly assigned to one of three experimental treatment groups.

The groups were considered to be equivalent in that each subject had completed a standard orientation and job training program and an apprenticeship and had been employed for at least 1 year. In addition, the workers' educational and social backgrounds were similar. No control group was used; instead, each group's productivity during and after the 2-week experimental intervention was compared with the preexperiment production level. The dependent variable was the quantity of top-quality fabric produced. The experimental treatments were as follows.

1. *Extrinsic rewards.* In this group, workers were rewarded for greater productivity

Source: Based on D. H. B. Welsh, F. Luthans, & S. M. Sommer (1993). Managing Russian factory workers: The impact of U.S.-based behavioral and participative techniques. *Academy of Management Journal, 36,* 58–79.

with highly valued U.S.-made products, such as jeans, t-shirts with logos, soap, coffee, and music audiotapes.

2. *Behavioral management.* In this group, Russian supervisors were trained to administer social rewards (praise and recognition as positive feedback) when workers performed specific behaviors that contributed to high productivity, such as checking looms, doing repairs, monitoring fabric quality, and assisting co-workers. Supervisors were also instructed to offer corrections when they observed dysfunctional behaviors, such as working with dirty hands, but they were told not to make negative comments or threats of disciplinary action.

3. *Participatory democracy.* In this group, an American psychologist and a Russian translator met with workers to ask for their input on how to improve job performance. Supervisors were not present. The sessions were relaxed and open-ended, but the researcher framed the discussion in terms of core job characteristics of task identity, skill variety, task significance, autonomy, and feedback. Employee suggestions related to equipment design, work methods, and safety procedures. The researchers hoped that because suggestions for improvement had come from the employees and they had the authority to implement them, the employees would then be motivated to apply their ideas on the job.

The groups receiving extrinsic and social rewards showed increased productivity during the experimental period, but productivity fell once the interventions were removed. The participatory democracy group showed a significant decline in productivity during the experimental treatment and a slight rise in productivity once the intervention ceased.

Follow-up interviews with the Russian employees and managers revealed that when workers had been given opportunities in the past to express their views about job-related issues, their ideas had rarely been implemented. They may have perceived the current study as another sham, expecting that once again their suggestions would be rejected. By not improving their productivity or truly participating during the experimental period, they could save themselves the frustration and disappointment of being ignored. Had the experiment been doomed by cultural values and the state of labor-management relations?

Critical Thinking Questions

1. What are the limitations and weaknesses of this study? How would you design a study to investigate the usefulness of the participatory management approach in Russia?

2. What conditions promote worker participation in American industry? Were these conditions present or absent in the Russian factory?

3. Would the results have been different if Russian supervisors had been trained to conduct the participatory democracy intervention? Why?

4. If you were an American I/O psychologist hired to institute a quality-of-work-life program in a Russian factory, how would you go about it?

5. Why have some quality-of-work-life programs failed in U.S. companies?

SUMMARY

Organizational psychologists study organizational climates and styles and the ways they affect the employees. The classic organizational style is **bureaucracy,** intended to be a rational structure in which rules of conduct and lines of authority were fixed and in which subjectivity and personal bias had no place. Bureaucracies ignored the human element—the needs, values, and motivations of workers—and could not adapt easily to social and technological change.

The modern organizational style—a **high-involvement management** approach called participatory democracy—is more concerned with employees' intellectual, emotional, and motivational characteristics. Workers participate in decision making at all levels. **Quality-of-work-life** (QWL) programs restructure job and management requirements to enhance worker participation. In **quality control circles,** small groups of workers meet periodically to solve problems relating to quality and quantity of production. In **self-managing work groups,** a work team controls all aspects of the job.

Employees and managers may resist changes in work methods, equipment, or policies. If workers are allowed to participate in decisions about the change, they are more likely to support it. **Organizational development** (OD) involves techniques for introducing large-scale changes. The process is carried out by **change agents** who diagnose problems, devise appropriate strategies, and implement the interventions.

New employees undergo an adjustment period called **socialization.** A socialization program should involve a challenging job, appropriate training and feedback, a considerate supervisor, co-workers with high morale and organizational commitment, and a suitable orientation program.

Organizational culture is the pattern of beliefs, values, and expectations that guide the behavior of the organization's members. It is expressed on three levels: observable artifacts, values, and underlying assumptions. **Person-organization fit** refers to the congruence between an employee's values and the organization's values.

Membership in a **labor union** can affect job satisfaction and productivity and can satisfy lower-level needs through pay, job security, and fringe benefits. Membership can also satisfy belonging, esteem, status, and power needs.

Informal work groups, which influence employee attitudes and behavior, exist beyond management's control. They operate by their own standards with regard to productivity and worker/management relations. **Social loafing** is the idea that people do not work as hard in a group as they do when working alone. Organizational operations are affected by computer technology, leading to restructuring of work units, formalization of procedures, and shifts in decision-making authority, communication patterns, and employee empowerment.

Electronic brainstorming can generate more and better ideas than traditional face-to-face groups, and can also lead to greater job satisfaction.

KEY TERMS

bureaucracies
change agents
electronic brainstorming
group cohesiveness
grievance process
high-involvement management
informal work groups
organizational culture
organizational development (OD)
participative organizational style
person-environment congruence

person-organization fit
quality control circles
quality-of-work-life (QWL) programs
role ambiguity
role conflict
self-managing work groups
social loafing
socialization
survey feedback technique
team building technique

ADDITIONAL READING

Adkins, C. L. (1995). Previous work experience and organizational socialization: A longitudinal examination. *Academy of Management Journal, 38,* 839–862. Discusses research on measuring the variables that affect socialization and resocialization, beginning with the process of organizational entry. Considers task competence, work role clarity, realistic expectations, and interpersonal relationships.

Howard, A., & Associates (Eds.). (1994). *Diagnosis for organizational change: Methods and models.* New York: Guilford Press. Provides perspectives on organizational change, the role of the individual employee, and the characteristics of the high involvement workplace.

Lawler, E. E., III, Morhman, S. A., & Ledford, G. E., Jr. (1995). *Creating high performance organizations: Practices and results of employee involvement and total quality management in Fortune 1000 companies.* San Francisco: Jossey-Bass. Part of a continuing series of longitudinal research reports on employee involvement in the workplace. Surveys workers in both service and manufacturing industries, and in hourly/clerical, technical/professional, and supervisory/managerial jobs.

Wellins, R. S., Byham, W. C., & Dixon, G. R. (1994). *Inside teams: How 20 world-class organizations are winning through teamwork.* San Francisco: Jossey-Bass. Reviews the opportunities and challenges of selecting, training, and empowering work teams. Reports successful programs at companies such as Kodak, Pfizer, and Colgate-Palmolive.

Characteristics of the Workplace

We have discussed some of the effects of the social and psychological climate in which work takes place. The structure of the organization, its style of leadership, and the motivations of employees all influence productivity and job satisfaction. We turn now to more tangible aspects of the workplace—physical factors, working hours, safety issues, and concerns about physical and emotional health.

Chapter 10 deals with physical conditions of work, including light, noise, temperature, color, and music. Work hours and work schedules are discussed, along with psychological factors such as boredom and monotony. Accidents, violence, alcoholism, and drug abuse are covered in Chapter 11. Psychologists help to determine the causes of workplace accidents and violence, and ways to prevent them. Dependence on alcohol or illicit drugs is a personal tragedy and a personnel problem. Psychologists design employee assistance programs for troubled workers at all occupational levels. Chapter 12 considers the stresses that result from certain physical and psychological conditions of work. Psychologists have developed ways of preventing stress and of treating it on and off the job.

Working Conditions

The conditions under which we work can have a significant impact on our efficiency and productivity. Whether we are trying to study for this course, change the oil in our car, or access the Internet, our surroundings affect our skill, ability, and motivation to perform the task. If the environment is too hot or too cold, too noisy or too quiet, too isolated or too distracting, our job performance can be impaired. If the office is painted in depressing colors, if the work station is inconveniently laid out, or if there is too much glare on our monitor, then our desire to do our best may be affected.

An organization can recruit and select the best employees, train them thoroughly, provide outstanding leaders and an optimal organizational climate to maximize job performance, but if the physical working conditions are uncomfortable, productivity will suffer. Uncongenial work settings are related to decreased productivity and job satisfaction, increased errors and accidents, and greater absenteeism and turnover.

When a workplace is made more comfortable, or working hours more flexible, productivity usually increases, at least temporarily. But the I/O psychologist must be careful in interpreting such changes in performance. What, precisely, has caused the greater productivity? Was it the new air-conditioning system or brighter lighting or better soundproofing—the actual physical changes? Or more subtle psychological factors such as employees' positive attitude toward management for instituting the changes?

Although the results may be beneficial, whatever the cause, the psychologist and the organization need to be able to explain the reasons for any increase in productivity. Suppose it can be related to improved job satisfaction because the workers believe that the company sees them as human beings rather than cogs in a machine. If so, the company will want to know whether there are other ways to improve satisfaction and productivity without instituting expensive changes in the physical working conditions.

In many industries, people work at peak efficiency under what appear to be intolerable conditions. And there are many other instances of poor performance and low morale in well-equipped, lavishly decorated surroundings. The effects of physical changes in working conditions may be influenced or modified by how employees perceive, accept, and adapt to these changes. Therefore, physical working conditions must be considered in light of complex psychological factors.

Research with 641 blue-collar and white-collar employees in Australia suggested that the physical work environment may consist of several factors. This questionnaire study uncovered the following five dimensions (Carlopio, 1996):*

1. *Environmental design,* including lighting, air quality, and general atmosphere of the work area
2. *Facilities,* including restrooms, eating areas, and recreational facilities
3. *Work organization,* including work schedule and pace, and amount of time and information provided to do the job
4. *Equipment and tools,* including the design and efficiency of the tools and machines provided to do the job

*Dimensions 1–3 are discussed in this chapter. Dimension 4 (equipment and tools) is covered in Chapter 13. Dimension 5 (health and safety) is discussed in Chapter 11.

5. *Health and safety,* including organizational procedures to deal with physical safety issues, hazards, and other factors that may affect employee health

PHYSICAL WORKING CONDITIONS

The physical work environment includes many factors, from the parking lot and location of the building to the amount of daylight and noise in the work area. Inadequate parking spaces or a parking lot too far from the building can so irritate employees that their attitude toward the organization is negative before they even reach their work stations.

Work Sites

The location of the work site, whether in the downtown of a large city or a more remote suburban area, can also affect employees' satisfaction with their jobs. For example, suburban office parks are often isolated from the shops, restaurants, and other services found in cities. Some I/O psychologists have suggested that younger, single employees may be more satisfied living and working in cities, whereas married persons may prefer the quieter suburbs as better places to rear children.

Some office buildings and manufacturing plants have been so poorly designed that they present difficulties for people just trying to find their way around. You have probably been in a large medical park complex, trying to figure out where you are (or where you left your car), using a "you are here" map of the kind commonly found in shopping malls. Psychologists have determined that those kinds of displays tend to confuse people. Simple signs with arrows more effectively direct us from one place to another. In one experiment, college students found their destinations in a complex building in an average time of less than 1 minute by following signs with arrows. The "you are here" map required 6 minutes to decipher (Butler, Acquino, Hissong, & Scott, 1993).

Most of us learn how to get to our own workplace after only a short period on the job, but people with sales or delivery jobs, whose work takes them into many buildings in the course of a day, lose a great deal of time because of poor directions.

Child- and Dependent-Care Facilities

A growing number of companies have established day-care facilities and on-site schools for the young children of their employees. Such facilities are increasingly seen as a significant fringe benefit. At the turn of the century it is expected that more than two thirds of all new employees will be women, most of childbearing age. If organizations expect to attract and keep these employees, they must be prepared to provide day-care facilities for the children.

A survey conducted at a large electronics and communications firm of 952 employees who were parents of children 5 years of age or younger found that employees who were more satisfied with the quality of care for their young children (regardless of where that care took place) experienced less conflict between work and family responsibilities. This, in turn, reduced the rate of absenteeism (Goff, Mount, & Jamison, 1990). A study of 155 hospital employees who used on-site day-care facilities concluded that child-care programs helped in recruiting and retaining new employees but had no impact on their job performance (Kossek & Nichol, 1992).

A survey of 745 employees from several organizations found that those whose employers provided assistance with child care were significantly higher in organizational commitment and lower in intention to quit than employees whose companies did not provide help with child care (Grover & Crooker, 1995).

One problem older employees face involves caring for elderly parents. A survey at Travelers Insurance found that 20% of employees over the age of 30 provided some sort of assistance for an aging parent. Other surveys put the figure as high as 40%. These employees experience considerable financial and emotional strain in trying to balance the needs of work and family. As the general population ages, growing numbers of workers will confront this dilemma, a situation that can have an impact on productivity, absenteeism, and stress (see, for example, Goodstein, 1995; Hepburn & Barling, 1996).

Some employers have responded to this need by establishing in-house counseling programs, long-term-care insurance, generous paid leave policies, and on-site care for dependents of all ages. For example, IBM instituted a corporate eldercare program in 1988. By 1993, 31% of all U.S. employers had developed policies to deal with the issue. One problem with eldercare services, however, is that few people are using them. According to the National Council on Aging, employees are wary of giving the impression that family matters are diverting their attention from job performance.

Office and Workplace Design

Once inside our place of employment, we may find several physical features that can create dissatisfaction and frustration. One source of complaints is the ventilating, heating, and air-conditioning systems in glass-wall, fixed-window buildings. Temperatures are often uncomfortably hot on the sunny side of the building and too cool on the shady side. Other frequent irritants are slow elevators in high-rise buildings, the quality of the food in the company cafeteria, and inconvenient or poorly maintained rest rooms.

Office size and design affect employee satisfaction and productivity. The layout of a set of offices will influence the behavior of managers who rely on spontaneous encounters as a way of obtaining and exchanging information. The closer their offices, the more likely they are to meet throughout the workday. Physical separation, such as placing suites of management offices on different floors of a building, decreases the amount of contact. The usual practice of isolating high-level executives on the top floor of company headquarters, where they rarely have informal contacts with others, may not be the best policy.

The size of an office building can influence working relationships. The smaller the building, the closer the relationships among employees tend to be. In very large buildings, where employees can have fewer interactions, relationships tend to be more formal and impersonal. All these factors, none of which involves actual job tasks, can impair productive efficiency. An unpopular location, poor design, or inconvenient layout can reduce morale and foster negative attitudes.

Workplace design and location are especially critical for disabled employees who may be barred from certain jobs not because of lack of ability, but because they do not have access to the work area. Steep flights of stairs, narrow doorways, and inadequate rest rooms may prevent them from being employed. The 1973 Rehabilita-

Landscaped offices have no floor-to-ceiling dividers. Such a setting may enhance employee communication and social relations, but it is also noisy and distracting.

tion Act and the 1990 Americans with Disabilities Act require the removal of architectural barriers; all parts of a building must be accessible to persons in wheelchairs. Compliance with the laws has meant modifications to the physical plant, such as automatic doors, ramps and elevators, handholds, wider doorways and corridors, and lower wall telephones and speakerphones. Surveys show that 60% of these required changes cost less than $100, and 90% cost less than $1,000. Many disabled employees do not need any physical modifications of an office workspace. IBM, which has hired disabled workers for more than 35 years, took the lead in redesigning work stations to provide job opportunities for these employees.

Environmental Psychology

Beginning in the mid-1960s, the field of **environmental psychology,** concerned with the relationships between people and their physical environment,

Environmental psychology
Studies the effect of workplace design on behavior.

sparked a revolution in workspace design. Combining architecture and psychology, environmental psychologists are concerned with natural and built environments and their impact on work behavior. For example, research on office design and layout has focused on communications between and within departments, flow of job tasks among groups, relationships between managers and subordinates, and work group cohesiveness.

Landscaped Offices

Landscaped offices An office design that consists of a large open area with no floor-to-ceiling walls; employee work stations are separated by partitions.

One result of environmental psychology research was the **landscaped office.** In contrast to private, separated offices, the landscaped office consists of a huge open space with no floor-to-ceiling walls to divide the area into separate rooms. All employees—from clerks to corporate officers—are grouped into cubicles, functional work units that are set off from others only by planters, screens or partitions, or cabinets and bookcases.

Inexpensive to construct and maintain, landscaped offices are believed to facilitate communication and work flow. The openness is supposed to enhance group cohesiveness and cooperation and reduce psychological barriers between employees and managers. Research on employee reactions has revealed both advantages and disadvantages. Employees report that landscaped offices are pleasant and are conducive to forming and maintaining social relationships. Managers report improved communication. Complaints relate to lack of privacy, noise, and difficulty in concentrating. Because cubicles are typically separated only by low dividers, work areas tend to lack the personal touches—such as photographs, plants, posters, or souvenirs—that contribute to feelings of individuality and comfort.

Studies of large numbers of workers in a variety of organizations show consistently that landscaped offices, with their noise, lack of privacy, and potential for interruptions by co-workers are positively related to self-reports of job dissatisfaction. Other research demonstrates that private offices with doors and with walls high enough to prevent seeing co-workers have a significant positive correlation with job satisfaction (see, for example, Duvall-Early & Benedict, 1992; Oldham, Kulik, & Stepina, 1991; Sutton & Rafaeli, 1987).

Despite these problems with landscaped offices, many organizations have invested considerable money in them and are reluctant to bear the additional expense of reconverting to more private offices. For organizations with large numbers of employees at computerized work stations, the landscaped office has become standard.

In addition to studying general issues of workspace design, I/O psychologists have conducted extensive research on specific environmental factors such as lighting, noise, and temperature. We noted in Chapter 8 that these aspects of the work environment are analogous to the hygiene needs proposed by Herzberg. All of these environmental factors can affect job satisfaction.

Illumination

Continued exposure to inadequate illumination while reading or performing detailed operations can be harmful to one's eyesight. Research confirms that inadequate lighting is a source of distress. High glare, dim bulbs, and a lack of natural light have negative effects on job performance.

NEWSBREAK #18

Clothes Encounters: Relaxed Dress Codes Redefine the Workplace

You see it everywhere these days, in banks and brokerage houses, in county offices and prestigious law firms—employees breaking the formal dress code and showing up for work in casual clothing. It usually occurs on Friday, and it represents a radical transformation in the look of many workplaces.

At Arnold & Porter, one of Washington, DC's, most powerful law firms, the chairman wears a black pinstripe jogging suit. Across the Potomac River, in Alexandria, Virginia, the public affairs director of the Society for Human Resource Management sports wildly colored boots of pink, purple, orange, green, and yellow. A bank vice president dons a sweater with the bank logo, topping off knee-length shorts. Even IBM, long a holdout for the approved male uniform of somber dark suit, white shirt, and subdued tie, now allows casual dress once a week.

The percentage of companies now permitting employees to "dress down" has risen from 17% in 1992 to 42% in 1995. Why are they doing it, and what do they get for it?

Kathy Comptom, who wears the multicolored boots to work, put it this way: "Companies are looking for benefits that don't cost them more money and are popular with employees. You see people in suits Monday through Thursday. But on Friday, in walks a totally different person—the real person—with a different level of morale, friendlier, more relaxed, and informal."

Will the day come when we all dress casually for work all the time? Would you have confidence in a lawyer in a jogging suit? Or a dentist in shorts? Or is a uniform still necessary to command respect and authority in some jobs?

Source: E. Hoffman. Clothes encounters: New relaxed dress codes redefine the workplace. *USAIR Magazine*, June, 1995.

Intensity. Intensity, or level of brightness, is the most common factor associated with illumination. The optimal level of intensity varies with the nature of the task and the age of the worker. Older workers generally need brighter light than do younger workers for satisfactory performance of the same task. A job involving the precise manipulation of small component parts, as in electronics assembly, requires brighter light than an assembly line in a bottling plant. Lighting engineers have recommended minimum intensity levels for a variety of work areas (see Table 10–1).

Distribution of Light. Another important factor in illumination is the distribution of light over the work area. Ideally, light will be distributed uniformly

TABLE 10–1 Recommended Lighting Levels for Selected Workplaces

Job	Minimum Footcandles[a]
Aircraft manufacturing (welding)	2000
Assembly, extra fine (computer chips)	1000
Clothing industry (cutting, cleaning, inspecting)	500
Dairy products (bottle washing)	200
Tobacco grading and sorting	200
Bank teller stations	150
Candy making and decorating	100
Barber shops, beauty salons	100
Photo engraving	50
Hotel lobbies	50
Retail store interiors	30
Laundries	30
Iron and steel manufacturing plants	20
Corridors and stairways	20
Airplane passenger compartments	5

[a]A footcandle of light (a standard candle at a distance of one foot) is approximately the brightness produced by a 100-watt bulb held ten feet above your head on a dark night.

Note. Adapted from *Footcandles in Modern Lighting,* 1971, Cleveland, OH: General Electric.

throughout the visual field. Illuminating a work area at a much higher intensity than its surroundings leads to eyestrain because of the natural tendency of the eyes to move. When a person looks from a brightly lit area to a dimly lit area, the pupils of the eyes dilate. Returning the gaze to the brightly lit area causes the pupils to contract. This constant action of the pupils leads to eyestrain. When you are sitting at a desk, you should have overhead lighting as well as a desk lamp that is focused on your work. This arrangement will give a uniform distribution of light throughout the room. Similarly, it is less fatiguing to the eyes to have additional lighting in the room where you are watching television.

Uniform illumination throughout a work area can be provided by indirect lighting in which all light is reflected. Thus, no light will strike the eyes directly. In contrast, direct lighting, with bulbs located at various points in the ceiling, tends to focus or concentrate the light on specific areas, causing bright spots and glare.

Glare. Glare reduces visual efficiency and contributes to eyestrain. Glare is caused by light of a brighter intensity than that to which the eye is accustomed. This brightness may come from the light source or from reflective surfaces. Glare can lead to an increase in errors in detailed work in as short a time as 20 minutes. It can also obscure vision, something you may have experienced when driving at night and confronted by an oncoming car that has its high-beam headlights on. Glare is also a problem with video display terminals for computers. There are several ways to reduce or eliminate glare. Extremely bright light sources can be shielded or kept out of the visual field. Workers can be supplied with visors or eyeshades. Reflective or glossy surfaces can be painted with a dull, matte finish.

Natural Light.   There may be a psychological component with regard to natural versus artificial light. Research has shown that people who work in windowless offices express a strong desire for windows, regardless of the adequacy of the artificial illumination in their work area (Nagy, Yasunaga, & Kose, 1995). Most workers like to be able to see outside, and they also believe that natural light is better for the eyes than is artificial light. People may have a physiological need for a certain amount of full-spectrum or natural light. Several European countries have laws requiring employers to ensure that all employees can see natural light from their work areas.

Noise

Noise is a common complaint in modern life. Data show that overall noise levels have increased by 11% in the last decade and that noise pollution levels will continue to rise (Staples, 1996). Noise makes us irritable and nervous, interferes with sleep, and produces physiological effects such as hearing loss. Noise is a documented occupational hazard for employees such as riveters, boilermakers, aircraft mechanics, and foundry and textile workers. Businesses have been faced with employee claims of hearing damage that total millions of dollars each year.

The basic unit for measuring noise is the **decibel** (db), which is a measure of the subjective or perceived intensity of a sound. Zero db is the threshold of hearing, the faintest sound most of us can hear. Table 10–2 shows decibel levels in familiar situations. Some loudness levels are threats to hearing. A worker exposed regularly over a long period to decibel levels above 85 can expect to suffer some hearing loss. Exposure to levels over 120 db can cause temporary deafness. Brief exposure to levels in excess of 130 can cause permanent deafness. In 1971, the U.S. government established maximum permissible sound levels for industrial

Decibel (db) The basic unit for measuring noise levels.

Miners are subjected to noise levels that can cause hearing loss.

TABLE 10–2 Decibel Levels for Familiar Sounds

Source of Noise	Decibel Level
Breathing	10
Whisper from 5 feet away	30
Quiet office	40
Conversation 3 feet away	70
City traffic	80
Kitchen appliances	95
Average factory	100
Power lawnmowers	110
Crying babies	110
Pneumatic hammers 3 feet away	120
Electronically amplified rock band	140
Jet aircraft at takeoff	150

workers: exposure to 90 db for an 8-hour day, 100 db for a 2-hour period, and 110 db for a 30-minute period.

When people are exposed to sounds in the 95 to 110 db range, blood vessels constrict, heart rate changes, and the pupils of the eyes dilate. The constriction of the blood vessels continues for some time after the noise ceases, a condition that alters the blood supply throughout the body. Continuous exposure to loud noise is associated with high blood pressure and muscle tension. Psychologists have suggested that noise can impair emotional well-being and induce stress. One study found that employees who worked in extremely noisy environments were more aggressive, distrustful, and irritable than those who worked in quieter surroundings (Donnerstein & Wilson, 1976). More recent research on office workers found that more than half claimed to be so disturbed by the noise in their work environment that they were dissatisfied with their jobs (Sundstrom, Town, Osborn, Rice, Konar, & Brill, 1994).

Not all noises are equally annoying or harmful. Most of us can adapt to a constant or continuous sound, whereas an intermittent or irregular sound is more distracting. When the hum of a fan or an air conditioner is introduced into our environment, it is disturbing at first because it contrasts with the relative quiet that preceded it. However, after a while it becomes part of the background and we no longer notice it. When we fly in an airplane, we generally do not pay attention to the sound of the engines. But it is more difficult to adapt to noises that occur randomly, such as hammering from a neighboring office that is being renovated.

Adaptation to continuous noise occurs only at the conscious level. Factory workers may no longer notice the roar of production machinery, but physiological effects are still occurring. Hearing suffers, blood vessels constrict, and more energy is required to maintain the work pace. These bodily changes can lead to irritability and tiredness, even though workers are not consciously aware of the noise.

Noise interferes with communication. If the background noise is low (between 50 and 60 db), then two people can conduct a conversation without raising their voices at a distance of up to 5 feet. As the background noise level rises, workers must talk louder or must leave their work stations and come closer together to be heard. The decibel level of the average factory forces workers and supervisors to shout. It is likely that important information is lost in transmission.

It is reasonable to assume that high noise levels impair employee efficiency, but the issue remains unresolved. The question is complicated by variables such as type of work (for example, a proofreader may be more distracted by noise than a pneumatic drill operator), kind of noise, and the worker's personal characteristics. A review of empirical studies on noise showed that for some factory jobs, reducing the noise level did not improve productivity but did lead to a reduction in errors. Studies of the effects of noise on jobs that require sustained attention, such as watching a radar screen, have also yielded inconsistent results (Koelega & Brinkman, 1986).

Color

Exaggerated claims have been made about the benefits of color for homes, offices, and factories. It has been suggested that certain colors increase productivity, reduce accidents, and raise employee morale. These claims are not supported by empirical evidence, and there is no validity to any purported relationship between a specific color and productivity, fatigue, or job satisfaction.

However, there is a role for the use of color in the workplace. Color can provide a more pleasant working environment and can be an aid in safety. Color is used in many manufacturing plants as a coding device. Fire equipment is red, danger areas yellow, and first-aid stations green. Color coding allows these areas to be identified quickly. I/O psychologists recommend the use of color to prevent eyestrain because colors differ in their reflective properties. A white wall reflects more light than a dark one. Thus, the appropriate use of color can make a workroom or office seem brighter or darker. Colors also create different illusions of size. A room painted a darker color seems smaller than it actually is. Light-colored walls give the feeling of space and openness.

On the U.S. Navy submarine *USS Tennessee,* the 24 Trident missile tubes, which run through all four decks, are painted reddish-orange. The color is darker for tubes at one end of the ship than the other to create the illusion of depth. This makes the cramped quarters appear to be more spacious than they are. The captain told an interviewer: "That's the psychologists looking out for us" (quoted in Florida's *St. Petersburg Times,* May 5, 1990).

Interior decorators claim that blues and greens are cool colors and that reds and oranges are warm colors. Anecdotal evidence suggests that these colors influence our perception of temperature. In one example, an office was repainted from a drab brown to a bright blue. When winter approached, the employees complained that they were cold even though the indoor office temperature was the same as it had been in previous winters. The temperature was raised 5 degrees, but the complaints persisted. The office was repainted in warm colors, and the employees said they were too hot. The temperature was lowered 5 degrees to where it had been before, and complaints ceased.

Certain colors may convey symbolic information, especially in the uniforms some employees are required to wear. Psychologists have suggested that "The color brown of the UPS uniform, for example, may convey trust. Similarly, hospitals use white to convey purity and cleanliness, and police organizations use dark colors to convey power" (Rafaeli & Pratt, 1993, p. 35).

When a sample of 1,097 office workers in 21 locations were asked for color preferences for their workplace, the majority expressed a preference for cool colors (blues and greens) and for pastels (light blue and pale yellow) (Sundstrom, 1986). Decorators say that people are more excitable and animated in a warm-colored room and more relaxed and calm in a cool-colored one. However, there is little scientific evidence for this suggestion.

If a work area is dingy, then repainting it may improve employee morale. A fresh coat of paint in any color can make workers feel better about their environment. But there is little I/O psychologists can conclude with assurance about the effects of color on employee behavior.

Music

The use of music at work is as old as work itself. Workers traditionally sang on the job, even in noisy factories at the time of the Industrial Revolution. During the late 1800s and early 1900s, quieter industries, such as cigar-making, encouraged singing on the job. Some companies hired musicians to play for the workers, and by the 1930s many organizations supported their own bands and singing groups.

Many claims have been made about the effects of music on productivity and morale. Employees are supposed to be happier and more efficient when they listen to music at work. Studies conducted by firms that supply taped music support these claims, but such research often lacks scientific rigor and control. Early research on music showed that most employees liked the idea of having music during working hours and believed it would make them more productive. This finding depended in part on the kind of work involved. Music has been found to increase production slightly for assembly-line jobs that are reasonably simple and repetitive. Workers regard this type of job as monotonous and not sufficiently demanding to fully engage their attention. Thus, music can provide a focus for these workers, something to occupy the mind and to help the workday pass more quickly and enjoyably. For more demanding work, there is no evidence that music increases productivity because the complexity of the work requires more concentrated attention.

Most of the music piped into factories, offices, corridors, elevators, and waiting rooms is supplied by Muzak, which has been in business since 1934. The company estimates that its background music is played to 100 million people in more than a dozen countries and that it humanizes the work environment by giving people an emotional lift. A different program is created for each workday. The tempo corresponds to changes in mood and energy levels and is designed to be more stimulating at midmorning and midafternoon. Critics consider such music bland or even a form of noise pollution. However, the I/O psychologist on Muzak's board of scientific advisors said, "Why should you want to listen to our music? You should be doing your job!" (quoted in McDermott, 1990).

Temperature and Humidity

We have all experienced the effects of temperature and humidity on our morale, efficiency, and physical well-being. Some of us are happier and have more vital-

NEWSBREAK #19

Wear Your Walkman to Work

You see them on subways, city streets, jogging paths, the beach, and the college library. Young and old wear them all hours of the day and night. Personal stereos, best known by the trademark of the company that first developed them—the Sony Walkman—bring us music any time and place we want to listen to it.

What about in the workplace? The office or factory? Some employers permit workers to use personal stereos on the job. They claim it contributes to job satisfaction and morale. One large Illinois company wanted to test this idea, to find out what would happen if their office workers were allowed to tune in on the job. Because management wanted scientific proof, they called on a group of psychologists from the University of Illinois at Urbana-Champagne to do what psychologists do best: run a study.

For 4 weeks, 75 employees chosen at random used personal stereos at work, while 181 other employees did not. The psychologists administered questionnaires to measure moods (nervousness, relaxation, enthusiasm, and fatigue), and how the workers felt about their jobs and their employer. From supervisors, the psychologists obtained hourly performance rates for the workers as well as ratings of job complexity.

At the end of 4 weeks, the answers were clear. Those employees permitted to listen to music at work showed statistically significant improvements in job performance and satisfaction. Those who worked without music showed no change in performance or satisfaction. There was one confounding variable: Although the use of personal stereos improved job performance for all employees, it was most effective for workers in simpler, less demanding jobs. The psychologists reasoned that for more complex and demanding tasks, there was more potential for distraction. So, if you have a simple, repetitive job, it's OK to turn up the volume. You'll probably be happier, and so will your boss.

Source: Oldham, G. R., Cummings, A., Mischel, L. J., Schmidke, J. M., & Zhou, J. (1995). Listen while you work? Quasi-experimental relations between personal stereo headset use and employee work responses. *Journal of Applied Psychology, 80,* 547–564.

ity in cold weather, whereas others prefer hot weather. Some are depressed by rainy days, and others barely notice them. Most of us work in facilities where temperature and humidity are controlled. But workers in construction, shipbuilding, and other industries are frequently exposed to temperature extremes.

Uncomfortable climate conditions affect the quantity and quality of physical labor. A review of a number of studies showed that temperatures around 90 degrees F had no significant effect on mental or cognitive tasks but did correlate with lower performance levels on perceptual-motor tasks such as tracking or operating machinery (Ramsey, 1995). The negative effects of high temperatures were also demonstrated in a study comparing a strenuous motor task (lifting) with a sedentary motor task (typing). Subjects in both groups experienced a similar degree of heat stress, showing that even less physically demanding work can be affected by temperature (Chad & Brown, 1995).

Even if production levels hold steady, workers must expend more energy to maintain that output and will usually need more frequent rest pauses. Motivation is also a factor. Highly motivated workers are better able to maintain production under temperature extremes than are poorly motivated workers.

Automated office equipment has been found to influence temperature and humidity levels. A single computer terminal does not generate much heat, but when dozens of terminals, printers, and fax machines are operated in the same office, employee complaints about heat and static electricity increase. The drier air also irritates the eyes of employees who wear contact lenses.

TEMPORAL WORKING CONDITIONS: WORK SCHEDULES

A vital part of the overall work environment is the amount of time we spend on the job. The number of hours worked daily or weekly and the amount of rest allowed during working hours are capable of influencing job satisfaction and productivity. A number of alternative work schedules have replaced the traditional 5-day, 40-hour week in which all employees of an organization arrived and left at the same time. We discuss the standard workweek, shift work, and alternative schedules such as permanent part-time employment, the 4-day workweek, and flextime.

Working Hours

At one time in the United States, people routinely worked 10 hours a day, 6 days a week. The 5-day, 40-hour week became the norm in 1938 with the passage of the Fair Labor Standards Act. The United States became the first country to formally establish a 5-day, 40-hour workweek, but this is not necessarily the most efficient work schedule. Workers have accepted it as normal, but in the past they accepted 48 hours and 60 hours as normal.

Nominal working hours
The prescribed number of hours employees are supposed to spend on the job; not all of these hours are actually spent performing job tasks.

There is a difference between **nominal working hours** (the prescribed number of hours employees are supposed to spend on the job) and actual working hours (the amount of time employees devote to job duties). The two rarely coincide. Some I/O psychologists suggest that employees spend no more than half the workweek actually performing required job tasks. Some of the lost time is scheduled by the company as rest pauses, but most of it is unauthorized and beyond the control of the organization. When workers arrive at the workplace, it may take them a long time to begin work. They may shuffle papers, sharpen pencils, or oil machines (whether needed or not). Throughout the workday employees may visit with co-workers, exceed the length of the lunch break, or linger at the coffee machine. Managers lose time waiting for meetings to begin or for telephone calls to be completed, or using their E-mail for personal messages.

There is an interesting relationship between nominal and actual working hours. When nominal, prescribed working hours are increased, actual working hours decrease. In other words, the longer the workday or workweek, the lower

Some jobs require workers to punch a time clock at the beginning and end of each work shift.

the productivity. This finding holds even for highly motivated workers. In the early days of World War II in England, patriotic fervor reached a peak. Dangerously low in supplies and equipment, the country was fighting for survival. The government extended the workweek in defense plants from 56 to 69 1/2 hours. At first, productivity increased 10% but it soon fell 12% below the previous level. Other consequences of increasing nominal working hours included greater absenteeism and more frequent accidents. In the 69 1/2-hour workweek, actual working hours were only 51. With the shorter 56-hour workweek, actual working hours had been 53. A study conducted by the U.S. Bureau of Labor Statistics during World War II showed that the 7-day workweek that was adopted by many American companies during the war resulted in no greater production than the 6-day week. One day of the 7 days was lost time.

This relationship between nominal and actual working hours also applies to overtime when employees are asked to work beyond the normal workday for a markedly higher rate of pay. Much of the extra time is unproductive because people tend to adjust to the longer workday by performing at a slower pace. If productivity drops when the number of working hours is increased, will productivity rise if the workday is shortened? Some research indicates that it will, but other studies show that a decrease in nominal working hours has no effect on actual working hours. In a case of historical interest, during the Great Depression of the 1930s a manufacturing plant reduced nominal working hours by more than 9 hours a week, yet actual working hours fell only 5 hours a week. Another plant reduced the workweek by 10 1/2 hours, and hourly production rose 21%!

Permanent Part-Time Employment

Part-time or half-time employment is the most widespread form of alternative work schedule. Nearly 25% of the U.S. workforce holds part-time jobs. Part-time employment has grown faster than full-time employment, particularly in service and retail trades. This trend to part-time employment is expected to be maintained as companies continue to downsize. By shifting to part-time employment, organizations reduce the costs of keeping full-time staffs (which require higher salary and benefit packages) and increase their scheduling flexibility.

We noted that full-time employment does not mean that the organization is actually getting a full day's work from each employee. Further, management has recognized that much work, such as writing and independent research, can be performed satisfactorily part time. A lower-level assembly-line or clerical job can be performed by two persons, each working half time.

The U.S. Department of Health and Human Services found that supervisors of part-time employees were strongly in favor of part-time employment. A study of welfare caseworkers in Massachusetts who worked 20 hours a week showed that they had a lower turnover rate and a higher caseload contact than did full-time employees. State government agencies in Wisconsin found that actual working hours among permanent part-time social workers, attorneys, and research analysts equaled or exceeded the actual working hours of full-time employees.

Part-time employment is attractive to people with pressing family responsibilities and to disabled persons who have mobility problems. Some managers and professionals prefer part-time employment because it gives them the chance to return to school or to explore other opportunities. Part-time employees are primarily women and include the younger and older segments of the work force. They tend to be concentrated in lower-level jobs and receive lower rates of pay than do full-time employees. However, increasing numbers of professionals and managers are opting for part-time employment. Telephone surveys and personal interviews with part-time employees and with their managers, peers, and subordinates at 47 companies found that professionals and managers who chose part-time work were not viewed differently from full-time employees when being considered for promotion. Part-timers reported no discrimination as a result of their status. In addition, 68% of the companies—which included financial services, public relations, utilities, manufacturing, retailing, publishing, and transportation—reported that they were able to retain valuable employees by providing the chance for part-time employment. This was particularly true for women managers who wanted a better balance between work and family (Mattis, 1990).

The Four-Day Workweek

Another way to alter the workweek significantly is to reduce it to 4 days. This usually involves 4 days at 10 hours a day (a 40-hour week) or 4 days at 9 hours a day (a 36-hour week with no reduction in pay). Union leaders, management consultants, and most of the companies that have tried the 4-day workweek are enthusiastic about it. Typically, the initiative to shorten the workweek came not from employees but from management for several reasons: the possibility of increasing worker productivity and efficiency, the idea of using the shorter workweek as an incentive to recruit workers, and the hope of reducing absenteeism, which in many organizations is unusually high on Mondays and Fridays.

Comments from managers and employees on the 4-day workweek have been positive. They cite improved job satisfaction and productivity, reduced absenteeism, and easier work scheduling. Empirical research conducted on the job shows little effect on production, but surveys confirm that the 4-day schedule is popular with the majority of the employees who try it (Dunham, Pierce, & Castañeda, 1987).

The appeal of the 4-day week was supported by a Gallup Poll: 45% of the men surveyed indicated that they would like a 4-day schedule. Women who did not work outside the home opposed the 4-day workweek by a ratio of two to one. Women who did work outside the home were far more favorable to the idea of a 4-day workweek.

Some companies have tried variations of the 4-day workweek. For example, Texaco, Shell Oil, and Dow Chemical instituted a 9-80 schedule (9 hours a day Monday through Thursday, 8 hours on Friday, and every other Friday off, for a total of 80 hours over a 2-week work cycle). Research on this approach is incomplete, but anecdotal evidence suggests that employees like having the alternate 3-day weekends. However, some employees, fearing downsizing and layoffs, come to work anyway on their days off, wanting to be seen by their bosses as dedicated workers.

A coal-mining outfit in Canada instituted a 4-day workweek of 12 hours a day followed by 4 days off. Surveys of the workers before the change was introduced, and again 10 months later, showed overwhelming support for the new schedule and desirable effects on morale and absenteeism. No significant job performance decrements were recorded. Although some workers reported feeling fatigued by the end of the longer workday, physiological measurements did not support this reaction (Duchon, Keran, & Smith, 1994).

Flexible Working Hours

A more radical alternative work schedule permits employees to decide for themselves when to begin and end the workday. In the 1960s, several companies in Germany tried a flexible working hours **(flextime)** schedule to deal with traffic congestion at rush hours. Under this plan, the workday is divided into four segments, two of which are mandatory and two optional (see Figure 10–1). Employees can report to work any time between, say, 7:30 a.m. and 9:00 a.m. and leave any time between 4:00 p.m. and 5:30 p.m. The mandatory work periods are the morning hours from 9:00 a.m. until the lunch break and the afternoon hours from lunch to 4:00 p.m. Thus, employees work a minimum 6 1/2-hour workday. The optional daily maximum is 9 1/2 hours. How long each employee will work is established individually as a function of the company's needs.

Flextime A system of flexible working hours combining core mandatory work periods with elective work periods at the beginning and end of the workday.

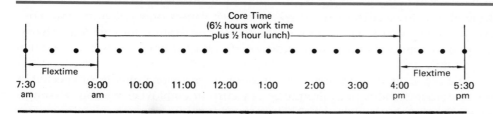

FIGURE 10–1. A typical flextime work schedule.

Flextime offers several advantages. Rush-hour traffic congestion around plants and offices has been reduced. Because employees spend less time and energy commuting, they are often more relaxed at work, more satisfied with their jobs, and more likely to begin work promptly. I/O psychologists have found that many workers make only minor changes in their work habits under a flextime schedule. In a survey of government workers in the United States and in Israel, employees began work, on the average, only 8 minutes later than before and remained on the job 22 minutes longer (Bridgwater, 1982). The researcher concluded that the inflexible demands of car pools, commuter timetables, and family life held the workers to schedules much like those they had before flextime. However, employees believed that having the choice of when to arrive and leave work enhanced their sense of personal freedom.

Some research has found no significant differences in productivity, employee satisfaction, or absenteeism as a result of a flexible working hours schedule. However, the plan does seem to be popular, and employees report improvements in family and social life. Surveys show that the majority of workers on flextime do not want to return to a fixed-hour schedule (Buckley, Kicza, & Crane, 1987; Dunham, Pierce, & Castañeda, 1987).

Flexible working hours appear to be most appropriate for jobs such as research and development, clerical and secretarial, and light and heavy manufacturing. For some assembly-line and shift-work operations, flextime is difficult to implement because of the interdependence of work teams. Overall, flextime is a fair, sensible, and low-cost alternative work schedule that is popular with employers and employees.

Rest Pauses

Ever since the Hawthorne studies, management has recognized the importance of authorized rest breaks. Their beneficial effects have been amply demonstrated, but there is a more insistent reason for granting them: Employees will take breaks whether or not the company sanctions them. If the time is going to be used anyway, the organization might as well appear beneficent and offer the rest pauses as a fringe benefit.

When authorized rest pauses are introduced, unauthorized breaks decline although they do not disappear. Other benefits of rest periods include increased morale and productivity and reduced fatigue and boredom—another instance of how a decrease in nominal working hours can result in an increase in efficiency.

Workers who engage in heavy physical labor need rest pauses because muscles in continuous use tire and become less effective. Rest pauses also reduce repetitive motion injuries to hands and wrists. For more sedentary and intellectual work, the change of stimulation provided by a rest break is helpful. It allows boredom to dissipate and provides the opportunity to think about something else or to socialize with co-workers. Rest pauses may result in more positive attitudes toward management. When a rest program is implemented, workers tend to believe that it is an expression of management's concern for them as individuals.

The rest pause has become a standard of organizational life. It is expected by new employees and is not relinquished by current employees without a comparable gain elsewhere, such as a shorter workweek.

Many jobs are repetitive and physically demanding, requiring workers to be on their feet throughout the workday. These employees should be given formal rest periods to reduce boredom and fatigue.

Shift Work

Many industries operate around the clock. For example, workers in electric and natural gas utilities, transportation, steel, automotive assembly, hospital services, and telecommunications networks typically work one of three shifts, usually 7:00 a.m. to 3:00 p.m., 3:00 p.m. to 11:00 p.m., or 11:00 p.m. to 7:00 a.m. Some companies assign workers to one shift permanently, whereas others rotate work assignments, switching workers each week or so to a different shift. Employees working evening or all-night shifts usually receive extra pay to compensate for the inconvenience of the working hours. Some 25% of the work force in the United States and in England does shift work. The jobs involve white-collar as well as blue-collar personnel.

How does **shift work** affect job performance? Research conducted in the United States and in Europe shows that workers are less productive on the all-night shift than on the day shift. They are more prone to make errors and have more serious accidents (Costa, 1996; Vidaček, Kaliterna, & Radošević-Vidaček, 1986). Nuclear power plant accidents in the United States and in Russia occurred during the night shift. A nuclear plant in Pennsylvania was closed by the Nuclear Regulatory Commission when night-shift control room personnel were found to be asleep on the job. An analysis of bus accidents in the Netherlands found that the accident rate was much higher on shifts that began in early morning than on shifts that began in late afternoon (Pokorny, Blom, Van Leeuwen, & Van Nooten, 1987).

The disruption of the normal sleep-wake cycle has physiological and psychological consequences. Humans develop a diurnal rhythm, a regular daily cycle of bodily activities that is consistent from one 24-hour period to the next. This means that most of us are more alert and productive during normal waking

Shift work Work periods for industries such as utilities or telecommunications that operate 24 hours a day.

hours. When the diurnal rhythm is disrupted, the body undergoes dramatic changes and sleep becomes difficult. The effect on sleep is the major complaint of employees on night-shift work; that is, they are unable to sleep during the day because of daylight and household routines. Family life suffers, and everyday activities such as shopping become difficult to schedule. Night-shift workers and those on a rotating-shift schedule report a high incidence of stomach disorders, sleep disorders, cardiovascular complaints, marital problems, and irritability. A study of 3,446 workers in the German chemical industry found that those on shift work had a significantly higher incidence of stress and psychosomatic complaints than did those not on shift work (Frese & Semmer, 1986).

Research with 20 firefighters on a rotating-shift schedule found that they slept significantly shorter periods when assigned to the night shift. Self-ratings also showed they were sleepier and experienced greater periods of negative moods on the night shift (Paley & Tepas, 1994). A study of 61 nurses in England and Wales found significantly lower moods, alertness, and performance on cognitive tasks on rest days following a night shift as compared to a day shift. Recovery from the negative effects of the night-shift schedule required longer than the 1 day off they received (Totterdell, Spelten, Smith, Barton, & Folkard, 1995).

I/O psychologists agree that fewer problems are encountered with the fixed-shift system than with the rotating-shift system, even when the fixed shift occurs at night. Surveys of 587 nurses and midwives in England and Wales found that those who worked the night shift permanently had fewer health, sleep, social, and family complaints than those who worked rotating shifts. The problems were further reduced for employees who had chosen the night shift voluntarily as compared to those arbitrarily assigned to the night shift (Barton, 1994). Thus, workers permanently assigned to one shift are more likely to adjust to a new diurnal rhythm. With the rotating-shift system, workers must readjust every week or so, whenever the shift schedule is changed, and this system does not give the body time to adjust to one schedule before being forced to begin another.

There are other ways to alleviate some of the problems associated with shift work. When the rotating-shift system must be used, the changes from one shift to another should be made as seldom as possible—for example, every month instead of every week. A 1988 *Psychology Today* survey reported the following changes when the police department in a large northeastern U.S. city altered its work schedule so that officers changed shifts every 18 days instead of every 8 days and worked 4 consecutive days instead of 6. After a year on the new schedule, officers reported decreased fatigue and sleepiness on the job and increased alertness and energy. They felt less irritable and got along better with their families. Automobile accidents on the job dropped by 40%, the use of sleeping pills and alcohol by 50%, and sick leave requests by 23%.

One way to ease the change from one shift to another is to lengthen the time off between shift changes. A longer interim period makes the change less abrupt and allows employees to rest before starting a new schedule. Because the night shift is the most difficult for the employee and the least productive for the employer, it could be shortened to make it less stressful.

A potentially harmful form of shift work is the erratic work schedule of commercial airline pilots, who often change from night flights to day flights and back, sleeping at irregular intervals and disrupting their bodily rhythms. Studies of civilian and military pilots and flight crews working unusually long and erratic hours (such as 10 to 24 hours continuously) confirmed the harmful effects of severe disruptions of diurnal rhythms. The subjects reported considerable fatigue, slept poorly following their work periods, and took unauthorized naps in the cockpit for up to 2 hours. Examinations of aircraft flight recorders (so-called black boxes) revealed that deviations in pilot performance correlated positively with subjective feelings of fatigue (Neville, Bisson, French, Boll, & Storm, 1994; Rosekind et al., 1994).

Research conducted by psychologists at NASA's Fatigue Countermeasures Program found that allowing pilots 40-minute rest periods during low workload portions of long flights resulted in significantly increased alertness. As a result of this finding, several airlines, including Swissair and Qantas, permit such cockpit rest breaks. Although the FAA does not permit U.S. flight crews to have in-flight rest periods, it is considering changing its policy (Azar, 1996b). This is another example of how psychological research findings can lead to significant positive changes in the workplace—in this case, changes that could affect your safety the next time you fly.

PSYCHOLOGICAL AND SOCIAL WORKING CONDITIONS

Other important factors in the work environment relate to the nature of the job and its impact on employees; that is, the intrinsic environment of the job. For example, does your job provide you with a sense of satisfaction and achievement, or does it make you tired, bored, and ill? We have noted that the design of your job can influence your motivation and satisfaction. Some quality-of-work-life programs have been successful in improving morale and motivation, but jobs designed to be so simple that they make no demands on intelligence, achievement, or attention will lead to boredom, fatigue, and inefficiency.

Job Simplification

Simplified, fragmented, and repetitive work affects mental and physical health. For example, assembly-line workers complain more about their physical health and visit company medical facilities more often than workers who do less repetitive work. Psychologists suggest that people who hold such jobs on a rigid work schedule are more anxious, depressed, and irritable than workers doing the same kinds of jobs on a more flexible schedule. Simplified and repetitive work can lead to the deterioration in cognitive or mental functioning usually associated with old age. These workers are prone to absentmindedness, forgetfulness, and disorientation.

The history of **job simplification** dates from the beginnings of mass production in the early 20th century. If relatively expensive consumer goods such as automobiles were to be produced cost-effectively in sufficient quantities to meet consumer demand, then old-style production methods, such as building each unit by hand, would have to change. Mass production called for product consistency and standardization so that parts would be interchangeable. It also required fractionation of job tasks. It was no longer economically or technically feasible for one person to make an entire product. The work had to be meticulously divided so that each worker produced only a small part of the finished

Job simplification The reduction of manufacturing jobs to the simplest components that can be mastered by unskilled or semiskilled workers.

product. The ideal was to reduce every manufacturing process to the simplest elements that could be mastered by an unskilled or semiskilled employee.

Job simplification offered tremendous economic advantages to industry and to consumers, permitting the lowest possible cost per unit produced. When Henry Ford established his automobile assembly line, he was able to sell cars at a price within reach of people who previously could not afford them. The same was true for other consumer goods. The factory-produced chair in which you are sitting costs considerably less than a chair handmade by a skilled furniture craftsperson. This was an additional advantage of job simplification: industry no longer had to rely on the skilled trades, the workers who required years of apprenticeship, expected high wages, and were apt to be independent of mind. The typical assembly line could be filled with workers who had little skill and could quickly be trained to perform the job. The process made workers more docile and easier to manage. Because they had few marketable skills, they knew they could easily be replaced. Workers were as interchangeable as the parts they produced.

There is no denying that job simplification had a stimulating impact on the American economy. More jobs became available, and people had more money to buy the plentiful consumer goods. The more people bought, the more factories had to be built, which, in turn, meant even more jobs. New products required additional businesses to advertise, sell, and service them. Such economic growth could not have occurred if production methods had remained limited to the handcrafted approach.

Assembly-line workers are paying a price for their role in this industrial development. The farther removed workers are from the finished product, the less meaning and value they attach to their jobs. The carpenter who shaped a table from a piece of lumber knew the pride and fulfillment of achievement and the challenge of using skill and imagination. There is little challenge and satisfaction in operating a machine that attaches automobile bumpers over and over, day after day, year after year. The worker is an adjunct to the machine, pressing a button or pushing a lever or watching in case something goes wrong. The work has little meaning and quickly becomes frustrating and monotonous. Workers grow apathetic, morale declines, and quantity and quality of production deteriorate.

Job simplification also affects white-collar and managerial jobs because computers have turned many offices into electronic assembly lines. In white-collar jobs, work is increasingly fragmented, simplified, and made repetitive. As a result, office workers are becoming cheaper to train and easier to replace.

We noted in Chapter 9 how jobs can be enlarged, enriched, and expanded to provide employees with greater responsibility and challenge. The quality-of-work-life programs we discussed are real-world examples of making jobs more complex rather than simpler. Let us consider two additional examples. The management of a high-tech electronics firm in England redesigned the job of tending computer-controlled manufacturing equipment to give workers greater autonomy, control, challenge, and responsibility. One result was that the duration of equipment failures was 10 hours less a week than previously. Also, workers reported greater intrinsic job satisfaction and less stress (Wall, Corbett, Martin, Clegg, & Jackson, 1990). Similar beneficial effects were found in a robot-controlled assembly line producing drill bits for the mining and construction industries. When the degree of worker responsibility for correcting operational faults was increased, production increased significantly and downtime was reduced (Wall, Jackson, & Davids, 1992). In both cases, expanding the job benefitted both employers and employees.

Boredom and Monotony

Two consequences of job fractionation and simplification—boredom and monotony—are important components of the psychological work environment. Boredom results from the continuous performance of a repetitive and uninteresting activity and can lead to restlessness, unhappiness, and tiredness, a draining of interest and energy. However, what is boring for one person may be exciting for another. Although most people find assembly-line work monotonous, for example, others do not. And some workers in jobs that appear challenging also report feelings of boredom. The relevant factor is motivation. The data-entry clerk who is highly motivated to process entries without making errors will be less bored than the worker who lacks this motivation.

One obvious way to alleviate boredom is to enlarge the scope of the job, to make it more complex, stimulating, and challenging. For jobs to which this technique can be applied, it can be successful in motivating employees and preventing boredom. Management can also alter physical, temporal, and social conditions of work to reduce boredom. Attention to noise reduction, lighting, and pleasant surroundings can help to combat the negative effects of repetitive and monotonous work. A congenial informal work group helps, as do rest pauses to provide a change of activity. The greater the change in activity during rest pauses or lunch breaks, the less disruptive will be the effects of boredom.

Some companies have tried job rotation, letting workers perform different tasks during the workday. However, job rotation is successful only if the alternate activity is sufficiently different from the original one. If the two jobs are similar, switching from one to the other provides little relief from boredom. If the jobs are too dissimilar, retraining may be required.

Another method of counteracting boredom is to teach workers the value and meaning of their jobs. Greater employee interest can be engendered if workers are told how their work, or the part they are producing, fits into the overall operation. This awareness can be easily taught in lectures or by a tour of the plant. These programs can help workers to develop pride in their jobs and a sense that their work is important. The resulting increase in motivation can lead to a greater tolerance for routine work.

Fatigue

I/O psychologists describe two types of **fatigue:** psychological fatigue, which is similar to boredom, and physiological fatigue, which is caused by excessive use of the muscles. Both types of fatigue can cause poor job performance and lead to errors, accidents, absenteeism, and turnover. Prolonged or heavy physical labor produces measurable physiological changes. Studies of heavy lifting and carrying tasks consistently show cardiovascular, metabolic, and muscle fatigue as well as a decline in the ability to maintain frequency of task performance (Mital, Foononi-Fard, & Brown, 1994).

Psychological or subjective fatigue is more difficult to assess but is no less disturbing to employees. We are all aware of experiencing strain, irritability, and

Fatigue Physiological and psychological tiredness that can lead to deterioration in job performance.

weakness when we are excessively tired, and we may find it difficult to concentrate, think coherently, and work effectively.

On-the-job research has shown that productivity levels parallel reported feelings of fatigue. High reported fatigue is a reliable indicator that production will shortly decline. With most physical work, employees say that they are most tired at the beginning of the work period, again just before the lunch break, and again at the end of the workday. Thus, fatigue does not build up over the course of the work period but appears and disappears throughout the working hours. This suggests that factors other than physical labor—motivation, for example—influence fatigue. It often happens that a person leaves the job at the end of the shift feeling exhausted but finds that the fatigue disappears on arriving home and anticipating some pleasurable activity.

Research on physiological fatigue indicates that greater amounts of physical labor can be undertaken when the work pace is more gradual. Too rapid a rate of heavy work dissipates the body's energy too quickly so that the worker must then function at a slower pace for the remainder of the work period. An analogy can be made with long-distance runners who pace themselves so that they do not consume all their energy before covering the desired distance.

Rest periods are necessary for jobs that involve heavy physical labor and should be taken before fatigue is complete. The greater the amount of fatigue at the time of the rest break, the longer the recovery period must be. For some jobs, more frequent rest breaks are needed. Rest periods must provide total relaxation, not merely a stoppage of work. It is the manual laborer, more than the office worker, who will benefit from canteens and comfortable lounges in which to relax.

To determine additional factors related to fatigue, the work records and self-report records (rating job challenge and supervisor quality) of 3,705 temporary employees who reported job fatigue were compared with data on 10,000 other employees who did not report fatigue on the job. All employees were performing clerical or light industrial tasks. Factors significantly associated with high job fatigue included the following (Finkelman, 1994):

- Low job challenge
- Poor supervision
- Low job control
- Low ratings by supervisors of job performance
- Low pay
- Low information-processing or cognitive demands (amount of judgment and decision-making ability required by the job)

Which factors do you think had the highest correlation with reported job fatigue? Low pay? Little challenge? A bad boss? No, it was low information-processing demand. The researcher concluded that the less mental challenge and stimulation the work provided, the more fatiguing it was for the workers.

Telecommuting: The Workplace at Home

We have noted the flexibility in work scheduling in recent years. Now that flexibility has come to characterize the workplace itself. Many employees work at home, thanks to advances in personal computers, telecommunications, and fax machines. This move toward **telecommuting**—the decentralizing of work—is already in effect at more than 600 U.S. companies in life insurance, data processing, financial services, airline and hotel reservations, and mail-order merchandising. These firms have placed computer or word-processing equipment in their employees' homes. The Bureau of National Affairs estimates that 15 million people are performing such jobs at home.

Telecommuting Using telecommunications to decentralize work and allow employees to perform work at home on personal computers.

The opportunity to work at home is becoming so widespread that some houses and apartment buildings are being constructed with computer connections built in as a selling feature. Telecommuting is particularly attractive to employees with day-care or dependent-care problems and to disabled workers. Approximately half of home-based employees are men and half are women.

Companies that provide for telecommuting cite gains in productivity, reduced costs for office overhead, and—obviously—a decline in absenteeism. People working at home may have fewer interruptions than people working in offices and may be able to concentrate better. Employees working at home can perform their job in bad weather or when feeling poorly whereas office-based employees might hesitate to come to work.

Los Angeles County administrators estimate that their telecommuting program involving 2,600 workers saves $11 million a year in increased productivity,

A typical telecommuter, this head of an advertising agency operates the business from his home.

reduced absenteeism, decreased overtime pay, and reduced office space. They also claim the program cut commuting time by 1.4 million hours, thus eliminating 7,500 tons of carbon monoxide from car exhausts.

A 1996 AT&T poll of 1,005 home-based employees found that 80% believed they were more productive than when working in the company offices. In addition, 61% said they got sick less often and 79% appreciated the chance to wear more casual clothes while working.

Surveys at other companies found increases up to 30% in productivity as well as a significant reduction in nonproductive time resulting from office socializing. Psychologists also noted that telecommuting did not appear to be related to any decrease in an employee's opportunity for promotion (Becker & Steele, 1995).

Not everyone likes the idea of working at home. Some people miss the social interaction. Others are not sufficiently disciplined to work steadily without supervision. Some managers believe they will lose their authority over subordinates if the subordinates are not physically present. Labor unions are concerned about the declining loyalty of members who do not work together on the job. Despite these objections, for many employees home is the workplace of the future.

Working the Night Shift by Choice

We saw in Chapter 10 that there are many harmful effects of shift work because it tends to disrupt the normal diurnal rhythm. People who work on rotating shifts are usually less productive and more prone to make errors on the night shift. In addition, they have trouble sleeping during the day and report a high incidence of physical, emotional, marital, and family problems.

Research has shown that employees who work on a permanent shift arrangement report fewer difficulties, even when that shift is at night. A British psychologist decided to investigate whether employees who volunteered to work at night experienced fewer problems than those who worked at night as part of a rotating shift arrangement.

To secure subjects, the psychologist contacted hospitals in England and Wales, inviting nurses and midwives to participate in the study. A total of 587 volunteered (530 females, 55 males, 2 unspecified). Of these, 240 employees served permanently on night-shift duty, and 347 worked on a rotating shift basis. The permanent night-shift subjects were significantly older than those on the rotating shift, with a mean age of 38 years versus 30 years. Also, 75% of the permanent night-shift subjects were married; only 59% of the rotating-shift workers were married.

The subjects were given the Standard Shift-work Index questionnaire, which contains items designed to assess the severity of health, sleep, and social disruptions experienced as a result of shift work. Six months later, the subjects completed additional questionnaires to assess several factors, including psychological and physical health, chronic fatigue, anxiety, neuroticism, sleep quality, job sat-

isfaction, "morningness" (a preference for morning rather than evening activities), and their reasons for working their particular shift arrangement.

The results showed that nurses on the rotating shift reported significantly more social disruptions and sleep problems than nurses on permanent night shifts. There were no consistent or significant differences between the two groups on any of the measures of psychological or physical health. Nurses on the permanent night shift did report significantly greater job satisfaction than those on the rotating shift.

Overall, subjects on permanent night-shift duty had fewer health, sleep, social, and domestic problems. Also, those who had chosen that shift had fewer problems than those who had been assigned to the shift. Thus, the psychologist suggested that employees who choose to work at night are better able to tolerate the effects of this arrangement than are those whose night-shift job is not their own choice.

Critical Thinking Questions

1. Describe the effects of shift work on job performance and on physical and psychological well-being, as reported by the other research discussed in this chapter.

2. How might the differences in age and marital status between the two groups in this study have influenced the findings?

3. If you were in charge of a factory that had to remain in operation 24 hours a day, what steps would you take to alleviate the problems related to shift work?

4. What characteristics of a job or its work environment might be altered to minimize the harmful effects of shift work?

5. Describe the consequences of the erratic and unusually long hours often worked by airline flight crews. What steps can be taken to relieve those problems?

Source: Barton, J. (1994). Choosing to work at night: A moderating influence on individual tolerance to shift work. *Journal of Applied Psychology, 79,* 449–454.

SUMMARY

Physical working conditions include factors such as the location of the factory or office building, parking facilities, heating and air-conditioning systems, elevators, eating facilities, and rest rooms. **Environmental psychology** is concerned with the impact of these workplace features on employee behaviors and attitudes. In the **landscaped office** employees are grouped in functional units with no floor-to-ceiling barriers.

Light distribution and glare must be considered in designing illumination for various work spaces. Noise in the work area can lead to deafness and to physiological effects such as increased muscle tension and blood pressure. Color is a useful coding device and can create different illusions of size and temperature and improve the aesthetic appearance of the workplace. Some employees like music on the job, but research shows that it does not influence productivity. Optimal temperature and humidity ranges have been established for different kinds of workplaces. The comfort level of a workspace also depends on humidity level and air circulation.

Temporal working conditions include the number of hours worked and how those hours are arranged. Much scheduled work time is lost to unauthorized breaks. When the **nominal working hours** are reduced, production tends to increase. Part-time employment offers opportunities to combine career, family, educational, leisure, and other pursuits, and may result in greater productivity. The 4-day workweek seems to result in lower absenteeism and higher morale but has little effect on productivity. **Flextime** is popular with employees but has little effect on productivity or job satisfaction. Rest pauses will be taken whether or not they are officially sanctioned. They are necessary in manual labor to rest the muscles. For sedentary workers, rest pauses provide a change of pace and help to alleviate boredom. **Shift work** disrupts the body's diurnal rhythm and can lead to social and psychological difficulties. In general, productivity is lower on the night shift; serious accidents and errors are higher.

Psychological working conditions relate to the design of the job and its effects on employees. Many jobs have been so simplified that they are boring and lead to psychological and physiological **fatigue** that reduces productivity. Repetitive, boring work is also tiring. Boredom can be relieved by enlarging the job scope, rotating jobs, improving working conditions, scheduling rest pauses, and communicating to employees the value and importance of their work. Computers and telecommunications have made **telecommuting** possible for many types of employees.

KEY TERMS

decibel (db)

environmental psychology

fatigue

flextime

job simplification

landscaped offices

nominal working hours

shift work

telecommuting

ADDITIONAL READING

Goodstein, J. (1995). Employer involvement in eldercare: An organizational adaptation perspective. *Academy of Management Journal, 38,* 1657–1671. Reviews the demands of caring for elderly dependents (usually parents), especially on women employees, and discusses attempts of employing organizations to accommodate the obligations of this work-family issue.

Hochschild, A. R. (1997). *The time bind: When work becomes home and home becomes work*. New York: Metropolitan/Henry Holt. Reports on a study of a large midwestern organization in which both men and women employees routinely put in 10-hour workdays and identified more with their colleagues and subordinates than with their own families. They also derived greater social support from office relationships than from relationships outside work.

Rafaeli, A., & Pratt, M. G. (1993). Tailored meanings: On the meaning and impact of organizational dress. *Academy of Management Review, 18*, 32–55. Reviews the effects of clothing on employee behavior and organizational image. Considers attributes of dress (color, style, type of material), similarity of dress among employees in an organization, and conspicuousness of dress (such as uniforms) compared to other organizations.

Schor, J. B. (1991). *The overworked American: The unexpected decline of leisure*. New York: Basic Books. Suggests that U.S. employees have longer working hours, relative to those of European employees, largely because of employer demand, unemployment, and dependence on compensation and benefits packages.

Staples, S. L. (1996). Human response to environmental noise: Psychological research and public policy. *American Psychologist, 51*, 143–150. Argues for environmental noise research that considers psychological issues such as individual differences in reactions to noise, factors that affect a worker's degree of annoyance, and the identification of groups prone to stress-related health effects of noise.

Safety, Violence, and Health in the Workplace

SUMMARY
KEY TERMS
ADDITIONAL READING

■   ■   ■   ■

The shops, offices, and factories in which we work can be dangerous places. In 1994, there were 6588 accidental deaths on the job, an average of 18 per day; most of the victims were men. This represents an increase of 4% over the previous year.

The number of disabling injuries on the job, although not fully documented, is thought to be in excess of 2 million each year. Research by the Bureau of Labor Statistics indicates that for every disabling work injury reported, 10 are not reported by companies seeking to hide a poor safety record. Thus, some 20 to 25 million employees each year may sustain injuries in job-related accidents.

Accidents extract a huge emotional toll on the victims' families and co-workers. The monetary cost of so many injuries is also staggering, not only to employees and their organizations, but also to the nation as a whole. Billions of dollars are forfeited through lost time and wages and paid out in medical benefits and workers' compensation claims.

The health of workers in some types of jobs can be undermined by their exposure to toxic chemicals in the workplace. Disabling illnesses acquired because of these on-the-job conditions generally do not kill or maim as suddenly or dramatically as accidents, but they impose emotional and economic costs as well, shortening the lives of thousands of workers.

Although accidents are the primary cause of death on the job for all workers, murder is the second; for women employees it is the leading factor, accounting for 42% of women's on-the-job fatalities. Injuries from deliberate acts of violence are becoming more widespread. In the 1-year period from July 1992 to July 1993, 2.2 million employees were physically attacked at their place of work, or were threatened with attack, and 16.1 million reported verbal or physical harassment (Martin, 1994).

In this chapter we examine these and other aspects of workplace health and safety, discussing what I/O psychologists have learned about accidents and violence on the job and what organizations are doing about the problems. We deal with alcohol and drug abuse, both of which have adverse effects on employee health, safety, and job performance, and with the concerns related to employees with AIDS. We also discuss health problems thought to be related to the use of computers in the workplace.

THE SCOPE OF EMPLOYEE HEALTH PROBLEMS

The toll from work-related diseases is as shocking as the accident rate. These illnesses are more insidious than a sudden, traumatic accident because they develop slowly over years before the worker experiences physical symptoms. For example, coal miners develop a unique respiratory condition called pneumoconiosis, or black lung disease, a progressively crippling disorder caused by the prolonged inhalation of coal dust. Chemical industries pose health perils to their workers, dangers that are not fully known. Up to 10 million workers are exposed daily to chemicals for which safe thresholds have not been established. The Environmental Protection Agency (EPA) has designated as toxic more than 16,000 chemical substances regularly used in the workplace. Some 150 of these are neurotoxins; that is, they cause damage to the human brain and nervous system.

NEWSBREAK #20

The Sick Building Syndrome

Many of us spend our working days sealed off from fresh air, trapped in closed environments. We can't open the windows—in most cases they're not designed to open—and we breathe only filtered cooled or heated air. The cooling and heating systems in modern office buildings may be cost-efficient to operate, but the results can be dangerous. What we inhale can make us sick.

According to the World Health Organization, the physical complaints brought on by these artificial environments include eye, ear, and throat irritations, dry nasal membranes, skin inflammations, fatigue, headaches, nausea, and dizziness. Consider a few examples. In a sealed office building in San Francisco, California, most of the 250 employees complained of headaches, sinus problems, allergic skin reactions, and general discomfort shortly after the building opened. The symptoms disappeared when the air-filtration system was modified to allow more fresh air to circulate. In another new building, workers became dazed and stuporous most afternoons, especially on hot days. The problem was traced to the roof, where melting tar released fumes that were drawn into the air-conditioning system and dispersed throughout the building. Bacterial infections have also been transmitted through ventilation and air-conditioning systems.

When hundreds of employees in a $37-million, 10-story county office complex in Florida developed symptoms of asthma, the building had to be abandoned. Experts concluded that construction flaws, a faulty air-conditioning system, a leaky roof, and vinyl wallpaper had combined to make the building a breeding ground for mildew and other contaminants.

Sealed buildings contain an alarming number of chemicals that are not dissipated or diluted by fresh air. Solvents, adhesives, cleaning fluids, fire-retardant materials, paint additives, formaldehyde in insulation, and chemicals in carpeting, wall coverings, and draperies can all be toxic. Copy machines produce ozone, which has been linked to headaches and upper respiratory tract infections. Solvents in carbonless paper are dangerous. Long-term exposure to electronic equipment has been related to headaches, eye problems, and neurological disorders. Harmful levels of microwaves and other sources of radiation have been linked to eye damage, memory loss, thyroid dysfunction, and leukemia. Perhaps some buildings should be labeled: Caution: Working here may be hazardous to your health.

Miners, mill workers, and shipyard workers are exposed to asbestos on the job, facing the danger of lung cancer at seven times the national rate. Textile workers are at risk for byssinosis, or brown lung disease, caused by inhaling cotton dust. Medical technicians face dangers from radiation exposure. Office workers face the potentially harmful effects of indoor pollutants. Table 11–1 lists some frequently used substances, their health effects, and the types of workers who are regularly endangered.

TABLE 11–1   Hazardous Substances and On-the-Job Diseases

Potential Dangers	Potential Diseases	Workers Exposed
Arsenic	Lung cancer, lymphoma	Smelter, chemical, oil-refinery workers; insecticide makers and sprayers—estimated 660,000 exposed
Asbestos	White-lung disease (asbestosis); cancer of lungs and lining of lungs; cancer of other organs	Miners; millers; textile, insulation and shipyard workers—estimated 1.6 million exposed
Benzene	Leukemia; aplastic anemia	Petrochemical and oil-refinery workers; dye users; distillers; painters; shoemakers—estimated 600,000 exposed
Bischloromethylether (BCME)	Lung cancer	Industrial chemical workers
Coal dust	Black-lung disease	Coal miners—estimated 208,000 exposed
Coke-oven emissions	Cancer of lungs, kidneys	Coke-oven workers—estimated 30,000 exposed
Cotton dust	Brown-lung disease (byssinosis); chronic bronchitis; emphysema	Textile workers—estimated 600,000 exposed
Lead	Kidney disease; anemia; central-nervous-system damage; sterility; birth defects	Metal grinders; lead-smelter workers; lead storage-battery workers—estimated 835,000 exposed
Radiation	Cancer of thyroid, lungs and bone; leukemia; reproductive effects (spontaneous abortion, genetic damage)	Medical technicians; uranium miners; nuclear-power and atomic workers
Vinyl chloride	Cancer of liver, brain	Plastic-industry workers—estimated 10,000 directly exposed

Note. Adapted from *Healthy People in Unhealthy Places: Stress and Fitness at Work* (p. 90) by K. R. Pelletier, 1984, New York: Delacorte.

EMPLOYEE ACCIDENT STATISTICS

We noted earlier that more than 6,000 workers are killed by accidents on the job every year, and that as many as 25 million are injured. These figures do not include those killed or injured commuting to and from the workplace. More than 90% of the employees killed on the job are men, though they constitute only 54% of the workforce. There is an obvious reason for this occurrence: more men than women work in construction and heavy industry, where an accident can have the most severe consequences. More men than women work as long-distance truck drivers, an occupation that contributes to 20% of all on-the-job fatalities every year. In fact, highway accidents are the leading cause of job-related accidental death.

In 1995, the *New York Times* estimated that falls accounted for 10% of deaths on the job, most notably among roofers, painters, and construction workers on bridges and high-rise buildings. Other causes included falling objects (9%), electrocution (5%), and fires and explosions (3%).

Obviously, some jobs are more dangerous than others, which means that some workers are subject to greater risk of injury or death at work. Not surprisingly, exposure to a hazardous work environment can be stressful. This was demonstrated clearly in a questionnaire study of 207 EMT (emergency medical technician) firefighters. The perceived riskiness of their work was significantly and positively related to symptoms of stress. Firefighters who reported themselves to be the most familiar with the risks of their jobs were also the least satisfied with their work (McLain, 1995). Thus, working in a risky job was shown to have emotional as well as physical costs.

Effects of Federal Legislation on Accidents

In 1970, the U.S. Congress passed the Occupational Safety and Health Act establishing the Occupational Safety and Health Administration (OSHA) in the Department of Labor. OSHA's purpose is to assure safe and healthful working conditions by developing and enforcing federal safety standards and by sponsoring research on the causes and prevention of accidents and diseases in the workplace.

Although progress has been made, OSHA has been so poorly funded that it has not been able to carry out its mandate to make the workplace safer. More than 25 years after OSHA was established, it has so few safety inspectors that on the average a company can expect to be visited only once every 84 years. In Florida alone, it would take 103 years for the OSHA staff to inspect the state's 320,000 businesses.

INTERPRETING ACCIDENT STATISTICS

We noted in Chapter 2 that statistics do not lie but that sometimes the people who use statistics distort ideas in their own interests, backing up the distortions with data. This is the situation with accident statistics. The problem is finding a precise, acceptable definition of an accident, which is not as ridiculous as it sounds.

How severe must an accident be for it to be included in an organization's accident statistics? Suppose a bakery worker drops a 100-pound sack of sugar. Is this an accident? Technically, yes. However, whether it is listed by the company as an accident depends on the consequences, not on the action itself. If the sack does not split and spill sugar all over the equipment and if no one is hurt, the episode will not be recorded as an accident. But what if the sack falls on the worker's foot and breaks a few bones? Is this considered an accident? Not necessarily. Many companies will not list this as an accident, even though the worker is injured and requires medical treatment. The injured worker may not be able to walk for a while, but if the company provides a desk job until the injuries heal, then the employee will not have lost work time. Here we have an accident that results in an injury, yet it will not be included in the accident statistics, and the company's safety record will remain intact. The definition of an accident in this case depends on whether the injured worker must be absent from work.

A few years ago, a large U.S. meat-packing firm was fined $2.59 million for failing to report in 1 year more than 1,000 job-related injuries among its workers. Statistics on railroad accidents investigated by a Washington-based journalist contradicted official government reports: Where Amtrak cited 494 injuries in 25 train wrecks, the independent journalist found 1,338. It is this failure to record all job-related injuries, not just those that keep workers off the job, that has led the Bureau of Labor Statistics to conclude that accidents are significantly underreported.

Incomplete reporting makes research on the causes and prevention of accidents more difficult. The statistics provided by business and industry show the results of only a small proportion of accidents and provide little information on their causes. By concentrating on lost-time accidents, the data provide an inaccurate picture of overall safety patterns or of patterns in specific work units and departments.

An organization likes to claim a good safety record. It shows that the company is a caring employer, doing all it can to promote a safe working environment for its employees. To preserve a good safety record and a favorable public image, a company may resort to extreme measures such as closed-door investigations, incomplete reporting, and outright distortion of facts. However, sometimes it is the employees who distort the facts. Some fail to report minor accidents for fear of acquiring a reputation as careless or accident-prone. Others fear disciplinary action if the accident was their fault because they failed to follow prescribed operating procedures or to activate safety devices.

This underreporting and cover-up of accidents has been documented in many countries. In Japan, workers tend to conceal evidence of job-related injuries because of personal shame. To avoid losing face, Japanese workers attempt to hide even major injuries such as broken bones or to insist that they occurred at home. Managers conspire to conceal workers' injuries because they represent negligence on their own part as well.

CAUSES OF ACCIDENTS

Human error is the factor responsible for most accidents, whether they occur at the workplace, on the highway, or in the home. For example, an analysis of accidents that occurred on the flight decks of U.S. Navy aircraft carriers (an unusually dangerous workplace) showed that 90% of them were caused by human error (Shappell, 1995). However, conditions of the work environment and the nature of the job tasks also contribute to accidents.

Workplace Factors

Workplace conditions studied by I/O psychologists include type of industry, hours of work, lighting, temperature, equipment design, and social pressure.

Type of Industry. The frequency and severity of accidents vary as a function of the type of industry. A steel mill provides more opportunities for accidents than does a bank. The greater the physical demands made on the worker, the higher the accident rate. Also, stressful and tiring work seems to result in more accidents.

Industries such as construction, highway transportation, timber, and mining are high in frequency and severity of accidents. Industries such as warehousing, aircraft and automobile manufacturing, and communications have a low frequency and severity of accidents. Cement and steel companies report a low frequency of accidents, but when accidents do occur, they are usually severe. Electric utilities also record few accidents, but these tend to be severe because of the high voltages involved. Wholesale and retail businesses have high accident rates, but lost-time injuries are rare. Data for high-risk industries are shown in Table 11–2.

Hours of Work. We might assume that the higher the number of hours worked, the higher the accident rate, but research does not provide clear support for this idea. However, shift work seems to be related to accident rates. In general, fewer accidents occur during the night shift than during the day shift, although night shift accidents, when they do occur, are usually more serious. This situation may be related to level of illumination. The artificial lighting provided at night can be better for work than the natural lighting conditions during the day.

An investigation of accidents in an iron and steel mill showed that 41% occurred on the 7:00 a.m. to 3:00 p.m. shift, 23% on the 3:00 p.m. to 11:00 p.m.

TABLE 11–2 High-Risk Industries

Industry	Injury Rate per 100 Full-time Workers
Meat packing plants	33.4
Mobile home manufacturing plants	29.8
Vending machine manufacturing plants	28.1
Wooden roof supports manufacturing plants	27.1
Sugarcane processing plants	26.2
Wood buildings prefabricators	26.0
Scrap rubber reclamation plants	25.7
Sawmills	25.4
Boat builders and repairers	24.2
Plumbing fixture manufacturers	23.5

Note. Data from Bureau of Labor Statistics.

shift, and only 16% on the 11:00 p.m. to 7:00 a.m. night shift. Two peak accident periods were documented—between nine and ten o'clock in the morning and between two and three o'clock in the afternoon. These peak accident periods may have been related to fatigue (Ong, Phoon, Iskandar, & Chia, 1987).

Research conducted on the U.S. nuclear power industry found that the more hours of overtime worked, the higher the frequency of safety problems and procedure violations, errors that could easily lead to serious accidents if not caught in time (Baker, Olson, & Morisseau, 1994).

Lighting.   Good lighting can lead to a reduction in accidents. The insurance industry estimates that one fourth of all industrial accidents are caused by poor lighting. Accidents are higher in plants that continue production through dusk before the nighttime lighting is turned on. Dusk is also a time of frequent automobile accidents. The relationship between level of illumination and accident rates in industry has been firmly established, and an alert management can easily correct the problem of a poorly lit work area.

Temperature.   Studies of factory workers show that accident rates are lowest when the workplace temperature is maintained at 68 to 70°F. Accidents increase when the temperature varies significantly, either warmer or cooler. Studies of coal miners show that minor accidents are three times more frequent under high temperatures (approaching 85°F) than under low temperatures (approaching 62°F). Workers seem to become more careless under the discomfort of higher temperatures. Older workers are more affected than younger workers by climatic extremes and are more likely to have accidents at higher temperatures.

Equipment Design.   Another physical factor related to accidents is the design of the tools, equipment, and machines used on the job. For example, if an engineer locates a stop button where it is difficult to reach, this can have deadly consequences for the worker who needs to shut down the machine immediately. Poor placement of switches and controls, inadequate warning lights for system malfunctions, and dials that are difficult to read have all been blamed for accidents.

Engineering psychologists strive to match equipment requirements with the capabilities of the human operators (see Chapter 13). Their work on safe workplaces and equipment has been highly effective, particularly with regard to cumulative trauma disorders and repetitive motion injuries such as carpal tunnel syndrome. These injuries are caused by continuous and repeated motions of hands and wrists and can affect shoulders and back as well. Repetitive motion injuries are prevalent among office workers using computer terminals and among certain types of factory workers. Redesigning tools and equipment, improving employee posture, and providing rest pauses are all effective in reducing repetitive motion injuries.

As an example of how equipment and tool redesign can reduce accidents, consider the case of a large meat packing plant. As shown in Table 11–2, meat packing plants have the highest injury rate of all industries, primarily because the work involves the constant use of knives. Joint management-worker teams were organized to investigate the jobs of all 800 workers in the plant, with the goal of reducing the number of accidents.

The teams altered the shape and sharpness of the knives and redesigned the handles to change the wrist position. They adjusted the height of the work sta-

A hazardous work environment such as a natural gas drilling plant must be designed so that emergency controls are within easy reach.

tions to reduce bending, designed conveyer systems to eliminate lifting and carrying, and provided floor mats to reduce the fatigue caused by standing throughout the work period. These changes resulted in significant reductions in the number and severity of cumulative trauma disorders, in lost production time, and in restricted duty days attributable to accidents (May & Schwoerer, 1994).

Part of the reason for the success of this program in the meat packing plant was the participation of the workers. They were actively involved in redesigning their work environment to make their jobs safer, less fatiguing, and easier to perform. As we have seen in many instances, change in the workplace is much better accepted when the workers participate in decisions regarding that change.

Cumulative trauma disorders are also seen in grocery store checkout clerks who are required to make frequent repetitive wrist movements using electronic scanners. Every product must be physically moved over or in front of the scanner so that the price of the item will be registered. A comparison of 19 combinations of scanners and checkout stands, using both experienced and inexperienced cashiers, showed that a checkout stand that allows the cashier to sit while working causes severe pressure on the back and shoulders.

The optimum workstation design for checkout clerks was found to be one in which the cashier stands and is able to use both hands interchangeably to distribute the workload between both wrists. This reduces the type of injury likely to ensue if only one hand is used (Marras, Marklin, Greenspan, & Lehman, 1995). The next time you are in a checkout line, notice if the cashier uses one hand or two when passing items by the scanner.

Safety Devices.   Also important in the design of safe machinery is the development of built-in safety devices and other aids to prevent accidents. They must function to keep a worker's hand away from sharp moving parts or to automatically disconnect the power supply in an emergency but must not interfere with the operation of the machine.

Personal equipment—such as respirators, safety glasses with shatterproof lenses, steel-tipped shoes, ear protectors, and padded gloves—can be provided to protect workers in dangerous jobs from injury, but too often they are not used. Sometimes the reasons are practical; for example, workers object to using a safety device that interferes with job performance. A respirator can hinder communication among workers. Thick gloves make it hard to press buttons on a control panel. Another reason safety equipment is not used is because it can be uncomfortable. Workers using respirators for jobs performed under high-temperature conditions may find that the device clamped to their faces causes skin irritations. A survey of 208 employees in an automobile glass factory revealed that 62% rated the safety devices uncomfortable; only 30% considered them tolerable enough to wear (Akbar-Khanzadeh, Bisesi, & Rivas, 1995).

Sometimes, personality characteristics affect the decision to use safety equipment. A study of 226 men working in a noisy factory in Israel found that those who scored high on a test measuring hostility were the least likely to wear ear protectors (Rabinowitz, Melamed, Feiner, Weisberg, & Ribak, 1996).

A study conducted in the Netherlands of workers in a lead-smelting factory found that differences in the levels of lead in the workers' blood were directly related to their use of protective devices such as respirators. The more frequently the workers used the devices, the lower the level of lead. (Meijman, Ulenbelt, Lumens, & Herber, 1996).

Social Pressure.   Accidents can be caused by the pressure to maintain a production schedule or adhere to a timetable. Workers often perceive the threat of disciplinary action or dismissal if they fail to keep to a schedule. Shutting down a production line or a power plant because they think conditions are unsafe costs the company huge sums of money. The employee or manager who assumes the responsibility for such an action may be punished. Airline pilots who refuse to fly in bad weather or because ice is forming on the aircraft's wings cause passengers to miss connecting flights and are responsible for reducing the company's on-time performance record. When pilots see their colleagues reprimanded for similar behavior, they feel considerable pressure to take off on time despite the weather.

Personal Factors

Proper attention to equipment design and to the physical and social conditions of the work environment can help to reduce the frequency and severity of accidents. Overall, however, the human element is the more important causal factor.

NEWSBREAK #21

Look Out! The Driver of the Truck Behind You May Be Asleep

That's a chilling thought to remember the next time you travel on an interstate highway. Take a look at those 40-ton 18-wheelers barreling along all around you, and then think of this statistic: 78% of all truck drivers have a sleep disorder. It's called obstructive sleep apnea, and it causes a sleeping person to stop breathing momentarily and to awaken briefly. Someone with this disorder can wake up literally hundreds of times each night and not know it. The next day, however, the person will be sleepy.

"If someone wakes up every 2 or 3 minutes throughout the night," said psychologist William Dement, director of the Sleep Research Center at Stanford University, "it's as though they had very little sleep or no sleep at all." And then that person climbs into the cab of a tractor-trailer and drives at speeds up to 80 miles an hour, trying to keep awake for the duration of a 10- or 12-hour workday. No wonder fatigue is a major factor in truck accidents, when three out of four drivers have such disturbed sleep.

In case you're wondering whether you might be suffering from obstructive sleep apnea, don't worry. The disorder is three times higher among truck drivers than in the general population. One cause may be irregular work and sleep patterns. Long-distance drivers may work half the night, sleep for 2 hours, then continue driving. Other factors are lack of regular exercise and a tendency to be overweight.

There are cures for sleep apnea, but first you have to know you have it. Most truck drivers don't know. They may wonder why they feel so tired during the day, but there is a natural tendency to shrug it off, gulp down another cup of coffee, and keep on trucking. That's their job.

Source: T. Hilchey. Sleeping disorder may affect many truckers, study shows. *New York Times,* May 14, 1995.

Some of the personal factors studied by I/O psychologists are alcohol and drug use, cognitive ability, health, fatigue, work experience, age, and personality characteristics.

Alcohol and Drug Use. Large numbers of employees use alcohol or illegal drugs on the job. An employee with a drinking or drug problem is much more likely to be involved in an accident than is an employee without such a problem.

Cognitive Ability. It seems reasonable to assume that workers with a lower measured level of intelligence would have more accidents than workers with a higher measured level of intelligence. However, research does not adequately support this idea. Some studies have found that cognitive ability is related to accident-free behavior only in certain jobs, such as those requiring judgment and decision making as opposed to those involving repetitive manual labor.

Tests of cognitive ability, perception, and selective attention were given to 71 transport drivers for a petroleum products company to determine factors that could predict loading and unloading errors and traffic accidents. (**Selective attention** is the ability to focus on one stimulus while excluding all other stimuli that may be competing for attention.) Individual differences in selective attention were found to predict driving accidents. Drivers with scores indicating that they were easily distracted had a greater number of accidents (Arthur, Barrett, & Doverspike, 1990).

Selective attention The ability to focus on one stimulus while excluding all other stimuli that may be competing for our attention.

Health. I/O psychologists have documented the relationship between health and accidents. Employees who are in poor health or who are frequently ill tend to be highly susceptible to accidents. Workers with physical disabilities, assuming that their overall health is good and that they have jobs commensurate with their abilities, do not have a disproportionate share of accidents. These disabled employees are usually highly motivated to work well and safely. One physical defect related to accidents is poor vision; in general, people who have fewer accidents have better eyesight than do people who have more accidents.

Fatigue. Fatigue causes a decrease in productivity and an increase in accidents. During a typical 8-hour workday, periods of increased productivity are accompanied by decreased accidents. In the 10-hour workday in many heavy industries, a sharp rise in the accident rate during the last 2 hours of the shift has been reported, presumably because of fatigue.

Fatigue is also a factor in highway accidents, a subject of study for I/O psychologists because highways are the workplace for bus and truck drivers. One research review concluded that fatigued bus and truck drivers were asleep at the wheel in 10% of the collisions involving other vehicles. Fatigue was also found to be the primary contributing factor in 25% of single-vehicle accidents, such as when a van runs off the road and hits a tree (I. D. Brown, 1994).

Work Experience. A shorter time on the job tends to result in a higher accident rate. A 7-year study of more than 35,000 accidents among shore-based U.S. Navy enlisted personnel found that 35% of the accidents occurred during the sailor's first month in a new job assignment. After that time, the accident rate dropped rapidly and continued to decline as time on the job increased, up to 10 months (see Figure 11–1).

The relationship between accidents and greater time on the job is not as clear. Although studies have reported fewer accidents among employees with greater work experience, these findings may be biased by self-selection. Workers who have had numerous job-related accidents are likely to have been fired or transferred or have quit to look for safer employment. Therefore, we cannot conclude that longer work experience, by itself, leads to a reduction in the accident rate. In some cases, the decrease in accidents among experienced workers can be explained by the fact that those who had more accidents have dropped out.

Age. The link between age and accidents is similar to the relationship between experience and accidents because there is an obvious relationship between age

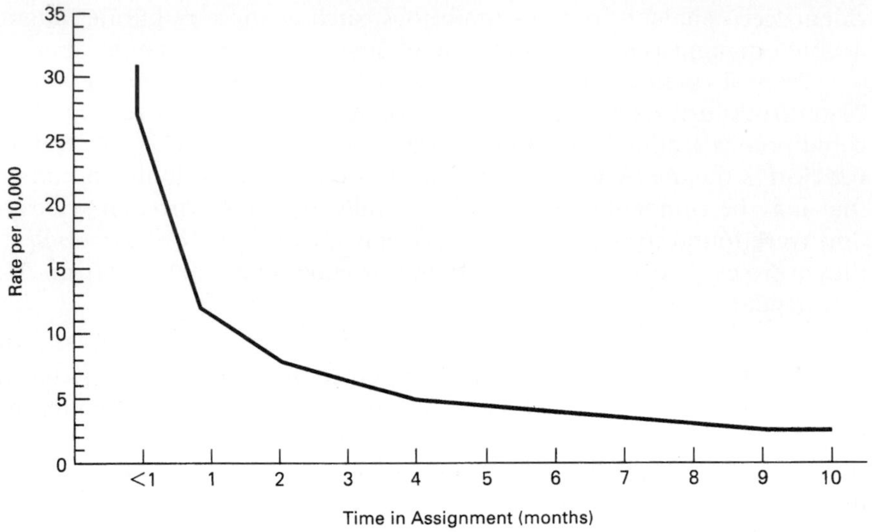

FIGURE 11–1. Accident and injury rate among U.S. Navy personnel. (Data from J. C. Helmkamp & C. M. Bone, "The effect of time in a new job on hospitalization rates for accidents and injuries in the U.S. Navy, 1977–1983." *Journal of Occupational Medicine*, 1987, 29, 654.)

and length of work experience. Other factors that interact with age are physical health and attitudes toward the job. Overall health, as well as specific abilities such as vision and hearing, deteriorate with age. However, older workers have greater job knowledge and more highly developed skills. Reaction time and eye-hand coordination may no longer be as good, but older workers usually have a more complete grasp of the job's demands. Their attitudes toward safety and other job characteristics tend to be more serious. A meta-analysis of research studies suggests that the frequency of accidents declines with age but that the severity of accidents increases with age (Rhodes, 1983). When older workers do have accidents, they are likely to be more costly in terms of physical consequences and time lost from work.

That finding was confirmed in a more recent study of 209 nuclear power plant workers. Researchers found that older employees (over age 50) took longer to recover from injuries and therefore lost more time from work. This study also confirmed that older workers took safety more seriously than younger workers and reported engaging in safe work practices far more often (Ringenbach & Jacobs, 1995).

Research conducted in Finland on the causal factors in 1,943 highway accidents in which there was at least one fatality found that truck drivers who fell asleep or whose fatigue contributed to their accident were more likely to be younger. Those in the youngest age group studied (18 to 35) suffered the most from nighttime fatigue and had far more accidents than nighttime drivers over the age of 56 (Summala & Mikkola, 1994).

A study of 4,179 on-the-job fatalities involving falls found that these accidents increased significantly after the age of 45. Also, it was shown that when the victim is an older worker (over age 45), his or her injury is likely to be more serious (Agnew & Suruda, 1993).

Personality Characteristics.   A popular belief is that people who have a great many accidents have some unique set of personality characteristics that distinguishes them from people who rarely have accidents. Research does not support this contention, although some studies have found that people who have a high number of accidents manifest such characteristics as neuroticism, hostility, anxiety, social maladjustment, and a sense of fatalism. However, any relationship between personality variables and accident frequency is not strong. There is no basis for concluding that people who have frequent accidents have a personality that is clearly different from that of accident-free individuals.

Temporary emotional states can contribute to accidents. The person who is angry with a spouse or boss or is preoccupied with money problems is likely to be less attentive on the job and hence more susceptible to accidents.

Accident Proneness.   The theory of **accident proneness** holds that certain people are more likely than others to have accidents and that most accidents are caused by or involve the same few people. The theory also assumes that accident-prone persons are likely to have accidents regardless of the type of situation. An effective way to test this theory is to compare accident records for the same people for two different periods to determine if the people who had accidents in one period also had accidents in the other. Correlations from these studies are low, indicating that a person's past accident record is not a valid predictor of future accidents.

Accident proneness The theory that certain people have personality characteristics that predispose them to have accidents, and that most accidents are caused by or involve the same few people; this theory is not supported by research.

In a now-classic study, one psychologist reexamined accident statistics that had originally been interpreted as supporting the accident-proneness theory (DeReamer, 1980). In analyzing driving records of 30,000 people, it was found that fewer than 4% of them accounted for 36% of the accidents over a 6-year period. These data suggested that a small group of drivers was involved in a large number of accidents. If they could be prevented from driving, then the accident rate could be cut by more than one third. The data were reanalyzed by comparing accident records for the first 3 years of the period with accident records for the second 3 years of the period. It was found that the accidents during the two periods did not involve the same drivers. Those identified as safe drivers during the first period accounted for more than 96% of the accidents in the second period, a finding that is highly damaging to the accident-proneness theory.

The theory no longer enjoys the credibility it once had, although evidence suggests that some workers may be predisposed to have more accidents in a particular type of work. Accident proneness may be specific to the situation and not a general tendency over all situations, which limits the theory's predictive value.

PREVENTING ACCIDENTS

There are several actions an organization can take to reduce accidents. These include proper reporting of accidents, attention to workplace design, safety training, management support, and safety publicity campaigns.

Accident Reports

I/O psychologists have found that an accident prevention program is no better than the quality of its accident reports. All accidents, regardless of the consequences, should be investigated and described in detail. A comprehensive accident report will include the following:

1. Precise time and location of the accident
2. Type of job and number of employees performing it

3. Personal characteristics of the accident victim
4. Nature of the accident and known or suspected causes
5. Results of the accident—personal injuries and damage to plant, equipment, and supplies

Workplace Design

Although most accidents are caused by human error, conditions in the physical work environment, as we have noted, are potential sources of accidents. Lighting in the workplace must be adequate for the job tasks, and temperature must be maintained at a comfortable level. Work areas should be clean and orderly; many accidents have been traced to poor housekeeping. Oil or grease spots on the floor, electrical cables underfoot, and equipment stored in hallways or stairwells can cause serious accidents that can easily be prevented. First-aid kits, fire extinguishers, and other safety equipment should be located conveniently throughout a work area and painted in vivid and easily identified colors.

Controls that are hard to reach or that require excessive force to operate and displays that are excessively complicated and so easily misread are design mistakes that are ready sources of accidents. Emergency controls must be made accessible and easy to operate.

Engineering psychologists suggest two general principles for the design of safety devices: (1) The machine should not function unless the safety device is engaged (for example, a power saw that will not work unless the hand guard is in place is designed to be as safe as possible); and (2) the safety device must not

Safety devices such as face shields should be easy to use and should not interfere with production.

interfere with production or cause the employee to work harder to maintain the same output.

Safety Training

Most organizational training programs devote time to accident prevention. Typically, workplace dangers and hazards are pointed out, and information is presented on the causes and results of past accidents. Rules for safe operating procedures are taught, along with the location of emergency and first-aid equipment. Periodic drills may be held to maintain awareness of safe working habits. When a company has an increase in accidents, retraining is often necessary. Experienced workers may become careless, and refresher courses are required. In general, companies that systematically continue safety training efforts are rewarded with substantial reductions in accidents and in hours lost from work. The money saved easily pays the cost of the safety training programs.

Management Support

Supervisors play a key role in any successful program for safety training and awareness. Because of their close association with workers, supervisors must be alert to unsafe working conditions and practices. Supervisors are in the best position to remind employees of safe working habits and to arrange proper maintenance of equipment and the work environment. They are also able to recommend when retraining is advisable. If supervisors do not insist on adherence to safe working procedures, then any safety training program will be less than maximally effective. By example as well as instruction, supervisors can maintain employee motivation to work safely and to prevent accidents.

However, supervisors cannot be expected to practice safety awareness unless their superiors reinforce that concern. If management tolerates sloppy accident reporting or expresses even a neutral attitude toward safety, this does not encourage or reinforce attention to safe practices. Active high-level management support of safety is a key dimension of an appropriate organizational climate. All levels of supervision must demonstrate to subordinates that safety is everyone's responsibility.

A study of 300 blue-collar employees at the U.S. plant of a multinational company confirmed that management support for safety programs significantly increased the employees' perception of the level of safe practices at their plant (Janssens, Brett, & Smith, 1995). In the chemical industry, an investigation of safe and unsafe working practices among 222 workers found that the company's perceived safety climate, as measured by a questionnaire, was significantly related to the accident rate. Employees who perceived stronger organizational support for safety engaged in fewer unsafe behaviors on the job (Hofmann & Stetzer, 1996).

Safety Publicity Campaigns

To motivate employees to follow the safe working practices they have been taught, many organizations conduct publicity and promotional campaigns with colorful posters and booklets, charts showing the number of accident-free days, and contests with appealing prizes.

Posters and Booklets. Posters are the most frequently used device, but their effectiveness depends on the kind of message depicted. Negative themes coupled with gruesome pictures of mangled bodies ("Don't do this—or this is what will happen") are particularly ineffective. These fear-oriented appeals create resentment and anger toward the company and the message. The most effective safety posters stress positive themes (for example, "Wear hard hat in this area" or "Hold on to railing").

Posters should be attention-getting with bright colors, sharply defined lettering, and visible placement. Psychologists recommend the following criteria for posters and warning signs:

1. *Signal word.* Warnings should have signal or key words that are appropriate to the level of danger—for example, *Danger, Warning,* or *Caution.*
2. *Hazard statement.* Warnings should tell clearly what the dangers are.
3. *Consequences.* Warnings should tell clearly the results of failing to comply.
4. *Instructions.* Warnings should tell workers what to do or what not to do to avoid the danger. The example in Figure 11–2 meets these criteria.

Research to examine the relative effectiveness of 84 potential signal words found that eight words aroused the highest perception of danger (from most to least effective): deadly, danger, warning, caution, careful, attention, notice, and note (Wogalter & Silver, 1990).

Additional research demonstrated significant differences in effectiveness between extreme terms, such as *deadly,* and less extreme terms, such as *note.* However, no significant differences were found among intermediate terms, such as *warning* and *caution,* which are the terms most likely to be used as signal words. Thus, the research showed they would be equally effective in conveying a warning. The study also confirmed the importance of signal words in increasing the perception of hazards (Wogalter, Jarrard, & Simpson, 1994).

Booklets of safety instructions and rules do not seem to be effective in encouraging safe working practices no matter how widely they are distributed. It is easy to ensure that all workers receive a booklet, but it is far more difficult to make them read it.

Safety Contests. Safety contests can be effective in maintaining interest in accident prevention. Some contests reward workers on an individual basis for accident-free work over a given period. Other contests operate on a group basis, rewarding a work crew or department. Contests can be competitive, pitting one work unit against another to see which has fewer accidents. Such contests may make workers more conscious of safe operating procedures and thus reduce accident rates, but the effects may not last much longer than the life of the contest. One solution is to hold continuous contests, changing the awards frequently enough to maintain employee interest. An obvious disadvantage of safety contests is that they encourage workers, supervisors, and managers to suppress the reporting of accidents.

FIGURE 11–2. An effective warning poster.

WARNING   (Signal word)
UNDERGROUND GAS LINE   (Hazard statement)
EXPLOSION AND FIRE POSSIBLE   (Consequences)
NO DIGGING   (Instructions)

VIOLENCE IN THE WORKPLACE

We noted earlier that murder was the second leading cause of death on the job and the primary cause of death for women. In addition, more than 2 million employees are physically assaulted at work, or threatened with assault, every year. The office and factory have become dangerous places.

The Scope of Workplace Violence

You have seen the stories on the television news. A disgruntled ex-employee who has been fired returns to the office or the factory and starts shooting, usually killing or wounding former co-workers and the supervisor who fired the employee. This has occurred with such disturbing frequency, particularly in the postal service, that the phrase "going postal" is used as a generic description of the phenomenon.

It is important to put such an event in perspective; you need not fear that the person at the next desk is looking at you suspiciously. Although disturbed workers have, indeed, gone on murderous rampages, fully three fourths of workplace fatalities involve deliberate robberies rather than random, vengeful acts. For example, of the 1,004 Americans killed on the job in 1992, 793 were murdered during attempted robberies.

Victims are typically taxi drivers, convenience store clerks, pizza delivery drivers, and owners of small inner-city grocery and liquor stores. Only one third of workplace homicides were found to have been committed by ex-employees or co-workers. More people are killed by lightning strikes than are murdered by co-workers.

Women are especially vulnerable to workplace violence, accounting for 42% of all homicide victims. Many of these are killed by boyfriends or husbands, who choose the women's workplaces as the sites of their actions. Some companies provide security for women employees who are being stalked by abusive partners. Others have offered to transfer women employees to other locations.

A telephone survey of 598 employed men and women revealed that in the previous 12 months, 8.7% had been victims of threats of violence or of actual violence in the workplace. Some 14.8% reported they had been attacked, and 21.2% said they had been threatened with attack at work. In this study, those most likely to have experienced threats or actual violence on the job included men and women under the age of 25, supervisors, employees who deal with the public, and people who work primarily at night. The victims were likely to experience significantly lower job satisfaction and greater job stress than other workers and were likely to consider changing jobs and carrying a weapon to work (Budd, Arvey, & Lawless, 1996).

Studying Workplace Violence

Violence in the workplace in the United States has become such a widespread concern to employers that I/O psychologists have developed various terms to describe it. Organization-motivated aggression refers to destructive behaviors caused by some factor within the organization, such as layoffs or reductions in force. Organization-motivated violence refers to the possible consequences, such as assault or homicide, that may result from the organization-motivated aggression (O'Leary-Kelly, Griffin, & Glew, 1996).

I/O research has identified a tendency toward deviance among the basic dimensions of work behavior. Supervisor ratings of specific job behaviors of 18,146 employees in 42 entry-level jobs (in retail sales, warehouses, nursing homes, courier services, and amusement parks) suggested eight dimensions or components of work behavior (Hunt, 1996). These include:

- Industriousness
- Thoroughness
- Attendance
- Adherence to rules
- Theft and drug misuse
- Unruliness
- Schedule flexibility
- Off-task behavior

Of relevance to our discussion of violence in the workplace is the dimension labeled *unruliness*, which includes the following aggressive and violent behaviors:

- Threatening or bullying other employees
- Punching, kicking, throwing, or damaging something in anger
- The loud and harsh use of profanity
- Exhibiting emotional and irrational behavior when thwarted
- Defacing or destroying company property

As you can see, none of these behaviors involves homicide or physical assault, yet the tendency toward unruliness may contribute to an atmosphere of violence and may even be found to become a significant precursor to violence.

Additional research presents a profile of three characteristics of persons believed to be most likely to commit murder in the workplace (Martin, 1994):

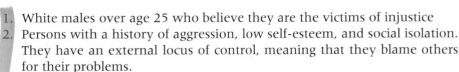

1. White males over age 25 who believe they are the victims of injustice
2. Persons with a history of aggression, low self-esteem, and social isolation. They have an external locus of control, meaning that they blame others for their problems.
3. Substance abusers with a history of disputes with management

Protecting Workers From Violence

Ideally, companies would not hire anyone who is prone to violence, but employee selection techniques are not yet sufficiently accurate to accomplish that goal. Even if human resources directors had the tools to identify infallibly applicants exhibiting the profile noted above, not all such persons would go on to commit an act of violence on the job. Indeed, none of them might do so if adverse organizational conditions, such as firing or a harsh reprimand, do not affect them.

I/O psychologists recommend several positive steps to deal with the issue of violence in the workplace. Managers can be trained to recognize potentially violent workers. Difficult employees can be offered counseling. Supervisors can be taught more tactful ways of communicating bad news, such as disciplinary actions or terminations.

More tangible suggestions for reducing workplace violence were released by OSHA in 1996. These guidelines include the installation of metal detectors, alarm systems, effective lighting, video surveillance cameras, and bulletproof barriers. They also recommend the hiring of more security guards (Martin, 1994; Minor, 1995). If these suggestions are implemented, the workplace may soon take on the characteristics—and the level of fear—that typify many other segments of society.

ALCOHOLISM IN THE WORKPLACE

More than 10 million people in the United States are known to be alcoholics, although the actual figure may be higher. The U.S. Public Health Service considers alcoholism to be a major health threat, along with heart disease and cancer. Alcoholism is defined as an illness characterized by an inability to control the consumption of alcohol to the extent that intoxication is inevitable once drinking has begun. Medically, alcoholism is an addiction, a pathological drug dependence that is harmful to health and that interferes with normal functioning.

Up to 10% of the American work force is estimated to be alcoholic at a cost to employers in excess of $100 billion a year. This cost is attributable to absenteeism, tardiness, errors and accidents, low productivity, inefficiency, and, often, the dismissal of valuable employees in whom money and training time was invested. Although there is no dispute that alcoholism is a serious problem for American business, not everyone agrees on the extent of alcoholism in the work force. It is possible that the problem is overstated by therapists, consultants, and directors of rehabilitation programs, the people whose livelihoods depend on the idea that alcoholism is rampant and that their programs can cure it.

Alcoholic employees can be found at all levels of organizational life. According to the National Institute on Alcohol Abuse and Alcoholism, more than 70% of known alcoholics are professional, semiprofessional, or managerial employees earning approximately $50,000 a year. More than half of all alcoholics have attended college. The greatest incidence of alcoholism is in the 35-to-55 age group.

The Drug Free Workplace Act of 1988 makes employers holding $25,000 or more in federal government contracts responsible for the prevention of substance abuse on the job. The law requires these employers to notify employees that the possession, sale, or use of alcohol or illegal drugs on the job is prohibited. If employees are convicted of alcohol or drug offenses, employers are required to impose disciplinary action such as mandatory treatment programs, suspension without pay, or discharge.

Effects of Alcoholism on the Job

Alcoholics tend to believe that drinking will not affect their behavior at work and that no one will detect a difference in the way they perform their jobs. This is untrue; the debilitating effects of excessive drinking are evident almost immediately. However, in the beginning stages only a trained observer will notice them.

Although behavioral changes occur gradually, after 3 to 5 years of steady drinking, job performance and efficiency will have deteriorated so greatly that the changes will be obvious to supervisors and co-workers. The downward path

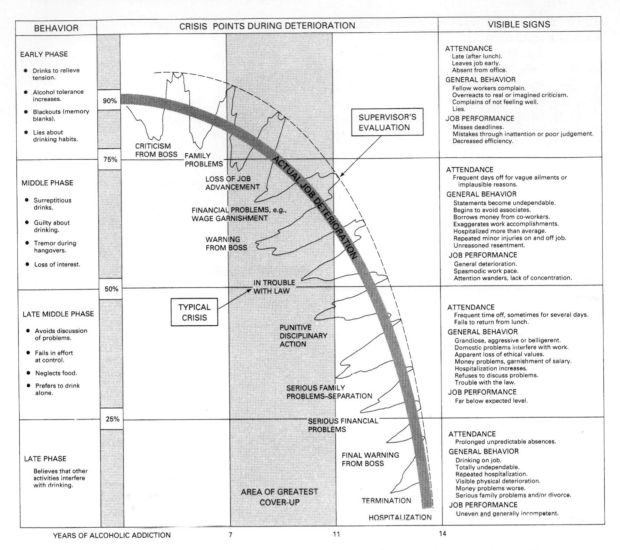

BEHAVIOR	CRISIS POINTS DURING DETERIORATION	VISIBLE SIGNS

EARLY PHASE

- Drinks to relieve tension.
- Alcohol tolerance increases.
- Blackouts (memory blanks).
- Lies about drinking habits.

MIDDLE PHASE

- Surreptitious drinks.
- Guilty about drinking.
- Tremor during hangovers.
- Loss of interest.

LATE MIDDLE PHASE

- Avoids discussion of problems.
- Fails in effort at control.
- Neglects food.
- Prefers to drink alone.

LATE PHASE

Believes that other activities interfere with drinking.

90%
75%
50%
25%

CRITICISM FROM BOSS
FAMILY PROBLEMS
LOSS OF JOB ADVANCEMENT
FINANCIAL PROBLEMS, e.g., WAGE GARNISHMENT
WARNING FROM BOSS
IN TROUBLE WITH LAW
TYPICAL CRISIS
PUNITIVE DISCIPLINARY ACTION
SERIOUS FAMILY PROBLEMS–SEPARATION
SERIOUS FINANCIAL PROBLEMS
FINAL WARNING FROM BOSS
AREA OF GREATEST COVER-UP
TERMINATION
HOSPITALIZATION

ACTUAL JOB DETERIORATION
SUPERVISOR'S EVALUATION

ATTENDANCE
Late (after lunch).
Leaves job early.
Absent from office.
GENERAL BEHAVIOR
Fellow workers complain.
Overreacts to real or imagined criticism.
Complains of not feeling well.
Lies.
JOB PERFORMANCE
Misses deadlines.
Mistakes through inattention or poor judgement.
Decreased efficiency.

ATTENDANCE
Frequent days off for vague ailments or implausible reasons.
GENERAL BEHAVIOR
Statements become undependable.
Begins to avoid associates.
Borrows money from co-workers.
Exaggerates work accomplishments.
Hospitalized more than average.
Repeated minor injuries on and off job.
Unreasoned resentment.
JOB PERFORMANCE
General deterioration.
Spasmodic work pace.
Attention wanders, lack of concentration.

ATTENDANCE
Frequent time off, sometimes for several days.
Fails to return from lunch.
GENERAL BEHAVIOR
Grandiose, aggressive or belligerent.
Domestic problems interfere with work.
Apparent loss of ethical values.
Money problems, garnishment of salary.
Hospitalization increases.
Refuses to discuss problems.
Trouble with the law.
JOB PERFORMANCE
Far below expected level.

ATTENDANCE
Prolonged unpredictable absences.
GENERAL BEHAVIOR
Drinking on job.
Totally undependable.
Repeated hospitalization.
Visible physical deterioration.
Money problems worse.
Serious family problems and/or divorce.
JOB PERFORMANCE
Uneven and generally incompetent.

YEARS OF ALCOHOLIC ADDICTION   7   11   14

FIGURE 11–3. Deterioration in behavior and job performance of an alcoholic as a function of time. (From A. Carding, "Booze and business." *Administrative Management*, 1967, *30*, 21. © Doyle Lindley, Bechtel Corporation. Reproduced by permission.)

of an alcoholic's behavior shows signs of altered job performance during the first few years (see Figure 11–3). These signs include excessive absenteeism, long lunch breaks, lies, errors, and low productivity. In the middle phase, gross changes are apparent that can no longer be overlooked. By this time, the alcoholic has usually received a warning from supervisors and is no longer being considered for promotion.

As the performance curve shows, everything goes downhill—career, family life, reputation, and financial stability. Ironically, each crisis precipitated by excessive drinking provides yet another reason to continue drinking. Unless the person recognizes the problem and accepts help, this cycle can lead to career failure, prison, hospitalization, or an early death. When a worker's superiors continue to ignore excessive drinking, mistakenly believing that they are being kind or helpful, they are only prolonging the problem. Intervention at an early stage is vital to an alcoholic's recovery.

The Alcoholic Executive

The plight of any alcoholic employee is tragic, but when the alcoholic is an executive, the cost to the company is greater. When an organization loses an executive because of a drinking problem, it is deprived of someone in whom it has invested considerable training, a high salary and fringe benefits, and significant responsibilities, a person whose judgment and decision-making abilities have been considered important to the organization's success.

Alcoholic executives, more than lower-level employees, are adept at concealing their problem for a longer period. They may be aided by their administrative assistants or their secretaries, who are often willing to cover up for their bosses' indispositions. Thus, alcoholic executives can escape detection longer than people in the accounting office, the warehouse, or on the assembly line.

There is another comfort for alcoholic executives. They are not as apt to be fired as are lower-level employees. The executive is more likely to be retained and given a make-work job until retirement. Although management recognizes the problem of alcoholism on the factory floor, it is more reluctant to admit that it exists in the office next door.

Rehabilitation of Alcoholics

Many federal government agencies and more than half the largest corporations in the United States sponsor formal alcoholic rehabilitation programs. These rehabilitation efforts return as much as 20 dollars for every dollar invested in them in terms of reduced absenteeism, reduced health care costs, and higher productivity. These organizational efforts are often referred to as **employee assistance programs** (EAPs). EAPs offer counseling services for various employee problems, but their major concerns are alcohol and drug abuse.

Employee assistance programs (EAPs) Counseling and rehabilitative services for various employee problems, notably alcohol and drug abuse.

Not all employees are willing to use the services of employer-provided EAPs, preferring instead to deal with their problems in more private ways (if at all). A questionnaire survey of 1,987 employees of a communications firm found that their tendency to use the company's EAP depended on several factors, most notably (1) the workers' perceptions of the program's confidentiality, credibility, and accessibility and (2) the workers' view of how strongly top management supported the EAP (Milne, Blum, & Roman, 1994). Once again we see the importance of the degree of support for the program provided by senior management as well as the importance of the employees' beliefs and perceptions. Regardless of the accuracy of those perceptions, they are likely to be the primary factor in choosing to use, accept, or implement a new program.

Employers can offer a greater motivation for alcoholic employees to seek treatment than can families or friends: Employers offer the hope of retaining a job. Psychologists and physicians who work with alcoholics agree that fear of losing one's job carries more weight than threats from spouses or the potential for an early death. To alcoholics, keeping their jobs may be their last defense against admitting that they have a drinking problem. When that defense is jeopardized, the desire to seek and accept help is usually great.

Most programs to combat alcohol abuse in industry follow a three-step process suggested by the National Council on Alcoholism.

1. *Education of managers and supervisors.* The purpose is to persuade management that alcoholism is not a moral or ethical issue but a medical problem, a treatable illness.
2. *Early detection of alcoholic employees.* Managers should be trained to detect the symptoms of alcoholism and the resulting behavioral and performance changes. Early detection improves the alcoholic worker's chances for recovery.
3. *Referral of alcoholic employees for help.* Some companies rely on in-house physicians and psychologists to supervise rehabilitation programs for alcoholic employees. Other companies refer employees to outside clinics. Most organizations provide for treatment on company time and continue the workers' salaries while they are in treatment programs.

An effective treatment approach involves co-workers who are members of Alcoholics Anonymous. That organization has a high success rate in dealing with alcoholism because its members know the effects firsthand.

There is some evidence, albeit weak, to suggest that recovering alcoholics become better workers. Their performance no longer suffers from their drinking, and they may expend extra effort, realizing that this is their last chance. However, even if the job performance of recovering alcoholics does not improve, at least the company has reclaimed experienced workers who would otherwise have been lost.

DRUG USE IN THE WORKPLACE

The use of illegal drugs in the workplace is a serious problem. Marijuana is the principal drug used; amphetamines, opiates, cocaine, and PCP have also been found on the job. In addition, prescription drugs such as tranquilizers, painkillers, and stimulants have the potential for abuse. Psychologists suggest that 1 out of every 10 current and prospective employees has used or will use drugs. The National Institute of Drug Abuse reports that the use of illegal drugs is higher among younger employees, specifically, that one third of 18- to 25-year-old workers regularly abuse drugs and nearly one fourth of workers of all ages use illicit drugs on the job (Wright & Wright, 1993).

Although drug abuse has been detected at all corporate levels, it is highest among skilled and semiskilled laborers and lowest among managerial and professional personnel. The overuse of prescription drugs is highest among middle-aged and older employees. Drug users are found in offices, medical facilities, media organizations, factories, and military bases. One nuclear power plant caught security guards using drugs. The U.S. Navy discovered that the majority of one aircraft carrier's crew regularly smoked marijuana. And an oil company learned that offshore drilling rig crews in the Gulf of Mexico were often under the influence of drugs.

An investigation at the U.S. Postal Service found that 10% of 5,465 job applicants tested positive for illicit drug use. Marijuana accounted for 65% of the positive tests, cocaine for 24%. Twice as many black applicants as white applicants tested positive. More persons between the ages of 25 and 35 tested positive than any other age group (Normand, Salyards, & Mahoney, 1990). A study of seven U.S. railroads found that 19% of their employees had a drug or alcohol problem. More than 50 train accidents have been traced to drug use, including the wreck of a passenger train that killed 16 people. Drug tests showed that the driver had been smoking marijuana shortly before the crash (Miller, 1991).

In one sense, the drug-dependent worker may present a more serious problem than the alcoholic worker in terms of the disruptive effects on production and efficiency. Drug users are potentially more dangerous because they may attempt to convert other workers in the hope of selling them drugs to finance their habit.

Effects of Drug Use on the Job

Behavioral effects of drug use on the job will vary with the type of drug taken. In general, however, the new user shows marked changes in behavior. There is a negligence about appearance, personal hygiene, and dress; some take to wearing dark glasses. Emotional outbursts are common, along with a tendency to borrow money. There is also likely to be impairment in judgment and reflexes, sluggishness of movement, dilation or contraction of the pupils of the eyes, bloodshot eyes, and, in extreme cases, needle marks on the arms or elsewhere on the body. These behavioral changes affect job performance.

In addition, drug abusers have been found to have four times the number of accidents, three times the number of absences, three times the number of health benefit claims, and five times the number of workers' compensation claims. They are far more likely to be late for work. They rate low in job satisfaction and exhibit more negative job behaviors that affect performance (Bass et al., 1996; Stein, Smith, Guy, & Bentler, 1993).

In the U.S. Postal Service study cited earlier, all applicants who performed well on the other selection procedures were hired so that the job behaviors of drug users and nonusers could be compared. After a year, applicants who had tested positive for drugs during the selection process had an absenteeism rate 60% higher and a dismissal rate 47% higher than applicants who had not tested positive for drugs. The researchers estimated that the cost to the Postal Service of the year of reduced productivity from hiring the drug users for the research study amounted to $4 million.

Depending on what there is to steal from an organization, drug use can lead to an increase in employee theft. Thus, drug users are likely to become marginal employees who are a burden to management and a threat to the morale and safety of co-workers. In hazardous occupations, such as construction and transportation, drug users, like alcoholics, can be a menace to the public. Proponents of on-the-job drug screening argue that public safety is the best reason for mandatory drug testing. The public has a right to expect that operators of buses, trains, and airplanes will not have their judgment or reaction time impaired by drugs.

Drug Testing

The chances are high that you will be tested for drug use when you next apply for a job. Nearly 80% of large U.S. corporations routinely screen job applicants for drug use, and the number is expected to rise. Most of the companies that test for drug use refuse to hire applicants who test positive. Drug testing is now part of the employee selection process, and the results of your drug test can override your performance on other selection measures.

Several studies have assessed the attitudes of undergraduate college students—future employees—toward drug testing and drug use in various occupations. The results showed that students who used drugs were less in favor of mandatory testing than were students who did not use drugs. Overall, however, more students viewed drug testing favorably than unfavorably. The students were most supportive of testing people who had a known history of drug use, and they favored testing all job applicants rather than testing at random. Drug testing was seen as more appropriate for occupations involving hazards to co-workers and to the public, such as airline pilots, air traffic controllers, police officers, and surgeons. (Drug testing was viewed as far less necessary for college professors.) College students reported a greater personal interest in applying to companies that did not have drug testing programs or did not appear to need them (Crant & Bateman, 1990; Murphy, Thornton, & Reynolds, 1990).

Attitude surveys of human resources managers and of medical laboratory technicians showed that employees had more positive attitudes toward drug testing when the programs had union support and when management gave employees the opportunity to express their opinions about the screening program. The right to appeal a career decision based on the results of a drug test was considered important, as was advance notice of drug tests. Testing programs without these features were related to decreased job performance and morale and to increased interest in quitting. The personnel managers expressed the belief that drug users should be given the same chance as alcoholics for treatment and rehabilitation (Gomez-Mejia & Balkin, 1987; Konovsky & Cropanzano, 1991).

A survey of 108 employees of an airline and a utility company, which routinely drug-tested workers in safety-sensitive jobs, found that those who perceived that their jobs involved danger believed punitive drug testing programs were less fair than programs that were not so punitive. Thus, the employees who had the most dangerous jobs held negative attitudes toward the programs in which they could be fired for drug use, even though using drugs on their jobs could endanger their lives and the safety of others (B. J. Tepper, 1994).

Psychologists have suggested the following guidelines to make drug testing programs as equitable as possible (Murphy, Barlow, & Hatch, 1988):

1. The organization should issue a statement to employees describing its policy on drug abuse and testing.
2. If employees belong to a union, the company's drug policies and testing procedures must be submitted to collective bargaining before being put into effect. Employers who refuse to bargain with the union are subject to charges of unfair labor practices.
3. Drug testing procedures should apply to all employees. No specific group should be singled out for testing.
4. Current employees should be tested only in documented cases of job impairment or because of other valid indications of probable cause.
5. Employees should be informed in advance of drug testing procedures, including the drugs being screened for, the types of tests, and the consequences of refusing to be tested.
6. All positive test results should be confirmed by a second test.
7. All results of drug tests should be kept confidential.

Drug testing is controversial. It can be argued that testing infringes on employees' rights to privacy and confidentiality and security from unreasonable search and seizure. Primarily for these reasons, some governments have been reluctant to institute widespread drug testing programs for employees and instead require organizations to reassign workers in dangerous jobs to alternative tasks if they are known to be drug users.

The validity of drug testing is also an issue. The Centers for Disease Control report that mass drug screening, particularly with inexpensive and unsophisticated tests, can incorrectly indicate the presence of drugs in up to two thirds of the cases. This high rate of false positives means that a disturbingly large number of job applicants and employees are mislabeled as drug users.

The lack of accuracy of the tests can be attributed to false readings, laboratory errors, and cheating by employees. Other substances in urine or blood samples can mimic the presence of drugs. Poppy seeds can falsely indicate the use of opiates. Marijuana can be inaccurately indicated by over-the-counter cough and cold products such as Contac or by painkillers such as Advil and Nuprin. An herbal tea that is a normal part of the diet of workers from certain South American countries can lead to a positive test for cocaine. Laboratory technicians can inadvertently mix up samples. Some years ago, the U.S. Army found that half the urine samples of a group of 60,000 soldiers had been so carelessly handled in the laboratory that none of the test results could be considered reliable.

People being tested for drug use may try to cheat the system by substituting someone else's drug-free urine or by adding an adulterant such as laundry bleach to mask traces of drugs. For this reason, most employers insist that employees urinate in the presence of an observer, a practice many people find offensive.

A newer and more accurate test for drugs, using 1½-inch long strands of hair, eliminates some of those problems. Fewer people object to having hair snipped from the back of their heads than to urinating in the presence of a company observer. Also, it is more difficult to substitute another person's hair or to add something to it to mask the presence of drugs.

The hair test, known as a **radioimmunoassay**, is more accurate than urinalysis. When a group of 800 job applicants submitted to both tests, the urine samples showed that 3% of the applicants tested positive for drugs. The hair test found that 18% of the same applicants tested positive. The presence of drugs can be detected in hair for up to 90 days after the last drug use, whereas drug traces in urine disappear after 3 or 4 days. This means that applicants or employees cannot simply abstain from using illicit drugs for a few days and expect to pass the test, as they can with urinalysis. Only a few major companies are using radioimmunoassay of hair today, but that is expected to increase as more employers learn of its advantages.

The first step taken by many organizations to deal with drug use on the job is a clear and direct statement to employees and job applicants about the policy concerning drug use, drug testing, and the consequences of violating that policy.

The second step is screening all job applicants, not only with drug testing but also by paying attention to gaps in employment history, criminal conviction records, dishonorable military discharges, and physical signs of addiction.

The third and most difficult step is to detect employees who are using or selling drugs on the job. One company hired an ex-addict who worked at various jobs throughout the plant and identified drug users. Another company hired private detectives who posed as employees. Some employers have used drug-sniffing

Radioimmunoassay A method of testing for drug use that involves analysis of hair samples.

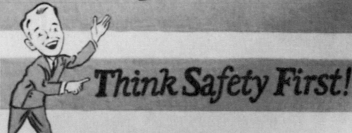

Drug users are highly likely to have accidents on the job. (Reproduced by permission of Partnership for a Drug-Free America.)

dogs to detect the presence of drugs in the workplace and in employees' cars in the company parking lot.

Most organizations differentiate between occasional users of soft drugs and addicts or pushers of hard drugs. If occasional users have a good job performance record and agree to accept help, companies will usually arrange for a treatment program. If users refuse help, they will usually be fired. Drug pushers are subject to arrest.

A survey of more than 1,000 organizations found that 70% of their employees who tested positive for drugs were referred for treatment and counseling and 10% were suspended or transferred. A study of 93 managers in public and private sector organizations who made nearly 3,000 disciplinary decisions with regard to drug use found that those who disciplined drug users thought that punishment rather than counseling was the best way to handle inappropriate behavior. These managers believed in retribution rather than correction. The retributive managers held highly negative personal attitudes toward drug use. Thus, a manager's way of dealing with drug users was influenced by his or her personal beliefs (Klaas & Dell'omo, 1991).

Workers who are treated successfully for drug problems and return to their jobs show reduced absenteeism, accidents, sick leave, and claims for health benefits. In general, EAPs report success rates of 75 to 80%, with success defined as remaining drug-free and maintaining satisfactory job performance for 1 year after treatment. A meta-analysis of other research is less optimistic, showing an overall abstinence rate for 25% of the users 1 year following treatment. Drug users who have intact families or other social support networks and who are able to retain their jobs show a 1-year abstinence rate of 50% (Reid, Murphy, & Reynolds, 1990). Once drug users have lost their jobs, the recovery rate drops to 5%, a clear indication of the importance of detecting and treating a worker's substance abuse problem while he or she is still employed.

HEALTH ISSUES OF COMPUTER USE

Some employees who work with computers report a high incidence of back pain, physical fatigue, and visual disturbances. These problems can often be eased by altering the design of the work area and by correcting poor lighting conditions. In 1990, the city government of San Francisco, California, passed legislation to regulate the use of video display terminals in the workplace in order to reduce eyestrain, muscle fatigue, and repetitive motion injuries. The law follows guidelines recommended by engineering psychologists and requires that workers be provided with adjustable chairs and adequate lighting and that computer terminals be equipped with detachable keyboards and adjustable screens. In addition, employees whose jobs do not include regular rest breaks must be given 15 minutes of alternative work every 2 hours.

Carpal tunnel syndrome, a repetitive motion disorder of the wrist, has plagued workers in certain occupations for decades. Any job that requires repeated identical or similar motions can lead to this painful, crippling nerve injury. Once reported mainly by blue-collar workers such as meat cutters, carpenters, jackhammer operators, assembly-line workers, sewing machine operators, and upholsterers, it received little recognition or publicity.

Carpal tunnel syndrome A repetitive motion disorder that may involve numbness, tingling, or pain in fingers, hands, and forearms.

It was only with the advent of computers—when white-collar workers, such as newspaper reporters and editors, started feeling those characteristic shooting pains in hands and forearms accompanied by tingling and numbness in the fingers—that carpal tunnel syndrome became famous. And when media people started hurting, they wrote articles about this new-found condition. Psychologists and medical researchers began to study it, and OSHA became alarmed.

Repetitive motion injuries are said to afflict more than 2 million people in the American workforce, many suffering damage to the point of needing surgery to relieve the pressure on the affected nerve. The condition can often be prevented by proper attention to engineering psychology guidelines of the kind legislated by the city of San Francisco.

There are additional health concerns for people who manufacture computer chips. This work is potentially dangerous because it exposes employees to arsenic, cyanide, acids, and noxious solvents. Some workers claim that the job causes headaches and loss of concentration, and they are concerned about long-term health effects. Research to date neither confirms nor refutes these charges. Nevertheless, companies such as AT&T have transferred pregnant women from computer chip manufacturing areas to other workstations. Other companies inform employees of the hazards of the job and offer the opportunity for a transfer.

Studies have shown a higher rate of miscarriages among pregnant women who work with computers more than 20 hours a week, compared to pregnant women who do other kinds of office work. Research on animals has related the low-frequency, pulsed, electromagnetic radiation emitted by video display terminals to miscarriages and birth defects. However, the evidence with human subjects is less certain.

Psychologists suggest that the source of the problem is the stressful assembly-line atmosphere in which many computer operators function rather than the radiation emitted by the display screens. In an investigation of pregnant women in several occupations, clerical employees had a higher miscarriage rate than did managerial and professional employees who spent a comparable amount of time working at a computer terminal. The jobs of the managerial and professional women employees may have been less stressful and more satisfying. Research on pregnant women workers in Finland and in Canada found no evidence of increased risk of miscarriages or birth defects from working with computers (Marriott & Stuchly, 1986; McDonald, Cherry, Delorme, & McDonald, 1986).

The issue raises a problem of discrimination. Some companies, such as AT&T in its computer chip operation, practice **protective exclusion,** barring women of childbearing age from certain jobs out of fear of lawsuits should it be shown that computer work is related to miscarriages, birth defects, or other health problems. In some companies, women job applicants have been asked to supply urine samples that were tested, without the applicants' knowledge or consent, for evidence of pregnancy. In instances where women were not hired on the basis of such a policy, it constitutes sex discrimination.

In 1991, the U.S. Supreme Court struck down this practice of protective exclusion as a form of sex discrimination and ruled that employers could not exclude women from jobs in which exposure to toxic substances might harm a developing fetus. The case before the court involved the Johnson Controls battery plant, which had excluded women of childbearing age (except those who could

Protective exclusion The idea of barring certain groups of employees, such as women of childbearing age, from potentially hazardous jobs because of fear of lawsuits.

prove they were sterile) from high-paying assembly-line jobs that exposed them to potentially harmful lead fumes. Some women had undergone surgery to be rendered sterile rather than transfer to lower-paying jobs. It is interesting that the company's fetal-protection policy had never been applied to men even though the men's sperm was at risk of becoming malformed, a condition that could lead to birth defects.

Computers emit other forms of radiation, including X-rays and infrared, magnetic, and electrostatic fields. The long-term effects of these emissions have not been determined.

AIDS IN THE WORKPLACE

AIDS has reached epidemic proportions in the United States and other countries. It is an employee health concern for several reasons. An AIDS sufferer or an HIV-positive person in a work group can have a profound effect on job performance and morale, engendering the fear of becoming infected among ill-informed co-workers. At a New England telecommunications company, 30 employees walked off their jobs when they learned that a co-worker had been diagnosed with AIDS. Some employees erroneously believe that all AIDS patients are gay men or lesbians or drug abusers.

Another problem confronting organizations is the increased cost of health insurance. AIDS is the first epidemic to occur since employer-paid health insurance became a standard fringe benefit. This insurance, already expensive, will become even more costly because the total medical bills of AIDS patients run to billions of dollars. Insurers are prohibited by law from excluding AIDS coverage in their policies.

Employers cannot discriminate against persons with AIDS in hiring or other career decisions, nor can they fire AIDS sufferers because of fear of contagion. The Centers for Disease Control has concluded that AIDS cannot be spread through casual contact at work and that people with AIDS do not present a danger to co-workers.

Only about one fourth of U.S. companies have policies and programs to deal with employees who are HIV-positive. Some companies educate employees about the disease by presenting factual information in newsletters, booklets, and videotapes. Informal question-and-answer sessions with medical experts are also helpful. Such company-sponsored educational programs can have the additional benefit of inducing employees to modify their behavior in ways that will reduce the risk of contracting or spreading the virus.

Substance Abuse and Job Behavior

Research shows that people who test positive for drug or alcohol use are not ideal employees. They exhibit social withdrawal behaviors (absenteeism, lateness, sick leave, turnover) and have frequent accidents and high workers' compensation claims. However, there is little direct evidence linking substance use with low productivity.

Laboratory studies have documented the harmful effects of drug use on various cognitive and motor skills tasks. Nevertheless, it is difficult to assess the relationship between drug use and task performance directly on the job because an employee's level of intoxication cannot always be measured precisely. Also, as we saw in Chapter 5 on performance appraisal, we cannot apply the same criteria to assess productivity on different jobs. The job performance of a college dean cannot be measured in the same way as the job performance of a bus driver. Is there some way to assess indirectly the job performance of substance abusers, by measuring work behaviors that are relevant for all types of jobs?

Two psychologists at Texas Christian University attempted to answer this question with a large-scale investigation of the relationship between substance abuse and those job behaviors that influence productivity. The subjects were 1,325 municipal employees from 109 work groups: 65% of the employees were Mexican-American, 27% were white, and 8% were black. The employees anonymously completed questionnaires dealing with personal background, drug and alcohol use on and off the job, job history, work environment, job behavior, and perception of substance use among co-workers.

Job behavior items included: (1) positive work behaviors (doing more than required, volunteering to work overtime, and attempting to improve working conditions); (2) psychological withdrawal behaviors (daydreaming, letting others do the work, socializing with co-workers, and spending work time on personal matters); (3) physical withdrawal behaviors (leaving early, taking a long lunch period or rest break, and falling asleep on the job); (4) antagonistic work behaviors (arguing with co-workers, disobeying supervisor's instructions, filing grievances, and spreading rumors about co-workers). These behaviors can affect job performance for most types of jobs.

A majority of the employees reported positive work behaviors and psychological withdrawal behaviors to some degree. Those who engaged extensively in psychological withdrawal behaviors were found to be less productive and were expected to have a negative impact on group morale. Employees who reported using alcohol or illicit drugs on or off the job tended to engage in more physical and psychological withdrawal behaviors and in more antagonistic work behaviors than employees who did not report substance abuse. The researchers concluded that substance abuse had a negative impact on job performance through the various withdrawal behaviors displayed.

Critical Thinking Questions

1. What criticisms can you make of this study? How would you investigate the effects of substance use on work behavior?
2. If you were a manager, how would you deal with subordinates who showed physical and psychological withdrawal behaviors associated with substance use?
3. Why do most organizations have different policies for alcoholics and for drug abusers?
4. Why are drug testing programs controversial? What do surveys show about the attitudes of college students and of employees toward drug testing?
5. What responsibility, if any, should organizations assume for employees who drink to excess or who use illegal drugs? How successful are treatment programs for alcoholics and for drug users?

Source: Based on W. E. K. Lehman & D. D. Simpson. (1992). Employee substance use and on-the-job behaviors. *Journal of Applied Psychology, 77,* 309–321.

SUMMARY

The Occupational Safety and Health Administration (OSHA) tries to enforce federal industrial safety standards. One problem with research on accidents is that many organizations distort accident data through incomplete reporting in an effort to maintain good safety records. Workplace factors that affect accidents are type of industry, work schedules, lighting, temperature, and equipment design. Personal factors contributing to accidents include alcohol and drug use, health, fatigue, work experience, age, and certain personality variables. The theory of **accident proneness** has little research support.

To prevent accidents, organizations should: practice complete reporting and analysis of accidents, consider the design of the job and the work environment, provide managerial support for safe work practices, provide safety training, and sponsor safety publicity campaigns.

Murder is the second leading cause of death in the workplace, but the majority of these killings occur during the commission of robberies. Women are vulnerable to workplace attacks by boyfriends or husbands.

Alcoholism on the job has been linked to lateness, absenteeism, low productivity, and emotional problems. Organizations try to assist alcoholic employees through **employee assistance programs** (EAPs) and by training managers to detect signs of alcoholism in their workers. Drug use on the job has been found at all occupational levels. In general, organizations treat drug users more severely than they do alcoholics. The use of drug testing in employee selection is increasing, although the tests may not be accurate and may violate privacy rights. AIDS can affect worker productivity and morale; co-workers of a person with AIDS may react negatively out of fear or ignorance. Effects on employee health of prolonged computer use are being investigated.

KEY TERMS

accident proneness

carpal tunnel syndrome

employee assistance programs (EAPs)

protective exclusion

radioimmunoassay

repetitive motion injuries

selective attention

ADDITIONAL READING

Janssens, M., Brett, J. M., & Smith, F. J. (1995). Confirmatory cross-cultural research: Testing the viability of a corporation-wide safety policy. *Academy of Management Journal, 38,* 364–382. Reviews differences among corporate cultures and societies in their concerns for their employees and their approaches to job safety. Studies safety priorities in employing organizations in the United States, France, and Argentina as a reflection of authoritarian versus participative management styles.

Macdonald, S., & Roman, P. (Eds.). (1994). *Drug testing in the workplace: Research advances in alcohol and drug problems.* New York: Plenum Press. Part of a continuing series on workplace drug testing. Includes literature reviews, research reports, and sociological perspectives, and covers labor union policies on drug testing, effects of drug use, legal issues, and testing methods.

Sonnenstuhl, W. J. (1996). *Worker sober: The transformation of an occupational drinking culture.* Ithaca, NY: ILR Press/Cornell. Relates the incidence of alcoholism on the job to specific occupations and organizational cultures.

VandenBos, G. R., & Bulatao, E. Q. (Eds.). (1996). *Violence on the job.* Washington, DC: American Psychological Association. Describes approaches to managing workplace violence in high-risk settings, the roles of hostility and perceived injustice in precipitating violence, the impact of domestic violence on the workplace, and employee assistance programs on violence prevention.

Stress in the Workplace

CHAPTER 12

We have described a number of ways in which work can be harmful to your health. Accidents and violence on the job and exposure to noxious chemicals in factories and sealed office buildings account for substantial numbers of injuries and deaths every year. There is another serious danger in many workplaces that affects millions of employees, but it operates in more silent and subtle ways. Whereas poorly designed chairs or toxic fumes are physical agents that affect health, productivity, and morale, stress is a psychological agent that affects physical and emotional well-being and our ability to perform our jobs.

Stress-related diseases are widespread among the U.S. population. One national survey, conducted by a life insurance company, found that 46% of employed adults considered their jobs to be extremely stressful. The proportion of stress-related disabilities increased from 6% in 1982 to 13% in 1991. One of every three Americans has seriously considered quitting their jobs because of stress. And 72% of those surveyed said that stress at work reduced productivity and adversely affected physical and mental health (Keita & Hurrell, 1994).

Psychosomatic disorders
Physical complaints caused by or related to emotional factors such as job stress.

As many as half of all visits to physicians are precipitated by stress. Further, a major share of physical complaints may be **psychosomatic**—that is, actual physical disorders caused by or related to emotional factors such as stress on the job. Physical problems associated with stress include ulcers, colitis, coronary heart disease, arthritis, skin diseases, allergies, headaches, neck and lower back pain, and cancer. Stress has been linked to an increase in infectious diseases and may be implicated in disorders that involve suppression of the immune function, which plays a vital role in fighting malignancies. Thus, it is no exaggeration to say that stress can kill.

Stress on the job is also costly to employers, as reflected in lower productivity, reduced motivation, and increased errors and accidents. High stress is also re-

With portable office equipment such as laptop computers, some employees are rarely free of job demands, even while traveling. This constant job-induced stress can reduce efficiency and lead to physical complaints.

lated to increases in turnover intentions and counterproductive behavior, such as theft and drug and alcohol abuse. Stress in the workplace contributes to spiraling health care costs. The estimated expenditures for only two stress-related diseases—coronary heart disease and ulcers—is approximately $45 billion a year, which makes stress more costly for organizations than accidents. For every worker killed in a job-related accident, at least 50 suffer some form of heart disease. Research on more than 960,000 workers in the United States and in Sweden reported that employees in high-stress jobs had a rate of heart disease four times greater than did employees in low-stress jobs.

Another investigation, involving 260 employees of a chemical company and a life insurance company, found that stressful job events, as measured by a self-report inventory, correlated positively with health care claims and costs. This relationship held for both 1-year and 2-year periods of study. In other words, employees who reported the greatest amount of job stress cost their employers significantly more in health care benefits than employees who reported experiencing little stress on the job (Manning, Jackson, & Fusilier, 1996a, 1996b).

The total cost of stress-related disorders has been put at $150 billion annually, including medical costs, absenteeism, and lost productivity. Stress-related workers' compensation claims now account for more than 14% of occupational disease claims, nearly triple the rate a decade ago.

Stress affects employees at all levels and types of jobs. It is unlikely that you can avoid the consequences of stress in your career, any more than you can avoid them in college. No matter what you do, where you work, or at what level you function, stress will probably affect the quality of your working life and, in turn, other aspects of your daily living.

THE NATURE OF STRESS

Some of us feel stress every time we take an exam. People undergo stress when a car runs a stop sign and almost hits them or when a shadowy figure chases them down a dark street. When something like that happens, we become anxious, tense, and fearful. **Stress** involves physiological and psychological responses to excessive and usually unpleasant stimulation and to threatening events in the environment.

Stress Physiological and psychological responses to excessive and usually unpleasant stimulation and to threatening events in the environment.

Physiological Effects of Stress

Dramatic physiological changes occur during stress. Adrenaline, released from the adrenal glands, speeds up all bodily functions. Blood pressure rises, heart rate increases, and extra sugar is released into the bloodstream. The increased blood circulation brings additional energy to brain and muscles, making the person stronger and more alert to cope with the threat. A stressful situation mobilizes and directs one's energy, boosting it beyond its normal level.

Most of us will not encounter extreme emergency situations, and few jobs expose people to threatening physical events such as those faced by police and firefighters. For the majority of us, the stresses we face on the job are psychological or emotional in nature, such as an argument with the boss, the belief that we have been treated unfairly, or concern about a promotion. These constitute what we commonly call hassles or insults of everyday life. Individually, they are low-level sources of stress, but they are hard on the body because they accumulate. Each stress adds to the previous one and can tax the body's energy reserves because of the physiological changes it produces. If stressors are frequently found in the workplace, the body remains in a state of high physiological arousal and alertness for long periods, a condition that can lead to physiological damage and illness.

For example, a study of 390 blue-collar workers tested under stressful laboratory conditions found that those who had worked in highly demanding jobs for 2 years demonstrated significantly greater increases in blood pressure, heart rate, and skin temperature than did workers in nondemanding jobs. The first group also showed a lower rate of recovery once the stressful laboratory condition was removed. This finding indicates an overall lower level of resistance as a function of being in demanding, stressful jobs for 2 years (Schaubroeck & Ganster, 1993). A review of some three dozen studies on stress and heart disease also showed a consistent positive relationship between job stress and the likelihood of developing heart disease (Landsbergis, Schnall, Schwartz, Warren, & Pickering, 1995).

Prolonged stress contributes to psychosomatic disorders. These disorders are not imaginary; they involve specific tissue and organ damage. Although their origin lies in psychological and emotional factors, they have a definite physical impact on the body. Further, the illnesses brought about by stress can serve as new sources of stress. When physical health has declined, resistance has been lowered, and bodily energy has been reduced, then motivation and job performance are likely to suffer.

Not all employees are affected by stress in the same way. Consider air traffic controllers, who are generally considered to have one of industry's most stressful jobs. Hour after hour they must exercise constant vigilance, tracking aircraft at various speeds and altitudes converging on or departing from the same point. Their work is hectic, difficult, and demanding, with the additional burden of being responsible for hundreds of lives throughout each workday. Research on the physiological functioning of air traffic controllers shows that their bodies reflect the pressures of the job. As the number of aircraft in their sector increases, coronary arteries become more constricted and blood pressure rises. The incidence of hypertension among air traffic controllers is three times higher than normal for their age group.

This would appear to be a classic example of the deadly effects of stress. We would guess that the rate of heart attacks, strokes, and other stress-related disabilities is many times higher among air traffic controllers than among the rest of the population. But research indicates that this is not so. On some measures, air traffic controllers are healthier than the general population. Although some air traffic controllers show a pattern of disease and early death, others are apparently unaffected.

Job Satisfaction and Control

What makes the difference? Why doesn't the stress of the job affect them all in the same way? The difference seems to lie in the level of job satisfaction controllers get from their work. Those who report being very satisfied with their jobs do not suffer from harmful effects of stress. Those who are very dissatisfied with their jobs do show stress-related effects.

Consider another high-stress occupation—that of corporate executive. It is widely assumed that executives experience considerable job stress and consequently have a higher rate of heart attacks than does the general population. Research does not support this position. High-level executives have 40% fewer heart attacks than do middle-level managers, who are popularly assumed to work under less stressful conditions.

NEWSBREAK #22

Stress Is Killing the Police of Paris

When you think of Paris, you probably don't imagine a fast-paced, high-stress lifestyle. If you know the place in person, or from the movies, you probably think of a beautiful city of great charm, of hours spent sipping coffee at sidewalk cafes or strolling along tree-lined boulevards. When we imagine a stressful city, most likely we think of New York. But in 1995, 60 police officers in Paris committed suicide, almost twice as many as in New York. One killed her three children before turning the gun on herself.

Why in that most beautiful of cities are the police so greatly stressed? Paris police officers have demanding jobs that get worse every year. They have minimal control over their working conditions and little support from their bosses. To make matters worse, the police force has traditionally been unpopular with the public. In schools, children of police officers are routinely taunted because of their parents' jobs. And the criminals with which the police must deal are becoming more difficult: militant teenagers, gangs, terrorists, strikers, and demonstrators.

With significant budget cuts, there are now fewer officers patrolling the streets. And they are underpaid in a city with extremely high living costs. They have nowhere to turn for assistance, for social and emotional support. France provides no employee assistance programs or counseling services like those considered routine in the United States. The Paris police union fights for economic issues such as wages and pensions but so far has failed to deal with psychological issues such as job stress.

"The police are under constant stress," said Guy Maurin, a police union official, "and they take their stress home, so there are a lot of domestic problems." Almost all the police stationed in Paris were recruited from elsewhere in the country, because Parisians are unwilling to accept these jobs; they know how bad things are. And so most of the police of Paris apply for transfer back home after only a short time on the job. "We're cut off from our family here," one said. "Cut off from our friends."

Some government assistance has recently been promised. The Interior Minister agreed to hire psychologists to help police officers deal with job stress and to train supervisors to be more supportive of the cop on the beat. Until then, job stress and its effects will continue to haunt the police of Paris. As Guy Maurin said of the latest police suicide, "He got no support or understanding from his superiors. They might well have saved his life."

Source: Simons, M. Suicide rates are rising for the unpopular, harassed police force in Paris. *The New York Times.* April 7, 1996.

The primary reason top executives are relatively less affected by job stress is that they have more autonomy and control over their work than do middle-level managers. Considerable research has shown that being able to control workplace events can significantly reduce perceived job stress. A study of 136 nurses found that their levels of objectively assessed job demands (ratings by their department head) and control over their work were significantly associated with two physiological measures of stress: blood pressure and adrenal gland responses. The higher the job demands and the lower the control over those demands, the higher were the measures of stress (Fox, Dwyer, & Ganster, 1993). A 3-year study of 76 postal workers in the Netherlands confirmed that lack of control over their jobs was a significant source of stress (Carayon, 1995).

The employee's degree of control, such as the authority to make decisions or the freedom to set work schedules, may also influence the risk for coronary heart disease in nonmanagerial personnel. A study of 5,000 nonmanagerial employees found that those whose jobs combined high stress and little control were two to three times more likely to have heart attacks than were those whose jobs combined high stress and greater control (Karasek & Theorell, 1990).

A longitudinal study conducted in Sweden followed the working careers of 25,287 men. The findings confirmed that the employees most likely to die of heart attacks had held jobs that involved routine work over which they had little or no control. Subjects who had held such jobs throughout their working lives were twice as likely to die of heart disease than subjects in jobs with a high degree of control. Also, men who had held high-control jobs but who had to change to low-control jobs during their career were three times as likely to die from heart disease. Losing control was apparently more harmful than never having it (Hancock, 1996).

Personal Factors in Stress

If we are to examine thoroughly the causes of stress on the job, then we must take account of personal factors that can render employees more or less vulnerable to stress. Not all stressors at work affect all people in the same way. A source of stress that can ruin the health of one worker may have no noticeable effect on that of a co-worker.

INDIVIDUAL DIFFERENCES IN REACTIONS TO STRESS

We have mentioned two factors that may reduce the effects of stress on the job: high job satisfaction and control over the conditions of one's work. Several other variables can influence our vulnerability to stress. One factor involved in coping with stress is social support—that is, our network of family and social ties. The person who lives alone or who is emotionally alienated from others is more vulnerable to the effects of stress than is someone who has strong ties to family, friends, and colleagues. Family support can help compensate for negative feelings about one's job and can enhance self-esteem, acceptance, and worth. Social support on the job, such as a cohesive work group or a good relationship with one's boss, can also reduce the effects of stress.

Lack of social support can increase the risk of heart disease; the lower the level of available social support, the greater the health risk. Variations in social support over the course of the workday have been found to affect blood pressure. Studies of men and women in various occupations showed that blood pressure rose when social support was low and dropped when social support was high (Theorell & Karasek, 1996).

Physical health is related to susceptibility to stress. People in better physical condition suffer fewer harmful effects from a stressful work environment than do people in poorer physical condition. Physical exercise is a good way to improve general physical well-being. Many companies provide exercise facilities to help employees alleviate stress.

Levels of knowledge, skill, and ability to perform the job can make an employee more or less resistant to stress. Employees with high skill levels usually find their work less stressful than do employees with lower skill levels. You may have noticed this effect in your college classmates. Students who are barely able to keep up with the coursework are usually more anxious about exams than are those who have less difficulty mastering the material.

The Type A Personality

Personality factors have been related to our ability to tolerate stress. This relationship is particularly apparent with **Type A** and **Type B personalities** and their differential susceptibility to heart disease, which, as we noted, is a major consequence of stress (Friedman & Rosenman, 1974). Although specific physical factors such as smoking, obesity, and lack of exercise are implicated in heart disease, they may account for no more than 25% of the cases. The rest may be linked to aspects of the Type A personality pattern. In contrast, Type Bs rarely have heart attacks before the age of 70, regardless of the nature of their job or their personal habits.

Two primary characteristics of the Type A personality are a high competitive drive and a constant sense of time urgency. Type As are described as being intensely ambitious and aggressive, always striving to achieve, racing against the clock, rushing from one self-imposed deadline to the next. They are attracted to high-stress, fast-paced, competitive, and demanding jobs. When Type As set out to accomplish something, it must be done immediately. Type A personalities are hostile, although they are successful in hiding that quality from others. They express their aggression through competitiveness, especially on the job. They are impatient and quick to get angry if they believe subordinates or colleagues are working too slowly. Type As are thought to be in a continual state of tension, perpetually under stress. Even when their work environment is relatively free of stressors, they carry their own stress as a fundamental part of their personality.

Type As also tend to be extraverted and high in self-esteem. They show a high level of job involvement and score high in the needs for achievement and power. A study of industrial hygienists, auditors, and registered nurses found that when Type As hold jobs in which they believe they can exert control over their work, they tend to be more productive and to experience greater job satisfaction than when they believe that their jobs offer little control (Lee, Ashford, & Bobko, 1990). Table 12–1 shows some typical Type A behaviors.

Type B personalities may be just as ambitious as Type As, but they have few of the other characteristics. Type Bs experience less stress at work and at leisure. They may work as hard and in equally stressful environments but suffer fewer harmful effects. These two personality types behave in different ways in response

Type A/Type B personalities Personality factors related to one's ability to tolerate stress; Type A persons have been associated with heart disease, anger, hostility, time urgency, and depression; Type B persons work as hard as Type As but show fewer stress effects.

TABLE 12–1 Are You a Type A Person?

Do you

_____ always do everything very rapidly? *Type A people eat, move, walk, and talk at a brisk pace. They speak with emphasis on certain words, and the ends of their sentences are spoken much faster than the beginnings.*

_____ become extremely impatient with the speed at which things are accomplished? *Type A people continually say "yes, yes" or "uh-huh" to whoever is talking to them, and even finish other persons' sentences for them. They become outraged by a slow car ahead of them or a slow-moving line in a restaurant or theater. When they read, they skim the material quickly and prefer summaries or condensations of books.*

_____ always think about or try to do two or more things at the same time? *For example, Type A people may think about one thing while talking to someone about something else, or they may try to eat and drive at the same time, in an effort to get more accomplished in a given period of time.*

_____ feel guilty when you are on vacation or trying to relax for a few hours?

_____ fail to be aware of interesting or beautiful things? *Type A people do not notice a lovely sunset or the new flowers of spring. If asked, they cannot recall the furnishings or details of an office or home they just visited.*

_____ always try to schedule more events and activities than you can properly attend to? *This is another manifestation of the sense of time urgency Type A people feel.*

_____ have nervous gestures or tics such as clenching your fists or banging on a desk to emphasize a point you are making? *These gestures point to the continuing tension at the root of the Type A personality.*

_____ consistently evaluate your worth in quantitative terms? *For Type A persons, numbers alone define their sense of accomplishment and importance. Type A executives boast about their salary or their company's profits. Type A surgeons tell how many operations they have performed, and Type A students report how many A's they have received in school. These people focus on the quantitative rather than the qualitative aspects of life.*

to prolonged stress over which they have little control. For example, Type As will struggle to master such a situation, but if they are not successful, they will become frustrated and give up. Type Bs in a similar situation will try to function as effectively as possible and will not give up.

The early research on the Type A and Type B personality dimensions, conducted in the 1960s and 1970s, described a clear link between Type A behavior and coronary heart disease. More recent research has failed to confirm that relationship consistently, although few psychologists are willing to state that there is no relationship at all. The difference between studies that support the relationship between Type A behavior and heart attacks and the studies that do not is related to how Type A behavior is assessed. Research that relies on structured interviews to uncover expressions of Type A behaviors supports Type A as a genuine risk factor in heart disease. Research that uses self-report inventories to measure Type A behaviors tends not to support the relationship (Evans, 1990).

A meta-analysis of 87 studies reported a modest relationship between Type A behavior and heart disease but a stronger relationship between heart disease and the emotions of anger, hostility, and depression. These researchers concluded that the coronary-prone personality "does not appear to be that of the workaholic, harried, impatient individual," but rather "a person with one or more negative emotions: perhaps someone who is depressed, aggressively competitive, easily frustrated, anxious, angry, or some combination" (Booth-Kewley & Friedman, 1987, p. 358).

Other studies discount the importance of depression and anxiety as contributory factors in coronary heart disease but support the role of hostility and a sense of time urgency (see, for example, Edwards & Baglioni, 1991; Ganster, Schaubroeck, Sime, & Mayes, 1991; Landy, Rastegary, Thayer, & Colvin, 1991; Matthews, 1988). We noted that Type A personalities are high in hostility, which they are adept at concealing from others. Thus, the relationship between heart disease and personality factors remains intact, but it may include psychological attributes other than those originally associated with Type A behaviors.

Some intriguing research conducted on infants within 2 days of birth, a condition that minimized the possible influence of environmental factors, found that babies of Type A mothers were more likely to exhibit an intense behavioral style, as measured by amount of crying, than were babies of mellower, or non-Type A, mothers (Turkington, 1992). Perhaps, the researcher suggested, Type A people are born that way?

Job Complexity

Measures of Type A behavior and of job complexity were obtained from 251 police officers and firefighters who had no previous history of heart trouble or high blood pressure. Seven years later, 177 of the subjects were reexamined. Job complexity, as assessed in the initial study, correlated positively with symptoms of heart disease found after 7 years' time, but only among those subjects previously identified as Type A personalities. Among Type B personalities, measures of job complexity correlated negatively with symptoms of heart disease (Schaubroeck, Ganster, & Kemmerer, 1994).

It is interesting that complex jobs—defined as high in mental demands and requiring high aptitude, skill, and creativity—should be linked to heart disease in Type A personalities. As we saw in Chapters 8 and 9, it is precisely those challenging and demanding complex jobs—the ones that have been enlarged and enriched—that provide the highest level of job satisfaction. This presents a dilemma for Type A individuals: The jobs they find the most stimulating, which fulfill their high competitive drive, may be the most harmful to their health.

Hardiness

Another personality variable that may account for individual differences in vulnerability to stress is **hardiness.** People characterized as being high in hardiness have attitudes that may make them more resistant to stress. They believe that they can control or influence the events in their lives. They are deeply committed to their work and to other activities they find of interest, and they view change as exciting and challenging rather than threatening.

Hardiness A personality variable that may explain individual differences in vulnerability to stress; hardy persons, who believe they can control the events in their lives, may be more resistant to stress.

Hardiness can be assessed by a 20-item scale designed to measure three components: control, commitment, and challenge. Research has shown that hardy persons develop fewer physical complaints under highly stressful conditions than do persons who are not hardy. Thus, hardiness may moderate the effects of stress through the way people appraise and interpret the events in their lives (Kobasa, 1979, 1982). For example, because hardy people tend to define a stressful situation in more positive terms, their efforts to cope with stress have fewer harmful effects. A study of women employees and homemakers ages 25 to 65 compared performance on the hardiness scale with physical illness, depression, and reaction to life change events (such as promotion, demotion, or troubles with one's boss). Nonhardy women reported that 40% of their life experiences were undesirable. Hardy women characterized only 27% of their life events as undesirable (Rhodewalt & Zone, 1989).

Studies of college undergraduates enrolled in introductory psychology courses found that hardy students interpreted stressful events that had occurred in the past month less negatively than did nonhardy students and that their health was less affected by those events. Hardy students also displayed a greater tolerance for frustration in a laboratory task and perceived it as less threatening than did nonhardy students (Roth, Wiebe, Fillingim, & Shay, 1989; Wiebe, 1991).

Researchers investigating the relationship between hardiness and Maslow's hierarchy of needs studied a sample of women ages 25 to 55 in various lifestyles. They found that hardiness was positively related to self-actualization and that both hardiness and self-actualization represented a high level of psychological health (Campbell, Amerikaner, Swank, & Vincent, 1989).

Positive effects of hardiness have been found in several research studies conducted in the workplace. Measures of stress, physical health, and personality were taken from male middle- and high-level executives in a large public utility. The executives were divided into two groups: those who functioned under highly stressful conditions who were low in illnesses, and those who functioned under highly stressful conditions who were high in illnesses. The high-stress, good-health executives were found to be higher in hardiness. The executives in the high-stress, poor-health group were lower in hardiness. The low-hardiness executives felt powerless to cope with stress, scored low in the need to achieve, reported little commitment to work, and viewed change as a threat (Kobasa, Maddi, & Kahn, 1982; Kobasa, Maddi, Puccetti, & Zola, 1985).

Locus of Control

Locus of control One's belief about the source of one's rewards; people with an internal locus of control believe that job performance, pay, and promotion are under their control and dependent on their own behavior; people with an external locus of control believe that such events are dependent on outside forces such as luck.

The personality variable of internal versus external **locus of control** influences a person's reaction to stress (Rotter, 1966, 1975). People who rate high on internal control believe that they can influence the forces and events that shape their lives. People who rate high on external control believe that their lives are determined by other people and by outside events and forces such as luck or chance. Managers high in internal control were shown to experience less stress than did managers in similar jobs who were high in external control. The researchers concluded that the belief in one's level of control, which is a component of hardiness, significantly reduces the negative effects of stress (Gemmill & Heisler, 1972). A study of 244 accountants conducted over a 1-month period confirmed that those with an internal locus of control and high social support were significantly less affected by stress than those with an external locus of control (Daniels & Guppy, 1994).

Self-Esteem

The concept of self-esteem refers to how we feel about ourselves, our assessment of how adequate and worthy we are in meeting life's challenges and demands. In the workplace I/O psychologists call this concept **organization-based self-esteem** (OBSE). People high in OBSE have a high sense of personal adequacy and see themselves as important, effective, and worthwhile members of their organizations.

OBSE has been studied in diverse occupational groups. For example, research conducted with firefighters and with professional administrative employees of a utility company revealed that persons low in OBSE were more affected by stress than those high in OBSE. Workers low in OBSE were found to be more susceptible to role conflict (a major workplace stressor), and to poor support from their supervisors. Low OBSE workers also tended to be more passive in coping with stress (Ganster & Schaubroeck, 1991; Pierce, Gardner, Dunham, & Cummings, 1993).

Organization-based self-esteem A personality dimension relating to our assessment of our adequacy and worth with regard to our place in the employing organization.

Negative Affectivity

Another personality characteristic that may influence our vulnerability to stress is **negative affectivity** (NA). NA is closely related to neuroticism, one of the so-called big five personality dimensions. People who measure high in negative affectivity are likely to experience distress and dissatisfaction in all areas of life, including on the job; to focus on the negative aspect of life events; and to dwell on their failures, weaknesses, and shortcomings.

Given these tendencies, it is not surprising that I/O psychologists have found that people high in NA are also more likely to show high levels of stress, as measured by self-report inventories, than are people low in NA (Burke, Brief, & George, 1993).

Negative affectivity A personality dimension characterized by a generalized life and job dissatisfaction and by a focus on negative aspects of life.

Type of Occupation

Stress levels differ as a function of occupation. The National Institute for Occupational Safety and Health (NIOSH) ranked 130 jobs in terms of the level of stress they engender. The jobs with the highest stress levels include laborer, secretary, clinical laboratory technician, nurse, first-line supervisor, restaurant server, machine operator, farm worker, and miner.

Other stressful occupations are police officer, firefighter, computer programmer, dental technician, electrician, plumber, social worker, telephone operator, and city bus driver. Physiological indicators of stress were found to rise markedly among Los Angeles, California, bus drivers as traffic congestion increased and perceived control decreased (Evans & Carrère, 1991). One of the least stressful jobs is college professor. In general, clerical and blue-collar workers suffer more stress than do managerial and professional employees, largely because they have less opportunity to make decisions about their work and less control over working conditions.

Gender Differences

Women managers face more stressors than do men managers, both at work and at home (see, for example, Parker & Aldwin, 1994; Trocki & Orioli, 1994). We noted in Chapter 7 some of the problems of women managers. In addition to job pressures, women cope with stressors such as sexual harassment, discrimination, stereotyping, lack of role models, and feelings of isolation.

Women in minority groups, in particular, face workplace discrimination. A survey of 1,301 black women employed in a variety of jobs ranging from day-

Construction work can be stressful not only because of physical hazards but also because of external factors such as completion deadlines or failure to receive materials on time.

laborer to upper-level manager found that perceived race-based discrimination was a major source of job stress. This stressor rated even higher among younger (ages 24 to 29) and better-educated black women (Mays, Coleman, & Jackson, 1996).

Studies of American, British, and Asian women managers showed that they reported significantly higher levels of stress with regard to conflicts between career and family than did men managers. Women managers also had more psychosomatic complaints and feelings of nervousness, tension, and tiredness. The researchers found that when men managers developed stress-related illnesses, these tended to be manifested in physical symptoms. When women managers developed stress-related illnesses, these tended to be manifested in emotional symptoms (Davidson & Cooper, 1987; Lam, Lee, Ong, Wong, Chow, & Kleevens, 1987).

Women homemakers were also found to experience high levels of stress. The stresses of family life and the roles of wife and mother can lead to overwork, to dissatisfaction and a sense of little control, and to conflict with the need to seek employment outside the home. Many women homemakers report feeling depressed, believing that more demands are placed on them than on women with paying jobs.

College professor is one of the least stressful jobs.

WORK-FAMILY CONFLICTS

Both men and women report conflicts between the demands of family and the demands of the job, but the difficulties are usually greater for women. This stressor is apparently independent of type of job and working conditions, and it affects growing numbers of managerial and nonmanagerial employees. Today, more than 60% of all women with children 6 years of age or younger are employed outside the home. These working women are essentially holding two full-time jobs: one in the office, shop, or factory and the other at home. Spouses may help out, but the primary responsibility for family life remains with women. It is typically the woman worker who is called when a child becomes ill or who must adjust her work schedule when an elderly parent needs care.

Research conducted in Sweden on 1,800 employed men and women confirmed that a greater proportion of women than men bore the primary responsibility for child care. Therefore, employed women with children have a total workload (defined as hours spent working on the job plus hours spent working at home) that is far greater than that of employed men. In this study, the total weekly workload for women with 3 or more children was 90 hours, compared with 70 hours for men (Lundberg, 1996).

Surveys of two large samples of employed parents in the United States (more than 1,100 workers combined) found no gender differences in reported work-family conflict. For both men and women, conflict was significantly and positively related to depression, poor physical health, and alcohol abuse (Frone, Russell, & Barnes, 1996). These findings were supported by a questionnaire survey of 94 mothers and 48 fathers in dual-earner families with at least one young child living at home. These results showed similar effects of work-family conflict;

no significant differences were found between men and women on measures of work and family stress (Schwartzberg & Dytell, 1996).

A questionnaire study of men and women parents in managerial and professional jobs, whose spouses held similar positions, found that both men and women reported difficulties in balancing work and family demands. However, the stress seemed greater for women. Those women who reported high job involvement (who wanted to spend more time at work or who thought about work while doing something else) experienced greater work-family conflict than women who reported low job involvement. Highly job-involved women also felt more anxiety and guilt about whether they were carrying out family responsibilities adequately. The researchers noted that women have "fewer options than men for achieving control over competing role demands" (Duxbury & Higgins, 1991, p. 71). Later research supported this link between high job involvement and work-family conflict among men and women in managerial and nonmanagerial jobs (Adams, King, & King, 1996).

Questionnaire surveys of men and women psychologists and senior-level managers revealed that the women believed their jobs interfered with family life, rather than the other way around. They reported little conflict between work and family roles, perhaps because (with an average age of 43) they were already established in their careers (Gutek, Searle, & Klepa, 1991).

Other research suggests that work-family conflict is more pronounced among blue-collar and nonprofessional women workers and is likely to affect moods and emotional states. Employed mothers of young children in day-care centers were fitted with wristwatches that were programmed to emit a beep at eight randomly selected times between 8:00 a.m. and 10:00 p.m., for an 8-day period. Subjects were asked to record in a diary what they were doing at the time of the beep. These activities were classified as work-related, family-related, or social. If a woman was doing more than one thing at a time, this busyness was considered to be evidence of role juggling. Multiple role juggling was related to daily mood states, as assessed by questionnaires. Multiple role juggling was concluded to be a stressor that had a negative impact on mood and emotional state and on enjoyment of the tasks being performed (Williams, Suls, Alliger, Learner, & Wan, 1991).

The same technique of responding whenever the subject's beeper sounded was used in a study of 41 working parents, both mothers and fathers. As in the research discussed above, multiple role juggling was associated with high levels of distress. The results also confirmed the importance of control in dealing with stress. Feelings of high control were associated with positive mood states; low control was linked to feelings of fatigue and distress.

In addition, the results revealed that unpleasant mood states carried over in both directions: from work to family life, and from family life to work. Although these carryover effects occurred with both men and women, they were significantly stronger for women. The distressed employee let that feeling affect his or her dealings with the family, and vice versa. Positive mood states, however, did not appear to transfer from one situation to the other. The person happy at home did not necessarily exhibit that happiness at work.

Finally, these working parents indicated that their jobs interfered with family life far more than their homelife interfered with their jobs, confirming the results reported for the research on the women psychologists and the senior managers (Williams & Alliger, 1994).

A review of research on employed mothers reported that their jobs enhanced feelings of self-esteem and self-efficacy and provided status and a sense of overall satisfaction with life. In general, women with paying jobs outside the home have been found to be physically and emotionally healthier than full-time homemakers, despite job stress and work-family conflict (Nelson & Hitt, 1992). However, other research has shown that for the majority of working men, their blood pressure falls after they leave the workplace and go home for the evening. For many employed women, their blood pressure does not fall, because they encounter additional stress at home with family and housekeeping demands.

Most college-educated women today expect to have both careers and families. A questionnaire study of the attitudes and occupational plans of black and white college women found that those with higher-level career aspirations (in terms of entry-level salary and perceived occupational status or prestige) expressed less traditional attitudes about the role of women as mothers and homemakers. They reported plans to delay marriage and children until their careers were established, and they perceived less conflict in combining work and family roles (Murrell, Frieze, & Frost, 1991). Thus, any work-family conflict these women may experience may be deferred to a time when they have greater emotional and financial resources to deal with it.

As I/O psychologists have continued their research on work-family conflicts, and as the data showing the potentially harmful effects accumulate, organizations have begun to institute measures designed to reduce these effects. For example, the provision of day-care facilities at the workplace can relieve some of the concerns of employees with young children. Other approaches include flexible work scheduling, telecommuting, and opportunities for part-time work.

A survey of 1,239 organizations identified several factors among the companies most likely to provide help with work-family problems. These companies tend to be larger, to have more women employees, and to follow the lead of other companies in their industry or geographical area (Goodstein, 1994). In a study of 727 organizations, psychologists confirmed the importance of a company's size and of its emulation of the practices of competitors and neighboring companies in helping employees deal with work-family stressors. However, this survey found that it was having a high proportion of women *managers*, not just of women employees in the workforce as a whole, that increased a company's responsiveness (Ingram & Simons, 1995).

How effective are such organizational efforts in reducing work-family conflicts? A study of 398 parents working as healthcare professionals found that flexible scheduling and supportive supervisors significantly increased employee perceptions of their degree of control over their work and family concerns. In turn, those perceptions of high control were significantly associated with lower levels of work-family conflict, job dissatisfaction, health complaints, and cholesterol levels. Thus, in this study, factors related to stress were found to be significantly reduced by two management practices—flexible scheduling and supportive supervisors—that are much easier and less expensive to implement than the establishment of child-care facilities (Thomas & Ganster, 1995).

Another way for organizations to help reduce work-family conflict is to provide a short period of maternity or paternity leave following the birth of a child. In 1993, the U.S. Congress passed the Family and Medical Leave Act, providing up to 12 weeks of parental leave. To investigate the effective of parental leave on job stress, 570 women (81.5% of whom were employed outside the home) were interviewed and asked to complete several questionnaires during their pregnancy about their emotional health. The same questionnaires were administered again 1 month and 4 months after the women gave birth. The majority of the women (60%) took formal maternity leave from their jobs.

The results showed no correlation between the length of the leave taken and symptoms of stress. A longer period away from the job was not necessarily more effective than a shorter leave in alleviating the stress of balancing the demands of a new baby with the demands of the job. The researchers did find that women with full-time jobs showed higher levels of anxiety, indicating greater work-family conflict, 4 months after giving birth than did women with part-time jobs, independent of the length of leave (Hyde, Klein, Essex, & Clark, 1995).

CAUSES OF STRESS IN THE WORKPLACE

Many aspects of the work environment can induce stress. These include work overload and work underload, organizational change, and role conflict and role ambiguity.

Work Overload and Underload

Work overload Too much work to perform in the time available or work that is too difficult to perform.

Psychologists use the term **work overload** to describe the common condition of overwork. They have identified two types: quantitative overload and qualitative overload.

Quantitative overload is the condition of having too much work to do in the time available. It is an obvious source of stress and has been linked to stress-related ailments such as coronary heart disease. The key factor seems to be the degree of control workers have over the rate at which they work rather than the amount of work itself. In general, the less control employees have over their work pace, the greater the stress. Qualitative overload involves work that is too difficult. Having insufficient ability to perform a job is stressful. Even employees with considerable ability can find themselves in situations in which they cannot cope with the demands.

Work overload has become an increasing problem as a result of the extensive downsizing that has occurred in recent years in American factories and offices. Simply stated: There are fewer people available to do the same amount of work. Some employees are now doing the work formerly done by two; obviously, this can bring increased stress.

A questionnaire survey of 418 employees in 143 different jobs in 65 organizations found that employees in complex jobs who believed their abilities were not high enough to meet the demands of their jobs experienced significantly higher stress than employees who believed their abilities matched their job demands. In short, employees in a situation of work overload who did not feel competent to cope with the required tasks reported a high level of stress (Xie & Johns, 1995).

This positive correlation between work overload and stress is not unique to businesses in the United States. A 5-year study of 1,100 factory workers in China found that increased pressure on the job (in the form of extended working hours and bonuses for extra production), combined with job insecurity during a period of layoffs, led to significant increases in the workers' blood pressure and cholesterol levels (Siegrist, 1996).

Another study of approximately 100 middle managers from each of 21 countries found higher levels of work overload in non-Western countries such as India, Indonesia, Korea, and Nigeria. These managers believed they had too much work to do it well (Peterson, et al., 1995). In other words, they believed their workloads and their levels of responsibility were excessive, a belief not shared to the same extent by middle managers from Western countries. This difference may relate to the greater focus on individual effort that characterizes Western cultures. Non-Western cultures tend to be more collectively oriented. Thus, the organizational climate forces non-Western managers to depend more on the abilities of their colleagues to solve work problems than on their own individual efforts. This, in turn, can increase the perceived demands and complexity of their jobs.

The opposite condition, **work underload**—having work that is too simple or is insufficient to fill one's time or challenge one's abilities—is also stressful. A study of more than 1,500 executives found that those experiencing very high stress and those experiencing very low stress had significantly more health problems than did those who reported a moderate level of job-related stress. The researchers suggested that a lack of stimulation (low stress) could be as harmful as excessive stimulation; in other words, boredom and monotony are as harmful as having too much to do (French, Caplan, & Van Harrison, 1982).

Work underload Work that is too simple or is insufficient to fill one's time or challenge one's abilities.

A study of blue-collar workers in Israel found that ratings of job satisfaction and psychological distress, as well as absences due to sickness, were directly related to the self-reported monotony of the work. The higher the monotony (the work underload), the lower the job satisfaction, the higher the distress, and the greater the number of absences due to sickness (Melamed, Ben-Avi, Luz, & Green, 1995).

A survey of 5,450 blue-collar workers in Finland also found a significant relationship between job monotony and increased psychological distress, such as anxiety, worry, and stress, as well as greater physiological symptoms of that stress. This relationship was strongest in men under the age of 35 and in women over the age of 35 (Kivimäki & Kalimo, 1996).

Thus, an absence of challenge in the workplace is not necessarily beneficial. A certain level of job stress can be stimulating, invigorating, and desirable. Our goal should be to find the optimum level under which we can function and remain in good health and to avoid the extremes of work overload and underload.

Organizational Change

Another stressor is change. Employees who see change as exciting and challenging are less vulnerable to stress than are those who view change as a threat. It is the way we perceive or respond to change, rather than the change itself, that is the source of the stress. Many people resist change, preferring the familiar so that they will know what to expect.

Consider the relationship between employees and supervisors. Once that relationship has been established, assuming it is positive, all parties feel comfortable with it because each knows what to expect from the other. The situation is predictable, safe, and secure. When the supervisor leaves and employees face a

new boss, they no longer know what behaviors will be tolerated, how much work will be expected, or how their job performance will be evaluated. Such changes in the work environment can be stressful.

Other stressful changes include revised work procedures, training courses, and new workplace facilities. Company mergers can lead to concerns about job security, new managers, and different organizational policies.

A 3-year study of 397 employees of a regional water authority agency in Britain, which was changing from public to private ownership, showed how stressful such an upheaval and reorganization can be. Three levels of employees were studied: administrative, management, and manual workers. All displayed declines in job satisfaction and in measures of mental and physical health. Those affected most by the change (who evidenced the greatest signs of stress) were the manual workers, the group that could exercise the least control over the situation (Nelson, Cooper, & Jackson, 1995).

A stressful change for many older employees is the growing number of younger workers, women workers, and workers of diverse ethnic backgrounds who may bring to the job various attitudes, habits, and cultural values. Participatory democracy and other changes in the organizational climate are stressful for employees and managers who are resistant to change.

Role Ambiguity and Role Conflict

Role ambiguity A situation that arises when job responsibilities are unstructured or poorly defined.

An employee's role in the organization can be a stressor. **Role ambiguity** arises when the scope and responsibilities of the job are unstructured or poorly defined. The employee is not sure what is expected or even what to do. This is particularly crucial for new employees, whose roles are apt to be unclear. A study of 380 British engineers in their first 3 years on the job found that role ambiguity was related to job dissatisfaction, depression, and difficulty in getting along with superiors and co-workers. Role ambiguity diminished by the fourth year on the job (Keenan & Newton, 1987). Adequate orientation and socialization programs for new employees can reduce role ambiguity.

A study of 102 accountants revealed that they considered role ambiguity (as well as role overload) to be a high job stressor because it threatened their reputations with their supervisors. With this sample of subjects, the stress of role ambiguity was also found to generate considerable anxiety at home as well on the job (Doby & Caplan, 1995). Two additional studies—one involving 795 adults employed at a variety of jobs, and the other of 63 nonfaculty university employees—showed that a high level of job involvement and role clarification training could significantly reduce the stressful effects of role ambiguity (Frone, Russell, & Cooper, 1995; Schaubroeck, Ganster, Sime, & Ditman, 1993).

I/O psychologists have proposed three components of role ambiguity (Breaugh & Colihan, 1994):

- Performance criteria ambiguity—uncertainty about the standards used to evaluate a worker's job performance
- Work method ambiguity—uncertainty about the methods or procedures appropriate to the successful performance of the job
- Scheduling ambiguity—uncertainty about the timing or sequencing of work

You can readily see how for most jobs it would not be too difficult for supervisors to alleviate role ambiguity by establishing and promoting consistent standards and procedures.

Role conflict arises when a disparity exists in job requirements or between the job's demands and the employee's values and expectations. For example, when a supervisor is told to allow subordinates to participate in decision making and at the same time is pressured to increase production, the supervisor faces an obvious conflict. To meet production goals immediately may require authoritarian behavior, yet meeting participation goals requires democratic behavior.

When the job requires behaviors that conflict with an employee's moral code, such as when a salesperson is asked to sell a product known to be inferior or dangerous, role conflict can develop. The salesperson can quit, but the threat of unemployment may be a greater stressor than the conflict.

Role conflict A situation that arises when there is a disparity between job demands and the employee's personal standards.

Other Stressors

Supervisors and managers can be major sources of stress to their subordinates. Studies of 65 emergency medical technicians and of 343 middle-level bank managers confirmed that poor leadership behaviors—such as when supervisors fail to be supportive of their employees or refuse to allow participation in decision making—can lead to stress (Offermann & Hellmann, 1996; Revicki & Gershon, 1996).

Problems of career development—such as when an employee fails to receive an anticipated promotion—may also lead to stress. If career aspirations are not satisfied, frustration can be intense. Overpromotion can be stressful when employees are advanced beyond their level of competence to positions with which they cannot cope, leading to qualitative overload. The fear of failure on the job can induce considerable stress.

Performance appraisal is a source of stress. Few people like being evaluated relative to others. Also, a poor evaluation can have a significant impact on one's career.

Taking responsibility for subordinates can be a stressor for supervisors and managers. Evaluating employees for salary, promotion, or termination decisions; providing incentives and satisfactions; and managing their output on a daily basis can lead to stress. Managers are much more likely to report stress-related physical complaints than are employees such as accountants whose daily responsibilities do not include supervising others.

A person otherwise free of stress on the job can be adversely affected by a boss or co-worker who is experiencing stress (a so-called stress carrier). The anxiety exhibited by one stressed employee can easily affect other people.

Assembly-line work is associated with stress because it is repetitious, monotonous, noisy, and lacks challenge and control. A study of 662 blue-collar workers in the Netherlands found that the percentage of workers in factory jobs, farming, and highway transport dealing with physical stressors, such as noise, is as high as 29% (Houtman & Kompier, 1995).

Other physical working conditions that are common stressors are temperature extremes, poor lighting, shift work, and indoor pollution. A study of 87 university employees in job categories such as dean, secretary, and research assistant found that working in landscaped offices was linked to more self-reported physical and mental strain than working in private or semiprivate offices (Gehlmann, 1992).

Computer-controlled work monitoring can be stressful. Machine pacing of mail sorting and other repetitive keyboard tasks increases stress and is related to absenteeism, poor performance, and muscle fatigue. Automated monitoring of keystrokes and keyboard time is stressful, like having an ever-vigilant supervisor constantly looking over one's shoulder.

We confront many recurring stressful events every day, at home and at work. In addition, our personal characteristics may predispose us to experience stress independent of our job. A study of 97 new employees—engineers at an oil-field servicing company, faculty members at a university, and support staff at an electronics firm—found that the stress-related physical complaints these employees reported before they started their jobs accounted for most of the stress symptoms they reported 9 months later. The researchers suggested that these people brought their stress-related complaints with them to the job (Nelson & Sutton, 1990). Another possible explanation is negative affectivity (discussed earlier in this chapter), which can predispose a person to reporting feelings of stress.

EFFECTS OF STRESS IN THE WORKPLACE

We have noted some of the long-term health consequences of stress, those psychosomatic disorders that arise from prolonged exposure to stressful conditions. In addition, there are long-term psychological consequences, such as tension, depression, irritability, anxiety, low self-esteem, resentment, psychological fatigue, and neuroticism. One research study linked high work-related stress to spouse abuse. Some husbands who physically abused their wives reported such stressful work events as being laid off or failing to obtain a promotion (Barling & Rosenbaum, 1986). Other research found that stress on the job is significantly associated with violence toward children (Dompierre & Lavoie, 1994). A study of 400 employees (attorneys, secretaries, librarians, bank tellers, and teachers) found a relationship between work stressors and aggressive behaviors on the job, such as hostility, threats of quitting, and sabotage (Chen & Spector, 1992).

A classic large-scale study of the effects of stress on physical and emotional health, behavior, and job performance was conducted with 2,000 employees of a large organization in Canada (Zaleznik, Kets de Vries, & Howard, 1977). Management asked a team of psychologists to study key personnel in management, staff, and operations jobs who were showing signs of stress. Stress reactions had appeared soon after the company had undergone a sweeping organizational change, itself a recognized source of stress. The psychologists found a wide range of stress symptoms and grouped them in five categories: emotional distress, medication use, cardiovascular illness, gastrointestinal distress, and allergic respiratory problems. Specific symptoms are listed in Table 12–2.

The three groups of employees (management, staff, and operations) showed differences in the extent to which they suffered from these complaints, even though all had been exposed to the same organizational change. Managers showed a lower incidence of stress reactions than did staff and operations personnel. The staff group reported the highest incidence of cardiovascular illness and gastrointestinal distress. The operations group had the highest incidence of emotional distress, medication use, and allergic respiratory problems.

TABLE 12–2 Frequency of Occurrence of Stress Symptoms

Symptom	Percentage Reporting Symptom
Emotional Distress	
Insomnia	24%
Restlessness and agitation	21
Fatigue	19
Irritability	13
Moodiness	11
Medication Use	
Vitamin pills	21
Prescription drugs	7
Sleeping pills	3
Cardiovascular Illness	
Rapid heartbeat	8
High blood pressure	6
Gastrointestinal Distress	
Digestion problems	11
Colitis	6
Allergic Respiratory Problems	
Hay fever	9
Respiratory difficulties	4

Note. Adapted from "Stress Reactions in Organizations: Syndromes, Causes, and Consequences" by A. Zaleznik, M. F. R. Kets de Vries, and J. Howard, 1977, *Behavioral Science, 22,* p. 154.

The psychologists concluded that the managers reported fewer stress symptoms because they were more familiar with organizational processes and thus had more control over them. They were better equipped to tolerate the period of uncertainty and role ambiguity that followed the company's reorganization. Power and control over their work situation enhanced their self-esteem and independence, rendering them less vulnerable to the effects of stress. In contrast, employees in staff and operations positions, with little or no control over organizational processes, had lower self-esteem and autonomy and less tolerance of role ambiguity. Thus we see additional evidence of the importance of control as a factor in limiting stress effects on the job.

Managers were also found to feel less threatened by the performance appraisal process. Staff and operations personnel have a high accountability for results, outcomes that can be quantified for their evaluations. Although they have responsibility for results, such as meeting production goals, they have little control over how the organization operates to achieve its goals. For many staff and operations people, this lack of authority is clearly a stressful situation.

Other characteristic effects of stress in the workplace include mass psychogenic illness, burnout, and some types of workaholism.

Mass Psychogenic Illness

Mass psychogenic illness A stress-related disorder manifested in a variety of physical symptoms that spreads rapidly among a group of workers; popularly called assembly-line hysteria.

A stress-related disorder among assembly-line workers is **mass psychogenic illness,** more popularly known as assembly-line hysteria. This stress-produced malady affects greater numbers of women than men. It strikes suddenly, spreading so quickly throughout a production line that the line may have to be shut down.

Consider the case of an electronics plant in Ohio. One morning, an assembly-line worker complained of dizziness, nausea, muscular weakness, and difficulty in breathing. Within minutes, nearly 40 employees went to the company health clinic with the same symptoms. The illness spread, and the plant had to be closed. Managers speculated that there was something wrong with the air—some chemical, gas, virus, or other infectious agent. Physicians, toxicologists, and industrial hygienists were called in to investigate. They found nothing in the factory to explain the problem. The cause was determined to be mass psychogenic illness, a stress-related disorder that has no physical origin and that spreads by contagion.

On another assembly line, employees were packing frozen fish in boxes for shipping. One employee remarked about a strange odor. Suddenly, workers began to choke, experiencing dizziness, nausea, and trouble in breathing. The plant was closed, and investigators were summoned to search the building. They found nothing, no toxic agent in the air, in the drinking water, or in the fish that the workers were processing. There was no apparent physical cause for the illness, yet there was no denying that the workers were physically sick.

Although there is no physical cause, such as a virus in the air-conditioning system or a contaminant in the drinking water, physical stressors in the workplace have been found to trigger the onset of mass psychogenic illness. For example, the noise, speed, poor lighting, variable temperatures, unpleasant odors, and work overload conditions common to assembly lines can lead to mass psychogenic illness. Often, employees have recently been pressured to increase production on the line. This pressure may involve considerable overtime work, which most employees are not in a position to refuse. Poor relations with supervisors can also be a factor. If management has not established formal procedures for dealing with employee grievances or if communication and feedback between employees and management are poor, then the resulting friction will be a source of stress.

Another stressor related to mass psychogenic illness is social isolation. Employees who are unable to communicate with one another because of the noise and the rapid work pace can experience feelings of isolation and loneliness and a lack of social support from co-workers. Work-family conflict, especially for women, can be an additional source of stress, which may help to explain why more women than men fall victim to assembly-line hysteria.

Burnout

Burnout A condition of job stress that results from overwork.

The effects of job stress that result from overwork can be seen in the condition called **burnout** (Cordes & Dougherty, 1993; Freudenberger, 1980). Employees suffering from burnout become less energetic and less interested in their jobs. They are emotionally exhausted, apathetic, depressed, irritable, and bored. They tend to find fault with all aspects of their work environment, including co-workers, and react negatively to the suggestions of others. The quality of their work deteriorates but not necessarily the quantity. An analysis of longitudinal data collected on teachers and school administrators in Canada found that burnout was responsible for reduced job satisfaction (Wolpin, Burke, & Greenglass, 1991).

Employees suffering from burnout tend to become rigid about their work, following rules and procedures compulsively because they are too exhausted to be flexible or to consider alternative approaches. In time, the burned-out employee will have an impact on the emotional health and efficiency of co-workers and subordinates. Advanced burnout is characterized by even lower energy, self-esteem, self-efficacy, and job involvement, as well as an increase in physical stress symptoms and social withdrawal at the very time social support is most needed. Deterioration in job performance becomes noticeable, and poor performance appraisals are usually the result.

Three components of the burnout syndrome have been described (Maslach, 1982):

1. Emotional exhaustion—the feeling of being drained and empty that is caused by excessive psychological and emotional demands, often brought about by work overload or unrealistically high expectations
2. Depersonalization—a feeling of callousness and cynicism and a reduced sensitivity toward others
3. Reduced sense of personal accomplishment—the feeling that one's actions and efforts are wasted and worthless

A study of 219 supervisors and managers of a government welfare agency suggested that emotional exhaustion and depersonalization were strongly associated with stress (Lee & Ashforth, 1990). These findings were supported by a later meta-analysis of 61 studies, which also showed that emotional exhaustion and depersonalization were associated with turnover intentions and organizational commitment (Lee & Ashforth, 1996).

The Maslach Burnout Inventory was developed to measure this condition (Maslach & Jackson, 1986). It consists of four subscales to assess the components of emotional exhaustion, depersonalization, and personal accomplishment, and a related factor called personal involvement. Studies show the test to have high reliability and validity. Research reviews have found that high scores on the burnout scale are related to exhaustion and work overload factors in various occupations (see, for example, Green & Walkey, 1988).

Women managers appear to show more frequent and intense effects from the emotional exhaustion component of burnout than do men managers. Single and divorced persons have been found to be more likely than married persons to experience emotional exhaustion. Emotional exhaustion has also been related to lack of opportunity for promotion. Burnout also typically strikes employees who are highly dedicated and committed to their work—those who work overtime, take work home, or come to the office on weekends. An early sign of burnout is when these employees put in more time but accomplish less because of their exhaustion.

Burnout victims may feel insecure and have unfulfilling personal lives. Because they lack self-esteem and recognition off the job, they may try to find it on the job. By working hard and making significant contributions to the company, they earn tangible rewards and also prove to themselves that they are worthwhile. The price for prolonged overwork is an accumulation of stress and depletion of the body's energy, faster than the body can replace it. This condition, in turn, leads to physical and psychological problems.

A comparison of 241 Mexican women factory workers and 729 U.S. human services workers (teachers, police officers, and nurses) found that burnout was experienced in different ways for different reasons. The most significant predictors of burnout for the factory workers were low life control and high economic concerns. The most significant predictors of burnout for the human services workers were work overload and role conflict.

The subjects also differed in their work goals and motivations; failure to satisfy these goals contributed to burnout. The authors of the study noted:

> For human service professionals, work provides an opportunity to make a significant contribution to the people they work with and to society at large. When work does not provide that, the result is burnout—a feeling that they have nothing left to give. For the blue-collar women, on the other hand, work provides an opportunity to escape conditions of dire poverty and to enhance their sense of self.... When work does not provide that, the result is burnout—feeling trapped, hopeless, and anxious (Pines & Guendelman, 1995, p. 16).

Nurses who work in intensive care units of hospitals, a highly stressful work environment, have a high likelihood of burnout. A study of 508 ICU nurses in the Netherlands (57% women, 43% men) confirmed significantly higher burnout symptoms than shown by nurses working in other parts of the hospital. The results also showed that qualitative overload was significantly related to burnout (Schaufeli, Keijsers, & Miranda, 1995).

Workaholism

Workaholism So-called addiction to work because of anxiety and insecurity or because of a genuine liking for the job.

Burnout victims are sometimes described as **workaholics,** employees who are addicted to their work (Machlowitz, 1980). However, not all workaholics strive to perform well because they are driven by anxiety and insecurity. Some workaholics genuinely like their work and derive satisfaction from it. To them, work is not an unhealthy compulsion that gradually wears them down. Rather, work provides a healthy, enriching, and stimulating focus for their lives. These workaholics are happy, well-adjusted people who enjoy their jobs. They seldom take vacations because they feel no need to escape from their work. However, because of their intense sense of commitment, they can be a source of stress to others.

Psychologists estimate that 5% of all employees are workaholics and that the majority of these are content. These healthy workaholics are likely to have supportive families, autonomy and variety on the job, and tasks that match their level of knowledge, skills, and abilities. Workaholics who lack these qualities tend to be discontented and dissatisfied. They are more susceptible to burnout and to the negative effects of stress.

We have a distinction, then, between healthy and unhealthy workaholism. Healthy workaholics, sometimes called *work enthusiasts,* are highly committed to and involved with their work and derive great enjoyment from it. Unhealthy workaholics (*true workaholics*) are also highly involved with their work but derive little, if any, satisfaction from it. Unhealthy workaholics have been found to be compulsive and driven to perform their job tasks. They also score significantly higher than work enthusiasts on measures of stress and significantly lower on measures of health (Spence & Robbins, 1992).

Unhealthy workaholics may have an undesirable effect on their company and their co-workers. It has been suggested that their compulsive addiction to work can lead to several negative situations (Porter, 1996):

- Rigidity in thinking and analyzing problems
- Setting unrealistically high work hours and performance standards for colleagues and subordinates
- Attempting to maintain total control over the work process

As a result, true workaholics find it difficult to delegate authority, to request help, or to function as team players. For all their effort and hard work, true workaholics may do more harm than good for their organizations.

TREATING STRESS IN THE WORKPLACE

Organizational stress-management interventions include altering the organizational climate and providing treatment under employee assistance programs (EAPs). Individual techniques for dealing with stress include relaxation training, biofeedback, and behavior modification.

Organizational Techniques

Controlling the Organizational Climate. Because one of the stressors of modern organizational life is planned change, the organization should provide sufficient support to enable employees to adapt to change. Stress can be prevented or reduced by allowing employees to participate in decisions about changes in work

---

NEWSBREAK #23

What Do *You* Do When You're Stressed Out?

Stress. It's everywhere—on the job, in the home, on the highway. Certainly in the classroom. Stress is something all of us experience at one time or another. With some people, the effects of stress come and go quickly. For example, a driver runs a red light in front of us, or our plane is forced to make an emergency landing. We may feel shaky for a while, but we're soon back to normal. Other people have stress in their lives most of the time. They are trapped in an unhappy marriage. Their children cut classes. The boss is a tyrant. Co-workers steal their ideas. They have chronic indigestion. The car has a rattle. The cat sheds on

(continued)

the computer. The roof leaks.... But for most of us, it's work that causes the greatest stress.

A survey conducted by the Northwestern National Life Insurance Company found that 27% of all American workers consider their jobs to be the single greatest source of stress.

How do people handle their stress? What do they do? What do *you* do? One magazine conducted a poll of women in the workforce, asking how they coped with job stress. Most of the respondents—57%—said they coped by talking to a friend about their problems; this is what psychologists call *social support*. Here are some of the reported ways of dealing with stress:

Talk to a friend	57%
Drink coffee or eat	42%
Exercise and sports	36%
Keep their worries to themselves	35%
Act as though nothing happened	30%
Engage in a hobby	27%
Smoke cigarettes	23%
Drink alcoholic beverages	15%
Take it out on somebody else	8%
Take drugs	8%

Some of these ways of coping with stress are not very healthy. Others, such as exercising or getting a hobby, are positive steps. The most important thing you can do is develop your own social support network, either at your workplace or through outside interests, activities that can bring challenges and satisfactions you may not be getting from your job. Try to arrange mini vacations to give yourself short breaks from job stress. Psychologists also recommend techniques such as meditation, relaxation training, biofeedback, and behavior modification, all of which require the assistance of a professional. And if all else fails, you may have to consider changing jobs. This advice may all sound like common sense, and much of it is. What you want to do is *something* that will put you back in control of at least part of your life.

Sources: Miller, J. D. (1994). Foreword. In G. P. Keita & J. L. Hurrell, Jr. (Eds.), *Job stress in a changing workforce: Investigating gender, diversity, and family issues.* Washington, DC: American Psychological Association. Stress on your job: A major national survey. *Ms.,* April, 1984, p. 86.

practices and in the organizational structure. Participation helps employees to accept change and aids in their adaptation to change by allowing them to express their opinions and air their complaints.

Providing Control.   The belief that we can exercise some control over our work greatly reduces the effects of stress. Organizations can improve employees' sense of control by enriching, enlarging, and expanding jobs to provide greater responsibility and decision-making authority.

Defining Employee Roles.   To reduce the stress caused by role ambiguity, managers should tell subordinates clearly what is expected of them and what their job responsibilities are.

Eliminating Work Overload and Underload.   Appropriate employee selection and training programs, equitable promotion decisions, fair distribution of work, and proper matching of job requirements with employee abilities can help to eliminate work overload and work underload as stressors.

Providing Assistance to Stressed Employees.   EAPs can include in-house counseling programs that teach individual stress-control techniques. Facilities for physical exercise programs are also beneficial.

Providing for Social Support.   Social support networks can reduce personal vulnerability to stress effects. Organizations can enhance social support by promoting cohesive work groups and by training supervisors to show empathy and concern for subordinates.

Psychologists have conducted considerable research on social support and have found that an increase in social support can alleviate many of the harmful effects of stress. However, a meta-analysis of these studies suggests that the findings are inconsistent in explaining precisely how the reduction in stress effects occurs (Haines, Hurlbert, & Zimmer, 1991). One hypothesis is that social support moderates the impact of stressors on a person's perception of being under strain, especially in situations of work overload and role conflict. Another view is that social support enhances a person's overall ability to cope with stress.

Some researchers suggest that the first-line supervisor, as the personification of the organization's social support network, is the most important buffer against effects of job stress. A study of 728 police officers used questionnaires to measure the degree of stress experienced on the job and the amount of social support received from family, co-workers, and supervisors. The stress questionnaire involved 89 job events, ranging from the highly stressful "being shot at in the line of duty" to the relatively unstressful "issuing a summons." Social support was assessed by measures of group cohesiveness, empathy, and feedback. The researchers concluded that social support from supervisors was the only effective buffer against the harmful impact of stressful job events (Greller, Parsons, & Mitchell, 1992).

Another study, comparing 463 white and 224 Hispanic nonfaculty university employees, found that social support on the job and at home was a primary factor in reducing stress effects for both groups (Gutierres, Saenz, & Green, 1994).

Evaluative research has been conducted on EAPs that teach individual stress management and inoculation techniques such as relaxation exercises, biofeedback, and cognitive restructuring. Studies show that these programs can reduce the levels of physiological arousal associated with high stress. Participants who master the behavioral and cognitive techniques report less tension and fewer sleep disturbances, and an improved ability to cope with workplace stressors (Parkes, 1990). A meta-analysis of 37 studies involving 1,837 participants showed that stress-inoculation techniques significantly reduced anxiety and enhanced job performance (Saunders, Driskell, Johnston, & Salas, 1996).

Organizational EAPs do not act on the causes of stress in the workplace, but they do enable employees to learn more effective ways of coping. The benefits of these programs to employees and employers far outweigh their costs (see, for example, Ivancevich, Matteson, Freedman, & Phillips, 1990; Pelletier, 1991).

The number of organizations offering wellness or fitness programs to promote occupational health increased from 60% in the mid-1980s to 81% in the 1990s. By enhancing physical and emotional well-being, it is thought that employees will be less vulnerable to the effects of stress. The focus is on counseling employees to change or modify unhealthy behaviors and to maintain a healthy lifestyle. Although such programs are sponsored by the organization, the responsibility for healthful behaviors—such as exercise, proper diet, and stopping smoking—rests with the employee.

Some corporate stress management programs are directed toward Type A executives in the hope of reducing the incidence of coronary heart disease. Xerox estimates that the cost to the company of the loss of an executive is $600,000. Stress reduction and behavioral change techniques are considerably less expensive. Exercises to alter Type A behaviors include speaking more slowly and learning not to interrupt others when they are talking. Executives can be trained in such management practices as delegating responsibility, establishing daily goals, setting priorities, and avoiding stress-producing situations.

Individual Techniques

Some individual techniques for dealing with stress can be taught in company-sponsored EAPs or stress reduction programs. Others can be adopted personally, such as a program of physical exercise. Exercise can increase stamina and endurance, reduce risk factors for coronary heart disease, and dissipate excess energy and tension. Many companies sponsor physical fitness programs and provide exercise facilities and running tracks at the workplace.

These facilities are expensive to establish and maintain, and they may not be worth the cost when only a few employees use them. A survey of participation rates for workplace wellness and fitness programs showed that only 15 to 30% of white-collar workers and 3 to 5% of blue-collar workers were involved (Gebhardt & Crump, 1990). A study at four automobile manufacturing plants found that the addition of a physical fitness facility at one plant produced no measurable reduction in health risks compared to the less expensive health education classes offered at the other plants. The fitness facility was the least cost-effective approach to managing employee stress (Erfurt, Foote, & Heirich, 1992).

Other individual techniques for reducing stress are relaxation training, biofeedback, and behavior modification.

Relaxation training A stress-reduction technique that concentrates on relaxing one part of the body after another.

Relaxation Training.   As early as the 1930s, a method of **relaxation training** was promoted as a way to reduce stress. Patients were taught to concentrate on one part of the body after another, systematically tensing and relaxing the muscles. By focusing on the sensations produced by the relaxed state, they could achieve progressively deeper relaxation.

Psychologists have proposed several refinements of this basic technique. In autogenic training, subjects learn to relax by imagining that their limbs are growing warm and heavy. In meditation, subjects concentrate on deep, regular breathing and the repetition of a phrase or sound. The relaxation-response approach combines these two techniques. The quieting reflex technique teaches subjects to achieve the relaxed state more quickly. Feedback on muscle tension can be combined with these approaches, along with self-measurement of blood pressure before and after relaxation exercises.

Relaxation training has been found to be an excellent way to reduce the effects of stress. Proponents of meditation claim that it results in a deeper and more restorative type of relaxation than merely resting, but research suggests that meditation is no more effective for altering physiological functioning than is sitting quietly.

Biofeedback. **Biofeedback** is a popular technique for dealing with stress effects. It involves the electronic measurement of physiological processes such as heart rate, blood pressure, and muscle tension. These measurements are converted into signals, such as flashing lights or beeps, which provide feedback on how a bodily process is operating. Using the feedback, people then learn to control their internal states. For example, suppose that a light is activated on a monitor whenever your heart is beating at a relaxed rate. With practice, you can learn to keep the light on by maintaining that relaxed heart rate. Precisely how you learn to do this has not been established, but with enough practice,

Biofeedback A stress-reduction technique that involves electronic monitoring of physiological processes such that people can learn to control muscle tension, blood pressure, and brain waves.

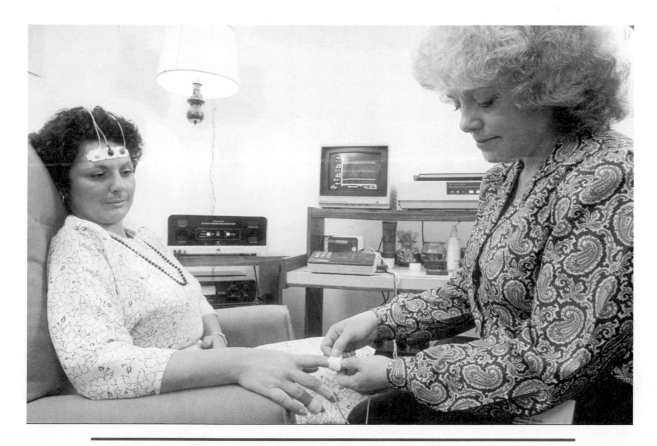

Biofeedback, a popular technique for dealing with stress, involves electronic measurement and control of bodily processes such as heart rate and muscle tension.

you can control your heart rate and soon will no longer need feedback from the light to do so.

Biofeedback can be used to control muscle tension, blood pressure, body temperature, brain waves, and stomach acid. By reducing the physiological changes that accompany stress, people can reduce the incidence of stress-related disorders.

Behavior modification A training program of positive reinforcement to reward employees for displaying desirable job behaviors. Behavior modification techniques are also effective in dealing with stress.

Behavior Modification.   **Behavior modification** techniques are effective in rendering Type A persons less vulnerable to stress. Characteristics that can be altered by behavior modification include intense drive, self-imposed deadlines, and a high rate of activity. Behavior modification involves the conditioning of positive emotional responses to stressful events.

Work Stress, Family Stress, and Psychological Well-Being

Conflicts between work and family have become an increasing source of stress for many working parents. We have seen that in dual-earner families, the woman usually has the greater share of responsibility for childrearing and household management. Thus, she essentially has two full-time jobs, because her spouse typically performs a lesser share of household duties.

To investigate how stress at work and at home affects the psychological well-being of dual-earner couples, a questionnaire survey was administered to 94 employed mothers and 48 employed fathers; all were from different households. The questionnaires were distributed to 350 elementary school children in a suburban New York school system, who were asked to give them to their parents. Half the fathers and one third of the mothers were in professional, technical, or management positions; the rest held clerical, service, or blue-collar jobs.

The questionnaires assessed the following factors:

- Depression and self-esteem
- Job-home interference, defined as the conflict between the demands of work and the demands of home
- Work stress: role ambiguity, role overload, lack of autonomy, nonchallenging work, work role insignificance, lack of resources on the job, and work environment discomfort
- Family stress: family role insignificance, family role overload, conflicting home demands, family role ambiguity, nonchallenge at home, lack of emotional support from spouse, lack of task sharing at home, and lack of emotional support from children

Source: Schwartzberg, N. S., & Dytell, R. S. (1996). Dual-earner families: The importance of work stress and family stress for psychological well-being. *Journal of Occupational Health Psychology, 1,* 211–223.

No significant differences between men and women were found on levels of work stress, family stress, job-home interference, and depression/self-esteem. However, there were significant differences in some of the dimensions of family stress.

Mothers reported higher levels of lack of task sharing at home, and fathers reported greater lack of challenge from their family role (nonchallenge at home). On the specific dimensions of work stress, fathers reported greater stress than mothers arising from dependency on others (a lack of autonomy).

The researchers found that for both men and women self-esteem was more affected by work stress, whereas depression was more affected by family stress. They concluded that the subjects derived pride from their accomplishments at work rather than at home. However, their emotional states of happiness or depression depended more on family relationships.

The results confirm other research findings showing that mothers employed outside the home experience higher levels of time pressure and time shortage than do fathers employed outside the home. As a result, these women seem greatly concerned about the amount of assistance they receive, or fail to receive, from their spouses.

The researchers referred to this effect as "Don't tell me I'm terrific. Tell me you'll do the laundry."

Critical Thinking Questions

1. Given the greater demands on women in dual-earner families, why do you think this and similar studies reported no gender differences in work-family conflict?
2. Is it possible that women are more reluctant than men to admit conflicts between their jobs and their families? If so, how would you explain this?
3. Why do you think work-family conflicts are greater among women with blue-collar jobs than among women managers and professionals?
4. How do the emotional and physical health of women who work outside the home compare

the emotional and physical health of women who are full-time homemakers?

5. What steps can employers take to reduce the stress of their employees' work-family conflicts?

SUMMARY

Stress in the workplace lowers productivity, increases absenteeism and turnover, and causes physiological changes. Prolonged stress can be a factor in the **psychosomatic** origins of illnesses, including heart disease, gastrointestinal distress, arthritis, skin diseases, allergies, headaches, and cancer. Factors that can reduce stress effects include high job satisfaction, control, high autonomy and power, social support, good health, job skills, and certain personality characteristics.

People identified as **Type A** may be more prone to heart attacks. They have a high competitive drive, a sense of time urgency, and high levels of hostility, aggression, anger, and impatience. **Type B** persons lack these characteristics and may be less vulnerable to stress effects. People high in **hardiness** (a belief that they can control life events, a commitment to work, and a view that change is stimulating) are less vulnerable to stress effects. Similarly, people high in internal **locus of control** and self-esteem are less vulnerable to stress.

Causes of stress include the following: **work-family conflicts, work overload, work underload,** change, **role ambiguity, role conflict,** career development problems, supervision, contact with stress carriers, machine-paced assembly-line work, and physical conditions of the workplace. Consequences of stress include long-term effects of psychosomatic disorders and short-term effects on health, behavior, and job performance.

Mass psychogenic illness affects more women employees than men employees and is spread quickly among co-workers. It is caused by physical and psychological stressors. **Burnout** is related to prolonged overwork and results in lower productivity, exhaustion, irritability, rigidity, and social withdrawal. Burnout victims are often **workaholics** who are compulsively driven to work hard out of insecurity and lack of fulfillment in their personal lives. Healthy workaholics derive satisfaction from work and are free of the stress effects of burnout.

Organizational techniques for coping with stress include emotional climate control, social support, redefinition of employee roles, and elimination of work overload and underload. Individual techniques include physical exercise, **relaxation training, biofeedback, behavior modification,** vacations, and quitting a highly stressful job.

KEY TERMS

behavior modification
biofeedback
burnout
hardiness
locus of control
mass psychogenic illness
negative affectivity
organization-based self-esteem
psychosomatic disorders

relaxation training
role ambiguity
role conflict
stress
Type A/Type B personalities
work overload
work underload
workaholism

ADDITIONAL READING

Geber, S. Z. (1996). *How to manage stress for success.* New York: AMACOM. A brief guide to assessing sources of job stress and to taking action to deal with the consequences.

Keitz, G. P., & Hurrell, J. J., Jr. (Eds.). (1994). *Job stress in a changing workforce: Investigating gender, diversity, and family issues.* Washington, DC: American Psychological Association. Covers research and theory on the effects of job stress on the individual employee as the U.S. economy shifts from manufacturing to service industries. Considers international competition, changing demographics, and family demands.

Koslowsky, M., Kluger, A. N., & Reich, M. (1995). *Commuting stress: Causes, effects, and methods of coping.* New York: Plenum Press. Examines psychological, physiological, and behavioral effects of driving to and from the job as a potential source of job stress.

Sauter, S. L., & Murphy, L. R. (Eds.). (1995). *Organizational risk factors for job stress.* Washington, DC: American Psychological Association. Reviews organizational culture as a source of job stress and relates the stress induced by particular occupations to specific diseases and physical conditions.

Engineering Psychology

Engineering psychologists are involved in the design of comfortable, safe, and efficient workplaces. From the adjustability of office chairs and the brightness level of the data on your computer monitor to the comfort of space shuttle interiors, psychologists study many aspects of working life to make jobs less stressful and employees more productive. Chapter 13 describes the contributions of engineering psychologists to the design of tools and equipment and the layout of work stations to ensure that these are compatible with the needs and abilities of employees.

Engineering Psychology

CHAPTER OUTLINE

We have discussed various ways in which I/O psychologists contribute to the organizational goal of increasing employee efficiency, productivity, and job satisfaction. We have seen how employees with the best abilities can be recruited and selected, trained for their jobs, and supervised and motivated effectively. We have also described techniques that can be applied to optimize the quality of work life and the conditions of the work environment. But we have mentioned only briefly a factor as influential as any of those discussed—the design of the machinery and equipment employees must use to do their jobs and the workspaces in which those jobs are performed.

Tools, equipment, and work stations must be compatible with the workers who use them. We may think of this as a team operation, a person and a machine functioning together to perform a task that could not be accomplished by either working alone. If the person and the machine are to work smoothly in this person-machine system, they must be matched so that each makes the best use of the strengths of the other and, where necessary, compensates for the weaknesses of the other.

Engineering psychology
The design of machines and equipment for human use, and the determination of the appropriate human behaviors for the efficient operation of the machines.

This pairing of operator and machine is the province of **engineering psychology,** also called **human factors,** or human engineering. British psychologists use the term **ergonomics,** which is derived from the Greek *ergon,* meaning work, and *nomos,* meaning natural laws. In conjunction with engineers, engineering psychologists apply their knowledge of psychology to the formulation of natural laws of work. Thus, engineering psychology is the science of designing or engineering machines and equipment for human use and of engineering human behavior for the efficient operation of the machines.

HISTORY AND SCOPE OF ENGINEERING PSYCHOLOGY

Until the 1940s, the design of machinery, equipment, and industrial plants was solely the responsibility of engineers. They made design decisions on the basis of mechanical, electrical, space, and size considerations. They paid little attention to the workers who would have to operate the machines. The machine was a constant factor, incapable of being changed to meet human needs. It was the employee who would have to adapt. No matter how uncomfortable, tiring, or unsafe the equipment, the operators—the only flexible part of the person-machine system—had to adjust, to make the best of the situation and fit themselves to the machine's requirements.

Adapting the worker to the machine was accomplished through time-and-motion study, a forerunner of engineering psychology, in which jobs were analyzed to determine how they could be simplified. Of course, this tendency to design machines while ignoring the needs of the people who operated them could not be maintained. Machines were becoming too complex and were requiring levels of speed, skill, and attention that threatened to exceed human capacities to monitor and control them.

The weapons developed for use in World War II placed greater demands on human abilities, not only muscle strength but also sensing, perceiving, judging, and making decisions. For example, pilots of sophisticated fighter aircraft were permitted little time to react to a dangerous situation, to decide on a course of action, and to initiate the appropriate response. Radar and sonar operators also required high levels of skill. In general, the wartime equipment worked well, but mistakes were frequent. The most precise bombsight ever developed was not leading to accurate bombing. Friendly ships and aircraft were being misidentified and fired upon. Whales were mistaken for submarines. Although the machinery seemed to be functioning properly, the system—the interaction of the person and the machine—clearly was not.

It was this wartime need that spurred the development of engineering psychology, similar to the way the screening and selection needs of the army in World War I gave rise to mass psychological testing. Authorities recognized that human abilities and limitations would have to be taken into account when designing machines if the overall system was to operate efficiently. Psychologists, physiologists, and physicians soon joined engineers in designing aircraft cockpits, submarine and tank crew stations, and components of military uniforms.

An example of this early work involved helping American pilots stay alive. During World War II, there was no consistent or standard arrangement of displays and controls within the cockpits of different models of aircraft. A pilot used to one type of plane who was suddenly assigned to another would be confronted by a different set of displays and controls. The lever to raise the wheels in the new plane might be in the same place as the lever to operate the flaps in the old plane. Imagine trying to drive a car in which gas pedal and brake pedal are reversed. In an emergency you would probably step on what you thought was the brake pedal and would step on the gas instead.

There was also no consistency in the operating characteristics of aircraft controls. Within the same cockpit, one control might be moved upward to turn something on and another switched downward to turn something on. A number of separate controls with identical knobs were often placed close together so that a pilot whose attention was diverted would not be able to distinguish among the controls by touch alone. As these problems were recognized, they were corrected, but many pilots were killed because their machines had been designed poorly, not aerodynamically, but from the reference point of the pilot, whose job it was to direct, control, and tame the aircraft's power.

Poor design also leads to other kinds of accidents. In 1979, a disastrous situation occurred at the nuclear power plant at Three Mile Island, Pennsylvania. The accident happened on the night shift, when the operators were less alert, but part of the problem involved a lack of attention to human needs. In the power plant's control room, instrument dials and controls had been placed too far apart. When operators detected a dangerous reading on one of the displays, valuable time was lost because the operators had to run to another part of the room to activate controls to correct the malfunction. To prevent a recurrence, the Nuclear Regulatory Commission ordered modification of nuclear power plant control rooms to consider the abilities of the human operators.

To deal with human factors in aircraft accidents, 66% of which can be traced to pilot error, the National Transportation Safety Board added engineering psychologists to the staff. Their job is to investigate pilot and crew fatigue, shift work schedules, health issues, stress, and equipment design, all of which can contribute to accidents.

Much human factors research has been conducted on passenger vehicles in an effort to make them safer. Variables studied include the brightness of automobile and motorcycle headlights; the position, color, and brightness of brake lights; and the layout of dashboard controls and displays. Since 1985, passenger cars driven in the United States have been required to have a brake light mounted in the rear window. This requirement is a result of human factors research on 8,000 vehicles that showed that a high-mounted brake light reduced the incidence of rear-end collisions by 50%.

Engineering psychologists are studying ways to make license plates and traffic signs more legible and noticeable at night. They also investigate the effects of alcohol on driver behavior, as well as driver reaction time—how drivers perceive and comprehend risky situations and make decisions about responding.

Engineering psychologists are also concerned about the effect on visibility of tinting or solar film on car windows, a practice becoming increasingly common around the United States. Research results show that the detection of objects—such as pedestrians or other cars—through the rear window while backing up is significantly reduced when that window is tinted (Freedman, Zador, & Staplin, 1993). In some cases such a window admits only 53% of the available light. Some states permit light transmission levels as low as 35%, whereas other states are regulating against the use of solar film. These and similar research results can be used to support future legislation on desirable levels of light transmission for safe visibility.

Research by engineering psychologists has demonstrated that using cellular phones while driving reduces reaction time, particularly among older drivers, and can lead to a higher accident risk among drivers of all ages (Alm & Nilsson, 1995; Violanti & Marshall, 1996).

Engineering psychologists contribute to the design of a variety of other products, including dental and surgical implements, cameras, toothbrushes, and bucket seats for cars. They have even been involved in the redesign of the mailbags used by letter carriers. Why? Because approximately 21% of letter carriers suffer from musculoskeletal problems such as low back pain from carrying mailbags slung over their shoulders. Preliminary research on a mailbag with a support strap at the waist and on double bags that distribute the weight on both shoulders has shown their potential for reducing muscle fatigue. The redesign of the mailbag is expected to save millions of dollars in disability payments (Bloswick, Gerber, Sebesta, Johnson, & Mecham, 1994).

Engineering psychologists also serve as expert witnesses in court cases involving claims against manufacturers for personal injury or property loss due to product defects and manufacturers' negligence. They have been called upon to testify in product liability cases to explain human behavior and expectations, assess design defects, and evaluate the effectiveness of written warning labels and instructions.

Because the field of engineering psychology is a hybrid, it is not surprising that its practitioners have diverse backgrounds. The membership of the Human Factors and Ergonomics Society consists primarily of psychologists and engineers but also includes professionals from medicine, sociology, anthropology, computer science, and other behavioral and physical sciences. At present there are about twice as many psychologists as engineers in the field, and there has been a rapid growth in the number of masters-level psychologists undertaking careers in engineering psychology. The growth of the field in the past few decades has been dynamic, and its work extends to many types of organizations.

TIME-AND-MOTION STUDY:
A PRECURSOR TO HUMAN ENGINEERING

Time-and-motion study was an early attempt to redesign work tools and to reshape the way workers performed their jobs. It developed from the effort of three pioneers who tried to make work more efficient. The first systematic attempt to study the way work was performed began in 1898 when Frederick W. Taylor, the promoter of scientific management, undertook an investigation for Bethlehem Steel of the task of shoveling. Taylor found that workers were using shovels of many sizes and shapes. As a result, the loads being lifted by each man ranged from 3 1/2 pounds to 38 pounds. By experimenting with different loads, Taylor determined that the optimum shovel, the one with which workers were most efficient, held 21 1/2 pounds. Heavier or lighter loads resulted in a decrease in total daily output. Taylor introduced shovels of different sizes for handling different materials, for example, a small one for heavy iron ore and a larger one for ashes. These changes may sound trivial, but Taylor's work saved the company more than $78,000 a year, an enormous sum at that time. With the new shovels, 140 men could accomplish the same amount of work that previously required 500 men. By offering an incentive of higher pay for greater productivity, the company allowed workers to increase their wages by 60% (Taylor, 1911).

Taylor's work was the first empirical demonstration of the relationship between work tools and worker efficiency. The next pioneers in the field were Frank Gilbreth, an engineer, and Lillian Gilbreth, a psychologist, who did more than anyone else to promote time-and-motion study. Whereas Taylor had been concerned primarily with tool design and incentive wage systems, the Gilbreths were interested in the mechanics of job performance. Their goal was to eliminate all unnecessary motion (Gilbreth, 1911).

It began when Frank Gilbreth at age 17 was an apprentice bricklayer. On his first day at work, he noticed that the bricklayers made many unnecessary motions in their work. He thought he could redesign the job to make it faster and easier, and within a year he was the fastest bricklayer on the job. Once he persuaded his co-workers to try his methods, the entire crew was accomplishing far more work without becoming exhausted.

Gilbreth designed a scaffold that could be raised or lowered so that the worker would always be at a height convenient to the work. By analyzing the hand and arm movements involved in laying bricks and changing to the most efficient ones, he found that workers could lay 350 bricks an hour instead of 120. This increase in productivity was not brought about by forcing men to work faster but by reducing the number of motions needed for laying each brick from 18 to 4 1/2.

Frank and Lillian Gilbreth organized their household and their lives around the principles of time-and-motion economy. Every activity was scrutinized for wasted motion. For example, Gilbreth always buttoned his vest from the bottom up because it took 4 seconds less than buttoning it from the top down. He used two brushes, one in each hand, to lather his face for shaving, a saving of 17 seconds. He tried shaving with two razors simultaneously but lost more time bandaging cuts than he had saved in shaving. The efforts to schedule the activities of the 12 Gilbreth children were recounted in the popular book and movie, *Cheaper by the Dozen.*

Time-and-motion study
An early attempt to redesign work tools and to reshape the way workers performed routine and repetitive jobs.

Time-and-motion engineers (sometimes called efficiency experts) have applied the Gilbreths' technique to many types of jobs, with the goal of reducing the number of motions required. The now-familiar operating room procedure of having nurses place each tool in the surgeon's hand is an outgrowth of time-and-motion analysis. Previously, surgeons sought out tools themselves, a practice that greatly increased operating time.

The most significant results of time-and-motion analysis have been with routine and repetitive work. In a typical motion study the worker's movements are recorded on film or videotape and analyzed frame by frame with a view toward modifying or eliminating inefficient and wasteful motions. (The same technique is applied by sports psychologists and coaches to analyze the performance of athletes.)

From years of research, psychologists have developed guidelines for efficient work. Some rules for increasing the ease, speed, and accuracy of manual jobs include the following:

1. Minimize the distance workers must reach to get tools and supplies or to operate machines.
2. Both hands should begin and end their movement at the same time. Movements should be as symmetrical as possible; the right hand should reach to the right for one item as the left hand reaches to the left for another item.

NEWSBREAK #24

"World's Greatest Woman Engineer"

Lillian Moller thought she was so plain that no one would ever marry her. So she decided she would have a career—an unpopular notion for a 22-year-old woman in the year 1900. She graduated from the University of California at Berkeley that year and was the first woman ever to be chosen as the school's commencement speaker. She stayed on at Berkeley to study for her PhD in English literature with a minor in psychology. In 1904, her plans were upset when she met a handsome, charismatic, wealthy owner of a construction company.

Frank Gilbreth was 10 years older than Lillian. He lived in Boston, where Lillian and some friends had stopped on their way to Europe. When they returned, Frank was waiting for Lillian at the dock with flowers. Before long, he traveled to California to meet her parents and set the date for the wedding. Frank wanted a wife, children, and all the pleasures of domesticity, but he also wanted a partner in his work. At his urging, Lillian changed her major to psychology and enrolled in graduate school at Brown University. She started working alongside him at construction sites, climbing ladders and striding across steel girders high in the sky. A fearless and fast learner, Lillian was soon helping Frank with decisions that would make construction work more efficient. She encouraged Frank to give up the construction business and become a management consultant, so they could apply their new ideas about work performance and efficiency to a broad range of jobs.

But the times decreed that women didn't do such things. That was made clear to her in many ways. In 1911, for example, Lillian and Frank wrote a book entitled *Motion Study*. The publisher refused to list her as co-author, claiming that a woman's name would detract from the book's credibility. The same thing happened a year later with their next book. In 1914, Lillian completed her PhD in psychology, but when she tried to publish her dissertation in book form, the publisher would not let her use her first name, insisting that a book on the psychology of management, written by a woman, would never sell to hard-headed businessmen. Consequently, the title page listed the author as L. M. Gilbreth.

Twenty years later, with a thriving consulting business to run and 12 children to raise, Lillian Moller Gilbreth found herself a widow. She tried to carry on their work, but most of the business executives for whom she had done consulting work for years cut her off. They had been willing to tolerate her as a wife helping out her husband but wanted nothing to do with her on her own.

If she could no longer continue to apply time-and-motion study to the workplace, the business she and Frank had built up, she decided to teach others how to do it. She organized workshops on industrial management, which attracted managers from many countries. These workshops, and the quality of the trainees she turned out, enhanced her reputation so that, eventually, business and industrial organizations began to seek her advice.

Over the years, Lillian Gilbreth became immensely successful and influential. She was awarded several honorary degrees, received appointments to presidential commissions, and won accolades from the male-dominated engineering community. One business leader in 1952 called her "the world's greatest woman engineer." She and Frank earned an additional measure of fame when the movie (*Cheaper by the Dozen*) was made about how they reared their 12 children according to their theory of scientific management.

Lillian Gilbreth died in 1972, in her nineties, still working in the field of scientific management. She applied her ideas to problems of efficient work in the home as well as the factory. The next time you open your refrigerator, notice the shelves on the inside of the door. That was her idea. Does your trash can have a foot-pedal to open the lid? That's easier to use than having to bend down to lift the lid, isn't it? That was her idea, too. Although these may seem like trivial examples to us today, Lillian Gilbreth's contributions in applying the principles of time-and-motion economy were so extensive that they touched jobs in the home, in factories, and in offices, making work for everyone a little easier.

Source: Kelly, R. M., & Kelly, V. P. (1990). Lillian Moller Gilbreth (1878–1972). In A. N. O'Connell & N. F. Russo (Eds.), *Women in psychology: A bio-bibliographic sourcebook* (pp. 117–124). New York: Greenwood Press.

3. The hands should never be idle except during authorized rest breaks.
4. The hands should never do tasks that can be performed by other parts of the body, particularly legs and feet. A foot control can often be used, thus relieving the hands of one more operation.
5. Whenever possible, work materials should be held by a mechanical device, such as a vise, instead of being held by hand.
6. The work bench or table should be of sufficient height that the job can be performed when standing or when sitting on a high stool. Alternating positions relieves fatigue.

You might think that these guidelines for simplifying jobs would be received with enthusiasm. After all, the company reaps a greater output and employees' jobs are made easier. Although management has generally been pleased with the results of time-and-motion study, workers and labor unions have been suspicious, even hostile. They have argued that the only reason for time-and-motion study is to force employees to work faster. This would lead to lower pay and to dismissals because fewer workers would be required to maintain production levels. These concerns do have some validity. Other worker complaints are that job simplification leads to boredom, to a lack of challenge and responsibility, and to low motivation, which is manifested in lower productivity.

Many satires have been written about attempts to reduce wasted motion and impose efficiency. One suggests a time-and-motion analysis of a symphony orchestra performance:

> For considerable periods the four oboe players had nothing to do. The number should be reduced and the work spread more evenly over the whole of the concert. . . . All the twelve violins were playing identical notes; this seems unnecessary duplication. The staff of this section should be drastically cut. . . . There seems to be too much repetition of some musical passages. . . . No useful purpose is served by repeating on the horns a passage which has already been handled by the strings. It is estimated that if all redundant passages were eliminated the whole concert time of 2 hours could be reduced to 20 minutes ("How to be Efficient," 1955, pp. 454–455).

Time-and-motion analysis is most applicable today to routine tasks such as assembly-line jobs. When operations, equipment, and functions are more complex and the total relationship between person and machine must be considered, a more sophisticated approach is needed.

PERSON-MACHINE SYSTEMS

Person-machine system A system in which human and mechanical components operate together to accomplish a task.

A **person-machine system** is one in which both components work together to accomplish a task. Neither part is of value without the other. A person pushing a lawnmower is a person-machine system. A person driving a car or operating a word processor is a more complex person-machine system. At a more sophisticated level, the Concorde supersonic airliner and its crew of specialists, each responsible for a different operation, is a person-machine system. An air traffic control network includes a number of separate person-machine systems, each an integral part of the whole. If one part—mechanical or human—fails, all other parts of the system will be affected.

In all person-machine systems, the human operator receives input on the status of the machine from the displays. On the basis of this information, the operator regulates the equipment by initiating some controlling action (see Figure 13–1). Suppose you are driving a car on a highway at a constant speed. You receive input from the speedometer (a display), process this information, and decide that you are driving too fast. Through the control action of easing your foot off the accelerator, you cause the computer-aided fuel injection system to reduce the flow of gasoline to the engine, which slows the car's speed. This decrease in speed is displayed on the speedometer for your information, and so the process continues.

Drivers also receive information from the external environment, such as a sign noting a change in the speed limit or a slow car blocking your lane. You process this information and dictate a change in speed to the machine. Verification of the altered status of the machine—the new speed—is displayed on the speedometer. The principle is the same for even the most sophisticated person-machine systems. It is the total system that is the starting point for the engineering psychologist's job.

Person-machine systems vary in the extent to which the human operator is actively and continuously involved. In flying an airplane or controlling traffic at a busy airport, operators are necessary most of the time. Even when an airplane is on automatic pilot, the flight crew must be prepared to assume control in an

An airplane cockpit is a complex person-machine system. Displays present information on the machine's status. The person processes the information and initiates action by operating the appropriate controls.

FIGURE 13–1.   A person-machine system. (Adapted from "Human Factors in the Workplace" by W. C. Howell, 1991. In M. D. Dunnette and L. M. Hough (Eds.), *Handbook of Industrial and Organizational Psychology*, 2nd ed., vol. 2, p. 214. Palo Alto, CA: Consulting Psychologists Press.)

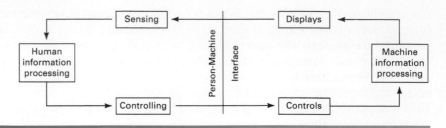

emergency. In other person-machine systems, humans interact less extensively. Many large-scale production processes, such as those in oil refineries, are highly automated. Some products and components can be assembled entirely by industrial robots. Although this automated equipment can operate itself, it cannot design, build, or maintain itself, or replace its own light bulb. Humans remain important components of such automated manufacturing systems even when they are not directly or continuously operating the equipment.

Automation has complicated the task of engineering psychologists. Employees who are required to monitor automated equipment find that job to be more fatiguing and boring than the job of actually running a machine. Engineering psychologists must design monitoring equipment to keep observers alert and vigilant so that they can detect errors and malfunctions and respond immediately and appropriately.

In general, the definition and requirements of person-machine systems are the same, regardless of the degree of involvement of the worker with the machine. No one has yet developed a machine that can design, build, and maintain other machines. Humans are still vital to the system.

Allocating Functions to Operators and Machines

The initial step in the design of a person-machine system involves making decisions about the division of labor between the human operator and the machine. To do that, each step or process in the functioning of the total system must be analyzed to determine its characteristics: the speed, accuracy, and frequency with which it is performed; and the stress under which it occurs. When this information is evaluated, the engineering psychologist can proceed to match the requirements of the system with the abilities of the person and of the machine. Each component—person and machine—has advantages and limitations.

Research by psychologists, physiologists, and physicians has revealed much information about human strengths and weaknesses, so they are aware of those functions for which humans are superior or inferior to machines (see, for example, Chapanis, 1965). In general, machines are superior to humans in performing the following functions:

1. Machines can detect stimuli such as radar wavelengths and ultraviolet light that are beyond human sensory capacities.
2. Machines can monitor reliably for lengthy periods as long as the stimulus in question is programmed or specified for the machine in advance.
3. Machines can make large numbers of rapid, accurate calculations.

4. Machines can store and retrieve huge amounts of information with a high level of accuracy.
5. Machines can apply greater physical force continuously and rapidly.
6. Machines can engage in repetitive activities with no performance deterioration as long as proper maintenance is applied.

Of course, machines are not perfect. They have several weaknesses and limitations. For example:

1. Machines are not very flexible. Even the most sophisticated computer can do only what it is programmed to do. When adaptability to meet changing circumstances is important, machines are at a disadvantage.
2. Machines cannot learn from errors or modify their behavior on the basis of past experience. Any change in operation must be built into the system or initiated by the human operator.
3. Machines cannot improvise. They are unable to reason or to examine unprogrammed alternatives.

It seems naive to talk, as some futurists do, about designing the human component out of the system. People can perform many vital functions that machines cannot. In other cases, people can perform functions at least as well as, and often cheaper than, machines. As long as machines lack flexibility and responsiveness, humans remain necessary to the operation of the system.

Some engineers believe that they should automate every possible function in a person-machine system, relegating the operator to a peripheral role. However, fully automated systems can fail, sometimes with disastrous results.

Consider modern mass transit systems. In some subway lines, drivers do not control the train's speed, nor do they bring it to a stop at station platforms. Those functions are computer controlled. In a study of the Metrorail system in Miami, Florida, trains failed to stop at stations 10% of the time, forcing the drivers to press an emergency button to stop the train quickly, usually overshooting the station platform (Howell, 1991). Without the driver to intercede, the train proceeded automatically to the next station, delivering its passengers to the wrong place.

Drivers in this system have been reduced to being monitors, acting only when the machine functions incorrectly or if the mechanism fails. They say they find it hard to remain alert when they have little to do but wait for something to malfunction. The job is boring, lacking in challenge and responsibility, and it rarely requires the drivers to use their skills. As the operators become more dependent on the computer-controlled equipment, they become less capable of making crucial decisions in emergencies. No matter how thoroughly they have been trained, if their job skills are rarely used, those skills will deteriorate.

WORKSPACE DESIGN

The harmful effects of poor workspace design can be seen in the U.S. Army's M-1 Abrams tank, which was built in the mid-1980s. The interior of a tank is the crew's workspace, and its design can influence job performance—in this case, the crew's fighting efficiency. The tank was designed without engineering psychology research and thus without regard for the human needs and characteristics of the crew. When it was tested, 27 of the 29 test drivers developed such severe neck and back pains that they required medical attention. Also, the drivers were unable to see the ground in front of the tank for a distance of 9 yards, making it difficult to avoid obstacles or cross trenches.

When the engine and turret blowers were operating, more than half the tank's gunners, loaders, and drivers reported that they could not hear one another well enough to communicate because the noise of the machinery was too loud. All crew members reported visibility problems at their work stations. When drivers and tank commanders rode with an open hatch, they found that the front fenders had been so poorly designed that they did not protect the crew from rocks, dirt, and mud churned up by the tank's treads. It was obvious that the designers of the M-1 tank had not considered the human factor.

In contrast, the cab of a locomotive built in Sweden was based on extensive human engineering research (Hedberg, 1987). Engineering psychologists collected data from 150 engine drivers about their complaints about neck, back, and shoulder pain experienced while working in the old locomotives. The psychologists found that only shorter drivers were reporting discomfort. Apparently, the seats and controls had been designed for taller drivers. Using this information, engineering psychologists and engineers designed the new cab to be comfortable and efficient for men and women drivers of various heights. They devised an adjustable seat and footrest so that drivers could operate the engine from standing or sitting positions and could change the height of the seat. The control panel was modified to place frequently used controls within easy reach and to make the speedometer display more visible (see Figure 13–2).

After a prototype locomotive was built, a representative sample of 50 drivers test-drove it and completed a questionnaire comparing their new and old workspaces. The majority of the drivers said they expected the redesigned cab to make their work safer, easier, and less fatiguing.

The effective design of the human operator's workspace—whether it be a bench for an electronic parts assembler, a display screen for a newspaper copywriter, or a locomotive cab for a driver—involves three established principles from time-and-motion study and engineering psychology research.

1. All materials, tools, and supplies needed by the workers should be placed in the order in which they are to be used so that the paths of the workers' movements will be continuous. The knowledge that each part or tool is always in the same place saves the time and annoyance of searching for it.

2. Tools should be pre-positioned so that they can be picked up ready for use. For example, for a job requiring the repeated use of a screwdriver, that tool can be suspended just above the work area on a coil spring. When it is needed, the worker can reach up without looking and pull it down ready for use.

3. All parts and tools should be within a comfortable reaching distance (approximately 28 inches). It is fatiguing for workers to change positions frequently to reach beyond the normal working area.

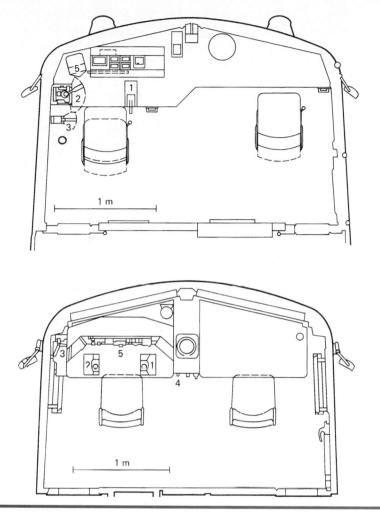

FIGURE 13–2.   Old (top) and redesigned (bottom) locomotive cabs.
(From "The Evaluation of the Driver's
Cab in the Rc5 Engine"
by G. Hedberg, 1987, *Applied Ergonomics, 18*(1), pp. 36, 37.)

As an example of good workspace design, see Figure 13–3, which illustrates
the workstation of a radar operator or power plant monitor. Typically, the
worker is seated before a panel or console of lights, dials, and switches. The job
involves monitoring and controlling the operation of complex equipment. The
monitoring console is designed so that operators can see and reach everything
necessary to successful job performance without leaving their chair or reaching
excessively beyond normal seated posture.

Sometimes it is necessary to change normal workspace design to accommodate workers' special needs. Consider the case of pregnant women employees
working at standup desks or worktables. At the latter stages of pregnancy, the
enlarged abdomen can force these women to stand farther away from the table
or to twist sideways, putting unusual pressure on the muscles of the back. A survey of 875 pregnant women workers in France revealed that more than half
were required to perform their jobs often or always in a standing position. A
study of 27 pregnant women workers in the Netherlands assigned to a manual
assembly-line task showed that women in the late months of pregnancy pre-

11 in.
Will Allow the Operator
to Reach the Corners

18 in.

FIGURE 13–3. Monitoring console work arrangement. (From *Human Engineering Guide for Equipment Designers* (p. 1:37) by W. Woodson, 1954, Berkeley, CA: University of California Press. Copyright © 1954 & 1964 by The Regents of the University of California. Reprinted by permission of the University of California Press.)

ferred a significantly lower table height for work in a standing position (Paul, Frings-Dresen, Sallé, & Rozendal, 1995). The psychologists who conducted the Netherlands study recommended that heights of all working surfaces be fully adjustable, not only to accommodate conditions such as pregnancy or overweight, but also to suit employees of different heights.

Another important consideration in workspace design is the size and shape of individual hand tools that must be used repeatedly. Applying engineering psychology principles can improve even basic tools such as hammers to make them easier, safer, and less tiring to use. Hand tools should be designed so that workers can use them without bending their wrists; hands are less vulnerable to injury when the wrists are kept straight. Research comparing the standard straight hammer with hammers that have handles angled at 20 degrees and 40 degrees found that for 3-minute sessions of continuous hammering the angled hammers decreased the incidence of wrist injuries, reduced muscle fatigue, and lessened workers' subjective judgments of discomfort (Schoenmarklin & Marras, 1989a, 1989b). Engineering psychology principles applicable to the design of pliers are shown in Figure 13–4.

The proper design of hand tools affects productivity, satisfaction, and physical health. The continuous use of tools that require bending the wrist while working can lead to nerve injuries, such as carpal tunnel syndrome, caused by the repetitive motion. Carpal tunnel syndrome can be painful and debilitating. It is also prevalent among people who spend a great deal of time playing the piano, knitting, or playing video games, a finding that may influence your choice of hobbies.

Human anthropometry A branch of engineering psychology concerned with the measurement of the physical structure of the body.

A branch of engineering psychology called **human anthropometry** is concerned with the measurement of the physical structure of the human body. Complete sets of body measurements have been compiled from a large, representative sample of the population in the performance of various activities. Specific data include height (standing and sitting), shoulder breadth, back height, chest depth, foot and hand length, knee angle, and so on (see Figure 13–5). These measurements are applied to the design of work areas to determine, for example, normal

Avoid short tool handles that press into the palm of the hand. The palm is very soft and easily damaged.

Avoid narrow tool handles that concentrate large forces onto small areas of the hand.

Tools and jobs should be designed so that they can be performed with straight wrists. Hands are stronger and less vulnerable to injury when the wrists are kept straight.

FIGURE 13–4. Application of human factors principles to the design of pliers. (From "Ergonomics," 1986, *Personnel Journal, 65*(6), p. 99.)

and maximum reaching distances, tool and desk height and arrangement, size and shape of seats, and viewing angles for video display terminals.

For the millions of people who work at a desk or work bench, the seats we use, if improperly designed, can cause back and neck pain and lead to fatigue, which, in turn, reduces productive efficiency. Research has been conducted on every conceivable aspect of the design of workplace seating, and guidelines are available for various kinds of jobs.

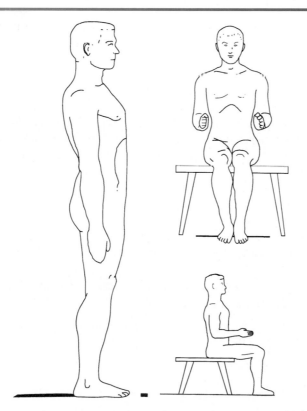

FIGURE 13–5. Typical postures used in gathering body measurements (anthropometric data). (From "Engineering Anthropometry" by K. H. E. Kroemer, 1987. In G. Salvendy (Ed.), *Handbook of Human Factors,* p. 160. New York: Wiley.)

We don't buy just any seats. We design them.

GM begins with detailed studies of the human body. Biomedical research. The kind of comprehensive investigation of anatomy da Vinci undertook in the 1500s.

As a leader in the field of Human Factors Engineering, we design interiors scientifically to minimize the possible distractions from your driving.

It may take us two years and countless clay models to arrive at a more comfortable, durable seat for new GM cars and trucks. But we think it's worth it.

And we believe old Leonardo would have thought so, too.

We believe in taking the extra time, giving the extra effort and paying attention to every detail. That's what it takes to provide the quality that leads more people to buy GM cars and trucks than any other kind. And why GM owners are the most loyal on the road.

That's the GM commitment to excellence.

Engineering psychologists help design components for various workspaces. (Reproduced by permission of General Motors Corporation.)

NEWSBREAK #25

Sitting Down On the Job
Is Easy, But Is It Safe?

Your office chair may be hazardous to your health. It can cause long-term back pain or damage the disks in your spinal column. It doesn't have to be that way. Not if you follow the advice of Richard Holbrook, an industrial designer in Pasadena, California, whose new office chair won the 1996 American Product Excellence Award. Holbrook believes chairs should be designed ergonomically, by having your work environment adapt to your personal characteristics. "What other product do you have such an intimate relationship with?" Holbrook asked. "A good chair can either hug you or beat you up." He offers the following tips on how to avoid being mugged by your chair.

- A chair should meet the contours and size of your body, so the torso rests on the proper muscles to support your weight.
- A chair should support your lumbar vertebrae (the lower part of the back and spine), restoring the natural S-shaped curvature of the spine and relieving pressure on the disks.
- Cushions should be firm but not hard. If they're too soft, you sink down, putting pressure on the hip joints. The contours should follow your body's, offering support to your upper back.
- Your feet should be flat on the floor when you are sitting naturally.
- Seat depth is important, particularly for short people. If the seat is too deep, it can cause circulation problems.

Check out your chair. It's a basic part of your work or study environment. Is it helping you or making your task harder?

Source: Posturing: Sitting pretty. *New York Times Magazine,* March 24, 1996, p. 23.

DISPLAYS: PRESENTING INFORMATION

In person-machine systems, operators receive inputs from the machine through the physical senses. For example, in driving a car you receive information on the operating status of the machine from visual displays (speedometer, temperature indicator, gas gauge) and from auditory displays (the chime alerting you to fasten the seat belt or remove the ignition key). More informally, you receive inputs tactually, such as when a balky engine causes the car to vibrate.

One of the earliest decisions to be made about the presentation of information in the design of a person-machine system is to select the most effective means of communication. Visual presentation of information, the mode most frequently used, is more appropriate in the following instances:

- The message is long, difficult, and abstract.
- The environment is too noisy for auditory messages.
- The auditory channels of communication are overloaded.
- The message consists of many different kinds of information that must be presented simultaneously.

The auditory presentation of information is more effective in the following instances:

- The information is short, simple, and straightforward.
- The message is urgent; auditory signals typically attract attention more readily than visual ones.
- The environment is too dark or otherwise does not allow for visual communication.
- The operator's job requires movement to different locations. The ears can receive messages from all directions, whereas the eyes must be focused on the display to receive messages.

Visual Displays

A common error made in the visual presentation of information is to provide more input than the operator needs to run the system. For example, most drivers do not need a tachometer to indicate engine rpm. Although this may not be a major concern in a passenger car, in an airplane, where large amounts of vital information must be displayed, any useless input adds to the display problem and is potentially confusing. The engineering psychologist must ask: Is this information necessary to the operation of the system? If the system can function without it, then that is one less item with which to confront the busy human operator. If the information is vital to the operation of the equipment, what is the most effective way to display it?

Three types of visual displays commonly used in person-machine systems are quantitative, qualitative, and check reading.

Quantitative visual displays Displays that present a precise numerical value, such as speed, altitude, or temperature.

Quantitative Displays. **Quantitative displays** present a precise numerical value. In situations dealing with speed, altitude, or temperature, for example, the operator must know the precise numerical value of a condition of the system. A pilot must know if the altitude is 10,500 feet, as dictated by the flight plan. An approximate indication of altitude instead of an exact one could lead the plane into the path of another aircraft or into a mountain in fog.

Five displays for presenting quantitative information and their relative reading accuracy are shown in Figure 13–6. You can see that the open-window display was read with the fewest errors. The vertical display was misread more than one third of the time. These results, from a now-classic research study, were obtained from a laboratory experiment on instrument dial shapes in which subjects were required to read displays in a brief fixed time period (Sleight, 1948).

A more recently developed quantitative display even easier to read than the open-window type is the digital display, or counter, in which actual numbers are shown. The familiar digital clock or wristwatch is an example of this type of display. Digital displays are common in consumer electronic products such as videocassette players and microwave ovens.

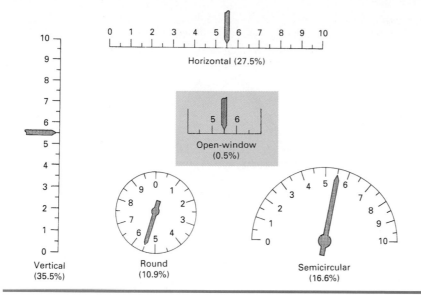

FIGURE 13–6. Percentage of errors in reading five types of quantitative display (From "The Effect of Instrument Dial Shape on Legibility" by R. Sleight, 1948, *Journal of Applied Psychology, 32,* p. 177. Copyright 1948 by the American Psychological Association. Reprinted by permission.)

Although digital displays can be read faster and with fewer errors than any other type of displays, they cannot be used in all situations. If the information being presented changes rapidly or continuously, a set of numbers may not remain in place long enough to be read and processed by the human operator. Digital displays are also unsuitable when it is important to know the direction or the rate of change—for example, whether temperature is rising or falling, or whether it is rising rapidly or slowly.

Visual displays in an air traffic control tower present information in words, symbols, and graphics.

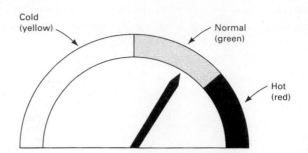

FIGURE 13–7.   A qualitative visual display. (Adapted from *Human Factors in Engineering and Design* (p. 76) by E. J. McCormick, 1976, New York: McGraw-Hill.)

Qualitative visual displays
Displays that do not present a precise numerical value; frequently used to show whether components, such as engine temperature, are in the safe or unsafe range.

Qualitative Displays.   **Qualitative displays** can be used when a precise numerical reading is not necessary. For example, most drivers do not need to know the precise temperature of their car's engine. All most of us want to know is whether the temperature is in the safe operating range. With many components of person-machine systems, the operator needs to know only whether the system is functioning within the proper range and whether the values are increasing or decreasing over time.

A typical qualitative display is shown in Figure 13–7. The operating ranges are often color coded with the dangerous, or hot, portion in red and the safe portion in green. Such a display permits quick, accurate verification of the system's status and reduces the amount of technical information the operator must absorb.

When several qualitative displays must be checked frequently, consistent patterning aids accurate reading (see Figure 13–8). Placing the dials so that they always face the same way in the normal operating range makes it easier to scan the display and detect an abnormal reading. Unpatterned displays force the operator to read each dial separately. Patterned displays are used in aircraft cockpits, power plant control rooms, and automated manufacturing plants.

Check reading visual displays   Displays that tell the operator in a person-machine system whether the system is on or off, safe or unsafe, or operating normally or abnormally.

Check Reading Displays.   **Check reading visual displays** are the simplest kind of visual display. They tell the operator whether the system is on or off, safe or unsafe, or operating normally or abnormally. For example, with the engine temperature gauge in your car, a warning light is sufficient to indicate whether

FIGURE 13–8.   Patterned and unpatterned dial displays. (From *Applied Experimental Psychology* (p. 151) by A. Chapanis, W. Garner, and C. Morgan, 1949, New York: Wiley. Reprinted by permission.)

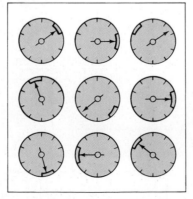

Unpatterned Dial Display

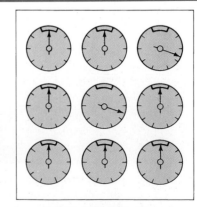

Patterned Dial Display

you can continue to drive safely or should stop because the engine is in danger of overheating. This kind of display is sometimes referred to as "go/no go." Either the system is in a condition to operate (to go) or it is not.

The most common check reading display is the warning light. When the light is not illuminated, the system is functioning satisfactorily. When the light comes on, it indicates a system malfunction serious enough to require the operator to take immediate corrective action.

Among the considerations in the design of warning lights is level of brightness. On a display panel that contains several sources of light, it is vital that a warning light be at least twice as bright as the background to get the operator's attention. Location of warning lights is also important. They should be centrally located within the operator's field of vision. Warning lights too far to one side of a console may not be noticed when the worker is attending to more centrally located displays and controls. Also, flashing lights attract attention more quickly than continuous warning lights.

Visual displays today include more than lights, dials, and gauges. Much information is displayed on video screens and in words, symbols, and graphics. The electronic flight information system used in aircraft and in air traffic control radar screens combines lines, numbers, and pictorial symbols to present precise information about location. Adding color to cockpit displays has been shown to reduce errors and response times for aircraft crew members in reading and processing information (Macdonald & Cole, 1988).

The U.S. Air Force and U.S. Navy use a different type of visual display in some of their jet fighters. These aircraft travel at speeds in excess of 800 miles an hour. Saving even a fraction of a second in the movement of a pilot's eyes can be crucial to a mission's success. At these speeds, it is difficult for pilots to watch a target through the windscreen and simultaneously scan the instrument panel for information. The new approach enables pilots to project the required data—such as fuel level or target display—directly onto the windscreen so that they do not have to shift their eyes from place to place. This is sometimes referred to as a **heads-up display** because it allows pilots to keep their head up while looking through the windscreen instead of glancing down to scan instruments.

Heads-up displays Visual displays used in aircraft that project data directly onto the windscreen so that pilots do not have to shift their vision to a control panel.

In flight simulators used to train military pilots in low-level flight, the external environment is presented in computer-generated lines and symbols depicting both the terrain and objects such as towers, trees, and buildings on the terrain. Research conducted by human factors psychologists for the U.S. Air Force showed that the speed and accuracy of detecting how high the trainee is flying above the terrain in this virtual environment varies with the density of objects presented in the scenes on the screen. Detection improved considerably with increases in the number or density of the objects. Adding detail to objects to make them appear more lifelike produced no consistent effect on performance (Kleiss & Hubbard, 1993).

Not all visual displays are so high-tech or intended for such limited use. For example, the common push/pull door signs are used every day by millions of people entering and exiting stores, factories, and office buildings. Some doors need to be pushed, others pulled. To find out how best to display this basic information visually, so that users would follow directions accurately, a study was conducted using 60 subjects under laboratory conditions and 1,100 subjects in the real world. Eleven different kinds of signs were tested. The most effective signs (those most quickly identified or eliciting the greatest compliance) combined a drawing of a hand with an arrow and the word *push* or *pull* displayed horizontally (see Figure 13–9) (Kline & Beitel, 1994). Thus, even a simple visual display can be improved through human factors research.

Auditory Displays

Auditory displays Alarms or warning signals in person-machine systems; auditory displays can be more compelling than visual displays.

An **auditory display** can be more compelling than a visual display for three reasons: (1) our ears are always open, but our eyes are not; (2) we can receive auditory information from all directions; and (3) our visual sense is often taxed to capacity. Table 13–1 presents the major types of auditory alarms.

An evaluation by engineering psychologists of the auditory warning signals used in U.S. Air Force planes revealed several potential problems from the standpoint of the human operator (Doll & Folds, 1986). First, auditory warning signals were found to be poorly standardized and inconsistent among aircraft, even among planes with similar combat roles. This violates a basic principle of engineering psychology: that displays and controls among similar types of machines be consistent.

Second, too many auditory warning signals were being used. For example, the F-15 fighter plane had 11 auditory signals (tones at various frequencies and with different numbers of repetitions), each signifying a separate condition—such as external threat, low altitude, or landing gear engaged. During combat missions, it would be easy for the pilot to confuse these signals and initiate the wrong control action. Many of the auditory signals sounded so similar that they would lead to confusion even under non-combat conditions.

FIGURE 13–9. Most effective and least effective door pull signs. (Adapted from T. J. B. Kline & G. A. Beitel, "Assessment of push/pull door signs: A laboratory and a field study." *Human Factors*, 1994, *36*, 688.)

Most effective (word plus symbol)

Least effective (symbol only)

TABLE 13–1   Characteristics of Auditory Alarms

Alarm	Intensity	Attention-Getting Ability
Foghorn	Very high	Good
Horn	High	Good
Whistle	High	Good, if intermittent
Siren	High	Very good, if pitch rises and falls
Bell	Medium	Good
Buzzer	Low to medium	Good
Human voice	Low to medium	Fair

Note. Adapted from "Auditory and Other Sensory Forms of Information Presentation" by B. H. Deatherage, 1972, *Human Engineering Guide to Equipment Design*, Washington, DC: U.S. Government Printing Office.

Third, the auditory warning signals did not provide any indication of the urgency of the situation. If two signals were activated close in time, the pilot would not necessarily know quickly enough which problem was the more important.

Sometimes, even the most carefully designed person-machine system does not work as intended because the human operator violates the conditions under which the system is supposed to function. On the night of May 17, 1987, aboard the navy frigate *USS Stark* on duty in the Persian Gulf, a radar operator was monitoring a complex system that was tracking all nearby radar signals. The system had visual and auditory warning devices to alert the operator if hostile radar was detected. The system designers believed that with both visual and auditory displays, there was no way the operator could miss a warning. If the operator was looking away from the visual display screen, the auditory signal—a rapid beeping—would surely be noticed.

Yet, when hostile radar was detected that night and the visual warning signal flashed on the screen, the operator was looking away and the auditory signal failed to sound. That operator, or an operator from an earlier shift, had disconnected the auditory alarm because he found it to be annoying. Because the ship was in enemy territory, the alarm was beeping frequently, and the operator had decided that it was bothersome.

With the auditory alarm disabled and the visual warning signal unseen, a jet fighter plane from Iraq fired an Exocet missile at the *Stark*, killing 37 American sailors. In this case the equipment portion of the person-machine system functioned satisfactorily, but the human operator did not.

Auditory signals may be used to transmit complex information. One example is the shipboard operation of sonar for detecting underwater objects. A high-frequency sound is transmitted from beneath the ship through the water. When it strikes a large enough object, the signal is reflected back to the ship and reproduced as the familiar pinging sound heard in old war movies. The job of interpreting the message or information that the sound conveys can be difficult. Extensive training is required to be able to discriminate among the sound's various qualities. With sonar, if the detected object is moving away from the ship, the reflected sound is of a lower frequency than is the transmitted sound. An object moving toward the ship provides a higher frequency of returning sound.

Humans can receive and interpret a variety of information through the auditory sense. We are capable of responding to formal signaling procedures (warning horns, whistles, and buzzers) and to informal cues (the misfire of a car engine, the wail of a mis-wound audiotape, or the beep of the computer that has lost your term paper).

CONTROLS: INITIATING ACTION

In person-machine systems, once human operators receive input through the displays and mentally process that information, they must communicate some control action to the machine. They transmit their control decisions through such devices as switches, pushbuttons, levers, cranks, steering wheels, mouses, trackballs, and foot pedals. Human factors decisions must be made about the choice, location, and shape of the controls. These decisions are based on the task's requirements; different tasks dictate different types of controls.

Engineering psychologists analyze the nature of the task to determine whether it involves, for example, turning on a light or activating some other system component. Does the task involve a fine adjustment, such as selecting one radio frequency from the spectrum of frequencies? Does it require frequent and rapid readjustment of a control, or is a single setting sufficient? How much force must the operator exert to accomplish the job? If the control must be activated in cold temperatures, will the wearing of gloves interfere with proper operation? If the control must be activated in conditions of low illumination, can it be easily identified by shape alone?

Guidelines for Controls.   After system designers have answered these questions, they select the best control for the task. Engineering psychology research offers general guidelines. For a task that requires two discrete settings of a control, such as "on" and "off," a hand or foot pushbutton is a suitable on/off switch. For four or more discrete settings, a group of finger pushbuttons or a rotary selector switch is preferred. For continuous settings, knobs or cranks are the best choice. For selecting elements on a computer display, devices such as a mouse, light pen, or touch pad can be used. A selection of controls and the actions for which they are appropriate are shown in Figure 13–10. In addition, controls should satisfy the following two criteria:

1. *Control and body matching.* Although, in theory, some controls could be activated with the head or the elbow, most of them use hands and feet. It is important that no one limb be given too many tasks to perform. The hands are capable of greater precision in operating controls, and the feet are capable of exerting greater force.
2. *Control-task compatibility.* A control action should imitate the movements it produces. For example, pulling an airplane's control column to the right pulls the plane to the right; the control movement and the machine's response are parallel. To lower aircraft flaps or landing gear, the control should move downward. Typically, we turn a control knob to the right (clockwise) to turn a machine on. Most people would have difficulty adjusting to a knob that turned to the left to activate a machine.

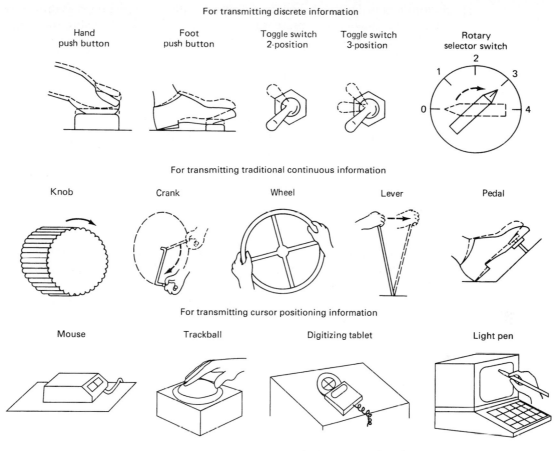

FIGURE 13-10. Control devices and the type of information they best transmit. (From M. S. Sanders & E. J. McCormick, *Human factors in engineering and design*, 6th ed., p. 261. New York: McGraw-Hill, 1987. Copyright 1987, McGraw-Hill Book Co. Used with permission.)

Combining Related Controls. Wherever possible, it is more efficient to combine controls that perform similar or related operations. For example, simple radios have three control functions—on/off, volume, and station selection—yet there are only two controls. The on/off and volume controls, which perform related functions, are combined to reduce the number of separate actions required of the human operator and to save space on the control panel.

Identification of Controls. Controls must be clearly marked or coded to assure their correct and rapid identification. Automobile manufacturers code instrument panels by using pictorial symbols to represent control functions (for example, a miniature wiper blade identifies the windshield wiper switch). On a crowded instrument panel, easily identifiable controls can minimize errors caused by activating the wrong control.

Another useful method of control identification is **shape coding.** Each knob on a console or control panel can be a recognizably different shape. Shape

Shape coding Designing knobs for control panels in recognizably different shapes so that they can be identified by touch alone.

coding allows for rapid visual identification of the correct control and permits identification by touch in low-lighting conditions or when the eyes must focus elsewhere. Sometimes the control's shape symbolizes its function. Engineering psychologists assisted U.S. Air Force engineers in shape coding aircraft control knobs. The landing flap control looks like a landing flap, and the landing gear control looks like a tire. Each control is unique in touch and appearance, and the control functions can be learned quickly. Standardizing these controls on all aircraft has reduced the opportunity for pilot error.

Placement of Controls.   Once the kind and shape of the controls have been selected, engineering psychologists determine their placement on the control panel. They also consider the control's relationship to an informational display. A primary requisite for control location is consistency or uniformity of placement. For example, we expect the gas pedal to be located to the right of the brake pedal on automobiles and the Enter key to be on the right side of the keyboard. The greater the standardization of control arrangement, the easier and safer it is for operators to work with different models of the same system. This sounds like common sense, but it took many years before engineering psychology research was accepted and before aircraft instrument panels achieved standardization. This basic principle is still being ignored in the design of many consumer products.

Consider the kitchen range. Typically, there are four burners on top and four knobs on a panel to control the burners. However, there is little consistency in the relationship between control knobs and burners. A survey of 49 electric and gas ranges revealed six knob-burner operating linkages. Although this does not create as serious a problem as lack of standardization in an aircraft cockpit, it can lead to burns and other accidents. With a gas range, we receive immediate feedback when we turn a knob to activate a burner, but with an electric range, we could touch a burner, thinking it was cold, to find out it had been turned on.

In the global marketplace, where a product manufactured in one country may be sold in many others, human engineers must be aware of cultural differences that may influence the product's use, such as the linkage between displays and controls. For example, subjects in Taiwan preferred a different burner/control linkage when operating a four-burner stove than subjects in the United States. They chose different knobs than the American subjects to control the same burners. The researchers suggested that this finding reflected the Taiwanese practice of reading characters vertically and from right to left, whereas English-speaking people read horizontally and from left to right. Thus, the so-called natural approach to the use of these controls differed for subjects in the two cultures (Hsu & Peng, 1993).

Controls that are associated with emergency functions must be placed in the normal line of sight where they can be distinguished from other controls. The operator should be able to reach emergency controls quickly. The controls should be protected with a cover or shield from accidental operation.

When displays are associated functionally with controls—such as a dial that must be set by turning a knob—they should be placed as close together as possible. It is desirable to group related displays and controls according to function. For example, in an aircraft cockpit displays and controls involving engine performance are grouped. When the order of operation is consistent, displays and controls can be grouped sequentially.

Design of Controls for Persons with Disabilities.   Human engineers must also consider whether the controls on consumer products can be operated easily and efficiently by persons who have physical limitations. Just as visual displays have been altered to accommodate visually impaired people (by presenting information in braille or in auditory formats, for example), so controls can be modified for use by people who are deficient in strength or in the ability to make precise muscle movements.

To determine the difficulty of operating the controls found on ordinary consumer products, 34 adults in the Netherlands were videotaped in their homes. Some 109 control operations were studied. The subjects were afflicted with arthritis or a muscular disease, such as muscular dystrophy, and all had difficulty manipulating objects with both hands. They attempted to operate washing machines, radios, stoves, alarm clocks, watches, refrigerators, coffee grinders, telephones, and kitchen and bathroom faucets. The primary difficulty detected was the amount of force required to push, pull, turn, or otherwise manipulate the controls. For persons with arthritis, the exertion of force was accompanied by pain.

The researcher offered several control design recommendations to make consumer products easier to use by persons with physical disabilities (Kanis, 1993):

- Controls should operate with the least amount of force possible.
- A physically impaired person should not have to perform simultaneous operations, such as pushing and turning at the same time (the kind of manipulation required to open safety caps on pill bottles).
- Pushing a control is better than having to turn or rotate a control; the latter operation requires manipulations with the fingers whereas pushing can be done with the whole hand.
- A control should not have to be held down for any length of time.
- If a control has to be gripped, it should be possible to do so with the whole hand or with both hands rather than with the fingers.
- There should be no obstructions that could interfere with reaching for and operating a control.

THE IMPACT OF COMPUTERS

Millions of employees use computer terminals on the job. Predictions call for computers in the workplace to soon be as common as telephones. When the human factors aspects of the design of computer terminals and computer furniture are ignored, the result is physical strain and discomfort. Concern about the effects of prolonged computer use on health began in the 1970s when two employees of the *New York Times* reportedly developed cataracts, which they attributed to working at video display terminals. Many computer users have since complained of blurred vision, eyestrain, and changes in color perception.

The organization Nine to Five, the National Association of Working Women, established a telephone hotline to take complaints from computer users. In a 2-month period, it received more than 3,000 calls, 17% of which concerned eye problems. However, the National Academy of Sciences concluded that there was no scientific evidence that computers caused visual damage. A study of computer users and non-users performing similar tasks found no differences between the two groups in visual complaints (Howarth & Istance, 1986).

Based on these and similar findings, engineering psychologists have concluded that most employee complaints about visual disturbances result not from the terminals but from equipment components and from the design of the work station. Equipment factors identified as potential hazards include the color of the phosphor in the cathode ray tube, the size of the screen, the degree of flicker of the characters on the screen, and the rate at which characters are generated.

In addition, level of illumination and glare in the workplace can be sources of eyestrain. Antiglare coatings and shields can be applied to reduce the problems. The overall lighting of the work area can be reduced and walls can be painted in darker colors. Fluorescent overhead lights can be replaced by indirect lighting. All these changes can enhance visual comfort for computer users.

There is evidence that people read more slowly from computer screens than from paper. Research has not identified specific factors in the display or the user—such as length of time spent at the terminal—but psychologists suggest that slower reading speed may be related to the quality of the image on the screen (size, type style, clarity, and contrast with background). Other complaints from computer users are fatigue and pain in wrists, hands, shoulders, neck, and back.

These complaints have been related to a lack of attention to human engineering concerns. For example, desks and chairs used with computer equipment are often poorly designed for jobs that involve sitting for long periods. Engineering psychologists have found that the best chair is an adjustable one, enabling computer operators to adapt it to their height, weight, and posture. Periodically changing position can reduce fatigue, and this is easier to do with an adjustable chair. Research showed that chairs designed for computer operators in the United States and in European countries were unsuitable for employees in Singapore. Asian workers were, on average, shorter in height and had shorter elbow-to-fingertip measurements. Also, they preferred a different seated posture (Ong, Koh, Phoon, & Low, 1988).

Separating the keyboard from the display screen has been found to increase user comfort. Desks with split and adjustable tops hold components at different heights. If the keyboard angle can be adjusted to individual needs, fatigue and back pain can be reduced (see Figure 13–11). Engineering psychology research has determined that the comfort range for keyboard operation is an angle of 7 to 20 degrees, which minimizes bending the wrists.

THE IMPACT OF INDUSTRIAL ROBOTS

Robots Computer-controlled mechanical manipulator arms that can be programmed to move parts, operate tools, and perform multiple routines simultaneously.

The use of **robots** to perform industrial jobs formerly done by humans has caused significant alterations in the work environment for many manufacturing jobs. Whereas computers affect jobs at all organizational levels from assembly line to corporate office, robots are changing the nature of blue-collar jobs. Workers most affected to date are mechanics, assemblers, welders, painters, assembly-line workers, and other semiskilled and unskilled industrial employees. Engineering psychologists estimate that within a decade, as many as 4 million factory jobs will be performed by robots.

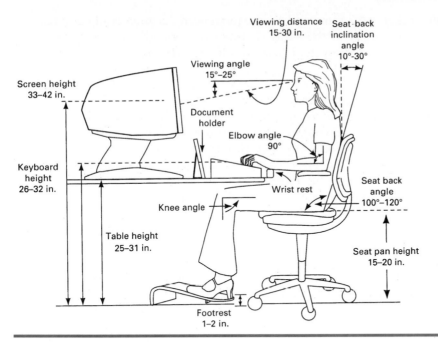

FIGURE 13–11. Guidelines for the design of computer work stations. (Adapted from M. S. Sanders & E. J. McCormick, *Human factors in engineering and design*, 6th ed., p. 358. New York: McGraw-Hill, 1987. Copyright 1987, McGraw-Hill Book Co. Used with permission.)

One fourth of the robots in U.S. companies are used in the automobile industry for welding and painting car bodies. The second largest use is in the manufacture of consumer appliances such as refrigerators and dishwashers. Robots are valuable in jobs that involve exposure to hazardous chemicals, such as spray painting epoxies on booster rockets.

Robots consistently perform better than humans in routine, repetitive work to produce more products of higher quality in a shorter time. For example, in one locomotive plant a team of eight unskilled workers and their robots can produce a locomotive frame in 1 day. Previously, it took 68 skilled machinists 16 days to produce a locomotive frame.

Robots work under difficult conditions, including extremes of noise and temperature, without any deterioration in performance. They are cheaper than human labor at an average cost of $5 an hour, compared to an average cost of $15 an hour per employee. Robots operate around the clock without fatigue or errors. They require no fringe benefits or vacations and have never been known to file a grievance or go on strike.

Aside from freeing employees from dangerous and uncomfortable work environments, most of the advantages of industrial robots accrue to management. Workers fear losing their jobs and being replaced by the machines, and they are concerned about having to match their work habits to the robot's pace.

Consider the situation at a General Motors automobile assembly plant in New Jersey. In modernizing the production facility, management installed more than 200 industrial robots for welding, painting, and sealing windows. The number of production workers was reduced by 26% and the number of first-line supervisors by 42%. However, an increase of 81% in the number of skilled electricians, machinists, and carpenters was required to maintain the new robots. Interviews with these skilled workers revealed that they experienced greater challenge and responsibility and more opportunities to upgrade their skills. The production workers who remained on the job reported a downgrading of responsibility and a reduction in the skills required to perform their jobs. They expressed the belief that they had become subordinate to the new equipment (Milkman & Pullman, 1991).

Thus, when robots are introduced into the workplace, the nature of the employees' jobs necessarily changes. In a robotized plant, it is also likely that employees will be separated by greater physical distances. This separation reduces their opportunity for social contact and group cohesiveness because more of the workday is spent alone. Some workers feel so threatened that they have engaged in sabotage. In a Russian industrial plant, high metal barricades had to be erected around the robots to protect them from angry workers.

At first glance it may appear that industrial robots are solely machines, but they are in fact person-machine systems. Once designed, built, programmed, and maintained, robots work with little human contact or intervention. But first, people are necessary to the system to design, manufacture, program, and maintain the machines.

Engineering psychologists are involved in the design of hardware and software for industrial robots. Hardware includes control panels (knobs, dials, warning signals), workspace features, operator seating, illumination, and other physical attributes of the person-machine system. Software aspects include computer

At this Nissan factory, most welding and car body assembly tasks are performed by industrial robots.

programs, computer language, and the means of presenting information on the display screen.

A critical issue for engineering psychologists is the division of labor—the allocation of functions—between industrial robots and human operators. Factors affecting this decision include the cost of developing the robot, the complexity of the task, safety concerns, space limitations, and the degree of accuracy required.

The growing use of industrial robots presents continuing challenges for engineering psychologists. Robots perform detailed and skilled factory jobs such as assembling computer components and undertaking maintenance operations in nuclear power plants. They are moving out of the factory and into service industries, operating in some plants and offices as tireless, vigilant security guards to patrol buildings at night and summon human guards when they sense intruders. Robot janitors are being developed to clean office buildings, programmed (we hope) to avoid bumping into the robot security guards. Fast-food chains are experimenting with robot-operated restaurants. A robot has already been developed to make pizza. Activated by voice commands and programmed to recognize spoken words such as "cheese" and "pepperoni," the machine was created to assist physically disabled workers operating franchise pizza restaurants. And a machine called McRobot has been developed to flip hamburgers.

In the years to come, I/O psychologists will confront problems of morale, job satisfaction, and retraining for the many employees forced to adapt to the robots in their workplace.

Physical Discomfort Among Computer Operators

Millions of people work at computer terminals. For many of them, the work leads to physical discomfort, eyestrain, and stress. The incidence of repetitive motion injuries (such as carpal tunnel syndrome) is increasing as is the number of complaints about visual disturbances and pain in shoulders, neck, and back. Most of these difficulties are related not to computer hardware but to the lack of attention to human engineering concerns in designing the work station.

How do workers' physical needs in the workplace relate to later physical complaints? To answer that question, human engineering psychologists from the University of Wisconsin and the National Institute for Occupational Safety and Health studied 905 data-entry video display terminal (VDT) operators employed by state government agencies. Some 90% of the subjects were women; all had been on the job at least 3 months.

The employees' job was to enter information from tax forms and traffic citations. The keyboards were located directly in front of the workers. The documents from which they obtained their data were placed either to the left of the keyboard or between the keyboard and the visual display. Workers manipulated the documents with the left hand and performed the keyboard entry task with the right hand.

Questionnaires asked the workers for information on age, height, weight, use of corrective lenses, weekly hours of VDT use, and job tenure. The questionnaires contained a body pictograph—a simple sketch of the human body divided by dotted lines into areas such as neck, upper back, shoulder, upper arm, forearm, wrist, hand, and so on. Subjects were asked to indicate on a scale of 0 (never) to 3 (almost constantly) the frequency of musculoskeletal discomfort (pain, tenderness, stiffness,

numbness, or tingling) experienced in each of the 18 body regions.

Forty subjects were selected at random for detailed ergonomic measurements taken on the job. These included relative keyboard height, upper arm angle, forearm angle, relative document distance, gaze angle to VDT, and head tilt. Measurements were also taken of the chairs while the employees were performing their data-entry tasks.

Almost constant back pain was reported by 33% of the workers, neck pain by 27%, shoulder pain by 15%, hand pain by 13%, and wrist pain by 12%. The pain rates were consistently higher on the right side of the body (where the hand operated the keyboard) than on the left side of the body.

The ergonomic measurements showed that greater discomfort was associated with longer reaches to the documents made with the left arm and with increased flexion of the right shoulder in operating the keyboard. Keyboard height and chair tilt were also linked with physical complaints.

The researchers concluded that discomfort could be reduced by lowering the keyboard to elbow level, elevating the backrest, and providing chairs in which workers' posture would be more erect. If these human engineering design considerations are applied to computer work stations, the incidence of physical complaints, absenteeism, sick leave, and errors could be reduced.

Critical Thinking Questions

1. In what other ways can proper human factors design reduce the strain of computer use?
2. What has engineering psychology research shown about the design of chairs, keyboards, and display screens for VDT users?
3. Do you think job-enrichment programs could reduce the physical complaints of VDT users? How?
4. What factors, other than those described, might have influenced the workers in this study?
5. Would rest pauses reduce discomfort among VDT operators? How would you design a study to investigate this variable?

Source: Based on S. L. Sauter, L. M. Schleifer, & S. J. Knutson. (1991). Work posture, workstation design, and musculoskeletal discomfort in a VDT data entry task. *Human Factors, 33,* 151–167.

SUMMARY

Engineering psychology is concerned with the design of tools, equipment, and workspaces to make them compatible with the abilities of employees. Psychologists consider the limitations and capacities of workers as well as the characteristics of the equipment to produce an efficient **person-machine system.** A precursor to engineering psychology was **time-and-motion study,** pioneered by Frederick Taylor and Frank and Lillian Gilbreth, which attempted to redesign tools and wage-incentive systems and to eliminate wasted motion on the job. Time-and-motion study is applied to routine jobs whereas engineering psychology focuses on sophisticated jobs involving complex systems.

The initial step in designing a person-machine system is allocating functions between human operators and machines. Humans are superior in detecting a range of stimuli, detecting rare or low-level stimuli from a confusing background, sensing and recognizing unusual or unexpected stimuli, recalling relevant information, using past experiences in making decisions, responding quickly to diverse situations, using inductive reasoning, and showing flexibility in problem solving. Machines are superior to humans in detecting stimuli beyond human sensory powers, monitoring for long periods, calculating rapidly and accurately, storing and retrieving large amounts of data, applying physical force, and engaging in repetitive tasks with no performance deterioration.

Workspace design involves principles of motion economy as well as data from **human anthropometry** (measurements of the body's physical structure). Three types of visual informational display are quantitative, qualitative, and check reading. **Quantitative displays** provide a precise numerical value. **Qualitative displays** provide an indication of relative operating conditions. **Check reading displays** tell whether a system is operating normally or abnormally or whether it is on or off. **Auditory displays** can attract attention more readily than can visual displays because the ears receive sound from all directions.

Controls to initiate action must be compatible with the task and the worker's abilities. Controls should be combined for similar or related operations and must be easily identifiable. Control identification can be aided by pictorial symbols or by **shape coding.** Controls may have to be modified for users from different cultures and for users with physical disabilities.

Computers are person-machine systems that may cause problems for the human operator. Computer use can lead to a downgrading of human skills, job dissatisfaction, boredom, and physical complaints including visual problems, fatigue, and pain in back, neck, shoulders, arms, and hands. **Robots** can perform better than humans can in routine, repetitive work. Robots can produce more products of higher quality without any deterioration in job performance.

KEY TERMS

auditory displays
check reading visual displays
engineering psychology
ergonomics
heads-up displays
human anthropometry
human factors

person-machine systems
qualitative visual displays
quantitative visual displays
robots
shape coding
time-and-motion study

ADDITIONAL READING

Carroll, J. M. (1997). Human-computer interaction: Psychology as a science of design. *Annual Review of Psychology, 48,* 61–83. Reviews two decades of research and applications in the field of human-computer interaction focusing on user-centered systems development.

Nickerson, R. (1992). *Looking ahead: Human factors challenges in a changing world.* Hillsdale, NJ: Erlbaum. Surveys economic, political, and technological trends to predict the direction of human factors psychology.

O'Brien, T. G., & Charlton, S. G. (Eds.) (1996). *Handbook of human factors testing and evaluation.* Hillsdale, NJ: Erlbaum. A sourcebook on assessing the components of person-machine systems.

Sanders, M. S., & McCormick, E. J. (1993). *Human factors in engineering and design* (7th ed.). New York: McGraw-Hill. A standard textbook on human factors and ergonomics design.

Wickens, C. D. (1992). *Engineering psychology and human performance* (2nd ed.). New York: HarperCollins. An engineering psychology text that focuses on how psychological processes—such as sensing, perceiving, thinking, and responding—can be related to machine systems ranging from household appliances and workplaces to technologically advanced space stations.

Consumer Psychology

Not everyone works for an organization, but all of us are consumers of the products and services of many organizations. We buy automobiles, cosmetics, food, clothing, and appliances. We vote for political candidates and express our opinions on issues in public opinion polls. We respond to appeals from charities and special interest groups.

We are bombarded by communications from all these organizations—messages from business, government, and other groups urging us to behave in one way or another. These thousands of advertising appeals appear on television and computer screens and billboards, and in the pages of our magazines and newspapers.

Consumer psychologists are concerned with the interactions between consumers and organizations. Advertisers spend billions of dollars to influence our choices, and many of their persuasive techniques were devised by psychologists. Consumer psychology is also important to you as an employee. If people do not buy what your company produces, then it will not be in business for long.

Chapter 14 deals with some of the major facets of the producer/consumer interaction—the ways of studying consumer behavior and preferences; the nature of advertising; the importance of packaging, trademarks, and product images; and the assessment of reactions to television programs.

Consumer Psychology

CHAPTER 14

THE SCOPE OF CONSUMER PSYCHOLOGY

Consumer psychology The study of the interactions between consumers and organizations that produce consumer products.

There is no escaping the influence of **consumer psychology.** Pick up a magazine, turn on the radio or TV, or drive down a highway, and almost everywhere you will be bombarded by up to 3,000 advertising messages every day, some 200 of them on television. Indeed, it is difficult to avoid commercial announcements, even on the Internet. Your telephone company probably sends advertising flyers with your monthly bill. Videotapes of popular films contain commercials for snack foods. Some city office buildings post ads in public rest rooms, on the inside of the stall doors.

Scented paper forces us to smell a product even if we do not look at the ad for it. Aromas of perfumes, chocolates, detergents, and the leather upholstery of the Rolls-Royce automobile fill the glossy pages of our magazines. More than a billion scent strips a year are distributed, creating severe problems for people who suffer from allergies. Thanks to microchips the size of a grain of salt, it is possible to hear advertisements in print. In 1987 Absolut Vodka spent $1 million on a Christmastime ad that played "Jingle Bells" when readers turned the page. The company claimed that the ad produced the largest holiday season sales in its history.

It is not possible for us to pay attention to or respond adequately to all the messages directed toward consumers, nor should we—if we want to maintain our sanity. We fail to perceive the majority of the messages that surround us, but even if we remain unaware of the details of many ads, we are certainly aware that the process of advertising is ongoing.

Consumer behavior has been of interest to I/O psychologists since the beginning of the field. In fact, it was the study of consumer behavior that launched I/O psychology. Industrial psychology can be said to have begun in the early 20th century with the work of Walter Dill Scott on advertising and selling. In 1921 John B. Watson, founder of the behaviorist school of psychology, began to apply his ideas about human behavior to the business world. He proposed that consumer behavior could be conditioned—and, therefore, predicted and controlled—just like any other kind of behavior. He brought the experimental and survey methods to marketing, and he insisted that advertisements should focus on style and image rather than substance and fact. He also pioneered the use of celebrity endorsements. Today, interest in consumer psychology continues to flourish. A new journal, the *Journal of Consumer Psychology,* was begun in 1992.

RESEARCH METHODS IN CONSUMER PSYCHOLOGY

Much of the research conducted by consumer psychologists relies on the techniques described in Chapter 2. The most frequently used empirical methods are laboratory experiments and surveys. Women and children are surveyed more often than are men. Consumer research is conducted in various settings, such as university laboratories, downtown intersections, homes, shopping centers, and the offices of manufacturers and advertising agencies.

Surveys and Public Opinion Polls

The premise underlying the use of surveys is simple—that is, most people can and will express their feelings, reactions, opinions, and desires when someone asks them. This assumption holds whether we are trying to determine reactions to a new brand of peanut butter or to a presidential candidate. We have only to recall how accurately most preelection polls have predicted election results or how successfully new products have been introduced on the basis of market testing to know that the survey method often works well. However, there have also been failures to predict election results or to forecast a product's success.

Part of the difficulty is the complex and changeable nature of human behavior. For example, some people will tell a poll-taker on Friday that they intend to vote Republican and then will vote Democratic on Tuesday, perhaps because of a sudden change in the economy. Respondents may tell an interviewer that they drink imported beer, but a glance inside their refrigerator would reveal cans of some generic light brand. They may have told the researcher that they buy the expensive brand because they thought it would enhance their status.

Searches of trash cans have revealed that on the average people drink twice the amount of beer and liquor than they report in consumer surveys. A long-term field study of garbage dumps carried out by anthropologists at the University of Arizona found that survey respondents consistently underreported the amount of junk food they consumed and overreported the amount of fresh fruit and diet soft drinks they ate. The scientists concluded that what people tell interviewers about purchases and consumption habits rarely corresponds with what is found in the garbage (Rathje & Murphy, 1992). People tend to respond to surveys and polls with statements that they think will boost their stature, and on such vagaries elections are lost and manufacturers go bankrupt.

In part for this reason, Japanese manufacturers do not survey large, random samples of consumers to assess intentions and preferences. Instead, they interview only those persons who have already purchased or used a particular product or one similar to it. For example, when Toyota wanted to know what American consumers desired in a small imported car, they questioned owners of the Volkswagen Beetle, a car that was similar to the one Toyota was planning, to ask what the owners liked and disliked about their cars.

Focus Groups

A widely used type of survey involves **focus groups,** which are small samples of consumers who meet in groups of 8 to 12 to describe their reactions to a product, package, or ad, or to the ideas and issues being promoted by a political candidate. Members of focus groups are usually paid for their participation and are selected to match the profile of the average voter or the consumer of a particular type of product. For example, only pet owners would be selected for a focus group on an ad for dog food. Only mothers of infants would be chosen to evaluate a new disposable diaper. Focus groups can be structured on the basis of age, income, educational level, or any other variable relevant to the product.

The focus group sessions are observed through one-way mirrors and videotaped for later analysis. The data produced by focus groups—the comments and responses of the participants—are more qualitative than are those obtained from questionnaires in large-scale empirical surveys. Sometimes, focus group members are not asked direct questions but are observed as they try to use a new product. In a session to evaluate a disposable razor, observers found that many men cut themselves while shaving because the package directions were not clear.

Focus groups A method of surveying public opinion through the paid participation of 8 to 12 group members who meet to describe their reactions to a product or advertisement or to specific issues.

Focus groups often reveal problems that developers and advertisers had not considered. One businessman hoped to start a pet care venture featuring dog washes, similar to car washes. He took the idea to a market research firm, and they assembled a focus group to determine reactions of dog owners. The participants quickly raised a major problem. The dog wash idea was fine, but it meant that owners would have to drive home with wet dogs in their cars. As a result, the idea was scrubbed.

Projective Techniques

Some consumer psychologists suggest that we cannot uncover human motivations by asking questions that permit people to mask or distort their true intentions and feelings. To probe these deeper motivations, psychologists recommend in-depth procedures such as projective techniques.

We described projective techniques in Chapter 4—for example, the Rorschach Inkblot Test, the Thematic Apperception Test, and the sentence completion test. Additional projective techniques used in market and motivation research are listed in Table 14–1. The theory behind the use of projective techniques is the same whether they are applied to employee selection or to consumer behavior. When people are presented with an ambiguous stimulus, it is assumed that they will project their needs, fears, and values onto the stimulus in the act of interpreting it.

The classic example of this approach to consumer research is the instant-coffee study (Haire, 1950). When instant coffee was a new product it met with considerable consumer resistance. To find out why, psychologists first tried the direct survey method. Shoppers were asked, "Do you use instant coffee?" When they said no, they were asked what they disliked about instant coffee. Most people said that they did not like the taste, but the researchers suspected other reasons. They then tried the indirect or projective approach.

Interviewers showed a shopping list to two groups of 50 women each. They asked the women shoppers to describe the personality of the homemaker who had compiled the list. The shopping lists were identical except that one included a jar of Nescafé instant coffee and the other included a pound of Maxwell House drip grind "real" coffee. The lists were a projective stimulus designed to reveal the respondents' feelings about the kind of person who would use real or instant

TABLE 14–1 Projective Techniques for Market Research

Technique	Instructions to Consumers
Role Playing	Imagine you are the manufacturer of this brand of athletic shoe . . .
Analogies	Describe yourself as a corn flake . . . Describe this brand of deodorant as a kind of flower . . .
Psychodrawings	Draw brown bread as compared with white bread.
Personifications	If jeans came to life as a person, who would it be?
Obituaries	Write an obituary for roach killer.

Adapted from J. Lannon. Asking the right questions: What do people do with advertising? In D. A. Aaker & A. L. Biel (Eds.), *Brand Equity and Advertising*. Hillsdale, NJ: Erlbaum, 1993, p. 169.

coffee. The shoppers were not asked directly to reveal their personal feelings, but they were expected to project those feelings onto their characterization of the fictitious shopper.

Solely on the basis of the type of coffee listed (recall that all the other items on the lists were the same), the subjects described the fictitious homemakers as having different personalities. Almost half described the person who would buy instant coffee as lazy and extravagant, someone who failed to plan her household purchases and schedules and was probably not a good wife. The shopper who would buy real coffee was described in much less negative terms. No one called her a spendthrift or a bad wife, and only a few described her as lazy.

The findings of this study reveal one reason why it took so long for instant coffee to be accepted by consumers. The unflattering image of the instant-coffee user was a projection of consumers' personal feelings about the product. They refused to purchase instant coffee because they were afraid that other people would think they were like the lazy person described in the study.

Another example of the use of projective techniques to study consumer behavior involved the reaction of low-income Southern women to a new brand of roach killer packaged in small plastic trays. Surveys had shown that consumers *said* they believed the new plastic trays were far more effective than the old-style sprays, yet they continued to buy the sprays. To determine the reasons for this inconsistency, groups of women were asked to draw pictures of roaches and to write stories about them. The researchers reported the following about the possible motivation of the women consumers:

> The results were very informative—all the roaches in the pictures were male, "symbolizing men who the women said had abandoned them and left them feeling poor and powerless." The women were said to be expressing their built-up hostility by spraying the roaches and watching them squirm and die! (Foxall & Goldsmith, 1994, p. 162).

Direct questioning would not have revealed this motivation.

In theory, the projective approach offers the same advantages as projective tests for employee selection—that is, the ability to reach deeper levels of motivation, to uncover feelings and desires that cannot be assessed by objective tests and questionnaires. However, projective tests are low in reliability and validity. Even the most highly trained and experienced clinical psychologists can disagree on the interpretation of projective test results. If the method is of doubtful validity in a clinical setting, it may be more questionable in consumer research where the practitioner may not be a trained psychologist. There have been successful uses of projective techniques to study consumer behavior, but because the advertising industry does not publicize its failures, it is difficult to determine the extent of that success.

OBSERVATIONS OF CONSUMER BEHAVIOR

Consumer surveys and projective techniques share a basic weakness. They reveal only what people *say* they believe or will do. These expressed intentions do not always coincide with behavior. Because of this discrepancy, some consumer psychologists believe that the most accurate way to investigate consumer behavior is to observe what people do when purchasing a product or when expressing their preference by selecting one brand over another.

Purchasing Behavior

Common sense suggests that acceptance of a new product or advertising campaign will be reflected in subsequent sales figures. For example, if sales of a toothpaste double in the 6 months following an ad campaign, then the campaign must have been successful. However, unless all other variables capable of influencing sales were controlled, we cannot conclude with certainty that the new advertising approach was solely or even partially responsible for the boost in sales.

Suppose the company's aggressive sales staff arranged for more prominent shelf display of the toothpaste during the 6-month period. That increased visibility could have contributed to higher sales, independent of the ad campaign. Or suppose the company's leading competitor was faulted in a government report for adding an allegedly harmful ingredient to its toothpaste formula. That criticism could contribute to higher sales for all other toothpaste manufacturers. Thus, sales data can reflect factors other than the one being evaluated, and without adequate control over all possible influencing variables, we cannot determine precisely what caused any increase or decrease in sales.

A more direct way to investigate purchasing behavior is to place observers in shops and supermarkets. For example, researchers have watched mothers with young children as they shopped for cereals and snack foods. More than 65% of the time, children ask for a particular product. More than 50% of the time, the mothers buy the products children demand. This kind of data is especially valuable because it indicates that children, not adults, should be the target of ads for cereals and snack foods. Had the mothers been questioned directly in a survey, however, they might have said that they were the ones to choose these products, not wanting to appear to be dominated by their children—or perhaps not realizing the extent of their children's influence.

Although observations of actual purchasing behavior can be useful, they are costly and time-consuming. There are other problems as well. One relates to adequate sampling of shopping behavior. Stores in different locations—such as inner city versus suburban—attract customers with different needs and income levels. Various types of shoppers can be found in the same store at different times of the day or week. People who shop in the evenings and on weekends may have different buying habits from those of people who shop during the day. The research design must compensate for this problem by providing for observations at an adequate sample of locations and shopping hours, but this increases the cost of the research.

Another problem with behavioral observations of purchasing behavior is the lack of experimental control over other influencing variables; this is a weakness of all types of observational research studies. In observing supermarket shopping patterns in urban and suburban locations, for example, it is difficult to determine whether the differences found are a function of socioeconomic level, ethnic composition, shelf arrangement, or inventory.

Scanner cable panels Groups of supermarket shoppers whose purchasing behavior is monitored electronically at checkout and who are later targeted for specific types of advertising via cable television.

Another way to observe purchasing behavior uses **scanner cable panels.** Groups are formed of approximately 2,500 shoppers who volunteer to have their food purchases monitored electronically. Biographical information on the shoppers, such as age, income, educational level, and ages of children, is obtained. Each person receives a plastic identification card that is given to the supermarket checkout clerk at each shopping trip. The card is read by the computerized scanner at the checkout register. A record is kept of the items purchased that will be analyzed later by researchers.

The purchasing information is made available to cable television producers to target advertising for different kinds of shoppers—for example, sending pet food commercials only to homes of people who have purchased pet food. Manufacturers can also test advertisements by sending different commercials for the same product to various homes in the cable sample. By recording subsequent purchases of that product by the panel shoppers, the manufacturer can determine which commercial is associated with a change in sales.

Brand Identification and Preference

Consumer psychologists are also interested in how well shoppers recognize, identify, or recall specific product brands. Much of this research focuses on the ability to discriminate among competing brands of a product. When all recognizable cues are removed—such as product name and distinctive packaging—can consumers truly distinguish, say, one brand of cola from another? Studies consistently demonstrate that many people cannot discriminate among brands of products such as soft drinks, cigarettes, beer, and margarine. Researchers have concluded that many consumer preferences and loyalties are based on factors other than the product's taste or other intrinsic qualities.

Consumer preferences are studied to determine reactions in advance of the release of a new product. Studies have been conducted on the feel of clothing fabrics, on preferences for shapes of soaps and shampoo bottles, even on the perceived crispness of breakfast cereals in different packaging.

Research has been conducted on perceived quality, reliability, wholesomeness, or status of brand names. A national research firm surveyed a representative sample of 2,000 adults and asked them to rate 190 familiar corporate names on the quality of their products or services. The top-ranking names were Disney, Kodak, Mercedes-Benz, Cable News Network (CNN), and Hallmark. With company mergers, acquisitions, and reorganizations so widespread, many companies have used information from these kinds of surveys to select a name that will present the most positive image for their product.

Testing for Advertising Effectiveness

A major research activity of consumer psychologists is testing the effectiveness of advertising and promotional campaigns. In television advertising alone, approximately 6,000 commercials are tested every year. Nearly two thirds are judged to be failures and are never aired. Psychologists use several techniques to determine ad effectiveness.

The most direct approach is to ask people for their reactions to an ad. Does the ad make them want to buy the product? Do they believe the ad? Which of two ads for a product do they find more interesting? It is necessary that the respondents be a representative sample of the population for whom the product is intended. Using single men or elderly women to pretest an ad for baby food is not likely to yield useful results.

Aided Recall.   The most popular technique to test advertising effectiveness is **aided recall,** which is used to determine the extent to which the contents of the ad can be remembered. Once an ad has appeared in a magazine or broadcast on radio or television, a sample of consumers is questioned—usually the following day—about whether they read the magazine or heard or saw the program in which the commercial appeared. If so, they are asked to tell as much of the selling message as they can recall. The interviewer asks specific questions about the nature of the ad; this aids the recall. A study that exposed subjects over a period of time to 20 radio commercials for blue jeans, soft drinks, deodorants, dairy products, and condiments found that aided recall was a reliable way of evaluating an ad's memorability. However, a high rate of recall for the ad's message did not necessarily lead the consumer to purchase the product (Higie & Sewall, 1991).

Aided recall technique A test of advertising effectiveness to determine the extent to which ad content can be recalled; the interviewer aids the recall by asking specific questions.

Recognition.   Another technique for testing the effectiveness of ads is **recognition.** People who have seen a particular television program or magazine are shown copies of the ads and are questioned about them. Do the consumers recognize the ad and remember where they saw it? Do they recall the name of the product? Had they read the message? Unfortunately, people may say that they have seen an ad or commercial even when they have not. When researchers showed people ads that had not yet appeared in the media, some respondents claimed to have seen them. A comparison of aided recall and recognition techniques showed that recognition was the more sensitive measure of memory for television commercials (Singh, Rothschild, & Churchill, 1988).

Recognition technique A technique for testing advertising effectiveness by asking people if they recognize a particular ad, where they saw it, and what they can recall about it.

Sales Tests.   Some psychologists argue that although these techniques provide information on how people feel about an ad or how much they recall, the only meaningful test of advertising effectiveness is whether the campaign results in higher sales. We have noted the limitations of using sales data as a measure of advertising success. The **sales test technique** is designed to reduce those limitations because it permits experimental control of extraneous variables. Sales tests have been found to be a highly accurate way of assessing the impact of advertising on sales.

Sales test technique A way of testing the effectiveness of an advertising campaign by introducing the new advertising in selected test markets.

In a sales test, an advertising campaign is introduced in selected test markets—certain neighborhoods, cities, or geographical areas. Other areas, chosen to be as similar as possible to the test markets, serve as controls; the new advertising is not presented in these control areas. If the test and control areas are comparable, then any change in sales within the test areas can be attributed to the advertising campaign. The control over possible influencing variables is the major advantage of sales tests. The researcher is not measuring interest in an ad or what subjects say they remember but whether they actually buy the product on the basis of the ad.

The use of sales tests for studying advertising effectiveness also has limitations. An adequate sales test is costly. It takes time to arrange, and it requires precise accounting of the purchasing behavior of a large number of people. Another problem involves the areas selected for the control group. By not exposing people in the control markets to the new ad campaign, the company risks losing sales to competitors.

Coupon Returns.   The effectiveness of magazine and newspaper advertising can be tested by evaluating coupon returns. When coupons are returned to the manufacturer to obtain a product sample or to enter a contest, they provide a measure of reader interest. When coupons are used to purchase a product or receive a discount (cents-off coupons), they measure actual buying behavior. However, if the inducement to return the coupon is attractive, such as when a West Coast mail-order retailer offered a free pair of sweat socks to introduce a house brand, there is the danger that people will respond even though they have no interest in the product but just want to get something free. There are also people who will return virtually any coupon because they like to get mail. It is difficult to determine how many coupon returns come from habitual coupon clippers and how many come from people who are genuinely interested in the product.

Coupon returns may indicate the attention-getting value of an ad, but they do not provide a direct measure of the ad's impact on sales. When coupons offer a reduced price for a product, they are effective in inducing people to change brands—at least temporarily. A price reduction obtained by redeeming a coupon at the supermarket promotes greater sales than an equivalent price markdown given at the store.

The marketing director of a direct-mail seller of wedding stationery conducted an experiment to determine the impact of coupons that could be redeemed for a free prize. The subjects were 30,000 people who had requested catalogs. Would the promise of a free-prize coupon produce larger catalog orders? The first 10,000 subjects were offered a coupon for a gift in return for any order. (The gifts were selected products from the catalog, such as 100 personalized napkins.) The second 10,000 subjects were informed that they would receive a gift for returning the coupon with their order, if they first completed a lengthy survey containing personal information. The third 10,000 subjects served as the control group; they did not receive a coupon offer or a survey.

Common sense might suggest that the first group would respond with the greatest number of orders because they did not have to make any extra effort to get their prize. To the company's surprise, significantly more orders were sent in by the second group, the one that had to complete the survey to receive the gift.

NEWSBREAK #26

Coupons: They Make a Lot of Cents

It started in 1895, more than 100 years ago, when Asa Chandler, of Atlanta, Georgia, distributed coupons for a free glass of Coca-Cola at his soda fountain. Today, an estimated 267 billion cents-off, free-product, and rebate coupons are distributed annually, an average of almost 3,000 for every U.S. household. We cut them out of newspapers and magazines and faithfully take them to stores to redeem for our purchases of soap, deodorant, and breakfast cereal. Pharmacies give them out for discounts on prescription drugs, and even cemeteries have offered dollars-off coupons for gravesites.

(continued)

Coupons can save real money. In 1994, the face value of the average coupon rose 6%, to 63 cents. The average family that uses coupons can count on saving approximately $650 a year, a payback of 15 to 16 dollars an hour for the time required to clip, assemble, and organize the coupons. Hard-core coupon users—who have been known to purchase several copies of the Sunday newspaper to get additional coupons—save even more money. These dedicated users, known in the trade as "couponers" rarely make any supermarket purchases unless they can use their coupons to get something off. Frequently, they will only shop on days when stores double their coupons.

Most people obtain their coupons from the Sunday newspapers; four out of five coupons are delivered that way. Soon you will be able to get them on the Internet. A company called Moneymailer announced plans to carry coupons. All you have to do is scan the site's listings of national and local advertisers and print out the coupons. Perhaps you will even be able to get coupons good for free computer time!

Sources: No more clipping. *Newsweek,* April 1, 1996. E. J. Martin. It all started with a coupon for a free coke. *St. Petersburg [FL] Times,* January 11, 1996. D. J. Morrow. 50 cents off! 2 for 1! But get them while you can. *New York Times,* March 17, 1996.

The experimenter concluded that any special promotion or free offer will be more effective when the customer must take some action to earn it. Otherwise,

> the customer will either impute a lower value to the product or suspect that the offer is "too good to be true." Requiring the customer to "work for" the offer apparently overcomes customer suspicion and significantly increases perceived value (Porter, 1993, p. 17).

TELEVISION PROGRAMMING RESEARCH

Millions of dollars are spent annually to develop television programs that will attract and hold a sizable portion of the viewing audience. Networks compete sharply for the considerable prize of the advertising dollar. The fact that 90% of all new programs are canceled before the end of the viewing season attests to the frequency with which television executives are unable to select winning programs. Several techniques are available to help predict the likelihood of success of a program or series, as well as audience size and composition.

Predicting Audience Reactions to New Programming.   Before a program is aired, samples of potential viewers are invited to screen previews or pilot programs. The usual procedure is for viewers to communicate their reactions continuously throughout the show. They are given a control device with two pushbuttons. When they like a particular scene, they press one button; when they dislike a scene, they press the other button. When they are indifferent or neutral, they do not press either button.

These studies of audience reaction can be an excellent way of predicting program acceptance, assuming the subjects are a representative sample of the intended viewing audience. Unfortunately, most viewer samples selected by television networks are composed of people chosen at random off the street. People who happen to be walking past a TV studio in New York or Los Angeles at a particular time of day can hardly be considered typical of the television viewing population as a whole.

Determining Audience Size and Composition. Ratings determine which programs remain on the air, and they are used as a basis for determining how much networks can charge advertisers for broadcasting their commercials. In telephone surveys, interviewers ask respondents about their television viewing during a recent period, such as the previous day or week, and inquire about the programs that were seen and the family members who watched each program. Interviewers may also ask what program, if any, is being watched at the moment of the telephone call.

Nielsen Ratings. Nielsen Media Research uses mechanical devices to assess audience size and composition. These devices eliminate the errors inherent in telephone surveys. A recorder called the Audimeter, installed in the houses of a viewer sample, notes the times the television set is on and the channels to which it is tuned. Although the Audimeter provides an accurate record of channel choice for all programming periods, it does not tell who is watching a particular program—or whether anyone is watching. Some people leave a TV set on much of the day as a babysitter for infants or because they like the sound.

Nielsen uses a diary system during periods of ratings sweeps in which 250,000 households are asked to record viewing choices. The bulk of Nielsen's ratings data comes from the People Meter, which looks like a standard remote control device. Each member of the sample of 5,000 households is assigned a personal code to enter when watching television. Thus, the People Meter registers who is watching what channel. When the viewer leaves the room, he or she is supposed to push appropriate buttons to tell the People Meter, but some viewers fail to do so. Some viewers will enter another family member's code as a joke. Viewers most likely to follow instructions on the use of the device are older persons who have only one television set.

Critics charge that few people in the Nielsen sample bother to push the appropriate buttons on the People Meter to indicate age and sex data, and that no more than half those who receive diaries bother to return them. Nielsen concedes that only half of their randomly selected families accept the offer of a People Meter, and it is not known how these families might differ from those who do not accept the offer. Despite such criticisms, Nielsen continues to dominate the television ratings industry.

Nielsen ratings are used by television programmers and sponsors in the United States, Canada, Australia, Finland, France, Japan, Mexico, and Norway. The company also offers a Hispanic ratings service in the United States, with the Telemundo and Univision networks, to help advertisers evaluate the audience for Spanish-language programming. Nielsen monitors television viewing in bars, truck stops, college dormitories, airports, health clubs, and doctors' offices.

THE SELLER

Let us examine some of the techniques the sellers of goods and services use to encourage, persuade, stimulate, or manipulate you, the consumer, to buy their products.

The Nature and Scope of Advertising

There are several different types of advertising. Although the most frequently used is the direct sell type, designed to elicit an immediate response from the consumer, other advertising is created for different purposes.

Consumer Awareness.   A second type of advertising is designed to create consumer awareness of a new product, an improved product or package, or a price change. This advertising also tries to reinforce the brand name. Because so much purchasing behavior is linked to brand names, companies spend considerable sums creating and maintaining public awareness of company and product names.

Product Image.   A third type of advertising tries to establish an image for a product or service. Many products cannot be distinguished from one another on the basis of ingredients or quality, so advertisers try to create differences in terms of images, symbols, or feelings. For example, an automobile must do more than provide transportation; a lipstick must provide more than color. It must, through its image, make the owners feel younger, sportier, or more attractive, or enhance their prestige and economic status. As the president of a firm that makes men's and women's fragrances said, "In the factory we make cosmetics. In the store we sell hope."

Institutional Advertising.   A fourth type of advertising is institutional advertising, the goal of which is to persuade the public that the company is a good neighbor and community benefactor. An example is the campaign conducted by an oil company to promote highway safety rather than simply to sell its brand of gasoline. Companies advertise that their products are good for the environment, that they contribute a share of their profits to charities, or that they support Little League baseball teams. Institutional advertising can build public good will, boost sales, help recruit employees, improve employee morale, and drive up the price of the company's stock.

A sample of 214 college students* rated a series of advertisements designed to show the environmental sensitivity of two major American corporations, Anheuser-Busch and Exxon. A previous sample of 79 students had evaluated a list of 30 large companies and had selected Anheuser-Busch as the most concerned with environmental issues and Exxon as the least concerned. As expected, the identical ads were rated significantly more positively when they were

---

*You will recall that using college student samples in simulated work settings to study various work behaviors presents problems of generalizability of the findings to employees actually on the job. However, because people of all ages, and from all socioeconomic groups, are consumers—including college students—it is appropriate here to discuss research studies that rely on college student subjects.

This direct-sell ad promotes consumer awareness of the product and tries to establish an image of luxury and fun. (Courtesy of Ford Motor Company.)

VISITORS TO MS. GAWEL'S CLASSROOM FIND OUT JUST HOW WILD IT REALLY IS.

To help awaken them to the plight of the world's rainforests, Julie Gawel's students created one of their own.

Julie, an art teacher at Killough Middle School in Houston, Texas, designed the multidisciplinary program for her students utilizing reading, writing, science, and art. After researching the rainforest environment, the students practiced drawing its inhabitants; learning about paint, color mixing, and texture in the process. Then they transformed their classroom with wall-size murals and papier-mâché trees filled with a menagerie of plants and wildlife.

Finally, the students invited parents and local business leaders to their rainforest, where the children made presentations and passed along the lessons they learned about conservation.

For teaching her students how to be wild about art – and the world's rainforests – Julie Gawel is our newest Good Neighbor Award winner.

State Farm is pleased to contribute $5,000 in her name to Alief Independent School District.

GOOD NEIGHBOR AWARD

STATE FARM INSURANCE COMPANIES
Home Offices: Bloomington, Illinois
www.statefarm.com

The Good Neighbor Award was developed in cooperation with the National Art Education Association.

Institutional advertising promotes the idea that the company is a good neighbor and community benefactor. (Reproduced by permission of State Farm Insurance Companies.)

associated with the company considered to be the most concerned with environmental issues. The messages were seen to be significantly more believable and indicative of a stronger environmental commitment when associated with the company with the stronger environmental image.

The same ads were seen as significantly less sincere and less believable when attributed to the company with the negative environmental image. Those ads were also rated as exhibiting a lower commitment to the environment. The only type of advertisement to boost that corporation's negative image noted major financial contributions to environmental funds or organizations. Thus, it was found to be possible to change a negative corporate image, but only with certain kinds of ads (Davis, 1994).

Comparative Advertising. In comparative advertising, one brand is compared with competing brands. Such ads highlight the advantages of the advertised product and the disadvantages of the competitors' products. This approach has not been found to be more persuasive than noncomparative advertising except when the ad is presented by a spokesperson with a high degree of credibility. For example, one study of comparative advertisements for two brands of videocassette recorder compared satisfied customer testimonials from a high-credibility source (an electrical engineer) and a low-credibility source (a car salesman). Subjects concluded that the engineer was the more knowledgeable and objective source of information about the product. They were more likely to accept the engineer's judgment about which brand to purchase (Gotlieb & Sarel, 1991).

Informational Advertising. Some advertising comes under the heading of informative advertising when it enables consumers to make more intelligent purchasing decisions. The type of information provided in such an ad can include price, quality, performance data, components or contents, availability, nutritional information, warranties, and safety record. The use of informative advertising has increased from an average of 20% of ads a decade ago to more than 65% today. Magazine ads tend to be more informative than television ads. More cable television commercials than network television commercials are informative. Advertising produced in England, Japan, and China was found to have a greater informational content than did advertising produced in the United States (Stern & Resnik, 1991).

Types of Advertising Appeals

The major way in which an ad campaign can persuade you to buy a product is through its appeal; that is, what it promises to do for you. Which human needs or motivations does the product promise to satisfy? Psychologists have identified many human needs: the innate or primary needs, such as food, water, shelter, security, and sex; and the learned or secondary needs, such as power, status, achievement, esteem, and affiliation. These secondary motivations depend on our personal experiences. They vary from one person to another and one culture to another.

To sell their products and services, advertisers must identify the relevant needs and direct their messages toward the appropriate segment of the population. Most ads attempt to satisfy more than one need. For example, an advertisement for imported beer can promise to quench thirst (a primary need) and to

Some advertisers attempt to appeal to emotional needs and feelings such as affection, romance, and beauty. (Reproduced by permission of Perugina Chocolates.)

satisfy the desires for status and affiliation (secondary needs). Ads for mouth-wash and deodorant promise to help us avoid embarrassing situations and thus be more likeable. If we use the right cologne, we are assured by advertisers that we will find love and thus fulfill the needs for social support and self-esteem. Driving the right car can provide power, prestige, achievement, and self-esteem along with the hope of attracting a mate. Advertisers use several techniques to appeal to these diverse human needs.

Celebrity Endorsements.   A product endorsed by a celebrity entertainer or sports figure invites the audience to identify with that person's achievements and success. Celebrities are often used to sell products, although there is little published evidence of the impact of celebrity endorsements on buying behavior unless the celebrity is believed to be qualified to promote the product. A study of college students investigated the influence of celebrity status, attractiveness, trustworthiness, and perceived expertise on their expressed intentions to pur-chase particular products. Only the perceived expertise of the celebrities was pos-itively related to buying intentions. For example, a tennis pro is considered to be a believable endorser of tennis rackets, a good-looking male movie star an effec-tive promoter of men's cologne, and a fashion model an appropriate spokesper-son for a line of designer jeans.

Some celebrities endorse more than one product. For example, basketball star Michael Jordan has appeared in ads for more than 14 different products. Does multiple endorsement affect a celebrity's credibility or effectiveness in sell-ing a product? To answer that question, a sample of 461 college undergraduates participated in an experiment in which some of the students were exposed to up to eight ads showing a movie star endorsing products such as cameras, tooth-paste, breath mints, and a major credit card. Under other experimental condi-tions, the subject groups viewed a single ad, two ads, or four ads featuring the same celebrity endorsing the products.

The results showed that as the number of products endorsed by the celebrity increased, the subjects' ratings of the celebrity's credibility and likability de-creased significantly. In addition, the students' attitudes toward the ad became significantly less favorable (Tripp, Jensen, & Carlson, 1994).

Positive and Negative Appeals.   Advertising appeals can be positive or nega-tive; the message can indicate that something pleasant will happen to you if you use the product or that something unpleasant will happen if you do not use the product. An ad for deodorant soap can show a room full of happy people who are obviously desirable because they used the soap, or it can show a person sit-ting at home alone, dateless and dejected because he or she failed to bathe with the soap. A related approach is to make the person feel guilty for not buying the product, a tactic that is particularly effective with mothers of young children.

Negative appeals are effective for certain kinds of products, but they do not work when the consequences are overly unpleasant. Pictures of gruesome auto-mobile accidents in campaigns to promote safe driving or depictions of diseased lungs in smoking cessation campaigns have been shown to be ineffective. Such fear-laden appeals distract people from the message. The same holds true for guilt appeals. Research has shown that strong appeals are significantly less effec-tive than moderate appeals in inducing feelings of guilt. The strong appeal made the subjects (mothers of young children) express anger toward the ad and the company that sponsored it (Coulter & Pinto, 1995). The most frequently used approach combines both types of appeal, first showing the negative consequences of not using the product and then showing the positive consequences of using the product.

Implied Superiority.   A widely used appeal is implied superiority, in which the superiority of one product over its competitors is not stated directly but is inferred by the consumer. For example, if all headache remedies take the same amount of time to bring relief, one product may claim that no competitor provides faster relief than Brand X. The claim is true, but the phrasing can lead people to conclude that Brand X is superior because it sounds as if it works faster. The ad also suggests indirectly that the claim is based on research that provides supporting data for the implied idea that Brand X works faster than do all other pain relievers.

Consumer research shows that 70% of the assertions made in television commercials for airlines, beer, deodorant, and shampoo rely on claims of implied superiority. Consumers tend to believe these claims and even to exaggerate them. In laboratory studies, a majority of subjects reported that the implicit claims had in fact been stated directly in the ads to which they had been exposed (Wyckham, 1987).

Trademarks

A familiar trademark can facilitate advertising effectiveness because it serves as a shorthand symbol of the feelings and images associated with the product (see Figure 14–1). Key aspects of the product come to be identified with and exempli-

FIGURE 14–1.   Trademarks. (Reproduced by permission of Chevron Corporation; AT&T Corporation; and Toyota Motor Sales USA, Inc.)

fied by the trademark. Most trademarks are brand names, for example, Coca-Cola, Kleenex, and Xerox. When a trademark is well established in the marketplace, it alone—without any other advertising message—can stimulate consumers to recall the product.

Research has shown that even incidental exposure to trademarks and brand names can lead to a favorable attitude toward a product. Familiarity with a brand "makes a stimulus easier to perceive . . . and increases the likelihood it will be seen on the store shelf" (Janiszewski, 1993, p. 390).

A leading consulting firm on brand name identity surveyed 5,000 people in the United States, selected as a representative sample of the population between the ages of 18 and 65. The resulting ranking of the best known brand names is shown in Table 14–2 (Owen, 1993).

Companies spend a great deal of time and money on the development of product trademarks and names. Identity consultants specialize in naming and re-naming products and companies. For example, California Airlines changed its name to AirCal when focus-group interviews revealed that the new name had greater consumer impact. Allegheny Airlines changed its name to USAir to make it sound more like a national than a regional carrier.

TABLE 14–2   Top 25 U.S. Brands

Brand	Age of Consumer				
	18–29	**30–39**	**40–49**	**50–59**	**60+**
Coca-Cola	1	2	1	2	2
Campbell's	2	3	2	1	1
Disney	6	1	4	9	12
Pepsi-Cola	4	4	3	4	7
Kodak	5	5	5	5	15
NBC	7	8	7	7	6
Black & Decker	10	10	6	3	3
Kellogg's	15	7	9	6	8
McDonald's	3	6	10	16	17
Hershey's	13	12	11	8	22
Levi's	8	11	8	25	48
GE	33	20	13	10	4
Sears	19	17	14	11	5
Hallmark	21	25	15	13	18
Johnson & Johnson	16	15	22	18	27
Betty Crocker	14	14	21	21	25
Kraft	18	16	17	19	62
Kleenex	29	22	20	14	13
Jell-O	30	24	19	12	14
Tylenol	9	18	24	24	42
AT&T	43	36	31	28	21
Crest	11	9	12	20	19
Duracell	27	26	28	41	43
IBM	40	29	30	42	69
Fruit of the Loom	26	30	25	32	26

From S. Owen. The Landor ImagePower Survey®: A Global Assessment of Brand Strength. In D. A. Aaker & A. L. Biel (Eds.), *Brand Equity and Advertising* (p. 21). Hillsdale, NJ: Erlbaum, 1993.

Research can also tell manufacturers how recognizable their product name is to the consuming public and what it means to the target audience, which is especially crucial for U.S. companies marketing products in other countries. Sometimes a trademark can have an unintended, or unfavorable, meaning in another language. The Chevrolet Nova, named for a star that suddenly increases in brightness and energy, became in Spanish "no va," meaning "doesn't go"—not a very good name for a car. Coca-Cola changed its product name in China when the company discovered that in Chinese it meant "bite the wax tadpole." One U.S. airline boasted in Spanish-language magazines about the leather upholstery on its seats; in translation the message meant "sit naked."

A trademark can be so effective that it comes to stand for all brands of a certain type of product. For example, kleenex is now used to mean any kind of facial tissue, and xerox any kind of photocopier. When this occurs, the company can lose its identifiability and its exclusive share of the market.

Trademarks that have worked successfully for years may have to be altered to reflect changes in the marketplace. The image of Betty Crocker, the fictional woman trademark for many of General Mills's food products, was updated in 1996 to reflect the greater racial and ethnic diversity of the American population. The new Betty Crocker is a computer-generated hybrid of 75 real American faces. Designed to represent many races, she now looks multicultural, in an attempt to depict more accurately American society.

Product Image

Often allied with a product's trademark is its image—the ideas, thoughts, and feelings associated with the product's personality. The development of a successful product image, one with which consumers want to identify, can bring a company from obscurity to prosperity. Indeed, the image can be more important than the qualities of the product itself.

Consider Marlboro cigarettes. When the brand was introduced in the 1920s, the packaging and advertising were oriented toward an elegant, feminine personality. Consumer response was low until 1955, when a new advertising campaign was launched to change the product's image. Cowboys, ranchers, and other rugged outdoor men sporting tattoos and riding horses were used in the ads. The image of the Marlboro Man in Marlboro Country was born. It became part of our lives, and the brand's sales took off.

Sometimes product image is transmitted by a symbol, such as the tiny alligator on some popular knit shirts. This symbol is said to represent the image of the person wearing the product. A classic study compared consumer perceptions of a person wearing a plain knit shirt and wearing shirts with alligator, fox, and polo player logos. The person wearing the plain shirt was judged to be self-confident, tolerant, satisfied, and friendly. The same person in the fox emblem shirt was described as self-confident, enthusiastic, and a leader. In the polo player shirt he was perceived as less self-confident, tolerant, enthusiastic, satisfied, and friendly than in any of the other shirts. In the alligator shirt, the same person was described as a preppy fellow who was neither a leader nor a follower. Of course, the shirt was identical in all cases; the only difference was the logo (Swartz, 1983).

The most difficult problem in developing a product image is not transmitting it to the public but deciding on the image or personality that will attract potential buyers. One technique for studying product image involves group interviews with selected samples of consumers in which they are questioned about their perceptions of various products. This in-depth approach attempts to elicit positive and negative feelings about the products.

A more objective approach involves the adjective checklist, which was used in the study of the shirts with the different logos. Consumers are given a list of descriptive adjectives and phrases and are asked to select those that characterize their feelings about the product or their conception of the person who would buy the product. A study using college students as subjects asked them to apply an adjective checklist to products marketed to the college population. The product personalities described for McDonald's fast food and Levi's jeans are shown in Table 14–3. Given the results of such research, advertisers can determine which qualities to emphasize or ignore in developing a product image.

Product Packaging

Another important aspect of an advertising campaign is the product's package, the part of the product that consumers see at the critical point of sale, the moment of deciding whether to purchase. Shoppers looking for a box of crackers on a supermarket shelf who are confronted by an array of competing brands may not remember the TV commercial they saw last night or the magazine ad they read last week. At the instant of purchase, the packaging may be the deciding factor.

There is an old saying about not judging a book by its cover, but many people make various decisions on that basis. We often evaluate people by their

TABLE 14–3   Descriptive Phrases Associated with Product Personality

Levi's Jeans
   Casual wear
   Faded look
   Rugged durability
   Blue color
   Shrinks to fit
   Slightly abrasive feel of denim on skin
   Leather patch
   Copper rivets
   Yellow stitches
   Reinforced seams
   Angle cut pockets

McDonald's Fast Food
   Golden arches sign
   Long, thin, salty french fries
   Mushy hamburger
   Noises of hissing fries
   Beige, orange, and brown decor
   Striped hats and shirts
   Milkshakes
   Smell of fry oil

Note. Adapted from "Product Drama" by J. F. Durgee, 1988, *Journal of Advertising Research, 28,* p. 46.

clothing or their car, and we make similar judgments about the products we purchase. Consumer psychologists have documented many instances of consumer attitudes that have been shaped not by the quality of the product but by the wrapping in which it was offered. For example, in another classic consumer study, two groups of people were questioned about the taste of coffee. For one group, the coffee was poured from an ordinary electric coffeemaker. For the other group, the coffee was served from an ornately engraved antique silver urn. The consumers rated the taste of the coffee poured from the antique urn much higher than the coffee from the electric coffeemaker. The coffee was the same in both cases. It was the container that accounted for the difference in the way people perceived the taste.

In other research on this concept, pills of two sizes were shown to groups of patients and physicians, who were asked to rate the potency of each drug. Both groups reported that they believed that the larger pill was the more potent. In fact, the larger pill was less than half as strong as the smaller pill.

Overall, the package must reinforce the product's image or personality as established by its advertising campaign. For example, a man's cologne should not be packaged in a pink tube with letters in script but in a sturdy box with bold stripes and colors. The design and matching of product and package are determined through consumer research. Consumers are asked to free-associate to the designs of current or proposed packaging, telling researchers the positive or negative images elicited by the designs. Surveys and projective techniques can also be used to determine packaging impact and preference.

Packaging is an expensive part of the manufacturing and marketing process, accounting for more than one-third of the cost of most supermarket items. For every dollar you spend on food, drugs, toiletries, and cosmetics, approximately 35 cents goes for the container, not for what is in it. Packaging also adds to environmental pollution. Consumer groups and manufacturers are working to eliminate unnecessary packaging and to design containers that are more environmentally friendly. McDonald's replaced polystyrene hamburger boxes with less bulky and more flexible wrapping papers. The L'eggs plastic trademark egg for women's pantyhose has been replaced by a biodegradable cardboard package.

Sears reduced packaging by 25%, eliminating 1.5 million tons of waste. Hand tools such as hammers and screwdrivers are now displayed without packaging instead of being mounted on cardboard and encased in hard plastic. Producers of compact discs reduced the size of their cartons. The movement for a safer, cleaner environment has been altering consumer and manufacturer attitudes about packaging.

Sex in Advertisements

The use of attractive and scantily clad models of both sexes is popular in advertising. We might assume, therefore, that its effectiveness is beyond question. However, the value of sexy images in advertising has been accepted on faith, with little empirical research support. Sex appeal in ads does have a high attention-getting value. Studies using the eye camera show that most consumers reading magazines, when confronted with several ads on a page, will immediately look at the ad that contains an element of sex. But what then? In general, the information in the ad that features provocative pictures of women is read more often by women than by men. Men look at the pictures, but women read the message, which usually means that the ad is communicating with the wrong audience. Similar results have been found with ads featuring pictures of attractive men; the messages are read more often by men than by women, again attracting the wrong audience.

More discouraging is research evidence suggesting a very low rate of recall for information that accompanies sexy illustrations. One company published two versions of a magazine ad, each containing a mail-in coupon for additional information. One ad showed a bikini-clad young woman; the other ad did not. Coupon returns were significantly higher for the ad without the sexy model.

Laboratory research supports the field observations. In one study, male subjects viewed several ads. Some of the ads had sexy illustrations and some did not. The subjects were then shown the same ads with the brand names deleted and were asked to identify the product or advertiser. They were questioned again 24 hours later. There was no difference in the rate of recall for the sexy and non-sexy ads. After 7 days, the subjects had forgotten significantly more of the sexy ads than the non-sexy ads.

It appears, then, that the wrong audience reads the messages accompanying sexy ads, and although many people enjoy looking at the ads, they are not likely to remember the product. However, advertisers continue to rely on the shock value, and their promotions—especially for fragrances, underwear, and jeans—grow more daring every year.

Women in Advertisements

Women are often depicted in print advertisements and television commercials as sex objects, housewives, and mothers—people who are seen as inferior and subordinate to men. A mailed questionnaire survey of 296 women in a large metropolitan area surveyed their attitudes about the portrayal of women in ads, their image of the company sponsoring the ads, and their intentions to purchase the products offered in the ads. The average age of the subjects was 47, and the group fit the profile of upscale women in terms of formal education and income. They represented various occupations (homemaker, student, blue-collar worker, white-collar professional, and retiree), and diverse groups (white, black, Hispanic, Native American, and Asian American).

In general, the respondents were highly critical of the portrayal of women in advertisements. Although they believed that advertising was changing in terms of its treatment of women, they thought that most ads still showed women as being dependent on men, reinforcing the view that women do little of importance and that their proper place is in the home (Ford, LaTour, & Lundstrom, 1991).

Although the majority of television commercials show women in traditional roles, a growing number are featuring them in the business world and in positions of authority. Increasing numbers of women are heads of households responsible for purchasing items formerly bought almost exclusively by men, such as automobiles, home repair products, and travel services. There has also been an increase in the number of men purchasing products for cooking, housecleaning, and child care. Some advertisers have recognized these changes in the social climate and have responded accordingly, designing their commercials and advertising campaigns for different segments of the male and female buying public.

Some advertisers recognize the buying power of women for products that are beyond the scope of the traditional homemaker role. (Reproduced by permission of Samsonite Corporation.)

Success of Advertising Campaigns

The most important question for the seller is whether the advertising campaign is effective in increasing sales. In many cases, neither the advertising agency nor the company knows the answer, because effectiveness is difficult to determine. Further, companies are reluctant to broadcast their failures and are apt to exaggerate their successes.

Research on the success of television advertising campaigns has not been supportive. Nationwide surveys of viewers consistently show that most people dislike TV commercials. Television viewers watch fewer than half the commercials broadcast. They leave the room during commercial breaks, turn off the sound or switch channels with the remote control device, and erase or fast forward through commercials on video recorded programs.

Advertising agencies today usually assume that most people are not sitting through or paying attention to television ads. They refer to viewers as "nomads," wanderers or surfers from one channel to another. Consumer psychologists have suggested three types of viewers (Kaufman & Lane, 1994):

1. Channel nomads: people who surf from channel to channel looking for a program of interest. In New York City, viewers in households with remote control devices change channels on the average of every 3 minutes 26 seconds.
2. Mental nomads: people busy with other activities (such as preparing dinner, talking on the telephone, or playing with their children) who occasionally glance at the television set.
3. Physical nomads: people busy in other parts of the home who watch snatches of programs when they wander in and out of the room containing the television set.

Such nomadic behavior has also been found to characterize radio listeners. For example, research has shown that drivers who listen to the car radio avoid half of all advertising by switching stations (Abernethy, 1991).

In laboratory test situations, where people watching TV commercials were unable to tune them out, channel surf, or leave the room, subjects misunderstood or forgot approximately one third of what they had seen when questioned immediately after viewing the ads. A day later, the subjects had forgotten or misunderstood three fourths of what they had seen. The figure was higher for magazine ads.

The trend toward briefer television commercials (15-second spots instead of 30-second spots) may render advertising even less effective. One study questioned more than 1,000 viewers after they had seen a pilot for a new situation comedy along with a dozen commercials for national brands of window cleaner, mouthwash, cough drops, car wax, and other common household products. Some subjects were exposed to commercials in a 15-second format, others in a 30-second format. A third group saw some commercials of each type. The results showed that for the 15-second ads recall was lower and attitudes toward the product were less favorable. Consumers described the briefer commercials as less informative, less believable, and more irritating (Patzer, 1991).

In a laboratory study, 78 graduate and undergraduate students watched a television program with three commercial breaks. One of the breaks featured two 15-second commercials and one 30-second ad. When questioned after the program, the subjects demonstrated consistently lower recall for the 15-second commercials than for the 30-second ad (Ward, Oliva, & Reibstein, 1994).

The trend toward shorter and more frequent television commercials, combined with greater numbers of national and local newsbreaks, has led to what consumer psychologists describe as "clutter." Research conducted in the 1970s and 1980s, when clutter was considerably less, showed that recall for commercials and brand names decreased as clutter increased. However, more recent research has not found recall or brand name recognition to be significantly affected by further increases in clutter. Perhaps, as the researchers suggest, the baseline for television clutter was already so high that additional increases have had little effect (Brown & Rothschild, 1993).

The attempt to present even more advertising messages through subliminal advertising—presenting messages so quickly or faintly that they are not consciously recognized—attracted a great deal of publicity when first attempted in the 1950s. The idea has been revived periodically over the years, but research continues to demonstrate that it is not effective (see, for example, Smith & Rogers, 1994).

Advertising effectiveness may depend on the context in which an ad appears. For example, it has been suggested that the emotional tone of a television program can affect viewer response to commercials. To test this hypothesis, one group of adult subjects viewed a segment of a happy program (*Real People*) about how people were trying to teach frogs to improve their self-image. Another group of viewers watched a sad program, a segment of *60 Minutes* about the murder of a child. The viewers watching the happy program demonstrated a higher recall of ad content and rated the ads as being more effective than did viewers watching the sad program. There was no difference between the groups on stated intentions to purchase the products advertised (Goldberg & Gorn, 1987).

With magazine or newspaper advertising, a second exposure to an ad will sometimes increase its effectiveness. In one study, 240 business school graduate students were shown eight print ads of various levels of complexity. They were shown the same ads a week later. For the more complex ads, the second exposure resulted in a more positive evaluation of the ads' effectiveness and a substantially greater liking for the product (Cox & Cox, 1988).

Many advertisements compete for our attention, and the sheer number and variety can interfere with our ability to recall them. Laboratory studies on magazine ads have shown that ability to recall ads is more difficult when we are exposed to ads for a number of products or to ads for competing brands of the same product (see, for example, Burke & Srull, 1988; Keller, 1987, 1991). The researchers suggested that this may explain why so many people are unable to remember ads, even ads seen only a few moments before.

Another factor that can influence the effectiveness of print advertisements is the national literacy rate. At the present level of illiteracy in the United States, 33% of the population cannot fully comprehend advertising copy written at an eighth-grade level. "When people cannot read and process information, they cannot respond appropriately to marketing communications" (Harrison-Walker, 1995, p. 54).

Computer Advertising

The World Wide Web provides a new way for advertisers to spread their messages. To date, the effort is small, but it has the potential to grow rapidly. In

NEWSBREAK #27

Here's a Tip for You

Consumer psychologists try to amass as much information as possible about human behavior and motivation. Where we shop. What we purchase. Why we buy it. What ads we like. Which ads turn us off. There's not much that escapes the scrutiny of consumer psychologists, even leaving a tip in a restaurant. To the people who serve meals and clear tables, the tips we leave can compose the bulk of their income. Therefore, the amount you decide to leave for their service is vital to them.

Do you tend to tip excessively? Do you tip only a token amount and hurry to leave the restaurant before the waitperson notices? Consumer research has identified several factors that influence the size of your tips. Here's what they have learned:

- *How big was your bill?* Bill size is the single best predictor of tip size. The larger the bill, the larger the tip.
- *How friendly was your server?* This should be the first thing a new server learns. The friendlier they are, the larger tip they earn. Waitpersons who smile and introduce themselves by name tend to make more money than those who don't.
- *How professional was the service?* This may surprise you. Studies show a weak relationship between customer evaluations of the quality of service and the size of the tip. Thus, smiling may compensate for making a mistake with the order.
- *How attractive was the server?* As with many other social activities, more attractive people fare better than less attractive people. In this case, they tend to receive larger tips, though the amount was not significant.
- *What is your sex?* This is not a trick question. Gender can determine the size of the tip. Research shows that men are bigger tippers than women.
- *How many in your party?* Do you expect to leave a bigger tip when you are eating alone or when you're with a group? The research evidence is unclear. Some studies show that the larger the party, the smaller the individual tip, but not all research confirms this.
- *How often do you eat there?* Regulars at a restaurant tend to tip more than first-time customers or people who eat there only occasionally. Apparently, people feel differently about tipping when they expect to patronize the restaurant again.
- *Cash or charge?* In this case, the data are clear. People who charge meals leave larger tips than those who pay cash. Perhaps it doesn't seem like "real money" when you're using plastic. Also, even when paying cash, diners leave bigger tips when the bill is presented on a tray that bears a credit card company logo. This cue seems to serve as a stimulus to tip more than when the bill is presented on a blank tray.

(continued)

> ■ *What's the weather like?* Hotel room-service waiters receive larger tips on pleasant days when they can tell customers the weather is sunny than on cloudy days when they say it is raining.
>
> One final point about tipping, though there's no psychological research to back it up. Bartenders at establishments around the Capitol Hill area of Washington, D.C., whose bars are frequented by members of Congress and their staffs, report that Republicans are bigger tippers than Democrats!
>
> *Sources:* Daley, S. (1996, May). Hey, big spender. *Washingtonian Magazine*, p. 194. Lynn, M., Zinkhan, G. M., & Harris, J. (1993). Consumer tipping: A cross-country study. *Journal of Consumer Research, 20,* 478–488. McCall, M., & Belmont, H. J. (1996). Credit card insignia and restaurant tipping: Evidence for an associative link. *Journal of Applied Psychology, 81,* 609–613. Rind, B. (1996). Evidence of beliefs about weather conditions for tipping. *Journal of Applied Social Psychology, 26,* 137–147.

1995, American companies spent $37 million for advertising on the Web. (While this may sound like a lot of money, it accounted for only a fraction of the $60 billion companies spent that year on advertising in other media.) Still, in the 11 months from May, 1995, to April, 1996, more than 500 major corporations established Web sites to sell their products.

Advertising on the Web is more expensive than traditional outlets. For example, a 30-second ad on a television network news program can cost $65,000, and it will reach an audience of up to 12 million potential customers, for an average cost of $5.42 per 1,000 customers. A 1-month ad on the World Wide Web, at current rates, costs an estimated $75 per 1,000 customers. Advertisers believe the cost will drop sharply as more companies sign up for Web sites. They also expect Web advertising to be more effective because it will reach a targeted audience of people interested in the product. Ads for, say, computers or beer shown on a television program will be sent to many people who have no interest in those products, much less in the particular brands.

It is too soon to evaluate the effectiveness of Internet advertising. Although it is possible to count the number of times a specific Web site has been accessed, it is not yet possible to determine the characteristics of the person who hit there (age, level of education, or income, for example), or how long they browsed. In time, surveys of regular on-line users will provide this kind of demographic data. The World Wide Web represents the most exciting new medium for advertisers to promote their products since the advent of television.

THE CONSUMER

Consumers can be influenced by marketplace factors other than advertising when they make their purchasing decisions. A store's atmosphere and cleanliness, the ease of parking, the length of the aisles—all these things can affect shopper behavior. For example, research on supermarket shopping behavior has found that shoppers will look down short aisles rather than walk down them. They are much more likely to walk down long aisles and to make more impulse buys as a result. In addition, products more likely to be purchased on impulse are those at the ends of the aisles and around the checkout lanes (Foxall & Goldsmith, 1994). You can readily see where manufacturers would want to shelve their products for maximum visibility.

Another in-store factor that influences shopper behavior, independent of advertising, is providing free samples of a product. A 3-day behavioral observation study of 300 customers at a California chocolate shop in a regional shopping mall showed that nearly all those who received a free food sample purchased chocolates. Of those who did not receive a free sample, only two thirds purchased chocolates (Lammers, 1991).

Personal factors that affect consumer behavior include the standard biographical variables—age, sex, educational level, socioeconomic status, and ethnic origin—along with cognitive variables such as perceived time available for shopping, attitudes toward shopping, purpose of the shopping trip, and the shopper's mood and personality. For example, people whose personality includes a high degree of self-consciousness in public (being overly concerned about the impression they make on others and about what others think of them) have been found to be concerned about the labels on the products they buy. A study of 160 college students and 160 older consumers found that those who scored high on a test of public self-consciousness rated food labels of national brands significantly higher in brand preference than store brand labels for the same food product. Those who scored lower on self-consciousness gave significantly higher preference ratings to the less expensive store brands (Bushman, 1993).

Other aspects of consumer behavior of interest to psychologists are buying habits, brand loyalty, and the effect of product pricing.

Buying Habits and Brand Loyalty

Many of the stores in which we shop and the products we select are chosen on the basis of habit. Once we have found a product we like, it is simpler to continue to buy it than to select a new one. To demonstrate the strength of shopping habits, a supermarket rearranged its display of canned soups. The soups had been grouped by brand name but were changed to alphabetical order by type of soup, intermixing brands. Although signs were posted to explain the arrangement, more than 60% of the customers were fooled. Habit led them to the space on the shelf where they had previously gotten the desired soups. When questioned, customers said that the soups had been stocked in their usual order. They were amazed to find the wrong cans in their shopping cart! When consumers shop in new stores, where habit does not automatically lead them to the shelf locations of the usual products, they tend to buy many more different brands than in the past (Park, Iyer, & Smith, 1989).

A study of 173 college freshmen asked them to choose among eight brands of peanut butter. The students were inexperienced shoppers and had never purchased peanut butter for themselves. Subjects with no particular brand awareness tended to sample more brands. Those who were aware of a particular brand because of a national advertising campaign tended to select that brand. Although subsequent taste tests showed that brand to be of inferior quality, the subjects who had chosen it remained loyal to it over a series of five trials (Hoyer & Brown, 1990).

The design of an advertising campaign to change persistent buying habits presents a challenge. One study found that consumer loyalty to 50 major brands remained unchanged over an 8-year period (Johnson, 1984). Sixteen brands that were top sellers in their product category in 1923 retained their primacy 60 years later; these included Campbell soup, Lipton tea, Kodak cameras, and Wrigley chewing gum. These findings reinforce the importance to advertisers of establishing brand preferences in childhood. Once caught, consumers may remain loyal to a particular brand for many years and pass that loyalty on to their children.

It is sometimes difficult for researchers to distinguish between buying habits and brand loyalty. Both can be defined in terms of repeat purchase behavior, and the result is that the consumer is relatively impervious to ads for competing brands.

Product Pricing

The price of a product can be an important influence on buying behavior, independent of advertising and product quality. Consumers frequently use price as an index of quality on the assumption that the more an object costs, the better it must be. Some manufacturers capitalize on this belief and charge a higher price than their competitors do for a product of equal quality. Identical products, differing only in price, are often judged solely by their cost, with the more expensive product rated higher in quality.

Some consumers do not consider price when shopping for certain items. Observations of supermarket shoppers revealed that most do not pay attention to price information when shopping for staples such as breakfast cereal, coffee, and

Supermarket shoppers may judge certain products to be superior solely on the basis of price.

soft drinks, and they cannot accurately report current prices. Because of different package weights and sizes, shoppers are often unable to make the calculations necessary to determine which of several brands is the best buy. When supermarkets provide unit pricing information, such as cost per serving or cost per item, shoppers use this information extensively in making purchasing decisions.

A popular technique to gain sales for a new product or package is to charge a low price as an introductory offer. The idea is that once shoppers purchase the product, they will continue to do so out of habit, even when the price is raised to the level of competing products. Research does not support this notion. Sales are usually high during the introductory price period but drop when the price is raised. In stores that do not lower the price during the introductory period, sales typically remain stable.

Rebates are an effective way of offering a price reduction as an inducement to purchase. A price decrease in the form of a rebate usually produces higher sales than an equal point-of-sale price reduction. A survey of 495 shoppers found that frequent rebate users showed a high awareness of current prices and bought many products they did not need. They were enticed to make a purchase by a smaller rebate amount than were less frequent rebate users (Jolson, Wiener, & Rosecky, 1987).

Advertising to Ethnic Groups

There are important differences in consumer values, attitudes, and behaviors among people of different ethnic groups. Researchers have documented preferences for certain products among whites, blacks, Hispanics, and Asian Americans. Blacks constitute more than 12% of the U.S. population. In many large cities, they account for up to 90% of the residents—a sizable market with considerable purchasing power. Research suggests that blacks tend to spend more money than whites with comparable incomes for clothing but less for food, housing, and medical care. They purchase more milk and soft drinks but less coffee and tea. Also, they tend to favor national brands over private label house brands.

Consumer research has shown that black spokespersons are more effective than white spokespersons in reaching black consumers. In one study, 300 college student subjects of both races examined professionally produced full-color advertising storyboards for five products: a portable word processor, a laundry detergent, a cordless telephone, a popcorn popper, and a frozen fruit beverage. The researcher found that blacks recalled more ad content and expressed a more favorable attitude toward an ad when it featured a black rather than a white actor. The reactions of white subjects varied with their level of prejudice, as measured by a questionnaire on racial attitudes. Low-prejudiced whites exhibited higher recall of ads that featured black actors than did high-prejudiced whites (Whittler, 1991).

Advertising expenditures for the Spanish-speaking consumer market, representing some 9% of the U.S. population, have increased significantly in the past decade. Because nearly half of these consumers speak limited English, they cannot be reached effectively by mainstream mass-market advertising. Therefore, some national advertising is being targeted at Spanish-language publications and cable television networks. Among neighborhood businesses, which are preferred by the majority of Mexican American shoppers, there is a greater reliance on word-of-mouth communication and in-store advertising posters. Spanish-speaking consumers show a high degree of brand loyalty, especially to brands imported from their homeland.

The degree of assimilation into mainstream U.S. culture has been found to affect decision-making behavior in Hispanic families with regard to major consumer purchases such as automobiles and houses. A study of 227 married couples of Hispanic background living in Texas showed that the higher the degree of identification with the parent culture, the more dominant was the husband in making such decisions. Consumer decision-making power had shifted to the wife in families with a low identification with the parent culture. Thus, the higher the degree of assimilation, the more influential the wife's opinion in major purchasing decisions (Webster, 1994).

Advertising to Children and Adolescents

The 4-to-12 age group contains 34 million children with control over approximately $14 billion in disposable income. The fastest-growing spending categories for these young consumers are shoes and clothing. One explanation psychologists have advanced for the children's high degree of purchasing power is parental guilt. Consumer psychologists suggest that in single-parent families, in families with both parents employed outside the home, and in families in which parents have postponed childbearing until their thirties instead of their twenties, the children have been indulged with more money to spend and more influence over family purchasing decisions.

Marketing to children uses techniques such as placing products on lower supermarket shelves, airing cartoon commercials on children's television programs, and distributing in schools pencils, cups, and book covers featuring a product's name or logo.

A substantial portion of the advertising directed toward children appears on television. It is estimated that 11-year-olds watch 25,000 TV commercials a year. By the time most children in the United States reach age 18, they have watched in excess of 15,000 hours of television. So powerful is the influence of television advertising that children as young as 2 have been found to hold firmly established brand name preferences (Hitc & Hite, 1995; Minow & LaMay, 1995).

Television commercials oriented toward children have generated a great deal of controversy, and complaints have been voiced by parents and consumer groups. A survey of 690 adults revealed that they held highly negative opinions about child-oriented advertising. The majority of these adults believed that advertising stifled creativity, promoted materialism, and encouraged poor nutritional habits (Hite & Eck, 1987).

Young children can develop negative attitudes about commercials, attitudes that strengthen as they grow older and discover that many advertising claims are false. A study of 102 9- and 10-year-olds found a high level of mistrust of ads and a strong effort to resist their entreaties. More than 45% of the children questioned expressed negative feelings about the ads they were shown, saying that ads trick people and do not tell the truth (Brucks, Armstrong, & Goldberg, 1988).

However, television is an effective medium for reaching children with advertising messages. This large audience spends more time watching television than it spends in school. Laboratory and observational field studies report that television commercials increase young consumers' motivation to acquire many of the products displayed. Other research has shown that 5-year-olds acquire information significantly better when it is presented through televised words and pictures than when they simply hear the same message (words with no pictures) (Peracchio, 1993).

Consumer psychologists asked 250 mothers to keep diaries for 4 weeks, noting each request their children made for a specific product. The women were trained to make accurate records and were contacted weekly to ensure that the diaries were being prepared correctly. The ages of the children studied were 3 to 4, 5 to 7, and 9 to 11. Over the 4-week period, the average number of requests per child was 13 1/2, with the greatest number coming from the youngest children and the smallest number from the oldest children. The data suggested to the researchers that parents usually know what older children want and will buy those products regularly. Older children also often have money to make purchases on their own.

Most of the requests from older children were made at home, whereas requests from younger children were made more frequently during shopping trips. This finding may indicate that younger children are more likely to accompany their mothers on shopping trips. When the mothers were asked the reason for a child's request, 26% said the child had seen the product in a store, 21% said the child had seen an ad for the product, and 20% said a sibling or friend had bought the product. Most mothers acceded to their children's requests and purchased the desired products (Isler, Popper, & Ward, 1987).

Researchers detected changes in the consumer behavior of adolescents beginning in the 1980s, which they have attributed to the increase in the number of mothers employed outside the home. Only 25% of teenagers live in a traditional household in which the mother is a full-time homemaker and the father is employed outside the home. Teenagers spend an estimated $30 billion a year on clothing, cosmetics, and other personal items such as audiotapes and CDs. They

Many teenage shoppers are responsible for household grocery purchases.

have also assumed responsibility for much household spending. Many adolescents compile the household grocery list, make decisions about specific brands, and do the family marketing. More than 60% of teenage girls and 40% of teenage boys are believed to do routine grocery shopping.

While the rapidly growing number of single-parent households has changed the shopping habits of their children, it appears not to have affected their eating habits. A comparison of the families of 210 single mothers and 310 married mothers revealed no significant differences in the use of convenience foods or the number of meals eaten in full-service and fast-food restaurants (Ahuja & Walker, 1994).

Advertisers appeal to the adolescent market through magazine ads and cable television music channels and have in recent years increased their targeted ads for foods and household products. Although advertising obviously influences their buying behavior, when adolescents are asked to respond to questionnaires about advertising tactics, they report high levels of skepticism and disbelief about advertising claims (Boush, Friestad, & Rose, 1994).

Advertising to Older Persons

Changing demographic trends have produced another important market for advertisers: working people over the age of 50. This consumer segment, growing in numbers and affluence, will, by the year 2020, constitute more than one third of the population. The over-50 group now includes the first of the baby boomers, who began turning 50 on January 1, 1996. This vanguard of 76 million represents a huge not-yet-old but no-longer-young market with a large disposable income that they are used to spending freely.

The over-50 age group market share of the national income is approximately 40%, representing a multi-billion-dollar market for goods and services. Many advertisers have responded to this trend by revising their image of older people in advertisements and by eliminating stereotypes about the older consumer. Ads featuring attractive older models now promote cosmetics, hair care products, luxury travel, automobiles, clothing, jewelry, and health clubs.

Retired people over age 65 are another active consumer group. Although their incomes are usually lower, they constitute a large market for clothing, home furnishings, travel, entertainment, and health care products and services. Older consumers tend to read more newspapers and magazines than do younger consumers. Their television preferences include news and sports programs. They rely on mass media advertising for information more than younger people do, and they are critical of ads suggesting that young people are the only ones who have fun. They also rely on salespersons more than do younger shoppers.

A study of 111 women consumers over the age of 65 led psychologists to propose two types: the self-sufficients and the persuadables (Day, Davis, Dove, & French, 1988). Self-sufficients were described as being high in internal locus of control. They were also more independent, cosmopolitan, outgoing, and influential in dealing with others. They were more likely to read books, go shopping, attend concerts and sporting events, and eat in restaurants. Persuadables were described as being high in external locus of control. They were also more easily persuaded by advertisements and had little confidence in their own opinions. They preferred to stay at home rather than engage in outside activities. The self-sufficients read more magazines and watched less television, whereas the persuadables watched a great deal of daytime television. These findings suggest that advertisers can reach the self-sufficient market segment with print ads and the persuadable market segment with TV commercials.

Some elderly consumers resent being treated as a separate segment of the marketplace on the basis of their age. They resist participating in programs that use terms such as "golden years" or "senior citizen," even when it would save them money. A study of 113 people over the age of 50 delineated three levels of age segregation (K. Tepper, 1994):

- Ages 50–54: highly unlikely to use a senior citizen's discount, because doing so would mean admitting to being old.
- Ages 55–64: more likely than the previous group to use a senior discount.
- Ages 65 and older: totally accepting of a senior discount and of the label "senior citizen."

Consumer researchers suggest that people in these categories will respond to different kinds of ads and advertising appeals, based on their rejection or acceptance of their age status.

Advertising to Gay Men and Lesbian Women

An increasingly vocal and visible consumer group, gay persons are better educated and more affluent than the general population. A survey of 20,000 homosexuals that was conducted by a Chicago opinion polling firm found that approximately 60% of gay men and women were college graduates, compared to about 20% of the U.S. population as a whole. The survey estimated that the group represents a large potential market of people with high discretionary incomes.

Advertising to Disabled Persons

Another substantial consumer group with financial clout is the 43 million people in the United States who are disabled. Advertisers now use disabled persons as models in catalog ads and print ads and in television commercials. Companies such as McDonald's and Nike and retailers such as Nordstrom, Target, Lands End, and Kmart, have shown people in wheelchairs, persons with artificial limbs, and children with Down's syndrome. The companies report that such advertising has a positive effect on sales and enhances their public image.

This awareness of disabled persons was heightened by the Americans with Disabilities Act that mandated accessibility of public places, including stores, restaurants, and shopping centers. As a result, more disabled persons are becoming active shoppers. Also, more companies are responding to the needs of disabled persons with products to extend their strength and mobility and to compensate for their limitations. These items range from easy-to-fasten clothing to easy-to-grasp kitchen utensils. One popular mail-order catalog calls its products "designs for independent living."

Manufacturers and advertisers respond to changing markets with new products and marketing techniques. Consumers should be aware of the varied nature of advertising—sometimes valuable and informative and sometimes manipulative and deceptive. As a consumer, you should remember one of history's oldest lessons: *caveat emptor.* Let the buyer—of ideas, political philosophies, values, theories, research findings, and even psychology textbooks—beware.

Guilt Appeals in Advertising

Advertisements are designed to appeal to many human needs. Some ads appeal to the needs for sex, status, power, or achievement. Others to esteem and affiliation. Many appeal to more than one need at the same time. Some advertising messages use positive appeals, promising that something good will happen to you if you use the right product. Others threaten terrible consequences—such as never having a date—if you are foolish enough to reject what they are selling. And some ads use guilt appeals to try to persuade you that you will be a worthless person or a failure if you do not follow the advertiser's advice.

The major target audience for guilt appeals is mothers who have jobs outside the home, some of whom may already feel guilty because they are not staying at home full time with their children. To investigate the effect of guilt appeals on these working mothers, two marketing professors conducted a study in three phases. In Phase 1, 80 undergraduates identified three ads they believed were intended to create guilt. They described the ads in terms of components they perceived to be guilt-inducing, such as facial expressions, postures, and the wording of the ad copy.

In Phase 2, the two professors and a research assistant analyzed ads in women's and parents' magazines, identifying copy and pictures they believed were capable of inducing various levels of guilt. They based their judgments on the guilt-inducing components identified by the subjects in Phase 1.

Using the data from Phases 1 and 2, the researchers wrote advertising copy for two fictitious products (bread and dental floss) at three levels of guilt. For example, the Phase 3 ads for bread are as follows:

- Low guilt appeal: Whoever said "Children will eat anything" had to be joking.... Children have taste too!
- Moderate guilt appeal: Moms who don't teach their children to eat good meals have

children who don't always learn. You shape your child's eating habits, so don't let your family down.
- High guilt appeal: It's YOUR responsibility to make sure that your kids have healthy eating habits. The pressure is on YOU, so don't make any mistakes.... DO IT RIGHT!

Next, the researchers matched appropriate photographs with each of the guilt appeals. They selected 12 photos of a mother and son, depicting various facial expressions and postures, and asked 10 working mothers to judge the photos that seemed most appropriate for each of the three ads for each product. The picture-ad combinations were pretested to determine whether they induced the appropriate levels of guilt. A new sample of 20 working mothers rated the three ads on a 5-point scale as to how much guilt they induced. The results confirmed that the high guilt ad copy and picture induced the most guilt, the low guilt ad induced the least guilt, and the moderate guilt ad was rated midway between the other two.

A sample of 60 mothers with jobs outside the home was shown the three ads and asked to complete questionnaires assessing their emotional responses to the ads, their attitudes toward the company promoting the product, and their intention to purchase the brand advertised. The results showed that the moderate guilt appeal elicited significantly more guilt than the high and low guilt appeals. The high guilt appeal generated significantly more negative feelings (anger and irritation), and a lower intent to purchase the product, than did the other two levels of guilt appeals.

The researchers concluded that the high guilt appeal was counterproductive, leading to anger and negative feelings toward the company. It reduced the consumers' intention to purchase the product and did not induce as high a level of guilt as did the moderate appeal.

Critical Thinking Questions

1. With what kinds of products, and with what kinds of people, do you think guilt appeals would be most effective?

Source: Coulter, R. H., & Pinto, M. B. (1995). Guilt appeals in advertising: What are their effects? *Journal of Applied Psychology, 80,* 697–705.

2. Why do you think the high-guilt-appeal ads generated so much anger and irritation among the subjects while engendering less guilt than the moderate appeal?
3. What are the advantages and disadvantages of questionnaire and survey data in consumer psychology research?
4. What weaknesses can you find in the research methodology of this study? What strengths?
5. How would you design an advertising campaign to induce guilt feelings sufficient to motivate people to donate to a charitable cause? Give examples using both positive and negative appeals.

SUMMARY

Consumer psychology studies consumer behavior through surveys, **focus groups,** in-depth procedures, and behavioral observations including **scanner cable panels.** Testing for advertising effectiveness is done through direct questioning, aided recall and recognition, sales tests, and coupon returns. Television programming research uses viewer panels to screen programs, and Nielsen ratings to estimate audience size and composition. Advertising types include direct sell, product image, consumer awareness, institutional, and comparative. Advertising appeals can be positive, negative, or mixed. Many ads involve claims of implied superiority, which consumers tend to believe.

Trademarks can be effective advertising aids, as can the product's image. Packaging can also be influential at the point of purchase. Sexy images are commonly used in ads; they attract people to the ads but do not seem to influence how much of the advertising message is recalled. The image of women in advertising is changing; although women are increasingly shown in positive roles outside the home, they are still portrayed in traditional homemaker roles and as sex objects. Most people dislike TV commercials, avoid watching them, and fail to remember three fourths of the ads they see. The trend toward 15-second commercials contributes to the clutter on television nowadays. Illiteracy reduces the effectiveness of print ads. Brand loyalty can render buyers immune to advertising for competing products. Product price is often used as an indication of quality.

Much advertising directed toward children is effective in persuading them to want the products advertised, but children become increasingly distrustful of ads as they grow older. Ethnic groups, older persons, disabled persons, and gay persons are being targeted as market segments with specific needs and preferences.

KEY TERMS

aided recall technique
consumer psychology
focus groups

recognition technique
sales test technique
scanner cable panels

ADDITIONAL READING

Clark, E. M., Brock, T. C., & Stewart, D. W. (Eds.). (1994). *Attention, attitude, and affect in response to advertising.* Hillsdale, NJ: Erlbaum. A collection of papers on how people process persuasive communications and how such information produces changes in their attitudes and behavior.

Hine, T. (1995). *The total package: The evolution and secret meanings of boxes, bottles, cans, and tubes.* Boston: Little, Brown. Covers the history and development of product packaging and how packages influence purchasing and consumption decisions.

Mayer, M. (1991). *Whatever happened to Madison Avenue? Advertising in the '90s.* Boston: Little, Brown. Examines changes in the advertising industry of the 1970s and 1980s and describes problems confronting advertisers in the 1990s.

Minow, N. W., & LaMay, C. L. (1995). *Abandoned in the wasteland: Children, television, and the First Amendment.* New York: Hill and Wang. Discusses the history of television broadcasting, deregulation, and broadcasters' responsibility for serving the public interest, especially with regard to children's programming.

Rathje, W., & Murphy, C. (1992). *Rubbish!* New York: HarperCollins. Describes anthropologists' work on consumption habits as reported by consumers in interviews and as documented by examinations of trash containers.

Tybout, A. M. (1994). Consumer psychology. *Annual Review of Psychology, 45,* 131–169. Discusses research on how people process and make judgments about advertising information and how they respond to different types of pricing policies and sales promotion initiatives.

References

Abernethy, A. M. (1991). Differences between advertising and program exposure for car radio listening. *Journal of Advertising Research, 31*(2), 33–42.

Adams, G. A., King, L. A., & King, D. W. (1996). Relationships of job and family involvement, family social support, and work-family conflict with job and life satisfaction. *Journal of Applied Psychology, 81*, 411–420.

Adams, J. S. (1965). Inequity in social exchange. In L. Berkowitz (Ed.), *Advances in experimental social psychology* (vol. 2). New York: Academic Press.

Adkins, C. L. (1995). Previous work experience and organizational socialization: A longitudinal examination. *Academy of Management Journal, 38*, 839–862.

Agnew, J., & Suruda, A. J. (1993). Age and fatal work-related falls. *Human Factors, 35*, 731–736.

Ahuja, R. D., & Walker, M. (1994). Female-headed single parent families: Comparisons with dual parent households on restaurant and convenience food usage. *Journal of Consumer Marketing, 11*(4), 41–54.

Aiello, J. R., & Kolb, K. J. (1995a). Electronic performance monitoring and social context: Impact on productivity and stress. *Journal of Applied Psychology, 80*, 339–353.

Aiello, J. R., & Kolb, K. J. (1995b). Electronic performance monitoring: A risk factor for workplace stress. In S. L. Sauter & L. R. Murphy (Eds.), *Organizational risk factors for job stress* (pp. 163–179). Washington, DC: American Psychological Association.

Aiello, J. R., & Shao, Y. (1993). Electronic performance monitoring and stress: The role of feedback and goal setting. In M. J. Smith & G. Salvendy (Eds.), *Human-computer interaction: Applications and case studies* (pp. 1011–1016). Amsterdam: Elsevier Science.

Akbar-Khanzadeh, F., Bisesi, M. S., & Rivas, R. D. (1995). Comfort of personal protective equipment. *Applied Ergonomics, 26*(3), 195–198.

Albaum, G. (1987). Do source and anonymity affect mail survey results? *Journal of the Academy of Marketing Science, 15*(3), 74–81.

Alderfer, C. (1972). *Existence, relatedness and growth: Human needs in organizational settings.* New York: Free Press.

Allen, N. J., & Meyer, J. P. (1990). Organizational socialization tactics: A longitudinal analysis of links to newcomers' commitment and role orientation. *Academy of Management Journal, 33*, 847–858.

Alm, H., & Nilsson, L. (1995). The effects of a mobile telephone task on driver behaviour in a car-following situation. *Accident Analysis and Prevention, 27,* 707–715.

American Psychological Association (APA). (1992). Ethical principles of psychologists and code of conduct. *American Psychologist, 47,* 1597–1611.

American Psychological Association (APA). (1996). Statement on the disclosure of test data. Washington, DC: American Psychological Association.

Anastasi, A. (1986). Evolving concepts of test validation. *Annual Review of Psychology, 37,* 1–15.

Anderson, N., & Schackleton, V. (1986). Recruitment and selection: A review of developments in the 1980s. *Personnel Review, 15*(4), 19–26.

Antonioni, D. (1994). The effects of feedback accountability on upward appraisal ratings. *Personnel Psychology, 47,* 349–356.

Applebaum, E., & Batt, R. (1994). *The new American workplace.* Ithaca: ILR.

Armstrong, S. S. (1991). Another note on survey return rates. *Journal of Consumer Marketing, 8*(3), 57–62.

Arthur, W., Jr., Barrett, G. V., & Doverspike, D. (1990). Validation of an information-processing-based test battery for the prediction of handling accidents among petroleum-product transport drivers. *Journal of Applied Psychology, 75,* 621–628.

Arvey, R. D., Bouchard, T. J., Jr., Segal, N. L., & Abraham, L. M. (1989). Job satisfaction: Genetic and environmental components. *Journal of Applied Psychology, 74,* 187–192.

Arvey, R. D., & Campion, J. E. (1982). The employment interview: A summary and review of recent research. *Personnel Psychology, 35,* 281–322.

Arvey, R. D., & Faley, R. H. (1988). *Fairness in selecting employees.* Reading, MA: Addison-Wesley.

Arvey, R. D., Strickland, W., Drauden, G., & Martin, C. (1990). Motivational components of test taking. *Personnel Psychology, 43,* 695–716.

Ash, P., Slora, K., & Britton, C. (1990). Police agency officer selection practices. *Journal of Police Science Administration, 17,* 258–269.

Ashford, S. J., & Black, J. S. (1996). Proactivity during organizational entry: The role of desire for control. *Journal of Applied Psychology, 81,* 199–214.

Ashforth, B. E., & Saks, A. M. (1996). Socialization tactics: Longitudinal effects on newcomer adjustment. *Academy of Management Journal, 39,* 149–178.

Atkinson, J. W., & Feather, N. T. (1966). *A theory of achievement motivation.* New York: Wiley.

Atwater, L. A., Roush, P., & Fischthal, A. (1995). The influence of upward feedback on self- and follower ratings of leadership. *Personnel Psychology, 48,* 35–59.

Atwater, L. A., & Yammarino, F. J. (1992). Does self-other agreement on leadership perceptions moderate the validity of leadership and performance predictions? *Personnel Psychology, 45,* 141–164.

Avolio, B. J., Waldman, D. A., & McDaniel, M. A. (1990). Age and work performance in nonmanagerial jobs: The effects of experience and occupational type. *Academy of Management Journal, 33,* 407–422.

Azar, B. (1996, May). Naps lead to safer piloting, study shows. *APA Monitor,* p. 22.

Baker, B. R., & Cooper, J. N. (1995). Fair play or foul? A survey of occupational test practices in the U.K. *Personnel Review, 24*(3), 3–18.

Baker, K., Olson, J., & Morisseau, D. (1994). Work practices, fatigue, and nuclear power plant safety performance. *Human Factors, 36,* 244–257.

Baldwin, T. T., Magjuka, R. J., & Loher, B. T. (1991). The perils of participation; Effects of choice of training on trainee motivation and learning. *Personnel Psychology, 44,* 51–65.

Bamberger, P., Admati-Dvir, M., & Harel, G. (1995). Gender-based wage and promotion discrimination in Israeli high-technology firms: Do unions make a difference? *Academy of Management Journal, 38,* 1744–1761.

Bangert-Drowns, R. L. (1986). Review of the developments in meta-analytic method. *Psychological Bulletin, 99,* 388–399.

Banker, R. D., Field, J. M., Schroeder, R. G., & Sinha, K. K. (1996). Impact of work teams on manufacturing performance: A longitudinal field study. *Academy of Management Journal, 39,* 867–890.

Barber, A. E., Daly, C. L., Giannantonio, C. M., & Phillips, J. M. (1994). Job search activities: An examination of changes over time. *Personnel Psychology, 47,* 739–766.

Barber, A. E., Hollenbeck, J. R., Tower, S. L., & Phillips, J. M. (1994). The effects of interview focus on recruitment effectiveness: A field experiment. *Journal of Applied Psychology, 79,* 886–896.

Barber, A. E., & Roehling, M. V. (1993). Job postings and the decision to interview: A verbal protocol analysis. *Journal of Applied Psychology, 78,* 845–856.

Barling, J., & Rosenbaum, A. (1986). Work stressors and wife abuse. *Journal of Applied Psychology, 71,* 346–348.

Barnum, P., Liden, R. C., & Ditomaso, N. (1995). Double jeopardy for women and minorities: Pay differences with age. *Academy of Management Journal, 38,* 863–880.

Barr, S. H., & Hitt, M. A. (1986). A comparison of selection decision models in manager versus student samples. *Personnel Psychology, 39,* 599–617.

Barrett, M. W. (1995). Dual-earner dads may be the latest victims of salary discrimination. *Academy of Management Executive, 9*(2), 71–72.

Barrick, M. R., & Alexander, R. A. (1987). A review of quality circle efficacy and the existence of positive-findings bias. *Personnel Psychology, 40,* 579–592.

Barrick, M. R., & Mount, M. K. (1991). The big five personality dimensions and job performance: A meta-analysis. *Personnel Psychology, 44,* 1–26.

Barrick, M. R., & Mount, M. K. (1993). Autonomy as a moderator of the relationship between the Big Five personality dimensions and job performance. *Journal of Applied Psychology, 78,* 111–118.

Barrick, M. R., & Mount, M. K. (1996). Effects of impression management and self-deception on the predictive validity of personality constructs. *Journal of Applied Psychology, 81,* 261–272.

Barrick, M. R., Mount, M. K., & Strauss, J. P. (1993). Conscientiousness and performance of sales representatives: Test of the mediating effects of goal setting. *Journal of Applied Psychology, 78,* 715–722.

Barrick, M. R., Mount, M. K., & Strauss, J. P. (1994). Antecedents of involuntary turnover due to a reduction in force. *Personnel Psychology, 47,* 515–535.

Bartol, K. M., & Martin, D. C. (1988). Influences on managerial pay allocations: A dependency perspective. *Personnel Psychology, 41,* 361–378.

Bartol, K. M., & Martin, D. C. (1990). When politics pays: Factors influencing managerial compensation decisions. *Personnel Psychology, 43,* 599–614.

Barton, J. (1994). Choosing to work at night: A moderating influence on individual tolerance to shift work. *Journal of Applied Psychology, 79,* 449–454.

Bass, B. M. (1985). *Leadership and performance beyond expectations.* New York: Free Press.

Bass, B. M. (1997). Does the transactional-transformational leadership paradigm transcend organizational and national boundaries? *American Psychologist, 52,* 130–139.

Bass, B. M., & Avolio, B. J. (1993). Transformational leadership: A response to critiques. In M. M. Chemers & R. Ayman (Eds.), *Leadership theory and research: Perspectives and directions* (pp. 49–80). San Diego: Academic Press.

Bass, B. M., & Avolio, B. J. (1994). Shatter the glass ceiling: Women may make better managers. *Human Resource Management, 33,* 549–560.

Bass, B., & Yammarino, F. J. (1991). Congruence of self and others' leadership ratings of naval officers for understanding successful performance. *Applied Psychology: An International Review, 40,* 437–454.

Bateman, T. S., & Crant, J. M. (1993). The proactive component of organizational behavior. *Journal of Organizational Behavior, 14,* 103–118.

Becker, F., & Steele, F. (1995). *Workplace by design: Mapping the high-performance workscape.* San Francisco: Jossey-Bass.

Becker, T. E. (1992). Foci and bases of commitment: Are they distinctions worth making? *Academy of Management Journal, 35,* 232–244.

Becker, T. E., Billings, R. S., Eveleth, D. M., & Gilbert, N. L. (1996). Foci and bases of employee commitment: Implications for job performance. *Academy of Management Journal, 39,* 464–482.

Becker, T. E., & Colquitt, A. L. (1992). Potential versus actual faking of a biodata form: An analysis along several dimensions of item type. *Personnel Psychology, 45,* 389–406.

Begley, T. M., & Czajka, J. M. (1993). Panel analysis of the moderating effects of commitment on job satisfaction, intent to quit, and health following organizational change. *Journal of Applied Psychology, 78,* 552–556.

Bernardin, H. J. (1986). Subordinate appraisal: A valuable source of information about managers. *Human Resource Management, 25,* 421–439.

Bernardin, H. J., & Cooke, D. K. (1993). Validity of an honesty test in predicting theft among convenience store employees. *Academy of Management Journal, 36,* 1097–1108.

Bernardin, H. J., Dahmus, S., & Redmon, G. (1993). Attitudes of first-line supervisors toward subordinate appraisals. *Human Resource Management, 32,* 315–324.

Billimoria, D., & Piderit, S. K. (1994). Board committee membership: Effects of sex-based bias. *Academy of Management Journal, 37,* 1453–1477.

Blakley, B. R., Quiñones, M. A., Crawford, M. S., & Jago, I. A. (1994). The validity of isometric strength tests. *Personnel Psychology, 47,* 247–274.

Blau, G. (1988). An investigation of the apprenticeship organizational socialization strategy. *Journal of Vocational Behavior, 32,* 176–195.

Blau, G. (1993). Further exploring the relationship between job search and voluntary individual turnover. *Personnel Psychology, 46,* 313–330.

Blau, G. (1994). Developing and testing a taxonomy of lateness behavior. *Journal of Applied Psychology, 79,* 959–970.

Blocklyn, P. L. (1987). The aging workforce. *Personnel, 64*(8), 16–19.

Bloswick, D. S., Gerber, A., Sebesta, D., Johnson, S., & Mecham, W. (1994). Effect of mailbag design on musculoskeletal fatigue and metabolic load. *Human Factors, 36,* 210–218.

Bluen, S. D., Barling, J., & Burns, W. (1990). Predicting sales performance, job satisfaction, and depression using the Achievement Strivings and Impatience-Irritability dimensions of Type A behavior. *Journal of Applied Psychology, 75,* 212–216.

Bogg, J., & Cooper, C. (1995). Job satisfaction, mental health, and occupational stress among senior civil servants. *Human Relations, 48,* 327–341.

Bommer, W. H., Johnson, J. L., Rich, G. A., Podsakoff, P. M., & Mackenzie, S. B. (1995). On the interchangeability of objective and subjective measures of employee performance: A meta-analysis. *Personnel Psychology, 48,* 587–605.

Booth-Kewley, S., Edwards, J. E., & Rosenfeld, P. (1992). Impression management, social desirability, and computer administration of attitude questionnaires: Does the computer make a difference? *Journal of Applied Psychology, 77,* 562–566.

Booth-Kewley, S., & Friedman, H. S. (1987). Psychological predictors of heart disease: A quantitative review. *Psychological Bulletin, 101,* 343–362.

Borman, W. C., & Cox, G. L. (1996). Who's doing what: Patterns in the practice of I/O psychology. *The Industrial-Organizational Psychologist, 33*(4), 21–29.

Borman, W. C., Hanson, M. A., & Hedge, J. W. (1997). Personnel selection. *Annual Review of Psychology, 48,* 299–337.

Borman, W. C., White, L. A., & Dorsey, D. W. (1995). Effects of rater task performance and interpersonal factors on supervisor and peer performance ratings. *Journal of Applied Psychology, 80,* 168–177.

Borman, W. C., White, L. A., Pulakos, E. D., & Oppler, S. H. (1991). Models of supervisory job performance ratings. *Journal of Applied Psychology, 76,* 863–872.

Borman, W. C., Hanson, M. A., Oppler, S. H., Pulakos, E. D., & White, L. A. (1993). Role of early supervisory experience in supervisor performance. *Journal of Applied Psychology, 78,* 443–449.

Bouchard, T. J., Jr., Arvey, R. D., Keller, L. M., & Segal, N. L. (1992). Genetic influences on job satisfaction: A reply to Cropanzano and James. *Journal of Applied Psychology, 77,* 89–93.

Boush, D. M., Friestad, M., & Rose, G. M. (1994). Adolescent skepticism toward TV advertising and knowledge of advertiser tactics. *Journal of Consumer Research, 21,* 165–175.

Bouzid, N., & Cranshaw, C. M. (1987). Massed versus distributed word processor training. *Applied Ergonomics, 18,* 220–222.

Bracken, D. W. (1994, September). Straight talk about multirater feedback. *Training & Development,* pp. 44–51.

Brannick, M. T., Michaels, C. E., & Baker, D. P. (1989). Construct validity of in-basket scores. *Journal of Applied Psychology, 74,* 957–963.

Bray, D. W. (1964). The Management Progress Study. *American Psychologist, 19,* 419–420.

Bray, D. W. (1982). The assessment center and the study of lives. *American Psychologist, 37,* 180–189.

Breaugh, J. A., & Colihan, J. P. (1994). Measuring facets of job ambiguity: Construct validity evidence. *Journal of Applied Psychology, 79,* 191–202.

Brett, J. F., Cron, W. L., & Slocum, J. W., Jr. (1995). Economic dependency on work: A moderator of the relationship between organizational commitment and performance. *Academy of Management Journal, 38,* 261–271.

Bretz, R. D., Jr., Boudreau, J. W., & Judge, T. A. (1994). Job search behavior of employed managers. *Personnel Psychology, 47,* 275–301.

Brickner, M. A., Harkins, S., & Ostrom, T. M. (1986). Effects of personal involvement: Thought-provoking implications for social loafing. *Journal of Personality and Social Psychology, 51,* 763–769.

Bridgwater, C. A. (1982, August). Inflexible flextimers. *Psychology Today,* p. 13.

Broad, W., & Wade, N. (1982). *Betrayers of the truth: Fraud and deceit in the halls of science.* New York: Simon & Schuster.

Brockner, J., Grover, S. L., & Blonder, M. D. (1988). Predictors of survivors' job involvement following layoffs: A field study. *Journal of Applied Psychology, 73,* 436–442.

Brockner, J., & Hess, T. (1986). Self-esteem and task performance in quality circles. *Academy of Management Journal, 29,* 617–623.

Brown, B. K., & Campion, M. A. (1994). Biodata phenomenology: Recruiters' perceptions and use of biographical information in resume screening. *Journal of Applied Psychology, 79,* 897–908.

Brown, D. C. (1993). Target Stores settle out of court in Soroka v. Dayton Hudson. *The Industrial-Organizational Psychologist, 31*(2), 88–89.

Brown, D. C. (1994a). EEOC releases ADA testing guidance. *The Industrial-Organizational Psychologist, 32*(2), 66–67.

Brown, D. C. (1994b). Subgroup norming: Legitimate testing practice or reverse discrimination? *American Psychologist, 49,* 927–928.

Brown, I. D. (1994). Driver fatigue. *Human Factors, 36,* 298–314.

Brown, T. J., & Rothschild, M. L. (1993). Reassessing the impact of television advertising clutter. *Journal of Consumer Research, 20,* 138–146.

Brucks, M., Armstrong, G. M., & Goldberg, M. E. (1988). Children's use of cognitive defenses against television advertising: A cognitive response approach. *Journal of Consumer Research, 14,* 471–482.

Buch, K., & Spangler, R. (1990). The effects of quality circles on performance and promotions. *Human Relations, 43,* 573–582.

Buckley, M. R., Kicza, D. C., & Crane, N. (1987). A note on the effectiveness of flextime as an organizational intervention. *Public Personnel Management, 16,* 259–267.

Budd, J. W., Arvey, R. D., & Lawless, P. (1996). Correlates and consequences of workplace violence. *Journal of Occupational Health Psychology, 1,* 197–210.

Burke, M. J. (1984). Validity generalization: A review and critique of the correlation model. *Personnel Psychology, 37,* 93–115.

Burke, M. J., Brief, A. P., & George, J. M. (1993). The role of negative affectivity in understanding relations between self-reports of stressors and strains: A comment on the applied psychology literature. *Journal of Applied Psychology, 78,* 402–412.

Burke, M. J., & Day, R. R. (1986). A cumulative study of the effectiveness of managerial training. *Journal of Applied Psychology, 71,* 232–246.

Burke, M. J., & Normand, J. (1987). Computerized psychological testing: Overview and critique. *Professional Psychology, 18,* 42–51.

Burke, R. R., & Srull, T. K. (1988). Competitive interference and consumer memory for advertising. *Journal of Consumer Research, 15,* 55–68.

Burnette, E. (1994, November). Psychology makes top 10 of country's hottest careers. *APA Monitor,* p. 10.

Bushman, B. J. (1993). What's in a name? The moderating role of public self-consciousness on the relation between brand label and brand preference. *Journal of Applied Psychology, 78,* 857–861.

Butcher, J. N. (1994). Psychological assessment of airline pilot applicants with the MMPI-2. *Journal of Personality Assessment, 62*(1), 31–44.

Butler, D. L., Acquino, A. L., Hissong, A. A., & Scott, P. A. (1993). Wayfinding by newcomers in a complex building. *Human Factors, 35,* 159–173.

Bycio, P., Hackett, R. D., & Allen, J. S. (1995). Further assessments of Bass's (1985) conceptualization of transactional and transformational leadership. *Journal of Applied Psychology, 80,* 468–478.

Cable, D. M., & Judge, T. A. (1994). Pay preferences and job search decisions: A person-organization fit perspective. *Personnel Psychology, 47,* 317–348.

Cameron, K. S., Freeman, S. J., & Mishra, A. K. (1991). Best practices in white-collar downsizing: Managing contradictions. *Academy of Management Executive, 5*(3), 57–58.

Campbell, J. M., Amerikaner, M., Swank, P., & Vincent, K. (1989). The relationship between the Hardiness Test and the Personal Orientation Inventory. *Journal of Research in Personality, 23,* 373–380.

Campbell, R. J., & Bray, D. W. (1993). Use of an assessment center as an aid in management selection. *Personnel Psychology, 46,* 691–699.

Campbell, W. J. (1996). Lessons from the field. *The Industrial-Organizational Psychologist, 33*(3), 102–103.

Campion, M. A. (1991). Meaning and measurement of turnover: Comparison of alternative measures and recommendations for research. *Journal of Applied Psychology, 76,* 199–212.

Campion, M. A., Campion, J. E., & Hudson, J. P., Jr. (1994). Structured interviewing: A note on incremental validity and alternative question types. *Journal of Applied Psychology, 79,* 998–1002.

Campion, M. A., Cheraskin, L., & Stevens, M. J. (1994). Career-related antecedents and outcomes of job rotation. *Academy of Management Journal, 37,* 1518–1542.

Campion, M. A., & McClelland, C. (1991). Interdisciplinary examination of the costs and benefits of enlarged jobs: A job design quasi-experiment. *Journal of Applied Psychology, 76,* 186–198.

Campion, M. A., & McClelland, C. (1993). Follow-up and extension of the interdisciplinary costs and benefits of enlarged jobs. *Journal of Applied Psychology, 78,* 339–351.

Campion, M. A., Medsker, G. J., & Higgs, A. C. (1993). Relations between work group characteristics and effectiveness: Implications for designing effective work groups. *Personnel Psychology, 46,* 823–850.

Campion, M. A., Papper, E. M., & Medsker, G. J. (1996). Relations between work team characteristics and effectiveness: A replication and extension. *Personnel Psychology, 49,* 429–452.

Campion, M. A., Pursell, E. D., & Brown, B. K. (1988). Structured interviewing: Raising the psychometric properties of the employment interview. *Personnel Psychology, 41,* 25–42.

Carayon, P. (1993). Effect of electronic performance monitoring on job design and worker stress: Review of the literature and conceptual model. *Human Factors, 35,* 385–395.

Carayon, P. (1995). Chronic effect of job control, supervisor social support, and work pressure on office worker stress. In S. L. Sauter & L. R. Murphy (Eds.), *Organizational risk factors for job stress* (pp. 357–370). Washington, DC: American Psychological Association.

Carlopio, J. R. (1996). Construct validity of a Physical Work Environment Satisfaction Questionnaire. *Journal of Occupational Health Psychology, 1,* 330–344.

Carnevale, A. P. (1995). Enhancing skills in the new economy. In A. Howard (Ed.), *The changing nature of work* (pp. 238–251). San Francisco: Jossey-Bass.

Carrier, M. R., Dalessio, A. T., & Brown, S. H. (1990). Correspondence between estimates of content and criterion-related validity values. *Personnel Psychology, 43,* 85–100.

Cascio, W. F. (1993). A message from your president. *The Industrial-Organizational Psychologist, 30*(4), 5–7.

Cascio, W. F. (1995). Whither industrial and organizational psychology in a changing world of work? *American Psychologist, 50,* 928–939.

Chad, K. E., & Brown, J. M. M. (1995). Climatic stress in the workplace. *Applied Ergonomics, 26,* 29–34.

Chalykoff, J., & Kochan, T. A. (1989). Computer-aided monitoring: Its influence on employee job satisfaction and turnover. *Personnel Psychology, 42,* 807–830.

Chandler, A. D., Jr. (1988). Origins of the organization chart. *Harvard Business Review, 66*(2), 156–157.

Chao, G. T., O'Leary-Kelly, A. M., Wolf, S., Klein, H. J., & Gardner, P. D. (1994). Organizational socialization: Its content and consequences. *Journal of Applied Psychology, 79,* 730–743.

Chapanis, A. (1965). On the allocation of functions between men and machines. *Occupational Psychology, 39,* 1–11.

Chatman, J. A. (1991). Matching people and organizations: Selection and socialization in public accounting firms. *Administrative Science Quarterly, 36,* 459–484.

Chatman, J. A., & Jehn, K. A. (1994). Assessing the relationship between industry characteristics and organizational culture: How different can you be? *Academy of Management Journal, 37,* 522–553.

Chen, P. Y., & Spector, P. E. (1992). Relationships of work stressors with aggression, withdrawal, theft, and substance use: An exploratory study. *Journal of Occupational and Organizational Psychology, 65,* 117–184.

Childs, A., & Klimoski, R. J. (1986). Successfully predicting career success: An application of the biographical inventory. *Journal of Applied Psychology, 71,* 3–8.

Christiansen, N. D., Goffin, R. D., Johnston, N. G., & Rothstein, M. G. (1994). Correcting the 16PF for faking: Effects on criterion-related validity and individual hiring decisions. *Personnel Psychology, 47,* 847–860.

Church, A. H. (1995a). Organizational downsizing: What is the role of the practitioner? *The Industrial-Organizational Psychologist, 33*(1), 63–74.

Church, A. H. (1995b). Performance appraisals: Political tools or effective measures? *The Industrial-Organizational Psychologist, 33*(2), 57–64.

Clegg, C., Wall, T., & Kemp, N. (1987). Women on the assembly line: A comparison of main and interactive explanations of job satisfaction, absence, and mental health. *Journal of Occupational Psychology, 60,* 273–287.

Cohen, S. G., & Ledford, G. E., Jr. (1994). The effectiveness of self-managing teams: A field experiment. *Human Relations, 47,* 13–43.

Conway, J. M., Jako, R. A., & Goodman, D. F. (1995). A meta-analysis of interrater and internal consistency reliability of selection interviews. *Journal of Applied Psychology, 80,* 565–579.

Corderey, J. L., Mueller, W. S., & Smith, L. M. (1991). Attitudinal and behavioral effects of autonomous group working: A longitudinal field study. *Academy of Management Journal, 34,* 464–476.

Corderey, J. L., & Sevastos, P. P. (1993). Responses to the original and revised Job Diagnostic Survey: Is education a factor in responses to negatively worded items? *Journal of Applied Psychology, 78,* 141–143.

Cordes, C. L., & Dougherty, T. W. (1993). A review and an integration of research on job burnout. *Academy of Management Review, 18,* 621–656.

Cornelius, E. T., III, Schmidt, F. L., & Carron, T. J. (1984). Job classification approaches and the implementation of validity generalization results. *Personnel Psychology, 37,* 247–260.

Costa, G. (1996). The impact of shift and night work on health. *Applied Ergonomics, 27,* 9–16.

Coulter, R. H., & Pinto, M. B. (1995). Guilt appeals in advertising: What are their effects? *Journal of Applied Psychology, 80,* 697–705.

Cox, D. S., & Cox, A. D. (1988). What does familiarity breed? Complexity as a moderator of repetition effects in advertisement evaluations. *Journal of Consumer Research, 15,* 111–116.

Crant, J. M. (1995). The Proactive Personality Scale and objective job performance among real estate agents. *Journal of Applied Psychology, 80,* 532–537.

Crant, J. M., & Bateman, T. S. (1990). An experimental test of the impact of drug-testing programs on potential job applicants' attitudes and intentions. *Journal of Applied Psychology, 75,* 127–131.

Crohan, S. E., Antonucci, T. C., Adelmann, P. L., & Coleman, L. M. (1989). Job characteristics and well-being at midlife. *Psychology of Women Quarterly, 13,* 223–235.

Cron, W. L., Dubinsky, A. J., & Michaels, R. E. (1988). The influence of career stages on components of salesperson motivation. *Journal of Marketing, 52,* 78–92.

Cron, W. L., & Slocum, J. W., Jr. (1986). The influence of career stages on salespeople's job attitudes, work perceptions, and performance. *Journal of Marketing Research, 23,* 119–129.

Cropanzano, R., & James, K. (1990). Some methodological considerations for the behavioral genetic analysis of work attitudes. *Journal of Applied Psychology, 75,* 433–439.

Crouch, A., & Yetton, P. W. (1988). Manager-subordinate dyads: Relationships among task and social contact, manager friendliness and subordinate performance in management groups. *Organizational Behavior and Human Decision Processes, 41,* 65–82.

Cunningham, M. R., Wong, T. D., & Barbee, A. P. (1994). Self-presentation dynamics on overt integrity tests: Experimental studies of the Reid Report. *Journal of Applied Psychology, 79,* 643–658.

Dalessio, A. T., & Silverhart, T. A. (1994). Combining biodata test and interview information: Predicting decisions and performance criteria. *Personnel Psychology, 47,* 303–315.

Daley, S. (1966, May). Hey, big spender. *Washingtonian Magazine.*

Dalton, D. R., & Mesch, D. J. (1991). On the extent and reduction of avoidable absenteeism: An assessment of absence policy provisions. *Journal of Applied Psychology, 76,* 810–817.

Daniels, K., & Guppy, A. (1994). Occupational stress, social support, job control, and psychological well-being. *Human Relations, 47,* 1523–1544.

Davidson, M. J., & Cooper, C. L. (1987). Female managers in Britain: A comparative perspective. *Human Resource Management, 26,* 217–242.

Davis, B. L., & Mount, M. K. (1984). Design and use of a performance appraisal feedback system. *Personnel Administrator, 29*(3), 91–97.

Day, E., Davis, B., Dove, R., & French, W. (1988). Reaching the senior citizen market(s). *Journal of Advertising Research, 28,* 23–30.

Deadrick, D. L., & Madigan, R. M. (1990). Dynamic criteria revisited: A longitudinal study of performance stability and predictive validity. *Personnel Psychology, 43,* 717–744.

DeAngelis, T. (1991, December). Sexual harassment common, complex. *APA Monitor,* pp. 29–30.

DeNisi, A. S., Cornelius, E. T., III, & Blencoe, A. G. (1987). Further investigation of common knowledge effects on job analysis ratings. *Journal of Applied Psychology, 72,* 262–268.

Denison, D. R. (1990). *Corporate culture and organizational effectiveness.* New York: Wiley.

Denison, D. R. (1996). What is the difference between organizational culture and organizational climate? A native's point of view on a decade of paradigm wars. *Academy of Management Review, 21,* 619–654.

Dennis, A. R., & Valacich, J. S. (1993). Computer brainstorms: More heads are better than one. *Journal of Applied Psychology, 78,* 531–537.

DeReamer, R. (1980). *Modern safety and health technology.* New York: Wiley.

Derven, M. G. (1990). The paradox of performance appraisals. *Personnel Journal, 69,* 107–111.

de Vaus, D., & McAllister, I. (1991). Gender and work orientations: Values and satisfaction in Western Europe. *Work and Occupations, 18,* 72–93.

Dictionary of occupational titles (4th ed., rev.). (1991). Washington, DC: Government Printing Office.

Dobbins, G. H., & Platz, S. J. (1986). Sex differences in leadership: How real are they? *Academy of Management Review, 11,* 118–127.

Dobbins, G. H., & Russell, J. M. (1986). The biasing effects of subordinate likeableness on leaders' responses to poor performers: A laboratory and a field study. *Personnel Psychology, 39,* 759–777.

Doby, J. J., & Caplan, R. D. (1995). Organizational stress as threat to reputation: Effects on anxiety at work and at home. *Academy of Management Journal, 38,* 1105–1123.

Doll, T. J., & Folds, D. J. (1986). Auditory signals in military aircraft: Ergonomics principles versus practice. *Applied Ergonomics, 17,* 257–264.

Dompierre, J., & Lavoie, F. (1994). Subjective work stress and family violence. In G. P. Keith & J. J. Hurrell, Jr., (Eds.), *Job stress in a changing workforce: Investigating gender, diversity and family issues* (pp. 213–227). Washington, DC: American Psychological Association.

Donnerstein, E., & Wilson, D. W. (1976). Effects of noise and perceived control on ongoing and subsequent aggressive behavior. *Journal of Personality and Social Psychology, 34,* 774–781.

Dorfman, P. W., Stephan, W. G., & Loveland, J. (1986). Performance appraisal behaviors: Supervisor perceptions and subordinate reactions. *Personnel Psychology, 39,* 579–597.

Dougherty, T. W., Turban, D. B., & Callender, J. C. (1994). Confirming first impressions in the employment interview: A field study of interviewer behavior. *Journal of Applied Psychology, 79,* 659–665.

Drakeley, R. J., Herriot, P., & Jones, A. (1988). Biographical data, training success, and turnover. *Journal of Occupational Psychology, 61,* 145–152.

Drazin, R., & Auster, E. R. (1987). Wage differences between men and women: Performance appraisal ratings versus salary allocation as the locus of bias. *Human Resource Management, 26,* 157–168.

Dreher, G. F., & Ash, R. A. (1990). A comparative study of mentoring among men and women in managerial, professional, and technical positions. *Journal of Applied Psychology, 75,* 539–546.

Dreher, G. F., & Bretz, R. D., Jr. (1991). Cognitive ability and career attainment: Moderating effects of early career success. *Journal of Applied Psychology, 76,* 392–397.

Dreher, G. F., & Cox, T. H., Jr. (1996). Race, gender, and opportunity: A study of compensation attainment and the establishment of mentoring relationships. *Journal of Applied Psychology, 81,* 297–308.

Driskell, J. E., Copper, C., & Moran, A. (1994). Does mental practice enhance performance? *Journal of Applied Psychology, 79,* 481–492.

Duarte, W. C., Goodson, J. R., & Klich, N. R. (1994). Effects of dyadic quality and duration on performance appraisal. *Academy of Management Journal, 37,* 499–521.

Duchon, J. C., Keran, C. M., & Smith, T. J. (1994). Extended workdays in an underground mine: A work performance analysis. *Human Factors, 36,* 258–268.

Dunham, R. B., Grube, J. A., & Castañeda, M. B. (1994). Organizational commitment: The utility of an integrative definition. *Journal of Applied Psychology, 79,* 370–380.

Dunham, R. B., Pierce, J. L., & Castañeda, M. B. (1987). Alternative work schedules: Two field quasi-experiments. *Personnel Psychology, 40,* 215–242.

Dunn, W. S., Mount, M. K., Barrick, M. R., & Ones, D. S. (1995). Relative importance of personality and general mental ability in managers' judgments of applicant qualifications. *Journal of Applied Psychology, 80,* 500–509.

Dunnette, M. D. (1989). Validation of selection tests for electrical power plant operators. In B. J. Fallon, H. B. Pfister, & J. Brebner (Eds.), *Advances in industrial and organizational psychology* (pp. 377–387). New York: Elsevier/North-Holland.

Duvall-Early, K., & Benedict, J. (1992). The relationships between privacy and different components of job satisfaction. *Environmental Behavior, 24,* 670–679.

Duxbury, L. E., & Higgins, C. A. (1991). Gender differences in work-family conflict. *Journal of Applied Psychology, 76,* 60–74.

Dvir, T., Eden, D., & Banjo, M. L. (1995). Self-fulfilling prophecy and gender: Can women be Pygmalion and Galatea? *Journal of Applied Psychology, 80,* 253–270.

Eagly, A. H., Ashmore, R. D., Makhijani, M. G., & Longo, L. C. (1991). What is beautiful is good . . . : A meta-analytic review of research on the physical attractiveness stereotype. *Psychological Bulletin, 110,* 109–129.

Eagly, A. H., & Johnson, B. T. (1990). Gender and leadership style: A meta-analysis. *Psychological Bulletin, 108,* 233–256.

Eagly, A. H., Karau, S. J., & Makhijani, M. G. (1995). Gender and the effectiveness of leaders: A meta-analysis. *Psychological Bulletin, 117,* 125–145.

Eagly, A. H., Makhijani, M. G., & Klonsky, B. G. (1992). Gender and the evaluation of leaders: A meta-analysis. *Psychological Bulletin, 111,* 3–22.

Earley, P. C., & Lituchy, T. R. (1991). Delineating goal and efficacy effects: A test of three models. *Journal of Applied Psychology, 76,* 81–98.

Eden, D. (1990). Pygmalion without interpersonal contrast effects: Whole groups gain from raising manager expectations. *Journal of Applied Psychology, 75,* 394–398.

Eden, D., & Aviram, A. (1993). Self-efficacy training to speed reemployment: Helping people to help themselves. *Journal of Applied Psychology, 78,* 352–360.

Edwards, J. R., & Baglioni, A. J., Jr. (1991). Relationship between Type A behavior patterns and mental and physical symptoms: A comparison of global and component measures. *Journal of Applied Psychology, 76,* 276–290.

Eisenberger, R., Fasolo, P., & Davis-LaMastro, V. (1990). Perceived organizational support and employee diligence, commitment and innovation. *Journal of Applied Psychology, 75,* 51–59.

Eklund, J. A. E. (1995). Relationships between ergonomics and quality in assembly work. *Applied Ergonomics, 26*(1), 15–20.

Elton, C. F., & Smart, J. C. (1988). Extrinsic job satisfaction and person-environment congruence. *Journal of Vocational Behavior, 32,* 226–238.

Ely, R. J. (1995). The power in demography: Women's social constructions of gender identity at work. *Academy of Management Journal, 38,* 589–634.

Erffmeyer, E. S., & Mendel, R. M. (1990). Master's level training in industrial/organizational psychology: A case study of the perceived relevance of graduate training. *Professional Psychology, 21,* 405–408.

Erfurt, J. C., Foote, A., & Heirich, M. A. (1992). The cost-effectiveness of worksite wellness programs for hypertension control, weight loss, smoking cessation, and exercise. *Personnel Psychology, 45,* 5–27.

Evans, G. W., & Carrère, S. (1991). Traffic congestion, perceived control, and psychophysiological stress among urban bus drivers. *Journal of Applied Psychology, 76,* 658–663.

Evans, P. D. (1990). Type A behaviour and coronary heart disease: When will the jury return? *British Journal of Psychology, 81,* 147–157.

Eyring, J. D., Johnson, D. S., & Francis, D. J. (1993). A cross-level units-of-analysis approach to individual differences in skill acquisition. *Journal of Applied Psychology, 78,* 805–814.

Fagenson, E. A. (1990). Perceived masculine and feminine attributes examined as a function of individuals' sex and level in the organizational power hierarchy: A test of four theoretical perspectives. *Journal of Applied Psychology, 75,* 204–211.

Fagenson, E. A. (1993). Is what's good for the goose also good for the gander? On being white and male in a diverse workforce. *Academy of Management Executive, 7*(4), 80–81.

Farh, J. L., Dobbins, G. H., & Cheng, B. S. (1991). Cultural relativity in action: A comparison of self-ratings made by Chinese and U.S. workers. *Personnel Psychology, 44,* 129–147.

Feather, N. T. (1990). The effects of unemployment on work values and motivation. In U. Kleinbeck, H. H. Quast, H. Thierry, & H. Häcker (Eds.), *Work motivation* (pp. 201–229). Hillsdale, NJ: Erlbaum.

Feeney, E. J. (1972). Performance audit, feedback, and positive reinforcement. *Training and Development Journal, 26*(11), 8–13.

Feingold, A. (1992). Good-looking people are not what we think. *Psychological Bulletin, 111*, 304–341.

Fiedler, F. E. (1978). The contingency model and the dynamics of the leadership process. In L. Berkowitz (Ed.), *Advances in experimental social psychology*. New York: Academic Press.

Fiedler, F. E., & Garcia, J. E. (1987). *New approaches to effective leadership: Cognitive resources and organizational performance*. New York: Wiley.

Fiedler, F. E., Murphy, S. E., & Gibson, F. W. (1992). Inaccurate reporting and inappropriate variables: A reply to Vecchio's (1990) examination of cognitive resource theory. *Journal of Applied Psychology, 77*, 372–374.

Field, R. H. G. (1982). A test of the Vroom-Yetton normative model of leadership. *Journal of Applied Psychology, 67*, 523–532.

Field, R. H. G., & House, R. J. (1990). A test of the Vroom-Yetton model using manager and subordinate reports. *Journal of Applied Psychology, 75*, 362–366.

Fields, M. W., & Thacker, J. W. (1992). Influence of quality of work life on company and union commitment. *Academy of Management Journal, 35*, 439–450.

Finkelman, J. M. (1994). A large database study of the factors associated with work-induced fatigue. *Human Factors, 36*, 232–243.

Finkelstein, L. M., Burke, M. J., & Raju, N. S. (1995). Age discrimination in simulated employment contexts: An integrative analysis. *Journal of Applied Psychology, 80*, 652–663.

Fleishman, E. A., & Harris, E. F. (1962). Patterns of leadership behavior related to employee grievances and turnover. *Personnel Psychology, 15*, 43–56.

Ford, J. B., LaTour, M. S., & Lundstrom, W. J. (1991). Contemporary women's evaluation of female role portrayals in advertising. *Journal of Consumer Marketing, 8*(1), 15–28.

Ford, J. K., Smith, E. M., Sego, D. J., & Quiñones, M. A. (1993). Impact of task experience and individual factors on training-emphasis ratings. *Journal of Applied Psychology, 78*, 583–590.

Fowler, A. (1991). An even-handed approach to graphology. *Personnel Management, 23*(3), 40–43.

Fox, M. L., Dwyer, D. J., & Ganster, D. C. (1993). Effects of stressful job demands and control on physiological and attitudinal outcomes in a hospital setting. *Academy of Management Journal, 36*, 289–318.

Fox, S., & Dinur, Y. (1988). Validity of self-assessment: A field evaluation. *Personnel Psychology, 41*, 581–592.

Foxall, G. R., & Goldsmith, R. E. (1994). *Consumer psychology for marketing*. London: Routledge.

Freedman, M., Zador, P., & Staplin, L. (1993). Effects of reduced transmittance film on automobile rear window visibility. *Human Factors, 35*, 535–550.

French, J. R. P., Jr., Caplan, R. D., & Van Harrison, R. (1982). *The mechanisms of job stress and strain*. New York: Wiley.

Frese, M., & Semmer, N. (1986). Shiftwork, stress, and psychosomatic complaints: A comparison between workers in different shiftwork schedules, non-shiftworkers, and former shiftworkers. *Ergonomics, 29*, 99–114.

Freudenberger, H. J. (1980). *Burnout: The high cost of achievement*. Garden City, NY: Doubleday.

Fricko, M. A. M., & Beehr, T. A. (1992). A longitudinal investigation of interest congruence and gender concentration as predictors of job satisfaction. *Personnel Psychology, 45,* 99–117.

Fried, Y. (1991). Meta-analytic comparison of the Job Diagnostic Survey and Job Characteristics Inventory as correlates of work satisfaction and performance. *Journal of Applied Psychology, 76,* 690–697.

Fried, Y., & Ferris, G. R. (1986). The dimensionality of job characteristics: Some neglected issues. *Journal of Applied Psychology, 71,* 419–426.

Fried, Y., & Ferris, G. R. (1987). The validity of the job characteristics model: A review and meta-analysis. *Personnel Psychology, 40,* 287–322.

Fried, Y., & Tiegs, R. B. (1995). Supervisors' role conflict and role ambiguity differential relations with performance ratings of subordinates and the moderating effect of screening ability. *Journal of Applied Psychology, 80,* 282–291.

Friedman, M., & Rosenman, R. H. (1974). *Type A behavior and your heart.* New York: Alfred A. Knopf.

Frone, M. R., Russell, M., & Barnes, G. M. (1996). Work-family conflict, gender, and health-related outcomes: A study of employed parents in two community samples. *Journal of Occupational Health Psychology, 1,* 57–69.

Frone, M. R., Russell, M., & Cooper, M. L. (1995). Job stressors, job involvement and employee health: A test of identity theory. *Journal of Occupational and Organizational Psychology, 68,* 1–11.

Fullagar, C. J. A., Gallagher, D. G., Gordon, M. E., & Clark, P. F. (1995). Impact of early socialization on union commitment and participation: A longitudinal study. *Journal of Applied Psychology, 80,* 147–157.

Gallupe, R. B., Cooper, W. H., Grisé, M. L., & Bastianutti, L. M. (1994). Blocking electronic brainstorms. *Journal of Applied Psychology, 79,* 77–86.

Gallupe, R. B., Dennis, A. R., Cooper, W. H., Valacich, J. S., Bastianutti, L. M., & Nunamaker, J. F., Jr. (1992). Electronic brainstorming and group size. *Academy of Management Journal, 35,* 350–369.

Ganster, D. C., & Schaubroeck, J. (1991). Role stress and worker health: An extension of the plasticity hypothesis of self-esteem. *Journal of Social Behavior and Personality, 6,* 349–360.

Ganster, D. C., Schaubroeck, J., Sime, W. E., & Mayes, B. T. (1991). The nomological validity of the Type A personality among employed adults. *Journal of Applied Psychology, 76,* 143–168.

Gattiker, U. E., & Larwood, L. (1990). Predictors for career achievement in the corporate hierarchy. *Human Relations, 43,* 703–726.

Gaugler, B. B., Rosenthal, D. B., Thornton, G. C., III, & Bentson, C. (1987). Meta-analysis of assessment center validity. *Journal of Applied Psychology, 72,* 493–511.

Gebhardt, D. L., & Crump, C. E. (1990). Employee fitness and wellness programs in the workplace. *American Psychologist, 45,* 262–272.

Gehlmann, S. C. (1992). Individual differences in employee stress as related to office environment and individual personality factors. In J. C. Quick, L. R. Murphy, & J. J. Hurrell, Jr. (Eds.), *Stress and well-being at work: Assessments and interventions for occupational mental health* (pp. 225–234). Washington, DC: American Psychological Association.

Gemmill, G. R., & Heisler, W. J. (1972). Fatalism as a factor in managerial job satisfaction, job strain, and mobility. *Personnel Psychology, 25,* 241–250.

George, J. M. (1990). Personality, affect, and behavior in groups. *Journal of Applied Psychology, 75,* 107–116.

George, J. M. (1992). Extrinsic and intrinsic origins of perceived social loafing in organizations. *Academy of Management Journal, 35,* 191–202.

George, J. M., & Brief, A. P. (1992). Feeling good—doing good: A conceptual analysis of the mood at work—organizational spontaneity relationship. *Psychological Bulletin, 112,* 310–329.

Gilbert, G. R., Collins, R. W., & Brenner, A. (1990). Age and leadership effectiveness: From the perceptions of the follower. *Human Resource Management, 29,* 187–196.

Gilbreth, F. B. (1911). *Motion study.* Princeton, NJ: Van Nostrand.

Giles, W. F., & Mossholder, K. W. (1990). Employee reactions to contextual and session components of performance appraisal. *Journal of Applied Psychology, 75,* 371–377.

Gist, M. E., & Mitchell, T. R. (1992). Self-efficacy: A theoretical analysis of its determinants and malleability. *Academy of Management Review, 17,* 183–211.

Gist, M. E., Schwoerer, C., & Rosen, B. (1989). Effects of alternative training methods on self-efficacy and performance in computer software training. *Journal of Applied Psychology, 74,* 884–891.

Goff, S. J., Mount, M. K., & Jamison, R. L. (1990). Employer supported child care, work/family conflict, and absenteeism: A field study. *Personnel Psychology, 43,* 793–809.

Goffin, R. D., Rothstein, M. G., & Johnston, N. G. (1996). Personality testing and the assessment center: Incremental validity for managerial selection. *Journal of Applied Psychology, 81,* 746–756.

Goldberg, L. R., Grenier, J. R., Guion, R. M., Sechrest, L. B., & Wing, H. (1991). *Questionnaires used in the prediction of trustworthiness in pre-employment selection decisions: An APA task force report.* Washington, DC: American Psychological Association.

Goldberg, M. E., & Gorn, G. J. (1987). Happy and sad TV programs: How they affect reactions to commercials. *Journal of Consumer Research, 14,* 387–403.

Goldstein, I. L., & Gilliam, P. (1990). Training system issues in the year 2000. *American Psychologist, 45,* 134–143.

Gomez-Mejia, L. R., & Balkin, D. B. (1987). Dimensions and characteristics of personnel manager perceptions of effective drug-testing programs. *Personnel Psychology, 40,* 745–763.

Goodman, P. S., & Leyden, D. P. (1991). Familiarity and group productivity. *Journal of Applied Psychology, 76,* 578–586.

Goodstein, J. (1994). Institutional pressures and strategic responsiveness: Employer involvement in work-family issues. *Academy of Management Journal, 37,* 350–382.

Goodstein, J. (1995). Employer involvement in eldercare: An organizational adaptation perspective. *Academy of Management Journal, 38,* 1657–1671.

Gopher, D., Weil, M., & Baraket, T. (1994). Transfer of skill from a computer game trainer to flight. *Human Factors, 36,* 387–405.

Gordon, G. G., (1991). Industry determinants of organizational culture. *Academy of Management Review, 16,* 396–415.

Gordon, J. (1992). Work teams—How far have they come? *Training, 29,* 59–65.

Gordon, M. E., & Bowlby, R. L. (1988). Propositions about grievance settlements: Finally, consultation with grievants. *Personnel Psychology, 41,* 107–123.

Gordon, M. E., Slade, L. A., & Schmitt, N. (1986). The "science of the sophomore" revisited: From conjecture to empiricism. *Academy of Management Review, 11*, 191–207.

Gordon, R. A., Rozelle, R. M., & Baxter, J. C. (1988). The effect of applicant age, job level, and accountability on the evaluation of job applicants. *Organizational Behavior and Human Decision Processes, 41*, 20–33.

Gotlieb, J. B., & Sarel, D. (1991). Comparative advertising effectiveness: The role of involvement and source credibility. *Journal of Advertising, 20*(1), 38–45.

Gottfredson, G. D., & Holland, J. L. (1990). A longitudinal test of the influence of congruence: Job satisfaction, competency utilization, and counterproductive behavior. *Journal of Counseling Psychology, 37*, 389–398.

Gottfredson, L. S. (1992). Dilemmas in developing diversity programs. In S. E. Jackson (Ed.), *Diversity in the workplace: Human resources initiatives* (pp. 279–305). New York: Guilford Press.

Gottfredson, L. S. (1994). The science and politics of race-norming. *American Psychologist, 49*, 955–963.

Graen, G., Novak, M., & Sommerkamp, P. (1982). The effects of leader-member exchange and job design on productivity and satisfaction: Testing a dual attachment model. *Organizational Behavior and Human Performance, 30*, 109–131.

Graen, G., Scandura, T. A., & Graen, M. R. (1986). A field experimental test of the moderating effects of growth need strength on productivity. *Journal of Applied Psychology, 71*, 484–491.

Graen, G., & Schliemann, W. (1978). Leader-member agreement: A vertical dyad linkage approach. *Journal of Applied Psychology, 63*, 206–212.

Graen, G., & Wakabayashi, M. (1986). The Japanese career progress study: A 7-year follow-up. *Journal of Applied Psychology, 69*, 603–614.

Graves, L., & Karren, R. J. (1992). Interviewer decision processes and effectiveness: An experimental policy-capturing investigation. *Personnel Psychology, 45*, 313–340.

Green, D. E., & Walkey, F. H. (1988). A confirmation of the three-factor structure of the Maslach Burnout Inventory. *Educational and Psychological Measurement, 48*, 579–585.

Greenberg, J. (1986). Determinants of perceived fairness of performance evaluations. *Journal of Applied Psychology, 71*, 340–342.

Greenberg, J. (1988). Equity and workplace status: A field experiment. *Journal of Applied Psychology, 73*, 606–613.

Greenberg, J. (1990). Employee theft as a reaction to underpayment inequity: The hidden cost of pay cuts. *Journal of Applied Psychology, 75*, 561–568.

Greenberg, J. (1994). Using socially fair treatment to promote acceptance of a work site smoking ban. *Journal of Applied Psychology, 79*, 288–297.

Greenhaus, J. H., Parasuraman, S., & Wormley, W. M. (1990). Effects of race on organizational experiences, job performance evaluations, and career outcomes. *Academy of Management Journal, 33*, 64–86.

Gregersen, H. B., & Black, J. S. (1992). Antecedents to commitment to a parent company and a foreign operation. *Academy of Management Journal, 35*, 65–90.

Greller, M. M., Parsons, C. K., & Mitchell, D. R. D. (1992). Addictive effects and beyond: Occupational stressors and social buffers in a police organization. In J. C. Quick, L. R. Murphy, & J. J. Hurrell, Jr. (Eds.), *Stress and well-being at work: Assessments and inverventions for occupational mental health* (pp. 33–47). Washington, DC: American Psychological Association.

Griffin, R. W. (1991). Effects of work redesign on employee perceptions, attitudes, and behaviors: A long-term investigation. *Academy of Management Journal, 34,* 425–435.

Griffith, T. L. (1993). Teaching big brother to be a team player: Computer monitoring and quality. *Academy of Management Executive, 7*(1), 73–80.

Grover, S. L., & Crooker, K. J. (1995). Who appreciates family-responsive human resource policies: The impact of family-friendly policies on the organizational attachment of parents and non-parents. *Personnel Psychology, 48,* 271–288.

Groves, R. M. (1990). Theories and methods of telephone surveys. *Annual Review of Sociology, 16,* 221–240.

Guinn, K. A., & Corona, R. J. (1991). Putting a price on performance. *Personnel Journal, 70,* 72–77.

Guion, R. M., & Gibson, W. M. (1988). Personnel selection and placement. *Annual Review of Psychology, 39,* 349–374.

Gutek, B. A., Searle, S., & Klepa, L. (1991). Rational versus gender role explanations for work-family conflict. *Journal of Applied Psychology, 76,* 560–568.

Gutierres, S. E., Saenz, D. S., & Green, B. L. (1994). Job stress and health outcomes among White and Hispanic employees: A test of the person-environment fit model. In G. P. Keita & J. J. Hurrell, Jr. (Eds.), *Job stress in a changing workforce: Investigating gender, diversity and family issues* (pp. 107–125). Washington, DC: American Psychological Association.

Guzzo, R. A., & Dickson, M. W. (1996). Teams in organizations: Recent research on performance and effectiveness. *Annual Review of Psychology, 47,* 307–338.

Gyllenhammar, P. G. (1977). *People at work.* Reading, MA: Addison-Wesley.

Haberfeld, Y. (1992). Employment discrimination: An organizational model. *Academy of Management Journal, 35,* 161–180.

Hackett, R. D. (1990). Age, tenure, and employee absenteeism. *Human Relations, 43,* 601–619.

Hackman, J. R., & Oldham, G. R. (1975). Development of the Job Diagnostic Survey. *Journal of Applied Psychology, 60,* 159–170.

Hackman, J. R., & Oldham, G. R. (1976). Motivation through the design of work: Test of a theory. *Organizational Behavior and Human Performance, 16,* 250–279.

Hackman, J. R., & Oldham, G. R. (1980). *Work redesign.* Reading, MA: Addison-Wesley.

Haines, V. A., Hurlbert, J. S., & Zimmer, C. (1991). Occupational stress, social support, and the buffer hypothesis. *Work and Occupations, 18,* 212–235.

Haire, M. (1950). Projective techniques in marketing research. *Journal of Marketing, 14,* 649–656.

Haleblian, J., & Finkelstein, S. (1993). Top management team size, CEO dominance, and firm performance: The moderating roles of environmental turbulence and discretion. *Academy of Management Journal, 36,* 844–863.

Hall, F. S., & Hall, E. L. (1994). The ADA: Going beyond the law. *Academy of Management Executive, 8*(1), 17–26.

Hall, J. A., & Briton, N. J. (1993). Gender, nonverbal behavior, and expectations. In P. D. Blanck (Ed.), *Interpersonal expectations* (pp. 276–295). Cambridge, England: Cambridge University Press.

Hammer, E. G., & Kleiman, L. S. (1988). Getting to know you. *Personnel Administrator, 33*(5), 86–92.

Hammer, T. H., & Turk, J. M. (1987). Organizational determinants of leader behavior and authority. *Journal of Applied Psychology, 72,* 674–682.

Hancock, E. (1996, February). High control at work makes for a healthy heart. *Johns Hopkins Magazine,* p. 31.

Harder, J. W. (1991). Equity theory versus expectancy theory: The case of major league baseball free agents. *Journal of Applied Psychology, 76,* 458–464.

Harn, T. J., & Thornton, G. C., III. (1985). Recruiter counseling behaviors and applicant impressions. *Journal of Occupational Psychology, 58,* 57–65.

Harper, S. C. (1992). The challenges facing CEOs: Past, present, and future. *Academy of Management Executive, 6*(3), 7–25.

Harris, M. M., & Fink, L. S. (1987). A field study of applicant reactions to employment opportunities: Does the recruiter make a difference? *Personnel Psychology, 40,* 765–784.

Harris, M. M., & Schaubroeck, J. (1988). A meta-analysis of self-supervisor, self-peer, and peer-supervisor ratings. *Personnel Psychology, 41,* 43–62.

Harris, M. M., Smith, D. E., & Champagne, D. (1995). A field study of performance appraisal purpose: Research- versus administrative-based ratings. *Personnel Psychology, 48,* 151–160.

Harrison, D. A., & Shaffer, M. A. (1994). Comparative examinations of self-reports and perceived absenteeism norms: Wading through Lake Wobegon. *Journal of Applied Psychology, 79,* 240–251.

Harrison-Walker, L. J. (1995). The import of illiteracy to marketing communication. *Journal of Consumer Marketing, 12*(1), 50–62.

Hartel, C. E. J. (1994). Vantage 2000: Humanizing work and the workplace. *The Industrial-Organizational Psychologist, 32*(2), 25–29.

Hatcher, M. A. (1991). The corporate woman of the 1990s: Maverick or innovator? *Psychology of Women Quarterly, 15,* 251–259.

Hater, J. J., & Bass, B. M. (1988). Superiors' evaluations and subordinates' perceptions of transformational and transactional leadership. *Journal of Applied Psychology, 73,* 695–702.

Healy, M. C., Lehman, M., & McDaniel, M. A. (1995). Age and voluntary turnover: A quantitative review. *Personnel Psychology, 48,* 335–345.

Heaney, C. A., Israel, B. A., & House, J. S. (1994). Chronic job insecurity among automobile workers: Effects on job satisfaction and health. *Social Science and Medicine, 38,* 1431–1437.

Hedberg, G. (1987). The evaluation of the driver's cab in the Rc5 engine. *Applied Ergonomics, 18*(1), 35–42.

Hedge, J. W., & Borman, W. C. (1995). Changing conceptions and practices in performance appraisal. In A. Howard (Ed.), *The changing nature of work* (pp. 451–481). San Francisco: Jossey-Bass.

Heilman, M. E., Block, C. J., & Lucas, J. A. (1992). Presumed incompetent? Stigmatization and affirmative action efforts. *Journal of Applied Psychology, 77,* 536–544.

Helmreich, R. L., Sawin, L. L., & Carsrud, A. L. (1986). The honeymoon effect in job performance: Temporal increases in the predictive power of achievement motivation. *Journal of Applied Psychology, 71,* 185–188.

Heneman, H. G., III, & Schwab, D. P. (1985). Pay satisfaction: Its multidimensional nature and measurement. *International Journal of Psychology, 20,* 129–141.

Hepburn, C. G., & Barling, J. (1996). Eldercare responsibilities, interrole conflict, and employee absence: A daily study. *Journal of Occupational Health Psychology, 1,* 311–318.

Hershberger, S. L., Lichtenstein, P., & Knox, S. S. (1994). Genetic and environmental influences on perceptions of organizational climate. *Journal of Applied Psychology, 79,* 24–33.

Herzberg, F. (1966). *Work and the nature of man.* Cleveland: World.

Herzberg, F. (1974). Motivator-hygiene profiles: Pinpointing what ails the organization. *Organizational Dynamics, 3*(2), 18–29.

Higie, R. A., & Sewall, M. A. (1991). Using recall and brand preferences to evaluate advertising effectiveness. *Journal of Advertising Research, 31*(2), 56–63.

Hill, L. A., & Elias, J. (1991). Retraining midcareer managers: Career history and self-efficacy beliefs. *Human Resource Management, 29,* 197–217.

Hinkin, T. R., & Schriesheim, C. A. (1988). Power and influence: The view from below. *Personnel, 65*(5), 47–50.

Hirsh, H. R., Northrop, L. C., & Schmidt, F. L. (1986). Validity generalization results for law enforcement occupations. *Personnel Psychology, 39,* 399–420.

Hite, C. F., & Hite, R. E. (1995). Reliance on brand by young children. *Journal of the Market Research Society, 37*(2), 185–193.

Hite, R. E., & Eck, R. (1987). Advertising to children: Attitudes of business versus consumers. *Journal of Advertising Research, 27,* 40–53.

Hoffman, C. C., Nathan, B. R., & Holden, L. M. (1991). A comparison of validation criteria: Objective versus subjective performance measures and self- versus supervisor ratings. *Personnel Psychology, 44,* 601–619.

Hofmann, D. A., & Stetzer, A. (1996). A cross-level investigation of factors influencing unsafe behaviors and accidents. *Personnel Psychology, 49,* 307–339.

Hogan, E. A. (1987). Effects of prior expectations on performance ratings: A longitudinal study. *Academy of Management Journal, 30,* 354–368.

Hogan, J. (1991). Structure of physical performance in occupational tasks. *Journal of Applied Psychology, 76,* 495–507.

Hogan, R., Curphy, G. J., & Hogan, J. (1994). What we know about leadership: Effectiveness and personality. *American Psychologist, 49,* 493–504.

Hogan, R., Hogan, J., & Roberts, B. W. (1996). Personality measurement and employment decisions: Questions and answers. *American Psychologist, 51,* 469–477.

Hollenbeck, J. R., & Klein, H. J. (1987). Goal commitment and the goal-setting process: Problems, prospects, and proposals for future research. *Journal of Applied Psychology, 72,* 212–220.

Hollenbeck, J. R., & Williams, C. R. (1986). Turnover functionality versus turnover frequency: A note on work attitudes and organizational effectiveness. *Journal of Applied Psychology, 71,* 606–611.

Hollingworth, H. L. (1929). *Vocational psychology and character analysis.* New York: Appleton.

Honts, C. R., Raskin, D. C., & Kircher, J. C. (1994). Mental and physical countermeasures reduce the accuracy of polygraph tests. *Journal of Applied Psychology, 79,* 252–259.

Hough, L. M., Eaton, N. K., Dunnette, M. D., Kamp, J. D., & McCoy, R. A. (1990). Criterion-related validities of personality constructs and the effect of response distortion on those validities. *Journal of Applied Psychology, 75,* 581–595.

House, R. J. (1971). A path-goal theory of leader effectiveness. *Administrative Science Quarterly, 16,* 321–338.

House, R. J., & Mitchell, T. (1974). Path-goal theory of leadership. *Journal of Contemporary Business, 3,* 81–97.

Houtman, I. L. D., & Kompier, M. A. J. (1995). Risk factors and occupational risk groups for work stress in the Netherlands. In S. L. Sauter & L. R. Murphy (Eds.), *Organizational risk factors for job stress* (pp. 209–225). Washington, DC: American Psychological Association.

How to be efficient with fewer violins. (1955). *American Association of University Professors Bulletin, 41,* 454–455.

Howard, A. (1986). College experiences and managerial performance. *Journal of Applied Psychology, 71,* 530–552.

Howard, A. (1990). *The multiple facets of industrial-organizational psychology: Membership survey results.* Arlington Heights, IL: Society for Industrial and Organizational Psychology.

Howard, A. (1995). A framework for work change. In A. Howard (Ed.), *The changing nature of work* (pp. 3–44). San Francisco: Jossey-Bass.

Howard, A., & Bray, D. W. (1988). *Managerial lives in transition: Advancing age and changing times.* New York: Guilford.

Howarth, P. A., & Istance, H. O. (1986). The validity of subjective reports of visual discomfort. *Human Factors, 28,* 347–351.

Howell, J. M., & Avolio, B. J. (1992). The ethics of charismatic leadership: Submission or liberation? *Academy of Management Executive, 6*(2), 43–54.

Howell, J. M., & Avolio, B. J. (1993). Transformational leadership, transactional leadership, locus of control, and support for innovation: Key predictors of consolidated-business-unit performance. *Journal of Applied Psychology, 78,* 891–902.

Howell, W. C. (1991). Human factors in the workplace. In M. D. Dunnette & L. M. Hough (Eds.), *Handbook of industrial and organizational psychology* (2nd ed.) (vol. 2, pp. 210–269). Palo Alto, CA: Consulting Psychologists Press.

Hoyer, W. D., & Brown, S. P. (1990). Effects of brand awareness on choice for a common, repeat-purchase product. *Journal of Consumer Research, 17*(2), 141–148.

Hsu, S. H., & Peng, Y. (1993). Control/display relationship of the four-burner stove: A reexamination. *Human Factors, 35,* 745–749.

Huffcutt, A. I. (1990). Structured interviews emerge: The new technique of the 1990s? *The Industrial-Organizational Psychologist, 27*(3), 83–84.

Huffcutt, A. I., & Arthur, W., Jr. (1994). Hunter and Hunter (1984) revisited: Interview validity for entry-level jobs. *Journal of Applied Psychology, 79,* 184–190.

Hunt, S. T. (1996). General work behavior: An investigation into the dimensions of entry-level hourly job performance. *Personnel Psychology, 49,* 51–83.

Hunter, J. E. (1980). *Validity generalization for 12,000 jobs: An application of synthetic validity and validity generalization to the General Aptitude Test Battery (GATB).* Washington, DC: U.S. Employment Service.

Hunter, J. E. (1986). Cognitive ability, cognitive aptitudes, job knowledge, and job performance. *Journal of Vocational Behavior, 29,* 340–362.

Hunter, J. E., & Hunter, R. F. (1983). *The validity and utility of alternative predictors of job performance.* Washington, DC: U.S. Office of Personnel Management.

Hunter, J. E., & Schmidt, F. L. (1983). Quantifying the effects of psychological intervention on employee job performance and workforce productivity. *American Psychologist, 38,* 473–478.

Huseman, R. C., Hatfield, J. D., & Miles, E. W. (1987). A new perspective on equity theory: The equity sensitive construct. *Academy of Management Review, 12,* 222–234.

Hutchison, S., & Sowa, D. (1986). Perceived organizational support. *Journal of Applied Psychology, 71,* 500–507.

Hyde, J. S., Klein, M. H., Essex, M. J., & Clark, R. (1995). Maternity leave and women's mental health. *Psychology of Women Quarterly, 19,* 257–285.

Ibarra, H. (1995). Race, opportunity, and diversity of social circles in managerial networks. *Academy of Management Journal, 38,* 673–703.

Idaszak, J. R., & Drasgow, F. (1987). A revision of the Job Diagnostic Survey: Elimination of a measurement artifact. *Journal of Applied Psychology, 72,* 69–74.

Ingram, P., & Simons, T. (1995). Institutional and resource dependence determinants of responsiveness to work-family issues. *Academy of Management Journal, 38,* 1466–1482.

Irving, P. G., & Meyer, J. P. (1994). Reexamination of the met-expectations hypothesis: A longitudinal analysis. *Journal of Applied Psychology, 79,* 937–949.

Isler, L., Popper, E. T., & Ward, S. (1987). Children's purchase requests and parental responses: Results from a diary study. *Journal of Advertising Research, 27,* 28–39.

Ivancevich, J. M., Matteson, M. T., Freedman, S. M., & Phillips, J. S. (1990). Worksite stress management interventions. *American Psychologist, 45,* 252–261.

Jackall, R. (1983). Moral mazes: Bureaucracy and managerial work. *Harvard Business Review, 61*(5), 118–130.

Jackson, D. N., & Kovacheff, J. D. (1993). Personality questionnaires in selection: Privacy issues in the Soroka case. *The Industrial-Organizational Psychologist, 30*(4), 45–50.

Jackson, P. R., Wall, T. D., Martin, R., & Davids, K. (1993). New measures of job control, cognitive demand, and production responsibility. *Journal of Applied Psychology, 78,* 753–762.

Jackson, S. E., & Schuler, R. S. (1995). Understanding human resource management in the context of organizations and their environments. *Annual Review of Psychology, 46,* 237–264.

Jago, A. G., & Vroom, V. H. (1980). An evaluation of two alternatives to the Vroom-Yetton normative model. *Academy of Management Review, 23,* 347–355.

Janiszewski, C. (1993). Preattentive mere exposure effects. *Journal of Consumer Research, 20,* 376–392.

Janssens, M., Brett, J. M., & Smith, F. J. (1995). Confirmatory cross-cultural research: Testing the viability of a corporation-wide safety policy. *Academy of Management Journal, 38,* 364–382.

Jaros, S. J., Jermier, J. M., Koehler, J. W., & Sincich, T. (1993). Effects of continuance, affective, and moral commitment on the withdrawal process: An evaluation of eight structural equation models. *Academy of Management Journal, 36,* 951–995.

Jaroslovsky, R. (1988, July/August). What's on your mind, America? *Psychology Today,* pp. 54–59.

Jeanneret, P. R. (1991). Growth trends in I/O psychology. *The Industrial-Organizational Psychologist, 29*(2), 47–52.

Johns, G. (1993). Constraints on the adoption of psychology-based personnel practices: Lessons from organizational innovation. *Personnel Psychology, 46,* 569–592.

Johns, G. (1994a). Absenteeism estimates by employees and managers: Divergent perspectives and self-serving perceptions. *Journal of Applied Psychology, 79,* 229–239.

Johns, G. (1994b). How often were you absent? A review of the use of self-reported absence data. *Journal of Applied Psychology, 79,* 574–591.

Johnson, B. T., Mullen, B., & Salas, E. (1995). Comparison of three major meta-analytic approaches. *Journal of Applied Psychology, 80,* 94–106.

Johnson, T. (1984). The myth of declining brand loyalty. *Journal of Advertising Research, 24*(1), 9–17.

Jolson, M. A., Wiener, J. L., & Rosecky, R. B. (1987). Correlates of rebate proneness. *Journal of Advertising Research, 27,* 33–43.

Jones, R. G., & Whitmore, M. D. (1995). Evaluating developmental assessment centers as interventions. *Personnel Psychology, 48,* 377–388.

Judge, T. A. (1993a). Does affective disposition moderate the relationship between job satisfaction and voluntary turnover? *Journal of Applied Psychology, 78,* 395–401.

Judge, T. A. (1993b). Validity of the dimensions of the Pay Satisfaction Questionnaire: Evidence of differential prediction. *Personnel Psychology, 46,* 331–355.

Judge, T. A., Boudreau, J. W., & Bretz, R. D., Jr. (1994). Job and life attitudes of male executives. *Journal of Applied Psychology, 79,* 767–782.

Judge, T. A., Cable, D. M., Boudreau, J. W., & Bretz, R. D., Jr. (1995). An empirical investigation of the predictors of executive career success. *Personnel Psychology, 48,* 485–519.

Judge, T. A., & Ferris, G. R. (1993). Social context of performance evaluation decisions. *Academy of Management Journal, 36,* 80–105.

Judge, T. A., & Locke, E. A. (1993). Effect of dysfunctional thought processes on subjective well-being and job satisfaction. *Journal of Applied Psychology, 78,* 475–490.

Judge, T. A., & Watanabe, S. (1993). Another look at the job satisfaction–life satisfaction relationship. *Journal of Applied Psychology, 78,* 939–948.

Judge, T. A., & Welbourne, T. M. (1994). A confirmatory investigation of the dimensionality of the Pay Satisfaction Questionnaire. *Journal of Applied Psychology, 79,* 461–466.

Kalleberg, A. L., & Leicht, K. T. (1991). Gender and organizational performance: Determinants of small business success and survival. *Academy of Management Journal, 34,* 136–161.

Kalleberg, A. L., & Moody, J. W. (1994). Human resource management and organizational performance. *American Behavioral Science, 37,* 948–962.

Kane, J. S., & Bernardin, H. J. (1982). Behavioral observation scales and the evaluation of performance appraisal effectiveness. *Journal of Applied Psychology, 35,* 635–641.

Kane, J. S., Bernardin, H. J., Villanova, P., & Peyrefitte, J. (1995). Stability of rater leniency: Three studies. *Academy of Management Journal, 38,* 1036–1051.

Kanis, H. (1993). Operation of controls on consumer products by physically impaired users. *Human Factors, 35,* 305–328.

Karasek, R. A., & Theorell, T. (1990). *Healthy work: Stress, productivity, and the re-construction of working life*. New York: Basic Books.

Karau, S. J., & Williams, K. D. (1993). Social loafing: A meta-analytic review and theoretical integration. *Journal of Personality and Social Psychology, 65,* 681–706.

Karren, R. J., & Graves, L. M. (1994). Assessing person-organization fit in personnel selection: Guidelines for future research. *International Journal of Selection and Assessment, 2*(3), 145–156.

Kaufman, C. F., & Lane, R. M. (1994). In pursuit of the nomadic viewer. *Journal of Consumer Marketing, 11*(4), 4–17.

Keenan, A., & Newton, T. J. (1987). Work difficulties and stress in young professional engineers. *Journal of Occupational Psychology, 60,* 133–145.

Keita, G. P., & Hurrell, J. J., Jr. (1994). Introduction. In G. P. Keita & J. J. Hurrell, Jr. (Eds.), *Job stress in a changing workforce: Investigating gender, diversity, and family issues* (pp. xiii–xix). Washington, DC: American Psychological Association.

Keller, K. L. (1987). Memory factors in advertising: The effect of advertising retrieval cues on brand evaluations. *Journal of Consumer Research, 14,* 316–333.

Keller, K. L. (1991). Memory and evaluation effects in competitive advertising environments. *Journal of Consumer Research, 17,* 463–476.

Keller, L. M., Bouchard, T. J., Jr., Arvey, R. D., Segal, N. L., & Dawis, R. V. (1992). Work values: Genetic and environmental influences. *Journal of Applied Psychology, 77,* 79–88.

Kelley, P. L., Jacobs, R. R., & Farr, J. L. (1994). Effects of multiple administrations of the MMPI for employee screening. *Personnel Psychology, 47,* 575–591.

Kelloway, E. K., & Barling, J. (1993). Members' participation in local union activities: Measurement, prediction, and replication. *Journal of Applied Psychology, 78,* 262–279.

Kelloway, E. K., & Watts, L. (1994). Preemployment predictors of union attitudes: Replication and extension. *Journal of Applied Psychology, 79,* 631–634.

Kelly, R. M., & Kelly, V. P. (1990). Lillian Moller Gilbreth (1878–1972). In A. N. O'Connell & N. F. Russo (Eds.), *Women in psychology: A bio-bibliographic sourcebook* (pp. 117–124). New York: Greenwood Press.

Kemery, E. R., Roth, L., & Mossholder, K. W. (1987). The power of the Schmidt and Hunter model of validity generalization. *Journal of Applied Psychology, 72,* 30–37.

Keys, B., & Case, T. (1990). How to become an influential manager. *Academy of Management Executive, 4*(4), 38–51.

Kilduff, M., & Day, D. V. (1994). Do chameleons get ahead? The effects of self-monitoring on managerial careers. *Academy of Management Journal, 37,* 1047–1060.

King, M., Murray, M. A., & Atkinson, T. (1982). Background, personality, job characteristics, and satisfaction with work in a national sample. *Human Relations, 35,* 119–133.

King, W. C., Jr., & Miles, E. W. (1995). A quasi-experimental assessment of the effect of computerizing noncognitive paper-and-pencil measurements: A test of measurement equivalence. *Journal of Applied Psychology, 80,* 643–651.

Kirkpatrick, S. A., & Locke, E. A. (1996). Direct and indirect effects of three core charismatic leadership components on performance and attitudes. *Journal of Applied Psychology, 81,* 36–51.

Kivimäki, M., & Kalimo, R. (1996). Self-esteem and the occupational stress process: Testing two alternative models in a sample of blue-collar workers. *Journal of Occupational Health Psychology, 1,* 187–196.

Klaas, B. S., & Dell'omo, G. G. (1991). The determinants of disciplinary decisions: The case of employee drug use. *Personnel Psychology, 44,* 813–835.

Klaas, B. S., Heneman, H. G., III, & Olson, C. A. (1991). Effects of grievance activity on absenteeism. *Journal of Applied Psychology, 76,* 818–824.

Klein, J. A., & Posey, P. A. (1986). Good supervisors are good supervisors—anywhere. *Harvard Business Review, 64*(6), 125–128.

Kleiss, J. A., & Hubbard, D. C. (1993). Effects of three types of flight simulator visual scene detail on detection of altitude change. *Human Factors, 35,* 653–671.

Klimoski, R. J., & Brickner, M. (1987). Why do assessment centers work? The puzzle of assessment center validity. *Personnel Psychology, 40,* 243–260.

Kline, C. J., & Peters, L. H. (1991). Behavioral commitment and tenure of new employees: A replication and extension. *Academy of Management Journal, 34,* 194–204.

Kline, T. J. B., & Beitel, G. A. (1994). Assessment of push/pull door signs: A laboratory and a field study. *Human Factors, 36,* 684–699.

Kluger, A. N., & Colella, A. (1993). Beyond the mean bias: The effect of warning against faking on biodata item variances. *Personnel Psychology, 46,* 763–780.

Kobasa, S. C. (1979). Stressful life events, personality, and health: An inquiry into hardiness. *Journal of Personality and Social Psychology, 37,* 1–11.

Kobasa, S. C. (1982). The hardy personality: Toward a social psychology of stress and health. In G. Sanders & J. Suls (Eds.), *Social psychology of health and illness* (pp. 3–32). Hillsdale, NJ: Erlbaum.

Kobasa, S. C., Maddi, S. R., & Kahn, S. (1982). Hardiness and health: A prospective study. *Journal of Personality and Social Psychology, 42,* 168–177.

Kobasa, S. C., Maddi, S. R., Puccetti, M. C., & Zola, M. C. (1985). Effectiveness of hardiness, exercise, and social support as resources against illness. *Journal of Psychosomatic Research, 29,* 525–533.

Koelega, H. S., & Brinkman, J. A. (1986). Noise and vigilance: An evaluative review. *Human Factors, 28,* 465–481.

Komaki, J., Zlotnick, S., & Jensen, M. (1986). Development of an operant-based taxonomy and observational index of supervisory behavior. *Journal of Applied Psychology, 71,* 260–269.

Konovsky, M. A., & Cropanzano, R. (1991). Perceived fairness of employee drug testing as a predictor of employee attitudes and job performance. *Journal of Applied Psychology, 76,* 698–707.

Koppes, L. L. (1991). I/O psychology master's-level training: Reality and legitimacy in search of recognition. *The Industrial-Organizational Psychologist, 29*(2), 59–67.

Koppes, L. L., Landy, F. J., & Perkins, K. N. (1993). First American female applied psychologists. *The Industrial-Organizational Psychologist, 31*(1), 31–53.

Kossek, E. E., & Nichol, V. (1992). The effects of on-site child care on employee attitudes and performance. *Personnel Psychology, 45,* 485–509.

Kraiger, K., Ford, J. K., & Salas, E. (1993). Application of cognitive, skill-based, and affective theories of learning outcomes to new methods of training evaluation. *Journal of Applied Psychology, 78,* 311–328.

Kravitz, D. A., & Platania, J. (1993). Attitudes and beliefs about affirmative action: Effects of target and of respondent sex and ethnicity. *Journal of Applied Psychology, 78,* 928–938.

Kristof, A. L. (1996). Person-organization fit: An integrative review of its conceptualizations, measurement, and implications. *Personnel Psychology, 49,* 1–49.

Laabs, J. L. (1991). The golden arches provide golden opportunities. *Personnel Journal, 70*(7), 52–57.

Lam, T. H., Lee, P. W. H., Ong, S. G., Wong, C. M., Chow, W. K., & Kleevens, J. W. L. (1987). Mental health and work stress: A comparison of response patterns in executives and clerical workers in Hong Kong. *Journal of Occupational Medicine, 29,* 892–897.

Lammers, H. B. (1991). The effect of free samples on immediate consumer purchase. *Journal of Consumer Marketing, 8*(2), 31–37.

Lance, C. E., LaPointe, J. A., & Stewart, A. M. (1994). A test of the context dependency of three causal models of halo rater error. *Journal of Applied Psychology, 79,* 332–340.

Landsbergis, P. A., Schnall, P. L., Schwartz, J. E., Warren, K., & Pickering, T. G. (1995). Job strain, hypertension, and cardiovascular disease: Empirical evidence, methodological issues, and recommendations for future research. In S. L. Sauter & L. R. Murphy (Eds.), *Organizational risk factors for job stress* (pp. 97–112). Washington, DC: American Psychological Association.

Landy, F. J., Rastegary, H., Thayer, J., & Colvin, C. (1991). Time urgency: The construct and its measurement. *Journal of Applied Psychology, 76,* 644–657.

Landy, F. J., Shankster, L. J., & Kohler, S. S. (1994). Personnel selection and placement. *Annual Review of Psychology, 45,* 261–296.

Landy, F. J., & Vasey, J. (1991). Job analysis: The composition of SME samples. *Personnel Psychology, 44,* 27–50.

Langan-Fox, J., & Roth, S. (1995). Achievement motivation and female entrepreneurs. *Journal of Occupational and Organizational Psychology, 68,* 209–218.

Latané, B., Williams, K. D., & Harkins, S. (1979). Many hands make light the work: The causes and consequences of social loafing. *Journal of Personality and Social Psychology, 37,* 822–832.

Latham, G. P., & Frayne, C. A. (1990). Increasing job attendance through training in self-management: A review of two field experiments. In U. Kleinbeck, H. H. Quast, H. Thierry, & H. Häcker (Eds.), *Work motivation* (pp. 169–187). Hillsdale, NJ: Erlbaum.

Latham, G. P., & Wexley, K. N. (1977). Behavioral observation scales for performance appraisal purposes. *Personnel Psychology, 30,* 255–268.

Latham, G. P., & Wexley, K. N. (1981). *Increasing productivity through performance appraisal.* Reading, MA: Addison-Wesley.

Lautenschlager, G. J., & Flaherty, V. L. (1990). Computer administration of questions: More desirable or more social desirability? *Journal of Applied Psychology, 75,* 310–314.

Law, K. S., & Myors, B. (1993). Cutoff scores that maximize the total utility of a selection program: Comment on Martin and Raju's (1992) procedure. *Journal of Applied Psychology, 78,* 736–740.

Lawler, E. E., III. (1986). *High-involvement management: Participative strategies for improving organizational performance.* San Francisco: Jossey-Bass.

Lawler, E. E., III, & Porter, L. W. (1967). The effect of performance on job satisfaction. *Industrial Relations, 7,* 20–28.

Lee, C., Ashford, S. J., & Bobko, P. (1990). Interactive effects of Type A behavior and perceived control on worker performance, job satisfaction, and somatic complaints. *Academy of Management Journal, 33,* 870–881.

Lee, R. T., & Ashforth, B. E. (1990). On the meaning of Maslach's three dimensions of burnout. *Journal of Applied Psychology, 75,* 743–747.

Lee, R. T., & Ashforth, B. E. (1996). A meta-analytic examination of the correlates of the three dimensions of job burnout. *Journal of Applied Psychology, 81,* 123–133.

Lee, T. W., Mitchell, T. R., Wise, L., & Fireman, S. (1996). An unfolding model of voluntary employee turnover. *Academy of Management Journal, 39,* 5–36.

Lefkowitz, J. (1970). Effect of training on the productivity and tenure of sewing machine operators. *Journal of Applied Psychology, 54,* 81–86.

Lefkowitz, J. (1994). Race as a factor in job placement: Serendipitous findings of "ethnic drift." *Personnel Psychology, 47,* 497–513.

Lehman, W. E. K., & Simpson, D. D. (1992). Employee substance use and on-the-job behaviors. *Journal of Applied Psychology, 77,* 309–321.

Lengnick-Hall, M. L. (1995). Sexual harassment research: A methodological critique. *Personnel Psychology, 48,* 841–864.

Levine, E. L., Cannon, J. A., & Spector, P. E. (1985). *Generalizability of test validities for selection in skilled and semiskilled craft jobs.* Bell Communications Research Technical Report.

Levine, E. L., Sistrunk, F., McNutt, K., & Gael, S. (1988). Exemplary job analysis systems in selected organizations: A description of process and outcomes. *Journal of Business and Psychology, 3,* 3–21.

Levine, E. L., Thomas, J. N., & Sistrunk, F. (1988). Selecting a job analysis approach. In S. Gael (Ed.), *Job analysis handbook for business, industry, and government* (pp. 339–352). New York: Wiley.

Lewis, J., & McLaverty, C. (1991). Facing up to the needs of the older manager. *Personnel Management, 23*(1), 32–35.

Liden, R. C., & Parsons, G. K. (1986). A field study of job applicant interview perceptions, alternative opportunities, and demographic characteristics. *Personnel Psychology, 39,* 109–122.

Liden, R. C., Wayne, S. J., & Stilwell, D. (1993). A longitudinal study on the early development of leader-member exchanges. *Journal of Applied Psychology, 78,* 662–674.

Lin, T. R., Dobbins, G. H., & Farh, J. L. (1992). A field study of race and age similarity effects on interview ratings in conventional and situational interviews. *Journal of Applied Psychology, 77,* 363–371.

Liou, K. T., Sylvia, R. D., & Brunk, G. (1990). Non-work factors and job satisfaction revisited. *Human Relations, 43,* 77–86.

Locke, E. A. (1968). Toward a theory of task motivation and incentives. *Organizational Behavior and Human Performance, 3,* 157–189.

Locke, E. A. (Ed.). (1986). *Generalizing from laboratory to field settings: Research findings from industrial-organizational psychology, organizational behavior, and human resource management.* Lexington, MA: Lexington Books.

Locke, E. A., & Latham, G. P. (1990b). *A theory of goal setting and task performance.* Upper Saddle River, NJ: Prentice Hall.

Locke, E. A., Latham, G. P., & Erez, M. (1988). The determinants of goal commitment. *Academy of Management Review, 13,* 23–39.

Locke, E. A., & Schweiger, D. M. (1978). Participation in decision-making: One more look. In B. M. Staw (Ed.), *Research in organizational behavior.* Greenwich, CT: JAI Press.

London, M., & Smither, J. W. (1995). Can multi-source feedback change perceptions of goal accomplishment, self-evaluations, and performance-related outcomes? Theory-based applications and directions for research. *Personnel Psychology, 48,* 803–839.

London, M., & Wohlers, A. J. (1991). Agreement between subordinate and self-ratings in upward feedback. *Personnel Psychology, 44,* 375–390.

London, M., Wohlers, A. J., & Gallagher, P. (1990). A feedback approach to management development. *Journal of Management Development, 9*(6), 17–31.

Lord, R. G., & Hohenfeld, J. A. (1979). Longitudinal field assessment of equity effects in the performance of major league baseball players. *Journal of Applied Psychology, 64,* 19–26.

Lowe, R. H. (1993). Master's programs in industrial/organizational psychology: Current status and a call for action. *Professional Psychology: Research and Practice, 24,* 27–34.

Lubinski, D., Benbow, C. P., & Ryan, J. (1995). Stability of vocational interests among the intellectually gifted from adolescence to adulthood: A 15-year longitudinal study. *Journal of Applied Psychology, 80,* 196–200.

Lundberg, U. (1996). Influence of paid and unpaid work on psychophysiological stress responses of men and women. *Journal of Occupational Health Psychology, 1,* 117–130.

Lykken, D. T., Bouchard, T. J., Jr., McGue, M., & Tellegen, A. (1993). Heritability of interests. *Journal of Applied Psychology, 78,* 649–661.

Lynn, M., Zinkhan, G. M., & Harris, J. (1993). Consumer tipping: A cross-country study. *Journal of Consumer Research, 20,* 478–488.

Macan, T. H. (1994). Time management: Test of a process model. *Journal of Applied Psychology, 79,* 381–391.

Macan, T. H., Avedon, M. J., Paese, M., & Smith, D. E. (1994). The effects of applicants' reactions to cognitive ability tests and an assessment center. *Personnel Psychology, 47,* 715–738.

Macan, T. H., & Dipboye, R. L. (1990). The relationship of interviewers' pre-interview impressions to selection and recruitment outcomes. *Personnel Psychology, 43,* 745–768.

Macdonald, W. A., & Cole, B. L. (1988). Evaluating the role of color in a flight information cockpit display. *Ergonomics, 31,* 13–37.

Machlowitz, M. (1980). *Workaholics: Living with them, working with them.* Reading, MA: Addison-Wesley.

Mael, F. A., & Ashforth, B. E. (1995). Loyal from day one: Biodata, organizational identification, and turnover among newcomers. *Personnel Psychology, 48,* 309–333.

Magjuka, R. J., & Baldwin, T. D. (1991). Team-based employee involvement programs: Effects of design and administration. *Personnel Psychology, 44,* 793–812.

Major, D. A., Kozlowski, S. W. J., Chao, G. T., & Gardner, P. D. (1995). A longitudinal investigation of newcomer expectations, early socialization outcomes, and the moderating effects of role development factors. *Journal of Applied Psychology, 80,* 418–431.

Manning, M. R., Jackson, C. N., & Fusilier, M. R. (1996a). Occupational stress and health care use. *Journal of Occupational Health Psychology, 1,* 100–109.

Manning, M. R., Jackson, C. N., & Fusilier, M. R. (1996b). Occupational stress, social support, and the cost of health care. *Academy of Management Journal, 39,* 738–750.

Manz, C. C., Keating, D. E., & Donnellon, A. (1990). Preparing for an organizational change to employee self-management: The managerial transition. *Organizational Dynamics, 19*(2), 15–26.

Markham, S. E., & McKee, G. H. (1991). Declining organizational size and increasing unemployment rates: Predicting employee absenteeism from within—and between—plant perspectives. *Academy of Management Journal, 34,* 952–965.

Markham, S. E., & McKee, G. H. (1995). Group absence behavior and standards: A multilevel analysis. *Academy of Management Journal, 38,* 1174–1190.

Marlowe, C. M., Schneider, S. L., & Nelson, C. E. (1996). Gender and attractiveness biases in hiring decisions: Are more experienced managers less biased? *Journal of Applied Psychology, 81,* 11–21.

Marras, W. S., Marklin, R. W., Greenspan, G. J., & Lehman, K. R. (1995). Quantification of wrist motion during scanning. *Human Factors, 37,* 412–423.

Marriott, I. A., & Stuchly, M. A. (1986). Health aspects of work with visual display terminals. *Journal of Occupational Medicine, 28,* 833–848.

Martin, S. (1994, October). Workplace is no longer a haven from violence. *APA Monitor,* p. 29.

Martin, S. L., & Raju, N. S. (1992). Determining cutoff scores that optimize utility: A recognition of recruiting costs. *Journal of Applied Psychology, 77,* 15–23.

Martin, S. L., & Terris, W. (1991). Predicting infrequent behavior: Clarifying the impact on false-positive rates. *Journal of Applied Psychology, 76,* 484–487.

Martocchio, J. J. (1989). Age-related differences in employee absenteeism: A meta-analysis. *Psychology and Aging, 4,* 409–414.

Martocchio, J. J. (1994). Effects of conceptions of ability on anxiety, self-efficacy, and learning in training. *Journal of Applied Psychology, 79,* 819–825.

Martocchio, J. J., & Dulebohn, J. (1994). Performance feedback effects in training: The role of perceived controllability. *Personnel Psychology, 47,* 357–373.

Maslach, C. (1982). *Burnout: The cost of caring.* Upper Saddle River, NJ: Prentice Hall.

Maslach, C., & Jackson, S. E. (1986). *Maslach Burnout Inventory manual* (2nd ed.). Palo Alto, CA: Consulting Psychologists Press.

Maslow, A. (1970). *Motivation and personality* (2nd ed.). New York: Harper & Row.

Mathieu, J. E. (1991). A cross-level nonrecursive model of the antecedents of organizational commitment and satisfaction. *Journal of Applied Psychology, 76,* 607–618.

Mathieu, J. E., & Zajac, D. M. (1990). A review and meta-analysis of the antecedents, correlates, and consequences of organizational commitment. *Psychological Bulletin, 108,* 171–194.

Matthews, K. A. (1988). Coronary heart disease and Type A behaviors: Update on and alternative to the Booth-Kewley and Friedman (1987) quantitative review. *Psychological Bulletin, 104,* 373–380.

Mattis, M. C. (1990). New forms of flexible work arrangements for managers and professionals: Myths and realities. *Human Resource Planning, 13*(2), 133–146.

Maurer, S. D., & Fay, C. (1988). Effect of situational interviews, conventional structured interviews, and training on interview rating agreement: An experimental analysis. *Personnel Psychology, 41,* 329–344.

Maurer, T. J., & Tarulli, B. A. (1994). Investigation of perceived environment, perceived outcome, and person variables in relationship to voluntary development activity by employees. *Journal of Applied Psychology, 79,* 3–14.

Maxwell, S. E., & Arvey, R. D. (1993). The search for predictors with high validity and low adverse impact: Compatible or incompatible goals? *Journal of Applied Psychology, 78,* 433–437.

May, D. R., & Schwoerer, C. E. (1994). Employee health by design: Using employee involvement teams in ergonomic job redesign. *Personnel Psychology, 47,* 861–876.

Mays, V. M., Coleman, L. M., & Jackson, J. S. (1996). Perceived race-based discrimination, employment status, and job stress in a national sample of Black women: Implications for health outcomes. *Journal of Occupational Health Psychology, 1,* 319–329.

McCall, M., & Belmont, H. J. (1996). Credit card insignia and restaurant tipping: Evidence for an associative link. *Journal of Applied Psychology, 81,* 609–613.

McCall, M. W., Jr., & Lombardo, M. M. (1983, February). What makes a top executive? *Psychology Today,* pp. 26–31.

McCauley, C. D., Ruderman, N. M., Ohlott, P. J., & Morrow, J. E. (1994). Assessing the developmental components of managerial jobs. *Journal of Applied Psychology, 79,* 544–560.

McClelland, D. C. (1961). *The achieving society.* New York: Free Press.

McClelland, D. C. (1975). *Power: The inner experience.* New York: Irvington.

McClelland, D. C. (1987). *Human motivation.* Glenview, IL: Scott, Foresman.

McClelland, D. C., Atkinson, J. W., Clark, R. A., & Lowell, E. L. (1953). *The achievement motive.* New York: Appleton-Century-Crofts.

McClelland, D. C., & Boyatzis, R. E. (1982). Leadership motive pattern and long-term success in management. *Journal of Applied Psychology, 67,* 737–743.

McDaniel, M. A., Whetzel, D. L., Schmidt, F. L., & Maurer, S. D. (1994). The validity of employment interviews: A comprehensive review and meta-analysis. *Journal of Applied Psychology, 79,* 599–616.

McDermott, J. (1990, January). If it's to be heard but not listened to, it must be Muzak. *Smithsonian,* pp. 70–82.

McDonald, A. D., Cherry, N. M., Delorme, C., & McDonald, J. C. (1986). Visual display units and pregnancy: Evidence from the Montreal survey. *Journal of Occupational Medicine, 28,* 1226–1231.

McEnery, J., & McEnery, J. M. (1987). Self-rating in management training needs assessment: A neglected opportunity? *Journal of Occupational Psychology, 60,* 49–60.

McEvoy, G. M., & Buller, P. F. (1987). User acceptance of peer appraisals in an industrial setting. *Personnel Psychology, 40,* 785–797.

McEvoy, G. M., & Cascio, W. F. (1987). Do good or poor performers leave? A meta-analysis of the relationship between performance and turnover. *Academy of Management Journal, 30,* 744–762.

McEvoy, G. M., & Cascio, W. F. (1989). Cumulative evidence of the relationship between employee age and job performance. *Journal of Applied Psychology, 74,* 11–17.

McGregor, D. (1960). *The human side of enterprise.* New York: McGraw-Hill.

McLain, D. L. (1995). Responses to health and safety risk in the work environment. *Academy of Management Journal, 38,* 1726–1743.

McNeely, B. L., & Meglino, B. M. (1994). The role of dispositional and situational antecedents in prosocial organizational behavior: An examination of the intended beneficiaries of prosocial behavior. *Journal of Applied Psychology, 79,* 836–844.

Meglino, B. M., DeNisi, A. S., & Ravlin, E. C. (1993). Effects of previous job exposure and subsequent job status on the functioning of a realistic job preview. *Personnel Psychology, 46,* 803–822.

Meijman, T. F., Ulenbelt, P., Lumens, M. E. J. L., & Herber, R. F. M. (1996). Behavioral determinants of occupational exposure to chemical agents. *Journal of Occupational Health Psychology, 1,* 85–91.

Melamed, S., Ben-Avi, I., Luz, J., & Green, M. S. (1995). Objective and subjective work monotony: Effects on job satisfaction, psychological distress, and absenteeism in blue-collar workers. *Journal of Applied Psychology, 80,* 29–42.

Mellor, S. (1990). The relationship between membership decline and union commitment: A field study of local unions in crisis. *Journal of Applied Psychology, 75,* 258–267.

Mellor, S. (1992). The influence of layoff severity on postlayoff union commitment: The moderating effect of perceived legitimacy of a layoff account. *Personnel Psychology, 45,* 579–600.

Mellor, S. (1995). Gender composition and gender representation in local unions: Relationships between women's participation in local office and women's participation in local activities. *Journal of Applied Psychology, 80,* 706–720.

Mellor, S., Mathieu, J. E., & Swim, J. K. (1994). Cross-level analysis and the influence of local union structure on women's and men's union commitment. *Journal of Applied Psychology, 79,* 203–210.

Mental measurements yearbook, twelfth. (1995). Lincoln: Buros Institute of Mental Measurements, University of Nebraska Press.

Meyer, H. H. (1991). A solution to the performance appraisal feedback enigma. *Academy of Management Executive, 5*(1), 68–76.

Meyer, J. P., & Allen, N. J. (1991). A three-component conceptualization of organizational commitment. *Human Resource Management Review, 1,* 61–98.

Meyer, J. P., Allen, N. J., & Smith, C. A. (1993). Commitment to organizations and occupations: Extension and test of a three-component conceptualization. *Journal of Applied Psychology, 78,* 538–551.

Meyer, J. P., Paunonen, S. V., Gellatly, I. R., Goffin, R. D., & Jackson, D. N. (1989). Organizational commitment and job performance: It's the nature of the commitment that counts. *Journal of Applied Psychology, 74,* 152–156.

Miceli, M., Jung, I., Near, J. P., & Greenberger, D. B. (1991). Predictors and outcomes of reactions to pay-for-performance plans. *Journal of Applied Psychology, 76,* 508–521.

Miles, E. W., Hatfield, J. D., & Huseman, R. C. (1994). Equity sensitivity and outcome importance. *Journal of Organizational Behavior, 15,* 585–596.

Milkman, R., & Pullman, C. (1991). Technological change in an auto assembly plant: The impact on workers' tasks and skills. *Work and Occupations, 18*(2), 123–147.

Miller, A. B. (1991). *Working dazed: Why drugs pervade the workplace and what can be done about it.* New York: Plenum Press.

Miller, C. S., Kaspin, J. A., & Schuster, M. H. (1990). The impact of performance appraisal methods in employment act cases. *Personnel Psychology, 43,* 555–578.

Miller, E. C. (1978). GM's quality of work life efforts. *Personnel, 55*(4), 11–23; *55*(5), 64–69; *55*(6), 21–26.

Miller, K. I., & Monge, P. R. (1986). Participation, satisfaction, and productivity: A meta-analytic review. *Academy of Management Journal, 29,* 727–753.

Milliken, F. J., & Martins, L. L. (1996). Searching for common threads: Understanding the multiple effects of diversity in organizational groups. *Academy of Management Review, 21,* 402–433.

Milne, S. H., Blum, T. C., & Roman, P. M. (1994). Factors influencing employees' propensity to use an employee assistance program. *Personnel Psychology, 47,* 123–145.

Miner, J. B., Smith, N. R., & Bracker, J. S. (1994). Role of entrepreneurial task motivation in the growth of technologically innovative firms: Interpretations from follow-up data. *Journal of Applied Psychology, 79,* 627–630.

Minor, M. (1995). *Preventing workplace violence: Positive management strategies.* Menlo Park, CA: Crisp Publications.

Minow, N. W., & LaMay, C. L. (1995). *Abandoned in the wasteland: Children, television, and the first amendment.* New York: Hill & Wang.

Mital, A., Foononi-Fard, H., & Brown, M. L. (1994). Physical fatigue in high and very high frequency manual materials handling: Perceived exertion and physiological indicators. *Human Factors, 36,* 219–231.

Mohrman, S. A., & Cohen, S. G. (1995). When people get out of the box: New relationships, new systems. In A. Howard (Ed.), *The changing nature of work* (pp. 365–410). San Francisco: Jossey-Bass.

Morrison, E. W. (1993a). Longitudinal study of the effects of information seeking on newcomer socialization. *Journal of Applied Psychology, 78,* 173–183.

Morrison, E. W. (1993b). Newcomer information seeking: Exploring types, modes, sources, and outcomes. *Academy of Management Journal, 36,* 557–589.

Morrison, E. W., & Bies, R. J. (1991). Impression management in the feedback-seeking process: A literature review and research agenda. *Academy of Management Review, 16,* 522–541.

Morrow, C. C., Jarrett, M. Q., & Rupinski, M. T. (1997). An investigation of the effect and economic utility of corporate-wide training. *Personnel Psychology, 50,* 91–119.

Motowidlo, S. J., Dunnette, M. D., & Carter, G. W. (1990). An alternative selection procedure: The low-fidelity simulation. *Journal of Applied Psychology, 75,* 640–647.

Mount, M. K., Barrick, M. R., & Strauss, J. P. (1994). Validity of observer ratings of the big five personality factors. *Journal of Applied Psychology, 79,* 272–280.

Mount, M. K., Sytsma, M. R., Hazucha, J. F., & Holt, K. E. (1997). Rater-ratee race effects in developmental performance ratings of managers. *Personnel Psychology, 50,* 51–69.

Mowday, R. T., Porter, L. W., & Steers, R. M. (1982). *Employee-organization linkages: The psychology of commitment, absenteeism, and turnover.* New York: Academic Press.

Mulvey, P. W., Veiga, J. F., & Elsass, P. M. (1996). When teammates raise a white flag. *Academy of Management Executive, 10*(1), 40–49.

Münsterberg, H. (1913). *The psychology of industrial efficiency.* Boston: Houghton Mifflin.

Murphy, B. S., Barlow, W. E., & Hatch, D. D. (1988). Employers required to negotiate drug tests. *Personnel Journal, 67*(1), 27–28.

Murphy, K. R., & Constans, J. I. (1987). Behavioral anchors as a source of bias in rating. *Journal of Applied Psychology, 72,* 573–577.

Murphy, K. R., Jako, R. A., & Anhalt, R. L. (1993). Nature and consequences of halo error: A critical analysis. *Journal of Applied Psychology, 78,* 218–225.

Murphy, K. R., Thornton, G. C., III, & Reynolds, D. H. (1990). College students' attitudes toward employee drug testing programs. *Personnel Psychology, 43,* 615–631.

Murray, B. (1996, May). Work-study: Training in the trenches. *APA Monitor,* p. 44.

Murrell, A. J., Frieze, I. H., & Frost, J. L. (1991). Aspiring to careers in male- and female-dominated professions. *Psychology of Women Quarterly, 15*(1), 103–126.

Nagy, E., Yasunaga, S., & Kose, S. (1995). Japanese office employees' psychological reactions to their underground and above-ground offices. *Journal of Environmental Psychology, 15,* 123–134.

Nathan, B. R., & Alexander, R. A. (1988). A comparison of criteria for test validation: A meta-analytic investigation. *Personnel Psychology, 41,* 517–535.

Nathan, B. R., Mohrman, A. M., Jr., & Milliman, J. (1991). Interpersonal relations as a context for the effects of appraisal interviews on performance and satisfaction: A longitudinal study. *Academy of Management Journal, 34,* 352–369.

Nathan, B. R., & Tippins, N. (1990). The consequences of halo "error" in performance ratings: A field study of the moderating effect of halo on test validation results. *Journal of Applied Psychology, 75,* 290–296.

Neisser, U., Boodoo, G., Bouchard, T. J., Jr., Boykin, A. W., Brody, N., Ceci, S. J., Halpern, D. F., Loehlin, J. C., Perloff, R., Sternberg, R. J., & Urbina, S. (1996). Intelligence: Knowns and unknowns. *American Psychologist, 51,* 77–101.

Nelson, A., Cooper, C. L., & Jackson, P. R. (1995). Uncertainty amidst change: The impact of privatization on employee job satisfaction and well-being. *Journal of Occupational and Organizational Psychology, 68,* 57–71.

Nelson D. L., & Hitt, M. A. (1992). Employed women and stress: Implications for enhancing women's mental health in the workplace. In J. C. Quick, L. R. Murphy, & J. J. Hurrell, Jr. (Eds.), *Stress and well-being at work: Assessments and interventions for occupational mental health* (pp. 164–177). Washington, DC: American Psychological Association.

Nelson, D. L., & Sutton, C. (1990). Chronic work stress and coping: A longitudinal study and suggested new directions. *Academy of Management Journal, 33,* 859–869.

Nemetz, P. L., & Christensen, S. L. (1996). The challenge of cultural diversity: Harnessing a diversity of views to understand multiculturalism. *Academy of Management Review, 21,* 434–462.

Neter, E., & Ben-Shakhar, G. (1989). Predictive validity of graphological inferences: A meta-analytic approach. *Personality and Individual Differences, 10,* 737–745.

Neville, K. J., Bisson, R. U., French, J., Boll, P. A., & Storm, W. F. (1994). Subjective fatigue of C-141 aircrews during Operation Desert Storm. *Human Factors, 36,* 339–349.

Newton, T., & Keenan, T. (1991). Further analyses of the dispositional argument in organizational behavior. *Journal of Applied Psychology, 76,* 781–787.

Noe, R. A., & Schmitt, D. (1986). The influence of trainee attitudes on training effectiveness: Test of a model. *Personnel Psychology, 39,* 497–523.

Noe, R. A., & Steffy, B. D. (1987). The influence of individual characteristics and assessment center evaluation on career exploration behavior and job involvement. *Journal of Vocational Behavior, 30*(2), 187–202.

Noe, R. A., & Wilk, S. L. (1993). Investigation of the factors that influence employees' participation in development activities. *Journal of Applied Psychology, 78,* 291–302.

Norcross, J. C., Hanych, J. M., & Terranova, R. D. (1996). Graduate study in psychology: 1992–1993. *American Psychologist, 51,* 631–643.

Normand, J., Salyards, S. D., & Mahoney, J. J. (1990). An evaluation of pre-employment drug testing. *Journal of Applied Psychology, 75,* 629–639.

Northcraft, G. B., Griffith, T. L., & Shalley, C. E. (1992). Building top management muscle in a slow growth environment: How different is better at Greyhound Financial Corporation. *Academy of Management Executive, 6*(1), 32–41.

O'Driscoll, M. P. (1987). Attitudes to the job and the organization among new recruits: Influence of perceived job characteristics and organizational structure. *Applied Psychology: An International Review, 36*(2), 133–145.

Offermann, L. R., & Hellman, P. S. (1996). Leadership behavior and subordinate stress: A 360-degree view. *Journal of Occupational Health Psychology, 1,* 382–390.

Ohlott, P. J., Ruderman, M. N., & McCauley, C. D. (1994). Gender differences in managers' developmental job experiences. *Academy of Management Journal, 37,* 46–67.

Oldham, G. R., Cummings, A., Mischel, L. J., Schmidke, J. M., & Zhou, J. (1995). Listen while you work? Quasi-experimental relations between personal-stereo headset use and employee work responses. *Journal of Applied Psychology, 80,* 547–564.

Oldham, G. R., Kulik, C. T., & Stepina, L. P. (1991). Physical environments and employee reactions: Effects of stimulus-screening skills and job complexity. *Academy of Management Journal, 34,* 929–938.

Olea, M. M., & Ree, M. J. (1994). Predicting pilot and navigator criteria: Not much more than g. *Journal of Applied Psychology, 79,* 845–851.

O'Leary-Kelly, A. M., Griffin, R. W., & Glew, D. J. (1996). Organization-motivated aggression: A research framework. *Academy of Management Review, 21,* 225–253.

O'Leary-Kelly, A. M., Martocchio, J. J., & Frink, D. D. (1994). A review of the influence of group goals on group performance. *Academy of Management Journal, 37,* 1285–1301.

O'Neill, H. M., & Lenn, D. J. (1995). Voices of survivors: Words that downsizing CEOs should hear. *Academy of Management Executive, 9*(4), 23–24.

Ones, D. S., Viswesvaran, C., & Reiss, A. D. (1996). Role of social desirability in personality testing for personnel selection: The red herring. *Journal of Applied Psychology, 81,* 660–679.

Ones, D. S., Viswesvaran, C., & Schmidt, F. L. (1993). Comprehensive meta-analysis of integrity test validities: Findings and implications for personnel selection and theories of job performance. *Journal of Applied Psychology, 78,* 679–703.

Ones, D. S., Viswesvaran, C., & Schmidt, F. L. (1995). Integrity tests: Overlooked facts, resolved issues, and remaining questions. *American Psychologist, 50,* 456–460.

Ong, C. N., Koh, D., Phoon, W. O., & Low, A. (1988). Anthropometrics and display station preferences of VDU operators. *Ergonomics, 31,* 337–347.

Ong, C. N., Phoon, W. O., Iskandar, N., & Chia, K. S. (1987). Shiftwork and work injuries in an iron and steel mill. *Applied Ergonomics, 18*(1), 51–56.

Oppler, S. H., Campbell, J. P., Pulakos, E. D., & Borman, W. C. (1992). Three approaches to the investigation of subgroup bias in performance measurement: Review, results, and conclusions. *Journal of Applied Psychology, 77,* 201–207.

O'Reilly, C. A., III, Chatman, J. A., & Caldwell, D. F. (1991). People and organizational culture: A profile comparison approach to assessing person-organization fit. *Academy of Management Journal, 34,* 487–516.

Organ, D. W., & Ryan, K. (1995). A meta-analytic review of attitudinal and dispositional predictors of organizational citizenship behavior. *Personnel Psychology, 48,* 775–802.

Ottaway, R. N., & Bhatnagar, D. (1988). Personality and biographical differences between male and female managers in the United States and India. *Applied Psychology: An International Review, 37*(2), 201–212.

Overton, R. C., Taylor, L. R., Zickar, M. J., & Harms, H. J. (1996). The pen-based computer as an alternative platform for test administration. *Personnel Psychology, 49,* 455–464.

Owen, S. (1993). The Landor Image Power Survey: A global assessment of brand strength. In D. A. Aaker & A. L. Biel (Eds.), *Brand equity and advertising: Advertising's role in building strong brands* (pp. 11–30). Hillsdale, NJ: Erlbaum.

Owens, W. A. & Schoenfeldt, L. F. (1979). Toward a classification of persons. *Journal of Applied Psychology, 65,* 569–607.

Oz, S., & Eden, D. (1994). Restraining the Golen: Boosting performance by changing the interpretation of low scores. *Journal of Applied Psychology, 79,* 744–754.

Paley, M. J., & Tepas, D. I. (1994). Fatigue and the shift-worker: Firefighters working on a rotating shift schedule. *Human Factors, 36,* 269–284.

Park, C. W., Iyer, E. S., & Smith, D. C. (1989). The effects of situational factors on in-store grocery shopping behavior: The role of store environment and time available for shopping. *Journal of Consumer Research, 15,* 422–423.

Parker, R. A., & Aldwin, C. M. (1994). Desiring careers but loving families: Period, cohort, and gender effects in career and family orientations. In G. P. Keita & J. J. Hurrell, Jr. (Eds.), *Job stress in a changing workforce: Investigating gender, diversity, and family issues* (pp. 23–54). Washington, DC: American Psychological Association.

Parkes, K. R. (1990). Coping, negative affectivity, and the work environment: Additive and interactive predictors of mental health. *Journal of Applied Psychology, 75,* 399–409.

Pate, L. E., & Heiman, D. C. (1987). A test of the Vroom-Yetton decision model in seven field settings. *Personnel Review, 16*(2), 22–26.

Patzer, G. L. (1991). Multiple dimensions of performance for 30-second and 15-second commercials. *Journal of Advertising Research, 31*(4), 18–25.

Paul, J. A., Frings-Dresen, M. H. W., Sallé, H. J. A., & Rozendal, R. H. (1995). Pregnant women and working surface height and working surface areas for standing manual work. *Applied Ergonomics, 26*(2), 129–133.

Pelletier, K. R. (1991). A review and analysis of the health and cost-effectiveness outcome studies of comprehensive health promotion and disease prevention programs. *American Journal of Health Promotion, 5,* 311–315.

Peracchio, L. A. (1993). Young children's processing of a televised narrative: Is a picture really worth a thousand words? *Journal of Consumer Research, 20,* 281–293.

Peters, L. H., Hartke, D. D., & Pohlmann, J. T. (1985). Fiedler's contingency theory of leadership: An application of the meta-analytic procedures of Schmidt and Hunter. *Psychological Bulletin, 97,* 274–285.

Peterson, M. F., et. al. (1995). Role conflict, ambiguity, and overload: A 21-nation study. *Academy of Management Journal, 38,* 429–452.

Pfeffer, J. (1995). Producing sustainable competitive advantages through the effective management of people. *Academy of Management Executive, 9*(1), 55–70.

Phelps, S., & Mason, M. (1991). When women lose their jobs. *Personnel Journal, 70*(8), 64–69.

Phillips, A. S., & Bedeian, A. G. (1994). Leader-follower exchange quality: The role of personal and interpersonal attributes. *Academy of Management Journal, 37,* 990–1001.

Pierce, J. L., Gardner, D. G., Dunham, R. B., & Cummings, L. L. (1993). Moderation by organization-based self-esteem of role condition—employee response relationships. *Academy of Management Journal, 36,* 271–288.

Pines, A., & Guendelman, S. (1995). Exploring the relevance of burnout to Mexican blue collar women. *Journal of Vocational Behavior, 47,* 1–20.

Pingitore, R., Dugoni, B. L., Tindale, R. S., & Spring, B. (1994). Bias against overweight job applicants in a simulated employment interview. *Journal of Applied Psychology, 79,* 909–917.

Pion, G. M., Mednick, M. T., Astin, H. S., Hall, C. C. I., Kenkel, M. B., Keita, G. P., Kohout, J. L., & Kelleher, J. C. (1996). The shifting gender composition of psychology: Trends and implications for the discipline. *American Psychologist, 51,* 509–528.

Piotrowski, C., & Armstrong, T. R. (1989). The CEO: An analysis of the CNN telecast "Pinnacle." *Psychological Reports, 65,* 435–438.

Pokorny, M. L. I., Blom, D. H. J., Van Leeuwen, P., & Van Nooten, W. N. (1987). Shift sequences, duration of rest periods, and accident risk of bus drivers. *Human Factors, 29,* 73–81.

Porter, A. L. (1993). Strengthening coupon offers by requiring more from the customer. *Journal of Consumer Marketing, 10*(2), 13–18.

Porter, G. (1996). Organizational impact of workaholism: Suggestions for researching the negative outcomes of excessive work. *Journal of Occupational Health Psychology, 1,* 70–84.

Posner, B. Z., & Schmidt, W. H. (1988). Government morale and management: A survey of federal executives. *Public Personnel Management, 17*(1), 21–27.

Powell, G. N. (1990). One more time: Do female and male managers differ? *Academy of Management Executive, 4*(3), 68–75.

Powell, G. N. (1991). Applicant reactions to the initial employment interview: Exploring theoretical and methodological issues. *Personnel Psychology, 44,* 67–83.

Powell, G. N. (1993). *Women and men in management.* Newbury Park, CA: Sage.

Powell, G. N., & Butterfield, D. A. (1994). Investigating the "glass ceiling" phenomenon: An empirical study of actual promotions to top management. *Academy of Management Journal, 37,* 68–86.

Prewett-Livingston, A. J., Feild, H. S., Veres, J. G., III, & Lewis, P. M. (1996). Effects of race on interviewer ratings in a situational panel interview. *Journal of Applied Psychology, 81,* 178–186.

Prussia, G. E., Kinicki, A. J., & Bracker, J. S. (1993). Psychological and behavioral consequences of job loss: A covariance structure analysis using Weiner's (1985) attribution model. *Journal of Applied Psychology, 78,* 382–394.

Puffer, S. M. (1987). Prosocial behavior, noncompliant behavior, and work performance among commission salespeople. *Journal of Applied Psychology, 72,* 615–621.

Pulakos, E. D., & Schmitt, N. (1995). Experience-based and situational interview questions: Studies of validity. *Personnel Psychology, 48,* 289–308.

Quiñones, M. A. (1995). Pretraining context effects; Training assignment as feedback. *Journal of Applied Psychology, 80,* 226–238.

Quiñones, M. A. (1996). Training and development in organizations: Now more than ever. *Psychological Science Agenda, 9*(2), 8–9.

Rabinowitz, S., Melamed, S., Feiner, M., Weisberg, E., & Ribak, J. (1996). Hostility and hearing protection behavior: The mediating role of personal beliefs and low frustration tolerance. *Journal of Occupational Health Psychology, 1,* 375–381.

Rafaeli, A., & Pratt, M. G. (1993). Tailored meanings: On the meaning and impact of organizational dress. *Academy of Management Review, 18,* 32–55.

Ragins, B. R., & Cotton, J. L. (1991). Easier said than done: Gender differences in perceived barriers to gaining a mentor. *Academy of Management Journal, 34,* 939–951.

Ragins, B. R., & Scandura, T. A. (1994). Gender differences in expected outcomes of mentoring relationships. *Academy of Management Journal, 37,* 957–971.

Ramsey, J. D. (1995). Task performance in heat: A review. *Ergonomics, 38,* 154–165.

Rathje, W., & Murphy, C. (1992). *Rubbish!* New York: HarperCollins.

Rauschenberger, J., Schmitt, N., & Hunter, J. E. (1980). A test of the need hierarchy concept by a Markov model of change in need strength. *Administrative Science Quarterly, 25,* 654–670.

Raza, S. M., & Carpenter, B. N. (1987). A model of hiring decisions in real employment interviews. *Journal of Applied Psychology, 72,* 596–603.

Redman, T., & Snape, E. (1992). Upward and onward: Can staff appraise their managers? *Personnel Review, 21*(7), 32–46.

Ree, M. J., Carretta, T. R., & Teachout, M. S. (1995). Role of ability and prior job knowledge in complex training performance. *Journal of Applied Psychology, 80,* 721–730.

Ree, M. J., Earles, J. A., & Teachout, M. S. (1994). Predicting job performance: Not much more than g. *Journal of Applied Psychology, 79,* 518–524.

Reid, L. D., Murphy, K. R., & Reynolds, D. H. (1990). Drug abuse and drug testing in the workplace. In K. R. Murphy & F. E. Saal (Eds.), *Psychology in organizations: Integrating science and practice* (pp. 241–265). Hillsdale, NJ: Erlbaum.

Reilly, R. R., Smither, J. W., & Vasilopoulos, N. L. (1996). A longitudinal study of upward feedback. *Personnel Psychology, 49,* 599–612.

Rentsch, J. R. (1990). Climate and culture: Interaction and qualitative differences in organizational meanings. *Journal of Applied Psychology, 75,* 668–681.

Revicki, D. A., & Gershon, R. R. M. (1996). Work-related stress and psychological distress in emergency medical technicians. *Journal of Occupational Health Psychology, 1,* 391–396.

Rhodes, S. R. (1983). Age-related differences in work attitudes and behavior: A review and conceptual analysis. *Psychological Bulletin, 93,* 328–367.

Rhodewalt, F., & Zone, J. B. (1989). Appraisal of life changes, depression, and illness in hardy and nonhardy women. *Journal of Personality and Social Psychology, 56,* 81–88.

Rice, R. W., Phillips, S. M., & McFarlin, D. B. (1990). Multiple discrepancies and pay satisfaction. *Journal of Applied Psychology, 75,* 386–393.

Rind, B. (1996). Effects of beliefs about weather conditions on tipping. *Journal of Applied Social Psychology, 26,* 137–147.

Ringenbach, K. L., & Jacobs, R. R. (1995). Injuries and aging workers. *Journal of Safety Research, 26*(3), 169–176.

Roberson, M. T., & Sundstrom, E. (1990). Questionnaire design, return rates, and response favorableness in an employee attitude questionnaire. *Journal of Applied Psychology, 75,* 354–357.

Robertson, I. T., & Downs, S. (1989). Work sample tests of trainability: A meta-analysis. *Journal of Applied Psychology, 74,* 402–410.

Robinson, S. L., Kraatz, M. S., & Rousseau, D. M. (1994). Changing obligations and the psychological contract: A longitudinal study. *Academy of Management Journal, 37,* 137–152.

Rodgers, R., & Hunter, J. E. (1991). Impact of management-by-objectives on organizational productivity. *Journal of Applied Psychology, 76,* 322–336.

Rodgers, R., Hunter, J. E., & Rogers, D. L. (1993). Influence of top management commitment on management program success. *Journal of Applied Psychology, 78,* 151–155.

Roethlisberger, F. J., & Dickson, W. J. (1939). *Management and the worker: An account of a research program conducted by the Western Electric Company, Chicago.* Cambridge, MA: Harvard University Press.

Rosekind, M. R., Gander, P. H., Miller, D. L., Gregory, K. B., Smith, R. M., Weldon, K. J., Co, E. L., McNally, K. L., & Lebacqz, J. V. (1994). Fatigue in operational settings: Examples from the aviation environment. *Human Factors, 36,* 327–338.

Rosen, B., & Jerdee, T. H. (1990). Middle and late career problems: Causes, consequences, and research needs. *Human Resource Planning, 13*(1), 59–70.

Rosenthal, R., & Jacobson, L. (1968). *Pygmalion in the classroom: Teacher expectations and pupils' intellectual development.* New York: Holt.

Rosin, H., & Kobarik, K. (1995). Organizational experiences and propensity to leave: A multivariate investigation of men and women managers. *Journal of Vocational Behavior, 46,* 1–16.

Ross, J. E., & Unwalla, D. (1988). Making it to the top: A 30-year perspective. *Personnel, 65*(4), 70–78.

Rosse, J. G., Miller, J. L., & Stecher, M. D. (1994). A field study of job applicants' reactions to personality and cognitive ability testing. *Journal of Applied Psychology, 79,* 987–992.

Roth, D. L., Wiebe, D. J., Fillingim, R. B., & Shay, K. A. (1989). Life events, hardiness, and health: A simultaneous analysis of proposed stress-resistance effects. *Journal of Personality and Social Psychology, 57,* 136–142.

Rothstein, H. R. (1990). Interrater reliability of job performance ratings: Growth to asymptote level with increasing opportunity to observe. *Journal of Applied Psychology, 75,* 322–327.

Rothstein, H. R., Schmidt, F. L., Erwin, F. W., Owens, W. A., & Sparks, C. P. (1990). Biographical data in employment selection: Can validities be made generalizable? *Journal of Applied Psychology, 75,* 175–184.

Rotter, J. B. (1966). Generalized expectancies for internal versus external control of reinforcement. *Psychological Monographs, 80*(1, Whole No. 609).

Rotter, J. B. (1975). Some problems and misconceptions related to the construct of internal versus external control of reinforcement. *Journal of Consulting and Clinical Psychology, 43,* 56–67.

Rouiller, J. Z., & Goldstein, I. L. (1993). The relationship between organizational transfer climate and positive transfer of training. *Human Resource Development Quarterly, 4,* 377–390.

Rowe, D. C., Vazsonyi, A. T., & Flannery, D. J. (1994). No more than skin deep: Ethnic and racial similarity in developmental process. *Psychological Review, 101,* 396–413.

Russell, C. J., Settoon, R. P., McGrath, R. N., Blanton, A. E., Kidwell, R. E., Lohrke, F. T., Scifres, E. L., & Danforth, G. W. (1994). Investigator characteristics as moderators of personnel selection research: A meta-analysis. *Journal of Applied Psychology, 79,* 163–170.

Rynes, S. L., Bretz, R. D., Jr., & Gerhart, B. (1991). The importance of recruitment in job choice: A different way of looking. *Personnel Psychology, 44,* 487–521.

Rynes, S. L., & Connerley, M. L. (1992). Applicant reactions to alternative selection procedures. *Journal of Business Psychology, 7,* 261–278.

Rynes, S. L., & Gerhart, B. (1990). Interviewer assessment of applicant "fit": An exploratory investigation. *Personnel Psychology, 43,* 13–34.

Rynes, S. L., & Rosen, B. (1995). A field survey of factors affecting the adoption and perceived success of diversity training. *Personnel Psychology, 48,* 247–279.

Rynes, S. L., Tolbert, P. S., & Strausser, P. G. (1988). Aspirations to manage: A comparison of engineering students and working engineers. *Journal of Vocational Behavior, 32,* 239–253.

Saavedra, R., & Kwun, S. K. (1993). Peer evaluation in self-managing work groups. *Journal of Applied Psychology, 78,* 450–462.

Sackett, P. R., & DuBois, C. L. Z. (1991). Rater-ratee race effects on performance evaluation: Challenging meta-analytic conclusions. *Journal of Applied Psychology, 76,* 873–877.

Sackett, P. R., DuBois, C. L. Z., & Noe, A. W. (1991). Tokenism in performance evaluation: The effects of work group representation on male-female and white-black differences in performance ratings. *Journal of Applied Psychology, 76,* 263–267.

Sackett, P. R., & Wilk, S. L. (1994). Within-group norming and other forms of score adjustment in preemployment testing. *American Psychologist, 49,* 929–954.

Sackhaim, K. K. (1991). *Handwriting analysis and the employee selection process.* Westport, CT: Quorum.

Saks, A. M. (1995). Longitudinal field investigations of the moderating and mediating effects of self-efficacy on the relationship between training and newcomer adjustment. *Journal of Applied Psychology, 80,* 211–225.

Salgado, J. F. (1997). The five factor model of personality and job performance in the European community. *Journal of Applied Psychology, 82,* 30–43.

Saunders, T., Driskell, J. E., Johnston, J. H., & Salas, E. (1996). The effect of stress inoculation training on anxiety and performance. *Journal of Occupational Health Psychology, 1,* 170–186.

Sauter, S. L., Schleifer, L. M., & Knutson, S. J. (1991). Work posture, workstation design, and musculoskeletal discomfort in a VDT data entry task. *Human Factors, 33,* 151–167.

Scandura, T. A. (1992). Mentorship and career mobility: An empirical investigation. *Journal of Organizational Behavior, 13,* 169–174.

Scandura, T. A., & Graen, G. (1984). Moderating effects of initial LMX status on the effects of a leadership intervention. *Journal of Applied Psychology, 60,* 428–436.

Scandura, T. A., & Schrieshcim, C. A. (1994). Leader-member exchange and supervisor career mentoring as complementary constructs in leadership research. *Academy of Management Journal, 37,* 1588–1602.

Scarpello, V., & Campbell, J. P. (1983). Job satisfaction: Are all the parts there? *Personnel Psychology, 36,* 577–600.

Schaubroeck, J., & Ganster, D. C. (1993). Chronic demands and responsivity to challenge. *Journal of Applied Psychology, 78,* 73–85.

Schaubroeck, J., Ganster, D. C., & Kemmerer, B. E. (1994). Job complexity, "Type A" behavior, and cardiovascular disorder: A prospective study. *Academy of Management Journal, 37,* 426–439.

Schaubroeck, J., Ganster, D. C., Sime, W. E., & Ditman, D. (1993). A field experiment testing supervisory role clarification. *Personnel Psychology, 46,* 1–25.

Schaubroeck, J., May, D. R., & Brown, F. W. (1994). Procedural justice explanations and employee reactions to economic hardship: A field experiment. *Journal of Applied Psychology, 79,* 455–460.

Schaufeli, W. B., Keijsers, G. J., & Miranda, D. R. (1995). Burnout, technology use, and ICU performance. In S. L. Sauter & L. R. Murphy (Eds.), *Organizational risk factors for job stress* (pp. 259–271). Washington, DC: American Psychological Association.

Schippmann, J. S., Prien, E. P., & Katz, J. A. (1990). Reliability and validity of in-basket performance measures. *Personnel Psychology, 43,* 837–859.

Schliefer, L. M., Galinski, T. L., & Pan, C. S. (1995). Mood disturbance and musculoskeletal discomfort effects of electronic performance monitoring in a VDT data-entry task. In S. L. Sauter & L. R. Murphy (Eds.), *Organizational risk factors for job stress* (pp. 195–203). Washington, DC: American Psychological Association.

Schmidt, F. L., Hunter, J. E., Outerbridge, A. N., & Goff, S. (1988). Joint relation of experience and ability with job performance: Test of three hypotheses. *Journal of Applied Psychology, 73,* 46–57.

Schmidt, F. L., Hunter, J. E., Outerbridge, A. N., & Trattner, M. H. (1986). The economic impact of job selection methods on size, productivity, and payroll costs of the federal work force: An empirically based demonstration. *Personnel Psychology, 39,* 1–29.

Schmidt, F. L., Law, K., Hunter, J. E., Rothstein, H. R., Pearlman, K., & McDaniel, M. (1993). Refinements in validity generalization methods: Implications for the situational specificity hypothesis. *Journal of Applied Psychology, 78,* 3–12.

Schmidt, F. L., Ones, D. S., & Hunter, J. E. (1992). Personnel selection. *Annual Review of Psychology, 43,* 627–670.

Schmit, M. J., & Ryan, A. M. (1993). The big five in personnel selection: Factor structure in applicant and nonapplicant populations. *Journal of Applied Psychology, 78,* 966–974.

Schmit, M. J., Ryan, A. M., Stierwalt, S. L., & Powell, A. B. (1995). Frame-of-reference effects on personality scale scores and criterion-related validity. *Journal of Applied Psychology, 80,* 607–620.

Schmitt, N., Gilliland, S. W., Landis, R. S., & Devine, D. (1993). Computer-based testing applied to selection of secretarial applicants. *Personnel Psychology, 46,* 149–165.

Schmitt, N., & Robertson, I. (1990). Personnel selection. *Annual Review of Psychology, 41,* 289–319.

Schner, J. A., & Reitman, F. (1993). Effects of alternate family structures on managerial career paths. *Academy of Management Journal, 36,* 830–843.

Schoenmarklin, R. W., & Marras, W. S. (1989a). Effects of handle angle and work orientation on hammering: I. Wrist motion and hammering performance. *Human Factors, 31,* 397–411.

Schoenmarklin, R. W., & Marras, W. S. (1989b). Effects of handle angle and work orientation on hammering: II. Muscle fatigue and subjective ratings of body discomfort. *Human Factors, 31,* 413–420.

Schriesheim, C. A., Hinkin, T. R., & Podsakoff, P. M. (1991). Can ipsative and single-item measures produce erroneous results in field studies of French and Raven's (1959) five bases of power? An empirical investigation. *Journal of Applied Psychology, 76,* 106–114.

Schriesheim, C. A., Tepper, B. J., & Tetrault, L. A. (1994). Least preferred co-worker score, situational control, and leadership effectiveness: A meta-analysis of contingency model performance predictions. *Journal of Applied Psychology, 79,* 561–573.

Schwartzberg, N. S., & Dytell, R. S. (1996). Dual-earner families: The importance of work stress and family stress for psychological well-being. *Journal of Occupational Health Psychology, 1,* 211–223.

Schweiger, D. M., & DeNisi, A. S. (1991). Communicating with employees following a merger: A longitudinal field experiment. *Academy of Management Journal, 34,* 110–135.

Scott, S. G., & Bruce, R. A. (1994). Determinants of innovative behavior: A path model of individual innovation in the workplace. *Academy of Management Journal, 37,* 580–607.

Scott, W. D. (1903). *The theory and practice of advertising.* Boston: Small.

Scott, W. D. (1915). The scientific selection of salesmen. *Advertising and Selling, 25,* 5–6, 94–96.

Seashore, S. E., & Bowers, D. G. (1970). Durability of organizational change. *American Psychologist, 25,* 227–233.

Seppa, N. (1996, May). Keeping a job can be stressful, too. *APA Monitor,* p. 38.

Settoon, R. P., Bennett, N., & Liden, R. C. (1996). Social exchange in organizations: Perceived organizational support, leader-member exchange, and employee reciprocity. *Journal of Applied Psychology, 81,* 219–227.

Shaffer, G. S. (1987). Patterns of work and nonwork satisfaction. *Journal of Applied Psychology, 72,* 115–124.

Shaffer, G. T., Saunders, V., & Owens, W. A. (1986). Additional evidence for the accuracy of biographical data: Long-term retest and observer ratings. *Personnel Psychology, 39*, 791–809.

Shamir, B., House, R. J., & Arthur, M. B. (1993). The motivational effects of charismatic leadership: A self-concept based theory. *Organization Science, 4*, 577–594.

Shappell, S. A. (1995). Naval flight deck injuries: A review of Naval Safety Center data, 1977–1991. *Aviation, Space, and Environmental Medicine, 66*, 590–595.

Shenhav, Y. (1992). Entrance of blacks and women into managerial positions in scientific and engineering occupations: A longitudinal analysis. *Academy of Management Journal, 35*, 889–901.

Sheridan, J. E., Slocum, J. W., Jr., Buda, R., & Thompson, R. C. (1990). Effects of corporate sponsorship and departmental power on career tournaments. *Academy of Management Journal, 33*, 578–602.

Shore, L. M., Barksdale, K., & Shore, T. H. (1995). Managerial perceptions of employee commitment to the organization. *Academy of Management Journal, 38*, 1593–1615.

Shore, L. M., & Tetrick, L. E. (1991). A construct validity study of the Survey of Perceived Organizational Support. *Journal of Applied Psychology, 76*, 637–643.

Shore, L. M., Tetrick, L. E., Sinclair, R. R., & Newton, L. A. (1994). Validation of a measure of perceived union support. *Journal of Applied Psychology, 79*, 971–977.

Shore, L. M., & Thornton, G. C., III. (1986). Effects of gender on self- and supervisory ratings. *Academy of Management Journal, 29*, 115–129.

Shore, L. M., & Wayne, S. J. (1993). Commitment and employee behavior: Comparison of affective commitment and continuance commitment with perceived organizational support. *Journal of Applied Psychology, 78*, 774–780.

Shore, T. H., Shore, L. M., & Thornton, G. C., III. (1992). Construct validity of self- and peer-evaluations of performance dimensions in an assessment center. *Journal of Applied Psychology, 77*, 42–54.

Siegrist, J. (1996). Adverse health effects of high-effort/low-reward conditions. *Journal of Occupational Health Psychology, 1*, 27–41.

Singh, S. N., Rothschild, M. L., & Churchill, G. A., Jr. (1988). Recognition versus recall as measures of television commercial forgetting. *Journal of Marketing Research, 25*, 72–80.

Sleight, R. (1948). The effect of instrument dial shape on legibility. *Journal of Applied Psychology, 32*, 170–188.

Smith, K. H., & Rogers, M. (1994). Effectiveness of subliminal messages in television commercials: Two experiments. *Journal of Applied Psychology, 79*, 866–874.

Smith, P. C., Kendall, L. M., & Hulin, C. L. (1969). *The measurement of satisfaction in work and retirement*. Chicago: Rand McNally.

Smith, P. C., Kendall, L. M., & Hulin, C. L. (1987). The revised JDI: A facelift for an old friend. *The Industrial-Organizational Psychologist, 24*(4), 31–33.

Smith-Jentsch, K. H., Jentsch, F. G., Payne, S. C., & Salas, E. (1996). Can pre-training experiences explain individual differences in learning? *Journal of Applied Psychology, 81*, 110–116.

Smither, J. W., London, M., Vasilopoulos, N. L., Reilly, R. R., Millsap, R. E., & Salvemini, N. (1995). An examination of the effects of an upward feedback program over time. *Personnel Psychology, 48*, 1–34.

Smither, J. W., Reilly, R. R., Millsap, R. E., Pearlman, K., & Stoffey, R. W. (1993). Applicant reactions to selection procedures. *Personnel Psychology, 46,* 49–76.

Snell, A. F., Stokes, G. S., Sands, M. M., & McBride, J. R. (1994). Adolescent life experiences as predictors of occupational attainment. *Journal of Applied Psychology, 79,* 131–141.

Solomon, E. E. (1986). Private and public sector managers: An empirical investigation of job characteristics and organizational climate. *Journal of Applied Psychology, 71,* 247–259.

Spector, P. E., Brannick, M. T., & Coovert, M. D. (1989). Job analysis. In C. L. Cooper & I. T. Robertson (Eds.), *International review of industrial/organizational psychology.* New York: Wiley.

Spector, P. E., & Jex, S. M. (1991). Relations of job characteristics from multiple data sources with employee affect, absence, turnover intentions, and health. *Journal of Applied Psychology, 76,* 46–53.

Spence, J. T., & Robbins, A. S. (1992). Workaholism: Definition, measurement, and preliminary results. *Journal of Personality Assessment, 58,* 160–178.

Spera, S. P., Buhrfeind, E. D., & Pennebaker, J. W. (1994). Expressive writing and coping with job loss. *Academy of Management Journal, 37,* 722–733.

Spillman, J., & Spillman, L. (1993). The rise and fall of Hugo Münsterberg. *Journal of the History of the Behavioral Sciences, 29,* 322–338.

Sproull, L. S. (1986). Using electronic mail for data collection in organizational research. *Academy of Management Journal, 29,* 159–169.

Spychalski, A. C., Quiñones, M. A., Gaugler, B. B., & Pohley, K. (1997). A survey of assessment center practices in organizations in the United States. *Personnel Psychology, 50,* 71–90.

Staples, S. L. (1996). Human response to environmental noise: Psychological research and public policy. *American Psychologist, 51,* 143–150.

Steel, R. P., & Rentsch, J. R. (1995). Influence of cumulative strategies on the long-range prediction of absenteeism. *Academy of Management Journal, 38,* 1616–1634.

Stein, J. A., Smith, G. M., Guy, S. M., & Bentler, P. M. (1993). Consequences of adolescent drug use on young adult job behavior and job satisfaction. *Journal of Applied Psychology, 78,* 463–474.

Steiner, D. D., & Gilliland, S. W. (1996). Fairness reactions to personnel selection techniques in France and the United States. *Journal of Applied Psychology, 81,* 134–141.

Stern, B. L., & Resnik, A. J. (1991). Information content in television advertising: A replication and extension. *Journal of Advertising Research, 31*(3), 36–46.

Stevens, C. K., & Kristof, A. L. (1995). Making the right impression: A field study of applicant impression management during job interviews. *Journal of Applied Psychology, 80,* 587–606.

Stewart, G. L., Carson, K. P., & Cardy, R. L. (1996). The joint effects of conscientiousness and self-leadership training on employee self-directed behavior in a service setting. *Personnel Psychology, 49,* 143–164.

Stokes, G. S., Hogan, J. B., & Snell, A. F. (1993). Comparability of incumbent and applicant samples for the development of biodata keys: The influence of social desirability. *Personnel Psychology, 46,* 739–762.

Stone, D. L., & Colella, A. (1996). A model of factors affecting the treatment of disabled individuals in organizations. *Academy of Management Review, 21,* 352–401.

Stone, E. F., Stone, D. L., & Gueutal, H. G. (1990). Influence of cognitive ability on responses to questionnaire measures: Measurement precision and missing response problems. *Journal of Applied Psychology, 75,* 418–427.

Stout, S. K., Slocum, J. W., Jr., & Cron, W. L. (1987). Career transitions of superiors and subordinates. *Journal of Vocational Behavior, 30,* 124–137.

Stout, S. K., Slocum, J. W., Jr., & Cron, W. L. (1988). Dynamics of the career plateauing process. *Journal of Vocational Behavior, 32,* 74–91.

Straus S. G., & McGrath, J. E. (1994). Does the medium matter: The interaction of task type and technology on group performance and member reactions. *Journal of Applied Psychology, 79,* 87–97.

Stroh, L. K., Brett, J. M., & Reilly, A. H. (1992). All the right stuff: A comparison of female and male managers' career progression. *Journal of Applied Psychology, 77,* 251–260.

Summala, H., & Mikkola, T. (1994). Fatal accidents among car and truck drivers: Effects of fatigue, age, and alcohol consumption. *Human Factors, 36,* 315–326.

Sundstrom, E. (1986). *Work places: The psychology of the physical environment in offices and factories.* New York: Cambridge University Press.

Sundstrom, E., Town, J. P., Osborn, D., Rice, R. W., Konar, E., & Brill, M. (1994). Office noise, satisfaction, and performance. *Environmental Behavior, 26,* 195–222.

Super, D. E., & Hall, D. T. (1978). Career development: Exploration and planning. *Annual Review of Psychology, 29,* 333–372.

Sutton, R. I., & Rafaeli, A. (1987). Characteristics of work stations as potential occupational stressors. *Academy of Management Journal, 30,* 260–276.

Sutton, R. I., & Rafaeli, A. (1988). Untangling the relationship between displayed emotions and organizational sales: The case of convenience stores. *Academy of Management Journal, 31,* 461–487.

Swartz, T. A. (1983). Brand symbols and message differentiation. *Journal of Advertising Research, 23*(5), 59–64.

Sweeney, P. D., McFarlin, D. B., & Inderrieden, E. J. (1990). Using relative deprivation theory to explain satisfaction with income and pay level: A multistudy examination. *Academy of Management Journal, 33,* 423–436.

Taber, T. D. (1991). Triangulating job attitudes with interpretive and positivist measurement methods. *Personnel Psychology, 44,* 577–600.

Taber, T. D, & Taylor, E. (1990). A review and evaluation of the psychometric properties of the Job Diagnostic Survey. *Personnel Psychology, 43,* 467–500.

Tang, T. L., Tollison, P. S., & Whiteside, H. D. (1987). The effect of quality circle initiation on motivation to attend quality circle meetings and on task performance. *Personnel Psychology, 40,* 799–814.

Tannenbaum, S. I., Mathieu, J. E., Salas, E., & Cannon-Bowers, J. A. (1991). Meeting trainees' expectations: The influence of training fulfillment on the development of commitment, self-efficacy, and motivation. *Journal of Applied Psychology, 76,* 759–769.

Tannenbaum, S. I., & Yukl, G. (1992). Training and development in work organizations. *Annual Review of Psychology, 43,* 399–441.

Taylor, F. W. (1911). *Scientific management.* New York: Harper.

Taylor, M. S., & Bergmann, T. J. (1987). Organizational recruitment activities and applicants' reactions at different stages of the recruitment process. *Personnel Psychology, 40,* 261–285.

Taylor, T. O., Friedman, D. J., & Couture, D. (1987). Operating without supervisors: An experiment. *Organizational Dynamics, 15,* 26–38.

Tenopyr, M. L. (1992). Reflections of a pioneering woman in industrial psychology. *Professional Psychology: Research and Practice, 23,* 172–175.

Tepper, B. J. (1994). Investigation of general and program-specific attitudes toward corporate drug-testing policies. *Journal of Applied Psychology, 79,* 392–401.

Tepper, K. (1994). The role of labeling processes in elderly consumers' responses to age segmentation cues. *Journal of Consumer Research, 20,* 503–519.

Tett, R. P., Jackson, D. N., & Rothstein, M. (1991). Personality measures as predictors of job performance: A meta-analytic review. *Personnel Psychology, 44,* 703–742.

Tett, R. P., & Meyer, J. P. (1993). Job satisfaction, organizational commitment, turnover intention, and turnover: Path analyses based on meta-analytic findings. *Personnel Psychology, 46,* 259–293.

Thacker, J. W., & Fields, M. W. (1987). Union involvement in quality-of-worklife efforts: A longitudinal investigation. *Personnel Psychology, 40,* 97–111.

Tharenou, P., Latimer, S., & Conroy, D. (1994). How do you make it to the top? An examination of influences on women's and men's managerial advancement. *Academy of Management Journal, 37,* 899–931.

Theorell, T., & Karasek, R. A. (1996). Current issues relating to psychosocial job strain and cardiovascular disease research. *Journal of Occupational Health Psychology, 1,* 9–26.

Thomas, L. T., & Ganster, D. C. (1995). Impact of family-supportive work variables on work-family conflict and strain: A control perspective. *Journal of Applied Psychology, 80,* 6–15.

Thompson, C. A., Kopelman, R. E., & Schriesheim, C. A. (1992). Putting all one's eggs in the same basket: A comparison of commitment and satisfaction among self- and organizationally-employed men. *Journal of Applied Psychology, 77,* 738–743.

Tornow, W. W. (1993). Perceptions or reality: Is multi-source perspective measurement a means or an end? *Human Resource Management, 32,* 221–230.

Totterdell, P., Spelten, E., Smith, L., Barton, J., & Folkard, S. (1995). Recovery from work shifts: How long does it take? *Journal of Applied Psychology, 80,* 43–57.

Tracey, J. S., Tannenbaum, S. I., & Kavanagh, M. J. (1995). Applying trained skills on the job: The importance of the work environment. *Journal of Applied Psychology, 80,* 239–252.

Tripp, C., Jensen, T. D., & Carlson, S. (1994). The effects of multiple product endorsements by celebrities on consumers' attitudes and intentions. *Journal of Consumer Marketing, 20,* 535–547.

Trocki, K. F., & Orioli, E. M. (1994). Gender differences in stress symptoms, stress-producing contexts, and coping strategies. In G. P. Keita & J. J. Hurrell, Jr. (Eds.), *Job stress in a changing workforce: Investigating gender, diversity, and family issues* (pp. 7–22). Washington, DC: American Psychological Association.

Tubbs, M. E., Boehne, D. M., & Dahl, J. G. (1993). Expectancy, valence, and motivational force functions in goal-setting research: An empirical test. *Journal of Applied Psychology, 78,* 361–373.

Tuckel, P. S., & Feinberg, B. M. (1991). The answering machine poses many questions for telephone survey researchers. *Public Opinion Quarterly, 55*(2), 200–217.

Turban, D. B., Campion, J. E., & Eyring, A. R. (1995). Factors related to job acceptance decisions of college recruits. *Journal of Vocational Behavior, 47,* 193–213.

Turban, D. B., & Dougherty, T. W. (1994). Role of protégé personality in receipt of mentoring and career success. *Academy of Management Journal, 37,* 688–702.

Turkington, D. (1992, June). Are Type A babies simply born that way? *APA Monitor,* p. 43.

Valacich, J. S., Dennis, A. R., & Connolly, T. (1994). Idea generation in computer-based groups: A new ending to an old story. *Organizational Behavior and Human Decision Processes, 57,* 448–467.

Vancouver, J. B., & Schmitt, N. (1991). An exploratory examination of person-organization fit: Organizational goal congruence. *Personnel Psychology, 44,* 333–352.

Van de Vijver, F. J. R., & Harsveld, M. (1994). The incomplete equivalence of paper-and-pencil and computerized versions of the General Aptitude Test Battery. *Journal of Applied Psychology, 79,* 852–859.

Van Velsor, E., & Leslie, J. B. (1995). Why executives derail: Perspectives across time and cultures. *Academy of Management Executive, 9*(4), 62–72.

Varma, A., DeNisi, A. S., & Peters, L. H. (1996). Interpersonal affect and performance appraisal: A field study. *Personnel Psychology, 49,* 341–360.

Vecchio, R. P. (1990). Theoretical and empirical examination of cognitive resource theory. *Journal of Applied Psychology, 75,* 141–147.

Vecchio, R. P. (1992). Cognitive resource theory: Issues for specifying a test of the theory. *Journal of Applied Psychology, 77,* 375–376.

Veres, J. G., III, Green, S. B., & Boyles, W. R. (1991). Racial differences on job analysis questionnaires: An empirical study. *Public Personnel Management, 20*(2), 135–144.

Vevea, J. L., Clements, N. C., & Hedges, L. V. (1993). Assessing the effects of selection bias on validity data for the General Aptitude Test Battery. *Journal of Applied Psychology, 78,* 981–987.

Vidaček, S., Kaliterna, L., & Radoševič-Vidaček, B. (1986). Productivity on a weekly rotating shift system: Circadian adjustment and sleep deprivation effects. *Ergonomics, 29,* 1583–1590.

Vinokur, A. D., Van Ryn, M., Gramlich, E. M., & Price, R. H. (1991). Long-term follow-up and benefit-cost analysis of the Jobs Program: A preventive intervention for the unemployed. *Journal of Applied Psychology, 76,* 213–219.

Violanti, J. M., & Marshall, J. R. (1996). Cellular phones and traffic accidents: An epidemiological approach. *Accident Analysis and Prevention, 28,* 265–270.

Vroom, V. H. (1964). *Work and motivation.* New York: Wiley.

Vroom, V. H., & Jago, A. G. (1988). *The new leadership: Managing participation in organizations.* Upper Saddle River, NJ: Prentice Hall.

Wagel, W. H. (1987). Working (and managing) without supervisors. *Personnel, 64*(9), 8–11.

Wagner, J. A., III (1994). Participation's effects on performance and satisfaction: A reconsideration of research evidence. *Academy of Management Review, 19,* 312–330.

Waldman, D. A., & Avolio, B. J. (1991). Race effects in performance evaluations: Controlling for ability, education, and experience. *Journal of Applied Psychology, 76,* 897–901.

Wall, T. D., Corbett, J. M., Martin, R., Clegg, C. W., & Jackson, P. R. (1990). Advanced manufacturing technology, work design, and performance: A change study. *Journal of Applied Psychology, 75,* 691–697.

Wall, T. D., Jackson, P. R., & Davids, K. (1992). Operator work design and robotics system performance: A serendipitous field study. *Journal of Applied Psychology, 77,* 353–362.

Wanberg, C. R., Watt, J. D., & Rumsey, D. J. (1996). Individuals without jobs: An empirical study of job-seeking behavior and reemployment. *Journal of Applied Psychology, 81,* 76–87.

Wanous, J. P., Poland, T. D., Premack, S. L., & Davis, K. S. (1992). The effects of met expectations on newcomer attitudes and behaviors: A review and meta-analysis. *Journal of Applied Psychology, 77,* 288–297.

Wanous, J. P., & Zwany, A. (1977). A cross-sectional test of need hierarchy theory. *Organizational Behavior and Human Performance, 18,* 78–97.

Ward, S., Oliva, T. A., & Reibstein, D. J. (1994). Effectiveness of brand-related 15-second commercials. *Journal of Consumer Marketing, 1*(2), 38–44.

Warr, P., & Bunce, D. (1995). Trainee characteristics and the outcomes of open learning. *Personnel Psychology, 48,* 347–375.

Waung, M. (1995). The effects of self-regulatory coping orientation on newcomer adjustment and job survival. *Personnel Psychology, 48,* 633–650.

Wayne, S. J., & Ferris, G. R. (1990). Influence tactics, affect, and exchange quality in supervisor-subordinate interactions: A laboratory experiment and field study. *Journal of Applied Psychology, 75,* 487–499.

Wayne, S. J., & Liden, R. C. (1995). Effects of impression management on performance ratings: A longitudinal study. *Academy of Management Journal, 38,* 232–260.

Weber, M. (1947). *The theory of social and economic organization.* New York: Oxford University Press.

Webster, C. (1994). Effects of Hispanic ethnic identification on marital roles in the purchase decision process. *Journal of Consumer Research, 21,* 319–331.

Weisband, S. P., Schneider, S. K., & Connolly, T. (1995). Computer-mediated communication and social information: Status salience and status differences. *Academy of Management Journal, 38,* 1124–1151.

Weiss, D. J., Dawis, R. V., England, G. W., & Lofquist, L. H. (1967). *Manual for the Minnesota Satisfaction Questionnaire.* Minneapolis: University of Minnesota.

Weiss, R. J., & Craiger, J. P. (1997). Traveling in cyberspace: Computer-based training. *The Industrial-Organizational Psychologist, 34*(4), 70–75.

Welsh, D. H. B., Luthans, F., & Sommer, S. M. (1993). Managing Russian factory workers: The impact of U.S.-based behavioral and participative techniques. *Academy of Management Journal, 36,* 58–79.

Wentland, E. J. (1993). *Survey responses: An evaluation of their validity.* San Diego, CA: Academic Press.

Werner, J. M., & Bolino, M. C. (1997). Explaining U.S. Courts of Appeals decisions involving performance appraisal: Accuracy, fairness, and validation. *Personnel Psychology, 50,* 1–24.

Whittler, T. E. (1991). The effects of actors' race in commercial advertising: Review and extension. *Journal of Advertising, 20*(1), 54–60.

Wiebe, D. J. (1991). Hardiness and stress moderation: A test of proposed mechanisms. *Journal of Personality and Social Psychology, 60,* 89–99.

Wiersema, M. F., & Bantel, K. A. (1992). Top management team demography and corporate strategic change. *Academy of Management Journal, 35,* 91–121.

Wiersema, M. F., & Bantel, K. A. (1993). Top management team turnover as an adaptation mechanism: The role of the environment. *Strategic Management Journal, 14,* 485–504.

Wiersema, M. F., & Bird, A. (1993). Organizational demography in Japanese firms: Group heterogeneity, individual dissimilarity, and top management team turnover. *Academy of Management Journal, 36,* 996–1025.

Wiersma, U., & Latham, G. P. (1986). The practicality of behavioral observation scales, behavioral expectation scales, and trait scales. *Personnel Psychology, 39,* 619–628.

Wiesner, W. H., & Cronshaw, S. F. (1988). A meta-analytic investigation of the impact of interview format and degree of structure on the validity of the employment interview. *Journal of Occupational Psychology, 61,* 275–290.

Wiggenhorn, W. (1990). Motorola U.: When training becomes an education. *Harvard Business Review, 68*(4), 71–83.

Wilk, S. L., Desmarais, L. B., & Sackett, P. R. (1995). Gravitation to jobs commensurate with ability: Longitudinal and cross-sectional tests. *Journal of Applied Psychology, 80,* 79–85.

Williams, C. R., Labig, C. E., Jr., & Stone, T. H. (1993). Recruitment sources and posthire outcomes for job applicants and new hires. A test of two hypotheses. *Journal of Applied Psychology, 78,* 163–172.

Williams, C. R., & Livingstone, L. P. (1994). Another look at the relationship between performance and voluntary turnover. *Academy of Management Journal, 37,* 269–298.

Williams, K. J., & Alliger, G. M. (1994). Role stressors, mood spillover, and perceptions of work-family conflict in employed parents. *Academy of Management Journal, 37,* 837–868.

Williams, K. J., Suls, J., Alliger, G. M., Learner, S. M., & Wan, C. K. (1991). Multiple role juggling and daily mood states in working mothers: An experience sampling study. *Journal of Applied Psychology, 76,* 664–674.

Winefield, A. H., & Tiggemann, M. (1990). Employment status and psychological well-being: A longitudinal study. *Journal of Applied Psychology, 75,* 455–459.

Winefield, A. H., Tiggemann, M., Winefield, H. R., & Goldney, R. D. (1991). A longitudinal study of the psychological effects of unemployment and unsatisfactory employment on young adults. *Journal of Applied Psychology, 76,* 424–431.

Wogalter, M. S., Jarrard, S. W., & Simpson, S. N. (1994). Influence of warning label signal words on perceived hazard level. *Human Factors, 36,* 547–556.

Wogalter, M. S., & Silver, N. C. (1990). Arousal strength of signal words. *Forensic Reports, 3,* 407–420.

Wolpin, J., Burke, R. J., & Greenglass, E. R. (1991). Is job satisfaction an antecedent or a consequence of psychological burnout? *Human Relations, 44,* 193–209.

Wood, R. E., & Bandura, A. (1989). Social cognitive theory of organizational management. *Academy of Management Review, 14,* 361–384.

Wood, R. E., Mento, A. J., & Locke, E. A. (1987). Task complexity as a moderator of goal effects: A meta-analysis. *Journal of Applied Psychology, 72,* 416–425.

Wright, P. M., George, J. M., Farnsworth, S. R., & McMahan, G. C. (1993). Productivity and extra-role behavior: The effects of goals and incentives on spontaneous helping. *Journal of Applied Psychology, 78,* 374–381.

Wright, P. M., Lichtenfels, P. A., & Pursell, E. D. (1989). The structured interview: Additional studies and a meta-analysis. *Journal of Occupational Psychology, 62,* 191–199.

Wright, R. S., & Wright, D. G. (1993). *Creating and maintaining the drug-free workforce: A manager's guide to confronting alcohol and drug problems.* New York: McGraw-Hill.

Wyckham, R. G. (1987). Implied superiority claims. *Journal of Advertising Research, 27,* 54–63.

Xie, J. L., & Johns, G. (1995). Job scope and stress: Can job scope be too high? *Academy of Management Journal, 38,* 1288–1309.

Yu, J., & Murphy, K. R. (1993). Modesty bias in self-ratings of performance: A test of the cultural relativity hypothesis. *Personnel Psychology, 46,* 357–363.

Yukl, G., & Falbe, C. M. (1991). Importance of different power sources in downward and lateral relations. *Journal of Applied Psychology, 76,* 416–423.

Yukl, G., & Taber, T. (1983). The effective use of managerial power. *Personnel, 60*(2), 37–44.

Zaleznik, A., Kets de Vries, M. F. R., & Howard, J. (1977). Stress reactions in organizations: Syndromes, causes, and consequences. *Behavioral Science, 22,* 151–162.

Zedeck, S., & Cascio, W. F. (1984). Psychological issues in personnel decisions. *Annual Review of Psychology, 35,* 461–518.

Zeffane, R. (1994). Patterns of organizational commitment and perceived management style: A comparison of public and private sector employees. *Human Relations, 47,* 977–1010.

Zickar, M., & Taylor, R. (1996). Income of SIOP members in 1994. *The Industrial-Organizational Psychologist, 33*(6), 63–70.

Glossary

Accident proneness   The theory that certain people have personality characteristics that predispose them to have accidents, and that most accidents are caused by or involve the same few people; this theory is not supported by research.

Achievement motivation   McClelland's theory that emphasizes the need to accomplish something, to do a good job, and to be the best.

Adverse impact   When a minority group of applicants or employees is treated markedly worse than the majority group in personnel decisions.

Aided recall technique   A test of advertising effectiveness to determine the extent to which ad content can be recalled; the interviewer aids the recall by asking specific questions.

Alcoholism   An illness characterized by an inability to control the consumption of alcohol to the extent that intoxication is inevitable once drinking has begun.

Application blanks   A technique for compiling biographical information about a job applicant.

Appointed leadership   Leadership imposed on a group by an outside force, such as higher management.

Apprenticeship   A training method for skilled crafts involving classroom instruction and on-the-job experience.

Aptitude tests   Tests to measure specific abilities such as mechanical or clerical skills.

Assessment centers   A method of selection and training that involves a simulated job situation in which candidates deal with actual job problems.

Attribution   A potential source of error in performance appraisal in which raters attribute or assign positive or negative explanations to an employee's behavior.

Auditory displays   Alarms or warning signals in person-machine systems; auditory displays can be more compelling than visual displays.

Authoritarian leadership   The situation in which the leader makes all decisions and tells followers what to do.

Average rating error   In performance appraisal, the reluctance of a rater to assign very good or very poor ratings. Consequently, most ratings fall in the middle of the rating scale.

Banding A controversial practice of grouping test scores for minority job applicants to equalize hiring rates.

Behavior modeling An approach to management training in which trainees rehearse and attempt to imitate the behaviors of successful leaders as presented on videotape.

Behavior modification A training program of positive reinforcement to reward employees for displaying desirable job behaviors. Behavior modification techniques are also effective in dealing with stress.

Behavioral approach A way of understanding why good leaders behave differently from poor leaders on the job; this approach is based on the assumption that if effective leadership behaviors can be identified, then they can be taught.

Behavioral expectation scales (BES) A performance appraisal technique in which appraisers rate critical employee behaviors in terms of expectations.

Behavioral observation scales (BOS) A performance appraisal technique in which appraisers rate the frequency of critical employee behaviors.

Behaviorally anchored rating scales (BARS) A performance appraisal technique in which appraisers rate critical employee behaviors.

Biofeedback A stress-reduction technique that involves electronic monitoring of physiological processes such that people can learn to control muscle tension, blood pressure, and brain waves.

Biographical inventories An employee selection technique covering an applicant's past behavior, attitudes, preferences, and values; these questionnaires are longer and more extensive than standard application blanks.

Bureaucracies A formal, orderly, and rational approach to organizing business enterprises.

Burnout A condition of job stress that results from overwork.

Business games A training method that simulates a complex organizational situation to encourage the development of problem-solving and decision-making skills.

Career development and planning A lifelong learning approach to planning personal development opportunities throughout an employee's career.

Carpal tunnel syndrome A repetitive motion disorder that may involve numbness, tingling, or pain in fingers, hands, and forearms.

Case studies A method of executive training in which trainees analyze a business problem and offer solutions.

Central tendency In statistics, a quantitative representation of a group of raw scores.

Change agents Organization development facilitators who work with business groups to implement change and develop group confidence and effectiveness.

Charismatic leadership A leadership style characterized by a self-promoting personality, a high energy level, and a willingness to take risks; charismatic leaders stimulate their followers to think independently.

Check reading visual displays Displays that tell the operator in a person-machine system whether the system is on or off, safe or unsafe, or operating normally or abnormally.

Cognitive ability tests Tests of intelligence or mental ability.

Cognitive processes   Our processes of thought and judgment; in performance appraisal, a rater's cognitive processes can influence the judgments made about the employees he or she is evaluating.

Cognitive resource theory   An approach to leadership that focuses on the interaction between a leader's cognitive resources (intelligence, technical competence, and job-related knowledge), job performance, and stress.

Comparable worth   The idea that jobs that require comparable or equivalent skills should receive comparable compensation.

Computer-assisted instruction (CAI)   A computer-based training method in which trainees learn material at their own pace and receive immediate feedback on their progress.

Computer-assisted tests   A means of administering psychological tests to large groups of applicants in which an applicant's response determines the level of difficulty of succeeding items.

Concurrent validity   A type of validity that involves administering a test to employees on the job and correlating their scores with job performance data.

Consideration functions   Leadership behaviors that involve awareness of and sensitivity to the feelings of subordinates.

Constant bias   A source of error in performance appraisal based on the different standards used by raters.

Construct validity   A type of validity that attempts to determine the psychological characteristics measured by a test.

Consumer psychology   The study of the interactions between consumers and organizations that produce consumer products.

Content validity   A type of validity that assesses test items to ensure that they adequately sample the skills the test is designed to measure.

Contingency theory   An approach to leadership in which leadership effectiveness is determined by the interaction between the leader's personal characteristics and aspects of the situation.

Control group   In an experiment, the group of subjects that is not exposed to the independent variable.

Cooperative education programs   Business-sponsored training programs in which college students alternate periods of full-time college instruction with full-time employment.

Correlation   The relationship between two variables.

Correlation coefficient   A measure of the strength and direction of the relationship between two variables.

Criterion-related validity   A type of validity concerned with the relationship between test scores and job performance.

Critical-incidents technique   A means of identifying specific actions or behaviors that lead to desirable or undesirable consequences on the job.

Decibel (db)   The basic unit for measuring noise levels.

Democratic leadership   A leadership style in which leader and followers discuss problems and make decisions jointly.

Dependent variable   In an experiment, the resulting behavior of the subjects, which depends on the manipulation of the independent variable.

Descriptive statistics   Ways of describing or representing research data in a concise, meaningful manner.

Dysfunctional turnover   The detrimental situation that arises in an organization when good employees quit their jobs.

Elected leadership   A leadership style in which leaders are chosen by group members.

Electronic brainstorming   The generation of ideas by a group in which interaction takes place through individual computer workstations instead of in a face-to-face meeting.

Emergent leadership   The emergence of one person as a leader within an informal work group.

Employee assistance programs (EAPs)   Counseling and rehabilitative services for various employee problems, notably alcohol and drug abuse.

Engineering psychology   Studies the design of comfortable, safe, and efficient workplaces.

Environmental psychology   Studies the effect of workplace design on behavior.

Equal Employment Opportunity Commission (EEOC)   The federal agency established to ensure that all job applicants, regardless of race, religion, sex, or national origin, are guaranteed equal opportunities for employment.

Equity theory   A theory that suggests that our motivation to work is influenced by our perception of how equitably or fairly we are treated by our employer.

Equivalent-forms method   A method for determining test reliability that involves administering similar forms of a new test to the same group of subjects and correlating the two sets of scores.

ERG theory   A theory of work motivation based on three categories of needs: Existence, Relatedness, and Growth.

Ergonomics   The design of machines and equipment for human use, and the determination of the appropriate human behaviors for the efficient operation of the machines.

Existence needs   Physical survival needs, satisfied on the job through pay, fringe benefits, a safe working environment, and job security.

Experimental group   In an experiment, the group of subjects exposed to the independent variable.

Experimental method   The scientific way to determine the effect or influence of a variable on the subjects' performance or behavior.

Face validity   A subjective impression of how well the items on a psychological test appear to be related to the requirements of the job.

Fatigue   Physiological and psychological tiredness that can lead to deterioration in job performance.

Feedback   Knowledge of results given to job trainees to indicate their level of progress.

First-line supervisors   The first level in the management hierarchy.

Fixed-alternative survey questions   Similar to multiple-choice questions; respondents must limit their answers to the choices or alternatives presented.

Flextime   A system of flexible working hours combining core mandatory work periods with elective work periods at the beginning and end of the workday.

Focus groups   A method of surveying public opinion through the paid participation of 8 to 12 group members who meet to describe their reactions to a product or advertisement or to specific issues.

Forced-choice technique   A merit rating technique of performance appraisal in which raters are presented with groups of descriptive statements and are asked to select the phrase in each group that is most or least descriptive of an employee.

Forced-distribution technique   A merit rating technique of performance appraisal in which supervisors rate employees according to a prescribed distribution of ratings; analogous to grading on a curve.

Frequency distribution   A graphic representation of raw data that shows the number of times each score occurs.

Functional turnover   The situation that arises when poor employees quit their jobs; this type of turnover is not necessarily detrimental to the organization.

Grievance process   A formal mechanism for airing and resolving complaints between unionized employees and management.

Goal commitment   The strength of our determination to achieve our goals; an aspect of the goal-setting theory of motivation.

Goal-setting theory   A theory of motivation based on the idea that our primary motivation on the job is defined in terms of our desire to achieve a particular goal.

Graphology   The study of handwriting; although proponents claim that graphology is a valid predictor of job success, scientific research does not support this claim.

Group cohesiveness   The degree of closeness within a work group.

Group tests   Tests designed to be administered to a large number of people at the same time.

Growth needs   The needs for personal growth and development, satisfied on the job through the maximum use of our knowledge, skills, and abilities.

Halo effect   The tendency to judge all aspects of a person's behavior or character on the basis of a single attribute.

Hardiness   A personality variable that may explain individual differences in vulnerability to stress; hardy persons, who believe they can control the events in their lives, may be more resistant to stress.

Hawthorne studies   A long-term research program at the Hawthorne, Illinois, Western Electric Company plant that illustrated the influence of managerial and organizational factors on employee behavior.

Heads-up displays   Visual displays used in aircraft that project data directly onto the windscreen so that pilots do not have to shift their vision to a control panel.

High performance cycle   A theory of motivation and job satisfaction that suggests that goals affect level of job performance, depending on the kind of task and the abilities of the worker.

High-involvement management   The management style necessary for the modern organizational approach of participatory democracy.

Human anthropometry   A branch of engineering psychology concerned with the measurement of the physical structure of the body.

Human factors Another term for engineering psychology.

Human relations approach The approach to leadership that regards employee needs as a legitimate corporate responsibility.

Human resources psychology The study of personnel issues including employee recruitment, selection and placement, training, and performance evaluation.

Hygiene needs Characteristics of the work environment—such as company policy, quality of leadership, and salary—which are external to a job's actual requirements and can lead to job dissatisfaction.

Impression management Acting deliberately to make a good impression, to present oneself in the most favorable way.

In-basket technique An assessment center exercise that requires job applicants to process memos, letters, and directives found in a typical manager's in-basket.

Inadequate information error A potential source of error in performance appraisal in which supervisors rate their employees even though they may not know enough about them to do so fairly and accurately.

Independent variable In an experiment, the stimulus variable that is manipulated to determine its effect on the subjects' behavior.

Individual tests Psychological tests designed to be administered to one person at a time.

Industrial/organizational (I/O) psychology The application of the methods, facts, and principles of the science of psychology to people at work.

Inferential statistics Methods for analyzing research data that express relationships in terms of probabilities.

Informal work groups Cohesive groups within an organization that are not sanctioned or controlled by management.

Initiating structure functions The leadership behaviors concerned with organizing, defining, and directing the work activities of subordinates.

Integrity tests Paper-and-pencil tests to predict and detect employee dishonesty.

Interest tests Psychological tests to assess a person's interests and preferences; used primarily for career counseling.

Interpersonal affect Our feelings or emotions toward another person; in performance appraisal, interpersonal affect—the emotional tone of the relationship between rater and employee—can influence the assigned ratings.

Job analysis The study of a job to describe in specific terms the nature of the component tasks performed by the workers.

Job congruence The match between one's abilities and the requirements of one's job.

Job enrichment An effort to expand a job to give employees a greater role in planning, performing, and evaluating their work.

Job involvement The intensity of one's psychological identification with the job.

Job rotation A management training technique that assigns trainees to various jobs and departments over a period of a few years.

Job satisfaction Our positive and negative feelings and attitudes about our jobs.

Job simplification   The reduction of manufacturing jobs to the simplest components that can be mastered by unskilled or semiskilled workers.

Job-characteristics theory   A theory of motivation that states that specific job characteristics lead to psychological conditions that lead to increased motivation, performance, and satisfaction, if employees have a high need for growth.

Landscaped offices   An office design that consists of a large open area with no floor-to-ceiling walls; employee work stations are separated by partitions.

Leader-member exchange   An approach to leadership that encompasses the ways in which the leader-follower relationship affects the leadership process.

Leaderless group discussion   An assessment center exercise in which job applicants meet to discuss an actual business problem under the pressure of time; usually, a leader emerges from the group to guide the discussion.

Leniency error   In performance appraisal, the reluctance of a rater to assign very good or very poor ratings. Consequently, most ratings fall in the middle of the rating scale.

Locus of control   One's belief about the source of one's rewards; people with an internal locus of control believe that job performance, pay, and promotion are under their control and dependent on their own behavior; people with an external locus of control believe that such events are dependent on outside forces such as luck.

Management by objectives (MBO)   A performance appraisal technique that involves a mutual agreement between employee and manager on the goals to be achieved in a given period.

Mass psychogenic illness   A stress-related disorder manifested in a variety of physical symptoms that spreads rapidly among a group of workers; popularly called assembly-line hysteria.

Matched group design   A method for ensuring similarity between experimental and control groups that matches subjects in both groups on the basis of characteristics (such as age, job experience, and intelligence) that could affect the dependent variable.

Mean   The arithmetic average; a way of describing the central tendency of a distribution of data.

Median   The score at the midpoint of a statistical distribution; half the scores fall below the median and half above.

Merit pay   A wage system in which pay is based on level of performance.

Merit rating   Objective rating methods designed to yield an objective evaluation of work performance.

Meta-analysis   The large-scale reanalysis of previous research studies.

Mode   The most frequently obtained score in a distribution of research data.

Most-recent-performance error   A source of error in performance appraisal in which a rater tends to evaluate a worker's most recent behavior rather than behavior throughout the period since the last appraisal.

Motivation   Workplace factors and personal characteristics that explain why people behave the way they do on the job.

Motivator-hygiene theory   A two-factor theory to explain motivation and job satisfaction in terms of job tasks and workplace features.

Motivator needs Work characteristics—such as job duties, level of responsibility, and organizational recognition—that motivate employees to maximum job performance.

Motor skills tests Tests of muscle coordination, finger dexterity, and eye-hand coordination.

Naturalistic observation The scientific observation of behavior in its natural setting, without any experimental manipulation of the independent variable.

Needs assessment An analysis of corporate and individual goals undertaken before designing a training program to achieve them.

Needs hierarchy theory A theory of motivation encompassing physiological, safety, belonging, esteem, and self-actualization needs.

Negative affectivity A personality dimension characterized by a generalized life and job dissatisfaction and by a focus on negative aspects of life.

Nominal working hours The prescribed number of hours employees are supposed to spend on the job; not all of these hours are actually spent performing job tasks.

Normal distribution A bell-shaped distribution of data in which most scores fall near the middle and few fall at the extreme low and high ends.

Normative decision theory A theory of leadership that focuses on the correct norms or standards of behavior for leaders to follow.

Objective tests Tests for which the scoring process is free of personal judgment or bias.

On-the-job training Training that takes place directly on the job for which the person has been hired.

Open-end survey questions Questions for which respondents state their views in their own words; similar to essay questions on college examinations.

Organization-based self-esteem A personality dimension relating to our assessment of our adequacy and worth with regard to our place in the employing organization.

Organization chart A graphic depiction of the position and status of all employees or departments in an organization's hierarchical structure.

Organizational commitment The degree of one's psychological identification with or attachment to the organization for which one works.

Organizational culture The organization's pattern of beliefs, expectations, and values as manifested in company and industry practices.

Organizational development (OD) The study and implementation of planned organizational changes.

Organizational psychology The study of the social and psychological climate of the workplace.

Outplacement counseling Counseling programs for employees who have lost their jobs, usually through mergers or downsizing.

Paired-comparison technique A performance appraisal technique that compares the performance of each worker with that of every other worker in the group.

Paper-and-pencil tests Psychological tests in printed form; answers are recorded on a standard answer sheet.

Participative organizational style   Emphasis on the behaviors and needs of employees instead of a rigid focus on job tasks.

Path-goal theory   A theory of leadership that focuses on the kinds of behaviors leaders should exercise to allow their subordinates to achieve personal and organizational goals.

Peer rating   A performance appraisal technique in which managers or executives at the same level assess one another's abilities and behaviors.

Performance appraisal   The periodic, formal evaluation of employee performance.

Performance audit   An analysis undertaken prior to implementing a behavior modification training program to determine the problems or employee behaviors that can be modified for more efficient job performance.

Performance tests   The assessment of complex skills, such as word processing or mechanical ability, for which paper-and-pencil tests are not appropriate.

Person-environment congruence   The match between an employee's perception of the job requirements and the actual requirements of the organization.

Person-machine system   A system in which human and mechanical components operate together to accomplish a task.

Person-organization fit   The degree of congruence between an employee's values and organizational values.

Personality tests   Assessments of personal traits and feelings.

Personnel psychology   The study of personnel issues including employee recruitment, selection and placement, training, and performance evaluation.

Polygraphs   So-called lie detector machines that purport to measure deception and dishonesty; they have no predictive value for employee selection.

Power tests   Tests that have no time limit; applicants are allowed as much time as needed to complete the test.

Predictive validity   An approach to establishing criterion-related validity in which a new test is administered to all job applicants; all applicants are hired, regardless of test scores, and at a later date their test scores are correlated with a measure of job performance.

Probability   The idea that the differences between the means of experimental and control groups could have occurred by chance.

Probability sampling   A method for constructing a representative sample of a population for surveys or polls; each person in the population has a known probability or chance of being included in the sample.

Programmed instruction   A teaching method in which the material to be learned is presented in small, sequential steps.

Projective techniques   A personality assessment technique in which applicants project their feelings onto an ambiguous stimulus such as an inkblot.

Prosocial behavior   Employee behaviors directed toward supervisors, co-workers, and customers that are helpful to an organization.

Protective exclusion   The idea of barring certain groups of employees, such as women of childbearing age, from potentially hazardous jobs because of fear of lawsuits.

Psychosomatic disorders   Physical complaints caused by or related to emotional factors such as job stress.

Push polls   A relatively new phenomenon used in political campaigning to determine whether negative information can push voters away from one candidate to support the candidate who is paying for the poll.

Pygmalion effect   A self-fulfilling prophecy in which managers' expectations about the level of their employees' job performance can influence that performance.

Qualitative visual displays   Displays that do not present a precise numerical value; frequently used to show whether components, such as engine temperature, are in the safe or unsafe range.

Quality control circles   Employee groups organized to deal with specific production problems.

Quality-of-work-life (QWL) programs   Organizational programs based on active employee participation in decision and policy making.

Quantitative visual displays   Displays that present a precise numerical value, such as speed, altitude, or temperature.

Quota sampling   A method for constructing a representative sample of a population for surveys or polls; because the sample must reflect the proportions of the larger population, quotas are established for various categories such as age, gender, and ethnic origin.

Race norming   A controversial practice, now outlawed, of boosting test scores for minority job applicants to equalize hiring rates.

Radioimmunoassay   A method of testing for drug use that involves analysis of hair samples.

Random group design   A method for ensuring similarity between experimental and control groups that assigns subjects at random to each group.

Ranking technique   A performance appraisal technique in which supervisors list the workers in their group in order from highest to lowest or best to worst.

Rating scales   A performance appraisal technique in which supervisors indicate how or to what degree each relevant job characteristic is possessed by a worker.

Rational validity   The type of validity that relates to the nature, properties, and content of a test, independent of its relationship to measures of job performance.

Realistic job previews   A recruitment technique that acquaints prospective employees with positive and negative aspects of a job.

Recognition technique   A technique for testing advertising effectiveness by asking people if they recognize a particular ad, where they saw it, and what they can recall about it.

Reinforcement   A reward for appropriate behavior.

Relatedness needs   The needs for social relationships that bring emotional support, respect, and recognition, satisfied on the job by interactions with co-workers and mentors.

Relaxation training   A stress-reduction technique that concentrates on relaxing one part of the body after another.

Reliability   The consistency or stability of a response on a test.

Repetitive motion injuries   Injuries, such as carpal tunnel syndrome, caused by continuous and repeated motions of hands and wrists.

Reverse discrimination   The phenomenon that may occur when recruiting, hiring, promotion, and other personnel decisions in favor of members of a minority group result in discrimination against members of the majority group.

Robots Computer-controlled mechanical manipulator arms that can be programmed to move parts, operate tools, and perform multiple routines simultaneously.

Role ambiguity A situation that arises when job responsibilities are unstructured or poorly defined.

Role conflict A situation that arises when there is a disparity between job demands and the employee's personal standards.

Role playing An assessment center technique in which job candidates act out the role of a manager or an employee in a simulated job situation.

Sales test technique A way of testing the effectiveness of an advertising campaign by introducing the new advertising in selected test markets.

Scanner cable panels Groups of supermarket shoppers whose purchasing behavior is monitored electronically at checkout and who are later targeted for specific types of advertising via cable television.

Scientific management A management philosophy concerned with increasing productivity that regarded workers as extensions of the machines they operated.

Scientific method A controlled, objective, and systematic approach to research.

Selection ratio The relationship between the number of people to be hired and the number available to be hired (the potential labor supply).

Selective attention The ability to focus on one stimulus while excluding all other stimuli that may be competing for our attention.

Self-actualization need The need for self-fulfillment, for achieving one's full potential and developing all one's abilities.

Self-efficacy One's feeling of adequacy and competence in coping with work and life demands.

Self-managing work groups Employee groups that allow the members of a work team to manage, control, and monitor all facets of their work, from recruiting, hiring, and training new employees to deciding when to take rest breaks.

Self-ratings A performance appraisal technique in which managers assess their own abilities and job performance.

Self-report personality inventories Personality assessment tests that include questions dealing with situations, symptoms, and feelings; applicants are asked to indicate how well each item describes themselves or how much they agree with each item.

Sensitivity training Group sessions for management trainees that focus on interpersonal communication.

Shape coding Designing knobs for control panels in recognizably different shapes so that they can be identified by touch alone.

Shift work Work periods for industries such as utilities or telecommunications that operate 24 hours a day.

Situational approach An approach to the study of leadership that focuses on the interactions between leaders and followers, the needs of the followers, and the problems confronting the group; based on the assumption that leadership is a function of a particular situation.

Situational interviews   Interviews that focus not on personal characteristics or work experience but on the behaviors needed for successful job performance.

Situational testing   An early term for the assessment-center approach to employee selection and performance appraisal in which subjects act in a simulated job setting so that their behavior under stress can be observed and evaluated.

Skewed distribution   An asymmetrical distribution of data with most scores at the high or low end.

Social loafing   The idea that people do not work as hard in a group as they do when working alone.

Socialization   The adjustment process by which new employees learn their role in the organizational hierarchy, their company's values, and the behaviors considered acceptable by their work group.

Speed tests   Tests that have a fixed time limit, at which point everyone taking the test must stop.

Split-halves method   A method for determining test reliability that involves administering a new test to a group of subjects, dividing in half the total number of items, and correlating the two sets of scores.

Standard deviation (SD)   A precise distance along the baseline of a distribution of data; a measure of variability.

Standardization   The consistency or uniformity of the conditions and procedures for administering a test.

Standardization sample   The group of subjects used to establish test norms; the scores of the standardization sample serve as the point of comparison for determining the relative standing of the persons being tested.

Statistical significance   The level of confidence we can have in the results of an experiment; based on the calculation of probability values.

Stress   Physiological and psychological responses to excessive and usually unpleasant stimulation and to threatening events in the environment.

Structured interviews   Interviews that use a predetermined list of questions that are asked of every person who applies for a particular job.

Subjective tests   Tests that contain essay questions; the scoring process can be influenced by the personal characteristics and attitudes of the scorer.

Survey feedback technique   An organizational development technique in which surveys are conducted periodically to assess employee feelings and attitudes; the results provide feedback to higher management.

Survey research methods   Interviews, behavioral observations, and questionnaires designed to sample what subjects say they think or how subjects say they will behave in a given situation.

Systematic bias   A source of error in performance appraisal based on the different standards used by raters.

Team building technique   An organizational development technique that works with small groups or work teams to enhance team morale and problem-solving abilities.

Telecommuting   Using telecommunications to decentralize work and allow employees to perform work at home on personal computers.

Test norms   The distribution of test scores of a large group of people similar in nature to the job applicants being tested.

Test-retest method   A method for determining test reliability that involves administering a new test twice to the same group of subjects and correlating the two sets of scores.

Theory X/Theory Y   The Theory X approach to management assumes that people are lazy and dislike work and therefore must be led and directed; Theory Y assumes that people find satisfaction in their work and function best under a leader who allows them to participate in working toward their goals.

Time-and-motion study   An early attempt to redesign work tools and to re-shape the way workers performed routine and repetitive jobs.

Trait approach   The approach to leadership that focuses on personality traits; based on the assumption that some people are born or natural leaders who possess unique characteristics.

Transactional leadership   Leadership that focuses on the social interactions between leaders and followers; based on followers' perceptions of and expectations about the leader's abilities.

Transfer of training   The carryover of skills mastered during the training program to the job itself.

Transformational leadership   Leadership in which leaders are not constrained by their followers' perceptions but are free to act to change or transform their followers' views.

Turnover   Employee quitting; dysfunctional turnover occurs when good performers leave; functional turnover, which is beneficial to the organization, occurs when poor performers leave.

Type A/Type B personalities   Personality factors related to one's ability to tolerate stress; Type A persons have been associated with heart disease, anger, hostility, time urgency, and depression; Type B persons work as hard as Type As but show fewer stress effects.

Unstructured interviews   Interviews in which the format and questions asked are left to the discretion of the interviewers.

Valence-instrumentality-expectancy (VIE) theory   A theory of motivation asserting that people make choices that are based on their perceived expectations that certain rewards will follow if they behave in a particular way.

Validity   The determination of whether a psychological test or selection device measures what it is intended to measure.

Validity generalization   The idea that tests valid in one situation may also be valid in another situation.

Variability   The spread of a distribution of data around the measure of central tendency.

Vestibule training   Training that takes place in a simulated workspace.

Wage-incentive systems   The primary pay system for production workers in which the more units produced, the higher the wage.

Work overload   Too much work to perform in the time available or work that is too difficult to perform.

Work sample   A short period of formal job skill training followed by a test of job performance in a training facility.

Work underload   Work that is too simple or is insufficient to fill one's time or challenge one's abilities.

Workaholism   So-called addiction to work because of anxiety and insecurity or because of a genuine liking for the job.

Photo Credits

Author Index

Subject Index